Books are to be returned on or before
the last date below.' ECTION

the

Books are to be returned on or before
the last date below

n

99

0 7 DEC 1990

# POLITICS: AN INTRODUCTION

'Let me express unqualified enthusiasm for a comprehensive introductory textbook which really does succeed. . . . It is challenging because it encourages students to think about issues and concepts in a fresh and analytically precise way. . . . It is superior in range, style and accessibility.'

Professor Robert Eccleshall, Queen's University, Belfast,
and co-author of *Political Ideologies*

This textbook is designed to meet the needs of students taking introductory courses in politics. It is accessible and exciting, and by taking the widest possible definition of what is political it offers an unrivalled coverage of the subject. Specially designed as an interactive text, it includes think points, exercises and extracts as well as a range of illustrative material to stimulate responses from the reader. The authors emphasise the role of the individual in politics, and the interplay between the personal, the national and the global. They introduce topical issues and examples to bring the subject to life.

Features and benefits of *Politics: An Introduction*:

- **Comprehensive**: includes chapters on political sociology, political institutions, the state, political parties and associations, political thought and a whole section on international and global politics

- **User-friendly**: includes marginal comments, key words and definitions, extensive cross-referencing and a glossary

- **Clearly written** by a team who are all actively involved in teaching undergraduates and whose enthusiasm for teaching and engaging with students is manifest

- **Encourages further study** through imaginative and annotated further reading sections at the ends of chapters and a consolidated bibliography

**Barrie Axford**, **Gary K. Browning** and **John Turner** are all Principal Lecturers in Politics at Oxford Brookes University. **Alan Grant** and **Richard Huggins** are both Senior Lecturers in Politics at Oxford Brookes University and **Ben Rosamond** is Lecturer in Politics and International Studies at the University of Warwick.

# POLITICS: AN INTRODUCTION

Barrie Axford, Gary K. Browning, Richard Huggins,
Ben Rosamond, John Turner, with Alan Grant

London and New York

First published 1997
by Routledge
11 New Fetter Lane, London EC4P 4EE

Simultaneously published in the USA and Canada
by Routledge
29 West 35th Street, New York, NY 10001

Typeset in Adobe Garamond and Franklin Gothic by Keystroke, Jacaranda Lodge,
Wolverhampton

Printed and bound in Great Britain by Bath Press PLC, Bath

*British Library Cataloguing in Publication Data*
A catalogue record for this book is available from the British Library

*Library of Congress Cataloging in Publication Data*
A catalogue record for this book has been requested

ISBN 0–415–11074–2 (hbk)
ISBN 0–415–11075–0 (pbk)

D
320
PoL

# Contents

# Figures

# Tables

# Preface

The idea for this book was hatched a few years ago and grew out of our experiences as teachers of politics at Oxford Brookes University. To some degree we were concerned that there were few (if any) texts which were usable for our first-year undergraduate programme. This was due in part to the way we sought to introduce incoming students to the study of politics as well as to the nature of a modular system which is now so widely used elsewhere. But this is not a local book designed to fit a particular cohort of students. Our more pressing concern was that the market lacked a lively introduction to political science that covered the spectrum of political studies as widely as possible. There were good texts on institutions, some fine books using systematic comparison and others introducing students to the study of political ideologies. Nothing really got to grips with our preferred approach to the foundation-level teaching of politics at university.

This approach can be summed up as follows: first, we aim to demonstrate why politics matters, and therefore why the subject should be studied. It is our belief that those new to the subject should be encouraged to think about themselves as political actors in a political world. Students come to the study of politics for a variety of reasons, and many treat 'the political' as a separate, and peripheral, sphere of human existence. But such a view is sustainable only by adopting a very restricted definition of politics. Our position is that politics is much more than a realm of human activity populated by legislators, cabinets, parties, activists and apparatchiks, and we say more about this in the introductory chapter. More important to stress here is our belief that the successful student of politics (or political science, government, or any other label for the subject) is not someone who has just accumulated a cache of facts about various political systems, or who has learned by rote the main principles of Thomas Hobbes's theory of government. Rather, studying politics involves acquiring concepts, analytical frameworks and ideas which make it easier to understand, interpret and (perhaps) to explain political life. It is about being able to understand argument and counter-argument over normative and analytical questions.

Our strategy as teachers – and now as writers of a textbook – has been to introduce the study of politics by asking students to confront their own experience of the political world and by asking them to think seriously about the boundaries of the political. While this may strike some as an approach slanted towards what is still generally, if a little unhelpfully, called political behaviour, it is not intended to endorse a behavioural view of politics. Our intention is to persuade students to see themselves as part of political life and as actors in it. This is why the earlier chapters in the book are concerned with the individual in politics. Later chapters concentrate upon corporate political actors and wider political processes to give a fuller picture of the complexities of government and politics.

Another method we use to demonstrate the wide-ranging scope and relevance of politics is to draw upon less conventional sources, but only as these are appropriate to the subject matter of different chapters. The point is to offer readers a more catholic range of illustrative and reading materials, which will help them to appreciate how politics both infuses all sorts of human activity and how the study of politics is illuminated by reference to, for example, literary genres like the novel, as well as film and theatre. So, at times, in the sections headed 'further reading' at the end of each chapter, we have interspersed standard academic references with somewhat more exotic fare.

It is also worth pointing out that the book is not an explicitly comparative textbook. This does not mean that it is dilatory in its use of illustrative materials of a comparative nature, or that it is Anglo-centric. Rather, the book does not adopt any systematic framework of comparison, least of all one which trades on the detailed comparison of a few political systems. Of course we are all aware of the advantages of comparison and of the extent to which much good social science is by definition comparative. But we want to avoid focusing on Britain, the USA and France, or on any other permutation of countries, because the main purpose of the text is the study of politics as an acacemic discipline. To complement our general approach we offer a broad range of illustrative case-studies and comparative materials throughout the text.

Finally, we wanted to write a book that students would find user-friendly, but not patronising. The use of 'think points' and 'exercises' throughout the text is not an attempt to spoon-feed the reader. They should be taken as opportunities to think more

deeply about the material introduced in the text and can be used by the individual reader or by the seminar group. As far as possible, we have tried to highlight the most important terms found in the text. These appear in bold as key words and reappear in a consolidated glossary at the end of the book.

The composition and production of the book owe much to the initial enthusiasm for the idea shown by Routledge and particularly by Caroline Wintersgill. Moira Taylor's advice has been invaluable in seeing the project to fruition, especially through its difficult final stages. Thanks are also due to a battalion of referees whose comments on the first draft were thoughtful and constructive. The alacrity of their collective response was a great help to us. We are grateful to Alan Grant for contributing the chapter on 'Politics below the nation-state' (Chapter 12) and for participating in our early discussions on the book. In addition, a number of our students made useful and sometimes salutary comments on different parts of the book in its draft stages. Several individuals made helpful contributions to the discussion of topics, chapters, illustrative materials and general student-centredness. In particular we would like to thank Jane Booth and Raia Prokhovnik for their continuing and active interest in the project.

Barrie Axford, Gary K. Browning
Richard Huggins, Ben Rosamond
John Turner

# Acknowledgements

Acknowledgements to extracts are printed on the page on which they are displayed and also in the Bibliography. Every effort has been made to contact rights-holders but in a few cases this has not been possible. Any omissions brought to our attention will be remedied in future editions if the author contacts Moira Taylor at Routledge.

# INTRODUCTION

*Barrie Axford and Gary K. Browning*

**Some features of the book**

**Explanation in politics**

**The language of politics**

**The organisation and contents of the book**

# Introduction

Politics is important. Even if we did not know this as a matter of intuition we would be left in no doubt after a day spent looking at television news programmes and from reading most newspapers. Life and death issues such as war and peace are shaped by political ideologies and decisions. The state is ever present in our everyday lives. Law and order, economic transactions, the values of a society and the myriad ways in which people of different nations interact with one another all involve political influences. Contested ideas of what is right and wrong and cultural identifications which give shape to people's notions of who they are reflect political allegiances. For all this, it is sometimes difficult to be entirely clear about what constitutes 'the political'.

---

**THINK POINT**

Consider if and how the following are political:
- A conversation about the crime rate in a bar.
- A tax on cigarettes.
- Taking part in a demonstration against the transport of live animals.
- Parents talking with children about the taking of drugs.

---

These may strike you as curious illustrations to use in a book about politics. But from the perspective of teachers of politics, we have found that students new to the academic discipline may have a rather narrow conception of 'the political'. Many seem to regard the political sphere as an arena largely populated by politicians, political parties, elections and the various institutions of government. Beyond these core actors and institutions lies a more shadowy world of pressure groups, the media and the ubiquitous 'social context' of politics, a potpourri of economic, cultural and social institutions and processes which provide the backdrop to political activity. This rough and ready conception of politics is confined, by and large, to what goes on inside territorial units of governance called nation-states, although sometimes it takes on board what goes on between them. Let us be quite clear here: we are not suggesting that this is wrong – no serious attempt to cover key aspects of political activity could dispense with these topics – rather that it is but one way to define politics and to delimit the field of study.

At this point, having thought about the four cases above, you might like to offer a definition of politics yourself. The sort of questions you should ask yourself are these:

- Is there an essence to political behaviour?
- If so, how does it differ from other sorts of behaviour?

For example, if having a conversation about crime rates in a bar is a political act, what makes it political? Is it something intrinsic to the act itself or is the act made political by the context in which it is taking place? Context does not mean just the bar, but things like the prevailing climate of opinion, the country in which the conversation is taking place, maybe even the frame of mind of the people involved. The same might be asked about writing a poem. On the face of it a private act of creativity does not look like a political act, but if we were to locate that activity in a certain kind of context, perhaps under a system of government in which any form of uncensored creativity is considered to be dangerous dissent, potentially regime-threatening, then it becomes a political act almost by default. For the student of politics these are important considerations because they either expand or limit the scope of what is studied and influence how it is studied.

If, as one recent textbook on the subject says, politics is the process by which groups make collective decisions (Hague, Harrop and Breslin, 1994), then it becomes a matter of both professional convention and judgement to decide what is entailed in trying to understand that process. Suppose we were to examine just such a process which involved one or more factions trying to affect a government's decision to build a new runway at an international airport. One way to proceed would be to look at the conflict as a battle between interests with different kinds of resources – money, membership and so on – and to see how effectively these resources were deployed to influence public authorities and established ways of making policy decisions. This would be perfectly legitimate and would undoubtedly fall within the rubric of the definition supplied above. If, however, we were more concerned with the motivations of those involved, perhaps in why they became activists, we would be better employed in looking at the relationships between their behaviour and factors which might have influenced it. At this point, the student of politics often has to draw upon seemingly non-political factors to aid explanation. Studying the leadership style and the policy impact of American Presidents or British Prime Ministers might require attention to their family background and psychological make-up as well as to the ways in which they are constrained by powerful sectional interests or foreign-policy commitments. Students of voting behaviour have always recognised the need to relate that eminently political activity of voting to the social and personal factors which affect it. In recent years feminists, among others, have also been responsible for pushing out the boundaries of political debate and language and therefore of the study of politics, by insisting that personal and particularly sexual relationships are inherently political. In doing so, they have challenged the status of the concept 'state' as the key unit for political analysis and the locus for political activity.

But while politics is in a sense everywhere and of undoubted significance in people's lives, if not always in their consciousness, it remains a very elusive activity. No single focus, no entire approach can provide all the answers to political questions. The purpose of this book is to provide, in an engaging manner, a comprehensive introduction to the study of politics. We have no illusions about the scale of this task and we have tried to combine accessibility with a robust examination of the main concepts, fields and issues in politics and a full appreciation of the various approaches to its study.

## Some features of the book

There are a number of features which make the book both accessible to the reader and useful as an interactive text for use between instructors and students:

- It covers a wide range of political activities in a wide variety of settings.
- It examines the various features of the political landscape by interspersing the narrative with a range of *extracts* reflecting aspects of political life and thinking, and *exercises* and *think points* designed to allow the reader to develop these topics more fully.
- The book is designed as an interactive text for use in class between instructors and students through the use of the exercises, think points and readings.
- Each chapter stands as an introduction to a topic in its own right, but there is extensive and systematic cross-referencing to the treatment of concepts and issues in other chapters, where this is appropriate, to demonstrate the connections between topics and chapters. For example, the reader is encouraged to think that a concept like individualism can be usefully dealt with under a number of headings.
- Thus the book may be read by people interested in particular themes, but also by those who are looking for a general treatment of the study of politics.
- Key words in the vocabulary of politics are highlighted in the text and short definitions are provided in the margins the first time they are used.
- A glossary of all the key words used is provided at the end of the book.
- In order to support readers who wish to find out more about the topics covered, in addition to the references made in the text itself, which include the labelling of key works, a short annotated further reading section is set out at the end of each chapter.
- The book is designed to show that the study of politics is about making links between its manifestations at a number of levels. For

this reason, we have tried to talk about the personal and the global, indicating connections between them, as well as with processes and institutions at the national and societal levels of analysis.

This seems to us to be an important consideration. Not all students see themselves as part of a political world, let alone as political animals, so it is part of the duty of a book of this sort to introduce people to the study of politics in ways that are intelligible and user-friendly. We have been at pains to explore the place of individuals in political life, both from the standpoint of certain strains of political philosophy and ideology which have a strong **normative** component and through the insights of **empirical** research into individual motivations and behaviour. There are two main reasons for doing this: (1) to show to readers that they too occupy a political space and possess some form of political identity and (2) to introduce a properly human dimension to the study of politics. This does not mean that we advocate an approach to the study of politics in which the individual is at the centre of inquiry and social and political structures are marginalised (arguments which are taken up in different ways in chapters 1–4), but that we want to demonstrate the ways in which individuals relate to and both affect and are affected by these larger structures, up to and including what many people now call the global level.

As for the latter concept, while the issues of inter- and transnationality are addressed in detail in Chapters 15 and 16, we have tried to infuse a global dimension into other chapters where this seemed appropriate. For example, the discussion of democracy and political participation in Chapter 4 makes explicit reference both to the impact of global communications technologies on participation and to the prospects for democracy within global institutions. The overall approach of the book is multi-dimensional in that it explores the relationships between political activity and economic and social factors and, where relevant, cuts across conventional divides – the individual, the societal and the global – the better to understand complex relationships between actors and institutions. The gathering pace of globalising pressures means that it is the world which is now becoming the appropriate **unit for analysis** as well as, perhaps rather than, national political systems. In doing all this we take full note of the methodological issues involved and debates about these are reported in full.

## Explanation in politics

The study of politics is fraught with issues for the would-be observer. Not only is there the distinction between what are called normative and empirical approaches to study, but there is also the question of whether to take as the unit for analysis the individual, the social or the global? Since the end of the Second World War the extent to which political study lends itself to 'scientific' methods has been hotly disputed, especially with regard

**Normative** The prescription of what should or ought to be the case as opposed to what, descriptively, is the case.

**Empirical** A term meaning sense or understanding derived from experience.

**Unit for analysis** The concrete object of inquiry: the individual, the primary group like the family, voluntary associations, formal organisations like political parties, whole societies, nation-states, even the world as a whole.

to aspects of political behaviour like voting and other areas of political participation. Whether or not an approach can be called scientific is still very much open to question. If the term means something as broad as gaining systematic knowledge of the world around us, both natural and human, then most students of politics would have little trouble with the statement that the discipline is scientific, or potentially so. Of course some normative theorists would argue that systematic knowledge is not enough and that the purpose of studying politics is to uncover information relevant to the achievement of a better, or even the best society or the good life. Others, who may or may not be wedded to normative theorising still doubt that politics can ever be studied scientifically if by that is meant any of the things outlined below.

## Theories of politics that can be disproved by empirical evidence

For example, it might be asked how you could 'disprove' that democracy is a better form of government than dictatorship? The point here is that some fundamental political questions do not lend themselves to claims of truth or falsity. On a more mundane basis, critics also argue that proof is also hard to come by given the difficulty of agreeing on the definition of key concepts, collecting data, controlling for all the different factors which may affect something like voting or deciding what impels people to bomb federal buildings in the United States, or Canary Wharf in London.

## The ability to replicate methods and results through laboratory experimentation and/or statistical methods

For both ethical and logistical reasons, social and political researchers are rarely able to conduct the kind of controlled experiments common in the natural and technological sciences. Where they are able to generate and manipulate large bodies of statistical data, issues about the representative-ness of the samples used and the integrity of data sources over time present major constraints on the use of rigorous scientific method. When comparative research is being conducted these problems are exacerbated due to the relatively small number of cases (for example, countries) which can be studied, the problem with establishing functional equivalence across different systems (would ritual beheading of a ruler be the equivalent of a presidential election in terms of securing the peaceful succession of elites?) and, as we shall see below, because of the need both to generalise about political phenomena and to remain sensitive to local context and local meanings.

## The ability to rely on the visible and the measurable to explain political phenomena

It may be possible to examine the relationships between, say, the social characteristics of Congressional Districts in the USA and their voting patterns over a long period of time. Collectable documentary evidence exists for such activities and so do reliable statistical packages for computer analysis. But the same may not be true of the 'proof' needed to explain some critical but less observable relationships in political life. Take, for example, the thesis that in capitalist societies the working classes are always in a state of '**false consciousness**', meaning that they either do not recognise their subordination to a dominant class, or else are persuaded to applaud or to rationalise it in some way. In both cases they are held to be 'falsely conscious' because they fail to recognise their own real interests. Now, if the concept of false consciousness were part of a research project, just how would you set about proving (i) that people are suffering from it and that (ii) as a result they do not act in their own best interests?

**False consciousness** A term associated with Marxist thought which maintains that individuals and the class to which they belong may well demonstrate a sense of social understanding that is predominantly 'false', in that it hides from them or prevents them from recognising the 'real' nature of their position within the social order and the extent to which they are exploited.

### *The ability to distinguish between and maintain the separation of fact and value*

The idea that a scientific study of politics would be value-free, that is, not just based on things being a matter of opinion, strikes many people as at best mistaken and at worse morally repugnant. Clearly there are important considerations here, not least for comparative research across nations. If we study something like legislatures across quite different political systems, it is often hard to abstain from making judgements on the basis of criteria which have little to do with the hard and 'neutral' evidence available to us. Thus we might observe that in democratic systems, legislatures are institutions for helping to keep governments accountable, while in authoritarian systems they are a convenient means of making the passage of laws appear legitimate. Classifying legislatures on the basis of the functions they perform is a proper task for political scientists; making statements about the propriety of the tasks performed by particular legislatures may be thought at best unprofessional, at worst unscientific. As with the normative–empirical distinction there are different views on this issue.

### *The ability to make lawlike assertions or specify invariant relationships or else establish clear limits to the explanatory power of a theory*

There are no laws in the social sciences, or, to be properly and scientifically cautious, there are no laws yet. For the most part students of politics have to be content with more humble achievements: cataloguing the incidence of phenomena, setting up schemes of classification (participatory democracy, liberal democracy, democratic–elitist and so on) and fitting cases into them. The widespread use of statistical methods has led to an empirical political science which uses the language of variables, which talks about degrees of association between them and looks for probabilistic and not causal relationships. As we shall see in Chapters 2, 3 and 4, the development of a political science made in this image is closely linked with the rise of what Heinz Eulau (1963) called 'the behavioural persuasion in politics', which revolutionised (some critics say trivialised) the study of individual political behaviour and entrenched the collection and analysis of numerical data at the heart of political research.

Political behaviour, ideas and institutions change over time and space, and often the study of politics consists in the historical tracing of these changes without adding general theories which supply explanations of why these changes took place. In this book the analysis of institutions and processes tries to reflect an historical and descriptive approach to the study of politics, as well as explicating various theoretical positions. Even in the absence of theorising, description is often supplemented by the use of **models**, which, while not supplying explanations or predictions of future behaviour, set out clear ways in which the logic of political action and institutional change can be understood. Of course, there are grand theories of the human condition, and some of them are rehearsed in the chapters which follow, notably Chapter 7.

**Model** A representation of events and processes which focuses on key aspects of what is going on in them.

## The language of politics

A focus upon the allegedly scientific nature of political study necessarily draws attention to the very language of politics. The study of politics is conducted mainly through language as the primary medium through which meaning is conveyed. Symbolic representation of the world around us is the key element in the construction of any language system. We use language not only to express and exchange common understandings, but also to tell others who we are. When journalists talk about politics as being 'a battle-ground' or use some theatrical metaphor for political conflict, they are not just describing a state of affairs, but locating it in a system of meaning where politics is understood as an adversarial pursuit, perhaps red in tooth and claw.

The point is that language is not a neutral medium of communication, even if it is a rich one. Many words carry messages which are very context-specific in their meaning. To describe someone as 'homely' in the USA is taken as a form of insult because of its associations with plainness, whereas in Britain the word carries overtones of warmth, cosiness and so on. Feminists believe that apparently neutral language, or terms which have been accepted as generic descriptions of things – '*man*kind', or '*His* will be done' to refer to the power of the Christian God – are symbolic devices in the subjugation of women. We can see something of the same thing when talking about political terms or words used in the study of politics. 'Terrorist' is not a neutral or unambiguous term that lends itself readily to simple classification. If we were to classify a 'terrorist' as someone who challenges the power of the government of an independent state through violent means, have we abrogated our duty to distinguish not only between types of terrorism, but also whether a regime is deemed legitimate or not? When does terrorism commute to legitimate opposition, or the terrorist become the liberator?

The use of descriptive political concepts for purposes of classification, model-building and analysis is also shot through with ambiguity and contested meanings. This is not, or not only, because commentators cannot agree on how to describe visible phenomena, but because they cannot agree on the various manifestations of the phenomena, or even on criteria by which they would be able to recognise them. The classic case of this is the key concept of 'power'. Some of the debates surrounding the use of the term 'power' are set down in Chapters 3, 13 and 14. For now it is enough to note that as a concept (and concepts are the building blocks of any body of knowledge) power is essentially contested, because there are different definitions of what power 'is' and therefore how it appears or is exercised.

Essentially contested concepts like 'power' or 'freedom' are sometimes difficult because they have normative aspects, that is they express values. Thinking about values in politics lends itself to distinct types of theorising and these are discussed in the chapters on political ideas and practice (Chapters 6, 7 and 8). Values cannot be settled by pointing to actual features of the political worlds in which we live. Values are supported by reasons which may be questioned or challenged, regardless of science. Philosophical analysis may clarify the nature of the values being discussed, but it cannot demonstrate in a knockdown fashion what is to be done. Values are, however, of considerable importance in political life, for they are what animate people, and political theorists and ideologists have offered a variety of justifications for selected political values as constituting important signposts for the direction of political practice.

## The organisation and contents of the book

This book is aimed at providing a general introduction to politics. In pursuit of this goal it does not deploy any single approach as offering the high road to truth. Neither does it privilege any one area of politics over another. We have not tried to undertake any systematic form of comparative analysis, although comparison is an integral part of all forms of knowledge generation. Comparisons are made, mainly across national societies and we have sought to take illustrative materials from a wide range of countries as they are appropriate to the topic under discussion. However, as the main purpose of the exercise is to vivify the discussion of concepts and different areas of politics, we have not attempted any overarching use of the many forms of the comparative method to, variously, describe variations in political phenomena, test hypotheses about them, establish classifications of political phenomena or make predictions on the basis of our observations. Rather, we have reported on the application of the comparative method by different sorts of theorists and investigators, including those who make detailed historical comparisons of the processes whereby the world has become modern, and we have reported summaries of comparative data to support discussions of topics as various as human rights and political participation.

A good deal of illustrative material is used because we believe that politics comes alive for the student when it can be seen how decisions and actions affect particular people at specific times. Theories are of interest in that they abstract from the particular, but it might be argued that they are only relevant and interesting insofar as they actually relate to specific cases. A good example of the cases cited in this book is the extended treatment of the policy process given in Chapter 14. Here the *Brent Spar* case is taken to illustrate environmental policy-making, which is seen as having implications for a variety of European states. Likewise in Chapter 6, 'Concepts and issues', general discussion of the nature of freedom is given focus by relating it to the very real dilemmas of the Salman Rushdie case. Here, the freedom of an author is challenged to the point of death by a belief system which rates fundamental truths higher than freedom of expression. The book as a whole aims to make the nature of politics graphic and relevant to everyday experience. Throughout the book we have tried to engage readers, so that they might reflect on or argue with what has been written. One obvious way we have tried to do this is by introducing think points along the way. These are designed to encourage reflection and argument about what has been written. In other words, they are meant to foster the reader's active engagement with the book. The think points are not answered directly in the text itself, partly because they do not admit of simple and obvious responses. Politics is a diverse set of activities; learning about politics is a process of thinking through arguments that are often difficult and seldom uncontested. The main aim of the use of think points is to contribute to this process.

The book covers four broad areas of discussion and these constitute the four parts of the book:

## Part I: People and politics, Chapters 1–5

In Chapter 1, without assuming answers to the disputed question about the nature and worth of politics, the concept of the individual is explored, along with the issue of how far it is possible to study politics without having to theorise about entities larger than the individual. The idea of the individual as this appears (or does not appear) in different types of society and different sorts of social theory is examined and the impact of the individual upon different forms of the collective is explored. The conclusion of the chapter points to a larger theme of the book, namely that politics is a multi-dimensional project in which institutions such as laws, moral rules, corporate and collective bodies all matter, just as individuals matter.

In Chapter 2 the area of political socialisation, or how people learn about politics and acquire political identities, is discussed. The various attempts by political scientists to understand these complex processes are reviewed. The conclusion of this chapter is that the individual who is socialised (by the family, the school and other key institutions and processes) does not get lost in a thicket of social roles. Individuals are presented as active subjects involved in, rather than conditioned by, the processes of socialisation. Readers are invited to reflect upon their own experiences of socialisation.

Chapter 3 moves from the individual experience of social learning to examine political cultures and collective identities. The analysis recognises that the relationships between individual behaviour and attitudes and social and political norms are interactive. It explores the constructed nature of political cultures and the fact that they change over time. It offers a critique of the the idea of political cultures as monolithic and emphasises the political importance of subcultures and hybrid identities. At the same time it acknowledges that relatively common frameworks of assumptions and values serve to anchor individual behaviour and give meaning to institutional forms like electoral systems. Other themes, such as the putative link between political culture and political stability and the ideological functions of cultural norms as elements in different forms of social control, are also rehearsed.

Chapter 4 continues the discussion of the interaction between individual behaviour and political and social contexts by looking at the area of political participation. A variety of ongoing practices are observed, from the conventional to the exotic, and the place of participation in democratic and non-democratic systems is examined. The possibilities for new forms of democratic participation are canvassed through reference to the ideas of cyber-democracy and cosmopolitan democracy. Different theories of participation are advanced, drawing upon explanations used by economists to explain consumer behaviour, psychological theories of motivation and the more cautious attempts to associate different forms of political participation with various individual and social characteristics.

In Chapter 5 the book takes on something of a different hue, while still being concerned with the interaction between individuals and social and political structures. Here we examine questions related to the reproduction and change of social and political structures. For the first time in the book an explicitly historical approach to understanding political life is discussed, through a consideration of theories of modernisation and evolutionary and revolutionary change. Change at both the individual and systemic levels is examined and particular areas of change such as electoral change and the transformations in Central and Eastern Europe after 1989 receive further discussion.

### Part 2: Politics and ideas, Chapters 6–8

These chapters switch the focus of attention from the institutional and cultural settings of political behaviour to more general and evaluative forms of political thinking, which draw upon philosophical styles of thought, and explore their relevance to current issues in politics.

Chapter 6 takes various concepts and issues and looks at recent attempts to theorise about them. Justice and freedom, as key concepts, are examined, and leading normative theorists of politics such as Rawls, Nozick and Berlin are analysed. The chapter also relates the abstract discussion of political concepts to practical concrete issues such as the Rushdie case and the treatment of animals.

In Chapter 7 the variety of thinking and theorising which goes under the heading of political thought is discussed. The distinctiveness of Islamic political thought and the special questions thrown up by the treatment of women in political thought are examined. The rest of the chapter is devoted to looking at a number of classical political philosophers whose works have stood the test of time in opening up theoretical and evaluative perspectives on the meaning and purpose of political life. The nature and methodology of the history of political thought are examined as part of the process of reviewing the contributions of past political philosophers. At the same time, some of the most engaging and thoughtful scholarship of recent years in this area is also reviewed.

Chapter 8, on political ideology, concludes this part of the book. Political ideology is a style of thought of great importance, but a tricky subject to get to grips with. Ideologies are explained as mapping out large-scale visions of society and politics and as helping to orient individuals within a political culture. They are also seen as linking individuals to the structures of social and political life. Political ideologies are taken as being poised between theory and practice. A number of ideologies are reviewed and exemplified in the form of extracts.

## Part 3: Politics in action: Chapters 9–14

This segment of the book, which contains the largest number of chapters, continues the theme of making connections between the individual and the larger structures of state and society. The chapters explore the relations between citizens and different forms of state, the institutions of both national and local government and the manner in which various kinds of social and political groupings – parties and interest groups – try to exert influence over decison-makers. The place of the print and broadcast media in this process is also examined. The final chapter in this part looks at policy processes and at the ways in which resources are allocated and distributed.

Chapter 9 examines theories of the state. It covers state forms in liberal democratic, communist and fascist systems, reflecting upon theories of the state in each. The key concept of legitimacy is explored in this chapter, along with questions about the ways in which people come into contact with the state as subjects and citizens from birth to death.

Chapter 10 is the first of two chapters which examine different aspects of national government. In this chapter the formal national institutions of government are discussed in established and emerging democracies, author-itarian regimes and different types of developing nations. The increasing significance of political executives of different types is explored, along with the issue of executive–legislative relations, including that of accountability. The role of the judiciary in review processes and in 'informal' policy-making is considered.

In Chapter 11, which is the second of the 'national government' chapters, forms of bureaucratic politics are analysed, including the growth of quasi-state organisations as well as the more conventional bureaucratic apparatuses of the modern state. Here too the theme of the state is central, but light is also cast on the transformation of the state which is taking place 'from within'. In subsequent chapters (Chapters 15 and 16) we consider changes wrought from outside the territorial boundaries of the state.

Chapter 12 shifts the focus of analysis to sub-national politics and government, looking at the territorial distribution of power across different forms of state. Issues of sub-national rule in various sorts of unitary and federal system are explored, including the vexed question of the constitutional relationships between federating units, and between them and central governments. The legal and democratic status of local government in an era of big government is also considered.

Chapter 13 takes up what might be called the more informal aspects of politics and government, by examining important features of the politics of influence. Three main areas are discussed: the role of interest groups in articulating and sometimes in aggregating demands on government from sections of the population. Different systems of group representation and mediation are examined: the role of political parties as organised expressions of ideology and commitment and their functions as representative and governing agencies and, finally, the place of the communications media in producing an increasingly visual and a highly mediated form of politics in many countries.

Chapter 14, the last in this part of the book, uses the policy process as a way of highlighting important aspects of the working of different kinds of political systems. The examination of the highly topical policy networks debate not only casts light on the formal processes of resource allocation, but also illuminates more general discussions of the nature and distribution of power in societies. The nature of public policy is discussed and models and theories of the process examined. Some of these are very abstract, but the emphasis of the chapter is on exemplifying these debates through case-study material, such as media policy and the Brent-Spar incident.

## Part 4: Politics beyond the nation-state, Chapters 15 and 16

In these last two chapters of the book we look at politics beyond the nation-state. At points throughout the text we have alluded to the global dimension of an increasing amount of political, economic and cultural activity; these two chapters set out to examine what the idea of politics beyond the state really means. In both chapters the nation-state is the conceptual point of departure.

In Chapter 15 some conventional thinking about the nature of national and international politics and governance is explored. Key concepts in the analysis of international relations, such as sovereignty, are outlined and various ways of theorising international politics are analysed, especially as these bear on the formation of international organisations and multilateral institutions. The United Nations and the European Union are discussed in greater detail to illustrate the particular nature of politics beyond the nation-state and to exemplify the features of nation-less forms of governance.

Chapter 16 picks up on the analysis of territorial forms of politics and government as a way into the discussion of globalising tendencies which are affecting the conduct of national politics and the integrity of the territorial state. The vexed question of what is meant by globalisation is examined and different theories of the development of the global system described. Globalisation is presented as a contested phenomenon in terms of its impact upon individual, local, organisational and national identities, and one which is contributing to a redefinition of social and political life.

At the end of this substantial book the reader will feel, we hope, that s/he has been offered a digestible and thorough introduction to the diverse areas of political life and to the ways in which these are studied. We have tried to present politics and the study of politics as being not just about institutions or processes or ideas but about all of these, and as being more than just a study of discrete topics. There is no doubt that whatever the merits of this book, students of politics will still feel somewhat at sea given the scope and complexity of the subject being studied, but then uncertainty is a useful intellectual state and an endemic political one.

# PART 1 PEOPLE AND POLITICS

# 1 INDIVIDUALS: IS POLITICS REALLY ABOUT PEOPLE?

*Barrie Axford*

## Introduction

*Three questions for analysis*
*Parts or wholes: should we study individuals or structures?*

## The modern individual

*Individuals as utility maximisers: the myth of 'economic' man*

## Individualism in action

*Individuals and rights*
*Individualism and collectivism*
*Communitarianism*
*Beyond individualism and collectivism: the postmodern condition*

## Individuals and the capacity for meaningful political action

## Conclusion

## Further reading

# Individuals: Is politics really about people?

## Introduction

In the Introduction to this volume we learned that the concepts and ideas which are at the heart of political study are themselves intellectual battle-grounds. Key terms like 'power' are linguistic, and often moral, minefields over which the student of politics has to pass with great care, and it is easy to confuse, or else conflate, the normative with the empirical or to trans-gress seeming rules about the basis of scientific inquiry. So in the study of politics very little can be taken for granted, and this caveat extends to what we study and how we study it.

In this chapter we will begin our examination of the nature of political inquiry and the scope and content of politics by looking at the place of the individual in political life. The term 'individual' is in common use, so much so that we tend to take its meaning for granted. We are all individuals in the sense that we are single human animals, but while this is a necessary starting point for analysis, it is not sufficient to explain the importance of the concept in much political and social science. The idea of the individual and the quality of individuality suggest uniqueness and originality. Each of us is unique in certain definable ways but, perhaps more significantly, in undefinable ways too. What makes each of us different is very hard to explain, despite a great deal of research into what contributes to the making of an individual's 'personality'. A good deal of scientific (and not so scien-tific) debate has centred on whether personality is innate (genetic) or made through social intercourse and social learning. The important point for our purposes lies not so much in explanations of individuality, but in the status ascribed to the individual in political and social theory, as well as in everyday life. For example, a society, or any collectivity, which sees itself as made up of individuals is likely to be one where the virtues of independence are strongly embedded in custom and law. In such societies expressions of individuality will be generally applauded, and attempts to constrain the free choices of individuals in lawful pursuit of their interests would require careful justification. In influential strands of Western political philosophy, the status of the individual has been enshrined in belief systems which assert both the *centrality* of the individual in explanations of social life, and the *primacy* of the individual relative to any or all collective forms – the group, the nation, the state and so on. Needless to say such doctrines have been hotly contested, both because of their theoretical premises and because of their political implications. As such we will look not only at expressions of individualism but also consider the status of the individual as the appropriate unit for analysis in the study of politics, as well as discussing the pros and cons of pitching inquiry at the individual **level of analysis**.

Of course, in a discipline where little can be taken for granted, choosing the individual as a starting point for analysis is contentious, despite the commonsense assumption that in politics, as in life, people are at the centre of things. But we should not be misled by the appeal of commonsense assumptions and explanations. While the study of politics is necessarily a blend of sophisticated common sense, normative judgement and scientific knowledge or professional technique, it is also, in Thomas Kuhn's (1970) expression, 'pre-paradigmatic', or lacking in agreement on the fundamental questions for inquiry and on the rules under which knowledge can be generated. Starting with the idea of the individual, and with what motivates and influences political behaviour, and then examining individuals as members of groups, political parties, legislatures and nation-states, is a valuable approach to the study of politics but by no means the only one. But how could it be otherwise?

## Three questions for analysis

There are three main issues about the individual and politics which will be addressed in this chapter. Some of the points discussed here will be re-examined in later chapters from different perspectives. The issues are:

First, the key question of the relationships between the individual (sometimes termed the agent or the subject) and wider social processes and institutions (called structures). Individualistic or agent-centred accounts of social and political life argue that 'social wholes', that is, institutions like social classes or nations, are reducible to or explained by the motives and actions of individuals. At the other extreme, structure-centred positions believe that individual identities and behaviour are formed and take place within social relations which are governed by rules, or by 'history encoded into rules', as the sociologists March and Simon (1958) say. Because of this, to edit Karl Marx slightly, while people may make their own history, they do so in circumstances over which they have had little or no control. Between these poles lie a range of would-be explanations which try to reconcile individualistic and holistic theories.

Second, the extent to which the concept and status of the individual, along with related ideas about individual rights, are rooted in a particular intellectual tradition known generally as **Enlightenment** philosophy and associated with a particular historical pattern of social and political development, usually called **modernity**.

---

**Level of analysis** For our purposes, the difference between studying individuals and collectives of different sorts. Choosing one level of analysis as opposed to another determines the sort of inferences which can be made from data of various sorts.

**Enlightenment** The eighteenth-century Enlightenment 'project' was based on a belief in the universality of reason and the power of scientific explanation. The individual was at the centre of the philosophical and political project, with human emancipation seen as following from the spread of rational inquiry and decision-making.

**Modernity** The distinct way of life found in 'modern' societies. A process beginning in Western Europe in about the fifteenth century, the idea of modernity achieved an intellectual flowering during the Enlightenment. It is usual to tie modernity, or becoming modern, to the emergence of the nation-state, industrialism and the institution of private property. Modernity is also linked to the growth of bureaucratic organisations and secular and individualist ideas.

The spread of ideas and institutions associated with the Enlightenment around the world has been a feature of the ways in which many societies have become modern, but not all have embraced its precepts fully. For example, societies and political systems influenced by Marxism-Leninism, like those of the former Soviet Union and the People's Republic of China, have preferred to subsume individuality in wider collective identities and purposes – those of 'the State', 'the Party' or the idea of 'the People' as a whole. Even within those mainly Western countries where individualism has flourished there are significant variations on how the individual is perceived, and in how far individualism is incorporated into constitutional rights, or in ideas like consumer sovereignty. It may even be that the dominant ideology of Enlightenment individualism is giving way in the West to a **postmodern** version of individuality and new forms of politics to accompany it. This shift is sometimes discussed in terms of the transformation of modernity into postmodernity.

**Postmodern** Literally, beyond the modern, and suggesting a fragmentation of modernist beliefs, identities and certainties.

Third, the extent to which the individual retains the capacity for meaningful political action under present conditions and in different parts of the world. This is not just a matter of showing that under certain types of government, or in some political cultures, people are freer to express dissent or influence political decisions than in others. Clearly this is important, but equally so is the question of access to the kinds of resources that may be useful coin in the political realm – money, of course, but also information, weight of numbers, expertise and so on. We should also consider the possibility that the individual's ability to intervene effectively as a political actor may be affected by the relocation of decision-making from one level of government to another, a process which can be seen in the transfer of power from national governments to bodies like the European Community. At such a pass the possibility of face-to-face interaction, or of any kind of intimate connections between governors and governed becomes very remote, and individuals have to rely upon forms of mediated interaction – pressure groups, political parties, newspapers, faxes, telephones or computer communication – to exercise their power as individuals.

Let us examine each of these issues in some detail.

## Parts or wholes: should we study individuals or structures?

This is one of the fundamental questions of political and social analysis, and one which appears in different ways throughout this book. The agency–structure divide referred to above points up apparently fundamental differences in assumptions about and approaches to the study of political and social life. Because of this it is quite common to find radically different positions in the literature about the value of one approach relative to another. We can identify three main positions on this issue.

The first, which we will call *mutual exclusivity* requires that one studies *either* individuals *or* structures, but not both, and insists that studying one does not allow inferences to be made about the other. Attempts to do so merely end up with fallacious inferences being made about complex and possibly causal relationships. Thus, it is crucial to avoid discussing collectives, for example political parties or parliaments, in terms of the characteristics of the individuals who populate them. This *individualistic fallacy* treats institutions as no more than individuals writ large. On the other hand, it is equally important not to discuss individuals as if they simply take on the characteristics of the organisations of which they are members. This constitutes the *ecological or systemic fallacy*. Attention to the appropriate level of analysis makes for good social science, or so it is often argued. However, the rigid separation of individual and systemic levels of analysis is now increasingly subject to criticism, and we shall look at some of this below under the third approach to agency–structure relations.

The second strand, which we will call *reductionist*, holds that one set of variables can be explained wholly or in part by reference to another set. Thus, inquiry couched at the individual level of analysis might take collective or structural concepts, like the state or the **political system**, or the middle class, to be no more than expressions of the aggregate behaviour and attitudes of individuals at a particular time and in a particular place. Structural accounts of political life reduce individual motivation to an effect of pre-existing social, economic, cultural and political forms, or else remove individuals (agency) from any constitutive part in the making of social life, save as the players of predetermined historical roles. As we shall see below, there are many variations on these stark positions.

The third, which we will label *structurationist*, following the example of the sociologist Anthony Giddens, attempts to bridge the divide by arguing that what others call structures are in fact the product of the day-to-day interaction of individuals with each other and with the institutions of daily living with which they are in contact. For example, from a structurationist perspective, the structure or institutions of democracy are reproduced through both routine and dramatic actions by individuals when they vote, stand as candidates, follow courses in current affairs, or take to the streets in protest against a government policy. To take a different example, the reproduction of capitalism as a worldwide system of production and exchange is reliant upon mundane actions like shoppers buying goods in a supermarket. These shoppers are not consciously reproducing capitalism when they buy a tin of dogmeat or an avocado pear, but the effect is the same as if they were. In both cases the point is that structure of any sort is not external to individuals, but is given form and meaning through routine social practices by individuals or by individuals in concert. Structures are, therefore, *socially constructed* by the very people who engage in social practice. At the same time, structures are not just reducible to individual motivations and actions, since they often pre-exist and outlast individual actors and thus achieve a sort of permanence – or, as Giddens says, 'objectivity' – for many people because of this. So actors make (or reproduce) structures, but they are also informed and constrained by them.

**Political system** An expression sometimes used as a synonym for 'country', but which technically refers to the relationships, processes and institutions which make up a distinct political universe. Thus, the French political system consists of 'inputs' from society to the formal institutions of government, in the form of public opinion, pressure group activity and so on, while the institutions of government process these inputs to produce 'outputs' in the form of laws, policies and even norms and values. For a critical discussion of this concept applied to the policy process, see Chapter 14.

A. Giddens (1993) *New Rules of Sociological Method*, 2nd edn, Cambridge: Polity.

### Forms of individualist analysis

Using individuals as the unit for analysis is strongly associated with particular types of political and social inquiry. These cluster under the broad heading of **methodological individualism** but show some important differences of emphasis, as well as deriving from different intellectual traditions. Positions which are entirely voluntarist regard social life as mutable, no more than the outcome of the unconstrained choices and actions of individuals. Some strands of economic theorising applied to political life offer a particularly stark theory of human motivation which takes as axiomatic the self-interested behaviour of individuals, and this is explored more fully below in the section on 'The modern individual' (see pp. 22–46).

**Behaviouralist** assumptions about individuals as units for analysis seldom go this far. Behaviouralists are concerned with personal needs and motivations and concentrate upon attitude formation, perceptions and social learning processes which involve the internalisation by individuals of cultural values and norms. Much of this sort of work involves studying what people actually do – as voters, members of voluntary associations or family members – by employing a range of research techniques including sample surveys, oral interviews and detailed observation of individuals and small groups.

Other variants of the individualist approach to politics and social life, sometimes clustered under the title *subjectivist or interpretative sociology*, reject the behaviouralist claim that studying what people do or how they acquire identities and learn roles is a very fruitful way to understand either the complexities of individual psychology or the patterns of social life. Instead, they argue that researchers should look for the meanings which underlie action, so that each individual's experience and perceptions become the appropriate subject matter for the study of politics (Berger and Luckmann 1966). Unlike the behaviouralists, who sought to make the study of politics systematic, even scientific, by looking for regularities across the sum of individual behaviours, and also tried to identify the laws which might follow from such observations, subjectivists believe that it is impossible to generalise from individual experience.

### Forms of functional and structural analysis

Like those of their individualist counterparts, accounts which privilege structures as the right units of and level for analysis also differ about what phenomena they study and in the kind of questions they ask about them. By and large, structure-centred arguments concentrate upon whole societies, nations, government institutions, organisations or social groupings like class,

**Methodological individualism**
A philosophical and empirical focus on the individual and individual behaviour.

**Behaviouralism** A movement in postwar political science, concerned with both the generation of law-like generalisations about the political world and shifting the emphasis of political studies away from its traditional legal-institutional manifestation. With a focus upon individual behaviour, the 'behaviouralist approach', as it is called, is linked with quantitative research techniques designed to generate testable hypotheses about measurable attitudes and observable behaviour, thus rendering the study of politics more scientific.

*These ideas are discussed extensively in Chapters 2 and 3.*

but also take in social institutions like that of private property or marriage. Most, though by no means all, structural accounts believe that social phenomena can be explained without reference to the motivations and expectations of individuals. For example, functionalism seeks to uncover the requisites which are necessary for the maintenance, modernisation and stability of social and political systems. Basically these involve the ways in which individuals are socialised into roles and how they adapt to changing circumstances in their pursuit of socially sanctioned goals. We return to this question in Chapter 5 when discussing theories of political change.

**Marxism** There are various interpretations, although, essentially, emphasis is placed on the way in which the economic process shapes social and class relations and power in the policy-making process.

**Marxism**, as a body of doctrine, appears mainly structuralist, in that it too is exercised by the large-scale and long-term forces which shape societies – class conflict, technological developments and property conventions – and not by the personal histories of individuals (Althusser, 1969). Yet some debates over the canonical status of Marx's thought depict him as a humanist, very aware of the role of individuals in making history. But even in this guise he is never a fully paid-up voluntarist, but rather a theorist attuned to the idea that social life can be explained by charting the strong currents in world history, but also by taking note of the scurryings of human actors who are not entirely preconditioned.

Structurationist arguments start from the point that structures do not subsist automatically, they have to be made (and reproduced) by individual actors. This, says the philosopher Roy Bhaskar (1976) is not always, or often for that matter, a case of people consciously deciding to reproduce something – democracy, capitalism or marriage – although it can be. More often reproduction results from people simply doing routine things – witness our supermarket shopper – and having unintended, or perhaps unthought of consequences, following from their actions. At the same time, actions can only have meaning for individuals when they are set in meaningful contexts – indeed some actions, perhaps voting or getting a passport, are only possible within very particular and recognisable structures, like elections and laws on nationality.

---

**THINK POINT**
- These are rather abstract ideas; look through them again, perhaps making more detailed reference to some of the authors cited. You should be able to see how these ideas can be translated into more concrete matters relating to the study of politics and maybe in relation to your own experience.

---

## The modern individual

The concept of modernity, which we defined earlier, is a complex one referring to an historical period, a cluster of institutions which are usually understood as being typically modern, and a body of philosophical thought. The institutional forms are industrialism, market capitalism, the nation-state and the international system of nation-states. The political sociologist Goran Therborn talks about modernity being an 'epoch turned to the future' (Therborn 1995: 4), while Anthony Giddens says that modernity refers to 'modes of social life and organisation which emerged in Europe from about the sixteenth century onwards and which subsequently became more or less worldwide in their influence' (Giddens 1990: 1). Of most direct concern to this chapter is the whole body of cultural and philosophical knowledge which is the heritage of the European Enlightenment.

The Enlightenment took place during the period when the various structures of modern societies were being laid down in Europe, and so its impact upon the ways in which people perceived these processes, how they explained them and how they came to understand their own place in the wider scheme of things is seminal. Enlightenment thought emphasised the possibility of individual and social progress through the use of science. In this scheme of things, the individual subject is central, because the individual is the (rational) agent of change and thus the main engine of social progress. Above all, the individual subject is said to be 'indivisible' and to possess certain innate characteristics which are unique and unchanging. Chief among these is the capacity for reason or rational thought. The political ideology known as liberalism also places great stress on the capacities of the rational individual as both a key political and economic actor.

*Liberalism as an ideology is examined in Chapter 8.*

The modern age established a new and radical form of individualism, which came to a full flowering with the Enlightenment of the eighteenth century. In pre-modern times and in traditional societies the individual was seen as no more (though no less) than a figure subject to the overwhelming forces of history and of circumstance, hedged about by all manner of constraints – including those of birth, of status and rank, as well as by superstition and custom. **Renaissance** thought and Enlightenment rationality freed the individual from this great weight of history and tradition, at least in principle. No longer simply a small part of the medieval Great Chain of Being, the individual or human subject was reborn as sovereign or autonomous, ready and equipped to play a full part in the making of the world, but this time as a lead player. Raymond Williams, the philosopher and literary critic, has this to say on the making of the modern individual:

**Renaissance** A sixteenth-century movement in Europe which brought a more questioning and secular approach to art and literature and thus to the place of humans in the order of things.

> The emergence of notions of individuality in the modern sense can be related to the break-up of the medieval social, economic and religious order. In the general movement against feudalism there was a new stress on a man's personal existence over and above his place or function in a rigid hierarchical society. There was a related stress, in Protestantism, on a man's direct and individual relation to God, as opposed to this relation mediated by the Church. But it was not until the late seventeenth and eighteenth centuries that a new mode of analysis, in logic and mathematics, postulated the individual as the substantial category . . . from which other categories, and especially collective categories were derived. The political thought of the Enlightenment mainly followed this model. Argument began from individuals, who had an initial and primary existence, and laws and forms

> of society derived from them: by submission, as in Hobbes, by contract or consent, or by the new version of natural law in liberal thought. In classical economics, trade was described in a model which postulated separate individuals who . . . decided at some starting point to enter into economic or commercial relations. In utilitarian ethics, separate individuals calculated the consequences of this or that action which they might undertake.
>
> (R. Williams 1976: 135–6)

The Enlightenment creed outlined by Williams is very far from dead, but the history of modern societies has been anything but a linear progression towards the good society where rationality, self-development and individual autonomy hold sway. Liberal theories of government, based on individual rights and the consent of the governed, have had to come to terms with the phenomenon of mass politics, brokered by organised political parties and regulated by the bureaucratic structures of the nation-state. Modernism's claim to relegate the brutish and irrational side of human nature to the historical dustbin and to lead humankind to sunlit uplands peopled by rational beings who exercise a complete, though benign, mastery over nature, also looks somewhat threadbare in the light of much recent history. Any catalogue of this more drear account of the unfolding of modernity would have to include the random, but, tellingly, the more systematic, plundering of the idea that individuals possess universal qualities and enjoy 'inalienable' rights as a consequence of their very humanity. All lists are selective, but the following all point to a dark side of modernity in which the systematic exclusion (and worse) of people is justified on the basis of their imputed *collective* attributes, and through the use of stereo-types: the 'Terror' which followed the definitive modern event of the French Revolution in 1789; the near-genocide of the Native American peoples, carried out by those claiming to act in the name of freedom and a 'Manifest Destiny' to tame a savage frontier; and the horror of the extermination of Jews, homosexuals and Gypsies by the Nazis.

> The Utes are actual, practical Communists and the government should be ashamed to foster and encourage them in their idleness and wanton waste of property. Living off the bounty of a paternal but idiotic Indian Bureau, they actually become too lazy to draw their rations in the regular way but insist on taking what they want wherever they find it. Removed to the Indian Territory, the Utes could be fed and clothed for about one half what it now costs the government.
>
> Honourable N. C. Meeker, the well-known Superintendant of the White River agency, was formerly a fast friend and ardent admirer of the Indians. He went to the agency in the firm belief that he could manage the Indians successfully by kind treatment, patient precept and good example. But utter failure marked his efforts and at last he reluctantly accepted the truth of the border truism that the only truly good Indians are dead ones.
>
> (Denver politician William B. Vickers in the *Denver Chronicle* in 1877; quoted in Brown 1970: 376)

Now it might be argued that these examples are really aberrations, disfiguring the larger historical canvas of modernity but hardly destroying it. Clearly this is a difficult argument to address in any detail here, but the idea that in the making of the modern world darker forces are released as well as those expressing rationality and humanity is an important modification to Enlightenment thinking on the nature and status of the individual. The struggle of reason against more elemental forces like instinct, repression or neuroses of various sorts reveals a self which is more ambivalent, fragmented and uncertain than the confident, whole subject of the Enlightenment. Some sense of the variety of intellectual and practical objections to the rational individual capable of making free moral choices is conveyed in the following extract:

> The entire thrust of modern natural science and philosophy since the time of [Emmanuel] Kant and [Friedrich] Hegel has been to deny the possibility of autonomous moral choice, and to understand human behaviour entirely in terms of sub-human and sub-rational impulses. What once appeared to Kant as free and rational choice was seen by Marx as the product of economic forces, or by Freud as deeply hidden sexual urges. According to Darwin, man literally evolved from the sub-human, more and more of what he was understandable in terms of biology and bio-chemistry. The social sciences this century have told us that man is the product of his social and environmental conditioning, and that human behaviour, like animal behaviour operates according to certain deterministic laws. . . . Modern man now sees that there is a continuum from the 'living slime', as Nietzsche puts it, all the way up to himself. . . . Autonomous man, rationally able to follow laws he created for himself, was reduced to a self-congratulatory myth.
>
> (Fukuyama 1992: 297)

Fukuyama's argument here is in some measure critical of the tendency which he discerns in both the social and the natural sciences to equate humankind with all animal life. But the debate about the allegedly unique nature of humans and the notional 'rights' of non-human animals, which is the subject of a fully fledged politics in some parts of the world (and which is taken up in Chapter 8), still leaves us to address the matter of how far the model of the rational individual explains certain social and political phenomena, and to what extent we need to look to other explanations, where individual action is embedded in the customs, morals and habits of the communities and societies in which it occurs. We will examine these issues by looking at the application of the model of the rational individual to economic life (and by extrapolation to political life as well) and by seeing how unfettered individualism is tempered by cultural factors.

### *Individuals as utility maximisers: the myth of 'economic' man*

Much of the reasoning behind the concept of the rational individual derives from the classical ideas of liberalism and from modifications to liberal dogmas in the form of mathematical public choice theory, with its theoretical emphasis on the self-interested behaviour of individuals, who make choices in market situations based on their own preferences. In addition, it has been influenced by some variants of economic thinking devoted to economic liberalism as the justification for free-market principles. In both strands of thinking (see Dunleavy and O'Leary 1987) individual decisions are responsible for societal outcomes. Only individuals have goals, wants and needs, not collective entities like 'society' or 'the state'. In its most pristine form, seen particularly in public choice theory, proponents of this view claim to have uncovered fundamental and universal truths about human nature and individual behaviour, whether in economics, politics or any other area of human existence.

The intellectual basis for much of this reasoning is the claim that human beings are rational utility-maximising individuals. In other words, humans behave selfishly by trying to get as much of the things they want, thus maximising the benefit to themselves, at the same time as they minimise the costs incurred in actually getting those things. Such 'rational' calculation narrows motivation to what course of action or inaction is most likely to serve one's own preferences. Social life thus becomes a series of market-places in which individuals exercise what economists call 'effective demand', by demonstrating their willingness or reluctance to pay for goods or services. From the point of view of political behaviour, the decision to vote or not to vote, or to join a voluntary organisation, or (if we were to take nation-states as personified collective actors) to become part of a security alliance, would all be taken on the basis of whether they maximised our utility, or, as the nineteenth-century philosopher Jeremy Bentham (1843) rather more eloquently put it, whether or not they contributed to the achievement of pleasure and the avoidance of pain.

Now one of the consequences of this line of reasoning, at least in its pure form, is that what we normally call 'society' – the sum of various interactions between individuals, involving both loving and hating and subject to all sorts of rules governing behaviour – largely disappears, to be glimpsed only fleetingly as the sum of the negotiations between self-interested individuals in markets, to create a sort of society-effect.

As a justification for limited governmental intervention in the rational, market-driven behaviour of individuals these precepts have been used in a variety of ways by political elites in quite different systems. The economic and social policies of Margaret Thatcher in the UK or Ronald Reagan in the United States during the 1980s are 'strong' versions of the thesis, but elsewhere, for example on the self-styled 'intelligent island' of Singapore and in other Asian fast developers, the unfettered working of the free market has been compromised by the willingness of governments to intervene by protecting domestic industries from foreign competition, restricting foreign investment, funding local research and development and subsidising local industries.

These are important insights on the purity of liberal economics applied to real-world situations. But let us consider in more detail the whole question of utility as the cornerstone of the model of economic man. The most well-known definition of utility is Bentham's pleasure over pain principle, referred to above, which has the considerable merit of being intelligible and, apparently, full of common sense. The following extract contains what you might call a Benthamite theory of voting, courtesy of work based on the theory of economic democracy formulated by Anthony Downs (1956):

> Political parties are assumed to be homogeneous groups of politicians, which function as single, unitary actors. They formulate ideologies, or packages of policies, to reduce the cost of voters of collecting and evaluating the vast amount of information necessary to make an optimal voting decision. . . . Parties' policies can be arranged upon a single ideological dimension, which more-or-less corresponds to the familiar left–right dimension. . . . Voters vote for the party which occupies the position closest to their own most preferred position. . . . If the voters are rational and if voting involves some cost (in the form of information gathering, decision-taking, shoe leather and general mental distress during election campaigns) then a real benefit must accrue from the act of voting. Despite this the influence that a particular voter wields . . . is likely to be extremely small. In all but the smallest electorates the voter is likely to have an almost infinitesimal effect. . . . The difference between the various (party political) packages on offer may be quite large, but it is likely that each voter, considering the tiny chance of actually bringing about a change, will not expect a worthwhile return on his investment . . . the consequences of voting are so unlikely to offset the costs that it would not seem rational to vote at all.
>
> (Laver 1981: 102)

In similar vein, the theory of the calculating individual would suggest that it is not rational to join organisations which are striving to produce benefits that would be available to people whether or not they are members of the organisation. These benefits, called 'public goods', to distinguish them from benefits only available to those who are members, or who pay for them, would include things like clean air or universal welfare benefits, from which individuals could not be excluded even though they had incurred no costs or paid no dues to acquire them. In Mancur Olson's well-known book *The Logic of Collective Action* (1965) this problem is referred to as the phenomenon of the 'free-rider', a concept which has figured widely in discussions of the difficulty of mobilising and sustaining certain types of interest groups.

---

*THINK POINT*
- Consider your own motives for voting or not voting.
- Would you fit the model of the rational voter?
- Would you join a group devoted to pursuing the public interest?
- If not, why not?

---

**Political competence** A
person's political competence is
both a formal status, in the
sense that as a citizen one has
the right to vote, and a practical
skill, for example in terms of
organising a demonstration or
writing to a member of
Congress or Parliament.

Well and good, there is a neatness about this sort of explanation of
individual action or inaction. But there are still the obvious facts that many
people do vote and that some people seem to pursue goals that have nothing
to do with personal utility. The evidence, seemingly, is all around us. People
join organisations like Friends of the Earth or donate money to charity
without the expectation of personal material reward. Others intervene to
prevent old ladies being mugged, while some, in places like Tiananmen
Square in Beijing, are prepared to stand in the way of armoured vehicles
and tanks, and when they do their reasons are couched in terms of honour,
religion, justice, freedom and love, not self-interest. Are these people acting
irrationally, at least according to the lights of utilitarian reasoning, and if
they are, does it matter?

Downs (1956) offers a mitigating circumstance in which the strict
definition of rationality might be stretched to cover such eventualities. He
suggests that if no one voted democracy would collapse because there would
be no challenges to incumbents in office, and thus no approximation of
the market competition necessary to keep politicians and parties on their
toes and to ensure an adequate supply of public goods. So every (rational)
citizen is still prepared to shoulder some costs in order to insure themselves
against the even higher costs which would accrue should societal breakdown
occur. Other theorists, like Riker and Ordeshook (1968), offer a different
slant on the calculus of voting. They argue that voters derive *positive satisfactions* from complying with the ethical imperative implied in the status
of citizen, which status is consummated by the act of voting. The actual
act then becomes a symbolic reaffirmation of a voter's allegiance to the
political system, to a particular party or to the very idea of democracy,
as well as an expression of a citizen's **political competence**. Writing about
public sanitation in the United States, Matthew Crenson (1987) has
suggested that individuals may well be persuaded to join public interest
groups where it can be made clear that their failure to participate will result
in group failure and the deleterious effects of a 'public bad'. He has also
argued that people are more likely to contribute to the prevention of a
collective 'bad' – dirty air or poor sanitation – than to the securing of
a collective good – a better environment and so on. People, it seems, are
more easily mobilised in response to threats than in response to promises
(see also Jordan and Maloney 1996).

Now all this is a considerable relaxation of the rationality principle,
allowing that the concept of interests may not be as narrow as writers like
Downs and Olson believe and that people can derive pleasure from things
like 'doing one's duty as a citizen' or get satisfaction – psychic pleasure if
you like – from helping others. The strong concept of 'utility' now becomes
another way of describing whatever preferences people have, or of saying
that people do what they want to do. Without too much effort this less
rigorous definition of utility could be extended to the 'satisfactions' experienced by a suicide bomber in a busy street in Tel Aviv, seeking a 'marriage'
with death. There is also the sense that not all behaviour or choices need

be considered as rational, where that means making a calculation based on having access to all relevant information and then seeking to maximise utility. There must be occasions when the costs of acquiring perfect information would have to be considered too costly, and thus irrational. In such circumstances the individual, faced with the need to choose, falls back on habit or appeals to tradition, or even expediency.

All this suggests a more complex and messy model of the nature of individuality than can be contained in the economic version. People are embedded in a variety of social and cultural groups and what they think, feel and do is often intimately related to their rootedness in these identities. As Francis Fukuyama says, 'social and therefore moral behaviour co-exists with self-interested, utility-maximising behaviour . . . human beings act for non-utilitarian ends in a-rational, group-oriented ways' (Fukuyama 1995: 21). These aspects of sociability modify the force of simple cost-benefit calculations, and the desire to fulfil our own interests is mediated by the variable intensity of our social relationships and moral obligations as parents, workers, members of a softball club or activists in a single-isssue pressure group dedicated to the protection of the Newfoundland seal. The rational actor of economic theory is only a pale shadow of her/his flesh and blood counterpart, who is making decisions in situations which are encumbered by history, cultural values and imperfect information.

B. Barry (1970) *Sociologists, Economists and Democracy*, London: Collier Macmillan.

---

**THINK POINT**
● In sum, how convincing do you find the concept of the rational actor?

---

## Individualism in action

The difficulty with economic reasoning applied to the motivations of individuals is that while it may explain a good deal of human behaviour, it runs into difficulties explaining those acts which are non-utilitarian, at least without a good deal of conceptual stretching. As a theory of individual motivation, therefore, it is like the curate's egg, only good in parts. Even Adam Smith, the eighteenth-century father of what is often called neo-classical economics, believed that economic life is firmly embedded in social life and that individual motivations and behaviour have to be understood in relation to the customs, morals and habits of the society in which they take place.

This argument raises an important point about the very idea of individualism and about the status of the individual in modernity. Because human action is embedded in social and cultural life, it follows that the concept of the individual, and the intellectual and moral qualities attached to that status, are themselves socially constructed and culturally sanctioned. In other words, they are not the innate characteristics of human beings

## Exercise

Below is a well-known exercise in rational choice and the problems of collective action. It is called the 'prisoner's dilemma'.

*The scenario*: Bill and Ted are prime suspects in bank robbery. The police have circumstantial evidence that both are involved, including possession of safe-breaking equipment, baseball bats which could be used as weapons, and so on, but no actual witnesses. What they need is a confession from either or both of the suspects. At the police station the prisoners are separated and each is presented with the same deal, which is that if they make a full confession which implicates their partner they will be granted immunity from prosecution while their accomplice will carry all the blame and go to gaol for a long time. If they refuse, they may well end up taking all the blame themselves. Having no knowledge of how their partner is reacting, each has to make up his mind how to respond.

Their options, set out in the form of a game-play matrix, are shown in Figure 1.1. The entries in each cell of the matrix show how many years each prisoner will receive as his sentence. Bill's sentence is shown in words, Ted's using numbers:

|  | Bill's options | |
|---|---|---|
|  | stay silent | confess |
| **Ted's options** | | |
| stay silent | one, 1 | none, 5 |
| confess | five, 0 | three, 3 |

*Figure 1.1* The prisoner's dilemma

Both Bill and Ted are old hands at this sort of thing. They can see the options quite clearly. In particular, they do not know what the other may be doing. Given the same scenario, how would you read the options and what would you decide to do?

(despite what classical economics says) but are made and reproduced by people in the context of particular cultural rules and expectations. Where rules and expectations about the status of the individual exist, one might expect to find widespread evidence of individualism in both political theory and constitutional forms, as well as in the self-perceptions of ordinary people.

For example, the Constitution of the United States and the Declaration of Independence which preceded it are documents redolent with the spirit of individualism and individual rights. Although the American revolutionaries of 1776 sought to enhance the public good, it is the political theory of liberalism, with its insistence on the independence of people from each other and from 'primitive' attachments, that is most readily associated with

'American-ness'. Political authority, particularly governmental authority, had to be fitted into a society of individuals. Curiously, or so you might think, dedication to an individualistic value system and to the liberal creed has been a feature of the cohesion and stability of American society, at least until recently, legitimating the competitive instinct, entrepreneurship, thrift and the other qualities of 'rugged individualism' as *cultural* norms. So it comes as no surprise that the typical American hero is a combination of individualism without eccentricity, charm without sophistication and, of course, wholehearted patriotism. John Wayne springs to mind as the embodiment of these virtues, but so does the archetypal loner in the guise of practically all Clint Eastwood's 'Western' characters, along with the maverick Randle McMurphy in Ken Kesey's novel *One Flew Over the Cuckoo's Nest*. In fact, the pantheon is very large and contains some unexpected figures who lack the physical presence and glamour of Hollywood film stars. The appeal of the rank outsider Ross Perot as a candidate in the 1992 presidential election, was based on his opposition to 'big government' in Washington and the fact that he exemplified many of the qualities of American individualism, being a self-made billionaire and an advocate of self-help. Perot's much quoted aphorism 'Eagles don't flock; you have to find them one at a time' could be taken as a convenient summary of American individualism. The 'Unabomber' too, who for nearly two decades waged a one-man war in the USA against what he saw as the evils of the mass-consumption society, evoked an ambivalent response among a public shocked at his disregard for human life and romanced by his lone crusade.

French individualism also displays some of the features of the American strain, but, unlike its 'New World' counterpart, it has an almost anarchistic character. In France cultural and political values associated with the French Revolution of 1789 have produced a highly fragmented society where the individual citizen is suspicious both of the government and of many types of collective action. As a consequence the French seem far less inclined to participate in social organisations than, say, the British or Americans, except where this involves spontaneous and direct action against the French state, for example by students or farmers anxious to protect their livelihoods.

So, robust individualism abounds in France and the United States, but it would be foolish to suggest that there are no individuals in countries like Russia or Japan, or even Italy, if by that we mean that it would be hard to find people who have a strong sense of their own place in life or who are imbued with an independence of spirit and a critical cast of mind when it comes to evaluating the role of government in the affairs of citizens. In Alexander Solzhenitsyn's account of life in the prison camps of the Soviet Gulag, *One Day in the Life of Ivan Denisovitch*, the hero shows exactly the same wiles of stubbornness and inventiveness as those used by Randle McMurphy in his guerrilla war with authority inside the mental hospital where he is a voluntary patient. The difference is that in the United States, as in many other countries in the West, the status of the individual at the centre of social life has been institutionalised in thought and custom, as

*'We hold these truths to be self-evident, that all men are created equal, that they are endowed by their Creator with certain inalienable rights, that among these are Life, Liberty and the Pursuit of Happiness.' (American Declaration of Independence, 1776).* See also pp. 275–6.

well as in law. Because of this there is a culturally sanctioned expectation that individuals will behave as social critics as well as utility-maximisers.

---

**THINK POINT**
- Do you think of yourself in this way?
- What does being or acting as an 'individual' mean to you?

---

### Individuals and rights

The protection of individuals in many societies has often taken the form of translating rights-based political theory into laws and public policy, or else of appropriating the language of rights as political slogans – the right to work or the right to have control over one's body – which are sometimes translated into an organised politics. In practice, the articulation and codifying of rights takes different forms across the globe. More often than not, these forms have been expressed as rights associated with **citizenship** of particular countries and have not been extended to non-nationals. But after the Second World War in Western Europe, attempts were made to establish a system of rights which transcends national boundaries. These efforts were part of the broader processes of European unification and were particularly evident in the setting up of the Council of Europe in 1949 and in the adoption, in 1950, of a United Nations-inspired European Convention for the Protection of Human Rights and Fundamental Freedoms. The latter was given some judicial teeth in the form of the European Court of Human Rights (1959), which hears appeals from individuals and from collective bodies. The Council of Europe system of supranational rights includes rights to life, liberty and both the individual and collective pursuit of happiness. Freedom of conscience and of religion are guaranteed, along with freedom of expression and association.

By prohibiting torture and the use of the death penalty in peacetime, the Council of Europe has tried to exclude authoritarian regimes in Western Europe and, until after the fall of communism, those in eastern Europe too. As a sign of the changed or changing times, Russia was formally admitted to the Council of Europe in 1996, although the issue of human rights continues to be one of the crucial barriers to the full membership of Turkey. The language of rights also finds its way into the Social Chapter of the Maastricht Treaty on European Union, signed in 1991 and ratified by the member states over the subsequent three years. In the following extract some of the 'rights' contained in the treaty are set out, though many of them are little more than generalised statements of intent. Maastricht also laid down the skeleton of a European citizenship, among other things extending to all citizens of member states of the European Union the right to stand as candidates for election to the European Parliament in any Euro-constituency in the Union.

**Citizenship** Literally, membership of a particular state and the rights attaching to that status, despite the fact that modern conceptions of citizenship stress universal rights and obligations and there is now a transnational doctrine of human rights.

*Supranational means, literally, 'above the national', but see Chapters 15 and 16 for an extended discussion.*

ARTICLE 8

1. Citizenship of the Union is hereby established.

Every person holding the nationality of a Member State shall be a citizen of the Union.

2. Citizens of the Union shall enjoy the rights conferred by this Treaty and shall be subject to the duties thereby.

ARTICLE 8a

1. Every citizen of the Union shall have the right to move and reside freely within the territory of the Member States, subject to the limitations and conditions laid down in this Treaty and by the measures adopted to give it effect.

2. The Council may adopt provisions with a view to facilitating the exercise of the rights referred to in paragraph 1; save as otherwise provided in this Treaty, the Council shall act unanimously on a proposal from the Commission after obtaining the assent of the European Parliament.

ARTICLE 8b

1. Every citizen of the Union residing in a Member State of which he is not a national shall have the right to vote and to stand as a candidate at municipal elections in the Member State in which he resides, under the same conditions as nationals of that State. This right shall be exercised subject to detailed arrangements to be adopted before 31 December 1994 by the Council, acting unanimously, on a proposal from the Commission and after consulting the European Parliament; these arrangements may provide for derogations where warranted by problems specific to a Member State.

2. Without prejudice to Article 1 38(3) and to the provisions adopted for its implementation, every citizen of the Union residing in a Member State of which he is not a national shall have the right to vote and to stand as a candidate in elections to the European Parliament in the Member State in which he resides, under the same conditions as national of that State. This right shall be exercised subject to detailed arrangements to be adopted before 31 December 1993 by the Council, acting unanimously on a proposal from the Commission and after consulting the European Parliament; these arrangements may provide for derogations where warranted by problems specific to a Member State.

ARTICLE 8c

Every citizen of the Union shall, in the territory of a third country in which the Member State of which he is a national is not represented, be entitled to protection by the diplomatic or consular authorities of any Member State, on the same conditions as the nationals of that State. Before 31 December 1993, Member States shall establish the necessary rules among themselves and start the international negotiations required to secure this protection.

ARTICLE 8d

Every citizen of the Union shall have the right to petition the European Parliament in accordance with Article 1384.

Every citizen of the Union may apply to the Ombudsman established in accordance with Article 138c.

> ARTICLE 8c
> The Commission shall report to the European Parliament, to the Council and to the Economic and Social Committee before 31 December 1993 and then every three years on the application of the provisions of this Part. This report shall take account of the development of the Union.
> On this basis, and without prejudice to the other provisions of this Treaty, the Council, acting unanimously on a proposal from the Commission and after consulting the European Parliament, may adopt provisions to strengthen or to add to the rights laid down in this Part, which it shall recommend to the Member States for adoption in accordance with their respective constitutional requirements.
>
> (Maastricht Treaty in European Unity; Part Two Citizenship of the Union, Brussels, 12 February 1992)

Rights are also part of the language of international relations, but quite often as part of the rhetoric of praise and blame rather than as a commitment to those whose rights have been violated. The Gulf War of 1991 was fought in part over the issue of Saddam Hussein's violation of the independent status of Kuwait, but humanitarian concerns and attention to the rights of individuals and groups of people sometimes suffer out of respect for the *rights* of nation-states in international law and convention. Looking at the Gulf War, it is the failure to intervene on behalf of the Marsh Arabs in the south of Iraq, who were also the recipients of Saddam's displeasure, which points up the limits of intervention in pursuit of human rights. Early in 1996 the Nigerian military government executed the poet Ken Saro-Wiwa, following a suspect trial. International outcry was not matched by action on the part of governments and international bodies.

Goran Therborn (1995) identifies two areas of basic rights associated with the protection and enhancement of the status of the individual. These are rights which are *claims* upon the state and its resources, and rights to *act* in relation to other members of society as well as vis-à-vis the state. The first set includes rights to membership – the grounds on which people are allowed into a country as visitors, migrants and settlers, and the rules which govern their treatment as sojourners; it also includes rights to welfare, pensions and other social entitlements. Such rights were introduced at different points during the often protracted transition to modernity, and there is wide variation in their application across different social and political systems. Here is an extract from Therborn's book (1995) which deals with the variations in rights to membership:

> The importance of state membership was reinforced . . . with the new turn of migration into Europe.
> The legal tradition contains two major criteria for state membership, for citizenship, namely 'soil' or 'blood'. . . . The former means that you acquire your citizenship by the place where you were born, and the latter that it depends on who your parents (or ancestors) were. By and large, settlement countries – the New Worlds – and empires, like the British and the French, have tended to opt for soil, the other European countries for blood. . . .
> In fact the blood or soil distinction does not adequately capture post-World

War II varieties in Europe and the trajectories of their general tendency towards restrictiveness. The UK has, since 1971, increasingly narrowed the gate for entrants from the non-white Commonwealth, while keeping, in spite of IRA terrorism, an open door on Irish immigration. Irish residents in the UK have the same rights as British citizens. . . . Germany has been in many ways more restrictive. Labour imports were conceived as 'Gastarbeiter' [guest-workers] and denied any rights to permanent residence. Until 1990 people who were unable to claim German descent had no right to citizenship, however long they had been in Germany. . . . Since that date, fifteen years of residence, or in the case of youngsters aged between 16 to 23, eight years of residence and six years of school, entitles a claim to citizenship.

On the other hand, blood-rights have allowed a large number of Eastern Europeans to enter (West) Germany claiming German descent.

Political rights are most accessible in Britain, and since 1984, in Ireland. . . . Sweden gave foreign residents the right to vote in local elections in 1976, followed by Denmark and Norway, and by Iceland and Finland, but only with regard to other Nordic citizens . . .

In Eastern Europe postwar citizenship lost one of its otherwise most important accessories, the passport. . . . With the exception of the Yugoslavs since the mid-1950s, the Hungarians since the mid-1980s and, to a more limited extent, the Poles since the mid-1970s, a passport to Eastern Europeans was not a right but a special privilege, earned by loyal service or by post-retirement age. On the other hand, Eastern European regimes such as that of the USSR and the GDR, used their power to deprive citizens of their citizenship rights. Alexander Solzhenitsyn and Wolf Biermann were the most famous, or notorious cases.

After the war, the individual right to vote was an issue only by exception. . . . Greek women joined their Balkan sisters in 1952. . . . But Swiss women had to wait for recognition of their political maturity till 1971 and most Iberian women till the end of the dictatorships in the mid-1970s. . . .

The political distance between Finland and the Iberian peninsula, in terms of female enfranchisement, turned out to be about seventy years, between France (1946) and Norway (1913), somewhat above thirty years.

(Therborn 1995: 86–8; reproduced with the permission of Sage Publications Ltd)

---

**THINK POINT**
- What inferences can you draw from these comparative data?

---

Therborn's data are drawn from the continent of Europe, but similar, if not greater, variations in rights as entitlements can be seen in other parts of the world. In the United States civil rights extended to erstwhile black slaves after the Civil War of 1861–5 remained entirely notional for large sections of black America until well into the 1960s, due to entrenched local sentiments and the contested power of individual states to pass and impose discriminatory legislation. Australia and New Zealand enfranchised women long before most European countries, while military regimes in Argentina and Chile between the 1960s and 1980s sytematically degraded the rights

*In George Orwell's book* Nineteen Eighty-Four *the authorities systematically rewrote the language, giving new meanings to words, outlawing the use of others and establishing usage as either correct or incorrect, depending on the context and the climate of official opinion.*

of individual citizens in their quest to stamp out political opposition. Before the fall of the apartheid system in 1994, South Africa was an unhappy blend of respect for individual rights and the rule of law, extended to the white population, and both legal and customary discrimination against black people and other people of colour. It is clear that contrary to the tenets of individualism and sometimes regardless of legal requirements, in some regimes certain rights have been advanced or witheld on the basis of the possession of collective attributes like sex or race, regardless of the singular qualities of individuals. But in a curious inversion of this offensive practice, the stereotyping of individuals recently has achieved a certain political correctness when applied in appropriate contexts, although this sometimes smacks of an Orwellian regard for the subtleties of 'Newspeak'. Thus in movies like Disney's *Pocahontas* the English are subject to 'acceptable stereotyping' as arch colonialists.

The second category of rights mentioned by Therborn is that of *rights to act*. Rights to act define the legitimate scope of actions and include freedom of association, freedom of expression and voting rights. Some sense of the considerable variation in introducing measures which require at least a mathematical equality in the form of rights can be seen in Table 1.1. Other areas which fall under the rubric of rights to act are those concerning discrimination and harassment, the rights of workers to dispose of their labour freely and to enjoy rights relating to safety at work or job security. In the industrial economies of Western capitalism, these sort of rights have often conflicted with the rights of property-holders, in the form of owners of industrial or financial capital, to deploy their assets in ways likely to maximise profits. Where such conflicts have arisen, the state, in either judicial or bureaucratic guise, has usually intervened to mediate disputes between capital and labour, or with respect to the extension or limitation of the welfare state.

*Table 1.1* The introduction of universal franchise – selected countries

| country | universal male suffrage | universal adult suffrage |
|---|---|---|
| Belgium | 1894 | 1948 |
| Netherlands | 1918 | 1922 |
| France | 1848 | 1946 |
| Germany | 1871 | 1919 |
| Ireland | 1918 | 1923 |
| UK | 1918 | 1928 |
| Denmark | 1849 | 1918 |
| Norway | 1900 | 1913 |
| Switzerland | 1848 | 1971 |

*Source*: Pierson (1991)

### Individualism and collectivism

In his great study *Democracy in America* (1954) Alexis de Tocqueville noted that never had there been a country so committed to individual wants as opposed to collective needs as the United States. As we have noted, individual liberty is an often proclaimed American value, the stock-in-trade of election speeches by presidential hopefuls and from those politicians with less lofty ambitions. For all this, over the years the emphasis upon individual rights has been qualified to accommodate the interests of certain collective groups, such as ethnic minorities and women. The civil rights legislation enacted during the 1960s was interpreted first by federal government officials and then by the courts as endorsing the use of affirmative action and sometimes positive discrimination (special preferences or quotas in education, employment, etc.) for members of specifically defined disadvantaged groups – women, blacks, Hispanics and Native Americans. For the first time, and contrary to Tocqueville's dictum, American federal policy was defined in terms of rights and privileges for groups rather than individuals. This redefinition remains a source of important constitutional and political dispute in the USA and finds echoes in the politics of countries with quite different legal and cultural traditions.

Other forms of collectivism, particularly those associated with the expansion of the welfare states in Western Europe after the Second World War, sought to harness the use of public power to further social and economic freedoms, especially of those categories of people who might be relatively powerless. Examples of this can be seen in Scandinavian legislation passed in the early 1980s, whereby parents are forbidden to smack their children, schools having been barred from administering corporal punishment in the years following the Second World War. State action to protect or enhance the rights of individuals (and particularly children and wives) in societal groupings like the family also flowered under aggressively interventionist communist regimes in the Soviet Union and the German Democratic Republic (which today is part of a reunified Germany). It is of course a paradox that these same regimes systematically restricted the rights of citizens in other important respects, for example with regard to freedom of movement or freedom of association.

---

**THINK POINT**
- On what sort of grounds do you think the state/public authorities could intervene legitimately to protect individual interests?

---

Even in countries with a considerable distrust of government and a public philosophy that societies should be judged on the basis of how well they do in making individuals happy – the United States is again the obvious example – individual freedoms, like the freedom to smoke in public spaces or to drive an automobile without a seat-belt, are proscribed in the name of the public interest, or of knowing what is in the best interests of individuals. Much intervention of this sort is justified on the grounds that the function of government is not just to uphold the rights of the individual to do something, but to ensure that people in general are protected from unfettered individualism, where those freedoms may create passive smokers, victims of the playing of loud music in apartment blocks or abused children. The philosophical debates which underlie such practical and political questions are taken up again in Chapters 6 to 8

**Anarchy** A term often used rather loosely as a synonym for disorder, but which in fact refers to the doctrine which counsels the absence of formal government.

For some libertarians and all **anarchists** there are great dangers in governments assuming a moral responsibilty for the physical and mental well-being of their citizens, to the point where explicit guidance (counselling) may be given on what to eat and drink, or how and with whom to make love. These sorts of objections turn on what constitutes the legitimate scope of of government intervention and on why a civil society made up of sovereign individuals, or of individuals who have entered freely into associations with each other, should be free from restrictions imposed by the state. The difficulties, both morally and with respect to the use of legal enforcements, lie in the interpretation of what is meant by undue constraint, and in where the balance between freedom *to* and freedom *from* should rest. In the UK in the case of *Brown v. Regina* in 1994, the House of Lords, in its capacity as a court of appeal, ruled that forms of sexual preference involving degrees of physical violence (sadomasochism) between consenting adults are illegal on the grounds that their actions infringed against the Offences Against the Person Act of 1861. When the federal authorities in the United States laid siege to the compound of the religious sect the Branch Davidians, in Waco, Texas, in 1993, they justified their actions as needful (i) to control the stockpiling of weapons said to be taking place there and (ii) to protect those members allegedly menaced by the actions of the cult's leader, David Koresh, and his apocalyptic visions. Opponents of intervention, however, saw the actions as a further example of the expansion of federal power and the willingness of government to intervene in the affairs of private individuals and organisations.

From these observations we can see that the competing claims of individualism and different forms of collectivism (ranging from voluntary associations, informal organisations like families, larger social and cultural categories like social classes or ethnic groups, to the state itself) can lead to substantively different prescriptions about the nature and extent of government action. At the same time it is necessary to recognise that in many countries strains of individualism and collectivism do co-exist. This is not to deny that some societies are more individualistic or more collectivist than others, but just to note that we should beware of simple categories and stereotypes. Furthermore, when considering forms of collectivism it is important to distinguish between those societies which place a great deal of stress upon communal identities and activities, or on the important social functions of voluntary associations of private individuals, and those which privilege the state as the regulator of all social activity and the arbiter of individual morality. Let us look at some of these distinctions more closely.

While Americans may take pride in being individualists, a belief in the virtues of collective action is also an established part of their cultural and political tradition. Some 60 per cent of Americans belong to one or more voluntary associations. These cover a wide spectrum of American life and include social clubs, fraternal and charitable bodies like the Shriners, the Buffalos and the Rotarians; organisations representing the professions, such as the American Bar Association; and educational associations, for example parent–teacher associations (PTAs), and college fraternities and sororities. 'Economic' groups representing business, labour and agriculture, as well as 'cause' groups devoted to the promotion of a whole range of public interest issues, vie for the ear of decision-makers. In fact, one of the Founding Fathers of the American Republic, James Madison, wrote that groups of various sorts can be the product of 'the most frivolous and fanciful distinctions' (1961: 79).

---

**THINK POINT**
- What about your own experience?
- How many groups are you a member of?
- What about your parents and friends?

---

Japan, by contrast, is often spoken of as a society which is not very individualistic and in which there is a high degree of respect for the state. While it is true that the Japanese state plays a larger role in the life of its citizens than does the state in the USA, as the following extract makes clear, the Japanese are also joiners of private associations which make up that broad area of civil society between the family on the one hand and the state on the other.

> Like the United States, Japanese society supports a dense network of voluntary organisations. Many of these are what the Japanese call 'iemoto' groups, centred around a traditional art or craft like Kabuki theatre, flower arranging, or classical tea ceremony. These groups are hierarchical, like families, with strong vertical ties between masters and disciples, but they are not based on kinship and are entered into on a voluntary basis. Iemoto organisations . . . pervade Japanese society, extending far beyond the traditional arts to encompass religious, political and professional organisations.
> . . .
> It is more accurate to say that the Japanese have a group-oriented rather than a state-oriented culture. While most Japanese respect the state, their primary emotional attachments – the loyalties that make them stay in the office until ten at night or miss weekends with their families – are to the private corporations, businesses or universities which employ them.
>
> (Fukuyama, 1995: 54–5)

The robustness of civil societies populated by self-regarding individuals and by associations of various sorts, and which are separate from and formally ungoverned by the state, is often taken as a sign of the health of democratic systems. Although it is quite common for the influence of (some kinds of) voluntary associations to be criticised as being too great, even undemocratic, support for thriving, pluralistic civil societies usually stresses the value

*See Chapter 13, on the politics of influence.*

of intermediate associations in constraining both the harsher side of individualism and the power of the state. For example, the famous German sociologist Max Weber wrote favourably that it was a 'characteristic . . . of the specifically American democracy that it did not constitute a formless sand heap of individuals, but rather a buzzing complex of strictly exclusive, yet voluntary associations' (Weber 1946: 310). One of the main effects of state socialism in countries modelled on the Soviet system was to damage the institutions and associations of civil society, from churches to newspapers and down to the family itself. The following extract, from a family history of three generations of Chinese women, and told by the youngest, gives some indication of the almost pathological fears or paranoia felt by leaders of the Chinese Communist Party during the period known as the 'Cultural Revolution' under Chairman Mao Zedong, which made them try to root out opposition and see potential threats to their security throughout the fabric of Chinese society:

> Mao's Red Guards:
>
> Mao wanted the Red Guards (mostly young people, intensely loyal to Mao alone) to be his shock troops. He could see that most people were not responding to his repeated calls to attack the capitalist-roaders. . . . If he was to get the population to act, Mao would have to remove authority from the Party and establish absolute loyalty and obedience to himself alone. To achieve this he needed terror — an intense terror that would block all other considerations and crush all other fears. He saw boys and girls in their teens and early twenties as his ideal agents. They had been brought up in the fanatical personality cult of Mao and the militant doctrine of 'class struggle'. They were endowed with the qualities of youth — they were rebellious, fearless, eager to fight for a 'just' cause, thirsty for adventure and action. They were also irresponsible, ignorant and easy to manipulate — prone to violence. Only they could give Mao the immense force that he needed to terrorize the whole society. . . . One slogan summed up the Red Guard's mission: 'We vow to launch a bloody war against anyone who dares to resist the Cultural Revolution, who dares to oppose Chairman Mao'. . . .
>
> To arouse the young to mob violence, victims were necessary. The most conspicuous targets in my school were the teachers, some of whom had been victimised by work teams and school authorities in the last few months. Now the rebellious children set upon them. . . . In practically every school in China, teachers were abused and beaten, sometimes fatally. Some school children set up prisons in which teachers were tortured.
> (Chang 1993: 375–6; reproduced with permission from Jung Chang, *Wild Swans: Three Women of China*, London: HarperCollins)

From another source we can see the effects of a different kind of collective fervour on expressions of individualism. Read the following extract, which looks at the symbolism carried in revolutionary posters in the year following the Iranian revolution of 1979, when the Shah was overthrown by a combination of religious, nationalist and communist political groups, including supporters of a return to a more authentic Islamic lifestyle and an Islamic form of government.

> On the reverse [of the poster] was an allegorical painting of blood and revenge. In the foreground there was a flat landscape . . . bisected by a straight black road. . . . On this road a veiled woman, seen from the back, lay half collapsed. . . . The woman had a bloodied back. . . . Out of that blood . . . giant red tulips had grown; and above the tulips, in the sky, was the face of [Ayatollah] Khomeini, the saviour, frowning. Khomeini saved and avenged. . . . Also in this allegory of the revolution, personality had been allowed only to the avenger. The wounded woman . . . was veiled and faceless.
>
>   In one election poster, a faceless crowd – the veiled woman reduced to simple triangular outlines – held up photographs of the candidates of a particular party. . . . In [another] poster, Khomeini himself had been faceless, his features [within the outline of turban, cheeks and beard] replaced by a clenched fist. . . . Facelessness had begun to seem like an Islamic motif.
>
> (Naipaul 1982: 28)

Of course, these are highly personal accounts of much wider social and political events and processes, but they do draw attention to some of the salient features of those political systems which have tried to eradicate social and cultural **pluralism** in the name of revolutionary unity or religious purity. But it is not only in such determinedly singular or monistic regimes that there is a dearth of voluntary associations. In southern Italy, Spain and many of the nations of Latin America the gap between the individual or the family unit of loyalty and the state was not, and to some extent still is not, bridged by a rich seam of private associations. The drive towards sociability which so marks countries like the USA, Britain and Japan is much less apparent and has led some observers to suggest that such countries are less stable, maybe less democratic, than those with many intermediate associations.

This is clearly a contentious argument and turns on the idea either that individuals are forced to confront the state more directly in the relative absence of organisations which mediate their demands, or else that they are not shielded from the full force of state power by a pluralistic civil society. Francis Fukuyama (1995) goes further, suggesting that in those societies with strong familial traditions – Latin Catholic societies, or the Chinese, where the family-oriented tenets of Confucian philosophy run deep – trust in people outside the family and in extended social relationships is low.

Of course in all societies the reasons why individuals join voluntary associations are likely to be very complex. We have seen already that elegant, but oversimplified rational choice arguments do not capture this complexity. Neither does the assumption which is usually attributed to pluralist accounts of group formation, that groups will form almost spontaneously because individuals share goals or values and wish to see these enhanced or protected. The issue of why individuals engage in different forms of political participation, including joining things like protest groups, is taken up in Chapter 4. Here we should just note that different individual needs are met through membership or other forms of support for such bodies, and that these embrace both self-interested and non-material – or, as they are sometimes called, *expressive* – desires.

**Pluralism** The belief that there is, or else there should be, diversity. Political pluralism recognises and encourages variety in social, cultural and ideological forms and processes. Pluralist theories examine the influence of social groups in contributing and having access to the making of public policy, with competition for group influence.

**Totalitarianism** An all-encompassing system of political rule in which political control is exerted over all aspects of life.

Highly pluralistic political systems often reflect the richness of civil society and are also a means of defending it against what Harold Laski (1948), the English socialist writer, called the power of the state – 'the one compulsory association'. But for some, pluralism is not only a defence against monism or **totalitarianism** but also against the threats to sociability posed by unbridled individualism. Thus, much of the concern of early pluralist thought was to reject individualism since it encouraged the 'free-riding' syndrome of which we spoke earlier. The rejection of aggressive individualism is apparent too in ways of thinking about the organisation of societies and the place of individuals in them which are called communitarian.

### Communitarianism

Communitarian thought, which has become very fashionable since the late 1980s, due in part to the writing of sociologists like Amitai Etzioni in the United States and to its take-up by politicians seeking to offset the growing disenchantment with conventional politics, falls somewhere between the poles of liberal individualism and statist collectivism.

For communitarians like Richard Rorty (1992), the individual is firmly embedded in the cultural and social institutions of a society. The individual is socially situated and so is neither isolated nor selfish, and certainly not alienated from others. On the contrary, people are connected through patterns of friendship, communities of trust and reciprocity and networks of power. Just what communitarians mean by the term 'community' is not always clear, but what seems to be implied is the primacy (both theoretical and practical) of group or associative identities, with their complex mix of rights and duties. After the unfettered free-market liberalism of the 1980s in both Britain and the United States, some politicians, for example Tony Blair, the leader of the Labour Party in Britain, have turned to communitarian thinking to signal a shift in the direction of politics in the 1990s. In Italy, Silvio Berlusconi, leader of the new political movement Forza Italia has also expressed sympathy with the principles of communitarian thinking. The downsides of this sometimes romanticised version of associative identities and local governance are the accompanying dangers of sectarianism, 'group-think', and possibly the sort of 'we-feeling' which tips over into a strong distrust of outsiders. At this point euphemisms like 'ethnic cleansing' begin to look like acceptable items for a political agenda concerned to defend or promote group or local identities.

### Beyond individualism and collectivism: the postmodern condition

For all that communitarianism offers us a way of understanding the place of the cultural and the social in making the individual, it could be argued that it represents another side of the modernist tradition, albeit one with a cosy feel to it through its attempts to combine respect for the individual with older sentiments praising the value of collective identities. Set against both are a range of positions which have become known as postmodernism, to distinguish them from the tenets and claims of modernist (Enlighten-ment) thinking. Postmodernist ideas arose out of a great disenchantment with both the rationalist and collectivist arguments about the nature of the individual and of social life in general. Instead of assuming that identities are fixed, because human nature is like that – as in economic reasoning – or because social forces or cultural values impose rigid and unchanging identities on people (as members of a social class, as an ethnic group or the denizens of a local community) postmodernists like Lyotard (1984) argue that identity can be formed or re-formed more or less at will, and around any sort of focus or stimulus. The point is that in a postmodern world there are no absolutes, and so identity formation becomes a matter of choice and circumstance. In a more radical version of pluralism, cultural and political differences are applauded.

---

**THINK POINT**
- Does this make sense to you?
- How easy would it be for you to take on new identities at will?
- Is changing your allegiance to a particular band or style of dress of the same order as changing your political allegiance or your sexual preference?

---

If this suggests pluralism run riot, from a political standpoint its implications are enormous, although a fully fledged postmodern politics is hardly in evidence in any part of the world, least of all in those parts just emerging from authoritarian rule. Postmodernist claims about the nature of the individual and the fluidity of social life do legitimate a blossoming of all sorts of political demands and positions which were previously suppressed in some countries, or less than central to the political and policy agenda in others. Areas like gender politics or the specific demands of people of colour are good examples, but more exotic forms of what some people call the 'new' politics of identity are prepared to make fat a political issue or offer levitation as a means of getting in touch with who you are. In fact, some forms of ethnic identity or ultra-nationalism, say in Bosnia or Rwanda, seem to intimate a return to pre-modern conflicts and identities. It is also something of an irony that those who wish to undo modernist politics often couch their demands in the language of rights which is the legacy of liberalism and of the Enlightenment they so despise. Strands of feminist thinking have been particularly critical of the moral and intellectual bankruptcy of modernist thought, preferring to see notions of individualism, and even community, as part of a male-centred realm of discourse – only masquerading as universal traits – which left women marginalised or unequal in terms of status and of power.

---

**THINK POINT**
- What would you see as the advantages and disadvantages of a postmodern politics of difference?

---

There is now a great profusion of organisations claiming to represent or act on behalf of all sorts of interests and identities. Some of them, perhaps those advocating gender equality, have actually moved from the margins of political debate somewhere closer to the centre in some countries of the West. On the other hand, the greater public awareness of racial and gender inequalities may have served only to glamorise or entrench their status as victims.

## Individuals and the capacity for meaningful political action

*For more on the processes of globalisation, see Chapter 16.*

As individuals and as social beings we live in an increasingly complex world. This is not just because government is big, or because of vast business corporations, but also because we have to come to terms with flows of information, knowledge and power which are global rather than local. People have to confront not just local or national rules about the appropriate way to organise their life, but ones originating in institutions like the European Union or the World Trade Organisation.

When individual citizens express their grievances about litter on the streets, noise from a local factory or basing national defence on nuclear weapons, we might say that their chances of success, or just of making a decent fist of it, vary with the following sorts of factors:

- The extent to which expressions of dissent or difference are allowed or encouraged, both culturally and in law. In some regimes dissent of any kind to the claim that the party, the Führer or the absolute monarch fully represents or embodies the will and interests of the people would be circumscribed or prevented. But even the most draconian action on the part of rulers seldom eradicates opposition completely, although quite often this opposition is driven underground, to surface through dissident magazines and songs or in forms of dress.
- The extent to which apparently 'open' systems are really accessible to ordinary citizens. It is one thing to believe that strategically endowed actors like cabinet ministers or four-star generals, or even members of an internationally famous rock band, can influence the course of events, quite another to extend this reasoning to John and Jane Doe. All political systems and decision-making processes include some kinds of demands and issues and exclude others. The key issues are the basis on which inclusion and exclusion take place and whether some people or groups are systematically favoured or disadvantaged. We take up these questions more fully in Chapters 4, 13 and 14, where both political participation and the policy processes are examined.
- The sorts of resources available to the individual. It is likely that the relevance or use of a resource – money, status, expertise, communication

skills and so on – will vary from system to system and probably from issue to issue (although this is a point hotly contested in discussions about the distribution and exercise of power). There is also the question as to whether the possession of some resources, say mastery of a technical skill, might be offset by the fact that an individual is evaluated solely on the basis of her/his membership of a collectivity like an ethnic group. The ease and effectiveness with which particular resources can be brought to bear may be affected by the weight of cultural norms and institutionalised practices which either facilitate or hinder individual action.

> In 1970, Kate Jenkins was a junior civil servant in Whitehall, when she was reprimanded by an offended mandarin (senior civil servant) for her 'inappropriate' behaviour in failing to wear her wedding ring to work. Although she progressed in the service, her next promotion, to a job in the Employment Minister's private office, was only assured when, as she puts it, 'I had reassured the Establishment that I wouldn't be rushing home early every night to cook my husband's supper'.
>
> Today, and against all the gender odds, Kate Jenkins has become one of Britain's top civil servants. But her story is not typical. Recent research suggests that women have made only minor inroads into the male redoubts of the senior civil service in Britain. Survey data reveal that only 65 of 600 top officials in the top three civil service grades are female. Six departments in Whitehall employ no senior women, including 10 Downing Street and the Cabinet Office.

The matter of resources is a very complex one. In trying to understand whether an individual or a group has been an effective actor we should not assume that all outcomes are dependent on the mobilisation of effective resources, any more than we should believe that all decisions made by individuals are rational. An apparent lack of resources may not leave an individual without influence, and certainly does not leave her/him without value. Where there is a generalised expectation that individuals – ordinary people – will or ought to behave as social critics, even their most limited and infrequent intervention, say through the act of voting, will have symbolic worth, both for each individual and for the political universe of which s/he is a part. But the chances of individuals affecting outcomes has to be very limited, unless we are talking here about matters which involve mainly private and local exchanges and negotiations bearing on their own lives as mothers, fathers, students or members of the local volleyball team. When intervention has to be made with respect to issues that are not local but international or transnational the opportunities for effective action may be more limited. However, this does not mean that individuals are simply moulded by bigger forces or unable to act except in parochial matters. For one thing, they may join groups which are not only better endowed with resources, but may also be dedicated to the piecemeal or wholesale transformation of society. Amidst all the evidence to the contrary, affirmations of individuality are not hard to find. Occasionally politicians resign on matters of principle, conscientious objectors refuse to enlist in the armed forces of a country and workers flout the 'dress codes' now much in evidence as part of the expression of corporate cultures. 'Whistle-blowers' risk jobs, status and sometimes much worse to bring information about the conduct of businesses, charities and government departments and agencies to the attention of the wider public. These examples and others you might think of are not without moral overtones, but for the purposes of this chapter they are best understood as demonstrations of the symbolic and substantive aspects of individuality. In the rest of this book some of these issues and themes will be revisited to inform topics as various as feminism and globalisation.

## Conclusion

The message to take from this opening chapter is that the study of politics cannot dispense with the concept of the individual, but that we often need to see the individual acting in the context of wider social, political and cultural structures which both enable and constrain action. In other words, the study of political life requires a multi-dimensional approach which is sensitive to the place of the individual in political life and aware of the importance of larger social, cultural and political structures. Different theoretical traditions privilege different units and levels of analysis, in the same way that different political and cultural traditions emphasise either individuality or collectivism of one sort or another. In the next chapter we examine the ways in which individuals learn about politics and acquire political identities.

## Further reading

Bellah, R. M., Madson, R., Swidler, A. and Tipton, S. (1985) *Habits of the Heart*, Berkeley, Ca.: University of California Press. Elegaic account of the values of community and smallness applied to American society.

Hirschman, A. O. (1970) *Exit, Voice and Loyalty*, Cambridge, Mass.: Harvard University Press. The application of rational choice theory to a variety of social situations; it is quite fun to use the concepts to examine your own choices and what affects them.

Peake, M. (1972) *Titus Groan*, Harmondsworth: Penguin. This, the first volume of Peake's gothic masterpiece, tells the story of the boyhood of Titus Groan, heir to Gormenghast and to its ageless, stifling traditions, which inhibit initiative and change.

Pirsig, R. M (1974) *Zen and the Art of Motorcycle Maintenance*, New York: Bodley Head. Pirsig's cult classic of the 1970s is a marvellous compression of some of the main debates in Western philosophy, including the place of the individual, as well as a sort of intellectual 'Easy Rider'.

Wolfe, T. (1970) *The Electric Kool-Aid Acid Test*, London: Fontana. Examines the tensions between rampant individualism and the communitarian impulses of the early hippy drug culture in California in the 1960s.

# 2 LEARNING ABOUT POLITICS

*Ben Rosamond*

# Learning about politics

## Introduction

How do people learn about politics? What are the origins of their political views? At first sight these questions might seem quite banal. In response one might say that we learn about the political world from a fairly predictable range of sources; the media – newspapers, television, radio – spring to mind. Then there are those – the readers of this book perhaps – who learn about politics in a relatively formal way. Others learn about politics through being participants in the political process. Presumably a certain amount of political knowledge is the initial stimulus for political action, but active participation in pressure groups and political parties provides opportunities for the deepening of political knowledge. The same may be true for individuals whose careers take them into public office, as representatives or bureaucrats perhaps. Such people develop an understanding of how politics operates that the ordinary citizen cannot hope to match.

However, like most issues in political science, the question of how people learn about politics is far from simple. After all, what is political knowledge? Is it simply a matter of knowing about the main institutions of government in a country, along with having an idea of the platforms of the main political parties and a sense of what the main political issues of the day might be? Or does it concern a more subtle set of cognitions about authority and human relations which do not apply exclusively to the world of formal political activity? Might it be that 'what we know' about politics is intimately related to 'what we know' about our families or our working lives and so on. In other words, the nature of *what* people learn about politics and *what* constitutes knowledge about politics is a matter of debate.

So to return to our original question, to ask *how* people learn about politics presupposes that we agree about the matter of politics. Anyone who has read the introduction to this volume will realise that this is a far from easy question. In addition, the mechanism through which political knowledge is acquired is also much disputed. There are those who see families as the main seedbed of political views; others point to education, while others still would argue that the process of learning about politics is influenced decisively by the various experiences that life might bring. Going deeper still, there is the question of the psychology of political learning: the mental processes which are involved in conveying and receiving political information.

Finally, there is the question of *when* people learn about politics. The preceding discussion should give a clue to the main lines of the debate. In essence there is an argument about the importance of pre-adult experiences in fixing political views versus the impact wrought by changes in circumstance throughout life.

This chapter seeks to unpack these questions by reflecting upon the ways in which political scientists have sought to come to terms with the question of the acquisition of political knowledge and political views. Beginning the substantive content of the book with a chapter on political learning is a deliberate decision. After all, we could have started with a discussion of political institutions or with an analysis of the main strands in political thought over the centuries. To start with the issue of learning about politics, or **political socialisation**, gives you a chance to reflect upon your own socialisation, your own political views and your own experience of politics.

**Political socialisation** The process, or set of processes, through which people learn about politics and acquire political values. There is much dispute about which processes are significant and about when in the life cycle the most important socialisation takes place.

## Political socialisation

Political socialisation is the term applied by political scientists to embrace the debates sketched out in the opening paragraphs of this chapter. Political socialisation is an important concept because people are not born with an innate knowledge of politics. We do not begin our lives with an in-built sense of political tradition. Neither our role in the political life of our society nor our particular political views are genetically pre-programmed. Thus, as Michael Rush puts it:

M. Rush (1992) *Politics and Society: An Introduction to Political Sociology*, Hemel Hempstead: Harvester Wheatsheaf.

> Political socialisation may be defined as the process by which individuals in a given society become acquainted with the political system and which to a certain degree determines their perceptions and their reactions to political phenomena.
>
> (Rush 1992: 92)

Three questions emerge from this basic definition:

1. What is the purpose of political socialisation?
2. What can we say about the processes by which individuals become acquainted with politics?
3. What can be said about the implied connection between socialisation, on the one hand, and the formulation of political views and types of political behaviour, on the other?

These three questions form the guiding thread of this chapter and, to some extent, of the two chapters that follow.

> **THINK POINT**
> - What about you? A very good place to start is with your own experience of political socialisation. Pause for a few moments to consider your political views, your level of political activism and your general level of knowledge about the political process of your country. We will call this your 'political profile'.
> - Now consider the acquisition of that political profile.
>   Why is it that you think about politics in the way that you do?
>   What do you think motivates you to act politically? ('Acting politically' may mean that you are an aloof or apathetic bystander as well as a fully fledged activist.)
> - How and why did you come to know so much (or so little) about the political process?

## What is political socialisation for?

This question cuts to the heart of political science. It might be rephrased as: Why do people have to be political? Aristotle (384-322 BC) argued in *The Politics* that 'man is by nature a political animal' (Aristotle 1988: 3). By this, Aristotle meant that people, by virtue of their natural propensity to congregate, need to be part of a state in order to flourish as human beings. It follows that since humans are political in the most basic sense of that term, they need to acquire political skills to take part in the most complete expression of human community – the state. Projecting from Aristotle's insight, the first argument would be that political socialisation is required because it is an essential component of being a person. The thinking of Aristotle is echoed in the influential strands of democratic thought which argue that a fully functioning democratic polity requires a politically literate citizenry. Individual self-development is then best served by the active pursuit of and engagement with political knowledge.

Aristotle (1988) *The Politics*, ed. by Stephen Everson, Cambridge: Cambridge University Press.

Such reasoning tends to work outwards from the citizen. Alternatively, we might turn the argument on its head and suggest that any regime requires mass political socialisation into certain regime-friendly norms if it is to survive. From this vantage point, socialisation becomes (arguably) a more sinister process where individuals are moulded into particular roles whose primary function is to serve the system. Of course, the degree to which this process is sinister or oppressive will largely be related to the nature of the regime. Put another way, if we opt to understand political socialisation as serving the functional needs of the regime, then our *perception* of the regime becomes all-important. Let us take the example of the regime which characterises much of the industrialised and post-industrial Western world. We will call it *capitalist liberal democracy*. The extracts below give two alternative accounts of the nature of the regime in such systems. These are followed with respective deductions about the purpose of political socialisation.

## VERSION 1

### The system

Liberal democracy is a system which maximises the freedom of individuals in society. The state is receptive to the demands made upon it by the diversity of groups within society and public policy is largely a synthesis of those demands. In a system of democratic governance, ultimate authority rests with individuals. Moreover, the state does not intervene excessively in civil society, and thus enables individuals to go about their business as they please within the rule of law.

### Political socialisation

This is the mechanism by which people acquire the values, norms and habits which enable them to maximise their individual liberty within a system of pluralist liberal democracy. Socialisation is about (i) learning to be an individual and (ii) acquiring the political knowledge and habits which might optimise that individuality through participation in the liberal democratic polity.

## VERSION 2

### The system

Liberal democracy is a political system which underpins exploitative capitalist relations of production. This supports the concentration of power and wealth in the hands of a privileged ruling group or elite and results in the economic exploitation of the vast majority of the population. Liberal notions of freedom are an ideological mask for these deep, systemic inequalities.

### Political socialisation

This is a mechanism of control which largely indoctrinates the vast majority of the population into belief systems and acceptable forms of behaviour which support (or at least do not threaten) the interest of the ruling groups. This involves the legitimation of inequality and the dispersion throughout society of the view that the current regime is somehow natural or irreplaceable. Socialisation diverts oppressed groups from their real interests by teaching individuals that they are atomised individuals and by masking the inequalities of the system as a whole.

Now these are two polar positions which rather caricature particular sorts of argument. But the crucial point for our analysis is that perspective is everything. If we think of political socialisation in terms of Version 1, then it is quite easy to reconcile the 'individual-up' view with the idea that regimes require socialisation to function properly. Version 2, on the other hand, provides a strong basis for the view that political socialisation usually works against the 'real' interests of people. Here socialisation is about the reinforcement of power rather than the empowerment of the individual.

Either way, it would appear to be true that socialisation is necessary because it provides the social glue that binds the citizen to her/his political system. Regimes of any kind do not last for long without political support. Political support relies upon people recognising the validity of their political arrangements. As one writer puts it, '[p]residents are not respected, laws are not obeyed, taxes are not paid, political stability does not prevail – unless people believe' (Jaros 1973: 7).

So far we have been thinking of the relationship between socialisation and ongoing or longstanding regimes. However, we also need to pay attention to the role that political socialisation may play in the *transformation* of regimes. In such situations incoming political elites are confronted with the difficulty of 'educating' their population about the ways of the new regime. The problem, of course, is that socialisation into a new political system requires the 'un-learning' of old political values, traditions and habits. Examine the extract below, which considers these problems in relation to post-Apartheid South Africa.

It was the start of a new school year in South Africa, and of a new era in its schools. From January 11th to 17th, once-white state schools opened their registers to children of all races. There were neat queues of eager black parents at white suburban schools, but also plenty of confusion. The education minister for Gauteng, the region around Johannesburg, had promised that no child whose parents lived or worked in the feeder area of a school would be turned away because the parents could not afford the fees. On the first day of registrations alone, however, his service received 300 complaints from disgruntled black parents.

The main trouble arose at what are known as 'model-C' schools. These were set up by the previous government under FW de Klerk to offer parents more say in the running of state schools, in return for modest school fees. Most of the formerly segregated white schools have since become model-C schools. Some have used their new rights to admit blacks; about 100,000 black pupils were in model-C schools already by the end of last year. But in others the new fees have kept blacks out.

Black radicals regard model-C schools as thinly disguised bastions of white elitism. When some still refused admission to black children last week, angry black parents accused them of racism. Not always rightly. Most rejections had come on reasonable grounds: the school was already full, the parents neither lived nor worked in the area, or the aspirant pupils were too old. (Schools cannot admit pupils aged more than three years above the average for the class; one school turned away a young man of 20 seeking to join a standard-six class, for 13-year-olds.)

Weightier complaints concerned schools teaching in Afrikaans, a language not spoken by most blacks. One Afrikaans primary school, fearing a flood of black children, asked all applicants to agree to be tested for AIDS; it hastily withdrew the demand after angry complaints. A black reporter posing as a would-be pupil at an Afrikaans school was told the rolls were full; a white colleague queuing at the same school was let in.

Many blacks believe that these schools use language requirements as a proxy for those of race. Yet since most blacks also regard Afrikaans as the language of apartheid, few were expected to register at them. In fact, many did. Some blacks demanded that Afrikaans schools with room to spare become 'parallel medium schools', teaching Afrikaner pupils in Afrikaans, and black ones, in next-door classrooms, in English.

There has been anguish among Afrikaners at the idea of opening white classrooms to blacks. They tend to see integration as a threat to their language and culture, a fear sharpened by the dwindling number of Afrikaners of school age. In Ventersdorp, heartland of extreme Afrikaner politics, the town's white primary school and secondary one were both short of pupils. Both feared they would have to accept blacks. So the primary school upped sticks and moved to an empty part of the secondary-school building. It worked. Only five blacks got into the joint result. But Ventersdorp did not escape change: a new black school was set up in the old white primary-school building, in the middle of the white town.

Overall, though, most model-C schools seem to have accepted some black pupils. But South Africa's real problems remain. Even if every once-white classroom is integrated and every desk filled, blacks will still face a chronic shortage of good education. Township schools are overcrowded. Nearly 60% of black teachers are not fully qualified. Many black children retain a hostility to education born in apartheid days. Only 48% of black pupils who took the school-leaving exam at the end of 1994 passed it, compared with 97% of whites. 'The blame lies with apartheid,' says Mary Metcalfe, Gauteng's education minister. 'But the responsibility for clearing up the mess is ours.'

('New Year, New Schooling: A New Era for Education in south Africa';
reprinted by permission of *The Economist*, 21 January 1995)

Therefore, socialisation may also be about the clash between different value systems. We may not be born with a ready-made set of orientations towards things political, but any shift in patterns of socialisation is likely to encounter the legacy of old patterns.

This dilemma is particularly prevalent in post-communist Central and Eastern Europe. Communism (or state socialism) provided a distinctive mode of political organisation in which a single party (the communist party) ruled without any permissible opposition. Most political activity and virtually all significant career paths were directed through the party hierarchy. Social, political and economic life tended to be directed centrally by the state. It is also worth pointing out that communism was a model of politics that had been more or less imposed upon the countries of Central and Eastern Europe after 1945. As many writers on the left were eager to point out, the communism which dominated the eastern half of the European continent for forty years was a Soviet-style communism that on the whole bore little resemblance to indigenous varieties of socialism and social democracy in those countries.

The dramatic events of 1989 and after resulted in the astonishingly rapid collapse of communist regimes. In the euphoria which followed there was much talk of a transition to both liberal democratic polities and market-based capitalist economies. This was even dubbed by one writer, the American foreign policy analyst Francis Fukuyama (1992), as the 'end of history' because of what he saw as the inevitability of the spread of Western liberal democratic market values. But if a transition was to take place, communism would have to be 'un-learned' and replaced by the values,

F. Fukuyama (1992) *The End of History and the Last Man*, London: Hamish Hamilton.

norms, information and skills that might be necessary in the post-communist environment. This fact was not lost on policy-makers within the ex-communist countries and there was no shortage of outside agencies willing to provide assistance and aid to facilitate the so-called transition. To take one of many examples, the European Commission's aid package PHARE (Poland and Hungary Assistance for Restructuring the Economy, later expanded to several other countries in the region), which began in 1989, was devised with the explicit aim of *transferring* knowledge and skills. As the Commission's literature put it, the package was designed to bring about 'fundamental changes in attitudes, values and behaviour, as well as the means to acquire specific occupational and management skills' (cited in Axford and Booth 1995: 120).

So can individuals, be they managers, workers, civil servants or whatever, be educated in the ways of the West? Can they be taught not only how to restructure their economies along market-capitalist lines and how to build the institutions of liberal democratic political systems, but also how to acquire the value sets which underpin them?

There are, of course, plenty of debates about the propriety or otherwise of Western organisations offering a model of modernisation to post-communist countries. Our task, however, is to focus on the idea of knowledge- and value-transfer.

The research that has been conducted by scholars from a variety of disciplines does seem to suggest that the modernising perspective of aid, assistance and training packages from the West to Eastern Europe is fundamentally naive. Most obviously, the legacy of the communist period is evident. The communist experience had generated certain patterns of behaviour and expectations among mass populations which, it is argued, have been involved in the transformation process in quite complex ways. Poland provides a good example. The sociologist Zygmunt Bauman has cautioned against the assumption that the breakdown of communism arose simply because of a mass disillusionment with the system combined with a widespread desire for its replacement by capitalist liberal democracy. Bauman notes that:

> at the height of popular disaffection in Poland, during the heyday of Solidarity [an independent trade union movement] and the years of its legal suppression, research after research found that a large (and growing!) majority of the population wanted the state to deliver more of its, *specifically communist*, promise.
>
> (Bauman 1994: 20; emphasis mine)

In other words, opinion surveys were showing that Poles had not straightforwardly exchanged their preference for a centralised state-administered regime for an alternative Western-style model founded upon notions of individual responsibility. Thus, if we accept that communist regimes did not necessarily fall because of a desire to replace them with something 'better', it follows that communist attitudinal patterns were not purged by the 'revolutions' of 1989 and after. More recent surveys of opinion show that Poles tend to display apparently inconsistent beliefs about economic restructuring. So, for instance, declining support for the privatisation of state-owned enterprises combines with the view that privatisation is proceeding at too slow a pace (Kolarska-Bobinska 1994). The point is that what we might call incoming narratives (things like private enterprise, private property, individualism and democracy) are not simply absorbed. Their interaction with previously learned sets of values will transform them and displace their meanings. Indeed, as Eva Hoffman points out, it is important to understand not only the legacy of communism:

> Eastern Europe today is haunted by its various pasts, pursued equally by its memories, its amnesias, and its wilful deletions. There is the immensely complex legacy of the communist era, of course, but also the palpable presence of earlier periods, whose ghosts were supposedly slain by communism.
>
> (Hoffman 1994: xv)

We might even speculate that the experience of being socialised into new patterns of behaviour and alternative values is not new to the people of countries like Poland. The historical experience of having external models imposed is likely to generate a sense of cynicism about the resocialisation process.

This brief discussion about post-communist Eastern Europe ought to act as a warning against jumping to premature conclusions in political science. Broad generalisations about the place of socialisation and value-transfer in this context cannot hope to do justice to the complexity and nuance of the situation. What is evident is the dissonance between intention and outcomes. It is true that there are those who would seek to resocialise populations and key groups in such countries with the intention of producing eventual market economies and liberal democratic polities, but in such situations prior patterns of socialisation would appear to intervene in unpredictable ways.

## The processes of political socialisation

So far we have established that socialisation is likely to be an important component of regime stability and that it is something which cannot be administered with the expectation of predictable consequences. The task now is to begin to address the 'when' and 'how' questions raised in the introduction to this chapter.

### When?

The 'when' question has been a matter of lively debate in the literature on political socialisation. Dennis Kavanagh labels the two sides of the debate the *primacy* and *recency* schools. The titles are suggestive of the emphasis given to the critical period of political socialisation. Adherents of the primacy

D. Kavanagh (1983) *Political Science and Political Behaviour,* London: Allen & Unwin.

school emphasise the importance of childhood (and early childhood in particular), whereas analysts from the recency perspective point to the importance of the ongoing socialisation and resocialisation processes which occur throughout life. However, it is important to remember that this is more than simply a debate about when political learning takes place. It is sometimes forgotten that the primacy and recency schools are based upon very different assumptions and thus represent thoroughly different ways of thinking about the world in general and human learning in particular.

Primacy theory draws upon that branch of psychology which places emphasis upon the centrality of the early years to individual development. The key concept of the 'critical period' becomes useful here. The best-known example of the critical period emerged from studies of species of duck which revealed that the birds would not develop 'normally' unless certain sorts of information were acquired within a few hours of hatching. In human terms, the argument would be that the brain is best equipped for the receipt of certain sorts of information at certain critical (or 'sensitive') periods in early childhood. Studies of language acquisition reveal that it is extremely difficult for a person to learn basic linguistic skills in the period beyond childhood. This is thought to be because children are physiologically and psychologically ready to respond to external stimuli in a way which leads them to obtain the knowledge and skills associated with language. So individuals are likely to be socialised to certain sorts of key political information in a critical period in early childhood, probably in the environment provided by immediate family and guardians. Obviously infants and young children will not have the mental equipment to develop fully formulated opinions on the pressing political issues of the day. Neither will they arrive at sophisticated notions of voting preference. The argument of primacy theorists is that the sorts of values which are embedded in the early stages of childhood 'kick in' during later life as the individual becomes acquainted with the public world of politics.

Recency approaches to political socialisation are built around the view that political learning is an ongoing process which relates to changing experiences throughout the life cycle. This position draws on psychological studies of identity formation which suggest that how people define and understand themselves is subject to change. In particular, there is a sense in which the development of a 'mature' identity involves the rejection of earlier influences. In terms of political learning, the argument appears to be that the results of socialisation are never fully embedded, that changing circumstances can produce crises of political identity and resocialisation into new habits, norms and beliefs.

---

***THINK POINT***
- Think about your own experience of politics.
- Which of the two frameworks outlined above, primacy or recency, seems best placed to explain your political socialisation?

H. Hyman (1959) *Political Socialization: A Study in the Psychology of Political Behavior*, New York: Free Press.

D. Easton and J. Dennis (1964) *Children and the Political System: Origins of Political Legitimacy*, New York: McGraw Hill.

Both positions have been supported by empirical research. The first classic study in this area was Herbert Hyman's *Political Socialization*. Hyman's data appeared to support the claim that children in the United States tended to acquire the political preferences of their parents. This could be taken as evidence of the transmission of political values in childhood. In their research reported in *Children and the Political System* David Easton and Jack Dennis studied the acquisition of political values in childhood. They concluded that childhood political socialisation occurred as a four-stage process in which children learned about authority. In the first stage children would recognise that certain individuals were somehow endowed with authority. So, a parent would be able to stipulate bedtime or a police officer would be able to arrest miscreants. Second, children would realise that authority has both public and private faces. Here it would become apparent that the type of authority exercised by the parent is qualitatively different from that of the police officer. In the third stage children would recognise that authority can be embedded in institutions such as governments, parliaments and courts. The final and most sophisticated stage would occur at the point when children understood that institutions have an existence that is separate from the individuals who work within them.

The third and fourth stages in the Easton–Dennis model constitute recognition of what is commonly understood to be the political world: the domain of authoritative institutions. What is interesting is that Easton and Dennis would appear to understand the process of learning about politics as beginning *prior to* a formal understanding of politicians, parties, parliaments and so on. From this viewpoint, it is not necessary to be able to understand oneself in relation to 'political' objects in order to be socialised politically. Moreover, what is learned early matters:

> What enters the mind first remains there to provide lenses and categories for perceiving and sorting later perceptions. Furthermore, early learning occurs during the period of plasticity and openness: the assumptions acquired in childhood frequently appear to be absorbed in an unquestioned fashion. Such assumptions can become inarticulate major premises which then exercise a background effect on thought and overt behaviour precisely because they are not made sufficiently conscious to become open to challenge.
>
> (Greenstein et al.; 1970 cited in Kavanagh 1983: 45)

Support for the recency school is frequently found in accounts of the ways in which individuals adapt to new (political) environments. For example, in the UK politicians elected to Parliament frequently speak of the club-like atmosphere of the House of Commons, which imposes particular and peculiar rules and practices upon the new member. Effective political behaviour in such an environment is unlikely to be accomplished without a thorough learning of these quirks of procedure. To give some idea of the peculiarities of the House of Commons which every new Member of Parliament (MP) must learn, take a look at the extract below written by the political scientist and Conservative MP Nigel Forman.

Another interesting aspect of parliamentary culture in the House of Commons is the extent to which the institutionalised party conflict is organised, even ritualised, by the party Whips working through what are known as 'the usual channels'. This phrase is a euphemism for the sometimes heated and vigorous discussions which take place every day that the House is sitting behind the scenes and off the record between the Leader of the House and the Chief Whip for the Government and the Leader of the Opposition and the Opposition Chief Whip for the official Opposition. Without the benefit of these discussions, which often include Ministers, Whips and their opposite numbers on the opposition front bench, the whole place would probably grind to a halt. As it is, the essential deal between the two sides is based upon two assumptions: that the government must get its business done . . . and that the Opposition must have its full opportunities to oppose. . . . Indeed the co-operative principle is reflected in the attitudes and behaviour of individual MPs who all strive very hard, as soon as they get to Westminster, to secure 'a pair' – that is a member on the other side who will agree on specific occasions to stay away from the division lobbies when the votes are called, so that the overall result of the vote is not affected. . . . A final aspect of parliamentary culture which is worth mentioning is the fondness of MPs in all parties, but especially on the Conservative side, for dining clubs and informal political gatherings of all kinds. . . . In the Labour Party, the various factions usually like to meet, talk and perhaps plot in the Tea Room. In the Conservative Party they prefer the Members' Dining Room or private rooms on the terrace level or even their own London homes. . . . The views of such groups, as and when they are clarified, are then propounded and taken forward by the MPs concerned, who lose little time in passing on the essence of their discussions either to the party whips or sometimes, in suitably veiled form, to lobby journalists. It is in these ways and in these *symposia* (in the Greek sense of the word) that much political opinion at Westminster is moulded and developed.

(Forman, 1991: 154–5)

From Forman's account, we may draw the conclusion that the political values of an individual are subject to heavy mediation, especially in situations where that individual enters into a new environment. This mediation has several aspects. The norms embedded in institutions such as the British House of Commons provide 'rules of the game'. This means that the pursuit of one's political values has to be accommodated within these norms; to 'get on' in Parliament, an MP has to play by the rules of a very long-established political game. However, the process of learning these new rules may also involve the transfer of new values, be they the values residing in Parliament or those of the relevant parliamentary party. Some varieties of institutionalist political science warn the student against the assumption that actors bring ready-made sets of values and interests into institutional settings. Participation within institutions is seen as a generator of values and understandings. Such views have much in common with recency approaches to political socialisation.

### How?

From the discussions above, it should be clear that learning about politics is more than the conscious and deliberate induction into the world of

institutions, parties and issues. If some of the evidence unveiled by empirical research is correct, then it would be fair to argue that the boundaries
set by parents for their children may be as important, if not more important, to political learning than reading a textbook or attending formal
lectures about the functions of government. In short, we are not always
going to be conscious of political socialisation.

That is not to say that political socialisation is never deliberate. Recent
history is littered with authoritarian regimes that have sought to teach appropriate values and norms to their populations from an early age. Communist
political systems again provide some useful exhibits. In such regimes,
centralised syllabuses in schools and higher education were seen as a vital
component in the creation of citizens equipped for the task of building
communism. In the USSR public authorities laid down firm guidelines for
the moral education of the young. One report from 1964 described how
school children in the Soviet Union were taught about

> the inevitability of the end of capitalism and the victory of socialism and
> communism and the leading and organising role of the Communist Party of
> the Soviet Union in the building of communism in our country. History
> and society study are important means of bringing the pupils up in a spirit
> of selfless love for, and devotion to, their socialist motherland, in a spirit
> of peace and friendship among the nations in a spirit of proletarian
> internationalism.
>
> (cited in Lane 1978: 497)

The authorities in the USSR clearly saw a linkage between the development
of a certain moral code amongst the young and long-term regime stability.
It is also interesting to note the way in which children's literature and school
workbooks were laced with ideological messages. Take the examples of mathematics problems used in Soviet education quoted by Michael Rush:

> The first cosmonaut was a citizen of the Soviet union, Comrade Yuri Gagarin.
> He made a flight around the earth in 108 minutes. How many hours and
> how many minutes did the first flight around the earth last?
>
> A brigade of oil workers must drill 6 kilometres 650 metres per year. In the
> first half of the year it drilled 4 kilometres 900 metres, and in the second
> 1 kilometre 50 metres less. Did the brigade fulfil its annual plan? If it over-
> fulfilled it, by how much?
>
> (Rush 1992: 94)

In the German Democratic Republic, a system of 'polytechnic' secondary
schooling was introduced in 1958. Pupils in this system were to be trained
for the practicalities of manual labour in a society striving for the achievement of communism. According to the official justification, the curriculum
took the following form:

> In handicraft classes, which are taken from the first to the sixth grade, the
> children learn to handle simple tools, work with various materials and produce
> useful objects. . . . From the seventh grade onwards, children go once a week
> to a factory for what is known as polytechnical instruction. This consists of
> a theoretical part, comprising the two subjects 'Introduction to socialist

production' and 'Technical drawing', and in practical participation in the production process of the factory, under the heading of 'Production work'. . . .
They learn to work steadily and painstakingly, to be orderly and disciplined
and they realize the value of working together. *It is not so much their performance that is important, but the development of skills and character traits.*
(cited in Childs 1983: 174–5; emphasis mine)

---

**THINK POINT**
- What do you think of political socialisation through education as practised in the communist period in such countries?
- Is there something in the nature of communist regimes that required such overt educational political socialisation?
- Do you see any parallel processes occurring in your own country's educational system?

---

An immediate response from the vantage point of Western countries would be that such socialisation is a crass and abhorrent attribute of authoritarian governments with nothing in the way of democratic credentials.

Having said that, the United States and most Western European countries (although conspicuously not the United Kingdom) have developed pro-grammes of 'civics' education in schools. Programmes of this sort vary from country to country, but in general they tend to form a compulsory part of secondary education in which pupils are taught about basic constitutional principles and the functioning of political and legal processes.

Moreover, it is quite plausible to argue that the function of school curricula in Western countries is identical to that of the old communist countries: the induction of young people into regime-friendly values. The key difference would reside in the argument that control of the curriculum in the West is generally subject to forms of democratic control and popular input.

Some examples from school and university education in the United Kingdom should be enough to make this point. There has been much public debate about education in the UK over the years, but arguments have inten-sified since the mid-1980s. There have been two issues around which debate has turned. The first is the supposed link between the type of education that children receive and the achievement of skills which might be used fruitfully by industry in the quest for economic competitiveness. In essence, calls for the adjustment of the school curriculum to the needs of an advanced capitalist economy at the end of the twentieth century, combined with public policy measures such as the creation of a set of secondary-level City Technology Colleges suggest that what is taught to children may have wider systemic consequences. Similarly, the spectacular growth of university-level courses in subjects such as business and management is testimony to the dominant view that young people *need* to be taught practical, vocational skills rather than receive a conceptually rich but non-vocational training. The second element of the education debate in Britain turns on the issue of what children should be taught at school in terms of core values. On both sides of the argument education is seen as an avenue for the transmission of morality. For conservatives, teachers, in alliance with parents, have a responsibility for the moral induction of the young into, for example, unequivocal notions of right and wrong. The then Secretary of State for Education, John Patten, aroused much controversy in 1992 when he expounded his views on instilling a sense of discipline in the young. He argued: 'Dwindling belief in redemption and damnation has led to a loss of fear of the eternal consequences of goodness and badness. It has a profound effect on personal morality, especially on criminality' (*The Financial Times*, 15 August 1992).

So far we have looked largely at the alleged socialising effects of families and schools. In the literature on socialisation these are labelled **agents of socialisation**. The family and education are by no means the only agents of socialisation. We might look at the socialising impact of the workplace, social class, peer groups, leisure activities or membership of religious groups.

One agency worthy of deeper investigation here is the mass media. The mass media may be divided into print media (such as newspapers) and electronic media (such as film, radio, television and information technology). For the purposes of this discussion, we will attend briefly to the socialising role played by electronic media, particularly film.

Do we find values transmitted, or at least embedded, in films designed for children? An obvious test case would be the films made by the Disney Corporation. Disney acquired a reputation for the production of exquisitely animated feature-length productions, usually in the form of clearly plotted stories. From our point of view, it is interesting to look at these films in terms of the *values* which are being conveyed. The critically acclaimed *Fantasia* (1940) consists of a series of animated interpretations of pieces of classical music. In one of these sequences, a collection of flying horses, nymphs and various other mythological characters are animated to the music of Beethoven. To some eyes, this particular section of the film is most notable for its presentation of quite stark gender stereotypes. *Bambi* (1942) tells the story of a young male deer, brought up by his mother in a deeply idyllic woodland environment, who is taught the crucial lessons about life, responsibility and being a man by his (largely absent) father. More recently, *Pocahontas* (1995), the tale of a love affair between a native American Princess and an English colonial sea captain, juxtaposes the harmonious values of indigenous cultures with the barbarian tendency of supposedly civilising cultures. Yet the brief relationship between Pocahontas and John Smith is a testimony to the possibilities of congruous intercultural understanding.

Such media become important if we accept the view that core values are imprinted at an early age. A recency-based explanation could point to the role of movies and other media in shaping adult political sensibilities. After all, some films are the transmitters of overtly political messages. Take *Salvador* (1986), Oliver Stone's scathing critique of US foreign policy in Central America, or *Bob Roberts* (1992), Tim Robbins's cutting satire on fundamentalist neo-conservatism in the US. Some movies might not be directly

**Agents of socialisation**
Those individuals, groups or institutions which are responsible for the transmission of the information through which people acquire their socialistion.

'political', but may seek to convey particular sorts of values. Examples would include the compelling drama of *12 Angry Men* (Sidney Lumet, 1957), in which a liberal juror played by Henry Fonda seeks to overturn the prejudiced rush to convict a young murder suspect by the other eleven; or the feminist road movie *Thelma and Louise* (Ridley Scott, 1991).

At this point it is worth injecting a note of caution. To what extent do stimuli provided by the media alter perceptions or reinforce pre-existing cognitions? Unfortunately, there is no clear answer to this question, in spite of much research. As Hans Kleinsteuber puts it:

> [I]f we ask people whether media have any effect, we get an ambiguous answer: they accept an effect for people in general, but deny it in respect of themselves ... [W]ith political proselytising what is important is the previous attitude of the recipient: even the technically best advertising spot will not change a voter's mind if the party says nothing to him, the programme does not meet his expectations or the leading candidate seems untrustworthy.
>
> (Kleinsteuber 1995: 129)

Of course, it is very difficult to measure the impact of the media upon the cognitions of an individual, and herein lies one of the main problems of research into political socialisation. It is quite easy to establish the values which agents might be transmitting, but altogether more demanding to establish whether exposure to the agent actually has an effect. As Kleinsteuber's comment illustrates, asking someone whether or not they have been influenced is not likely to yield particularly reliable responses.

## The importance of political socialisation

The study of political learning or political socialisation is not an insulated discrete topic. That much should already be clear. To conclude this chapter it is worth addressing three particular questions about the wider implications of political socialisation for, respectively, political science, politics and the political system.

### What does political socialisation tell us about political science?

Why did political scientists become interested in socialisation? This is worthy of some lengthy discussion. Anyone who has seriously thought about politics would have contemplated either the relationship between political learning and political action or the way in which types of regime might be underpinned by certain sorts of formal or informal socialisation. We have seen that these ways of thinking go back at least as far as ancient Greece. But political socialisation as a concept which emerged very much in the environment of political science in the United States during the 1950s.

As most commentators acknowledge, the appearance of political socialisation as a serious subject of empirical enquiry was bound up with the so-called behavioural revolution in political science. In this view the main purpose of political, and for that matter, social science is the explanation of individual and collective behaviour. As David Sanders puts it, '[t]he central question that behaviouralists ask is: "Why do individuals, institutional actors and nation states behave in the way that they do?"' (Sanders 1995: 74). Framing the problematic of enquiry in this way suggests that behaviouralists are interested in establishing patterns of *causation*. The basic pattern of behavioural reasoning is illustrated in Figure 2.1. This raises a number of subsidiary questions which guide behaviourally oriented research. These might include:

D. Sanders (1995) 'Behavioural Analysis', in D. Marsh and G. Stoker (eds) *Theory and Methods in Political Science*, Basingstoke: Macmillan.

1. Why does stimulus $x$ produce response $y$ and not an alternative response?
2. How do the political systemic consequences $z$ of behaviour $y$ influence future political behaviour?

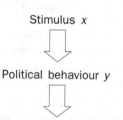

*Figure 2.1* Basic reasoning of behavioural political science

Furthermore, behaviouralists insist that we must be able to observe behaviour and test hypotheses empirically. The resulting body of empirical political theory will be open to verification or falsification. In other words, the behavioural movement was entangled with the quest to make the study of social phenomena more scientific. We have already addressed the question of whether the study of politics can be scientific, in the Introduction, and it might be worth thinking about that issue again now. For behaviouralists, the accumulation of empirical data from observable political phenomena in pursuit of particular hypotheses could lead to the tantalising prospect of law-like generalisations about the political world. But it was not just that the results of research would be scientifically valid; behaviouralists also believed that the ways in which they devised and conducted research projects should aspire to operate in the manner of the natural sciences.

The importance of political socialisation should be clear. If we are able to derive empirical generalisations about how, when and from whom people learn about politics, then we have a potentially powerful set of tools for explaining how people behave politically. Also, because of the behaviouralist concentration upon what is readily observable, enquiries into political socialisation have tended to concentrate on measurable sources of political information such as school curricula or the mass media or research into the patterns of learning among children across time.

---

**THINK POINT**

1 What do you make of behaviouralist approaches to the study of politics?
2 Do they have any obvious weaknesses?

---

For its advocates, behaviouralism had a number of advantages over other forms of political study. Perhaps the least controversial claim made on the approach's behalf was that it widened the scope of political science. Behaviouralism, argue its champions, focused attention away from the traditionally legalistic study of political institutions and constitutions towards the political actions of real people in all levels of the political system. More contentiously, behaviour is treated as the single most important unit of analysis in the study of politics; more important than institutional rules or norms. Doing political science in this way was made possible by advances in research methods which employed large-scale surveys amenable to sophisticated statistical analysis. Developments in computer hardware and software have made such techniques less burdensome on the researcher and enabled the collection and processing of enormous quantities of data.

For its opponents, behaviouralism was a deeply flawed approach to the study of politics for two reasons. The first line of criticism is that behavi-ouralism is likely to produce work that is overtly *empiricist*. In other words, the tenets of behaviouralism are said to encourage the asinine accumulation of facts. Generalisations emerge once regularities begin to form within a mass of accumulated empirical data. For many social scientists this approach is wrong-headed because it neglects the importance of devising theoretical and conceptual categories prior to the accumulation and manipulation of data (Sartori 1970). What we get is a political science based on phenomena that are amenable to easy measurement rather than those that are of theoretical importance. In his discussion of behaviouralism, Sanders (1995) argues that this tendency is likely to neglect potentially important explanations on the grounds that they might be difficult or impossible to organise. He points to studies of voting behaviour which have managed to achieve quite sophisti-cated analyses of individual motivations for voting based upon the interplay of various factors such as social position, ideological and party identification and economic perceptions. But there is no incorporation into voting studies of, for example, the ways in which individuals conceptualise themselves. As Sanders puts it, 'it is very hard to envisage how the responses to such questions – given the difficulty of measuring those responses systematically – could ever be incorporated into formal analysis. As a result they are largely excluded from the analytic frame' (Sanders 1995: 66).

The second and related point is that behaviouralist political science elevates the quantifiable and relegates the theoretical. Behaviouralist-influenced political scientists have a predisposition for measuring things. Data is valid if it can be measured. The other side of the coin is that data is not valid if it is not quantifiable. This betrays a rather contentious set of assumptions about the political world and how that world might be studied. For instance many critics note that the pseudo-scientific bent of behaviouralism leads many researchers to neglect the fact that they are actors in the social and political world themselves. Objectivity is not easily achieved. Of particular importance is the behavioural assumption that theory and observation can be separated. The researcher is portrayed as an objective onlooker who then builds empirical theory based upon what s/he has observed. But we can argue quite strongly that all observation is influenced by a pre-existing theoretical position. Thus how the researcher observes is likely to be subject to some sort of theoretical preconception. Indeed the selection of what is to be observed is equally likely to be conditioned in the same way. This *scientism* is also accused of neglecting the normative element of political enquiry. So-called value freedom is taken to be a good thing among behaviouralists, but the marginalising of values also potentially marginalises the great questions of political philosophy – questions about rights, freedom and justice.

The use of powerful arguments of this sort by critics has led to the abandonment of much of the most zealous and positivistic behaviouralism. Having said that, behaviouralism is still one of the most influential components of contemporary political science. A behavioural emphasis is central to the study of elections and voting, perhaps the best-known and most-publicised manifestation of the study of politics.

In the context of this volume, behaviouralism is important, not only because it provides a good case study of a particular way of 'doing' political science, but also because of the content of this chapter and of Chapters 3 and 4. As we will see, it is not necessary to be a behaviouralist to study political behaviour. But it very difficult to understand the work which has been done on socialisation, political culture and political participation without a basic grounding in behaviouralism.

### What does political socialisation tell us about politics?

This can be stated with more brevity. As indicated above, the work done on political socialisation rather suggests that politics is a very broad-based activity which is by no means confined to the world of formal political institutions. The study of political socialisation opens up the study of politics to both the analysis of political behaviour (how individuals and groups behave within the bounds set by institutions) and research into the factors which lie behind political action.

Moreover, one of the basic assumptions of much work on political socialisation is the idea that orientations to political objects are the product of the mobilisation of other sorts of values which we may learn in other arenas, whether as a child watching a Disney film or as an adult confronting problems in the workplace. So politics is not necessarily a separate sphere of human existence somehow apart from all other aspects of life. In many ways it is our life.

### *What does political socialisation tell us about the political system?*

The study of political socialisation raises some intrinsically interesting questions about the ways in which individuals acquire their political views and their orientations towards political objects. However, it is also worth drawing out some rather bigger issues which will be developed and argued through in the course of the next few chapters. Most prominently, there is the matter of the relationship between what we learn about politics and the stability or otherwise of the political system within which we live. Is what we learn about politics, in terms of particular chunks of knowledge as well as deeper values, somehow supportive of the regime? On the other hand, might it be possible to learn and mobilise around dysfunctional values? Also, what is it that we learn when we are socialised? This is very much the concern of Chapter 3. And, finally, does the way in which we are socialised influence the way in which we engage in political action (Chapter 4)?

Unfortunately, we will have to leave these questions hanging. Also, you should not expect to have any clear-cut answers to this issue by the time that you have finished reading this book. Unfortunately, political science is never that simple, but eventually you might be able to address these questions with greater conceptual sophistication.

## Conclusion

We all learn about politics, but not in ways that may be immediately obvious. How often do we think that a 6-year-old child sitting in a classroom, completing a writing exercise set by the teacher is being socialised politically? When we sit down to watch a film, do we imagine that it may propogate certain sets of values that reinforce or clash with our own? Of course, there is considerable dispute about whether either of these examples should be understood as an instance of the acquisition of political values and norms. Much depends upon what we think politics is all about and upon what we regard as politically relevant knowledge. The great advantage of studying socialisation is that it raises these difficult questions. With any luck it makes us less complacent about the subject that we study.

## Further reading

Bryant, C. G. A. and Mokrzycki, E. (eds) (1994) *The New Great Transformation? Change and Continuity in East-Central Europe*, London: Routledge. A collection of essays reflecting on post-communism in Europe, containing much valuable insight for the student of political socialisation.

Easton, D. and Dennis, J. (1969) *Children and the Political System: Origins of Political Legitimacy*, New York: McGraw Hill. The most famous study of pre-adult political socialisation.

## Exercise

Write a short statement of between 500 and 1,000 words reflecting on your own political socialisation experiences. Putting these thoughts down on paper should be a valuable exercise; it will help you to see the connections between personal experience and the study of politics. Remember you will not be writing about your views on particular political issues. Rather you should be thinking about where those views came from and the factors in your life which have had cause to influence or change your perspective on the poltiical world.

The following guidelines may be of help:

1. What are my political views? Not just which political party do I support but how do I feel about broader issues; indeed do I have any discernable political views?
2. Can I identify any agents of socialisation which may have acted as formative political influences? Here we are talking about parents, teachers, friends as well as the media.
3. At what points in my life do I think my key socialisation experiences occurred?: childhood, adolescence, adulthood?
4. Have my views about politics changed over time? If so, do these changes reflect new socialisation experiences brought about in new environments (such as moving to a new area, changing schools or starting a new job)?

Eulau, H. (1963) *The Behavioural Persuasion in Politics*, New York: Random House. A helpful discussion from a leading practitioner of behaviouralism.

Hyman, H. (1959) *Political Socialization: A Study in the Psychology of Political Behaviour*, New York: Free Press. Still worth a read. Usually regarded as the first systematic study of political socialisation.

Kavanagh, D. (1983) *Political Science and Political Behaviour*, London: Unwin Hyman. A clear critical discussion of the main themes of behavioural political science.

Rush, M. (1992) *Politics and Society: An Introduction to Political Sociology*, 2nd edn, Hemel Hempstead: Harvester Wheatsheaf. A clear introduction to an important subfield of political science.

Sanders, D. (1995) 'Behavioural Analysis', in D. Marsh and G. Stoker (eds) *Theory and Methods in Political Science*, Basingstoke: Macmillan. A very useful counterweight to blanket dismissals of behaviouralism. Clear and concise.

Young, H. (1990) *One of Us*, London: Pan. A biography of the former British Prime Minister Margaret Thatcher, notable for the attention that it pays to the formative impact of her early years.

# 3 POLITICAL CULTURE

*Ben Rosamond*

# Political culture

## Introduction

Put crudely, the previous chapter considered how human beings learn about politics. This chapter, to put it equally crudely, asks what it is that they learn. This is not simply what people are taught about politics in a formal sense, but also what they come to feel for and regard as natural about the society in which they live. The term used by students of politics to denote such values is **political culture**.

Culture is a rather elusive concept. Raymond Williams famously stated that '[c]ulture is one of the two or three most complicated words in the English language' (R. Williams 1976: 76). It is a term which is used in everyday discourse to connote at least two distinct things. The first is culture as 'high culture'. To say that a person is cultured suggests that s/he is well read or has been exposed with beneficial effects to the virtues associated with great music, literature or art. Here 'culture' is about personal or social improvement. The second sense in which 'culture' is commonly used relates to the depiction of difference. So it is frequently the case that disparities in habit, behaviour and outlook between two or more nationalities are explained by recourse to culture. So Germans are frequently portrayed as methodical, Australians as casual and flippant, the French as volatile and romantic, the English as reserved and soulless.

Reflection on national cultural stereotypes infuses a lot of the very best humour. The success of British comedy series such as *Monty Python's Flying Circus*, *Fawlty Towers* and *Yes Minister* is often ascribed to the way in which these programmes construct comic reflections upon British (or, more often English) cultural stereotypes. In the case of *Fawlty Towers* the writers, John Cleese and Connie Booth, created an English grotesque in the form of Basil Fawlty, a man of deeply reactionary sentiments who is cursed with the inability to control a world populated by (invariably) 'modern', cosmopolitan characters (a perfect metaphor for Britain in the mid-1970s perhaps). While humour with a 'cultural' foundation is frequently used in a self-deprecatory manner, it is also the case that cultural stereotyping can infect more pernicious forms of comedic discourse. Witness the stigmatisation

**Political culture** The set of values, beliefs and attitudes within which a political system operates.

R. Williams (1976) *Keywords: A Vocabulary of Culture and Society*, London: Fontana.

of ethnic minorities or other nationalities in much of what passes as humour.

So what is the use of 'culture' to the political scientist? After all, it is surely unseemly for supposedly detached members of the academic community to be engaging in the use of stereotypes. The answer lies partly with the empirical observation that there are notable variations in the ways in which politics is conducted from country to country. Therefore, the point of investigating politics through the lens provided by a cultural approach lies in the ways that culture can be used to give a conceptual grounding to the designation of difference. So if there is an assumption which underlies the work of those who use the concept of political culture, it is that distinct norms, rules, habits, traditions and belief systems sit at the heart of each political system, shaping the behaviour of the main participants in the political process.

Defining political culture is a controversial business. A famous paper written in the 1970s unearthed in excess of thirty meanings of the concept (Patrick 1976). Dennis Kavanagh has written widely on political culture. His preferred definition seems to be the following:

> For our purposes we may regard the political culture as a shorthand expression to denote the set of values within which a political system operates. It is something between the state of public opinion and an individual's personality characteristics.
>
> (Kavanagh, 1983: 49)

G. A. Almond and S. Verba (1963) *The Civic Culture: Political Attitudes and Democracy in Five Nations*, Princeton: Princeton University Press.

Another famous definition was that provided by the American political scientists Gabriel Almond and Sidney Verba in their major work *The Civic Culture*. They wrote of political culture as the 'pattern of orientations to political objects among the members of the nation' (Almond and Verba 1963: 15). By 'political objects', Almond and Verba meant institutions such as parliaments and political parties, as well as less tangible aspects of a nation's political life such as the conventional account of its history. Political culture is not simply to do with what we believe, but is also bound up with the ways in which we (particularly collectively) behave politically. So political culture can also be understood in terms of the political practices and rituals of a given community.

---

**THINK POINT**
- What are the components of your country's political culture?
- A useful way to engage with a new concept is to try it out for yourself. Spend a few minutes writing down what you consider to be the main elements of your country's political culture, taking into account the definition of the concept outlined above.
- Remember that you are not engaged in an exercise to describe the formal institutional make-up of your country. What you are briefed to do here is to think about the memories, traditions, habits, beliefs, norms and rules which inform political action by both elites and masses.
- You might also think about your place in your country's political culture. What are your orientations to political objects?

# The uses of political culture

Dennis Kavanagh has frequently stated in his work that 'political culture' is a new term for an old idea. Indeed a random trawl through the annals of political thought will yield multiple instances of thinkers who have contemplated the relationship between regimes and the value systems which underpin them.

We can go back to the writings of Plato (427–347 BC), commonly thought of as the founder of political thought, to find explicit statements about what we now know as political culture. In *The Republic* Plato stated:

> [g]overnments vary as the dispositions of men vary, and that there must be as many of one as there are of the other. For we cannot suppose that States are made of 'oak and rock' and not out of the human natures which are in them.
>
> (Plato 1945: 32)

Plato (1945) *The Republic*, trans. and with introd. by F. M. Cornford, Oxford and New York: Clarendon Press.

Plato's student Aristotle (384–322 BC) brought his taxonomic way of thinking into the study of political culture. In his *Politics* Aristotle tried to discern the most suitable form of human government. To achieve this end, he did not focus simply on institutions but also on social structures and their attendant value systems. What emerges is a celebration of the virtues of civility, consensus and partnership in politics which in turn is associated with a mixture of oligarchic and democratic characteristics and control by the 'middle classes' (in Aristotle's terms, those who are neither rich nor poor).

Aristotle (1985) *The Politics*, ed. by Stephen Everson, Cambridge: Cambridge University Press.

In modern political thought very few key writers failed to make the connection between the dispositions of people and the sorts of political system in which they lived. Jean-Jacques Rousseau, writing in the eighteenth century, wrote much on the importance of morality and custom as the basis of political stability. From a different perspective, the most famous critic of the French Revolution, Edmund Burke, placed considerable emphasis on the vital importance of tradition and the destructive consequences of the uprooting of well-established political norms. His *Reflections on the Revolution in France* (1790) is a quite devastating polemic against the use – as he saw it – of abstract theorising to displace long-standing institutions which rested on appropriate cultural foundations. To engineer a rupture with the past, as the French revolutionaries had done, was seriously misplaced. Progress, argued Burke, is best achieved in the context of continuity and with reference to past precedent and tradition.

Edmund Burke (1982) *Reflections on the Revolution in France*, Harmondsworth: Penguin.

There does seem to be a common theme throughout these diverse writings. The purpose of investigating what we now know as political culture has predominantly been to establish the nature of the relationship between regime *stability* and the structure of beliefs, values and traditions at any given time. The claim being made is that political culture filters our perceptions, influences our attitudes and has a large say in the extent and manner of our political participation (Dogan and Pelassy 1990). To be more precise, the relationship being proposed seems to take the form shown in Figure 3.1. Of course, we have to be careful with such grand schemes. As with all frameworks for analysis, there are certain assumptions being made. For example, the approach described in Figure 3.1 assumes that there is an identifiable political culture into which individuals are socialised. Moreover, the approach assumes that the constitution of a political culture will influence patterns of behaviour within a political system and that these behavioural patterns, in turn, have a major influence on the stability of a regime.

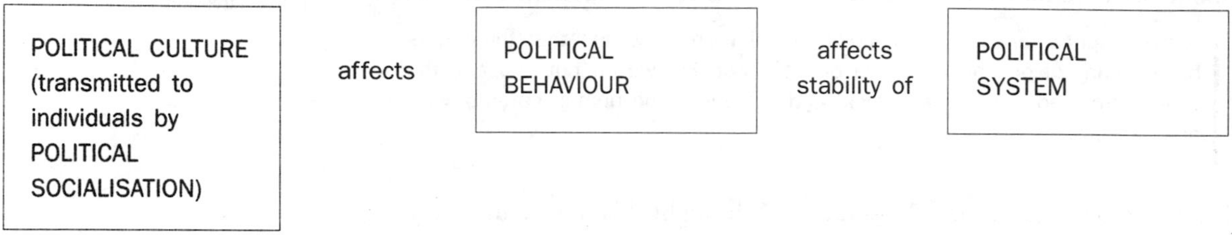

POLITICAL CULTURE (transmitted to individuals by POLITICAL SOCIALISATION)  →  affects  →  POLITICAL BEHAVIOUR  →  affects stability of  →  POLITICAL SYSTEM

Figure 3.1 Political culture and political stability

THINK POINT
- Take a close look at Figure 3.1. Can you think of any objections to the causal chain which is being proposed?
- To what extent do you think that it is possible to explain stability with reference to the underpinnings provided by political culture?

## The civic culture

The entry of the concept of political culture into the lexicon of political studies is most associated with the rise of the behavioural movement, discussed in Chapter 2. The attractiveness of the idea of political culture to behaviouralists should be obvious. The promise of finding correlations between certain sorts of cultural conditions and various levels of political stability dovetailed well with the behaviouralist's quest for scientific precision in explanation. Also, the study of attitudes and beliefs about politics amongst citizens was testimony to the behaviouralists emphasis on non-institutional forms of politics.

The paradigmatic example of the behavioural study of political culture remains *The Civic Culture*, by the American political scientists Gabriel Almond and Sidney Verba, which was first published in 1963. *The Civic Culture* was a report on an extensive survey carried out in five countries – the United States, the United Kingdom, Italy the Federal Republic of Germany and Mexico – in 1959. The methods used by Almond and Verba and their team of researchers say much about their understanding of political culture. The aim of the surveys was to acquire a mass of comparative data on public opinion from which conclusions about political culture could be made. Respondents – of whom there were roughly 1,000 in each country – were asked three sorts of questions about their attitudes to political objects. *Cognitive* questions were used to test the respondents' factual knowledge and beliefs about their respective political systems. *Affective* questions dealt with the ways in which those surveyed felt about those political objects – their attitudes to their political system. Finally, *evaluative* questions sought to ascertain opinions and judgements about the political objects, a test of wider political values.

---

**THINK POINT**
- Consider the description above of Almond and Verba's methodology. Does it seem to you to be a useful way of conducting research into political culture?
- Can you think of any problems with the methods used?
- Do you think that the methods used might pre-empt certain sorts of conclusion?

---

Armed with their data, Almond and Verba went on to make some influential and provocative statements about political culture. They identified three ideal types of individual and collective (national) political culture: parochial, subject and participant. A *parochial* political culture was characterised by general ignorance about political objects and a consequent lack of involvement in political activity. *Subject* political cultures were characterised by widespread knowledge about political processes, but a disinclination to participate in political activity, often because of feelings of powerlessness. *Participant* political cultures combined knowledge about politics with a willingness to participate in the political process. In such situations, people feel able to affect change; that their political activity will make a difference. It is important to remember two points. First, Almond and Verba regarded these types of political culture as the properties of both individuals and political systems as a whole. It was thought possible to aggregate individual orientations. The assumption, therefore, is that it is possible to link the micro and the macro aspects of politics. Second, the three categories are **ideal types**. This means that they represent an attempt to impose a classification upon the disordered and messy reality of the human world. This is said to aid investigation and to further knowledge by providing order to our thinking (see Burger 1976). Political culture would invariably appear as some sort of mixture of these ideal types and this is very much what Almond and Verba's research showed.

**Ideal type** A social scientific technique which imposes an analytical order on the social world and provides clear categories to guide further investigation.

In fact Almond and Verba concluded that all three ideal types would be unsatisfactory as cultural underpinnings for a stable democratic polity. Parochialism was a characteristic of 'traditional' societies and not of mature democracies, where developed institutions require a qualitatively different sort of value system. Subject political cultures were also deemed unsuitable. While citizens in such situations possessed the requisite political knowledge, they did not possess the sense that they could be effective democratic actors. On the other hand, a participant political culture carried with it the danger of a kind of democratic overload. Too many citizens trying to effect change through mass participation would be a source of instability which could seriously undermine the normative ideal of democratic stability.

Thus, in terms of their normative conclusions Almond and Verba argued that the best sort of political culture for a stable democratic system would involve a mix of subject and participant elements. They labelled this mixture the **civic culture**. In the civic culture, citizens would possess high levels of knowledge about the political process and feel empowered as political actors. Crucially, however, they would recognise the legitimacy of elites to make decisions on their behalf. At the same time, elites would be sensitive to the preferences of the mass population. The resultant system is a balance (a conclusion which echoes that of Aristotle, a point acknowledged by Almond (1980) himself). Almond and Verba argued that the political cultures of the United States and, particularly, the United Kingdom came near to the civic culture ideal.

**Civic culture** The type of political culture thought by some to provide the best environment for stable democratic politics to occur. It combines the optimum mix of subject and participant political attitudes.

### Criticisms of The Civic Culture

The work of Almond and Verba was subjected to much scrutiny. In particular, *The Civic Culture* appeared to be vulnerable to five sorts of criticism. While all of these were directed specifically at this one study, it is true that they could also be used to question various aspects of the cultural approach to politics.

The first, and perhaps most obvious, line of objection concerned the apparent Anglo-American bias of the study. In the concluding pages of *The Civic Culture* Almond and Verba argued that

> the development of a stable and effective democratic government depends upon more than the structures of government and politics: it depends upon the orientations that people have to the political process – upon the political culture. Unless a political culture is able to support a democratic system, the chances for the success of that system are slim . . . The civic culture appears to be particularly appropriate for a democratic political system. It is not the only form of democratic political culture, but it seems to be the one most congruent with a stable, democratic system.
>
> (Almond and Verba 1963: 498)

A few pages earlier, the explicit claim is made that the political systems of Germany, Italy and Mexico lack the necessary cultural basis for democratic stability (Almond and Verba 1963: 496). The US and Britain clearly have what it takes for democratic stability to prevail in the long term.

But not all stable political systems possess the qualities associated with the civic culture. Arend Lijphart noted that certain societies with explicitly non-consensual political cultures were able to achieve democratic stability. This suggested that the structure of political institutions could intervene to overcome divisiveness and hostility in the political culture. Lijphart's argument was that consensual behaviour among political elites with appropriate

A. Lijphart (1977) *Democracy in Plural Societies: A Comparative Exploration*, New Haven, CT: Yale University Press.

institutional support could ensure the effective governance of societies that were divided on religious, ideological, linguistic, regional, cultural, racial or ethnic lines. This form of democracy was labelled **consociational democracy** (Lijphart 1977, 1991). The two key criteria for the successful operation of a consociational democracy were identified as (i) the existence of a segmented society, where those segments are largely autonomous, and (ii) the existence of executive power-sharing among political elites. The major instances of consociational democracy identified by Lijphart are shown in Table 3.1. Apart from questioning a tendency towards the wholesale dismissal of continental European polities as unstable, Lijphart's important contribution also raises more profound questions of explanation in political science. In essence Lijphart is saying that institutions matter and can ameliorate the impact of political culture upon the political system, whereas Almond and Verba's version is that institutions are largely derived from a cultural base. For Lijphart there is no direct connection between the shape of a political culture and the stability of its governance. Of course, Lijphart did not jettison the idea of culture altogether. Power-sharing in consociational democracies is reliant upon a coalescent elite political culture. But then we need to ask what role the institutional environment plays in the promotion of coalescent attitudes among political elites. If it does play a role, culture becomes a derivative of institutions.

This last point touches on the second strand of criticism. This concerns the deeper-lying issue of the sorts of causal relationships that were being assumed by the authors of *The Civic Culture*. Some of the most cogent criticisms of the study argued that Almond and Verba had assumed that political structures could be explained with reference to political cultures. In other words, the allegation is that the authors of *The Civic Culture* understood degrees of democratic stability as being determined or caused by political culture. Two alternative positions exist. First, the chain of causation could be turned around so that we could explain the level of civic culture in a society with reference to the level of democratic stability. So, here, democratic stability creates and sustains what is understood as the civic culture. Second, there is the more complex position developed by Carole Pateman (1971), which argues that culture and structures are interdependent and mutually reinforcing. And in any case, how is democratic stability to be measured? While students of the relationship between culture and stability have drawn up elaborate schemes for the measurement of political culture, they would appear to have been less successful in the creation of criteria for measuring levels of stability in a given political system.

The third and fourth sources of criticism derive from the survey methodology used to obtain data about political culture. The third criticism of *The Civic Culture* compares the claims made about political culture to the size of the sample interviewed. In his critique of Almond and Verba, Dennis Kavanagh makes several challenging points along these lines. Around 1,000 individuals in each country were interviewed. This is a reasonably large sample, but not enough to allow the confident construction of a general

**Consociational democracy** A form of government said to characterise deeply divided, albeit stable, countries. It involves the creation of power-sharing institutions among coalescent political elites.

C. Pateman (1971) 'Political Culture, Political Structure and Political Change', *British Journal of Political Science* 1(3).

*Table 3.1* Cases of consociational democracy

Austria 1945–66
Belgium 1918–
Canada 1840–67; contemporary (partial)
Cyprus 1960–3
Israel 1948– (partial)
Lebanon 1943–75
Luxembourg *c*1917–67
Malaysia 1955–
Netherlands 1917–67
Netherlands Antilles 1950–1985
Surinam 1958–73
Switzerland 1943–

*Source:* Lijphart (1991)

D. Kavanagh (1980) 'Political Culture in Great Britain: The Decline of the Civic Culture', in G. A. Almond and S. Verba (eds) *The Civic Culture Revisited*, Boston: Little, Brown & Co.

theory of political culture. Kavanagh's argument is that such a sample size does not produce valid sample sizes of the various subgroups in each country. He dissects the British sample to prove the point:

> The British sample . . . contains only 24 respondents who had been to university . . . 58 members of the Labour Party, and only 58 from Wales and 94 from Scotland. This has always been a problem with representative British samples; over 80 percent of respondents live in England and three fifths share the characteristics of being English, white Protestant and resident in urban areas.
>
> (Kavanagh 1980: 131)

The broader point which is raised by Kavanagh's examination of the sampling deficiencies of *The Civic Culture* is the probable co-existence of a range of subgroups within any given country which may exhibit a plurality of political cultures and identities (see 'Subcultures' on pp. 88–91). The mistake may be to assume that there is such a thing as a national political culture which can be revealed through scientific measurement.

The fourth objection relates to the difficulty of establishing the meaning of responses to surveys. This is a perennial problem in survey work and is by no means a problem confined to Almond and Verba's investigations. The designer of the questionnaire has an agenda. The purpose of conducting surveys is to test hypotheses and so the questions seek to extract information from respondents that might help in the confirmation or refutation of those hypotheses. There are three particular dangers here. First, the respondent may also have an agenda and may interpret the questions in a way which is completely at variance with the purposes of the questionnaire. This clash of interpretations may not be revealed overtly; it may be invisible. The consequence is a distortion in the results. Second, the *Civic Culture* interviews asked people a very detailed list of questions about their political orientations (see Almond and Verba 1963: 526–49). The danger here is that the interview process may actually construct political orientations in individuals which may have been either not coherent or not present prior to the administration of the survey. Third, there is the possibility that the meaning of responses is non-fungible – that is to say, that the same response to the same question in different countries may not have equivalent meanings. This problem of functional equivalence is a major bugbear in comparative research. In some countries violence is eschewed as a method in politics; in others it is used on a regular basis, but may be regarded as a perfectly acceptable way of ordering political life. Observers brought up in a country like the UK, where general elections are infrequent occurrences have often regarded a country like Italy, where elections have tended to occur often, as a prime example of political instability. But such a view may mistake the local (Italian) function of elections, which might be described as reordering the executive in the same way as Cabinet reshuffles are used to reorder it in the British system – which, of course, are frequent occurrences.

The fifth and last point does not require elaboration, and does not really constitute a criticism because Almond and Verba were well aware of the issue when they did their work. Quite simply, political cultures evolve and any attempt, no matter how successful, to measure political culture can only be a snapshot of political culture at that particular time.

---

**THINK POINT**
- Go back to thinking about your country's political culture. Do you think that it might have changed over the last ten, fifty or 100 years?
- If so, how and, more importantly, why?

---

## An alternative approach: political culture and ideology

Much of the work done on political culture since the Second World War has followed from behavioural premises. However, that represents only one way of defining and using the concept of political culture from a range of alternative perspectives. By way of demonstration, we now turn to a very different way of 'doing' political science to see how notions of political culture might be employed. At first sight Marxism, with its emphasis on the economic dimensions of social life, may not be an obvious site for the discussion of things cultural. However, largely through the use of the concept of *ideology*, a number of Marxist and neo-Marxist thinkers have drawn up some striking and influential ideas about the operation of culture in politics.

To begin this discussion it is worth reflecting a little on the distinctive contribution made by Marxism to the understanding of ideology (for a much fuller elaboration, see Chapter 8). Marx and Engels tended to regard the dominant ideas of any historical epoch as an expression of the interests of the most powerful social groups. In other words, dominant attitudes and systems of political and cultural thought at any given time are rooted in a power relationship. The class which controls economic life disperses throughout society its attitudinal pattern and the belief systems which support it. This reveals two important attributes of the Marxist conception of ideology. First, ideology can be partially understood as *false consciousness*, which may mask the 'real interests' of the bulk of society. Broadly speaking, such real interests are defined as the overthrow of capitalism and its replacement with a system of social relations which does not rely on exploitation. The dominant ideas which we find in a capitalist society serve to legitimate the system of exploitation and inequality upon which capitalism depends for its survival. Second, ideas are expressions of material circumstances. So attitudes, cognitions, beliefs and ideologies are rooted in the structure of production relations in any given society. So those endowed with power in relation to the means of production possess the dominant value sets, although it is also true that countervailing revolutionary ideas develop in the material conditions of the mass urbanised working class that capitalism begets.

A major contribution in the Marxist tradition to the study of ideology (and, for our purposes, to the study of political culture) was made by the Italian Antonio Gramsci, who composed his most important works while a political prisoner of the Mussolini regime in the late 1920s and 1930s (Gramsci 1970). Among the questions which most preoccupied Gramsci was why there had not been a successful communist revolutionary overthrow of a regime in an advanced Western capitalist country. After all, Marxist theory appeared to suggest that the conditions would develop in capitalist societies for a revolutionary transition to communism. For Gramsci, the explanation resided in the ability of advanced capitalist regimes to rule by *consent* rather than by *coercion*. It was intellectual and moral leadership rather than military and police repression which explained the persistence of capitalist relations of production. The key concept here is the idea of **hegemony**. In the Gramscian sense, hegemony describes the non-coercive aspects of a ruling group's power over society. It is about the diffusion of a particular way of looking at the world, which in turn affects dominant mores, values and beliefs. What we normally regard as 'common sense' may in fact be bound up with the exercise of hegemony.

From this perspective, political culture becomes the prevailing value system and knowledge structure which is dispersed throughout society by the dominant classes at any given time (what Gramsci (1970) termed the 'historic bloc'). It follows that those seeking to transform economy and society in advanced capitalist countries need to attend to the development of a plausible counter-hegemony which replaces the 'common sense' of capitalism with an alternative value system. Of course, this cannot be imposed coercively; people cannot be forced to be communists – they must regard it as commonsensical to be part of a communistic, egalitarian social framework.

Gramsci's ideas were taken a stage further by the French structuralist Marxist Louis Althusser (1971), writing around thirty to forty years later. Althusser was interested in theorising about the ways in which hegemony actually worked. It is here that his provocative idea of *ideological state*

A. Gramsci (1970) *Selections from the Prison Notebooks,* London: Lawrence & Wishart.

**Hegemony** A term used to describe the non-coercive aspects of domination, the diffusion throughout society of the value and knowledge systems of a ruling group.

L. Althusser (1971) *Lenin and Philosophy and Other Essays,* London: New Left Books.

*apparatuses* (ISAs) is interesting. To begin with, Althusser maintained that in order to understand the persistence of capitalist relations of production we need to focus upon the power of the state. For Althusser, the state has two key components: repressive and ideological state apparatuses. The former, which includes the military and the police, functions via coercion in the last instance. ISAs, on the other hand, work ideologically. They are agencies for the dispersal of a particular hegemony throughout society. Althusser listed the ISAs as follows:

1. Religion.
2. Education.
3. Family.
4. Law.
5. Politics.
6. Trade unions.
7. Communications.
8. Culture.

The argument is that the ideological supports of state power, and therefore of capitalism, are deeply embedded in society in a variety of seemingly 'private' institutions.

The most obvious criticism to be levelled at this sort of approach is that it seems to lead to the conclusion that a whole host of institutions in civil society lack any autonomy. In the last instance, goes the counter-argument, it might be true that political parties, trade unions, religious institutions and prevailing literary customs might all lend support to the prevailing regime, but to paint with such a broad brush is to misunderstand the multiple conflicts which occur within and between the ISAs. So, a lot of meaningful politics may go on within the ISA structure. Indeed, what Althusser calls ISAs may be sites of resistance to the dominant knowledge and attitudinal patterns associated with capitalism.

Marxism has gone through something of a crisis in recent years, but one area where it remains strong is in its Gramscian manifestation. For example, some of the most influential writing on contemporary British politics (and in particular the phenomenon of Thatcherism) has been developed by the sociologist Stuart Hall, who admits a clear intellectual debt to Gramsci. Hall explained the ascendancy of Conservative governments in Britain after 1979 in terms of the ability of a conservative coalition to articulate 'authoritarian populist' themes which successfully latched onto various discontents felt by a people confronted by post-imperial economic decline. An important set of ideas in international relations theory is associated with the so-called neo-Gramscian school represented by scholars such as Robert Cox (1987, 1996) and Stephen Gill (1993). Here the emphasis is on the power of knowledge and ideas in the global political economy. From this point of view, the dominant organising principles of global economics and politics have become associated with the powerful script of neo-liberalism which emphasises the sanctity of free markets, the dangers of state intervention,

S. Hall (1988) *The Hard Road to Renewal: Thatcherism and Crisis of the Left*, London: Verso.

S. Gill (ed.) (1993) *Gramsci, Historical Materialism and International Relations*, Cambridge: Cambridge University Press.

the freeing of capital movements and the importance of free trade to the efficient allocation of resources on a global scale.

## Subcultures

One obvious objection to the idea of national political cultures is that such things do not exist. Rather, goes the argument, we should recognise that culture is important but also acknowledge that many political cultures may co-exist within any given political system. Our attention should be focused upon the interaction of different subcultures and the impact of that inter-action upon the political system as a whole. So the idea of subcultures becomes an important corollary to the ideas developed above about political culture. The term 'subculture' is frequently used as a shorthand for describing societal groups who possess a particular identity. This identity is often expressed through forms of behaviour and forms of expression such as fashion. A political subculture may be defined as a group of the population that possesses a distinct and consistent set of attitudes, beliefs and orientations to political objects.

The identification of political subcultures is complicated somewhat by the variety of possible ways in which such strata might be conceived. In his book *Political Culture* (1972), Dennis Kavanagh identifies four distinct bases on which subcultures develop:

1. Elite versus mass culture.
2. Cultural divisions within elites.
3. Generational subcultures.
4. Social structure.

Each of these ways of thinking about the basis of subcultural divisions produces particular sorts of investigation. The elite-versus-mass idea concentrates attention on the attitudinal differences which might obtain between the political class as a whole and the remainder of the population. The separation of elite from mass is useful because it hypothesises that exposure to particular sorts of knowledge and access to decision-making channels provides a common socialising experience for political elites. So rather than seeing elites as representative of the attitudes of particular sectors of the population, this approach treats the political elite as an investigable sub-culture in its own right. Indeed a number of classic empirical studies have argued that elites tend to be well versed in self-recruitment and that various political systems possess ways of socialising their elites into a distinct attitudinal pattern (Heath 1981; Mills 1956). The work by Prewitt (1970) in the United States suggested that political elites tended to develop a consensus upon basic norms and rules of the game.

The second way of thinking about subcultures is associated with the branch of political science which argues that the most important venue for politics is the zone populated by elite groups. Here, degrees of stability are not likely to be related to the prevailing 'macro'-political culture in society as a whole, but to the level of cultural consensus or divergence between elite groups. For Lijphart (1977), as we have seen, the nature of elite behaviour – particularly whether it is coalescent or adversarial – is the key to understanding the functioning of democratic polities.

The generational model of political subcultures takes us onto very different terrain. The argument here is that distinct political cultures belong to particular generations. The idea gives rise to the view that political culture possesses a dynamism. Political culture changes over time as particular generations become socialised into distinct value sets, reach political maturity in possession of those value sets and eventually die out to be replaced by a new generational political culture. The consequences for political systems should be clear. Agendas change in line with priorities that are derived from underlying values; political parties and political institutions need to adapt accordingly.

Such ideas are particularly associated with the work of Ronald Inglehart (1977, 1991), who maintained that Western societies in the 1970s were undergoing fundamental political changes thanks to generational shifts in prevailing values. The core argument revolved around what Inglehart saw as a transition from *materialist* to *post-materialist* values. Materialist values are defined in terms of the pursuit of economic and physical security as overriding priorities, whereas postmaterialist values are those which elevate self-expression, belonging and participation over basic material needs. The consequences for politics of such a transition would, of course, be quite profound. The traditional emphasis on military security and material economic welfare would be displaced by the 'new' politics of ecology, community and popular participation. Some empirical research in the 1970s appeared to confirm a definite difference between generations. Older generations seemed to be more firmly embedded in a structure of materialist values, while younger generations were clearly more amenable to post-materialist concerns.

Why does this transition take place? Inglehart makes clear the basis of his argument:

> The hypothesis of an intergenerational shift from materialist towards post-materialist values is based on two key concepts: people value most highly those things that are relatively scarce; though to a large extent, a person's basic values reflect the conditions that prevailed during his or her pre-adult years.
>
> (Inglehart 1991: 488)

So values are rooted in material circumstances, but Inglehart favours a model of political socialisation that emphasises the durability of pre-adult experiences. Those raised in the aftermath of the First World War, in the Great Depression or during the Second World War are much more likely to place a premium on values which emphasise the primacy of basic material needs. Those socialised during periods of rapid economic growth – with its

R. Inglehart (1977) *The Silent Revolution: Changing Values and Political Styles Among Western Publics*, Princeton: Princeton University Press.

attendant consumerism – and in conditions of peace do not regard basic material commodities as scarce resources. This creates a psychological space in which postmaterialist ideas can flourish.

---

**THINK POINT**
- What do you think of the Inglehart hypothesis?
- Can it be sustained?

---

Finally, there is much to be said for the approach which understands subcultures as derivatives of a nation's social structure. From this point of view, political subcultures are attitudinal expressions of the various class, religious, linguistic and ethnic divisions which characterise any country. So, for example, in most Western countries it is possible to speak of working-class culture which gives rise to certain sorts of beliefs and values which historically have been channelled into political systems by social democratic, labour and communist political parties. Some states are divided along religious lines. In the Netherlands, say, we might identify distinctive Catholic and Calvinist political cultures. Countries like Belgium and Switzerland are divided along linguistic lines. The elaborate features of the Swiss federal model are certainly comprehensible in terms of the various linguistic groups which form the social structure in Switzerland.

Political scientists (or perhaps more accurately political sociologists) who focus on social structure are interested in the relationship between the operation of the political system and the composition of the society which feeds it. One powerful and influential argument associated with the work of Stein Rokkan is that the pattern of political cleavages in any country can be understood with reference to the underlying foundations of the social structure.

S. M. Lipset and S. Rokkan (eds) (1967) *Party Systems and Voter Alignments: Cross National Perspectives*, New York: Free Press.

In his work with Seymour Martin Lipset (Lipset and Rokkan 1967), Rokkan developed a model of the evolution of cleavage structures in Western political systems. Lipset and Rokkan maintained that the origins of key social cleavages could be found in two important historical processes: nation-building (the 'national revolution') and industrialisation ('the industrial revolution'). This model is depicted in Figure 3.2.

The process of nation-building throws up two sorts of conflict involving the attempts of central elites to gain control over a given territory via the production of standardised norms and a common legal framework. The first is a clash with pre-existing religious forms of authority (the Church) over matters such as education; the second involves a series of conflicts with peripheral communities that may resist the centralising tendencies of the state elite. During industrialisation, conflicts develop between those engaged in pre-industrial forms of production, particularly agriculture, and the new urban bourgeoisie. Intensive industrialisation then creates the fourth line of social cleavage between the bourgeois classes and the social by-product of capitalism, the concentrated urbanised working classes. In each case and on each side of the cleavage line there develop distinct interests, identities and

| National Revolution | | Industrial Revolution | |
|---|---|---|---|
| Church | Centre | Primary economy | Worker |
| *versus* | *versus* | *versus* | *versus* |
| State | Periphery | Secondary economy | Owner |

*Figure 3.2* The Lipset and Rokkan model

value systems. Should these conflicts fail to be resolved by the time of democratisation, they will acquire institutional expressions in the form of political parties.

---

**THINK POINT**

What about gender? The argument about social subcultures is a very powerful one. It makes explicit the connection between social divisions and political cleavage patterns. Yet perhaps the most obvious and fundamental division in society is the gender divide. Now, while feminism has been an important political movement in most Western countries, gender has not become an issue around which politics in general, and party politics in particular, has revolved.

● Why do you think this is?
● What can we say about this issue in terms of political culture?
● Are there male and female political subcultures?
● If not, why not?

---

## Culture and political identity

So, there are many different ways of thinking about political culture. If anything unites the diversity of cultural approaches to the study of politics, it is that there is a connection between the framework provided by political culture and the sense of 'who we are' politically. In other words, the claim is that the scope and limits of political identity are shaped by the prevailing cultural framework. But it is not just that having a French identity is a product of exposure to French political culture. Rather, the components of French identity might be said to include a series of common assumptions, attitudes, dispositions and beliefs. The boundaries between political identity and political culture are not easily drawn.

If this all sounds a bit vague, that is because 'identity' is a very slippery concept. One writer even recommends that its use should be avoided as much as possible (Sparkes 1994: 251–2) and books have been written by the most eminent political scientists attempting to pin down 'identity' (Mackenzie 1978). Having said that, 'identity' is everywhere in the political world. We might even say that it is endemic to the human condition. As Craig Calhoun says, 'We know of no people without names, no languages or cultures in which some manner of distinctions between self and other, we and they are not made' (Calhoun 1994: 1). From this we can take it that identity is about the subjective concept one has of oneself ('who I am')

C. Calhoun (1994) 'Social Theory and the Politics of Identity', in C. Calhoun (ed.) *Social Theory and the Politics of Identity*, Oxford: Blackwell.

A. D. Smith (1991) *National Identity*, Harmondsworth: Penguin.

M. Githens, P. Norris and J. Lovenduski (1994) *Different Roles, Different Voices: Women and Politics in the United States and Europe*, New York: HarperCollins.

in relation to others, since part of understanding who one *is* is embedded in analysis of who one *is not*. Political identity, if it is to be defined at all, can be said to be about *collective* subjective expressions or individual associations with particular collectives ('I am French', or 'I am black', or 'I am Jewish', or 'I am a woman' and so on).

What is clear is that there are many possible bases for political identity. Anthony Smith argues that each person is made up of multiple identities and that these identities bring with them certain sorts of role. He mentions bases such as gender, social class, ethnicity, religion, territorial location and family. The identities which emerge from these bases may co-exist, so that it is possible to identify with a whole range of collectivities simultaneously. Of course it is also possible that the possession of multiple political identities may prevent an individual from assuming the purpose and role associated with a single political identity. A hypothetical example may clarify this. Imagine a country divided roughly equally along class and religious lines. This means that citizens of that country have two available bases for identification. Table 3.2 presents two possible scenarios for the distribution of the population among the available social categories. In scenario A divisions of class and religion reinforce one another, whereas in scenario B religious and socio-economic categories are cross-cutting. Thus, we might hypothesise that countries with scenario A will witness a more robust and polarised form of politics as Catholic and working-class identities work together to produce common causes against a more affluent Protestant middle class.

Alternatively, some identities would seem to prevail over others. The problem posed at the end of the previous section about gender offers a good entry point here. Why isn't gender – perhaps the most fundamental of all social divisions – the basis for mass political identities, which in turn structure political debate and produce political parties? The answer is much debated (Githens et al. 1994). Anthony Smith sums up the views of many analysts when he writes:

> [T]he very universality and all-encompassing nature of gender differentiation makes it a less cohesive and potent base for collective identification and mobilization. Despite the rise of feminism in specific countries, gender

Table 3.2 Possible relationships between social categories and political identities

**Scenario A**

|  | Catholic % | Protestant % |
| --- | --- | --- |
| Working class | 50 | 0 |
| Middle class | 0 | 50 |

**Scenario B**

|  | Catholic % | Protestant % |
| --- | --- | --- |
| Working class | 25 | 25 |
| Middle class | 25 | 25 |

> identity, which spans the globe, is inevitably more attenuated and taken for granted than other kinds of collective identity in the modern world. Geographically separated, divided by class and ethnically fragmented, gender cleavages must ally themselves to other more cohesive identities if they are to inspire collective consciousness and action.
>
> (Smith 1991: 4)

This may be true, but, as most feminists would argue, Smith's explanation leaves out the question of power – in this case the economic, social and ideological power exercised by men over women. Thus, the emergence of a given identity may reflect or be constrained by the exercise of power. It has often been suggested that early Marxists failed to take account of the powerful forces of nationalist sentiment. In abstract, as Marx and Engels argued, the working men (sic) may have had no country. In reality, however, millions marched to their deaths for their countries in the First World War.

This brings us to the question of where political identities come from. Political socialisation, as discussed in Chapter 2, is clearly important, and we may be able to identify particularly powerful agents of socialisation which propagate particular identities and subjugate or discourage others; but why individuals and groups coalesce around particular identities and roles is a matter of some dispute.

One way of thinking about identity-formation is to make a link between identity and material interests. Here, political identities become expressions of one's social location. For example, being working class means that a person has a set of objectively defined interests which are pursued optimally though the assumption of a socialist identity. Alternatively, being French implies allegiance to a certain set of 'national' interests. International politics, diplomacy and war might be understood as negotiations and conflicts between different national identities.

Such 'rationalistic' perspectives may be contrasted with what some call 'constructivist' approaches to identity. Here the concern is to reject the notion that identities are objectively determined or external to the inter-action of actors. Rather, identities are always socially constructed; they are products of interaction and subject to change. The historian Eric Hobsbawm has written about the 'invention of traditions', which he defines as 'a set of principles, normally governed by overtly or tacitly accepted rules and of a ritual or symbolic nature, which seek to inculcate certain values and norms of behaviour by repetition which automatically implies continuity with the past' (Hobsbawm 1992: 1). This kind of approach is useful for the deeper understanding of phenomena such as Scottish nationalism or the politics of the Jewish diaspora. Others within the constructivist perspective seek to explain the emergence of what has come to be known as 'identity politics' – the proliferation in recent years of new forms of politics around issues of ecology, lifestyle and the like. Anthony Giddens (1991) takes the view that such 'life politics' are explained by the appearance of globalisation (see Chapter 16) and greater risk which force the self to become 'reflexive'. In other words, confronted by contingency and uncertainty, individuals become

E. Hobsbawm (1992) 'Introduction: Inventing Traditions', in E. Hobsbawm and T. Ranger (eds) *The Invention of Tradition*, Cambridge: Cambridge University Press.
A. Giddens (1991) *Modernity and Self-Identity: Self and Society in the Late Modern Age*, Cambridge: Polity.

more prone to construct plausible narratives of who they are and what they should do.

By studying cultural questions and surveying changes in the political culture we get a better idea of how to confront the messy thicket of identity politics. Everybody is somebody. That would seem to be an inescapable fact about the political world. How they become who they are, and what happens when they realise who they are and what they should do accordingly are really what the study of politics is all about.

## Three case studies of political culture

We have seen already that the use of the term 'political culture' in the study of politics is highly contestable. To use the term and to apply it to the analysis of political situations is to accept certain sorts of assumptions about the importance of cultural phenomena. This section presents three case studies which deliberately use a cultural approach. This does not mean that 'political culture' is the only, or for that matter the best, way in which to make sense of the issues under discussion. However, the use of the cultural approach does allow the investigator to select data from the array of materials on offer and to develop and to interrogate particular sets of hypotheses. Like all frameworks, the cultural approach to politics tends to condition the sorts of question that we ask, governs our data collection and to some extent has an impact upon the kinds of explanation that we offer.

### The rise of the 'Asian Tigers': a cultural phenomenon?

The meteoric rise to prominence of newly industrialised economies in parts of Asia has been one of the most significant features of the global political economy in recent times. Inevitably, the attention of politicians, policy-makers and the media has been drawn to the factors which might underpin the remarkable growth rates of economies such as Japan and, more recently, those of Taiwan, Singapore, South Korea and Malaysia.

Like all phenomena in the political world, the rise of these so-called 'tiger' economies in Asia is amenable to explanation from a number of alternative approaches. One of the most popular explanations is built around the idea that cultural factors are at the heart of a proper understanding. A number of thinkers have suggested that the countries concerned possess cultures which are highly conducive to an impressively productive variant of capitalism.

In particular, it is the role played by so-called 'Confucian' values that has attracted the attention of Western commentators. The term is derived from the thought of the Chinese philosopher Kung Fu-tzu (Confucius in Latin) who is thought to have lived between 551 and 479 BC. Confucian thought is built around the advocacy of self-control and duty to others. This value structure, it is argued, remains deeply embedded in Asian societies, so that notions of 'community' and 'family' prevail over Western-style individualism.

In recent years the government of Singapore has been an enthusiastic sponsor of the teaching of Confucian values in schools. Lee Kuan Yew, Singapore's 'Senior Minister', put it like this: 'A Confucianist view of order between subject and ruler – this helps in the rapid transformation of society . . . in other words you fit yourself into society – the exact opposite of the American rights of the individual' (*The Economist*, 21 January 1995). The idea here is that a Confucian value infrastructure provides a solid basis for rapid industrialisation without the attendant breakdown of family life and the dislocating social consequences which follow. In the case of Singapore, there is an evident commitment to utilise the existing 'Eastern' cultural framework to avoid the mistakes of 'the West'. Such views are commonly expressed by opinion-formers and politicians across Asia. The 'Asian way' is portrayed as being a distinct route to modernity. Take this statement from Voice of Malaysia radio in May 1993:

> Datu Seri Dr Mahatir Mohamed [the Malaysian Prime Minister] has asked Malaysians not to accept western-style democracy as it could result in negative effects. The prime minister said such an extreme principle had caused moral decay, homosexual activities, single parents and economic slowdown because of poor work ethics.
>
> (*The Financial Times*, 5 March 1994)

Notice how politics and economics are being connected in this statement. It is not simply that the West's underlying value structure is inadequate. What is important is the application of 'liberalism', which has the effect of causing moral decay. This, in turn, is said to undermine productivity, economic growth and industrial advance.

None the less, some 'Western' analysts have concluded that there are important lessons to be learned. The British Conservative MP David Howell (1995) has argued that Western countries should contemplate a degree of what he calls 'Easternisation'. Howell argues that the core values of East Asian societies are central to economic success. In particular, the role of the family as the main provider of social security removes the need for an expansive and paternalistic welfare state. The Confucian culture provides cohesive moral standards which bind individuals into community networks. With such embedded security, individuals are able to pursue excellence in all aspects of their lives.

A less benign approach is offered in the recent work of American political scientist Samuel Huntington. In his provocative paper 'The Clash of Civilizations' Huntington argues that cultural differences are likely to be at the heart of future global conflicts. In that respect, 'Confucianism' as a value system represents one of the most profound challenges to the ideological hegemony of the West. However, Huntington's argument is not just that cultural alternatives exist, but also that these alternatives will collide with each other. They clash because modern information and communication technologies render people more mobile and reveal different cultures that might hitherto have been invisible.

S. Huntington (1993) 'The Clash of Civilizations', *Foreign Affairs* 72(3).

M. Weber (1930) *The Protestant Ethic and the Spirit of Capitalism*, London: Allen & Unwin.

**THINK POINT**
- Will cultures clash?
- What do you think of the Huntington hypothesis?
- Will civilisations come into conflict with one another because of cultural disparity?
- Or will the technologies he describes allow cultures to understand one another better and thereby reduce he threat of conflict?

What is interesting about the current debate about the alleged correlation between Asian/Confucian values and economic success is the way in which it recalls one of the most powerful social scientific theses ever devised. The German sociologist Max Weber famously accounted for the rise of capitalism as a system of production in Western Europe with reference to the work ethics associated with Protestantism. In *The Protestant Ethic and the Spirit of Capitalism*, written in 1904–5, Weber maintained that the variety of reformed Christianity which emerged in Europe after the fifteenth century developed a uniquely ascetic character which produced the accumulation strategies associated with capitalism. That is to say, values of hard work (as the main purpose of human life) and thrift (i.e. limited enjoyment of the fruits of one's labour) generated psychological and behavioural consequences which resulted in the emergence of capitalism as the European method of organising the production, distribution and exchange of goods. What is even more fascinating is that Weber dismisses Confucianism, seeing it as the cause of economic 'backwardness' in China!

The issues raised by this brief discussion are, of course, legion. First, and perhaps most obviously, there is the problem of cause and effect. The Confucian connection is an engaging hypothesis, but as social scientists we do not really have the wherewithal to go and test it with any degree of certainty. In some ways that problem does not matter, because the existence of the hypothesis has spilled over into an important debate which has interested key political actors both in Asia and the West. Whether Confucian values matter or not is secondary to the facts that Asian politicians are able to generate public support and legitimacy around the idea of a distinctive 'Asian way' (or for that matter a Singaporean way or a Malaysian way, etc.) and that Western policy-makers are consumed by the question of whether 'Easternisation' is the way in which to regain a competitive foothold in world markets.

The most powerful critical rebuttals of the Confucian thesis come from those who would argue that the emergence of capitalism in Asia denotes the spread of core 'Western' approaches to the organisation of economic and social life. It is of course true that capitalism will acquire distinctive local characteristics wherever it emerges, but the argument here would be that capitalism brings with it an inevitable and probably irresistible logic. As an illustration of this sort of thinking, take a look at the extract printed here from *The Financial Times* of 26 June 1995. The central argument of the piece is that while certain sorts of values may have helped Asian countries 'develop', these very values will be undermined by the powerful logic of industrial capitalism, thereby forcing the emergence of Western-style welfare institutions.

> Korea, perhaps more than any other east Asian nation, has prided itself on upholding the Confucian values of frugality and the importance of family ties. Traditionally, when Koreans hit hard times they relied on two things: substantial personal savings and the support of large, close-knit families. In the past, consequently, a Western-style state welfare system was considered both unwelcome and largely unnecessary. But now that Korea is becoming a fully developed country, there is a feeling that it needs a welfare system to match its advanced status. National health insurance, state pensions, unemployment insurance and other welfare measures have either already been introduced or are planned.
>
> The state is not about to do away with the role of the family or private savings. Children are still considered to have an obligation to support their parents, and vice versa. That attitude is not going to disappear overnight.
>
> Nonetheless, there is unease in some quarters about the innovations. Some Koreans complain that the introduction of social security is undermining the traditional family support system. But others argue that other social changes – urbanisation, lower birth rates, greater longevity, the trend towards nuclear families – were already having an impact on the traditional informal welfare system, and so a more organised approach is now necessary to fill the gaps.
>
> Another worry sometimes heard is that a state safety net will act as a disincentive to the high savings rates, which have played such an important role in Korea's industrial development. Savings rates have indeed slipped over the past few years – from about 39 per cent in 1988 to about 34 per cent now – but as wages have risen in real terms, it could be argued that a proportionally lower savings rate could still provide just as comfortable a cushion against misfortune. And to some extent, personal savings will be replaced directly with government organised savings in the form of the national pension scheme. Whether this will have a disproportionate impact on the savings rate will not become clear for some time.
>
> Korea is not alone in hoping to find a way to preserve the best aspects of the traditional system, while providing the kind of safety net necessary in a modern, urbanised society. Several other east Asian countries are working on the same task, but Korean bureaucrats and academics do not believe that anyone has yet found a perfect solution.
>
> The Korean approach has been to introduce welfare at a very basic level, and gradually increase its scope and level of benefits. This is based on the belief that once a level of welfare provision has been established, it is difficult to reduce it. The ministries involved are well aware of the perils of encouraging welfare dependency.
>
> One of the first elements of the welfare system to be introduced was a national health insurance scheme. From its start with employees of large companies in the late 1970s, the scheme now covers the entire population. However, insurance does not cover the full cost of inpatient or outpatient care, so it is still necessary to resort to personal savings for major treatment. There are special programmes providing free medical care for very low income or disadvantaged groups. As yet there is little private health insurance, but there is obviously scope for that market to expand. Welfare programmes for those

on very low incomes tend to focus on encouraging self-sufficiency through work, by offering retraining, places on government projects, or subsidised loans to set up small businesses. Cash payments and benefits in kind to those unable to work are very low, supporting a minimum standard of living well below the official poverty line. Benefits are expected to increase over the next few years, while maintaining incentives to work.

Unemployment is not yet a real problem in Korea. However, the first stage of a compulsory unemployment insurance scheme will be introduced this summer. The most significant measure currently being rolled out is the national pension scheme. Occupational pension schemes for civil servants and the military have existed since the 1960s, but it was not until 1988 that a general state scheme was introduced, starting with workplaces with more than 10 workers, and gradually expanding to cover smaller employers and the self-employed. This year the scheme is due to extend to the rural self-employed, and the final phase, taking in the urban self-employed, is due by 1998. As yet, the market for private pensions is underdeveloped. The current contribution level to the national scheme is 6 per cent of income, shared equally between employee, employer, and a transfer from the retirement fund which would previously have provided a lump sum in place of a pension. Contributions are due to be increased to 9 per cent, again divided equally between the three sources. Final pension payouts are linked to the recipient's average lifetime salary, and the formula used has an equalising effect, so that lower paid workers receive perhaps 60 per cent of their pre-retirement income, while higher earners receive only 30 per cent. The national pension funds are invested in the stock market, fixed interest securities and elsewhere, such as infrastructure projects. But there is some concern about the management of the substantial amounts of money being accumulated by the scheme. Asset allocation is decided by a government committee, dominated by ministers, with a few representatives from trade unions and the private sector.

The worry expressed by some outside the government is that funds can be directed into areas of government priority – whether infrastructure projects or propping up the stock market at politically sensitive moments – rather than into those investments which will produce the best return for scheme members. As the pot of money under management grows, the government may come under pressure to distance itself from the management.

One enthusiastic government official described the current plans for social welfare as Korea's 'Beveridge plan'. The Korean version, with its step-by-step approach, is far less radical than the UK original, though it may not seem so to die-hard Confucianists.

(B. Hutton 1995)

Another criticism would point to the way in which arguments about core Asian values might be used to lend legitimacy to authoritarian and non-democratic forms of government. So values and culture can be used politically not just by authoritarians in some Asian countries, but also by conservatives in the West.

### Northern Ireland: irreconcilable subcultures?

The recent history of Northern Ireland has been dominated by sectarian politics which has spilled over into terroristic violence. Readers, especially in the UK and Ireland, will be familiar with the near-daily catalogue of news stories reporting bombings, tit-for-tat killings and defiant statements by politicians on both sides of the nationalist–Unionist divide. The 'Troubles', as they are often rather euphemistically called, are a puzzle for outsiders and for politicians who might seek to secure a lasting peace in the province. They are also a challenge for political scientists. Might a cultural approach shed any light on the political situation in Northern Ireland? Can political science help find a solution to the violent entrenched politics of a deeply divided society?

To understand the present in Northern Ireland it seems to be important to understand the past. More precisely, what is important is to investigate the way in which different historical narratives are embedded in contemporary political identities. As the writer (and ex-politician) Gemma Hussey puts it:

> fear and hate which have their origins in the historical mists of battles for land and souls between the native Irish in Northern Ireland, the British Crown, and the imported Scottish Presbyterian and English Protestant landlords and smallholders of several centuries ago, still dominate in Northern Ireland.
>
> (Hussey 1995: 190)

The lines of political cleavage in Northern Ireland are fairly clearly drawn. On one side of the political divide sit Unionist political forces. The *raison d'être* of Unionism is to ensure that Northern Ireland remains part of the United Kingdom. The adherents of Northern Irish Unionism are overwhelmingly Protestant. Unionists are opposed by Nationalists (or Republicans) who seek to sever links with the UK to create a union with the Republic of Ireland. The bulk of Nationalist support comes from the minority Catholic community. As Figure 3.3 shows, the consequence is that

*Unionist Parties*

Official Unionist Party (OUP)
*9 seats won in the 1992 UK General Election*
Democratic Unionist Party (DUP)
*3 seats*
Ulster Popular Unionist Party (UPUP)
*1 seat*

*Nationalist Parties*

Social Democratic and Labour Party (SDLP)
*4 seats*
Sinn Fein
*0 seats*

*Other Parties*

The Alliance Party
*0 seats*

*Figure 3.3* The party system in Northern Ireland

the party system in Northern Ireland is almost entirely at variance with that of the mainland UK. The other significant component of Northern Irish politics is the existence of a variety of paramilitary organisations which claim to represent the interests of the respective Nationalist and Unionist communities. On the Republican–Nationalist side, the most significant organisation is the Provisional Irish Republican Army (IRA), although significant splinter groups such as the Irish National Liberation Army (INLA) have also been involved in terrorist activity. Pro-Unionist paramilitaries include the Ulster Freedom Fighters (UFF) and the Ulster Volunteer Force (UVF).

There are two key points to note. First, the dominant cleavage in the politics of Northern Ireland is built around the correspondence of religious division and polar positions on a particular historical-political issue. To that we might add that the cleavage also has a socio-economic dimension, with Catholics generally less affluent than Protestants. Second, this cleavage is not simply played out in the 'polite' arena of formal politics. This is not just about the operation of illegal terrorist organisations, but also about the refusal of politicians and political leaders on both sides of the argument to play the game of politics as it is normally understood. Republican groups such as Sinn Fein refuse to recognise the claims of the British state over what they would call the North of Ireland. Sinn Fein has had electoral success in British parliamentary elections, but winning candidates do not take their seats in the Westminster Parliament on the grounds that this would constitute an acknowledgement of the legitimacy of British sovereignty in Northern Ireland. Many Unionist politicians armed with slogans such as 'No surrender' and 'Ulster says no' flatly refuse to sit around the negotiating table with representatives of Sinn Fein.

The lack of accommodative politics and the routine use of violence in pursuit of political ends in Northern Ireland renders its political culture wholly dissimilar to the mainstream of UK politics. It is certainly the case that the roots of the 'Troubles' are very deep indeed and the way in which this history is read is crucial to the position adopted on the contemporary politics of Northern Ireland. The formal incorporation of Ireland into the UK was accomplished in 1801, but British dominion over the island stretched back several centuries. Significantly, waves of Scottish, English and Welsh settlers began to colonise Ireland, but particularly the north, from the sixteenth century. These largely Protestant settlers were the ancestors of today's Unionist community. The 'Home Rule' movement, demanding autonomy or independence, emerged in the nineteenth century and created major tensions amongst mainstream political parties in Britain. Pressures for a political settlement followed a series of violent conflicts in Ireland, exemplified by the Easter Rising of 1916, and the division of Ireland was accomplished with the passing of the Government of Ireland Act (1920) and the Anglo-Irish Treaty (1921). The bulk of the island of Ireland became the Irish Free State, while six counties of the north with Protestant majority populations remained in the United Kingdom. But this arrangement left a significant Catholic minority in the north and the legacy of territorial crisis remained:

> The fundamental defects in the . . . [post-1921] political structures and the impact of ensuing policy led to a system in the North of supremacy of the Unionist tradition over the nationalist tradition. From the beginning, both sections of the community were locked into a system based on sectarian loyalties.
>
> (*New Ireland Forum Report 1984*; cited in Hussey 1995: 189)

Catholic civil rights demonstrations in the late 1960s were met with concerted Protestant responses. British troops were sent to Northern Ireland to act as a broker between the two populations, but inter-communal violence and terrorism became more, rather than less, prevalent. Recent attempts to secure a peaceful settlement appeared to have achieved some mileage, including a relatively lengthy IRA ceasefire. However, by the middle of 1996 the so-called 'peace process' looked to have broken down, with Republican paramilitaries resorting to violent methods and leading Protestant politicians entrenched in characteristically uncompromising rhetoric.

As students of politics our task is not to participate in the argument but to try to interpret it. In situations such as this, one might like to argue that political science can be a useful tool. If political scientists are able to diagnose the Northern Ireland problem, then perhaps they might be able to suggest remedies, if not outright cures. The political science of the Northern Ireland question has been particularly amenable to an explanation which explores the issue in terms of political culture.

What is most evident is that Northern Ireland offers a clear case of subcultural hostility. Religious and social divisions together with a highly developed sense of historical identity in both camps have conspired to produce a deeply divided society. But note that Northern Ireland also appears to lack a consensual culture among its political elites. So rather than acting as brokers between two hostile subcultures, subcultural elites actually promote and enhance inter-communal hostility.

This, as Lijphart observed in a notable paper (Lijphart, 1975), constitutes a major infringement of the rules of accommodative, consociational politics. From the cultural perspective, the lack of inter-elite cooperation is the major barrier to peace in Northern Ireland.

A. Lijphart (1975) 'The Northern Ireland Problem: Cases, Theories and Solutions', *British Journal of Political Science* 5(1).

---

**THINK POINT**
- Do you agree with this point?
- You might consider 'testing' the argument by reading newspaper accounts of the so-called peace process in the mid-1990s.
- Was inter-elite cooperation the key, or do other factors matter?

---

### *European integration: creating a new political culture?*

As we will observe in Chapter 15, the European Union (EU) offers a remarkable set of institutions and political practices which seem to reside at a level higher than the traditional framework of the nation-state. There is an argument to suggest that the EU is developing the properties of a political system. for instance, there is a discernable – albeit complex – policy process with various inputs and outputs. Much work on the EU, and European integration more generally has been concerned with mapping the formal and less formal aspects of the system of EU institutions, as well as attending to their relationship with the institutions of (national) government in member states. The relationship between integration and the behaviour of pressure groups is another area of academic enquiry, as is more overtly theoretical work which tries to understand the dynamics of regional integration in Europe and the wider global political economy.

But we can also ask some very important questions about culture. Most obviously, does the evolution of a system of European institutions bring with it a corresponding European political culture? Also, to what extent are the norms, habits, attitudes and dispositions of political actors shaped by the processes of European integration?

The founders of what we now know as the European Union tended to regard political culture as a secondary phenomenon. Their purpose was to create a single market among member-state economies which would be presided over by a set of new institutions above the nation-state. The emphasis on the efficient, functional, technocratic management of economic life was given theoretical support by scholars of the neo-functionalist school, who argued that this elite-driven process would ultimately sell itself to pressure groups and mass publics alike. Both theorists and practitioners of European integration envisaged the transference of 'loyalties' (that is to say patterns of political behaviour) away from nation-states towards the new supranational European framework. So economic integration combined with the development of European-level institutions would produce a polity of sorts with its own norms.

There is some evidence to suggest that the EU policy process and the EU's institutions have developed their own distinctive cultures. The disparities between British political culture and that of the EU's institutions is explored by Stephen George (1994). For instance, the culture of the European Parliament came as something of a shock to British MEPs who had been schooled in the adversarial Westminster system:

S. George (1994) 'Cultural Diversity and European Integration: The British Political Parties', in S. Zetterholm (ed.) *National Cultures and European Integration: Exploratory Essays on Cultural Diversity and Common Policies*, Oxford: Berg.

> the most difficult thing that British members had to adjust to in the European Parliament was the constant talking around issues. It was . . . as though it was more important for everybody to have their say than it was to get on with the business in hand. The constant revision of drafts and reports to account for the views of minorities remained beyond the comprehension of some British MEPs, used to a system in which ritual denunciations of the proposals of political opponents were invariably ignored.
>
> (George 1994: 53)

The experience of European integration revealed further differences in elite political cultures. As George notes, there is a contrast between British and continental European approaches to decision-making which are rooted in different sorts of attitudes, norms and values. The British approach may be summed up as taking an incremental approach to problem-solving, whereas other European decision-making systems are more attuned to the setting of long-term goals prior to laying out the details of how these goals might be achieved. Consequently, disagreements, which often flare up in the inter-governmental forums of the EU, may not necessarily reflect different philosophical positions on a given issue, but may derive from alternative conceptions of how policy should be made and how issues should be negotiated.

In his study of British MEPs, Martin Westlake suggests that working in the environment provided by the European Parliament has tended to socialise these politicians away from the cultural norms of British party-political culture. Westlake's analysis of MEPs' attitudes over time seems to support the view that support for an expanded role for the Parliament and pro-integrationist attitudes more generally are the consequence of time spent working in the institution.

On the other hand, at the mass level there would appear to have been no large-scale process of loyalty transference from nation-states to European institutions (Sinnott and Niedermayer 1995). This suggests that in spite of the developments of a decision-making system and a set of political processes at the European level, mass publics in the member states have continued to identify first and foremost with their national political cultures. The process of loyalty transference would obviously lend legitimacy to the project of European integration, but, as most observers recognise, economic and political integration in Europe has always been an elite-led process. Perhaps, therefore, we should be looking for evidence of a European elite political culture. At first sight, this would seem difficult to establish.

Intergovernmental conflict has been a long-standing feature of the EU and its predecessors. However, some writers argue that there have been significant convergences of attitude and belief among significant groups of European elite actors (including governments, industrialists and officials working in European institutions) over matters such as the need for market liberalisation within the EC/EU (Sandholtz and Zysman 1989) and the nature of a future economic and monetary union (Dyson 1994).

Cultural convergence of this sort may create common economic institutions such as the liberalised economic space promised by the Single European Act of 1986. The aspiration of this legislation was the assurance of an economic area amongst member states in which there would be free movement of goods, services and persons and the removal of physical, technical and fiscal barriers to free trade. It is another thing entirely to expect an instant transformation of economic culture. The reconfiguration of economic institutions does not automatically portend the transformation of the consumption patterns of the French, the British or the Germans; nor does it stop advertisers from continuing to market products differently in different countries according to local cultural predilections (Niss 1994).

M. Westlake (1994) *Britain's Emerging Euro-Elite?* Aldershot: Dartmouth.

## Conclusion

The lessons to be learned from the analysis of political culture in its own right are clearly important for the student of politics. The centrality of attitudes, beliefs and orientations to political life in all of its manifestations is difficult to deny. The connections which can be made between levels of political stability and types of political culture provide the basis for much lively debate among political scientists. But this chapter has also delved a little deeper and in so doing has made a number of observations about the conduct of political science. The study of political culture reveals very clearly that political phenomena can be read from a variety of different perspectives. The 'cultural approach' is a clearly discernible subfield of political enquiry which chooses to investigate phenomena such as political stability, terrorism, regional integration and economic advance using culture as an independent variable (i.e. that which does the explaining). It is also true that the subject of political culture, as we have seen can be approached from radically different viewpoints. This point is important, not simply because there is a choice of ways of 'doing' political science. It is important for 'readers' of political science to appreciate that every piece of analysis has a theoretical homeland which does much to define the hypotheses which are generated and the agenda for research thereafter. The case study of *The Civic Culture* tells us much about the difficulties of inference in political science and the perils of constructing chains of causation. Such matters are not confined to the study of political culture; they pervade everything that you will read about in this book and everything that you will study subsequently.

## Exercises

1 This chapter includes three case studies in which contemporary issues are addressed through the lens of political culture. Your task is to write a similar short case study which thinks about any political issue in terms of culture. You can use newspapers and news magazines as your sources, but remember that you need to go beyond conventional journalistic treatments of issues. Your job is to re-read the issue using the concepts and ideas developed in this chapter.

2 The selection of the case study is obviously up to you and should reflect your own interests and knowledge. However, it might be useful to look for an instance of political conflict or for a situation where political actors are exposed to a new environment.

3 When you have completed the case study, take some time to think about how much – or how little – the use of political culture has told you about the issues in question. Has it enhanced or given a new angle to your understanding of your chosen issue? What else is there still to explain?

# Further reading

Almond, G. A. and Verba, S. (1963) *The Civic Culture: Political Attitudes and Democracy in Five Nations*, Princeton: Princeton University Press. A classic, if flawed, attempt to develop a classification of political culture. A very good example of political science in action.

Almond, G. A. and Verba, S. (eds) (1980) *The Civic Culture Revisited*, Boston: Little, Brown & Co. A collection of important critical essays on the concept of political culture.

Featherstone, M. (ed.) (1990) *Global Culture: Globalization, Nationalism and Modernity*, London: Sage. Sociologically inclined interrogations of the idea that 'globalisation' is inducing global cultural change. Some very important contributions, worthy of the attention of political scientists with an interest in culture.

Giddens, A. (1991) *Modernity and Self-Identity. Self and Society in the Late Modern Age*, Cambridge: Polity. An important contribution to understanding the psychological basis of 'identity politics' in the contemporary world.

Gramsci, A. (1970) *Selections from the Prison Notebooks*, London: Lawrence and Wishart. Astonishing set of reflections on history and politics, penned in the late 1920s and early 1930s. Enormously influential on subsequent 'alternative' formulations of political culture.

Inglehart, R. (1977) *The Silent Revolution: Changing Values and Political Styles Among Western Publics*, Princeton: Princeton University Press. Rigorous, if controversial, attempt to map the contours of generational politico-cultural change in Western societies.

Lijphart, A. (1977) *Democracy in Plural Societies: A Comparative Exploration*, New Haven, CT: Yale University Press. A telling rebuttal of simplistic characterisations of continental European political cultures which emphasises the mediating role of institutions.

Zetterholm, S. (ed.) (1994) *National Cultures and European Integration: Exploratory Essays on Cultural Diversity and Common Policies*, Oxford: Berg. Lively essays on the cultural dimensions of European integration.

# 4 POLITICAL PARTICIPATION

*Barrie Axford and Ben Rosamond*

**Introduction: what is political participation?**

**Political participation and democracy**

*Democracy: good or bad?*
*The idea of democracy*
*Indirect or representative democracy and participation*
*Elite theories of participation and democracy*
*Rethinking political participation and democracy*

**Who participates: some individual and social correlates of political participation**

*Selected variables and political participation: a brief inventory*

**Why do people participate in politics and why do some abstain?**

*Agency: political efficacy*
*Structure: the law, society and ideas*

**Conclusion**

**Further reading**

# Political participation

## Introduction: what is political participation?

Bringing together some of the insights from the previous two chapters, we might say that we all acquire knowledge about politics and that we all live within particular politico-cultural contexts. But how do we make use of our political socialisation and how to we behave in the context of our political culture(s)? On the face of it, it would appear that people express these aspects of their character in a variety of ways. Some individuals are highly active in politics; they may join political parties and canvass on behalf of particular candidates in elections or engage in administrative work in the cause of a local party organisation. Others may join single-issue pressure groups with the aim of advancing particular causes or demands; others still may become career politicians by successfully standing for public office. In complete contrast, other people would appear to abstain completely from political activity, refusing even to vote. The study of political participation is the examination of these kinds of activity (or non-activity).

---

**THINK POINT**
- What is the extent of your political participation?
- What activities have you undertaken in this area?
- Are you more or less politically active than your acquaintances?

---

The definition of **political participation** is far from straightforward. The problem is that the adoption of a definition automatically includes or excludes certain sorts of activity from the purview of political participation studies. For example, we might define political participation as those voluntary actions in which people seek to influence the making of public policy. The emphasis on 'voluntary' actions here threatens to exclude those forms of mass participation which are obligatory or coerced. The most obvious examples here would involve the requirement of shows of symbolic support for authoritarian regimes. But such a definition might also exclude the act of voting in democratic countries where voting is required by law. Aware of these difficulties,

**Political participation** A term to denote the actions by which individuals take part in the political process – debate centres on two issues: the value of political participation to individuals and the political system, and the causes of participation and non-participation.

G. Parry, G. Moyser and N. Day (1992) *Political Participation and Democracy in Britain,* Cambridge: Cambridge University Press.

the majority of students of political participation tend to opt for a more inclusive definition. The authors of a major study of political participation in Britain suggest that political participation consists of

> taking part in the process of formulation, passage and implementation of public policies. It is concerned with action by citizens which is aimed at influencing decisions which are, in most cases, taken by public representatives and officials. This may be action which seeks to shape the attitudes of decision-makers to matters yet to be decided, or it may be action in protest at the outcome of some decision.
>
> (Parry, Moyser and Day 1992: 16)

It is also worth noting that political participation is not confined to successful actions. Much (perhaps even the bulk) of the activity falling within this definition is fruitless. Moreover, while Parry and his colleagues do not examine more passive forms of behaviour, there are some political scientists who would regard conversations about political issues with friends, work colleagues or family along with the articulation of clear political attitudes as important types of participation in their own right.

A. H. Birch (1993) *The Concepts and Theories of Modern Democracy,* London: Routledge.

The next step in defining the concept is to classify the different types of political participation. In his book *The Concepts and Theories of Modern Democracy,* Anthony Birch lists what he understands as the main conventional types of political participation. The list is reproduced in Figure 4.1 (below). We might think of other specific examples of political participation. Other forms of human action might usefully be regarded as forms of political participation. Dressing in a particular way, choosing brand *x* over brand *y* when shopping, choosing which stories to read to one's child and fox-hunting are all actions with 'political' connotations. Indeed, if the feminist idea of the personal as political has any meaning, then a multiplicity of supposedly 'private' actions, such as negotiations over household chores, become politicised.

1 Voting in national elections.
2 Voting in referendums.
3 Canvassing or otherwise campaigning in elections.
4 Active membership of a political party.
5 Active membership of a pressure group.
6 Taking part in political demonstrations, industrial strikes with political objectives, rent strikes in public housing, and similar activities aimed at changing public policy.
7 Various forms of civil disobedience, such as refusing to pay taxes or obey a conscription order.
8 Membership of government advisory committees.
9 Membership of consumers' councils for publicly owned industries.
10 Client involvement in the implementation of social policies.
11 Various forms of community action, such as those concerned with housing or environmental issues of the day.

*Figure 4.1* The main types of political participation

*Source*: Birch (1993: 81)

But the crucial point is to think a little more deeply about the classification of the concept. In an important and influential early statement on the subject, Lester Milbrath (1965) developed an argument in which political participation was seen as a *hierarchical activity*. Milbrath arranged the American population along a one-dimensional hierarchy of political participation. Individuals could be located in one of three groups: 'gladiators', 'spectators' and 'apathetics'. Roughly one-third of the American public was located in the apathetics category. These were individuals who abstained from any form of political activity – even voting. Spectators – about three-fifths of the population – involved themselves minimally in politics. Most usually, these were people who did little more than vote in elections. This left as little as one-twentieth of the US public actively and widely involved in politics as gladiators.

While most studies have confirmed that intensive and committed political participation is a minority activity, research conducted after the first edition of Milbrath's study suggested that the hierarchical model of participation was in need of amendment. Milbrath's original hierarchy suggested that those in the upper echelons (gladiators) also engaged in the activities of spectators and less intensive gladiators. However, later studies pointed to a picture of *specialisation* in political participation. So, rather than arranging participants in a single hierarchy, it was necessary to develop classifications which acknowledged that the bulk of participation took place in relatively specialised domains. The path-breaking work originated again in the United States, but soon spanned out into comparative studies. The key work was done by Sidney Verba and Norman H. Nie in *Participation in America* (1972) and later by Verba, Nie and J.-O. Kim in *The Modes of Democratic Participation* (1971) and *Participation and Political Equality* (1978). The key insight to emerge from this work was the idea of *modes* (types) of political participation. This allowed a more sophisticated classification, such as that presented in Figure 4.2. There are various classifications available in the literature, but the crucial point to note is that the research conducted by Verba and his colleagues seemed to indicate that participants tended, with very few exceptions, to be *specialists* in a particular mode. So rather than being complete activists, so-called 'gladiators' would, for example, specialise in writing letters to politicians and public officials. This finding has been

L. Milbrath (1965) *Political Participation: How and Why Do People Get Involved in Politics?*, Chicago: Rand McNally.

S. Verba and N. H. Nie (1972) *Participation in America: Political Democracy and Social Equality*, New York: Harper & Row.
S. Verba, N. H. Nie and J.-O. Kim (1971) *The Modes of Democratic Participation: A Cross-National Comparison*, Beverly Hills: Sage; (1978) *Participation and Political Equality: A Seven Nation Comparison*, Cambridge: Cambridge University Press.

Protestors

Community activists (local issues)

Party and campaign workers

Communicators

Contactors (of politicians/officials on specific matters)

Voters

Inactive

*Figure 4.2* Modes of political participation

confirmed more recently in the work done on participation in Britain (Parry, Moyser and Day 1992: ch. 3).

*Citizenship*

## Political participation and democracy

So political participation is a minority sport almost regardless of how it is defined, and even in those countries with a 'participant' political culture and with a robust tradition of public involvement. For all this, the link between political participation and what many people think of as true **democracy** remains strong in thought, if less so in deed. But it will come as no surprise that there are competing ideas about the appropriate levels and intensities of participation in democratic systems.

However, like Mum and apple pie, nobody these days has a bad word to say about democracy as such. Indeed, as the French theorist Alan Touraine wrote in 1991, it has even made a spectacular comeback in recent years. He was not talking only about the democratic aspirations of people in Poland, Hungary, Czechoslovakia (now the Czech Republic and Slovakia), the former East Germany and, with rather less conviction, those in Russia, Bulgaria and Romania. In countries as various as Brazil, Chile, Nicaragua and Taiwan, free elections have taken place recently after years of despotism, repression, single-party or military rule, and resistance by governments which claimed to have replaced democracy with something more efficient, more unifying or more suited to hard times.

During 1996 forty states held national elections and according to the Inter-Parliamentary Union there were twenty-seven such contests held in the latter part of 1995 alone. Most of the polls conducted during 1996 seemed to offer some minimal degree of democratic choice. In South Korea, Taiwan and Uganda, the concept of people choosing leaders instead of leaders choosing themselves was introduced or reintroduced. The proliferation of elections has occurred at a time when politicians and politics itself seem to be held in low esteem by many people. In such a climate the growing popularity of elections can be explained by the explosion in the number of countries following the end of the Cold War and by the break-up of the Soviet empire. But there has also been something of an 'epidemic of democracy' in Latin America and, increasingly, in Africa. Parts of Asia still cling to other ways of choosing leaders, and China expressed her fear of popular democracy by trying to intimidate the Taiwanese during the run-up to the presidential elections on that island in 1996. None the less, in the years between 1986 and 1996, some sixty-nine nations across the globe moved to some kind of multi-party system.

But for much of what the historian Eric Hobsbawm calls the 'short twentieth century', which began with the revolt of the Russian navy at Petrograd in 1917 and ended with the tearing down of the Berlin Wall in 1989, the age has been one of revolutions and movements of national liberation, demanding not democracy but the destruction of *ancien régimes* and, of course, an end to capitalism.

**Democracy** From the original Greek, the term means, literally, rule by the people, or by the many. In modern political systems the term is usually linked with universal suffrage, free elections and with notions like the consent of the governed. In terms of modern democracies, an emphasis on human rights and the rules of law would also be key elements of any definition.

*Evidence of Democracy being better than other*

## Democracy: good or bad?

So in terms of general approbation, democracy has not always enjoyed such a good press as it does now, in the final years of the twentieth century. While writers like Aristotle were happy to applaud the value of popular participation in the affairs of the *polis* in ancient Greece, many of his contemporaries believed that rule by the 'demos' or the 'many' as it translates, was a recipe for disaster. Democracy (the rule of the many) was seen as only a little way from mob rule, and even Aristotle was ambivalent on this point. Of course the classical model of democracy contained in the ideal of the small Greek *polis* or city-state bears little resemblance to the large-scale mass democracies of the modern world, where voters are counted in tens of millions (or in India, the largest democracy, in hundreds of millions), but some of the same concerns voiced now echo those expressed by critics then. Basically these turn on a number of perennial issues:

- What does democracy mean? How is the idea of rule by the many to be translated into practice?
- Does 'real' democracy require the active participation of citizens?
- If it does, should the involvement be direct or indirect, frequent or infrequent?
- Does 'real' democracy need 'real' democrats?
- What should be the role of political elites in democracies?
- How is the accountability of political elites to the public to be ensured?

## The idea of democracy

Democracy means literally 'the rule of the many'. The classical notion of democracy idealised in the city-states of ancient Greece, like Athens, or, somewhat closer to the present day, in the town-hall meetings of small New England communities in the USA or in Swiss cantons (subnational units of local government), has as its core the idea of the direct and continuing involvement of citizens in the affairs of the community. Office-holding, if such is needed for the carrying-out of both routine and specialised tasks, devolves to members of the community by lot or rota. There are thus no politicians in the accepted sense of the term. Now of course, this version varied even among democratic city-states in Greece and, leaving aside for the moment the undemocratic nature of those 'participatory democracies' – they excluded women and slaves – there is the obvious difficulty of applying the model to contemporary democracies, namely the sheer numbers of people involved. None the less we might still express envy at the apparent ease with which 'professional' politicians were sidelined, but in our more complex age wonder about the possibilities of dismantling the machinery of government to the point where civil servants can be replaced by citizens taking a turn from mowing the lawn, taking the children ice-skating and holding down demanding jobs.

One response to this question might be that it depends on the context in which participation takes place. The definition of political participation quoted (see p. 110) above, talks about taking part in the formulation of public policies. The implication here is that participation is confined to the public arena of elections, or to activities aimed at influencing public officials and institutions. But need the reach of the idea be quite so limited? For example, could it be extended to include participation in the workplace through schemes for team-working, or to the university where students are 'empowered', to use a current expression, in matters relating to their course of study? These are contentious ideas which are affected by how we define 'political' activity, and they may overstretch the concept of participatory democracy. The question of whether IBM could be a democracy, with employees having the same status as citizens, is not in fact one which has exercised students of organisation or management studies too much, even if it is perfectly allowable in a discussion of democracy per se. Just as radical, but arguably more in line with the spirit of direct democracy, are attempts being made, primarily, though not solely, in the United States, to revitalise the ideal of direct or classical democracy through electronic means:

# Electronic Town Meetings:

Electronic town meetings (ETMs) intend to empower the citizens participating in them either directly, indirectly or at least experimentally. There must be information presented, deliberation of some sort and voting. . . . So the most primitive form of ETM format is that where, say, a TV news show presents a mini-documentary on an issue, has a few experts give their opinions on that issue and then asks the public to vote on it for a period of time. Another simple ETM might bring together a group of citizens to discuss an issue and vote on it in face-to-face groups but using electronic hand-sets to vote anonymously during the process. Some of the more interesting and more complex ETMs have a more sophisticated recipe and add such ingredients as a) scientific polling, b) computer-assisted democracy, c) different electronic media-mixes . . . for example:

### Reform Party of Canada ETM on Physician Assisted Suicide: Calgary 1994

In keeping with their electoral promises of 1992, when they won about 15% of the seats in Parliament, the national Reform Party of Canada decided to experiment with an ETM on the above issue. Here is the design: There are five parliamentary districts in the Calgary area represented by members of the Reform Party. They all agreed to pick a random sample of at least 400 constituents from each district and to ask them to become televoters in an ETM to be broadcast the next Sunday. Each televoter got a set of 8 telephone numbers to call: 1 for 'yes', 2 for 'no', with six other shades of agreement or disagreement. They also received a brochure with information about the issue and the voting procedures.

Perhaps the major innovation in this project was that each Reform MP stated in advance that if a significant consensus of their constituents voted in favour of the issue (legalising physician assisted suicide) they would be bound by the vote of their constituents even though these MPs were personally opposed. The results following the debate were that about 70% of voters in every district were in favour of the proposition.

(*Source*: adapted from Http://www.duc.auburn.edu/~tann/projectct4.htmlUnited)

Now several issues arise from this extract, which was itself adapted from an Internet source. The first is that although this ETM purported to be direct, it was in fact mediated in three ways: by having a sample of voters make the decision and not the electorate as a whole, which though more costly would be technically feasible; by having the proposition drawn up by activists or experts, so that the question of politicians setting the agenda for debate remains a potential concern; and by relying on disembodied or virtual interaction, which cannot be avoided and equally might be regarded as a strength, in that it allows unlimited numbers of people to participate provided that they have access to the technology.

The second issue, then, is the realistic possibility of creating digitally competent voters and of them getting routine access to the relevant technologies, as opposed to being used by sensitive or cynical politicians for the electronic equivalent of a photo opportunity. There may be a democratic world of difference between the routine and the exotic use of electronic media to influence policy-making. To some extent the issue of citizen competence has always dogged pleas for more democracy. Apologists for the continuation of colonial rule have often adopted and adapted the Augustinian mantra of 'let me be pure, Lord, but not yet' in the face of the claims of groups seeking self-rule and independence, recommending a longer period of education in the ways of democratic rule. Even in mature democracies like the United Kingdom, the use of the referendum is frowned upon by many politicians, not only because it allegedly suborns the legislative power of Parliament, but also because citizens are said to lack the understanding to make snap judgements on complex issues like whether Britain should be a partner to a single European currency.

The third issue bears more directly on this point and allows us to introduce rather different versions of a functioning democracy.

## Indirect or representative democracy and participation

The participatory strand canvassed above, with its normative stress on the direct involvement of citizens in collective self-government, is a world away from the the more routine practices in large-scale democracies. In these, the idea of indirect or representative democracy has become the dominant form, institutionalised through the medium of elections. As we shall see later in this chapter, the sort of electoral rules which operate in different systems can have a marked impact upon the participation of voters and on the outcome of elections, but all forms of indirect or representative democracy have a number of things in common:

- the exercise of the power of citizens at least one place removed from actual decision-making and where elected representatives stand in place of, or act on behalf of, voters;
- the use of periodic elections at all or most levels of government as a symbol of the sovereignty of the people and as a symbolic and sometimes substantive way of holding political elites accountable;
- the belief that elections are an efficient and democratic way of organising political succession;
- the belief that elections facilitate the limited but popular involvement of citizens in the above, securing popular consent for the system as a whole and approbation for the winners.

Some of these functions are common to electoral contests in both democratic and non-democratic systems, so an important caveat is necessary. In representative democracies political freedom involves the free choice of governors by the governed, in open elections contested by political parties, and by individuals of different shades of opinion. The whole operation is subject to general rules of conduct (electoral laws).

This definition of representative democracy makes political freedom the cornerstone of any functioning democracy, and without it the idea of democracy is little more than a sham. But, of course, the formal freedom to vote tells us very little about the quality or effectiveness of political participation. In fact it offers what has become known as a 'process' view of democracy, following the insights of Joseph Schumpeter in his book *Capitalism, Socialism and Democracy* (1976), who said that democracy is that 'institutional arrangement for arriving at political decisions in which individuals acquire the power to decide by means of a competitive struggle for the peoples' vote'. Political freedom, defined as the right to vote in a competitive political market is an important, perhaps *the* defining, characteristic of representative democracy, but we would need to know more about the conditions exisiting in particular countries before awarding them the accolade 'democratic' simply on this basis.

To some extent this has to be a normative judgement, but empirical data on what we might call the 'realities' which affect choice are often available. Some of these are examined in subsequent parts of this chapter, but it is worth noting here that effective choice, and thus effective participation, can only occur where individual concerns can be properly articulated and pursued in the public sphere. This is a matter not only of having formally free elections, but also of sustaining pluralistic civil societies where groups flourish, and participant political cultures. It is also a matter of ensuring that the rights of citizens are systematically protected.

Democracies in this sense, as well as in the more limited but probably more attainable Schumpeterian mould are pretty rare in human history (Fukuyama 1992). Table 4.1 gives some indication of the overall growth in numbers since the late eighteenth century.

*Table 4.1* Democracies worldwide, 1790–1990

| Country | 1790 | 1848 | 1900 | 1919 | 1940 | 1960 | 1975 | 1990 |
|---|---|---|---|---|---|---|---|---|
| US | • | • | • | • | • | • | • | • |
| Canada | | | • | • | • | • | • | • |
| Switzerland | • | • | • | • | • | • | • | • |
| UK | | • | • | • | • | • | • | • |
| France | • | | • | • | | • | • | • |
| Belgium | | • | • | • | | • | • | • |
| Netherlands | | | • | • | • | | • | • |
| Denmark | | | • | • | | • | • | • |
| Piedmont/Italy | | | • | • | | • | • | • |
| Spain | | | | | | | | • |
| Portugal | | | | | | | | • |
| Sweden | | | • | • | • | • | • | • |
| Norway | | | | • | | • | • | • |
| Greece | | | • | | | • | | • |
| Austria | | | | • | | • | • | • |
| W. Germany | | | | • | | • | • | • |
| E. Germany | | | | • | | | | • |
| Poland | | | | • | | | | • |
| Czechoslovakia | | | | • | | | | • |
| Hungary | | | | | | | | • |
| Bulgaria | | | | | | | | • |
| Romania | | | | | | | | • |
| Turkey | | | | | | • | • | • |
| Latvia | | | | | | | | • |
| Estonia | | | | • | | | | • |
| Lithuania | | | | | | | | • |
| Finland | | | | • | • | • | • | • |
| Ireland | | | | | • | • | • | • |
| Australia | | | | • | • | • | • | • |
| New Zealand | | | | • | • | • | • | • |
| Chile | | | • | • | | • | | • |
| Argentina | | | • | • | | | | • |
| Brazil | | | | | | • | | • |
| Uraguay | | | | • | • | • | | • |
| Paraguay | | | | | | | | • |
| Mexico | | | | | • | • | • | • |
| Colombia | | | | • | • | • | • | • |
| Costa Rica | | | | • | • | • | • | • |
| Bolivia | | | | | | • | | • |
| Venezuela | | | | | | • | • | • |
| Peru | | | | | | • | | • |
| Equador | | | | | | • | | • |
| El Salvador | | | | | | • | | • |
| Nicaragua | | | | | | | | • |
| Honduras | | | | | | | | • |
| Jamaica | | | | | | | • | • |
| Dominican Rep | | | | | | | | • |
| Trinidad | | | | | | • | • | • |

*Table 4.1* Continued

| Country | 1790 | 1848 | 1900 | 1919 | 1940 | 1960 | 1975 | 1990 |
|---|---|---|---|---|---|---|---|---|
| Japan | | | | | | • | • | • |
| India | | | | | | • | • | • |
| Sri Lanka | | | | | | • | • | • |
| Singapore | | | | | | | | • |
| South Korea | | | | | | | | • |
| Thailand | | | | | | | | • |
| Philippines | | | | | | • | | • |
| Mauritius | | | | | | | • | • |
| Senegal | | | | | | | • | • |
| Botswana | | | | | | | | • |
| Namibia | | | | | | | | • |
| Papua New Guinea | | | | | | | | • |
| Israel | | | | | | • | • | • |
| Lebanon | | | | | | | | |
| TOTALS | 3 | 5 | 13 | 25 | 13 | 36 | 30 | 61 |

*Key:* • means democratic prodecures in place at this date. Note for these purposes democracy was defined as a country with a market economy, representative government based on open elections, external sovereignty (i.e. being recognised by other countries) and juridical rights (the rule of law).
*Source:* adapted from Doyle (1983) and reported in Fukuyama (1992: 49–50).

---

**THINK POINT**
- What inferences can you make from these data? Notably, the table does not include either South Africa or Russia, which have been significant additions to the list of democratic countries in the intervening years.

---

**Liberal democracy** A doctrine, and sometimes a practice, which combines individual freedom with the idea of popular sovereignty.

Narrow as it is, Schumpeter's definition of representative democracy conveniently summarises the paradigm case of democratic theory and organisation in the modern world, that of **liberal democracy**. Political liberalism is a pre-democratic creed which emerged in Europe and North America at the time when countries were trying to establish forms of constitutional or limited government in which individuals were afforded protection from the potential (and often actual) tyranny of rulers with pretensions to absolutism. As such, liberal theory places a great deal of weight upon the rule of law and the recognition that certain rights – to property, conscience, assembly and speech – are sacrosanct. Democracy, as we have seen, enshrines the right of all citizens to have a vote and to be otherwise active in politics if they so choose. In Chapter 1 we reported on the considerable variations across countries in universalising this liberal right, especially with regard to women, but in principle all liberal democracies respect the doctrine of universal adult suffrage.

It is of course possible for a country to be liberal but not (or not yet) democratic. Early modern countries like eighteenth-century Britain fall into this category, but if we take liberalism to refer to economic liberalism or to a belief in the power of markets and consumer sovereignty as well as political liberalism, then countries like Singapore are liberal but not (yet) democratic. Francis Fukuyama (1992: 44) says that a country can also be democratic without being liberal, where that means having the right to vote but playing fast and loose with other individual rights. He mentions post-revolutionary Iran here, but Pakistan, Turkey and post-communist Russia would also fall into this category.

Liberal democracy *pace* Schumpeter is a combination of limited and regular popular participation through elections and rule by political elites. For some, especially committed democrats of the participatory school and those Marxists convinced that democratic procedures are a facade for ruling-class domination, this blend is a besetting weakness.

## Elite theories of participation and democracy

Classical **elitists** sounded a rather different alarm about the dangers of democracy, namely that it sought to undermine the natural order of things. In political terms elitism is the doctrine that government by a small ruling group is not only desirable, which was the claim of apologists for monarchical and aristocratic rule throughout the ages, but also inevitable. The classical elite theorists of the late nineteenth and early twentieth centuries – Gaetano Mosca (1939), Vilfredo Pareto (1935) and Roberto Michels (1959) – were entirely unconvinced by what they saw as the dangerous sham or 'fiction' of 'popular representation'. But even Mosca, whose works, along with those of Pareto and Michels, were taken up enthusiastically by the Italian fascists during the 1920s and 1930s, came to believe that systems of popular representation were healthy because they introduced a pluralist element into what would otherwise be an introverted and complacent ruling class.

Schumpeter's form of elitism has become known as 'democratic elitism' (Bachrach 1967) because, he reasoned, free elections introduced an element of competition among elite groups. C. Wright Mills's (1956) famous gloss on this argument was to identify what he called a 'power elite' in American society and in other industrialised societies. This elite was made up of those people who occupied key positions of authority in the state, including the military and in private organisations. However, even Mills's argument, which has been widely caricatured, acknowledged that the 'middle levels' and 'the masses' in industrial societies could still exercise power in all but key decisions, through elections, the activity of interest groups and by way of the (still pluralist) media of communication.

These modifications to the ideal-typical version of liberal democracy and others to be found in the plethora of work done on the nature and distribution of power in industrial societies (Dahl 1961, 1971; Domhoff 1979) paint a more depressing picture of the actual operation of liberal democracies than the standard version would allow. There are obviously many aspects to these critiques but, for the purposes of this chapter, one of the most telling is the claim that some interests, and therefore some forms of participation, are organised *into* the routines of liberal democratic politics and others systematically organised *out* (Bachrach and Baratz 1970; Crenson

**Elite** The best or the noble; in contemporary usage it is generally applied to those who have high status or high formal positions in politics, religion and society.

1971, 1987). For the most part this is not a matter of the proportionality or otherwise of electoral systems, or of anything to do with formal voting procedures; rather, it touches the very fabric of political and social life, and the value and legitimacy attached to different sorts of political activity, identity or demands. The suggestion is either that political elites deliberately marginalise certain kinds of demands and issues, or else that 'the way things are' effectively suppresses or excludes certain issues (Lukes 1974).

### Rethinking political participation and democracy

Much of what we have discussed above under the rubric of liberal democracy is part of a venerable academic and political debate on the nature of democracy and the relationships between political participation and democracy. However, we need to take into account the impact on these relationships of recent social, technological, political and, indeed, geopolitical forces. We will touch upon three significant developments.

### The prospects for cyber-democracy

Earlier in this chapter we discussed the potential for reinventing participatory democracy which resides in virtual communities like the electronic town meeting. Then we mentioned a North American experiment; but there are examples of the increased use of information and computer technologies (ICTs) across the globe as the vehicles for both conventional and less conventional forms of politics and social organisation. Political parties now make routine use of computerised mailing lists with customised messages for targeted voters, and local electronic networks (LENs) provide virtual forums for job exchanges and data bases for all sorts of local activities. In Denmark for example, the concept of the electronic village hall or information and community service centre (ICSC) has undoubtedly contributed to the revival of community identity in some remote areas and, arguably, to a greater sense of citizen empowerment.

It is, of course, very easy to become an uncritical cyber-enthusiast about these sort of developments, but even if we were to discount the rather nostalgic claim that interactive or face-to-face politics is in some way superior to cyber-politics there are still important issues about computer literacy and access. Whether putting an interactive terminal in every home would increase political and social awareness and participation rates or simply create more opportunities for discreet and overt surveillance and intrusion by authorities and corporations is open to discussion. However, as we go into the twenty-first century, the conduct of democratic politics is likely to become increasingly affected by these developments. A cynical view of the impact of electronic communications on democracy is provided by the Italian cartoonist Giannelli in his visual comment on the victory of the media tycoon Silvio Berlusconi in the Italian general election of 1994 (Figure 4.3).

### The emergence of what has been called the 'new pluralism'

Technological innovation is a critical part of the rapid changes that are

*Figure 4.3* Telecrazia
*Source: Corriere della Sera*, 30 March 1994:7.

taking place on a global scale at the present time. In other ways, too, what Ulrich Beck (1996) calls the 'reinvention of politics' is changing the face of contemporary politics. Many issues that have emerged on the political agenda in the last couple of decades – technological change itself, environmentalism, family and gender relations, and what is sometimes called 'lifestyle politics' – have upset the grand themes of ideological conflict (left versus right) which have dominated the politics of many liberal democratic societies. One effect of what Gregor McLennan (1995) calls the 'new pluralism' of the 1990s has been to widen the scope of democratic political participation and in at least some ways make it more difficult for a systematic bias or policy of exclusion to occur.

When Robert Dahl updated in 1987 his critique of liberal democracy, which, in 1971, he had originally called 'Polyarchy', he admitted that the practical merits of polyarchic societies (free elections, universal suffrage, associational freedoms, accountability of elites) constituted only the *necessary* components of a democratic society, but not a *sufficient* definition of a democracy. While still warning against the promise of participatory utopias and radical dreams of democracy, he argued that an approximation of a democratic society can only follow from a celebration of cultural complexity and a thoroughgoing political inclusiveness – a system in which anybody can play. The new politics of pluralism certainly has these things, but militant forms of feminism or ecologism may show less of the tolerance which Dahl also praised as a feature of pluralistic societies and democratic polities.

### The propects for global democracy

Most of the key modern assumptions about democracy have been predicated on the existence of the territorial state and the national society. This is hardly surprising given the centrality of the nation-state in the institutions of modernity, but it does ignore the growth of what David Held calls 'the diverse sites of social and economic power and the dense networks of regional and global interconnectedness' (Held 1995: ix), which are now spanning the globe and which are challenging the organisational forms of the nation-state and the ideological foundations of its autonomy. There are lots of manifestations of this and we will explore the question of globalisation more directly in Chapter 16. Here we can refer to the existence of a supranational *Some of the work of this court* body of law built up under the auspices of the European Court of Human *was discussed in Chapter 1.* Rights and elements of a 'postnational' citizenship contained in the Maastricht Treaty on European Union of 1991.

Nation-states remain central to the organisation and conduct of democratic practices, and citizenship rights are still given meaning largely within the confines of the territorial state, but this state of affairs is not immutable. Held talks about the possibility of establishing a 'cosmopolitian democracy', which recognises the nation-state level of competence but inserts a layer of governance that would limit national sovereignty. Cosmopolitan institutions would co-exist with states but would be able to override them in clearly defined areas of activity, like human rights. The practical difficulties with this sort of prescription are enormous, but from the narrower perspective of this chapter the question is how such changes would affect political participation. Having issues like human rights dealt with by cosmopolitan institutions would presumably widen the scope for participation, providing more points of access for those who wish to intervene. It is noteworthy that, even today, the international politics of human rights is reliant upon the activities of transnational interest groups to keep it buoyant, rather than the goodwill of national governments. In other respects, popular participation might well be unaffected unless it could be channelled into specific areas and issues, like having a global plebiscite on the death penalty or divorce, with the poll conducted through electronic means.

# Who participates: some individual and social correlates of political participation

In this and in the next section of this chapter we will look more closely at various factors which are related to political participation. You will note that we talk about 'related to' here as opposed to the much firmer 'caused by'; this is an important caution if students of politics are to avoid spurious generalisations and false inferences. We will be concerned with four different sorts of explanations or partial explanations for who participates in politics and why. They are not mutually exclusive, because in real life they all may be contributory factors to an actual decision to vote for a particular party or to stay at home watching *Baywatch*. Unfortunately there is no unified or general theory of political participation, and so what we have is a mixture of universal interpretations of behaviour, like the economic model of activism canvassed in Chapter 1 (see pp. 30–4), and less ambitious attempts to establish statistically valid relationships between variables – for example levels of education and type and intensity of political participation – in one or more countries.

Broadly speaking, in this section we will look at both personal and social characteristics associated with different forms of political participation across countries, asking the question 'who participates?' In the subsequent section we will explore both motivational (psychological and cultural) and structural factors which influence why people do or do not get involved in political activity. Because of the great variety of data available we have been quite selective in choosing illustrative material.

A number of general points should be made about who participates in politics and what is known about who participates:

- Much of the data collected has come from the Anglo-American democracies, although an increasing body of material is now available from other European democracies, Japan, India and the post-communist regimes of Eastern and Central Europe. The point to bear in mind is that some of the apparently general findings rely on a quite limited number of cases and types of political system.
- Information about individuals has come usually from large-scale survey analysis and sometimes from longitudinal studies of attitudes and behaviour conducted over a period of years. Other information has been produced by looking at the relationships between what are called 'aggregate statistics', like census data on the social make-up of parliamentary constituencies or voting districts, and notionally dependent political variables like the percentage of votes cast for extreme right-wing parties.
- A great deal of work on 'who participates' was conducted during the 1950s and 1960s and this has largely been corroborated, by studies done since then. However, it is always possible that significant social

and political trends may be missed or glossed over because data were collected at one point in time and inferences were made which were not followed through into subsequent investigations.

- All findings continue to show that political participation is a highly skewed activity, regardless of country. The more intense or select the activity (standing for office as opposed to voting), the more skewed is the social profile of those engaged in it and the fewer the numbers involved. There is also some evidence to suggest that different kinds of political and associational activity are strongly linked to certain social and individual characteristics. Data collected about the membership of civic organisations like Friends of the Earth (FoE) and Amnesty International's British Section (AIBS) reveal some interesting comparisons, some of which are reported in Table 4.2.

*Table 4.2* Characteristics of membership in selected voluntary organisations – UK data

|  | FoE % | AIBS % |
|---|---|---|
| *educated to degree level* | 35 | 26 |
|  | *n=238* | *n=98* |
| *household income £20,000 plus* |  |  |
| £20,001–£30,000 | 21 | 20 |
| £30,001–£40,000 | 11 | 14 |
| over £40,000 | 12 | 20 |
|  | *n=301* | *n=192* |
| *occupational categories* |  |  |
| clerical worker | 8 | 8 |
| professional | 49 | 53 |
| managerial | 11 | 15 |
|  | *n=455* | *n=271* |
| *self-perceived class* |  |  |
| working class | 21 | 23 |
| middle class | 74 | 71 |
|  | *n=644* | *n=341* |

*Source*: Adapted from Jordan and Maloney (1996).

---

**THINK POINT**
- What do these data tell us about the membership of the two organisations?

---

It is clear from these data that the middle class are the dominant social group in both organisations, but why should this be so? One possible explanation is that middle-class people have, or are more likely to have, greater disposable income than working-class people. There are some difficulties with this explanation however and they illustrate the problems with making inferences from data like these. There is an obvious discrepancy between the self-perceived middle-class position of some 74 per cent of members of FoE and the fact that only 35 per cent attended university and 44 per cent have incomes higher than the UK national average of some £18,000 (circa

1996 ). Although the figures are different for AIBS, the pattern is the same. At least a proportion of those calling themselves middle class must, on 'objective' or measurable criteria fall outside this class, being less well educated and less handsomely paid. They may of course rely on other factors to define their middle-classness, like the sort of newspapers they read, the political party they vote for, or the sort of wine they drink. Here, too, the data are not terribly helpful in establishing a profile of membership which fits some neat pattern of cause and effect. Parties of the left, centre-left and ecological fringe attract the vote of the self-assigned middle-class activists of FoE and AIBS, so that they vote 'out of their class'.

Membership of voluntary organisations (political parties, trade unions, churches, sports clubs, women's groups, etc.) varies considerably across countries, as Table 4.3 shows. Although it is possible to make some observations from these data, along the lines that the countries of southern Europe fall well behind all other groupings, except Japan, we would be hard put to explain these differences in terms of the social characteristic of the various populations, or, it seems, on the basis of their political history. All the countries of Eastern Europe have higher levels of associational activity than France, one of the members of the founding club of modern democracies. Nigeria, much criticised for its record on human rights, tops the league table. But we cannot make too many inferences from the figures, other than to describe them. It may be that cultural factors play a greater part in

*Table 4.3* The extension of civil society, 1990–1 (percentage of the population belonging to a voluntary organisation)

| | | | |
|---|---|---|---|
| *Germanic Western Europe* | 70 | E. Germany | 84 |
| Austria | 54 | Hungary | 54 |
| Belgium | 59 | Latvia | 68 |
| Britain | 53 | Lithuania | 60 |
| Denmark | 81 | Russia | 66 |
| Finland | 78 | | |
| Iceland | 90 | *North America* | 63 |
| Ireland | 49 | Canada | 65 |
| Netherlands | 84 | USA | 60 |
| Sweden | 84 | | |
| W. Germany | 68 | *New Latin World* | 41 |
| | | Brazil | 43 |
| *Latin Western Europe* | 35 | Chile | 45 |
| France | 39 | Mexico | 36 |
| Italy | 36 | | |
| Portugal | 34 | *Ex-colonial Zone* | |
| Spain | 30 | Nigeria | 86 |
| | | | |
| *Eastern Europe* | 67 | | |
| Bulgaria | 60 | Japan | 36 |
| Estonia | 73 | | |

*Source:* World Values Survey 1990–1 (directed by R. Inglehart), Institute for Social Research, University of Michigan (data file).

explaining the propensity of a population to join forms of collective action, but, as we saw in Chapter 3, this is a minefield for the unwary.

### Selected variables and political participation: a brief inventory

#### Gender

In recent years national and cross-national research into voting behaviour has identified a 'gender gap' in the political dispositions of women and men. The concept refers to a whole raft of phenomena, including differing rates of turnout, party identification, political attitudes on a range of policy issues, and even profoundly felt political values (Norris 1996; Mueller 1988 ). Much of the early research on voting patterns among men and women (Duverger 1955; and discussed in Randall 1987) indicated that, generally speaking, women were more inclined to vote for centre and right-wing political parties than men. The tendency for women to be politically conservative was explained by a number of factors, including their lower trade union membership, stronger religious observance and greater longevity (age, too, being associated with conservatism).

Table 4.4, however, modifies this finding quite substantially, while still showing marked variations between different countries. The table demonstrates that the conventional wisdom about women's greater conservatism is no longer valid, although, of themselves, the data do not reveal anything about the motivations of women (or men) voters or about the meaning that they attach to political allegiance. On 1994 figures, women are more left-wing than men in Portugal, Spain, Canada, the USA, Denmark and both Germanys (although Germany was united by this time, data remain disaggregated in this table). In Britain, Australia, Luxembourg, Italy, Ireland and France, women were more conservative. No significant differences can be seen in the other countries. There is also some recent evidence which indicates that there is an age factor operating, with younger women not only more left-wing than their sisters, but also more so than their male counterparts (Norris 1996)

#### Education

Almond and Verba (1963) suggested that education socialised citizens into the democratic political culture, although their data showed that this varied across systems. Generally speaking, those with higher education are more likely to participate in politics regardless of the activity, than those who are less well educated. Clearly there are problems with tying down indicators of educational attainment which would enable cross-national comparisons to be made and like to be compared with like (do terms like 'higher education' or 'further education' refer to the same thing in different countries? Where would vocational and post-experience education be located?). For all this, it seems that those with educational qualifications of any sort, and university graduates in particular, are not only more likely to participate, but are also more confident in their ability to understand politics. In Table

*Table 4.4* Percentage votes cast by men and women for parties of the right and left: selected countries, 1994

| | lwp % * | | | rwp % * | | L–R lead* | | |
| | W | M | Gap** | W | M | Gap** | W | M** |
| --- | --- | --- | --- | --- | --- | --- | --- | --- |
| Britain | 45 | 51 | –6 | 33 | 24 | 10 | 11 | 27 |
| Australia | 46 | 52 | –6 | 48 | 41 | 7 | –2 | 11 |
| Luxemb'rg | 28 | 30 | –2 | 44 | 34 | 10 | –16 | –4 |
| Italy | 7 | 8 | 0 | 71 | 67 | 5 | –64 | –59 |
| Ireland | 16 | 18 | –2 | 75 | 73 | 3 | –59 | –55 |
| France | 12 | 13 | –1 | 36 | 33 | 3 | –24 | –20 |
| Greece | 52 | 54 | –2 | 41 | 39 | 2 | 11 | 15 |
| Belgium | 30 | 27 | 3 | 31 | 29 | 3 | –1 | –1 |
| Netherlands | 30 | 30 | 0 | 45 | 46 | –2 | –15 | –17 |
| Denmark | 34 | 28 | 6 | 43 | 40 | 3 | –9 | –12 |
| W. Germany | 40 | 39 | 1 | 38 | 41 | –3 | 2 | –2 |
| Spain | 28 | 27 | 1 | 45 | 48 | 4 | –17 | –21 |
| USA | 46 | 41 | 5 | 37 | 38 | –1 | 9 | 3 |
| Portugal | 80 | 76 | 4 | 20 | 24 | –4 | 60 | 53 |
| E. German | 50 | 42 | 8 | 47 | 49 | –2 | 2 | –7 |
| Canada | 59 | 44 | 15 | 28 | 37 | –9 | 31 | 7 |
| All | 38 | 36 | 2 | 43 | 41 | 1 | –5 | –4 |

*Key:* * lwp = left-wing parties; rwp = right-wing parties; L–R lead = left–right lead

** W = women; M = Men; Gap = gender gap. A negative gender gap indicates that women are more right-wing. A positive gender gap shows that they are more left-wing

*Note:* Figures are rounded to the nearest decimal point.

*Source:* Eurobarometer, 1994, using Australian and Canadian general elections of 1993; US presidential election of 1992; major parties in European elections in 1994

*Table 4.5* Education and political participation – UK

| Activity | Graduates | Those with intermediate qualifications % | Those with no qualifications |
| --- | --- | --- | --- |
| contacted MP | 29 | 11 | 8 |
| signed petition | 52 | 37 | 29 |
| gone on protest | 17 | 7 | 2 |

*Source:* British Social Attitudes (1987)

4.5 the relationship between educational qualifications and different sorts of political activity is outlined, including more radical forms of activism like taking part in a demonstration.

Of course, higher education is not always a foolproof guide to involvement in what Milbrath called 'gladiatorial' activities. Recruitment to a leadership position in a political organisation which is conscious of its ideological integrity may mean that only those judged pure or loyal are eligible for office. In addition, there is often room for the maverick to challenge and some-times flout the usual rules governing elite recruitment, by taking advantage of circumstances, or through using other attributes to secure office – charm, communication skills and possibly money. By and large, the stereotype of the political activist and especially the elected representative, as male, middle-aged and married still holds good. Table 4.6 gives some comparative figures on this phenomenon and Figure 4.4 provides a nice piece of scurrilous political propaganda in the form of a campaign advertisement used by a female candidate in a mid-term contest for the US Senate (Upper Chamber of the US Congress) in 1986.

### Life-cycle transitions

Quite a lot of research on political participation indicates that critical points in a person's life history can affect (disrupt and reshape) past patterns and levels of political involvement (Stoker and Jennings 1996). For example, being married (or partnered) seems to produce both a marked convergence in the participation rates of partners and also a falling off in these rates, at least in the higher registers of activity. Research into other life-cycle influences, for example divorce or the death of a family member, have not been studied as much as the standard socio-economic variables of class,

*Table 4.6* Percentage of female Members of Parliament – selected European democracies

| France | 6% |
| --- | --- |
| Britain | 9% |
| Sweden | 41% |

*Figure 4.4* Why must a US Senator look like this?

occupation, income or sex, but given the significance of the networks of social and emotional interaction which centre on the family (or some surrogate for it), changes in close family circumstances may well have a formative and transformative impact on political participation.

Age differences in rates of participation have been studied to a much greater extent. Here the finding for the USA, Britain and France and for many of the other Western European liberal democracies is that between the ages of 50 and 60 political participation rates decline, except for those deeply involved as gladiators, but there is considerable variation across countries in the effects of age. In Germany, at least with regard to voting turnout, age is not a good predictor of activism, while what might be called unconventional forms of political participation are less obviously associated with the 'normal' pattern, which sees participation very low for those under 20, rising steeply into the mid-forties and falling off more erratically towards old age (Parry et al. 1993). The young are much more inclined towards different types of protest activity than any other age group The general finding, that political participation tends to rise and fall with age, would also have to be modified in the light of developments like the emergence of the 'grey lobby' in some Western countries, that is, of interest organisations devoted to articulating the demands of older people.

The discussion of standard personal and social variables goes some way towards building a profile of the factors associated with different kinds of political activism. Other explanations of activism concentrate upon the importance of 'resource variables' in predicting participation. Brady, Verba and Schlozman (1996), drawing upon American data, write about the significance of 'civic skills' acquired as a member of a religious organisation, or some non-political body, in disposing people towards political activism. Some of these skills, notably those derived from formal education, are related to a person's social and economic status in a community, but others are not. While this may be a particularly American slant on factors influencing participation, comparative data suggest that higher participation in voluntary associations is also linked with higher rates of political participation. In the next section of the chapter we address the question of why people participate in politics by looking more closely at motivational factors, which directs us to the psychology of politics or towards economic theories of activism.

## Why do people participate in politics and why do some abstain?

So far in this chapter we have explored the issue of whether or not political participation is 'a good thing'. We have also pointed to research findings that suggest that certain groups of people are more likely to be politically active than others and that those who participate in politics tend to specialise. This is all good insightful stuff, but the key question remains: why do people participate in politics?

As one might expect, there is considerable disagreement about how to answer this question. Ultimately, much will depend on the theoretical perspective being used. To illustrate, we will look again at the example of rational choice theory (see also Chapter 1).

Rational choice theory has become one of the most influential frameworks for the study of politics (see Ward 1995). It has been especially useful in the explanation of the engagement or non-engagement of people in the political process. The basic premise of rational choice theory is that those engaged in political activity aspire to achieve their aims via the most efficient means; they are – in the broadest sense of the term – self-interested. The genesis of rational choice approaches to politics is rooted in the history of political thought, in the work of writers such as Thomas Hobbes in the seventeenth century. However, the most compelling and systematic uses of the approach began to emerge in the 1950s. In *An Economic Theory of Democracy* (1957), the American political scientist Anthony Downs presented a ground-breaking application of microeconomic models to the study of politics in general and voting in particular. The analysis of Downs is built around the axiom that individuals base their electoral choice upon a calculation of costs and benefits. So the choice of whether or not to participate in politics hinges on whether the individual concerned feels that the act imposes costs or yields benefits. Notice that the whole approach is built around the idea that the individual is rational and calculative and that as a rule individuals seek to minimise personal cost. A favourite metaphor is that of politics as a supermarket. As Iain McLean puts it, 'when I go to vote I am doing something similar but not identical to what I do when I go shopping. In both cases I "buy" what I "want"' (McLean 1987: 9–10). Therefore, should an individual decide that her or his vote will make no difference to the outcome of an election, then that individual will not vote. Moreover, it is also possible that the benefits associated with a particular electoral outcome might accrue to the individual whether or not s/he votes. The individual may calculate that non-participation is rational in such situations. This is known as 'free-riding'.

Rational choice approaches provide a powerful script for those seeking to explore the reasons for any sort of political participation. Notice that, aside from being a particular brand of theoretical framework with its own basic assumptions, rational choice is also a largely *agent-centred* interpretation of participation or non-participation. The alternative would be to employ *structural* explanations which emphasise the conditioning effects of social, institutional and ideological environments upon human action. The structure–agency issue, as we noted in Chapter 1 is vital in the social sciences and it is not possible to do justice to the nuances of that debate here (for which, see Hay 1995). However, it is possible to think productively about the explanation for levels of political participation in structure–agency terms. We begin with some agent-based observations.

A. Downs (1957) *An Economic Theory of Democracy*, New York: Harper & Row.

## Agency: political efficacy

Why do some individuals participate in politics while others do not? Clearly, some individuals feel that by participating they will be able to make a difference or possibly even to change things. The polar opposite position in effect amounts to a shrug of the shoulders and saying 'why bother when my participation will make no difference?' In other words, feelings of **political efficacy** are important. It encompasses a wide variety of sentiments, feelings and aspects of human psychology. It is about the extent to which a person senses that s/he can make a difference politically as well as the degree to which that person feels politically literate or politically competent. Moreover, political efficacy is the way a person feels about the ability of the social groups with which s/he identifies to orchestrate change or achieve aims. A useful way of thinking about efficacy is to postulate the ways in which the possession of such feelings might affect political behaviour. Table 4.7 attempts to do this by deriving hypotheses from plotting efficacy feelings against the feeling of trust in the system.

**Political efficacy** The extent to which an individual feels that his or her participation in politics will be effective.

Consider the following passage, which is taken from the concluding pages of the autobiography of the South African President, Nelson Mandela. Mandela was a political prisoner of the apartheid regime in South Africa between 1964 and 1990. Here he describes the formation of his political views:

> It was only when I began to learn that my boyhood freedom was an illusion, when I discovered as a young man that my freedom had already been taken from me, that I began to hunger for it. At first, as a student, I wanted freedom for myself, the transitory freedoms of being able to stay out at night, read what I pleased, and go where I chose. Later, as a young man in Johannesburg, I yearned for the basic and honourable freedoms of achieving my potential, of earning my keep, of marrying and having a family – the freedom not to be obstructed in a lawful life.
>
> But then I slowly saw that not only was I not free, but my brothers and sisters were not free. I saw that it was not just my freedom that was curtailed, but the freedom of everyone who looked like I did. That is when I joined the African National Congress, and that is when the hunger for my own freedom became the hunger for the freedom of my people. It was this desire for the freedom of my people to live their lives with dignity and self-respect that animated my life, that transformed a frightened young man into a bold one, that drove a law-abiding attorney to become a criminal, that turned a family-loving husband into a man without a home, that forced a life-loving man to live like a monk.
>
> (Mandela 1995: 750–1)

*Table 4.7* Political efficacy and trust in the system

|  | High level of trust in the system | Low level of trust in the system |
|---|---|---|
| *High political efficacy* | Participation that is supportive of the regime. | Participation that is designed to reform or revolutionise the regime. |
| *Low political efficacy* | Voting and 'patriotic' support for the regime only. | Alienation and withdrawal from politics. |

At first sight this statement is the recollection of the main events of Mandela's political socialisation. But it is also the memoir of an individual remembering feelings of political efficacy in spite of being located in an institutional context which he did not trust. In terms of Table 4.7, it would seem appropriate to place Mandela in the top right-hand quadrant (low trust in the regime plus high political efficacy).

### *Structure: the law, society and ideas*

We turn now to consider some structure-based explanations for levels of political participation. One of the main determinants of political participation is the legal framework in any given state. In all countries certain sorts of political activity are proscribed by law whereas others are perfectly legitimate. Notice, though, that the proscription of forms of participation does not prevent groups of people from engaging in the banned activity. The distribution of dissident samizdat literature in the former communist states of Eastern Europe was technically illegal. Opposition to the regime in Nazi Germany was an illegal act (whereas putting people to death in gas chambers for no reason other than that they were Jewish was technically lawful). Terroristic activities are, by definition, beyond the bounds of acceptable participation, but much depends upon the nature of the regime that calls a particular form of activity 'terrorism'. Of course, other forms of political participation are deemed to be acceptable but are regulated in more subtle ways. Voting in elections provides an obvious example.

Elections may be defined as the way in which states allocate legislative power. In democratic countries legislative power is allocated on the basis of citizen choice and different forms of electoral system exist to translate citizen preferences into parliamentary seats. For the citizen, elections provide a particularly low-cost method of participating in the political process. Voting, not surprisingly, is the most common form of political participation.

Elections are heavily regulated and all countries place restrictions on who can vote. Non-adults, usually defined as under-18s, are normally denied the franchise, and some countries do not allow either prisoners or those in institutions and defined as mentally ill to vote. Otherwise, universal adult suffrage tends to apply, although this is a relatively recent phenomenon in most countries. For example, the granting of the vote to women lagged behind the achievement of full-scale male suffrage. A particularly stark example is Switzerland, where full female suffrage in federal elections was not achieved until 1971. Of course, in a number of countries the denial of voting rights to women produced mass movements demanding equality at the ballot box. So the denial of one form of political participation to women produced another form of political participation. In Britain the suffragette movement campaigned vigorously – often through programmes of civil disobedience – for votes for women in the years leading up to the First World War. The 1918 Representation of the People Act granted the vote to women householders over 30 years of age and to those over 35 who were the wives of householders. All women over 21 were granted the vote in

1928. In the United States a good deal of the impetus behind the black civil rights movement of the 1960s came from highly iniquitous electoral arrangements (see Piven and Cloward 1977). In theory, the Thirteenth, Fourteenth and Fifteenth Amendments to the US Constitution (passed in the wake of the Civil War) guaranteed racial equality. In practice, various devices such as extremely difficult literacy tests and poll taxes facilitated the exclusion of black people from the electoral register.

Therefore the boundaries set by electoral law can have an impact upon the types of participation practised by those who do not have the franchise. It is also the case that the precise nature of electoral law can have an effect upon the types of participation available within a political system. This is an issue which political scientists have debated for a long time. At issue is the impact of different sorts of electoral system. While each democratic country has its own distinctive electoral system and while the merits of each is subject to sophisticated discussion (Reeve and Ware 1992), the debate has revolved around the respective consequences of plurality and proportional representation systems of election. The main differences between these systems is described in Table 4.8. It is important to remember that the electoral systems described here are very much ideal types. The purpose of this discussion is not to discuss the pros and cons of electoral systems, but to understand how the *structure* of electoral law might influence the *agency* of political participation.

A. Reeve and A. Ware (1992) *Electoral Systems: A Comparative and Theoretical Discussion*, London: Routledge.

In his book *Political Parties*, Maurice Duverger argued that the single ballot, simple majority-system (plurality) favoured a two-party system (this has become known as Duverger's Law). Conversely, he hypothesised that PR systems were conducive to multi-party political systems. If it is correct that the electoral system structures the party system, then it follows that the range of choices available to the electorate is similarly conditioned. For example, the mechanisms of a plurality system where winner takes all is thought to favour the existence of inclusive parties spanning large portions of the political spectrum. In other words, there is an incentive for adjacent

M. Duverger (1964) *Political Parties: Their Organization and Activity in the Modern State*, London: Methuen.

---

*Table 4.8* Main types of electoral system

---

1. *Plurality*
   Countries are divided into electoral districts (constituencies). Each district elects a single member to the legislature. The candidate with the highest number of votes wins the election. A majority of the votes cast is not necessary to win the election in any given district.

2. *Proportional Representation (PR)*
   Seats in the legislature are usually allocated in accordance with the proportion of the vote cast for each party. The most common method for achieving this end is the use of multi-member constituencies where parties field lists of candidates. The number of representatives elected for that party will reflect the proportion of votes cast for that party in the constituency. PR systems frequently operate with the entire country as a single constituency. Thresholds sometimes operate. In such cases parties need to achieve a minimum proportion of the vote before representation is permitted.

---

political forces to coalesce into single parties. Small parties with limited electoral appeal tend not to prosper (unless they command significant regional concentrations of support). Conversely, in a PR system where seats are allocated in more or less strict proportion to the votes cast, smaller political parties representing narrow sectors of political opinion should be able to secure representation. One related feature of plurality systems is the phenomenon of *tactical voting*. In such situations, electors cannot necessarily vote for the party they favour the most because they know that it has no chance of winning. However, they do cast their votes for the party most likely to displace their least favoured party.

These examples suggest that the structure of the electoral system may place constraints upon the range of available opportunities for participation among the electorate. Other writers have presented evidence to suggest that the nature of the electoral system might have deeper consequences. Some researchers have suggested that PR systems facilitate the entry of women and members of ethnic minority groups into national parliaments, thereby broadening the social profile of the 'gladiators'. The work of Vicky Randall (1987) appears to confirm the impression that women are better represented in the parliaments of countries using PR systems than of those using plurality systems. The finding is confirmed by Kerstin Barkman (1995) who explains the constraints placed upon women by a plurality system such as that of the United Kingdom:

V. Randall (1987) *Women and Politics: An International Perspective*, Basingstoke: Macmillan.

> Women don't appear to lose votes . . . but on the other hand, if they managed to get selected as candidates, they are often taken on for 'hopeless' seats and are rarely given safe seats. . . . Party selection panels are not openly discriminatory; on the contrary most party headquarters profess themselves in favour of more women in parliament. Selection is decentralised though, and the ideological stance of the centre is often not reflected in the decisions made by constituency selection committees . . . the 'mental maps' of the selectors ensure that the chosen candidate conforms to a typical career pattern usually comprising higher education, a professional career and extensive political experience, all normally accomplished by the age of forty. This is a male pattern and unlikely to be feasible for most women, particularly if they marry and have children.
>
> (Barkman 1995: 141)

This commentary raises deeper structural questions about reasons for participation and non-participation. Studies of gender differences in participation tend to emphasise the role of two further sorts of structural constraint: social structure and dominant ideas.

Many have sought to explain levels and types of participation with reference to *social structure*. In such approaches researchers seek to establish whether categories such as class, religion, gender or ethnicity correlate with particular modes or intensities of participation. This method is frequently deployed in studies of voting behaviour, but clearly it has wider applications. It is relatively easy to identify correlations between social group and levels of political participation, but altogether more difficult to account for these trends. In their exhaustive study of political participation in Britain, Parry, Moyser and Day discovered that working-class people were less inclined to participate in politics than the salaried middle classes. This, they argue, may be attributable to the 'disadvantageous resource position' of the working class (Parry, Moyser and Day 1992: 131). A very powerful hypothesis, therefore, would suggest that certain groups in the population are better equipped to participate than others. Resources are a matter not simply of access to money, but also of access to political skills and political information.

*Ideas-based* explanations emphasise the ways in which dominant belief systems structure patterns of political preference and political behaviour across society. There are two ways in which such ideational structures might be thought to operate. First, certain patterns of belief offer disincentives to participate. Feminists would argue that patriarchal belief systems devalue the public role of women, who are treated predominantly as child-rearers and homemakers. The 'gendering' of ideas about politics dissuades women from entering (or for that matter challenging) what is understood as the conventional realm of politics. It also works on the perceptions of others, such as party selection panels, thereby producing discrimination (see Chapman 1993 for a much fuller discussion). It is often argued that a component of the oppression of particular social groups is the ideological masking of their 'real interests'. A classic literary statement of this view can be found in Robert Tressell's novel *The Ragged Trousered Philanthropists*, which was written in the early years of the twentieth century. In this extract, the book's main character, Owen, reflects on the failure of the majority of working-class people to engage in the sorts of participation necessary to overthrow the exploitative capitalist system in which they live and work:

> And the future, as far as he could see, was hopeless as the past; darker, for there would surely come a time, if he lived long enough, when he would be unable to work any more.
>
> He thought of his child. Was he to be a slave and a drudge all his life also?
>
> It would be better for the boy to die now.
>
> As Owen thought of his child's future there sprung up within him a feeling of hatred and fury against the majority of his fellow workmen.
>
> *They were the enemy.* Those who not only quietly submitted like so many cattle to the existing state of things, but defended it, and opposed and ridiculed any suggestion to alter it.
>
> *They were the real oppressors* – the men who spoke of themselves as 'The likes of us', who, having lived in poverty and degradation all their lives considered that what had been good enough for them was good enough for the children they had been the cause of bringing into existence.
>
> He hated and despised them because they calmly saw their children condemned to hard labour and poverty for life, and deliberately refused to make any effort to secure for them better conditions than those they had themselves.
>
> (Tressell 1965: 45–6)

> **THINK POINT**
> • Can you think of other ways in which ideas might structure political behaviour?

## Conclusion

It may be rather trite to say so, but without participation there would be no politics. It is not surprising, therefore, that much of the intellectual energy of political science has been taken up with trying to understand what motivates people to become involved in politics, what motivates others to abstain from the conventional political arena and what people do to express themselves politically. Our cumulative knowledge about these questions has increased considerably with the development of sophisticated survey methods and with advances in information technology which facilitate the processing of large data sets.

All well and good, but the study of political participation in isolation bars us from posing some interesting questions. In the context of this book, we would do well to reflect on the extent to which rates and types of participation in a given society can be understood in relation to that country's politico-cultural framework and/or to prevailing patterns of political socialisation. Moreover, it is always proper to think about the systemic consequences of participation. It is here that we touch on the highly charged normative debate about the relationship between participation and democracy. Is too much participation the cause of overload in the political system? Do too many demands make it impossible for political elites to govern effectively? Or does political participation represent the most effective means of expressing ourselves as human beings? Can we forego a little political stability in the interests of maximising citizen involvement in politics? These questions are not new; they are the mainstays of political philosophy and some of them are taken up in Part 2 of the book.

## Further reading

Birch, A. H. (1993) *The Concepts and Theories of Modern Democracy*, London: Routledge. An excellent discussion of the key questions of democratic theory.

Downs, A. (1957) *An Economic Theory of Democracy*, New York: Harper & Row. The classic, controversial rational choice account of why people vote (or don't vote) as they do.

Etzioni, A, (1993) *The Spirit of Community*, London, Crown Publishers. One of the bibles of the communitarian movement.

Milbrath, L. (1965) *Political Participation: How and Why Do People Get Involved in Politics?*, Chicago: Rand McNally. Perhaps the first systematic attempt to think about political participation. It develops the famous gladiators–spectators–apathetics hierarchy.

Milbrath, L. and Goel, M. (1977) *Political Participation: How and Why Do People Get Involved in Politics*, Chicago: Rand McNally. Rather more than a standard second edition. Read in conjunction with the 1965 volume, this careful reappraisal gives a good account of the development of US political science over a decade.

Parry, G. Moyser, G. and Day, N. (1992) *Political Participation and Democracy in Britain*, Cambridge: Cambridge University Press. Extensive report on a major research project. It also provides a state-of-the-art theoretical discussion.

Rheingold, H. (1994) *The Virtual Community: Finding Connection in a Computerised World*, London: Verso. Committed exploration of the up-side of the computer revolution in building community and improving democracy. It is both cyber-friendly and cyber-pretentious

Toffler, A. (1971) *Future Shock*, London: Bantam Books. An early source of writing on the democratic virtues of electronic plebiscites by a well-known futurologist.

# 5 POLITICS AND SOCIAL CHANGE

*Barrie Axford*

**Introduction**

**The study of political and social change**

**Key questions in the explanation of social and political change**

*What causal factors are privileged for explanatory purposes?*
*Does the theory seek to generalise about political and social change?*
*Does the theory emphasise order or change?*
*Is change continuous or discontinuous, evolutionary or revolutionary?*

**Modernisation and change: functionalism, evolutionism and teleological theories of change**

**Revolutionary change**

*Values and revolution – functionalist accounts*
*Revolutions and violence*
*Revolutions from above*
*Revolutions as a means of going back to the future*

**Two studies in political and social change**

*Short-term behavioural change: electoral change*
*Revolutionary change in East-Central Europe*

**Conclusion**

**Further reading**

# Politics and social change

## Introduction

So far in this book we have identified some of the ways in which people learn about politics and thus how they take on political identities. We have also looked at the ways in which they take part in political activity, or why they may be politically inactive. At least implicit in much of this discussion is the sense that while individuals are not free agents in influencing how they live, neither are they slavish followers of fashion and circumstance, nor simply moulded by larger social and political forces.

In this chapter we will examine political and social change, which will provide further insights into the relationships between agency and structures and introduce for the first time in this book an historical and temporal dimension to political analysis. We will try to unpick some of the issues surrounding theoretical explanations of social and political change and offer some detailed illustrations of different types of change. For example, Karl Marx's view of history and historical change saw it as an unfolding of basically exploitative relationships between social classes (slave and slave-owner, feudal peasant and landowner, or capitalist and wage-labourer) in which individuals are less important than the clash of great social forces. For him, social change comes about as the result of a necessary conflict between social classes, defined in terms of whether they own the means of production (for example different forms of capital or land or labour) or whether they are merely factors of production – hewers of wood, welders in a shipyard, agricultural workers or computer programmers – who are the direct producers of wealth. Political change, like the emergence of mass political parties in the twentieth century or the transition from dictatorship to democracy, is deemed by Marx to be an important facet of social change, but *influenced*, some Marxists would say *determined*, by economic factors. Until recently, some forms of Marxism depicted even major political changes, like the achievement of working-class male and full female suffrage as little more than historical footnotes.

Needless to say, this view of politics and of how social change comes about is not universally accepted. It is, however, one of the best-known

*Clearly it is impossible to refer to all of Marx's writings on the subject, but see, for example, the English edition of Das Kapital: K. Marx (1967) Capital, vol. 1, trans S. Moore and E. Aveling, New York: International Publishers.*

attempts to theorise social change and one of a small band of theories which attempt to provide a universal explanation of historical change. We will say more about its precepts below, but for the moment we need to define more tightly just what the concept of change means and then explore in detail a number of important questions about the nature of change and explanations of it.

To change means simply to alter or to make different. At first sight it might appear obvious, even banal, to note that change is a central concept in the social sciences. We are accustomed to saying that people and circumstances change, and sometimes we treat changes with apprehension or alarm, at other times with enthusiasm. Change comes with the package, and terms like evolution, development, movement, variation, transition, transformation and decay are testimony to the dynamism of all life. As individuals we may prefer to keep things as they are, to hanker after stability and not change, equilibrium not chaos, but, as the Greek philosopher Heraclitus said in about 500 BC, 'you cannot step twice into the same river, for other waters are continually flowing on'. In other words, nothing stays fixed, and the universe, including the social universe, is in a constant state of flux which embraces both permanence and change, stability and instability, order and disorder.

## The study of political and social change

This is all well and good, but if change is a characteristic of all existence, why is it such a contentious area of discussion in the social and political sciences? The answer is deceptively simple: as the sociologist Anthony Smith (1973) says, no theory of society could claim to be adequate if it failed to explain transformation and change in social life. The difficulty arises in deciding what passes for convincing explanation and whether it is possible to order the 'kaleidoscope of observable changes in history into a single, coherent framework; and more, to provide a unified theory of all social change' (Smith 1973: 1). To take an obvious example, Karl Marx's work, which was referred to earlier, does claim to provide an overarching theory of historical change. Like all great and complex theories, his is subject to different interpretations, but the basic elements of Marxism as a theory of large-scale and long-term change can be summarised as follows: Marx understood the course of human history to consist of a series of major conflicts, which he called social revolutions, that grow out of the objective *contradictions* (sources of tension and disruption) found in all class-divided societies. These contradictions are generic across all **modes of production** (slavery, feudalism and capitalism, plus their historical variants) but take on particular forms depending on historical circumstances. Contradictions arise within modes of production because of the necessary tensions between what Marx called the forces of production (types of technology and the primary division of labour) and the relations of production (ownership of property,

**Modes of production** A phrase usually associated with Karl Marx, and which refers to the way production is organised in society. It focuses upon the technology and social relations of production. The most essential part of social relations is control over productive forces and resources.

social class divisions and the means whereby the economic productivity of non-owners is extracted and used by the owning class). Through these tensions the essentially exploitative nature of the relationships between one class and another is revealed and exacerbated. Growing disjunctures are expressed in more intense class conflicts, and the seeds of a social revolution are sown as exploited classes achieve a consciousness and a unity which are then manifested in struggles against the dominant class. Conditions for social revolution are particularly ripe when the structures of a new mode of production – capitalism within feudalism or socialism within capitalism – create pressures which crystalise the revolutionary potential of nascent classes, like the middle classes in the period of early industrialisation or the industrial working class in capitalist modes of production. Writing about the "bourgeois revolutions" which heralded the end of feudalism in Europe after the French Revolution of 1789, Marx and Engels say that the bases of a commercial or even a proto-capitalist society were laid down during the feudal mode of production:

> Each step in the development of the bourgeoisie was accompanied by a corresponding political advance of that class. An oppressed class under the sway of the feudal nobility, an armed and self-governing association in the medieval commune, here independent urban republic (as in Italy and Germany), there taxable "third estate" of the monarchy (as in France) afterwards, in the period of manufacture proper, serving either the semi-feudal or absolute monarchy as a counterpoise against the nobility, and, in fact, corner-stone of the great monarchies in general – the bourgeoisie has at last, since the establishment of modern industry and the world market, conquered for itself, in the modern representative state, exclusive political sway.
>
> (Marx and Engels 1973b)

This is all very neat, but the course of history has rarely unfolded in quite so predictable, if occasionally tumultuous, a fashion. Marx himself might well have been surprised that Tsarist Russia was the site of the first socialist revolution in 1917, because it lacked a developed industrial base and an organised working class. Neither had it experienced a fully fledged bourgeois revolution to launch it on the road to industrial and political modernity. So, understood in terms of Marx's world-historical model of social change, the Soviet Union missed out on the penultimate stage of development by skipping the capitalist mode of production and jumping from feudalism to socialism. Japan, on the other hand, did become capitalist, but along a path which did not involve a bourgeois revolution; instead it followed a 'revolution from above', much influenced by a non-propertied, bureaucratic and warrior elite – the Samurai – who were crucial to the modernisation of that country (Trimberger, 1978).

*The Tsar was the imperial ruler of Russia before the revolution of 1917.*

## Key questions in the explanation of social and political change

For all its claim to generality, Marxism still leaves important questions about historical variation unanswered and this is true about all theories which have pretensions to tell the whole story. So when examining explanations of political and social change, we have to ask a number of key questions about theories of change.

### What causal factors are privileged for explanatory purposes?

Theories of change would seem to require causal analysis, that is, accounts which tell us what makes something happen over time, but this has always been a very contentious issue in the social sciences. As we discussed in the Introduction to this book, modern social scientists have been very wary about making statements of the order '*x* causes *y*' because of the deterministic feel of such pronouncements and also because any patterns of social causation (if such things exist) are likely to be very complex and probably not easily measurable. There is also the problem of deciding:

1 whether (or when) causation refers to a direct causal relationship between one thing and another (I tripped him, he fell down):
2 whether a more indirect link is implied, wherein causal factors are either contributory, or something which does not involve a direct relationship between discrete events (cause and effect);
3 whether there is a situation in which outcomes occur *necessarily* because of the properties of the objects involved (a bomb going off due to its combustible nature, a plane flying because of its aerodynamic qualities) but *contingently* due to the circumstances in which they are found (in a building or outside, in good or bad weather).

Thus social scientists are often more inclined to caution when making statements about relationships between variables, preferring to talk about 'tendencies' or 'probabilities', or 'degrees of association', especially where the nature of the relationship is to be shown using statistical analysis. When discussing political and social change two other issues need to be considered. The first, to use the language of statistics, is the explanatory power of different types of variables – that is, which variables are to be the independent and which the dependent variables. In many accounts of political change, political phenomena are often discussed as dependent variables. Eric Nordlinger's (1981) account of the factors which explain public policy outputs in democratic states examines the extent to which what he calls 'societalist' factors – like the degree of class conflict, or the power of interest groups, or the ethnic composition of a country – 'explain' what choices governments make. His notion of 'societalist' covers a wide spectrum of thought, taking in pluralist variants of democratic theory and Marxism.

*Independent variables are those which cause things to happen.*

*Dependent variables are those which are caused by something else.*

*We talked about democratic theory in Chapters 1 and 4.*

In his multi-volume study on the making of the modern world, Immanuel Wallerstein (1974, 1979, 1989) reduces political factors – the role of nation-states, war, ideological conflicts between governments and so on – to the basic effects of economic forces operating on a world scale. In this he has some weighty backing. As we have seen, Marx relegated most, if not all, political forms to the margins of explanatory power. But of late there has been a sustained attempt to reintroduce a more politically centred treatment of historical change, drawing upon the insights of major theorists like Max Weber, Émile Durkheim and Friedrich Hegel to construct alternative theoretical accounts to that of Marx and other 'societalists'.

Second, there is the question of whether change is caused by internal (or endogenous) factors or by external (or exogenous) forces. As we shall see, studies of social change and especially of **modernisation** in the Third World have often assumed that the level of a society's development is associated with factors internal to that society. From here it can be a fairly short step to the position that the relative 'backwardness' of some Third World countries is a consequence of their own history and culture – their societal genetics.

See, for example, M. Weber (1970) *The Protestant Ethic and the Spirit of Capitalism*, London: Allen & Unwin.

**Modernisation** Literally, the processes whereby society becomes modern.

## *Does the theory seek to generalise about political and social change?*

A generalisation is a measure (often an approximate measure) of the number of objects or cases which belong to some category, or a statement about the common properties of things. Thus we might say that $x$ per cent of people in Britain support the principle of capital punishment, or, more loosely, that 'most' young people under 18 prefer Blur to Bach. Generalisations do not, of themselves, give any clue to causation, they simply identify and record what things have in common and how many of them share certain characteristics. The difficulty with what might otherwise appear as a useful, indeed necessary, attempt to establish whether there are regularities in social life is that when it is applied to the allegedly common properties found in different societies over long periods of time, we run the risk of ignoring that which is particular, local and culturally unique. The idea that certain phenomena are invariant (unchanging) across time and space, which some theories of long-term, large-scale change, like Marxism, require, may understate the differences between objects. Here we run up against a version of what was introduced in Chapter 1 as the 'ecological' or 'systemic' fallacy, that is, the spurious inference of individual characteristics from common features.

All these points about the difficulties of studying change are important. They remain so regardless of the *scope* of what is being studied: world-historical change, societal change, particular features of societal change, like electoral behaviour or the development of political parties, and regardless of the *type* of change being studied: short term or long term, incremental, evolutionary or revolutionary.

The methods employed by students of political and social change are also various and range from (i) the use of statistical approaches which manipulate both survey data derived from individual respondents and aggregate data (which usually describe the characteristics of whole populations – income, car ownership and so on); (ii) case studies of particular societies, and (iii) comparative analysis of multiple states and societies and forms of comparative study which use smaller numbers of cases and owe much to the insights of historians as well as to the social sciences. Of particular note in this latter category is the monumental work of the historian Fernand Braudel (for example, 1975 and 1977), who painstakingly examined the relationships between economy and society between about 1400 and 1800 in Europe largely through reconstructing the day-to-day lives of its people, whether rural peasants or courtiers. Others of note in this broad church of comparative history are Barrington Moore (Jr) (1966), Immanuel Wallerstein (1974), Theda Skocpol (1978), Michael Mann (1986) and Charles Tilly (1975). We will refer to some of their arguments later in the chapter.

### Does the theory emphasise order or change?

We have suggested already that the idea of changing embraces both stability and variation, but the fact is that a good deal of social theory has tended to stress either one condition or the other. Marxism, broadly speaking, offers a theory of revolutionary conflict as the engine of change, but other strands of thinking, which sometimes cluster under the label of **functionalist**, have been much more concerned with the conditions under which order is achieved, describing the normal process of change as evolutionary not revolutionary (T. Parsons 1967). In such accounts, revolutionary change is often depicted as abnormal or dysfunctional, and the purpose of analysis is to discover the means by which societies reclaim equilibrium.

There is, of course, a good deal of room for caricaturing arguments in either camp, but it is worth noting that powerful (though sometimes hidden) normative positions are carried in analysis which purports to be objective and explanatory. For example, much of the work conducted during the 1950s and 1960s on the viability of democratic systems (see B. Barry 1970 for a masterly discussion of this work) during the height of the Cold War was concerned with the conditions for producing and maintaining stable democracy within a country (Almond and Verba 1963; Eckstein 1966; Lipset 1959). As we saw in Chapters 2 and 3, the importance of internalised normative constraints was central to these accounts. Leaving aside the vexed question of how important values actually are in explaining democratic stability, the normative burden of at least some of these arguments is that stability is a desired state of affairs and that certain ways of achieving it are preferable to others.

### Is change continuous or discontinuous, evolutionary or revolutionary?

This is not the same thing as saying that change is expected or unexpected from the standpoint of particular actors. It would be correct to say that

**Functionalist** A term used to describe a range of theories which stress the extent to which norms and values underlie social and political stability. Stable societies are seen as being able to carry out the basic 'functional' imperatives – socialisation, reproduction, education and so on – necessary for their survival.

events in Central and Eastern Europe and in the Soviet Union between 1989 and 1991 were unexpected, in the sense that the peaceful reforms already introduced by the then Soviet leader Mikhail Gorbachev were seen as adjustments to ensure the more efficient working of the Soviet political system and economy (*perestroika*) along with a little democratic mood music designed to show the West that the Soviet regime in particular could be more open (*glasnost*). The wholesale reconstruction of life without communism was not part of the agenda, and when it happened Western theorists were, figuratively speaking, caught napping. The question is whether what happened in state socialist societies like Poland, Hungary or the Soviet Union can be explained by existing theories of social change. Were events in the USSR after 1989 part of an evolutionary process of historical change, a revolutionary upheaval or an unlikely historical event subject only to the forces of contingency? We will assess some of the arguments about the changes in Central and Eastern Europe later in this chapter (see p. 161).

## Modernisation and change: functionalism, evolutionism and teleological theories of change

Social change is often seen as **teleological** or as having a particular direction or storyline. In a typical scenario, history begins with small mobile societies of hunter-gatherers and progresses to the modern, industrial societies of the Western world by way of the emergence of pastoral communities and the establishment of states based upon the power of landowners. All evolutionary theories depict social change as a succession of stages, each displaying a greater degree of social complexity and a more sophisticated division of labour than its predecessor. Most functionalist theories of social change are evolutionary, and so, in this respect, is Marxism, because it is a stage-based theory of history, albeit one which uses severe disruptions in the form of social revolutions, to explain the transition from one type of society to another. Here conflict, and not the striving for order, is seen as the main engine of social change.

As a variation on the evolutionary theme, some authors have stressed the cyclical quality of historical change. In his major work *The Rise and Fall of the Great Powers* (1988), the historian Paul Kennedy discusses the decline of American power in the last few decades of the twentieth century as part of a cyclical pattern of growth and decline largely caused by economic and technological factors. In his estimation, global or regional domination always goes to the strongest nation-state. But domination or hegemony is not permanent. Strong states flourish and may even become more powerful than any rivals, but in time they will be replaced by others, even stronger and more resourceful. Cyclical models of change also inform much of what has become known as *world-systems analysis*, particularly that associated with the pioneering work of Immanuel Wallerstein (1974, 1979, 1989). Like

**Teleology** A theory of the final causes of things, a story unfolding to a predetermined end.

*We shall have more to say about world-systems analysis in Chapter 16, where global issues are examined.*

**147**

Kennedy, Wallerstein sees the history of the modern world as one of ascending and declining hegemonies – those of the United Provinces (now called the Netherlands), Britain twice and, most recently, the United States.

Some evolutionary theories, however, go beyond seeing history as having an overall direction or a cyclical quality to propose a universal history; these accounts take the form of full-blown teleologies. Marx's universal history is a case in point, but Francis Fukuyama's (1992) treatise on the global triumph of liberalism and liberal democracy is one of the most recent and influential forays into a style of grand theorising which has largely gone out of fashion in contemporary social science and history. Fukuyama draws upon the work of the great philosopher Friedrich Hegel to construct a theory of the 'end of History', which, in a polemical article published in 1989, he described as 'the end point of mankind's ideological evolution and the universalisation of Western liberal democracy as the final form of human government' (Fukuyama 1992: 3). Fukuyama's universal history is one of fundamental conflict between ideologies as the engines of change. History is to be understood as a sequence of stages of consciousness or ideology which embody different views on the principles of social order and different conceptions of the human spirit. The latter is seen as either trapped or liberated by different kinds of social and political arrangements.

For Fukuyama, the sequence of historical stages represents a purposive and progressive route in the development of the human spirit and human potential. In the modern age and under market-oriented economic liberalism and liberal democracy, we have reached the final scene of this historical drama, since there are no longer any serious global challengers to these ideologies. Fascism and communism have failed and the message of Islam is most unlikely to have universal appeal. But the end of History does not signify the end of conflict. Intensely visceral and mostly local conflicts – between Jew and Muslim, Zulu and Khosa in South Africa, Serb and Croat in Bosnia, or Hutu and Tutsi in Rwanda – will in all probablity continue to disfigure the map of world politics. Various 'outsiders' – mostly in the Third World, or among disadvantaged or dispossessed populations inside the liberal heartlands of Western Europe and North America – will also present challenges to the complete universalisation of the dominant ideology.

---

**THINK POINT**
- Fukuyama's views have been widely discussed. How convincing do they seem to you?
- On what grounds could you object to his thesis?

---

The evolutionist slant of Fukuyama's argument lies in the mainstream of the Enlightenment traditions we referred to in Chapter 1. For Fukuyama, historical change involves an unfolding or diffusion of the main features of Western modernity or civilisation across the world. In this respect his thesis is a conscious attempt to revive an approach to the study of political and social change called modernisation theory, which emerged early on after the Second World War as a way of assessing whether Third-World and newly independent countries in Africa and Asia had the potential to become modern and democratic. Some of this work has its intellectual roots in the writings of Marx, with his emphasis upon capitalism as the main dynamic of social change in the modern world, but it owes more of a debt to the sociologists Émile Durkheim, who wrote extensively about industrialism, and Max Weber, who saw modernity as signifying the global spread of rationality and bureaucratic forms of decision-making.

In addition to the intellectual debt to major social theorists, students of modernisation were also concerned to ground their work on the relationships between political and socio-economic modernisation in rigorous empirical (scientific) investigation. As a consequence, much of the work tried to identify relevant indicators of key processes like development, industrialisation or modernisation, and to look for statistically significant relationships between notionally independent variables and notionally dependent ones using comparative methods and multiple cases.

In Seymour Martin Lipset's seminal study *Political Man* (1959) the basis of the investigation was the relationship between political democracy and high levels of economic development. Lipset examined data from well over fifty states for the period 1918–58. On the basis of these data he established a fourfold classification: English-Speaking Stable Democracies, of which there were 13; European and English-Speaking Unstable Democracies, which numbered 17; Latin-American Democracies which accounted for 7; and Latin-American Stable Dictatorships, of which there were 13. Democracy was defined procedurally, as open electoral competition between contenders for office. Levels of economic development were gauged against four indicators: wealth, industrialisation, education and urbanisation, with each broken down into component parts like levels of literacy, size of population catered for by medical practitioners and so on. Mean scores were computed for all indicators and components, and for each category of country. Lipset found that the average score was much higher for the democratic systems, and he concluded that high levels of socio-economic development (e.g. high gross national product – GNP) are strongly associated with democratic development. Where cases, like that of Nazi Germany, did not bear out this conclusion, he was prepared to allow that 'local' factors like culture and historical circumstances can make a significant difference to the path of development. But apart from historical anomalies, there are other substantial grounds on which one could object to Lipset's original thesis. Some of these are methodological – the limited size and representativeness of the sample, the conflation of the language of correlation (statistical association) with the language of causation, and the problems of locating countries in one category as opposed to another.

Other objections relate to the normative difficulties which many modernisation theorists encountered when they argued that industrial development followed a pattern of growth which would over time realise uniform social and political institutions across countries with widely differing histories and cultures. Countries like Britain and the United States, which had industrialised and democratised before any others, were studied to reveal the likely pattern of growth and change, and they were sometimes held up as exemplars of the modernisation process.

---

**THINK POINT**
- Are there any problems with this thesis, given that even Marx said that the country that is more developed industrially only shows, to the less developed, the image if its own future?

---

Now that you have thought about some of the central ideas of modernisation theory, you will have seen some obvious objections to its cental thesis. One of the main concerns has been the extent to which it offers a Euro-American slant on, or ideal version of the modernisation process, to the extent that these models of development are treated not only as typical, but as desirable. Although some writers, like Samuel Huntington (1968), have been prepared to argue that rapid economic development on the part of countries in the Third World can cause political instability in the form of riots, coups and revolutions, there is little work in this genre which acknowledges the possibility of alternative routes to modernity. So we must ask how far early modernisation theory can explain the process of change in places like Singapore or South Korea, neither of which are travelling the same route to economic and political modernisation as did the UK or the USA. The spectacular economic growth shown by many developing countries in recent decades has not always been matched by expected democratic changes. Spain managed the transition from authoritarian rule by 1990, but elsewhere, for example in Singapore, Taiwan and the Republic of Korea, some of the attributes of formal democracy (notably competitive elections) are not matched by liberality in the form of substantive regard for human rights. So the implied connection between advanced industrialisation and political liberalism has still to be be proved.

The linearity implied in modernisation theory and the teleology of Fukuyama's account is countered in the very influential work of the sociologist Anthony Giddens (1990, 1991), who is at pains to develop what he calls a 'discontinuist' interpretation of modern social development. Briefly, this involves the basic premise that modern social institutions (the nation-state, capitalism, industrialism) and modern patterns of thought (emphasis on rationality, respect for the individual) are in some critical respects distinct from all traditional forms of social order. The changes which have occurred in the last three or four centuries, says Giddens, have been so momentous that they are hardly traceable to pre-modern societies. Because of this, an evolutionist perspective on historical change is simply misleading.

# Revolutionary change

Modernisation means disturbance, the ending of old ways of doing things and the often conflict-ridden transition to new ways. The concept of **revolution** is in many ways a very modern concept. Because of the significance of revolutionary change in the modern world we will spend some time examining the phenomenon and attempts to explain it.

It is quite common to use the term revolution to apply to processes which take place over long periods of time, like the Industrial Revolution in the United Kingdom. But clearly some definitional caution is necessary here. Revolution implies deep change, and so it would be right to think of revolutionary change as transformational, where that means changing the whole identity or the organisational principles of a political system and society. Thus the overthrow of the Tsarist regime in Russia in 1917, the Iranian revolution in 1979 and the Cuban Revolution under Fidel Castro in 1959 are all instances of revolutionary change, not simply because they were dramatic, violent and of relatively short duration, but because they radically altered the nature of the societies and political systems in which they occurred.

This definition is very similar to one provided by Theda Skocpol in her book *States and Social Revolutions* (1978): which offers an historical comparison of what she calls 'social revolutions' in France, Russia and China. Skocpol's definition of a social revolution is that it involves 'rapid, basic transformations of a society's state and class structures, often accompanied by class based revolts from below' (Skocpol 1978: 26). This sort of change she refers to as 'structural change', to distinguish it from other sorts of conflicts and processes, which themselves may result in radical change but are not as comprehensive. So it is the coincidence of political and social transformation which marks out a revolution. On these criteria, what happened under the brutal stewardship of the Khmer Rouge in Cambodia (Democratic Kampuchea, as it was renamed) between 1975 and 1979, where the new regime symbolised its genesis in the slogan 'Year Zero', or in China after the Communist revolution of 1948 would count as a social revolution, but neither the 'Puritan Revolution' in England in the seventeenth century, nor the Portuguese revolution in 1974, which overturned the dictatorship of President Salazar, would count, because they left the class structures of those societies fairly intact. The military may seize power from civil authorities, and rebellions by disaffected warlords or uprisings by an aggrieved peasantry may all result in political change – the suspension of representative bodies like parliaments, the abrogation of free speech – but they do not necessarily transform social structures. By the same token, industrialisation, to which we referred above, can transform social structures, but without bringing about or following from political upheaval. It is not, says Skocpol, that revolutionary events do not share some characteristics with other transformative phenomena like coups or riots, but

**Revolution** A term which suggests profound change involving dramatic events over a short period of time, rather than evolution through stages or incremental adjustments to existing social, political and cultural arrangements.

T. Skocpol (1978) *States and Social Revolutions: A Comparative Analysis of France, Russia and China,* Cambridge: Cambridge University Press.

*It should be noted that there is still a lively debate about the former case in this respect.*

rather that they are distinguished by the potent combination of social *and* political change.

By contrast, Charles Tilly (1975, 1991), who has written extensively on modernisation and revolutions, is prepared to be more catholic in his definition of a revolution. He says that a revolution involves political discontinuity arising from challenges to the control of a government over a single, independent political system. The revolution ends when when there is a resolution to the challenge, one way or the other. On his account, what Skocpol would call coups or rebellions – for example the accession of Mustapha Kemal to power in Turkey in 1923 or the restoration of the Meiji dynasty in Japan in 1868 after two centuries of rule by the Shogunate (military warlords) and, presumably, the Chechnyan rebellion against the Russians in the mid-1990s – are all revolutions. Tilly acknowledges that there is a danger of erasing important distinctions between true revolutions and 'mere coups, bootless rebellions and simple brigandage' (Tilly 1991: 32) but argues that what appear to be separate categories often tend to run into each other in real life. All that is needed from the point of view of the analyst is to distinguish between political discontinuities on the grounds (i) of how far they change the structure of the polity in question, (ii) the make-up of the contending forces and (iii) the extent of (social) structural change which results from the revolution.

## Father of Turks

Mustafa Kemal once said that, had he the power, he would change social life in Turkey at one blow. By 1923, he had that power; by his death in 1938, he had not only changed its social life, but transformed its religious, economic and political foundations.

In 1923, when Turkey became a republic, Kemal became the first president and embarked on his radical programme of reform and modernisation. He eradicated Islam from the new republic's politics, founded secular schools, established the equality of the sexes and replaced Arabic dress, script and other Oriental trappings with European models, including the taking of surnames: he chose Atatürk (Father of the Turks).

(*Independent on Sunday*, 14 July 1996)

Skocpol is interested only in the structural aspects of revolutionary change and not in the ways in which people perceive change or contribute to it. Nor is she concerned with cultural and ideological factors. Nevertheless, ideas about transforming the organisational principles of societies and political systems do raise the matter of the place of individual actors in this process. In a well-known account of the relationships between revolutionary activity and individual motivation, Ted Gurr (1980) suggests that political instability is likely to develop when individuals experience a sense of relative deprivation, which is a psychological state that occurs when people perceive a gap between what they have and what they feel they should have – whether in politics, consumer goods or welfare benefits. This perception need not be attached to 'objective' or measurable criteria of deprivation and can be experienced even by those who are, relatively speaking, well off. When a sense of relative deprivation is both intense and widespread, the conditions for collective violence are present. Davis's (1962) contribution to the relative deprivation thesis was to describe the dangers for rulers which might follow from a failure to meet rising expectations among citizens and subjects. His 'J Curve' hypothesis charted the relationships between the rising aspirations of populations and the declining capacity of governments to deliver on them over time. Between the two there emerges a potentially revolutionary gap.

Now the problem with this sort of argument is that it still leaves too many questions unanswered, many of which seem to push explanation back towards structural factors, or towards some more sophisticated theory of the psychology of individuals and groups. These questions include: which segment of a population is more likely to rebel?; is discontent sufficient to trigger collective violence?; why do some discontented populations rebel, others not?; do revolutionary gaps occur where there is opportunity to express discontent through available political channels ?; and does it make a difference what sort of value system is dominant in society?

### Values and revolution – functionalist accounts

Key functionalist explanations of revolution, like those of Chalmers Johnson (1966) or Neil Smelser (1963) have tended either to privilege values as the basis of collective action or else to look more closely at the conditions in which revolutionary action takes place. Primarily, functionalist accounts are interested in the causes of what Smelser calls disturbance and strain in societies, and in how 'asynchronous changes' (Johnson 1966) caused by shifts in values and by alterations in the environments of communities and societies, can precipitate revolutionary activity and disturb societal equilibrium. Thus, during a period of change caused by factors like advances in technology or migration or conquest, a system may not be able to sustain its equilibrium, whether culturally, economically or otherwise. If the change is sufficiently rapid or intense, pressures for political elites to respond will grow accordingly and may not be met, since the demand for redress outstrips both the resources available and any government's capacity for action. The outcome is a massive loss of trust in the system and a lowering in the perception of the legitimacy of rulers. This 'power deflation', as Johnson calls it, in turn makes it more difficult for elites to introduce effective measures to restabilise the system. Growing violence and other forms of coercion exercised by state elites to retain some semblance of control lead only to further legitimacy deficits. It now requires only an immediate trigger or 'accelerator' – like a chance event, a massacre of protesters, an attempted coup by the military – to usher in a full insurrection.

Functionalist explanations of revolutionary change suffer from the same problems as functionalist explanations in general, that is, they are overly concerned with equilibrium and have a built-in tendency to interpret all change as causing disequilibrium. In addition, they either ignore psycho-logical factors relating to the motivations of actors or treat them in a rather cursory fashion. As we saw earlier, notions like relative deprivation rely heavily upon subjective perceptions for their explanatory use. The difficulty is that once this sort of subjectivity is introduced it becomes very hard to talk sensibly about the likelihood of whole populations engaging in violent, insurrectionary or revolutionary activities. Nor does the problem disappear if we adopt an approach more akin to the structurationist interpretation of social life which we covered in Chapter 1, although this does have the merit of providing a theoretical purchase on the questions 'when is a revolution complete?' or 'at what point does the identity of a system change?' In struc-turationist terms the answer would be that the identity of a system has changed when people living in it no longer conduct their own lives around the rules and conventions of the pre-revolutionary system.

Let us make this less abstract by looking at a recent example: people living in post-communist societies in Central and Eastern Europe are busily engaged in coming to terms with the marketisation of those societies and the democratisation of politics. For many this is proving to be an uncom-fortable transition in which the influence of old and hard-learned ways of doing things conflicts with newer styles and values. Some look back with nostalgia to the communist regimes with which they grew up; others have rushed to embrace Western mores and practices, as entrepreneurs or political activists. These people are living the revolution, whether they are resisting it or going with the flow. But the outcomes, both for them as individuals and for the types of post-communist societies in the making, are still very uncertain.

---

**THINK POINT**

- You should revisit Chapter 1 at this point, as Skocpol's (1978) analysis is clearly at odds with more agent-centred accounts of social life and it would be useful to rehearse the arguments set out there.

---

Because of these considerations the idea of the *rapid* transformation of whole societies also presents something of a definitional problem, and, when linked with the question of time scale, so does the idea of transformation itself. Does transformation mean complete transformation, and, if so, over how long a period? Marx, of course, allowed for, and in a theoretical sense even needed, the overlap of different modes of production or different organisational principles, to provide the groundsoil in which revolutionary momentum gathers pace. Skocpol, too, points to major continuities in structure, and even style, between the old monarchist regime and the revolutionary Bolshevik state in Russia, in that both were very centralised and coercive – *plus ça change, plus c'est la même chose.*

## *Revolutions and violence*

What we have discussed above are the basic criteria to be considered when examining revolutionary change, but there are others we should canvass. Revolutions are usually bloody, and violence is their stock-in-trade, but there have been exceptions to this rule, some of them quite recent. In the 'velvet' revolutions in Poland and the former Czechoslovakia in 1989, when the discredited communist regimes were overthrown, few heads were broken; but, as a rule, barricades are constructed, tanks roll and lives are lost. In Romania during the same *frisson* of revolutionary fervour, there was a good deal of bloodshed, including the execution of leading members of the ruling Ceauşescu family; while in Iran, following the successful overthrow of the Shah in 1979, the new government was zealous in both imprisoning and executing dissenters of various persuasions.

## *Revolutions from above*

In Skocpol's sense, social revolutions can be precipitated only from below, by the activities of a revolutionary class or movement, and there is a diffuse sense that all revolutions are popular uprisings, occasions for grand gestures, the stuff of theatre and the silver screen. Actual revolutions are not always so popular or so populous. Vanguard parties and revolutionary cadres often reduce the scope for popular involvement, seeing themselves as the guardians of the revolutionary spirit. Activists have often laboured long in the shadow of the secret police, produced underground newspapers to stir the masses and generally kept the torch of revolution alight. Less romantic is the phenomenon of revolution from above, such as occurred in Japan, Turkey or Peru (Trimberger 1978), where established political and social elites fought insider battles with others of that ilk for the shape of their country's future.

## *Revolutions as a means of going back to the future*

We spoke earlier of the link between revolution and modernisation. Put simply, modernisation is often seen as a process which involves either a smooth and evolutionary path to full modernity or else one which is rapid, violent and disjunctive. In both cases tradition (respect for the past, but also the ways in which the past plays a part in shaping how people think about the present and the future) declines in importance and eventually ceases to play a major role in the lives of most individuals. In his classic, though somewhat dated, account of the modernisation of Middle Eastern societies like the Lebanese, *The Passing of Traditional Society* (1958), Daniel Lerner writes about the ways in which traditional forms of power and authority relations were challenged by new communications structures and by the artefacts of Western living. Now, modernity is disruptive – theorists are all agreed on this, including Marx. But what is intriguing about Lerner's account of change in the Middle East is the question it leaves unasked, namely, why, in the face of powerful forces of change, does so much remain unchanged? One response is the answer we would expect to receive, that elements of traditional cultures and practices will always continue to subsist even after radical change has taken place; but we also need to give a rather different gloss to the idea of revolution and its relationship with change in general and modernity in particular. Lerner's chosen area of investigation, the Middle East, offers us an opportunity to provide such a gloss.

The development since the 1970s of a radical and highly politicised form of Islamic identity, sometimes called Islamic fundamentalism, as a response to Western modernisation, is a growing feature of the politics of many Middle Eastern and North African countries. In Algeria, Egypt and Turkey, the 're-Islamisation' of those societies from below has yet to result in the conquest of state power by revolutionary Islamic movements, but in Iran this is exactly what happened. The Iranian revolution, at least in the Islamic version which was ultimately successful, was a self-conscious attempt to halt the Westernisation of Iranian society under the Shah and to reintroduce the wholeness and purity of authentic Islamic lifestyles (and particularly those of the Shiites, the dominant Islamic group in Iran). Iran's is a clear case of revolutionary ideology seeking justification in the past, and of the revolution itself being seen as the bloody gateway to a form of individual and collective redemption. In Sudan, which underwent a military coup in 1989 and deposed the democratically elected president, Sadiq el-Mahdi, the radical Islamic government now in power has penetrated all areas of public and many areas of private life. Below is a summary of a journalist's account of some aspects of life in post-revolutionary Sudan.

## Hard Law

In Sudan, says Amanda Hutchinson, political parties and all independent newspapers have been banned by the fundamentalist regime. Freedom of speech is a thing of the past and strict curfews reign at night. The regime has tried to replace potentially dissident groups of trades unionists and students with more supine organisations, prepared to accept the writ of the government. Islamic law (Shar'ia) has been revived and applied with some vigour in certain areas of life. For example, Islamic banking, which forbids the earning of interest, is now in operation. In Khartoum (the capital city) police stop women if their heads are not covered, or if they are wearing jewellery. By and large, the more draconian forms of punishment – amputation or stoning – have been avoided.

To justify its actions, the regime tries to ground all its actions in holy writ. The civil war conducted against the Christian and animist denizens of the south of the country is interpreted and promoted as a holy war (a jihad). The miraculous nature of Islamic rule is reported on TV and radio, with talk of monkeys undertaking mine-clearing operations, miraculous rainstorms and martyrs who smell of musk and whose blood never clots.

(Amanda Hutchinson, *The Independent Magazine* 9 October 1993)

In Iran, the impetus towards revolution was crystallised by the failure of the imperial regime to establish a basis of legitimacy in anything but economic success and the promise of a leisured, Western-style economy and society. When this failed to materialise, or to materialise widely enough, due to the slowdown in Iran's fortunes after the oil crisis of 1973–4, the regime had little support to fall back on. By contrast, its religious opponents were drawing not only upon the current discontent, but also on the reservoir of tradition which religious leaders argued was being systematically undermined by the Shah. The interesting counterfactual question, and one of more general theoretical interest, is whether, or for how long, revolutionary opposition could have been averted by the continued successful 'delivery' of Western lifestyles which were already undermining the basis of traditional lifestyles.

In post-colonial societies where state power has been either peacefully transferred to new political elites or wrested bloodily from incumbents, there is often a need for the new regime to identify and legitimate itself through a process of **nation-building**, which might involve writing a new national anthem, designing new flags and conducting new public ceremonies, as well as collecting taxes and recruiting a standing army. It can also involve a deliberate appeal to and sometimes a creative invention of the past to show the longevity and underlying continuity of the nation, and its rootedness in ancient traditions. When Bulgaria embarked upon a deliberate policy of de-Russification, following the revolutions of 1989, it cast down the icons of communist rule in the form of statues of Lenin and busts of the discredited leadership, but also sought to reconstruct its past and the historiography of its past, stripped of the influence of Soviet ideology. New heroes were needed and new symbols of national unity to take the country forward to the bright(ish) new world of market capitalism. Where did they look? To those who had fought and sometimes died fighting the Russians as far back as the fourteenth century. So revolutions are also backward-looking, enabling a society to reinvent itself by appealing to its past.

**Nation-building** The processes through which a sense of national identity and belonging are effected. Sometimes these involve deliberate policy on the part of rulers, sometimes they are instigated through things like threat of invasion.

## Two studies in political and social change

### *Short-term behavioural change: electoral change*
The study of much social change is about long-term and far-reaching transformations. Quite often it is also about the causes and consequences of violent social upheavals. The methods deployed are a mixture of narrative history and comparative political sociology, and the techniques of social psychology and quantification. The study of elections and electoral behaviour belongs to another dimension of the study of political and social change. It is not that elections are always pacific affairs, since corruption, dirty tricks, intimidation and violence have frequently sullied their conduct. The outcome of elections has even precipitated rebellious or revolutionary activity by powerful but often disaffected interests in a country, who see their position challenged by the election of a rival or who feel undermined by the democratic process itself. In democratic systems particular elections

are sometimes described as 'critical', in the sense that they may usher in a new era in politics and government – the election of the National Socialist Party to power in Germany in 1933; the success of the reformist Labour Party in Britain in 1945; or that of President Franklin Roosevelt in Depression-hit America in 1934 – or one which breaks the mould of conventional party politics in some way, for example the election of the short-lived coalition under Silvio Berlusconi in Italy in 1994.

Although they perform various functions in different political systems elections are more often part of a more gradual or incremental process involving continuity as well as change, in the sense that they either confirm a leader or government in post or return a new incumbent to office. For the most part both these outcomes take place within established rules which are seen to be legitimate even by those who are the losers in the contest. Sometimes, however, changes in the rules which govern elections may be

Table 5.1 Votes and seats in UK general elections, 1945–92

| | Electorate and turnout | Total votes cast | Conservative[1] | Labour | Liberals[2] | Welsh & Scottish Nationalists | | Others (mainly Communist, N.Ireland etc) |
|---|---|---|---|---|---|---|---|---|
| 1945[3] | 73.3% | 100%–640 | 39.8%–213 | 48.3%–393 | 9.1%–12 | 0.2% | 0.49%–2 | 2.1%–20 |
| | 32,836,419 | 24,082,612 | 9,577,667 | 11,632,191 | 2,197,191 | 46,612 | 102,760 | 525,491 |
| 1950 | 84.0% | 100%–625 | 43.5%–299 | 46.1%–315 | 9.1%–9 | 0.1% | 0.3% | 0.9%–2 |
| | 34,629,770 | 28,772,671 | 12,502,567 | 13,266,592 | 2,621,548 | 27,288 | 91,746 | 262,930 |
| 1951 | 82.5% | 100%–625 | 48.0%–321 | 48.8%–295 | 2.5%–6 | 0.1% | 0.1% | 0.5%–3 |
| | 34,645,73 | 28,595,668 | 13,717,538 | 13,948,605 | 7,307,556 | 18,219 | 21,640 | 519,110 |
| 1955 | 67.8% | 100%–630 | 49.7%–345 | 46.4%–277 | 2.7%–6 | 0.2% | 0.1% | 0.8%–2 |
| | 34,858,263 | 26,760,493. | 13,311,936 | 12,404,970 | 722,408 | 57,239 | 33,114 | 230,807 |
| 1959 | 78.7% | 100%–630 | 49.4%–365 | 43.8%–258 | 5.9%–6 | 0.4% | 0.1% | 0.5%–1 |
| | 35,397,080 | 27,859,241 | 13,749,830 | 12,215,538 | 1,638,571 | 99,309 | 30,897 | 145,090 |
| 1964 | 77.1% | 100%–630 | 43.4%–304 | 44.1%–317 | 11.2%–9 | 0.5% | .0.2% | 0.6% |
| | 35,829,572 | 27,655,374 | 12,001,396 | 12,205,814 | 3,092,878 | 133,551 | 45,932 | 169,431 |
| 1966 | 75.8% | 100%–630 | 41.9%–253 | 47.9%–363 | 8.5%–12 | 0.7% | 0.2% | 0.7%–2 |
| | 35,964,684 | 27,263,606 | 11,418,433 | 13,064,951 | 2,327,533 | 189,544 | 62,112 | 201,032 |
| 1970 | 72.0% | 100%–630 | 46.4%–330 | 43.0%–288 | 7.5%–6 | 1.3%–1 | 0.1% | 1.7%–5 |
| | 39,342,013 | 28,344,798 | 13,145,123 | 12,178,295 | 2,117,033 | 381,818 | 37,970 | 486,557 |
| Feb '74 | 78.1% | 100%–635 | 37.8%–297 | 37.1%–301 | 19.3%–14 | 6.7%–9 | 0.1% | 3.1%–14 |
| | 39,770,724 | 31,340,162 | 11,872,180 | 11,646,391 | 6,058,744 | 804,554 | 32,743 | 958,293 |
| Oct '74 | 72.8% | 100%–635 | 35.8%–277 | 39.2%–319 | 18.3%–13 | 3.5%–14 | 0.1% | 3.1%–12 |
| | 40,072,971 | 39,189,178 | 10,464,817 | 11,457,079 | 6,346,754 | 1,005,938 | 17,426 | 897,164 |
| 1979 | 76.0% | 100%–635 | 43.9%–339 | 37.0%–269 | 13.8%–11 | 2.0%–4 | 0.1% | 3.2%–12 |
| | 41,093,264 | 31,221,361 | 13,697,923 | 11,532,218 | 4,313,804 | 636,890 | 16,858 | 1,043,755 |
| 1983 | 72.7% | 100%–650 | 42.4%–397 | 27.6%–204 | 25.4%–23 | 1.5%–4 | 0.04% | 3.1%–17 |
| | 42,197,344 | 30,671,136 | 13,012,314 | 8,456,934 | 7,780,949 | 457,676 | 11,606 | 951,656 |
| 1987 | 75.3% | 100%–650 | 42.3%–376 | 30.8%–229 | 22.6%–22 | 1.7%–6 | 0.02% | 2.6%–17 |
| | 43,181,321 | 32,536,137 | 13,763,066 | 10,029,778 | 7,341,290 | 543,599 | 6,078 | 852,368 |
| 1992 | 77.7% | 100%–651 | 41.9%–336 | 34.4%–271 | 17.8%–20 | 2.3%–7 | – | 3.5%–17 |
| | 43,249,721 | 33,612,693 | 14,092,891 | 11,559,735 | 5,999,384 | 783,991 | – | 1,176,692[4] |

Notes:
1. Includes Ulster Unionists 1945–70.
2. Liberals 1945–79; Liberal-SDP Alliance 1983–87; Liberal Democrats 1992.
3. The 1945 figures exclude University seats and are adjusted for double voting in the 15 two-member seats.
4. Other votes in 1992 included 738,338 for Northern Ireland parties, 170,368 for the Green Party, 62,807 for the Natural Law Party, and 64,744 for the Liberal Party.

taken as an indicator of significant shifts in political attitudes or in the political values of a country. The Italian general elections of 1994 were fought for the first time under new electoral laws which introduced simple majority voting for three-quarters of parliamentary seats, while a form of proportional representation was retained for the rest. Some people described this change as part of an 'electoral revolution' in Italy and said that the contest itself was a watershed or critical election in the history of postwar Italy. The demand for reform of the electoral system was part of a much wider concern about endemic corruption in Italian politics and about the tradition of ineffective government, which many critics blamed on the failure of general elections to produce strong, viable majorities in the Italian parliament.

So, by examining electoral data we can construct a picture of political change in a country, in two significant ways. The first produces a graph of what we might call ideological stability or change, charting the successes and failures of the main contenders for office, identifying new political forces and watching them wax and wane. Table 5.1 shows the outcomes of general elections in the United Kingdom for the period 1945–92.

## Exercise

What inferences can be drawn from the data in Table 5.1 about the nature of the UK party system, about stability and change, and about the general levels of popular support for democratic procedures in the UK?

Of course, looking at similar data for other countries might not reveal anything at all about the nature of ideological change, because there might be only one party in power over the whole period of study. Variations in electoral turnout might give some clue as to the legitimacy of the political system, but this is not a good indicator. High voter turnouts in authoritarian states could be an indication of electoral approval and legitimacy; on the other hand they may be a credit to the power of the state to mobilise expressions of popular support at critical junctures, through appeals to national unity, out of fear, or by using some form of coercion. By the same token, the notoriously low turnouts in USA presidential elections (averaging 51 per cent) might be taken as a sign of enduring and culturally sanctioned distrust of central government, but not of the overall illegitimacy of the system of government.

So this sort of indicator has a useful but arguably limited value in describing, let alone explaining, political change. The second use of electoral data in this respect is the insights they afford into the ways in which social and sometimes cultural changes are translated into political changes. Let us stay with the British example given above. One of the key questions asked about the outcome of the 1992 general election in the UK was how far it sealed the demise of the Labour Party and the shift to one-party domination by the Conservatives. Regardless of the particular issues surrounding any one general election, students of British electoral behaviour have been concerned with the ways in which changes in the social composition of British society have been affecting the levels of support for political parties in general, the intensity of support for particular parties and (most difficult of all) the meaning that party allegiances have in a changing electorate.

In their important study *Political Change in Britain* (1969) David Butler and Donald Stokes found that social class was still the strongest variable influencing electoral behaviour. This study examined at some length the phenomenon of 'working-class Conservatives', that is, those voters who opted to support a party of the right, thus ignoring their 'natural' allegiance to a party of the left. Butler and Stokes suggested that this propensity could be explained by values transmitted from parents to children and not by class location. Other writers on this theme (for example Nordlinger 1967) stressed different explanatory variables, including the importance of a sense-relative deprivation which might be felt by working-class voters with high expectations and a more pragmatic sense that Conservative politicians were better equipped to govern. By 1992, however, consternation about the phenomenon of working-class Conservatism had given way to a broader consideration of the ways in which changes in the class system, and, in particular, the rise of a 'new' working class of skilled manual workers, supervisory staff and people in clerical and technical occupations, had wrought considerable changes on the profile of party identification and voting. In Table 5.2, the significance of these categories is explored.

*These figures are also discussed in Chapter 13, when discussing the question of how political parties appeal to the electorate.*

*Table 5.2* Changes in the social basis of the Labour vote 1979 and 1992

|  | The new working class | | | | The old working class | | | |
|---|---|---|---|---|---|---|---|---|
|  | lives in South | owner occupier | non-union member | works in private sector | lives in North | council tenant | union member | works in public sector |
| CON | 46 | 44 | 40 | 38 | 29 | 25 | 30 | 32 |
| LAB | 28 | 32 | 38 | 39 | 57 | 57 | 48 | 49 |
| LIB DEM | 26 | 24 | 22 | 23 | 15 | 18 | 22 | 19 |

## Exercise

What, if anything, do these data tell you about the prospects for the Labour Party in the UK?

There are, of course a number of problems with using data like these as the basis upon which statements about the nature and direction of political change are based:

1. They may be confounded by the course of events. Dire prognostications about the demise of the Labour Party in the UK were based on its shrinking support among a traditional constituency which is disappearing because of social changes. Such a view does not take into account the ability of a party like Labour to reinvent itself and market its appeal to different audiences, nor the capacity of voters to change the basis of their allegiance. Here we have yet another replay of the dangers of taking only structural changes to be dominant.

2. Part of this problem may be overcome by collecting sufficient data over a long enough period. However, just what constitutes a long enough period is not always clear. Longitudinal studies of electoral behaviour are complex and expensive. There is also the problem that in many countries data are available only over a very short period of time. Studying electoral change in Russia was and still is a much more difficult task than in the UK, the USA or France.

3. Beyond these problems lies a more profound one. This is that the available data may tell only part of the story of change, perhaps the less interesting part. For example, the difficulty with using survey data (derived from questionnaire responses of a sample which is representative of an electorate) is that they often provide only superficial insights into key questions about the underlying meaning for the respondent of the vote which s/he casts. Thus it might not be too far-fetched to imagine a situation in which long-term analysis reveals apparent continuity in the outcome of elections and in the levels of party support, but which remains silent on the potentially substantial changes in meaning which voting for one party as opposed to another has for a member of the public. In Butler and Stokes's sense (1969), while you may vote for the party your parents supported, you may do so for quite different reasons than they did and, moreover, your identification with the party may be grounded in quite different motives.

### Revolutionary change in East-Central Europe

The events of 1989, when more or less bloodless 'revolutions' swept away the apparatuses of 'actually existing socialism' (Bahro 1981) in the Soviet satellite states in Central and Eastern Europe, changed the world. They also provide valuable reference points for the study of revolutions, and an opportunity to examine some of the theories about the nature of democratic transformations. It is, of course, wrong to depict what happened in 1989 as a single event, or even as 'an' event at all, as opposed to a common process which had moved along different time scales in the various countries involved, but which condensed in the year of revolutions, 1989.

In addition, the use of the term 'revolution' to describe what took place is not without problems. Below is an extract from a recent book on the changes which took place in the region:

> the revolution in Eastern Europe was always an odd one insofar as there was no new revolutionary idea whose time had come. Indeed insistent demands for liberal democracy and rather less insistent demands for a capitalist economy might have been thought more a counter-revolutionary demand for the restoration of pre-communist traditions – except that, Czechoslovakia apart, there was no tradition of democracy and little tradition of bourgeois capitalism to restore. Revolutions according to Skocpol are also 'accompanied by class-based revolts from below'. In Eastern Europe, however, one could speak variously of civil society against the party state, popular demonstrations, even national liberation, but not properly of class-based revolts. The collapse of communism was so quick, so dramatic and so complete, that references to revolution will no doubt continue, but . . . the term has the wrong connotations to capture the character . . . of the changes in 1989 and after. . . . Bruszt (1990) refers to the 'negotiated revolution' in Hungary. . . . Many Hungarians speak even less dramatically of 'rends-zervaltas' – an exchange of systems. . . . Similarly, the common description of a 'velvet revolution' in Czechoslovakia recalls a tradition of non-violence in that country.
>
> (Bryant and Mokrzycki 1994 : 1–2)

Tilly, as we have argued above (p. 152), would have no difficulty with the definition of these events as revolutionary, in that, on his reckoning, once there is a challenge to the government of a polity by a faction with claims which are completely at odds with those in control, a de facto revolutionary situation exists, since they are making claims antipathetic to the existing identity of the polity. In all the countries of East-Central Europe – Poland, Czechoslovakia, Hungary, Bulgaria, Romania, the GDR (East Germany) – the incumbent regimes were also unwilling or unable to suppress those opposing them, partly because of the evidence of widespread popular support for the opposition groups, partly because by then the massive failure of Soviet-model communism, both economically and politically, was apparent to all.

If we turn to the actual causes, with hindsight it can be said that the events of 1989 were the consequences of major changes in the wider European and world contexts. To a marked extent then, they were influenced by exogenous (external) factors. First there are economic considerations, which arose from the slowing down in the European and global economies during and after the oil crises of the 1970s. During the 'long cycle' of capitalist expansion between 1945 and the early 1970s, the wealth so generated also shored up the communist regimes in East-Central Europe. During this period, socialist economies like Hungary and Poland, but also the others to varying degrees, had opened their economies to the West, initiating just that 'revolution of rising expectations' among domestic populations written about by Smelser (1963), Davis (1962) and Johnson (1966). When the boom came to an end, these countries were particularly exposed and faced contracting markets, huge foreign debts and rampant inflation. Added to these woes was the growing technological gap between West and East in the shape of the computer revolution, which could not be bridged by economies tied to outdated production techniques often geared to military procurement and barely subsisting on low or non-existent domestic sources of investment. The upshot was growing frustration and unrest, exacerbated by chronic shortages in the supply of consumer goods. As a system of production and distribution, actually existing socialism appeared bankrupt.

Second, there are political and geopolitical factors. Some reformers felt that a 'liberalised' national communism might perhaps save the day for the *ancien régimes* and also salvage the crumbling communist system of economic and political governance. Gorbachev's experiments with *perestroika* and, to a lesser extent, with *glasnost* in the USSR after 1986 were the model for this sort of reasoning. However, on a practical level, all the states in East-Central Europe still feared the application of the Brezhnev Doctrine by the USSR. No radical form of communism could be tried while the implied threat of armed intervention existed. It is a supreme historical irony then that when Gorbachev abandoned the Brezhnev Doctrine he did not so much give *carte blanche* to innovative attempts to revitalise communism as remove the final and most telling barrier to jettisoning the whole system.

*The Brezhnev Doctrine was the doctrine that the Soviet Union had a right to intervene in the internal affairs of fraternal states in the interests of protecting the integrity of the socialist experiment.*

Again with hindsight, there does not appear to have been any real chance that a reformist strand in communism could have carried much popular support at the time, so that even if the Soviet military threat had not been lifted by Gorbachev, the result would have been a more violent challenge to the various regimes, whose sinews probably would have been stiffened by the knowledge that Soviet tanks were not far away. In the words of a Solidarity (Polish trade union-based movement in the vanguard of opposition to the communist regime since the early 1980s) poster of 1989:

> Where is there most bread and freedom? There is most bread and freedom in those states whose people in free elections choose their own rulers, to make the laws and form governments and parliaments.

These are sentiments not easily subject to bureaucratic tinkering with the existing state of affairs.

As we have seen, Theda Skocpol (1978), too, is anxious to stress the importance of external factors in explaining revolutions, notably war and external economic influences. But other interpretations of the demise of communism in East-Central Europe emphasise the contribution of internal or endogenous variables. One view, which has its intellectual roots in the evolutionist perspectives of writers like Talcott Parsons (1967), argues that state socialist societies failed because they lacked the adaptive capacity necessary to negotiate the uncertainties of a rapidly changing environment. Parsons felt that all societies progress through a series of what he called 'evolutionary universals' before they reach the stage of full modernity. These are an increasingly complex kind of social stratification, the development of a legitimated value system, the growth of money as a medium of exchange, and markets, bureaucracy and a universalistic legal system, along with what he calls 'democratic association'. It is the establishment of the last two features which makes a society fully modern. Indeed, they are the universally necessary preconditions if large-scale industrial societies are to become modern. So those industrial societies which have failed to achieve a pluralist, parliamentary democracy are not just different from Western capitalist societies, they are also, from an evolutionist perspective, much more *archaic*. The lack of participatory and pluralistic institutions and practices itself increased the rigidity of communist societies and diminished their adaptive capacity. Failure to adapt produced yet more dysfunctions within the societies and their growing marginalisation (primarily economic) in the modern world order. At this juncture, the evolutionary break-through necessary for further development begins to look more like a severe disjunction, even a revolution.

Parsons' views, which were branded as highly ideological and ethnocentric in the 1960s, have been revived in recent years to explain the rapid collapse of authoritarian regimes the world over, but as a complex theory of endogenous social change applied to the situations in East-Central Europe they still leave a great deal unexplained. For example, most theories of democ-ratisation, including those of Barrington Moore (1966) and Francis Fukuyama, place a great deal more weight upon the volitional aspects of change. Fukuyama stresses the longing for what he calls 'recognition' as a motive force in explaining why some countries achieve democracy and others do not. Moore, less anxious to offer ideological or cultural variables as explanatory, none the less falls back on just such a formula when he talks about the importance of the 'bourgeois impulse' in describing the propensity to democracy and liberalism. Both of these concepts are really quite vague and would be difficult to pin down as measurable indicators, but they do modify Parson's very structural interpretation of change which seems to take place without human agency and without passion.

B. Moore, Jr (1966) *The Social Origins of Dictatorship and Democracy*, Boston: Beacon Press.

Convergence theory, which enjoyed a vogue in the 1960s (Aron 1967), reasoned that there is a common logic of development in industrial societies which eventually will lead to the setting up of social structures which have much more in common than the differences between capitalism and communism would suggest. But what happened in 1989 was not the product of some logic of industrial societies which will produce hybrid institutions, but the exhaustion of the state-socialist economic system and the inability of its one-party regimes to resist the growing demands for transformative change. During the same period, Western capitalism was also changing, but not in the direction of collectivist forms of economic or political governance.

The 1970s and the 1980s saw a significant shake-up of the world's dictatorships and authoritarian regimes. In Europe, the southern countries of Portugal, Spain and Greece successfully threw off or superseded dictatorial and militaristic regimes, while in South America during the 1980s, authoritarian regimes in Argentina, Brazil, Uruguay, Chile and Paraguay were replaced by at least proto-democratic governments. In Skocpol's (1978) terms these 'transitions' were not revolutions, and that marks them out from the major political and social changes in train in East-Central Europe. But as 'social revolutions' they reverse the predicted flow of historical change found in teleological accounts like that of Marx. The transformation of socialism into capitalism rarely forms part of the theoretical agenda. As Bryant and Mokrzycki (1994) say, this is likely to be a messier process than most theoretical accounts allow, being a process of transformation but perhaps one without a storybook ending.

## Conclusion

In this chapter we have examined some of the issues involved in conceptualising and theorising different kinds of social and political change. Difficulties arise because of the sheer scope of the concept, and especially because of its temporal dimension. Data are often hard to come by, but this difficulty is compounded by the need to compare across both time and space. In conclusion it is perhaps necessary to restate the point with which we started the chapter, namely that while all self-respecting social theory has to deal with the question of change, providing a convincing explanation for any sort of change is remarkably difficult. In Part Two we turn to the realm of ideas in political life.

## Further reading

Giddens, Anthony (1994) *Beyond Left and Right: The Future of Radical Politics*, Cambridge: Polity. A book which assesses the impact of recent social and cultural changes upon the ideologies of left versus right and upon the political forces organised around those ideologies.

Hall, John (1986) *Powers and Liberties: The Causes and Consequences of the Rise of the West*, Harmondsworth: Pelican. A sociological and historical study of the origins of capitalism which looks not only at the rise of the West but also at its possible decline too.

Moore, Barrington, Jr (1966) *The Social Origins of Dictatorship and Democracy*, Boston: Beacon Press. A monumental, path-breaking study of different routes to modernity, and in many ways the intellectual base of Skocpol's work on social revolutions.

Pascale, Richard (1990) *Managing on the Edge*, Harmondsworth: Penguin. An interesting book by a professor of management theory, on the question of how organisations adapt to changing circumstances.

Tocqueville, Alexis de (1947) *The Old Regime and the French Revolution*, Oxford: Blackwell. The nineteenth-century French historian and political theorist Tocqueville employs a form of social psychology to explain the causes of the French Revolution.

# PART 2     POLITICS AND IDEAS

# 6 CONCEPTS AND ISSUES

*Gary K. Browning*

# Concepts and issues

## Introduction

In this chapter the concepts which underlie and determine the values of political life will be explored. At the same time, this conceptual exploration of political life will be related to the issues and disputes which colour the atmosphere of contemporary political debate and practice. In specific terms, the concepts of freedom, rights, justice and equality are examined. They are related to concrete problems, including the dilemmas of the Rushdie case, animal welfare and the welfare state. The practical questions arising out of these issues are shown to involve conceptual questions which render their theoretical analysis useful in a way which emphasises the vitality of political theory.

## Conceptual analysis

Conceptual analysis in contemporary political theory takes place in a number of different ways. In the immediate post-Second World War period in the Anglo-American world doubts were expressed about the procedures of political philosophy given that the criteria for determining values were recognised to be inherently controversial. There was a prevalent scepticism about the claims involved in the classic texts of political philosophy, where large-scale theorising incorporating grand claims about the human condition sustained accounts of the political expression of values such as justice and freedom. Grand theorising gave way to a more limited approach whereby analysis pointed up what concepts such as freedom and equality might be taken to mean. However, in the last quarter of the century there has been a revival of normative theorising in which analysis of concepts has gone hand in hand with justification of norms embedded in the concepts and intuitions upheld in prevailing political practices. The willingness to discuss substantive questions of, for example, justice and the political order has realigned contemporary Anglo-American political philosophers with the traditions of political philosophy.

A leading political theorist of modern times who has done much to restore the vitality of the discipline of political philosophy is John Rawls. His work *A Theory of Justice* (1971) set out a rigorously argued case for justifying a particular conception of justice as fairness by imagining potential citizens in an original position in which they would be unaware of particular attributes and social advantages they might possess. Based upon premises generated from this imaginative perspective, Rawls thereafter argued with great analytical rigour for a conception of justice informing political practices which would mesh with prevailing intuitions. Rawls's example of combining analytical rigour with the justification of values and intuitions has been followed by a host of celebrated theorists, including Nozick, Walzer and Taylor, who all invoke classical texts of political philosophy. The analytical approach has permeated a variety of traditions such as Marxism, where, for example in the works of Cohen (1978) and Elster (1985), an analytical style has been invoked to interrogate and justify Marxist conceptions. Likewise, feminist and postmodern thinkers, such as Lyotard (1984), have sought to combine rigorous analysis of concepts with particular interpretations of values and norms.

M. Walzer (1983) *Spheres of Justice*, Oxford: Blackwell.

C. Taylor (1989) *Sources of the Self: The Making of the Modern Identity*, Cambridge: Cambridge University Press.

R. Nozick (1974) *Anarchy, State and Utopia*, Oxford: Blackwell.

## Freedom

Freedom is a central concept of political life. Historic political philosophers, such as Mill, Rousseau and Hegel, have given celebrated, if controversial, accounts of its character, while practising politicians on the right and the left invoke the name of freedom to justify an array of policies. Berlin (1991) has produced perhaps the most notable analysis of freedom since the Second World War. He examined past accounts of freedom, analysed its deployment in political contexts and distinguished two distinct concepts of liberty or freedom. He distinguished between the concepts of **positive freedom** and **negative freedom**, which, he urged, had been put to radically different uses in the political arena.

**Positive freedom** A view which sees freedom as a condition to be achieved through positive actions.

**Negative freedom** A term taken as meaning freedom from state interference. It assumes that individuals should have an area of life where they are free to make decisions and behave as they wish as long as they do not interfere with the freedom of others.

Negative freedom, for Berlin, fits neatly with common-sense notions of freedom. He takes negative freedom to mean that a person is free if they are not subject to constraint or coercion. An individual on this model of freedom is free if s/he can make and act upon their own choices. The state is promoting freedom in so far as it leaves an area of life open to the decision-making of individuals. Within this account of freedom a state which concerned itself with the goal of promoting a more equal society might be undertaking a worthwhile goal but it would not be promoting freedom. Indeed, in so far as its promotion of equality involved disturbing the purposes and assets of individuals, it would undermine individual freedom.

Positive freedom, for Berlin, involves a different account of freedom from the negative variety, and this difference has been expressed and developed in the history of political thought. Berlin considers that a positive view of freedom assumes that freedom is not to be achieved by leaving individuals alone to get on with their lives. Rather, its point is to enable individuals to achieve self-mastery by the exercise of rational self-control over the irrational desires of the self. Freedom in a positive sense, for Berlin, entails overcoming obstacles to freedom which reside within individuals themselves. Hence, a positive conception of freedom can generate the paradox that in order to achieve freedom, coercion may need to be applied to individuals by the state. Berlin is sceptical of the endorsement of public coercion which he takes to be implicit in the positive model of freedom. According to Berlin, the positive model of freedom assumes that all individuals need to follow the same path of rational enlightenment and that political coercion can facilitate this process of enlightenment.

In a short-hand formulation of Berlin's (1991) account of the two concepts of liberty, negative freedom may be taken as freedom from constraints and positive freedom as the freedom to develop the rational self. Berlin's account has the merit of memorably underlining differences between classic accounts of freedom. For instance, Locke and Mill are taken as providing notions of 'negative' freedom where the concern is to allow individuals to develop their lives free from public coercion. Likewise, Rousseau, Hegel and Marx are seen as developing positive accounts of freedom where individuals find their true freedom in a shared community in which common goals are sought. Berlin also provides an incisive summary of the potential for tyranny implicit in positive accounts of freedom. Something of the flavour of Berlin's insightful and rhetorically persuasive writing is expressed in the following extract from his essay 'Two Concepts of Liberty', in which he highlights the dangers involved in the assumptions of positive theories of liberty.

> The common assumption of these thinkers (and of many a Schoolman before them and Jacobin and Communist after them) is that the rational ends of our 'true' natures must coincide, or be made to coincide, however violently our poor, ignorant, desire-ridden, passionate, empirical selves may cry out against this process. Freedom is not freedom to do what is irrational, or stupid, or wrong. To force empirical selves into the right pattern is not tyranny, but liberation. Rousseau tells me that if I freely surrender all parts of my life to society, I create an entity which because it has been built by an equality of sacrifice of all its members, cannot wish to hurt any one of them. ... Liberty so far from being incompatible with society becomes virtually identical with it.
>
> (Berlin 1991: 50–1)

## Exercise

1 According to Berlin how do theorists of positive freedom portray force as a means of freedom?
2 Consider how the language of Berlin is designed to persuade the reader that we should be wary of certain thinkers?

Berlin's analysis of freedom into the opposed notions of positive and negative freedom is a celebrated account, but it is not without critics. MacCallum Jr has argued against Berlin's position. He has urged that freedom is to be understood essentially as a single concept. For MacCallum, 'Whenever the freedom of some agent or agents is in question, it is always freedom from some constraint or restriction on, interference with, or barrier to doing, not doing, becoming, or not becoming something' (MacCallum 1991). According to MacCallum, there is a variation between specific conceptions of freedom, but accounts of freedom will always involve relations between the variables of agency, constraints and doing or development. According to this notion of freedom, undoubted differences exist between a theorist such as Rousseau, whom Berlin designates as a theorist of positive liberty, and, say, J. S. Mill, whom Berlin takes to be a theorist of negative liberty. These differences, however, are not seen as precluding a common adherence to a notion of freedom where persons are free due to their capacity to act free from restrictions. What counts as a restriction and what is signified as the agent and action/development differ in the thought of Mill from that of Rousseau, but MacCallum would suggest that the differences should be attended to in detail and should not be reduced to a general contrast between positive and negative conceptions of freedom.

In general, MacCallum is right to point to the shared character of conceptions of freedom when examined at a high level of abstraction. Equally, he is alert to the specific differences which distinguish particular notions of freedom and which resist easy classification under the general headings of positive and negative freedom. Berlin's essay itself had pointed to ways in which the division of the concept of freedom into negative and positive varieties might not be entirely clear cut. Berlin recognises that where 'negative' theorists of freedom see the individual as free in so far as her/his actions are not constrained by others, the notion of what counts as a constraint is problematic and might be specified in significantly divergent ways. Berlin is inclined to take a negative theory of liberty as equating constraining behaviour with either force or manifest coercion. None the less, he does admit the possibility that an economic system, alterable but not necessarily designed by agents, might be taken as a constraint on human freedom. If unplanned social and economic forms are taken as constraints on human freedom, then a negative theorist of freedom might advocate remedial state action on a scale sufficiently large to allow for the emergence of a tyranny he associates with positive freedom. The distance between negative and positive notions of freedom is therefore not so great as might at first be imagined.

Miller (1991) in his account of freedom, steers a course between Berlin and MacCallum. He considers that Berlin's account doesn't do justice to the variety of views on freedom. He distinguishes between three ways of formulating freedom: republican, liberal and idealist forms of freedom. Liberal freedom equates with Berlin's account of negative freedom. Republican freedom invokes the freedom citizens possess in participating in the public processes of government to shape their collective lives. Idealist freedom is envisaged as the process of liberation whereby a self overcomes internal constraints, such as drug addiction to realise an ideal freedom.

Miller's account of freedom certainly picks out important differences between theories of freedom. The sense in which collective political action can be said to constitute freedom is distinct from an individual's freedom to undertake actions unimpeded by others, which likewise differs from an individual freeing herself/himself from a habitual dependence upon alcohol. This division of freedom into three senses can also be said to make an important distinction which is not prevalent in Berlin's account. On the other hand, it can still be said that it assimilates too readily a number of distinct views on freedom to a model of three basic theories of freedom. MacCallum's account, in contrast, sees an abstract unity underpinning theories of freedom but at the same time highlights the importance of differences between them at the level of detail.

Perhaps what can be concluded is that the perspective on freedom which we take will be influenced by what we want to do. Berlin's account makes a sound and rhetorically convincing case for seeing an important division between theories of freedom. A number of theories can be seen as posing potential problems of tyranny at the individual and social level given their drive to promote freedom positively, whereas other theories are more concerned to ward off coercion and direct violence against persons. Likewise, Miller's model is useful in making more discriminating distinctions between theories of freedom, as it employs a more complex model. MacCallum's unitary concept of freedom provides a convincing overall account of freedom in that at a highly abstract level it makes conceptual connections between components of any account of freedom. It also signals that detailed attention should be paid to particular ways in which these elements of a view of freedom are to be connected in specific theories of freedom. While this unitary theory of freedom is therefore philosophically convincing at a general level, the rival accounts do perform useful jobs of work in connecting and contrasting specific theories of freedom.

## The Rushdie case

The Rushdie affair is an infamous case of recent years which has thrown up disturbing and challenging questions for any considered analysis of freedom. Some of the facts of the Rushdie case are reasonably well known. In 1989 Rushdie published *The Satanic Verses*, a complex work dealing with many themes such as migration, exile, death and resurrection in a style which is artful and resists any single line of interpretation. None the less, the centre of polemical attention upon the book quickly became its portrayal of Islam and Mohammed. Mohammed is depicted in ways which have been seen as disrespectful; for example, there are references to him as a shady businessman and as a debauchee who sleeps with many women. The general

For a balanced account of all the arguments in the Rushdie affair see B. Parekh (1990) 'The Rushdie Affair: Research Agenda for Political Philosophy', *Political Studies* xxxviii (4) (December).

tone of the book was quickly seen by many Muslims, skipping over tricky questions concerning the author's voice, as being disrespectful to their religion.

Soon after publication Muslims all over the world began to campaign against *The Satanic Verses*. The brunt of their complaints was that the book was inaccurate and insulting in its depiction of Islam and its representation of events recounted in the Koran (the sacred book of the Islamic religion) and was also designed to cause hurt to Muslims in general. This latter point was of particular relevance where Muslims were in a cultural minority, as they were, for instance, in Britain. The force of their argument was that where a specific community was in a minority and vulnerable to majority violence or disrespect, a book such as *The Satanic Verses* which insulted the cultural minority could do much damage in disempowering that minority culture and in fostering antagonism towards it.

---

**THINK POINT**
- Do you think that Muslims might have good grounds for objecting to the work of Salman Rushdie?
- What actions, if any, do you think might have been justifiably taken against Rushdie by the Islamic community?

---

In response to protests by Muslims, the late Ayatollah Khomeini of Iran intervened and declared a death sentence, or fatwa, against Rushdie. This fateful intervention changed and charged the cultural and political atmosphere. Many Muslims in Britain became more aggressive in their stance against Rushdie's novel. Soon Rushdie was forced into hiding to sustain himself against possible attack, and ever since he has been forced to resort to a shadowy half-life under security protection, as the Ayatollah's call for his death is recognised as providing a constant and real threat to his life.

For the most part, Rushdie has defended his right to have written *The Satanic Verses* as being part and parcel of the writer's right to freedom of expression. His defence of his own actions has been squarely based on a view of freedom and its significance. It's true that in the light of possible remission of the fatwa Rushdie did equivocate and entertain the possibility of a reconciliation with Islam, but for the most part he has stood by his writing and defended it in classical liberal terms. In an article in the *Independent* in 1990 Rushdie presented an eloquent summary of the liberal defence of his work. A short extract of this article is presented below:

> How is freedom gained? It is taken: never given. To be free you must first assume your right to freedom. In writing *The Satanic Verses*, I wrote from the assumption that I was and am a free man.
> What is freedom of expression? Without the freedom to offend, it ceases to exist. Without the freedom to challenge, even to satirise all orthodoxies, including religious orthodoxies, it ceases to exist.
>
> (Rushdie 1990)

The Rushdie case raises interesting questions about freedom and its theoretical analysis which highlight the practical relevance of abstract analysis. The threat to Rushdie's life eloquently demonstrates what can be at stake in questions of freedom. Rushdie himself can be seen as invoking what Berlin would term a negative account of freedom. For Rushdie freedom, crucially, is about the right to express oneself without being subject to restraint or coercion. In Rushdie's defence of freedom of expression what is being said is of less importance than the right to say it. It is 'negative' about what is being said. This negative aspect of freedom, however, is not seen as marking its shallowness. Rushdie sees this right to say what might be offensive as of the utmost importance.

In contrast to Rushdie's position, opponents of *The Satanic Verses* and its publication might and often do appeal, at least implicitly, to a positive view of freedom. Hence, the point about freedom of expression from such a perspective depends on what is being said. The positive things that are said about groups and cultures matter. The freedom of groups and individuals is related to how they are regarded and the status of people is intimately related to what is said about them; scurrilous remarks about a world religion can impair the freedom of its practitioners. This putative critique of Rushdie in terms of a positive view of freedom might also be articulated in the guise of Miller's (1991) notion of republican freedom. Here, the freedom of a cultural grouping can be seen as bound up with its defence and maintenance of its key doctrines, just as the freedom of a political community is maintained by participation in and maintenance of its key political institutions. Hence, from this perspective, it is detrimental to a cultural group's freedom if its doctrines and sacred writings are attacked and damaged.

The Rushdie case, then, can be seen as exhibiting ways in which contrasting views of freedom are expressed. It also points up ambiguities in interpretations of freedom. It was mentioned previously (p. 174) that what counts as a constraint upon freedom in Berlin's account of negative liberty is ambiguous. For Berlin, an individual is free in so far as s/he is free from constraints, but what counts as a constraint is not clear cut. Hence, outraged Muslims who see *The Satanic Verses* as wounding their sense of selfhood in so far as it undermines the Islam religion, the source of their selfhood, could construe this literary work as a constraint upon their freedom. Action consequently directed against Rushdie's work, even including the notorious fatwa itself, can therefore be seen as being supported by a negative view of freedom, albeit a version of negative freedom distinct from that assumed by Berlin. Recognition of the importance of the notion of constraint in a great variety of distinct and often conflicting views of freedom lies behind the conceptual manoeuvring of MacCallum Jr (1991) when he characterised freedom as a unitary concept which involves a plurality of interpretations of its basic terms.

The Rushdie case also throws up an interesting and challenging question about the identity of the agent or agents who are assumed to possess or express freedom. Rushdie himself can appear as a classical and tragic individual hero of freedom. This lone and wronged individual sticks to his words, risking his life for the cause of freedom. The predicament he faces, though, is a solitary one. On the other hand, the freedom of the Muslim community or communities in Britain and elsewhere can be seen to have been threatened by the abuse and disrespect shown to its religious heritage. Again, MacCallum, in his account of freedom notes that a persisting subject capable of action or development is presupposed by all theories of freedom but he observes that the nature of this subject/agent will vary radically from particular theory to particular theory.

In the light of our brief survey of the Rushdie case it will be evident that it presents a practical issue which invokes and involves theoretical perspectives. Differing practical vantage points on the issue of the Rushdie case can be seen as assuming differing *conceptual* understandings of freedom. Theoretical and practical controversies also underlie disputes about the phenomenon of political correctness. Political correctness is a movement emanating principally from American University campuses which seeks to challenge language and behaviour which are seen as defamatory and threatening to minority and vulnerable groups. Hence advocates of political correctness track language and behaviour taken as being offensive to, for example, blacks, Muslims, women, disabled people. They challenge the use of 'incorrect' language and campaign to change linguistic usage and modify offensive behaviour.

Opponents of political correctness see its concern to challenge the right of individuals to speak as they wish as infringing the freedom of individuals, who are depicted as having the 'negative' right to say what they like. Supporters of political correctness, on the other hand, might see freedom as involving the 'positive' respect for others' freedom and dignity. But, alternatively, supporters of political correctness might construe derogatory language against certain groups as constituting a barrier to the achievement of freedom on the part of the group. From this perspective a Polish or Irish joke may be funny but it may also serve as a constraint impairing the freedom of Irish and Polish people. If jokes constantly depict Irish people as stupid and violent, it makes it hard for an Irish person to enjoy the freedom to be taken seriously.

## Rights

Rights are important concepts in the world of politics. They are often encoded in laws and form legal safeguards of freedom, and appeals couched in the terms of rights are ubiquitous features of the current political scene. The experience of tyrannies in Nazi Germany, the Soviet Empire and Bosnia are graphic reminders of the human cost involved in the denial of rights. Rights function as a way of highlighting important attributes requiring protection by law. It is the lack of protection of attributes such as free speech, free movement, property and life itself which is the hallmark of the tyrannies identified above. In this sense the language of rights may be said to be the idiom in which criteria for a 'good' state are set out.

To say that rights are significant and generally held in high esteem by political commentators and publics is not to say that rights and their specification are uncontroversial. Rights are the subject of theoretical and practical debate, which we shall track in the ensuing pages. A central source of controversy about rights is the question of whether or not there are any natural rights. The historical background to natural rights theory lies in Ancient Greece, where the notion that an objective order of reason was responsible for both natural events and the values to which men should adhere took root. Subsequently, in medieval times, God was regarded as the author of a law of nature which prescribed the moral conduct man should follow. St Thomas Aquinas, the thirteenth-century theologian and philosopher, argued that there were distinct but interrelated kinds of law. In descending order, for Aquinas, there was the eternal law of God, the natural law rationally discernible by man and the positive law enacted by men. Aquinas urged that the world was framed according to the eternal plan of God, but that man could come to know something of this divine plan by invoking his reason to reflect upon his own rational nature and its consequent obligations.

In the modern world emerging in the European world of the sixteenth and seventeenth centuries, the 'natural rights' of man became central components of ethical and political reasoning. Theorists such as Hobbes and Locke and the constitutions and rhetoric of the American and French Revolutions emphasised the natural rights of individuals, which were to be upheld against other individuals and in most cases against the state itself. In the case of the theorists and situations cited above, God is invoked as the author and guarantor of the rights of man. While more recent theories of natural rights have tended to abandon express references to God as the author of rights, there remains a presumption of an underlying objectivity to the ascription of rights. The nature of men and, latterly, human beings in general is characteristically seen as underwriting basic claims on behalf of the individual, notwithstanding the accidental interplay of social and historical life. Generally the rational and free nature of human beings is invoked to justify classic claims to the rights of life, liberty and property, though in recent years there has been an expansion of the rights claimed, so that education, abortion and employment are frequently cited as key human rights.

The notion of natural rights has been challenged from a variety of perspectives. Utilitarians, Marxists and ethical relativists are amongst those who have attacked the notion that rights are natural. All political theorists who take history and historical development seriously, including Marxists, Hegelians and liberal progressivists like Mill, tend to question the presumption that 'human nature' can be isolated from the flow of events and be referred to as a fixed standard of 'right'. So-called basic individual natural rights are seen by theorists who stress the irreducibly social nature of man

**Logical positivism** A philosophical doctrine which maintains that a term is meaningful in so far as it is susceptible of verification.

(including, once again, Hegel and Marx) as parasitic upon specific forms of social development which recognise and support these rights. A hard-headed utilitarian such as Bentham insists that it is nonsense to talk of rights without reference to a positive framework of law in which such rights are inscribed. Again, **logical positivists**, who see meaningful discourse as being possible only in reference to observable phenomena, disparage reference to supposedly objective, natural rights. While the positivist impulse in philosophy has retreated in recent decades, there are many contemporary philosophers who recognise the inherent contestability of values. Values rely on contestable forms of justification according to this standpoint, and this contestability rules out the notion of objective, unchanging 'natural' rights.

While the notion of natural rights is a highly contestable one, it continues to elicit support. In the wake of war crimes of appalling horror in the civil wars in the countries of the former Yugoslavia, the appeal of designating certain crimes as transgressing objective human rights remains attractive. The torture of children and the massacre of peoples offend against any seemingly reasonable basis of human interaction, and thereby lend support to the argument for objective natural rights. While such an argument is appealing and informs and helps sustain justifiable campaigns against repression, its theoretical force is debatable. The 'natural' basis of rights would seem to imply their applicability in all circumstances, but it is not clear that the inviolability of property rights should be maintained in periods of famine and conflict when the redistribution of goods might be the only way of preserving lives.

While the validity of natural rights is a controversial subject, conceptual discussions of rights invariably take their bearings from Hohfield's classic study *Fundamental Legal Conceptions* (1919). Hohfield distinguished between distinct types of rights, namely liberties, claims, immunities and powers. The most important of these designated rights are liberty rights and claim rights. Liberty rights are those rights individuals are deemed to possess which do not involve distinct and matching claims on others, such as the right an individual may be said to have to whistle as s/he walks. Claim rights are distinct claims individuals may have on others. For instance, an employee may have distinct claims against a company. Immunity rights and powers are more specific kinds of rights. A Member of Parliament, for example, is granted immunity from prosecution for slander for what is said in Parliament. A person may also be granted specific powers to act as the guardian of another individual.

---

*THINK POINT*
- Do you consider that there are any natural rights?
- If so, which do you consider to be the most important of these rights?
- If not, explain the reasons why you reject them.

---

The distinction between liberty and claim rights set out by Hohfield informs the discussion about negative and positive rights. The distinction between negative and positive rights matches Berlin's (1991) separation of negative liberty from positive liberty. Norman Barry (1981) and Cranston (1973), in distinguishing between negative and positive rights, ape Berlin in privileging the negative variety. They see the rights of life, liberty and property as being negative insofar as they do not require positive action on the part of the state to promote them. Positive rights, on the other hand, are seen as demanding state action to implement them, and unlike negative rights are held to expand as social demands on the state are generated over time. Hence, the provision of positive rights such as the right to extended education, decent housing and nursery provision are characterised as responses to the development of contingent 'wants' in Western societies over the last two centuries. The extension of the range of rights has been resisted by those, like Cranston, who wish to privilege long-standing 'negative' rights. However, there seems no inherent reason why some rights should be privileged as being beyond debate and other claims are debarred from discussion. All rights, including negative ones, are socially acknowledged attributes of significance which are accorded legal status as being worthy of protection. The identification, and the range, of attributes awarded such protection is a proper object of human concern, discussion and legal enactment.

## Animal rights

In recent years the claims for animals to receive moral recognition by human beings have been advanced and there is a body of opinion which would like to accord 'rights' to animals. Supporters of animal rights argue that to deny rights to animals is tantamount to speciesism. Non-human animals, as well as human beings, are regarded by animal rights' theorists as having interests. These interests are taken to derive from all animals' capacities both to suffer and to experience pleasure. If all animals are seen as having interests, then to privilege humans over other species is to behave in a speciesist way, just as to discriminate against black people is to behave in a racist way. The capacity to suffer and experience pleasure is viewed by theorists such as Singer (1976) as being crucial in assigning moral consideration as it is taken as a more fundamental aspect of experience than, say, intellectual abilities.

While animal rights' theorists are busy trying to promote the rights of animals, their arguments do not receive universal acceptance. Resistance to animal rights turns upon the argument that humans are distinct from the rest of the animal kingdom in ways which are significant in the assessment of ethical worth. For instance, it is commonly held that the superior intelligence of human beings entitles them to receive moral consideration at the expense of animals. This point is a contestable one. It might well be argued that superior intelligence might qualify a species for greater moral consideration, but a relative superiority in intelligence seems a shallow basis for allowing one species to monopolise our moral concern. Moreover, there is an evident variety in intelligence amongst human beings. Various forms of mental illness and brain dysfunction impair the mental capacities of human beings. It would seem harsh and morally questionable to dismiss the rights of those suffering from such mishaps and to assign rights according to intelligence quotients.

Another manoeuvre made by those who resist ascribing rights to the rest of the animal kingdom is to maintain that animals other than humans should be excluded from our moral perspective as they cannot assume moral duties to match the putative rights they are to be assigned. This point poses questions. It is certainly true that we could not expect the rest of the animal kingdom to follow our moral example if we were to assign the right of life to animals. The rest of the animal kingdom does not operate according to moral concepts. But to say that other animals will operate differently from human beings is not to say that they should be denied rights. There is no necessary reason why recipients of rights must all behave in the same way. Children, for instance, are assigned special rights and they are seen as having different responsibilities from adults.

---

**THINK POINT**
- If all human beings became vegetarians, should we expect other animals to become vegetarians?
- Can we expect non-human animals to recognise moral obligations?

---

The need for animals to be assigned rights emerges most strongly consequent upon a recognition of the suffering which is inflicted upon animals by human beings. Perhaps the most serious forms of suffering are inflicted by the prevalent form of farming in the Western world, namely factory farming, and the practice of experimenting upon animals. While animals have been harnessed to farming since the beginnings of agriculture, they are now subject to intensive production techniques which render their conditions of life quite alien to their basic instincts and render them susceptible to disease and severe suffering.

Animal experimentation is extremely widespread. There are over five million experiments performed on animals each year in Britain alone. Experiments are especially prevalent in scientific establishments, notably psychological ones, where there is no prospect of the experiments yielding medical benefits. Experiments on animals are conducted for the purposes of cosmetics and defence, where the prospects of decided benefits to humans are remote. Even the experiments on animals conducted for the benefit of medical science are questionable. It is by no means clear that experiments need to be conducted on animals when simulations might do the job better, particularly when differences between humans and other animals render the knowledge gained through such experimentation problematic.

Of course, the issues of animal suffering and the need to protect animals by the provision of animal rights go beyond what has been discussed above. Animals are eaten by human beings and there is a case for humans changing their eating habits to stop killing animals. Animals are also subject to seemingly random acts of cruelty. Again, zoos often house animals in the most inhospitable conditions. The prospects for animals do not look good as new technological and scientific possibilities such as cloning emerge.

Speciesism – the word is not an attractive one, but I can think of no better term – is a prejudice or attitude of bias toward the interest of members of one's own species and against those of members of other species. It should be obvious that the fundamental objections to racism and sexism made by Thomas Jefferson and Sojourner Truth apply equally to speciesism. If possessing a higher degree of intelligence does not entitle one human to use another for his own ends, how can it entitle humans to exploit nonhumans for the same purpose? . . .

The racist violates the principle of equality by giving greater weight to members of his own race when there is a clash of interests between their interests and the interests of those of another race. The sexist violates the principle of equality by favouring the interests of his own sex. Similarly the speciesist allows the interests of his own species to override the greater interests of members of other species. The pattern is identical in each case. . . .

Most human beings are speciesists . . . ordinary human beings – not a few exceptionally cruel or heartless humans – allow their taxes to pay for practices that require the sacrifice of the most important interests of other species in order to promote the most trivial interests of our own species.

(Singer 1976: 7, 9, 10)

## Exercise

1 Do you agree that human beings are speciesist?

2 Is speciesism like racism?

3 To what relatively trivial human interests are the interests of other species sacrificed?

## Equality

The meaning of equality is disputed. How is the concept of equality taken to apply to social and political life? The idea that human beings are equal is a puzzling one. Consider some examples: are Frank Bruno, Woody Allen, your next-door neighbour and Mother Theresa equal? There are certainly important differences between them. If egalitarianism is taken to be the wholehearted concern to achieve concrete equality of outcome between these and other people, then it would appear to involve a degree of interventionism which is both breathtaking and monstrous. Plato was a philosopher of Ancient Greece who treated the issue of justice and equality in a spirit far removed from egalitarianism. He urged that justice involved treating people differently as justice consisted in giving each man his due, and he believed that there were significant differences between people which must be respected.

A core meaning of the term 'equality' in a social and political context is that equality should be seen as a basic presupposition of moral concern. On this basis, a fundamental presupposition of equality as a moral procedural principle informs the plea that all persons are entitled to equal consideration save where a special case can be made for differential treatment. In more concrete terms, this has been translated into a concern that people should receive equal consideration before the law, save where criminal behaviour leads to justifiable punishment. It has also led to a concern that voting rights are equal. Equality in these senses has now become a generally accepted norm in liberal democratic societies. The extension of the vote to women and an equalisation of property rights between men and women in Western countries, however, are fairly recent phenomena. In more recent years, there has also been pressure to extend the reach of the concept of equality to include other species than human beings. In the previous section, we traced the arguments seeking to justify the attribution of rights to animals.

While equal legal and voting rights have been accepted in Western and many non-Western societies, there is little agreement on the extent to which we should aim to achieve substantive equality in social and political life. The idea that social and political life should be organised to achieve material equality between people is controversial. It implies a concern to regulate outcomes rather than ensuring that rules apply equally to those who will achieve differing outcomes. One way of securing an equality of material outcome would be to ensure that all achieved the same level of well-being. Another way to achieve equality of outcome would be for all to satisfy their needs equally. The difficulties in the way of achieving either of these aims, however, are immense. To compute the needs or well-being of all and then to secure their equal provision would demand an enormous amount of governmental regulation. The ongoing problems of regulation are highlighted when it is considered that if resources were to be distributed equally, then steps would have to be taken so that arrangements would not be overturned by the dynamics of individual choice and behaviour.

Given the problems of attaining equality of outcome, some theorists sympathetic to the ideal of substantive equality have looked at ways of achieving a form of equality which would allow for the dynamics of individual choice and difference. Walzer (1983) has argued for what he terms 'complex equality', by which he means a form of just society where inequalities in the several spheres of society do not invade one another. On this view, inequalities in one sphere are not repeated in others. Wealth may dominate the business world, but health needs would trigger treatment in the health sphere and education would be organised according to the learning needs and capacities of individuals rather than wealth. Miller (1991) is another contemporary political theorist who has urged that a more subtle view of political equality is required. He urges that a just society would be one in which all citizens would have equal status, an ideal which would be undermined if citizens of great wealth were to dominate society. He considers that all citizens have the right to a certain level of welfare if all are to enjoy an equality of respect in society. Miller recognises, though, that the effort to secure any more substantive form of equality would jeopardise individual freedom.

The achievement of equality of opportunity is one way in which the concept of equality is held to be a political concern. Many politicians advertise their commitment to the establishment of equality of opportunity, but this notion of equality of opportunity raises questions. For one thing, it might lead to great inequality of outcome. Plato, in *The Republic*, subscribed to a form of equality of opportunity in which women were to receive the same opportunities as men, but he envisaged a form of society in which there would be large-scale differences between classes, including differential entitlements to rule. A meritocracy has been seen by some as a nightmare prospect in which differences of outcome would be all the more galling because they would be seen as being clearly deserved.

While the condition of equality of opportunity may be seen as possibly problematic, there are also difficulties surrounding the possibility of attaining it. For instance, can all the significant environmental factors which promote inequality of opportunity be eliminated? To establish equality of opportunity, all children would have to be given the same kind of schooling. In most Western countries, however, there are presently a range of schools. Even within similar schools teachers will vary and this variety will affect the future opportunities of children. Again, families vary in terms of the levels of support they are able and willing to offer their children, and it would seem difficult and undesirable to establish equality in this sphere. To get anywhere near the establishment of equal opportunities, radical changes would have to be effected and these changes would disrupt traditional and accepted patterns of family life and education. Even if equality of opportunity could be achieved, it would seem to exact an exorbitant price in terms of excessive regulation. Questions would also remain about genetic differences between individuals. If genetic patterns prove alterable, would it be reasonable to alter these patterns prior to birth so that all may have equal opportunities? Such a question probes deep into the concept of individual identity. Many would seek to resist genetic manipulation because they equate individuality with genetic foundations.

Questions about equality tend to generate ideological controversy and this is true of efforts to achieve positive or reverse discrimination. Schemes of positive discrimination aim to reverse or nullify historic forms of discrimination suffered by distinct groups in society – such as blacks, women, disabled people – by advantaging these groups in certain ways. These schemes are often operated in contexts where there is a palpable record of unequal treatment affecting particular groups. In these circumstances it might seem reasonable to advantage a group, for instance by establishing a quota of disabled people to be employed in public service posts when the previous record of their employment in such jobs has been low. However, when a particular group is advantaged, injustice might be seen as being inflicted upon other groups. Likewise, it is problematic to decide on which groups are to be selected and to decide which members of the group are to be so advantaged. It might happen that a person belongs to an historically dis-advantaged group while in other ways s/he may be categorised as advantaged, for example a wealthy, well-educated member of a minority cultural group. These problematic aspects of the question are what cause such schemes of positive discrimination to be hotly contested. Consider Minogue's views on egalitarianism set out below.

> Inequality is notoriously the common condition – one might well say 'the natural condition' – of mankind. An 'inegalitarian' as the opposite of an egalitarian would presumably be the partisan of some specific form of inequality – one based on blood for example. My disagreement with egalitarianism is thus both particular and general. I oppose not only the plan of equality, but any kind of plan at all. I take the state to be a specific type of association in which resourceful individuals recognize a sovereign power able to enforce the conditions of peace permitting the citizens to live their lives as they choose. To bend that power to the end of imposing any kind of abstract outcome, whether egalitarian or inegalitarian, seems to me something for which no serious reason could be given. Specific measures of redistribution – for the relief of poverty, for example – might well be publicly judged necessary, but any such measures both can and ought to be justified in specific terms, and not in terms of some overriding plan to be imposed on a whole society.
>
> (Minogue 1990: 100)

## Exercise

1  What problems does Minogue see with egalitarianism?
2  Why is Minogue against any kind of plan for society?
3  Why does Minogue not refer to himself as an inegalitarian?
4  How might an egalitarian respond to Minogue's arguments?

## Justice

Justice is a much-disputed concept which underpins many controversial social issues. It has been the object of rigorous analysis in recent years. Two of the most celebrated and controversial contemporary political philosophers, Rawls and Nozick, have done much to promote debate about the nature and understanding of justice. Rawls wrote *A Theory of Justice* in 1971 and Nozick responded with *Anarchy, State and Utopia* in 1974. These two works carved out distinct contrasting viewpoints on justice and, although both thinkers have advanced their thinking on justice in subsequent writings, these two works warrant a brief discussion as they set out engaging and distinct standpoints on justice.

Rawls develops in *A Theory of Justice* a rigorous analysis of what would constitute a just society understood as one embodying fair terms of social cooperation. To effect a framework for a basic structure of justice, Rawls conducts a thought experiment whereby he imagines heads of households in an original position in which they are behind a veil of ignorance which screens out knowledge of their particular characteristics and assets in society. They are to be equipped with knowledge of how any scheme of society which they uphold will work out, but they will not have knowledge of their own particular qualities and so cannot frame general conditions for fair cooperation which favour their own particular interests. The conditions for the basic structure of a society chosen in the original position are seen by Rawls as conditions respecting the equality and liberty of all, and thus enabling a fair mode of social cooperation to take place.

Rawls sees the framework of justice which will emerge from his analysis as one in which two principles will be highlighted, the first taking priority over the second. First, is the principle that each person in society is to have a right to as much freedom as is compatible with freedom for all. Second, social and economic inequalities are to be so arranged that they are to the greatest benefit of the least advantaged and attached to offices and positions open to all under fair conditions of equal opportunity.

It is Rawls's second principle of distributive justice which has generated acute controversy. By this principle, Rawls is, in effect, licensing the redistribution of wealth; indeed, differences in wealth are to be justified only in so far as they benefit the worst off. The perception of inequalities from the vantage point of Rawls's original position renders them separable from personal knowledge of one's own particular qualities and position in society. Such a perspective Rawls takes as promoting an interest in fairness and an overriding concern for the situation of the worst off. This Rawlsian perspective is the nub of Nozick's challenge to Rawls's theory of justice, however, in that Nozick, like other neo-liberal theorists, challenges the rationale of distributive justice.

Nozick begins his account of justice with a different thought experiment from that of Rawls. Whereas Rawls reworks the idea of a social contract between members of a political society, Nozick assumes a state of nature in which individuals with rights to life, liberty and property are imagined as acting and interacting with one another. In this imaginative picture Nozick sees individuals as being concerned to pursue their own goals and welfare and concludes that a state will be formed by the actions of a dominant protective agency to which individuals will resort in order to protect their interests in the inevitable disputes that will arise between individuals.

Nozick imagines a state being formed, but he does not bestow upon this state powers to override the rights of individuals. He sees the rights of individuals as being strong side constraints on actions. For Nozick, these rights of individuals are to be maintained, so that, for instance, the state should not interfere with property holdings as long as the holdings result from the voluntary actions of individuals. If property is gained through legitimate means of transfer, e.g. cash payments and inheritance, then there is no justification for state interference with the property arrangements that ensue. For Nozick, Rawls's theory of distributive justice involves an injustice in that the property of the better off might be redistributed by the state to benefit the worst off. The injustice would consist in the violation of the rights of the better off, who, for Nozick, would have gained their property through legitimate means.

Nozick's theory of justice is an entitlement theory which differs from Rawls's perspective in being backward-looking in its review of the legitimacy of property arrangements. Rawls's *A Theory of Justice* and Nozick's *Anarchy, State and Utopia* might be said to occupy different sites on the liberal landscape. Nozick's theory of justice is robustly individualistic. Individuals and individual rights are seen as being of primary importance, and the state is to be minimal, in that extensive interference is taken as diminishing individual rights. Rawls, like Nozick, is liberal in that he prioritises individual liberty. But he is concerned that the general patterns of poverty and prosperity accompanying a minimal state might derogate from the principles of freedom and equality he takes to be central for contemporary liberal democratic states. He adopts a perspective which allows for just decisions to be made about the overall distribution of wealth in society. He is therefore prepared to countenance some state intervention to develop a pattern of distributive justice.

The theoretical debate between Rawls and Nozick shadows a practical conflict between left and right liberals, who diverge over the extent of state intervention. This close relationship between theory and practice itself highlights one of the dimensions of criticism of both Rawls and Nozick which has been prevalent in recent years. Communitarian critics of both Rawls and Nozick have highlighted that individuals are always located in particular societies and communities and that theorising is always shaped by prevailing social norms and is inevitably tailored to certain types of community rather than others. Communitarian critics have objected to the nakedly individualistic perspective of Nozick. The communitarians are by no means united, but theorists such as Walzer (1983), Macintyre (1988), Taylor (1989) and Sandel (1984) can all agree that the individual cannot be separated from society and cannot be accorded explanatory priority. Individuals and societies are seen as correlative, and all would look to the importance of some community goods, such as culture and education, as necessary to generate flourishing forms of individuality.

Rawls has been criticised by communitarians on at least two counts. On the one hand, *A Theory of Justice* has been seen as too universalistic. Critics deny that it provides an overarching account of justice and note its relationship with particular features of a modern liberal society. It has also been criticised, notably by Sandel, for its alleged prioritising of socially disembedded individuals who are imagined in the original position as functioning without reference to their cultural homes. Rawls, in a series of articles and in a subsequent book, *Political Liberalism* (1993), has sought to clarify and revise the formulation of a conception of justice as fairness in *A Theory of Justice* in ways which bear upon the communitarian critique. Rawls observes that the original position is not and was not meant to function as a theory unrelated to a particular social and cultural setting. He explains it as functioning as a representative device whereby people like *us* (citizens of a democratic public culture) can model the basic principles allowing for fair social cooperation. Justice as fairness, Rawls accepts, is a theoretical exploration of the standpoint of a form of democratic society in which there will be reasonable disagreement on comprehensive moral, religious and philosophical beliefs. Rawls, then, accepts limitations of his project. His theory of justice is one that is limited by the form of prevailing public culture (his general theorising is taken as deriving from and harmonising with intuitions and principles held in a democratic public culture) and it is a specifically political conception of justice and not a metaphysical one.

The communitarian approach to justice has a number of attractive features. It recognises the difficulties of establishing a universal answer to the question of justice. It acknowledges man's social and changing nature. It suffers, however, from being rather vague on important questions concerning the nature of the type of community and framework of justice which are to be supported. In this sense it may be said to resemble post-modernism. Postmoderns such as Lyotard are suspicious of overarching theory purporting to be universalistic. They recognise the significance of differences and are sceptical of the capacity of general criteria to appraise practices. For Lyotard, even Rawls's limited project of establishing general principles to supply a framework for a reasonable conception of justice within a democratic public culture denies difference and experimentation (Lyotard 1984).

The issue of state intervention into the economy to achieve social justice is of ongoing importance and relates to the understanding of justice as a concept. The political history of the last two centuries in Western countries has much to do with this subject. Central to an understanding of British political and social history has been the gradual expansion of the welfare state. Pioneers of the welfare state such as Beveridge explicitly called for an expansion of the state's services to ensure a minimum of social justice. The language of contemporary politics in Europe and the USA is charged by conflict between those who seek to maintain the level of welfare services provided by the state and those who, inspired by neo-liberal doctrines such as those espoused by Nozick, wish to curtail state activity.

Below is an extract from Beveridge's *Full Employment in a Free Society* (1944) which laid the framework for the state provision of social welfare in Britain after the Second World War.

> Social security today can be made the subject of a definite Plan and of legislation to give effect to that Plan. It lies wholly within the power of each National Government; once the decision has been taken to abolish Want by comprehensive social insurance as the principal method, once a few issues of equity between older and newer contributors have been settled, the rest is administrative and actuarial detail: the Plan should be as definite as possible, so that every citizen, knowing just what he may expect from social insurance can plan his personal spending and saving to suit his special needs.
>
> 50. Prevention of idleness enforced by mass unemployment is a different task. Detailed legislation is neither needed nor useful. It is a problem of adjusting State action to the free activities of the citizens of that State and to the policies of other States. It involves one large decision of principle – acceptance by the State of a new responsibility to the individual – and the setting up of an agency of the State with powers adequate to the discharge of that responsibility.
>
> (Beveridge 1944: 38)

## Exercise

1 What do you think is meant by the problem of adjusting State action to the free activities of citizens?
2 Do you agree that providing a comprehensive Plan for social security is relatively straightforward?
3 What do you take to be the principal reasons behind the development of state provision of social welfare? Can it be supported by a convincing theory of justice?

## Conclusion

This chapter has put together conceptual analysis and the consideration of contested, practical issues in politics. In so doing, it has been concerned to signal the relevance of political theory for the life-and-blood activities of politics. The ascription of rights to animals raises questions about the meaning of a right, just as a death threat against an author dramatises the significance of freedom. Whereas forty years ago epitaphs for political theory were being coined (Laslett 1956), nowadays the subject is very much alive.

# Further reading

Bellamy, R. (ed.) (1993) *Theories and Concepts of Politics*, Manchester: Manchester University Press. An interesting and informative run through a number of concepts of political theory by a range of different authors.

Lyotard, J.F. (1988) *The Differend: Phrases in Dispute*, Manchester: Manchester University Press. Lyotard's most sophisticated attempt to establish the incommensurability of doctrines and standpoints, in which justice is seen as the attempt to bear witness to differends.

Macintyre, A. (1981) *After Virtue*, Guildford: Duckworth. A thoughtful exploration of different intellectual traditions on virtue.

Macintyre, A. (1988) *Whose Justice? Which Rationality?* London: Duckworth. A challenging account of differing notions of justice.

Nozick, R. (1974) *Anarchy, State and Utopia*, Oxford: Blackwell. This is a lively book which puts a strong case for a minimal state.

Rawls, J. (1971) *A Theory of Justice*, London: Oxford University Press. Classic status for a complex work which argues for a distributive theory of justice and has been the subject of relentless discussion.

Rawls, J. (1993) *Political Liberalism*, New York: Columbia University Press. Reworked essays and lectures which seek to clarify the theory of justice as fairness previously put forward by Rawls.

Sandel, M. (1984) *Liberalism and its Critics*, New York: New York University Press. A lively critique of Rawls and other liberal theorists from a communitarian perspective.

Walzer, M. (1983) *Spheres of Justice*, Oxford: Blackwell. A famous statement of a communitarian understanding of justice.

# 7 POLITICAL THOUGHT

*Gary K. Browning*

# Political thought

## Introduction

This chapter is devoted to exploring the tradition of political thought. It begins by examining how political thought is to be understood, recognising the diversity of ways in which politics and thought are related. It concentrates upon discussing political philosophy, in the guise of the classic texts of political philosophers. It analyses the relationship between the classic texts of traditional political philosophy and the more recent style of analytical political philosophising undertaken in the Anglo-Saxon world. Subsequently the character of the history of political thought is reviewed. The debate between contextualist historians and those who consider that the great texts of political philosophy can speak for themselves is examined. Thereafter, a number of specific political philosophies are reviewed. Finally, political Islam and issues of gender are looked at to highlight the ways in which the history of Western political thought is limited by contextual assumptions which render its analysis of politics less universal than is sometimes imagined.

*See Chapter 6.*

## Political thought

Political thinking can take place at many levels and in a variety of ways. Human life inevitably involves thought, and politics is a universal activity amongst human beings. Thinking is present in most recognisably human activities. To consider someone as acting for reasons and to see a person as taking part in activities which involve rules and conventions which have to be understood, are aspects of human identity which we assume or take for granted. In this sense, thinking is more or less fundamental to human activities. Again, politics is a constant factor in history. In the Introduction, politics was taken as involving collective decision-making, and the ubiquity of politics is signalled by the myriad ways in which people are concerned with the character and organisation of group activities. Systematic thought about politics has focused upon the politics of the most important of human associations, **states**. States are associations which literally lay down the laws

*See the Introduction for a general account of how this book regards politics and theories of politics.*

**State** A human association in which sovereign power is established within a given territorial area, and in which the sovereign power usually possesses a monopoly on the means of coercion.

*See Chapter 16.*

for all other groups and individuals. Recently the centrality of nation-states in political analysis has been challenged by theorists of globalisation who point to the involvement of nation-states in global patterns of development.

---

**THINK POINT**
- Consider the following human activities and note how thinking is involved in them: driving a car, doing housework, reading this book, debating in a legislature.
- Consider how politics is involved in the following group activities: deciding on expenditure in a family household, prioritising the objectives of a charity such as Oxfam, the introduction of tougher penal measures.

---

The institutions and practices of states presuppose language and thought; for example, lobbying, debate in legislatures, executive decision-making and administrative regulations are reflective activities. 'Political thought', as a term, however, conveys a sense of systematic reflection upon the practices and institutions of political life. As has been observed previously in this book (see Introduction), there are a variety of ways of theorising politics. Political science, in various styles, aims at achieving laws or plausible generalisations about political behaviour. Traditionally, however, political thought in academic commentary is taken to signify political philosophy. The study of the history of political thought, for example, generally focuses upon classic texts of political philosophy. The classic texts of political philosophy, such as Plato's *Republic*, and Hobbes's *Leviathan*, constitute broad-ranging explorations of politics which relate politics to the general conditions of experience. Hence Plato elaborated the nature of the relationship between truth, practical life and philosophical understanding.

*See the section on Plato later in this chapter (pp. 202–5).*

The classic texts of political philosophy continue to inform the way in which the meaning and value of politics are imagined. As was observed in Chapter 6, Anglo-Saxon political philosophers in the mid-twentieth century, under the spell of linguistic philosophy, tended to limit the scope of political philosophy to that of **conceptual analysis**. See also T. D. Weldon (1953) *The Vocabulary of Politics*, for the epitome of a conception of political philosophy as conceptual analysis. Contemporary political philosophers, however, while recognising the ineluctably controversial nature of judgments of value, are willing to undertake large-scale theorising about norms. Rawls (1971) and Nozick (1974), for example, have elaborated theories of justice which develop and justify contrasting accounts of just, substantive arrangements of society.

**Conceptual analysis** A practice and view of philosophy which takes philosophy to be concerned with the analysis and clarification of concepts rather than substantive issues.

*See Chapter 6 for a more detailed analysis of justice.*

In so far as contemporary political philosophers engage with the norms of political practice and work out schemes of political organisation, exhibiting substantive applications of political values, then the contemporary identity of political philosophy borders on political ideology and is in touch with the grand theorising of classic political philosophers such as that undertaken by Plato and Hobbes. Both political philosophy and political ideology are to be understood as developing conceptual explorations of politics involving value judgements. While political philosophy accents the critical examination of assumptions, political ideology emphasises a programmatic set of recommendations. The links between contemporary political philosophers and their predecessors is evident in the way they lean on the classic texts of political philosophy in constructing their arguments. Rawls, for instance, self-consciously works within the social contract tradition and looks to Kant as an exemplary moral philosopher. Nozick's justification of a minimal state owes much to a tradition of natural rights theorising, and to Locke's political thought in particular. Habermas, a leading contemporary continental political philosopher, theorises within the context of a reading of modern philosophy, as is evidenced in his book *The Philosophical Discourse of Modernity* (1987). The continuing influence of the classic texts of political philosophy signals their importance, and in the succeeding sections of this chapter a framework for their historical understanding will be explored and the arguments of several past political philosophers will be examined.

## The history of political thought

Thinking about politics, at whatever level and style it is undertaken, inevitably implies some engagement with history. Politics as a human activity takes place over time. Without people having lived together in communities there could be no theories of politics. Politics in the abstract would be a void. Political thought has to be based upon actual political behaviour. This dependence of theory upon practice applies to the most abstract kind of political thought, namely political philosophy, as well as to the most severely practical kind, such as a specific policy recommendation. On this reading, then, an historical understanding of the classic texts of political philosophy, which constitutes the most familiar treatment of political thought, must recognise that the texts are composed in relation to actual worlds of political experience.

---

**THINK POINT**
- Hegel, in *the Philosophy of Right*, urges, 'What is rational is actual and what is actual is rational' (Hegel 1971). If what Hegel is saying here amounts to the idea that the rational must be based on what has been developed in practice, do you agree with him?

---

The dependence of political philosophy on the prior practice of politics ensures that the subject has an historical dimension. As the practice of politics develops, so reflection upon politics changes. The relationship between theory and practice is not straightforward, however, and the meaning and consequences of Hegel's remark on the actuality of reason are controversial, for he did not equate actuality with existence. A political philosopher may be critical of political practice and s/he may also imagine a framework of political organisation distinct from present practices. For instance, Plato's recommendations on education and sexual equality do not reflect the traditions of Greek political life. Historic political philosophers, in framing their understanding of politics, theorise within the context of political practices but do not reflect them unthinkingly. Likewise, their thought is developed within an intellectual context. Marx employs concepts refined by the German philosophical tradition in diagnosing the condition of the proletariat in the mid-nineteenth century as alienated.

## The methodology of the history of political thought

There is a methodological dispute over whether the subject should accent the historical contexts in which political thinkers write or discuss the ideas of the texts of political thought themselves without paying close attention to their provenance in locally determined historical contexts. **Contextualists** argue that a text of political thought such as Hobbes's *Leviathan* must be related to a variety of contexts, notably the intellectual and political, referred to above, if its meaning is to be understood. Historians of political thought like Plamenatz (1963), on the other hand, consider that the classic texts of political philosophy can be read and understood with a minimum of contextual knowledge on the part of the reader.

The historian of political thought whose practice and methodological work have perhaps been taken as providing foundations for the contextual approach is Professor Skinner. There is an irony in Skinner's reputation as a contextualist in that his most famous methodological essay, 'Meaning and Understanding in the History of Ideas' (Skinner 1988), criticised contextualist readings of political thought which assimilated thinking to the context and ignored authors' intentions.

Skinner exposed what he took to be the weaknesses of a textual approach to the history of political thought, which assumed that the meaning of classic texts could be acquired without historical investigation of their meaning and point. For Skinner the point of a text in political thought, and its meaning, can only be captured if the intentions of the author can be understood. An author's intentions, for Skinner, are often puzzling and cannot simply be read off from the text. On the other hand, intentions cannot be reduced to some distinct context, such as the economic, for the point behind an author's deployment of concepts involves the conscious agency of the author. Notwithstanding Skinner's critique of this kind of contextualist approach, his emphasis upon recovering the historical intentions of authors and reading texts in the context of contemporary political debates and ideologies has been taken as a paradigm of a contextualist reading of the history of political thought (King 1996).

The contextualist approach to the history of political thought, exemplified in the works of Skinner, Pocock and Collini, has elucidated the texts of political thought by relating them to contemporary ideological debate and conceptual paradigms. If the nuances of historical context are ignored

**Contextualism** This stands for the view that the meaning of political ideas can be understood only by relating them to the historical contexts in which they were generated.

Significant 'contextualist' works include:
J. Tully (ed.) (1988) *Meaning and Context – Quentin Skinner and his Critics*. Cambridge: Polity (a collection of essays and commentaries on Skinner's work);
J. G. A. Pocock (1971) *Politics, Language and Time*, London: Methuen;
S. Collini, D. Winch and J. Burrow (1983) *That Noble Science of Politics*, Cambridge: Cambridge University Press.

there is certainly a tendency for texts to be misread. It would be a mistake, for instance, to assume that the term property holds the same meaning in Locke's texts as it does today. Property in the seventeenth century had a range of meanings, one of which was as an umbrella term for entitlements in general (Dunn 1984). A failure to respect the historical meanings of terms can lead to a serious misreading of a text. Likewise, a narrowly textual approach to the history of political thought has tended to encourage the misleading assumption that all texts in political thought will contain doctrines on a set of political principles and institutions.

The contextual approach to the history of political thought has broadened the scope of the subject in that its attention to ideological debate and conceptual paradigms has pointed to the historical interest of practical and rhetorical pieces of political thought. Again, it has revivified the historical study of the classic texts of political philosophy by disclosing the conditionality of even the most philosophical accounts of politics. Contextualists maintain that authorial purposes and the expectations of audiences of the most abstract texts cannot be assumed without historical research. Contextualism, however, is not a neat unproblematic recipe for the understanding of political thought. There is no easily specifiable context for a text. The context for Hegel's political thought, for example, ranges across centuries of philosophical exploration which he self-consciously assimilated, as well as the immediate inspiration of German idealism and youthful colleagues and the political and religious situation within Germany. Given the seemingly limitless character of this context, concentration upon the internal logic of his texts at least establishes a manageable field of enquiry.

An implication of the contextualist approach to which Skinner (1988) has drawn attention is that the historical specificity of political theorising precludes the assumption that there exist perennial problems and answers in the history of political thought. In the extract below he argues against the existence of perennial or unhistorical answers to philosophical problems and repudiates the notion that classic texts of political philosophy provide answers to the problems we set ourselves in the contemporary world of politics.

> This reformulation and insistence on the claim that there are no perennial problems in philosophy, from which we can hope to learn directly through studying the classic texts, is not of course intended as a denial of the possibility that there may be propositions (perhaps in mathematics) the truth of which is wholly tenseless. (This does not yet amount to showing that their truth is any less contingent for that.) It is not even a denial of the possibility that there may be apparently perennial questions, if these are sufficiently abstractly framed. All I wish to insist is that whenever it is claimed that the point of historical study of such questions is that we may learn directly from the answers, it will be found that what counts as an answer will usually look, in a different culture or period, so different in itself that it can hardly be in the least useful even to go on thinking of the relevant question as being 'the same' in

the required sense at all. More crudely: we must learn to do our own thinking ourselves.

It is by no means my conclusion, however, that because the philosophical value at present claimed for the history of ideas rests on a misconception, it must follow that the subject has no philosophical value in itself at all. For it is the very fact that classic texts are concerned with their own quite alien problems, and not the presumption that they are somehow concerned with our own problems as well, which seems to me to give not the lie but the key to the indispensable value of studying the history of ideas. The classic texts, especially in social, ethical, and political thought, help to reveal – if we let them – not the essential sameness, but rather the essential variety of viable moral assumptions and political commitments.

(Skinner 1988: 66–7)

## Exercise

1 Do you agree with Skinner that what counts as an answer to a 'perennial' question will vary according to culture and period?
2 Do you think that the classic texts of political thought are valuable in teaching us the essential variety of moral assumptions and political commitments?

## The value of the history of political thought

Skinner is representative of contextualism in general in disparaging the claim that classic texts in the history of political philosophy furnish answers to today's political problems. Answers about politics, for contextualists, are relative to time and place. Skinner suggests that if political thinkers were to be presented as answering the same question, then the question would have to be phrased in a very abstract manner which allowed for profound differences amongst the specific answers to the question. He is surely right to signal that political thinkers' 'answers' to a question like one exploring the best political order for a society would be framed according to diverse concepts and assumptions. None the less, it is worth emphasising that an awareness of the tradition of the history of political thought serves to open up a range of possible responses to a contemporary question about the best political order.

Again a newly formulated answer to a fundamental question considering the best organisation of social and political life does not guarantee its novelty, due to its ignorance of the history of political thought. Rather, political thinking invariably is informed by an ongoing tradition of thought, and contemporary political theorising such as that conducted by Rawls (1971), Nozick (1974), Habermas (1987) and Gadamer (1981) self-consciously builds upon past traditions of thought. In this way the political thought of

Hobbes, Locke and Hegel is relevant to ongoing, critical reflection on the order and justice of political life.

---

**THINK POINT**
- Consider reasons for and against the political thought of a past political philosopher such as Plato, Hobbes or Marx being relevant to us today.

---

## Key political philosophers

In this section a number of significant political philosophers of the Western political tradition are examined. Aspects of their contexts are explored together with the distinct contributions they have made to political thinking. Evidently, any selection of specific theorists is controversial, but the point has not been to include all or even most of the significant political philosophers of Western political thought. The aim is to focus on a number of thinkers whose political thought is of undeniable importance, and to show how their theories relate to particular contexts and yet can contribute to an ongoing engagement with politics.

### Plato

Plato has exerted a significant impact upon the subsequent history of Western political thought and practice. Seminal modern thinkers such as Mill, Hegel and Marx, and twentieth-century political theorists such as Gadamer, Collingwood and Strauss can scarcely be understood without reference to Plato's legacy. It would be a mistake, however, to ignore the relation of Plato's political thought to a distinct context, namely that of the Ancient Greek *polis* and, in particular, the culture and events of fifth-century Athens. Plato's biography and the details of the composition of his most famous texts remain disputable. His most famous political texts are *The Crito* (1961c), *The Republic* (1945), *The Statesman* (1961e) and *The Laws* (1961d). *The Republic* has proved endlessly fascinating. Rousseau has admired it as a masterly work of education, Hegel has seen it as an essay in the retrieval of the Greek political tradition and Popper has lambasted it as the negative tribal image of his ideal, open society.

### Context of Plato's thought

Plato was born in 428 BC to a noble Athenian family, and he died in 347. The Peloponnesian war between Athens and Sparta served as the disturbing background to Plato's early years. The *Letter VII* (1961a) purports to provide an autobiographical sketch of Plato's political development. Its authenticity is in doubt, but its account is plausible and coheres with what is known about Plato from other sources. It reviews Plato's reaction to events at the end of the Peloponnesian war. The aristocratic regime which came to power in the wake of the Athenian defeat in the war is presented as high-handed

G. K. Browning (1991b) 'Ethical Absolutism in Hegel and Plato's' *History of Political Thought* XII (3).

and partisan. The return of democracy to Athens, however, is depicted as catastrophic in that it leads to the trial and execution of Socrates, Plato's philosophical mentor. The execution of Socrates exerted a momentous impact upon Plato. The Platonic dialogues portray Socrates as a paragon of intellectual and moral virtue, and his trial and execution are depicted as tragic tokens of political corruption. Plato's own political philosophy can be seen as a sharp condemnation of Athenian political practice.

The immediate political context of the Athenian *polis* evidently shaped Plato's political theorising, but he was also moved by contemporary intellectual developments. Melling, in his book *Understanding Plato*, has referred to 'a marked degree of plasticity in the political and social ideas current in Plato's Athens. Rival models were canvassed, opposing ideologies argued out in drinking circles and dinner parties' (Melling 1987). Intellectual debate and the critical interrogation of traditions were undertaken by the sophists, intellectuals who purported to be able to teach virtues and rhetoric. Sophists were a diverse group of intellectuals, but many of them sought to deny a natural basis of morality and urged that morality was shaped by prevailing social conventions. Plato was opposed to these views and aimed to re-establish the bases of an objective system of values on a new philosophical basis. The sharpest dramatic scenes in his dialogues depict dramatic confrontations between Socrates and sophists such as Gorgias, Protagoras and Thrasymachus.

In his opposition to the political and intellectual currents in fifth-century Athens Plato also looked to the Greek philosophical context, and his works can be seen as reflecting and building upon Greek philosophical traditions. Socrates is the charismatic figure who enlivens the dialogues. Evidence of the actual historical figure of Socrates is fragmentary, and derives in large part from the artistry of Plato. Plato's artistry, however, is concerned to paint a picture of Socrates which develops his own philosophical enterprise. Given the image of Socrates which can be gathered from elsewhere, it would seem that the early dialogues of Plato reflect a more faithful portrait of the man than the later ones, where Plato constructs a distinct philosophy of his own. In the early dialogues Socrates is represented as a gadfly whose wisdom consists in awareness of his own ignorance and is coupled with an interrogative strategy whereby he questions the underlying assumptions of others' views about the moral virtues. The ideal of a philosophy which can stand the test of such questioning impels the later philosophising of Plato.

### Plato's political thought

The early dialogues of Plato are for the most part sceptical and do not present a definite set of doctrines. Socrates is depicted as engaging in conversations with a variety of people. Generals, politicians, rhetoricians and sophists, for example, are questioned about their views on the moral virtues. Their views are invariably found to lack adequate support. The negative outcome of these conversations offers a critique of the ethical and political condition of the contemporary Greek *polis*. Its leading representatives cannot provide reasoned justifications of its practices and are bereft of convincing accounts of the ethical virtues. The implication of these investigations is that an effective political world demands an organisation which is based upon demonstrably rational criteria. The problems of the contemporary *polis* are thrown into sharp relief in *The Apology* (1961b), where Plato portrays Socrates as the innocent if eloquent victim of contemporary political machinations. Plato's search for high ethical standards is at the same time flagged in *The Crito*, where Socrates is depicted as staying to face his death, notwithstanding his innocence, because of his commitment to Athens and its laws.

Plato's *Republic*, a dialogue from Plato's middle period of writings, provides a detailed and radical account of a just *polis*. It diverges markedly from contemporary practice. Plato sketches the outlines of a just city in which the association is divided into three classes: the rulers, the soldiers and those who engage in trade and productive activity. Justice is highlighted as consisting in each class performing the role for which it is suited. The class of citizens who are most suited to rule must, according to Plato, assume the duty of ruling. Similarly, those who are most courageous must assume the duty of defending the city.

The ideal commonwealth of *The Republic* contains a number of radical features. The rulers are to be socialised so that they assume a rational disinterested concern for the community. They are to receive an education which culminates in their practice of philosophical enquiry. Their philosophical education is held to enable them to understand the ethical virtues and to rule rationally. These guardians and the auxiliary soldiers are to share things in common so that they are not inspired to pursue their own selfish desires for material gain at the expense of the communal good. This communist impulse also inspires the proposed abolition of family life amongst the guardians. Children will be brought up communally, so that family interests will not prejudice political judgements. Plato also prescribes sexual equality ―in Greece for the guardians, in startling contrast with contemporary practice. Plato's rationalism leads him to recommend sexual equality because he can see no relevant difference between the sexes to preclude women from ruling.

Alongside the extraordinary measures Plato advocates for the ruling guardians, he also recommends that a highly authoritarian style of rule be imposed upon the remaining body of citizens. Art is to be severely censored and education is to be tightly controlled so that justice and truth can be inculcated by the ruling elite. *The Republic* is an endlessly fascinating work for reasons which go beyond the mere rehearsal of the kind of ideal regime Plato recommends. Plato provides a series of memorable images to depict his vision of what is involved in a philosphical turn of mind and vocation. Philosophers are those who perceive the light beyond the subterranean prison in which most of us are condemned to live. Plato, in his evocation of the distinctiveness and rarity of the philosophical individual, betrays a pessimism about the human condition which casts doubt over the practical possibility of achieving his ideal regime. This doubt inspires Plato's later political dialogues, *The Statesman* and *The Laws*, in which Plato is prepared to adapt

This reading of Plato is explored in G. K. Browning (1991a) *Plato and Hegel: Two Modes of Philosophising about Politics*, New York: Garland Press.

rather than abolish contemporary practices and conceives of the rule of law as a realistic safeguard against rank disorder. In *The Laws* Plato recommends a rigid adherence to the rule of law and a mixed form of sovereignty.

Next, said I [Socrates], here is a parable to illustrate the degrees in which our nature may be enlightened or un-enlightened. Imagine the condition of men living in a sort of cavernous chamber underground, with an entrance open to the light and a long passage all down the cave. Here they have been from childhood, chained by the leg and also by the neck, so that they cannot move and can see only what is in front of them, because the chains will not let them turn their heads. At some distance higher up is the light of a fire burning behind them; and between the prisoners and the fire is a track with a parapet built along it, like the screen at a puppet show, which hides the performers while they show their puppets over the top.

I see, said he [Glaucon, interlocuter of Socrates].

Now behind this parapet imagine persons carrying along various artificial objects, including figures of men and animals in wood or stone or other materials, which project above the parapet. Naturally, some of these persons will be talking, others silent.

It is a strange picture, he said [Glaucon], and a strange sort of prisoners.

Like ourselves, I replied; for in the first place prisoners so confined would have seen nothing of themselves or of one another, except the shadows thrown by the fire-light on the wall of the Cave facing them, would they?

(Plato 1945: 227–8)

## Exercise

1 Put into your own words Plato's image of the human condition as presented in this passage.
2 What political views might be inspired by this image of the human condition?

Nor again is it at all strange that one who comes from the contemplation of divine things (the philosopher) to the miseries of human life should appear awkward and ridiculous when, with eyes still dazed and not yet accustomed to the darkness, he is compelled, in a law-court or elsewhere, to dispute about the shadows of justice or the images that cast those shadows, and to wrangle over the notions of what is right in the minds of men who have never beheld Justice itself.

(Plato 1945: 231)

## Exercise

1 On the strength of what Plato writes in the passage above, consider whether or not he regards the achievement of philosophical rule as an easy task.
2 How does the above passage relate to events in the life of the actual Socrates?
3 How, according to Plato, would you come to see Justice itself?

## Thomas Hobbes

Hobbes is both a celebrated and an infamous figure in political philosophy. He is celebrated because there is almost universal respect for the power of his thinking and the systematic character of his reflection upon politics. He is infamous because of the severity of his conclusions and the absolute authority he accords the sovereign. An explanation of both the severity of his conclusions and the unusually disciplined nature of his thought is afforded by a review of the context in which he wrote. Hobbes's most famous text is *Leviathan*, which was published in 1651; it was preceded by earlier versions of his political theory, *Elements of Law* and *De Cive*, published in 1640 and 1641, respectively.

### The context of Hobbes's thought

Hobbes himself joked that his birth was premature on account of the arrival of the Spanish Armada, and that fear and anxiety thereafter fixed themselves as key components of his thinking. While this anecdote was told for amusement, it remains true that political events in the years preceding Hobbes's writing of *The Leviathan* played a notable part in impressing upon Hobbes's mind the need for security and unequivocal political authority. The English Civil War, between the King, Charles I, and Parliament, took place between 1642 and 1649 and demonstrated graphically the dangers of disputed political authority. Civil war is an extreme reminder of the dangers to civil order which can be unleashed when authority comes to be disputed. While Hobbes's political ideas were developed before the outbreak of the Civil War, the gathering tensions between monarch and Parliament and the resulting uncertainties of government throughout Charles I's reign contributed to Hobbes's recognition of the need for clear and undisputed sovereign authority.

Ideological and social tensions generated by the prevailing religious discord and the proliferation of religious sects also left a mark on Hobbes's thinking. Hobbes recognised the power of religion to move men's minds and passions. In particular, Hobbes perceived that fanatical puritan sects which followed and proseltysed for religious practices distinct from those of the Church of England threatened to unravel social and political ties. This recognition helps to explain his recommendation in the *Leviathan* of state control over the promulgation of religious doctrine.

The political and social context of Hobbes's early years sensitised him to the significance of signs of religious and political dissent. His intellectual background alerted him to rationalist developments on the continent of Europe. Hobbes was distinctly unimpressed by the traditional education he had received at the University of Oxford. From his school days Hobbes was a gifted linguist, but he was uninspired by the intellectual atmosphere of Oxford. The dominance of scholastic philosophy, which subscribed to an Aristotelian worldview and ignored the rise of the new science, dismayed Hobbes. Hobbes himself was inspired by the rigour and exactitude of Euclidean mathematics and was impressed by contemporary scientific developments. Indeed, the structure and composition of *The Leviathan* is modelled on geometry insofar as the object of explanation, the state, is decomposed into its component parts so that it can then be reconstituted deductively.

### Hobbes's political thought

Hobbes's *Leviathan*, the masterpiece of his political thought, is composed of four parts. 'Of Man', 'Of Commonwealth', 'Of a Christian Commonwealth' and 'Of the Kingdome of Darknesse'. By far the most important parts in the presentation of his account of politics and the basis of political authority are the opening two parts. Hobbes begins his account of politics and the state by examining the nature of man, the underlying assumption being that an explanation of a political association must rest upon an understanding of the elements of which it is composed. Hobbes's account of man is distinctive and challenging. He sees men mechanistically and individualistically, as a series of particular bodies in motion. Human action, for Hobbes, is the product of passions generated by a particular self's contact with external bodies. Particular selves, according to Hobbes, pursue their own desires and seek to avoid that which provokes discomfort.

The good, for Hobbes, in contrast to Plato is not something which philosophers can reach by a heightened form of understanding. Rather, he believes that each individual terms good what s/he finds desirable. There is no common, ethical world which human beings naturally inhabit. For Hobbes, each person pursues her/his own 'good'; individuals seek the felicity of generally being able to satisfy their desires. The achievement of felicity is no easy thing, however, and Hobbes, in drawing a logical picture of the natural condition of mankind, stresses the uncertain and dangerous predicament constituting the human condition. In seeking to satisfy their own desires men inevitably come into conflict with other men pursuing their own goals. Men and women, according to Hobbes, have a natural right to whatever they can obtain. Conflict is endemic given the tendency for rights to clash. Above all, human beings in this condition fear they will not be able to pursue their desires. They fear that their power to achieve their goals will be taken away. They fear death at the hands of another. A fear which is rational given the potential for conflict among human beings.

Hobbes identifies the human condition as constituting a predicament whereby man's desires and the desire to satisfy his desires lead to chronic insecurity. For Hobbes, however, reason can be used instrumentally to resolve this predicament. Rational rules can be framed to alter the situation. The first such rule is that men should seek the peace. Men, for Hobbes, can only secure peace by covenanting together to form a political association. To ensure conditions of peace they should mutually contract with one another to confer authority and power upon a sovereign who is not party to the covenant. The sovereign will be granted absolute authority and power to ensure that peace is achieved. According to Hobbes, agreement to these conditions generates a moral as well as a prudential obligation to obey the sovereign.

The sovereign, ideally a single person, is presumed to follow the rules of reason himself and so will want to rule according to law so as not to inflame discontent. Ultimately, however, a sovereign, for Hobbes, can legitimately do all that is required to secure the peace so long as he is presumed to be effective in this endeavour. This notion of sovereignty certainly involves the sovereign's authority over religious publications and practices and education.

Hobbes's standpoint is controversial and has aroused much hostility since its formulation. Many see the power he bestows upon the sovereign and the state as prejudicial to human freedom. The *Leviathan* certainly contrasts with J. S. Mill's subsequent eloquent defence of human individuality and liberty. It lacks Marx's impassioned concerned for equality and social justice. Feminists have also criticised its assumption of male rule within politics and the family (Pateman 1988). Nevertheless, it remains a remorseless investigation into the logic of public authority. The state of nature operates as a powerful reductio ad absurdum argument for the ubiquity and inescapability of a political world.

So that in the nature of man, we find three principal causes of quarrel. First, Competition; Second, Diffidence; Thirdly, Glory.

The first, maketh men invade for Gain; the second, for safety; and the third, for Reputation. The first use Violence, to make themselves Masters of other mens persons, wives, children, and cattell; the second, to defend them; the third, for trifles, as a word, a smile, a different opinion, and any other signe of undervalue, either direct in their Persons, or by reflexion in their Kindred, their Friends, their Nation, their Profession, or their Name.

Hereby it is manifest, that during the time men live without a common Power to keep them all in awe, they are in that condition which is called Warre; and such a warre, as is of every man, against every man.

(Hobbes 1968: 185)

#### Questions

1 How does Hobbes see the condition of human beings who live in a state of nature, without a state?
2 What does Hobbes see as the sources of conflict between men?
3 Do you agree with Hobbes's depiction of man's character and motivations?

### John Locke

Locke is a political theorist who was closely involved in the development of practical politics in Britain in the seventeenth century. His political thought was concerned to protect the subject from the practical dangers of absolutist kings and has subsequently inspired generations of liberal thinkers to think about the dangers of political despotism. While the precise meaning of the details of Locke's political theory can be difficult to pin down, the overall design is relatively clear in its evocation of a distinct social sphere in which the individual possesses rights which the political authority should not transgress. The notions of individualism and limited government in Locke are themes which can be seen as responses to a specific historical context, but they also relate to contemporary post-Soviet states which are seeking to build civil societies to anchor personal freedoms and to limit the power of their states.

Locke was born in Wrington, a small village in Somerset, in 1632. He was sponsored by a friend of his father's and attended Westminster School and Oxford University. Indeed, Locke was to achieve much in many spheres. He distinguished himself in philosophy and medicine, and developed political interests and a political career in assuming a variety of duties for the Earl of Shaftesbury from 1683. Shaftesbury was the leader of a section of the Whig Party which was opposed to Charles II and his drift towards absolutism and Catholicism. Matters came to a head between 1679 and 1683 when Shaftesbury's faction led a concerted effort to exclude Charles II's brother James, an acknowledged Catholic, from ascending to the throne. This exclusion crisis culminated in the failure of the Rye House plot of 1683, in which the kidnapping of James, the Duke of York, had been planned. Locke followed his patron Shaftesbury in leaving England in the wake of their implication in the act of treason. Following the successful overthrow of James II in 1688 by the so-called Glorious Revolution, however, Locke returned to England, and his *Two Treatises of Government* (1963) was published anonymously in 1689. The *First Treatise* is a rebuttal of Filmer's *Patriarcha*, which had been published in 1680, while the second develops Locke's own account of the nature of government.

Historical scholarship by Laslett (1963) and Ashcraft (1987), amongst others, has established that the *Two Treatises of Government* were in fact composed largely in the years before 1689. Hence Locke's texts were not designed simply to justify the accession of William and Mary in 1688, but to shape opinion so as to precipitate the removal of James II from the throne. Scholarship has thereby revealed a radical edge to the famous political work. Indeed, in Locke's keenness in the *Two Treatises of Government* to decry an overmighty and unlimited government which ignores the rights of property, he displays a very practical concern to limit the power of the prevailing Stuart dynasty. Locke's political interests influence his famous political work rather more than his scientific and philosophical doctrines. Locke's *Essay Concerning Human Understanding* plots limits of human knowledge from a philosophical standpoint, but his famous political work operates with a notion of natural rights which assumes a human capacity to intuit natural law.

## Locke's political thought

Locke is a theorist of a social contract, but he differs markedly from Hobbes in the way he deploys the notion of a social contract. The contract is a device which establishes a political association. Locke begins by imagining men and women in a state of nature, a condition without government. While it is a non-political condition, it is a moral condition. Men in a state of nature are conceived by Locke as equally free, rational and independent. Men can distinguish right from wrong and they can do so because they are conceived by Locke as being able to discern the natural law and the moral obligations deriving from God. The moral obligations deriving from natural law entail that men should respect one another's rights to life, liberty and (material) property, though at times Locke refers to property in a broader sense as a synonym for all entitlements.

The rights to life, liberty and property operate as constraints upon government as well as restrictions on behaviour in a state of nature. For Locke, men agree to form a political society because there are inconveniences in the state of nature, but they do not sacrifice fundamental rights in the transition to government. The inconveniences in the state of nature arising out of the somewhat uncertain enforcement of the law of nature are envisaged as persuading men to set up a government, but the authority of this government does not legitimate transgression against man's natural rights. Political authority, for Locke, is assumed to be a kind of trust whereby each man's right to interpret and enforce the natural law is entrusted to government. Locke, however, was mindful of the possibility of a government abusing this trust and rests the legitimacy of government on the ongoing consent of the people.

While the general outlines of Locke's concern to limit the power of governments are clear, the precise mechanism of how the consent of the people is to be elicited is left unclear. Likewise, the manner in which the people are to be represented politically and the scope of the franchise are not specified. Given the context in which Locke was writing, however, the lack of clarity on these matters is not surprising. Locke was animated by a distrust of the Stuart monarchy, and the *Second Treatise* was concerned to marshal support for his critique of that monarchy and its 'abuse' of power. It is plausible that Locke did not want to alienate potential support by spelling out the specifics of his political theory when he could maximise support by leaving matters vague. Locke concentrated upon constructing a case against a government which abused its trust by relying overly on executive power and transgressing against rights.

Locke's *Second Treatise of Government* is vague on some details, but nevertheless, expresses a powerful statement of limited government. The authority of government is limited by the supposed conditions of its emergence, so that there is to be a continuous recognition of the natural rights of man. Locke's focus upon the limits of government and the rights of man has been lauded by subsequent liberal theorists.

> ### Of the state of nature
>
> To understand political power aright, and to derive it from its original, we must consider, what state all men are naturally in, and that is, a state of perfect freedom to order their actions, and dispose of their possessions and persons, as they think fit, within the bounds of the law of nature, without asking leave, or depending upon the will of any other man . . .
>
> But though this be a state of liberty, yet it is not a state of licence: though man in that state has an uncontrollable liberty to dispose of his person or possessions, yet he has not liberty to destroy himself, or so much as any creature in his possession, but where some nobler use than its bare preservation calls for it. The state of nature has a law of nature to govern it, which obliges every one, and reason, which is that law teaches all mankind who will but consult it, that being all equal and independent, no one ought to harm another in his life, health, liberty, or possessions.
>
> (Locke 1963: 309)

### Questions

1. How does Locke conceive of the law of nature in the state of nature? How does it limit man's freedom to act?
2. Locke derives the rights of man from prohibitions arising out of the law of nature. Do you think there might be other rights besides those relating to life, health, liberty or possessions?

## Jean-Jacques Rousseau

Rousseau was a profound thinker whose radical critique of the tensions and dissonance within civilised society allied to his robust defence of participatory democracy disturbed contemporary social and political assumptions. Indeed, the question of whether or not men and women can be happy and harmonious within a complex materially advanced civilisation reverberates uneasily within today's world of global markets and continued social fragmentation. Likewise, the general sense of political alienation in today's world makes the prospect of radical popular democracy both disturbing and seductive. Rousseau's critique of advanced civilisation is expressed most tellingly in his *A Discourse on the Origin of Inequality*, published in 1755, and his conception of democracy is formulated elegantly and controversially in his *Social Contract* of 1762.

### Context of Rousseau's thought

Rousseau led an extraordinary life, producing a number of literary masterpieces which have exerted an impact on the subsequent development of the autobiographical novel, evident in the work of Proust and Joyce, and on social and political theory, notably in the development of the notion of alienation in the work of Hegel and Marx. Rousseau's heightened sensitivity is expressed most vividly in his reflections on his life and its stresses and strains in his *Confessions* of 1761, but his affective take on his own experience can be seen in his theoretical works.

Rousseau was born in Geneva in 1728, and he was to stay in the city until he was 16 years old, when he wandered off, at first into the arms of a benefactress and subsequently to find fame and notoriety in equal measure in Paris. Geneva and Switzerland were to exert a lasting impact upon his mind. He idealised the democracies which were established in the small cantons in Switzerland, and he savoured the disciplinary, republican regime in Calvinist Geneva. In his political thought he favoured participatory democracy in a small-scale state and the development of a disciplined, virtuous citizenry. Rousseau's republican sympathies, his love of democracy and his espousal of moral renewal through a disciplined ethical regime were also inspired by his sympathy for classical republican states such as Sparta and Rome, which had been nourished by the storytelling of his father.

In the France of the mid-eighteenth century in which Rousseau formulated his social and political thought, he was conscious of and reacted against Enlightenment thought and its celebration of reason. While Rousseau is a theorist who exemplifies a commitment to a life of reason, he is at the same time sensitive to problems which have emerged with the development of civilisation and does not accept the fashionable Enlightenment doctrine of progress. His critical attitude to Enlightenment values can be seen in the shock value of the triumph of his prize-winning essay of 1750, *A Discourse on the Arts and Sciences*, in the competition set up by the Dijon Academy. In the essay, Rousseau depicted the revival of the arts and science as so many garlands of flowers bestrewing the miseries and sickness of civilisation.

Rousseau, in his great work of political theory *The Social Contract*, shows an awareness of recent traditions and developments in political philosophy. The very title of the book intimates its relationship to the works of recent predecessors, Hobbes and Locke. While working with a familiar intellectual model, however, Rousseau refashions it to suggest something new and challenging. Whereas Hobbes had depicted the movement between the state of nature and the setting up of a political commonwealth as one in which covenanters would abstain voluntarily from an ongoing involvement in political decision-making, Rousseau sees the members of a rational and free political association as collectively determining the conditions of their on-going association. Rousseau's thought, however, resembles Hobbes's in so far as his citizens' freedom is a political achievement in which the conditions of a pre-political state of nature do not restrict the pull of democracy, in contrast to Locke's stipulation that a series of rights put moral limits on political action.

## Rousseau's political thought

A major theme within Rousseau's political thinking, and one which resonates in later theorists such as Hegel and Marx, is that of alienation. Rousseau had a profound sensitivity to inauthenticity in himself and others, and he diagnosed the modern world and civilised society as thwarting the free, authentic expression of individuality and identity. In his *A Discourse on the Origin of Inequality* Rousseau develops a history of civil society in terms of the story of human sickness. He posits a state of nature as a device to highlight the distorted condition of contemporary and civilised man. The state of nature is envisaged by Rousseau as a condition stripped of the artifices and conventions which characterise developed societies.

Men and women in the state of nature are seen as simple, free creatures at ease with themselves. Their limited wants are easily satisfiable, so that they are pictured as being content. Again, while men and women in the state of nature are self-regarding, they feel a compassion for the suffering of others. Human beings in the state of nature experience a relatively healthy form of self-love, *amour de soi*. This benign self-regard, though, is turned into a more sinister form of self-love, *amour propre*, in the development of more sophisticated societies. History, for Rousseau, is the story of corruption, whereby a healthy innocence gives way to a corrupt sophistication with the onset of farming and technology. A person's sense of self fragments as wants multiply in the context of a thoroughly social condition in which happiness and self-regard are measured comparatively. The transformation of a world of rough and rude equality into a sophisticated state of social inequality spells the ruin and fragmentation of mankind. A man becomes alien to himself.

The conundrum posed by social development is the context for Rousseau's *The Social Contract* and his *Emile*, an exploration of an ideal form of education, both written in 1762. *Emile* takes for granted the existing political conditions and outlines a form of education enabling the eponymous hero of the book to live well. It articulates a child-centred form of education whereby reason is progressively developed by its deployment in solving problems. At the same time, the child is sheltered from the dangers of easy acceptance of received ideas; he is educated so as to think for himself. None the less, his socialisation and development are structured carefully by his educator. Rousseau advocates a different form of education for women, one designed to refine their distinct sensibilities and prepare them for domestic tasks.

*The Social Contract*, Rousseau's major work of political philosophy, takes men as they are, and frames the logic of a form of political life which would enable men to be free and resolve the problems of social development as they had been diagnosed in the *Discourses*. The terms of a legitimate and free form of political association, set out in *The Social Contract*, amount to the conditions of radical popular sovereignty. The natural independence of man in a state of nature is exchanged for the public freedom of citizenship. Rousseau envisages that in assuming membership of a legitimate political association, men will grant all authority to the state. As it is for Hobbes, sovereignty is an absolute in Rousseau's vision of political association. For Rousseau, however, citizens will participate in the ongoing process of making collective decisions. Rousseau restricts active citizenship to men on account of his conception of the non-rational nature of women.

Rousseau sees the making of collective decisions as conducive to the achievement of a moral form of public freedom. In obeying the state, men are to achieve freedom, because they obey disinterested moral rules of their own making. They are to exercise a general will and not to pursue their own selfish ends. For Rousseau, the remedy for the problems of social life is itself a thoroughly social one. Men are to abandon their natural self-love and independence for the achievement of the social freedom of morality whereby they participate in framing a collective moral world. From this perspective, Rousseau imagines, freedom is not opposed to obedience to law, and he entertains the paradox that men might be forced to be free.

Rousseau's paradoxical formulation of the compatibility of freedom with social force has been criticised for its susceptibility to promote tyranny. The tyrannical tendencies of Rousseau's political thought are compounded by the role he envisages for a legislator whose advice the democratic legislature will follow and for the patriotism engendered by public religious ritual. None the less, Rousseau's clear separation of individual and group self-interest from the public, social good remains a compelling vision of political life. Likewise, his strictures against corporate interests and his espousal of a participative form of democracy continue to be relevant to democratic theory and practice.

*See the discussion of Berlin's (1991) account of positive freedom in Chapter 6.*

There is often a great deal of difference between the will of all and the general will; the latter considers only the common interest, while the former takes private interest into account, and is no more than a sum of particular wills: but take away from these same wills the pluses and minuses that cancel one another, and the general will remains as the sum of the differences.

If, when the people, being furnished with adequate information, held its deliberations, the citizens had no communications with one another, the grand total of the small differences would always give the general will, and the decision would always be good. But when intrigues arise, and partial associations are formed at the expense of great association, the will of each of these associations becomes general in relation to its members, while it remains particular in relation to the State: it may then be said that there are no longer as many votes as there are men, but only as many as there are associations. The differences become less numerous and give a less general result. Lastly, when one of these associations has to prevail over all the rest, the result is no longer a sum of small differences, but a single difference; in this case there is no longer a general will, and the opinion which prevails is purely particular.

(Rousseau 1973: 185)

## Exercise

1 Is there a common interest, distinct from all particular interests?
2 Why is Rousseau against the organisation of particular interest groups and associations? Are his fears about such interest groups plausible?
3 Can political decisions be guaranteed always to be good?

### J. S. Mill

John Stuart Mill was born in 1806, the son of James Mill, who was a friend of Bentham and a political theorist in his own right who subscribed to the doctrine of utility. Mill's life and work were a complex struggle to think through the conditions of his own age, incorporating insights from a wide range of writers. Mill's most celebrated works of political thought, *On Liberty* (1982) and *Considerations on Representative Government* (1972) (written in 1859 and 1861, respectively), offer an incisive analysis of the character of politics and the most pressing needs facing a 'modern age'. Mill's call for a dividing line between where government can legitimately regulate individuals' lives and where individuals are to be left free to pursue their own self-chosen ends resonates in contemporary discussions of the nature of the state.

### The context of J. S. Mill's thought

The context of J. S. Mill's thought reflects a quite deliberate attempt on the part of his father, James Mill, to nurture a thoughtful, reflective child who would be useful to society. J. S. Mill's *Autobiography* (1971), published posthumously in 1873, is an eloquent testimony to his own reaction to his upbringing. Mill recalls a hothouse education whereby he was reading Greek at the age of three, Plato's Dialogues at ten and from an early age was working with his father at logic and political economy. J. S. Mill diagnoses a subsequent personal crisis as arising out of this precocious development of his reason and which he was to overcome by turning to his under-developed emotional side and engaging with the Romantic poets. J. S. Mill did not reject the utilitarian code to which he subscribed from an early age, but he modified it, broadening its scope to take account of what he came to see as a complex many-sided world of experience.

J. S. Mill positively sought to assimilate a wide range of intellectual influences to enable him to understand a complex present, designating his mature standpoint 'practical eclecticism'. The early assimilation of political economists, notably Ricardo, and utilitarianism left permanent impressions on his thinking. He revised utilitarianism, however, to incorporate qualitative distinctions between types of pleasure, so that rational pleasures counted for more than bodily pleasures. He also allowed for the idea of progress so that he applied the principle of utility differentially to political societies at different stages of development.

His sensitivity to historical development was deepened by his reading of Comte and Carlyle. De Tocqueville's warnings about the dangers of conformity and repression in a 'modern age' of equality and von Humboldt's eloquent advocacy of individuality and individual freedom contributed to Mill's distinctive political standpoint, which emphasised the importance of cultivating individuality in an age of gathering social pressures upon the individual. From Coleridge he gained an understanding of the important role to be played by a rational elite who might trace pathways of enlightenment within society.

## Politics and society

Mill's most celebrated work of political theory is *On Liberty*, which is a masterpiece in terms of its economical and elegant defence of the importance of individual liberty and his analysis of where the line between legitimate governmental regulation and individual liberty is to be drawn. Mill defends individual liberty on the grounds that social freedom is required by the principle of utility, taking man as a progressive being, because he holds that without the liberty to experiment in lifestyles, conduct and thought there would be no possibility of progress in human affairs. His portrayal of individuality, however, is sketched in such glowing colours that it would seem to possess a value which supersedes reckoning in terms of its outcomes. Against a backdrop of recognition of the gathering dangers of social conformity, Mill articulates the ideal of personal autonomy.

Mill also proposes an economical criterion for distinguishing when an individual's actions should be subject to regulation by the laws. He urges that an individual should be free to do whatsoever s/he wishes save when her/his actions harm others. The notion of harming another's interests is invoked to stipulate when conduct should be subject to legal constraint, for if an action harms another it is manifestly not simply the business of the individual concerned. In framing this criterion for the legitimacy of the exercise of coercion by the state, Mill trades upon a controversial distinction between self-regarding and other-regarding actions. Self-regarding are those private actions of an individual which do not concern others, and other-regarding actions are those which impinge on the interests of others. This distinction is a notoriously tricky one to draw. In important senses no man is an island and seemingly private matters, for instance concerning jokes one might relate and tastes one might indulge, help to create a social climate which affects others. None the less, Mill's concern to designate a certain area of one's life distinct from the purview of government is attractive in a century which has witnessed grotesque political infringements of personal liberty.

Mill's views on liberty are complemented by his views on democracy. In *Considerations on Representative Government*, Mill urges that a representative democracy is the best form of government. It promotes rationality and public-spiritedness by calling upon the electorate to consider public issues in a rational spirit. Mill favours widespread and active involvement in politics at many levels. In the context of nineteenth-century Britain, however, he does not advocate complete popular franchise. He recommends that the test of literacy should be administered as a determinant of the right to vote to ensure that the electorate is able to engage in rational consideration of issues. Additionally, Mill stipulates that extra votes should be extended to the most rational sections of the electorate (graduates and property owners) to ensure that the many do not drown out the voices of the better-educated few. While Mill recognises representative democracy as the best form of government, he considers that it can only be the mode of government for a nation which has progressed to the point where its members are sufficiently educated to accept the responsibilities of citizenship. In the context of a society sufficiently developed to sustain representative democracy, Mill urges that women as well as men should have the vote. Indeed, Mill's work *The Subjection of Women* is a pioneering example of a feminist argument, in which women are presented as suffering from inequality in legal and political terms and it is seen as wholly against the general utility for women to be so discriminated against. Women, like men, are seen by Mill as capable of rational behaviour; their inherent rationality, however, has not been nurtured by an appropriate education.

Like other tyrannies, the tyranny of the majority was at first, and is still vulgarly, held in dread, chiefly as operating through the acts of the public authorities. But reflecting persons perceived that when society is itself the tyrant – society collectively, over the separate individuals who compose it – its means of tyrannising are not restricted to the acts which it may do by the hands of its political functionaries. Society can and does exercise its own mandates: and if it issues wrong mandates instead of right, or any mandates at all in things in which it ought not to meddle, it practises a social tyranny more formidable than many kinds of political oppression, since, though not usually upheld by such extreme penalties, it leaves fewer means of escape, penetrating much more deeply into the details of life, and enslaving the soul itself. Protection therefore against the tyranny of the magistrate is not enough: there needs protection also against the prevailing opinion and feeling; against the tendency of society to impose, by other means than civil penalties, its own ideas and practices as rules of conduct on those who dissent from them; to fetter the development, and, if possible, prevent the formation, of any individuality not in harmony with its ways, and compel all characters to fashion themselves upon the model of its own.

(Mill 1982: 63)

## Exercise

1 Why does Mill fear the tyranny of the majority?
2 In what ways can majority opinion assert itself?
3 Has the power of majority opinion decreased or increased since Mill's time?

### Karl Marx

Karl Marx has exerted a massive influence on modern social and political theory and practice. Revolutions have been carried out in his name, states have purported to be governed according to his principles and some of the most sophisticated and subtle theorists of the twentieth century, such as Adorno, Lukács and Sartre, have self-consciously theorised in a Marxist tradition. Marx combines intricate analysis of economic and social forms with clear-cut propagandistic messages to galvanise mass support. He relates politics to the structures of power within social and economic practices and offers a uniquely focused analysis and critique of the practices of work, which are generally overlooked in theories of politics.

## The context of Marx's thought

A useful shorthand formula to appreciate Marx's intellectual context is the celebrated notion of Lenin's that Marx combined German philosophy with English (Scots is a more apt depiction) economics and French politics. The German philosophical background imparts a holistic conceptual framework to his theorising in which rival positions are assimilated rather than merely negated. His detailed study of the classical political economists both promoted and reflected his close analysis of the economic system. French political thought and practice inspired the revolutionary impulse within his writings.

The specific context within which Marx operated at the outset of his intellectual career was the break-up of the Hegelian philosophical school. Hegel's philosophy had been balanced delicately between heaven and earth, the status quo and critique, and systemic determinism and openness. On his death the different sides of Hegelianism took wing. Right, or Old, Hegelians interpreted Hegelianism as supporting faith in Protestantism, maintaining an uncritical allegiance to an increasingly reactionary Prussian state and imagining that world history had ended, in the sense that there was no scope for further significant development. The Young, or Left, Hegelians looked at things differently. They saw the spirit of Hegelianism as a critical one in which existing political arrangements and forms of faith should be criticised. They did not see the present as the end of history but rather looked to the future and a reformed political life. Significantly, Feuerbach, of the Young Hegelians, turned his critical powers against Hegel's philosophy, and in his *Principles of the Philosophy of the Future* (1966) he condemned Hegel for reducing the status of man by making him the object of abstract Reason. For Feuerbach, man rather than God or Reason must be the subject of philosophy and social life. Feuerbach's humanism was an immediate inspiration for Marx's *Economic and Philosophical Manuscripts* of 1844, in which Marx brilliantly theorised the conditions of modern capitalism as constituting the alienation of man from his own activity and creations.

Marx, like Feuerbach, was keen to break with Hegel, but his ties with Hegel were never severed entirely. He developed a more historical perspective on social and political life than Feuerbach, and in so doing explicitly followed Hegel in seeing man as essentially an historical being. In *The German Ideology* of 1845–6 Marx presents himself as a materialist in contrast to Young Hegelians like Bauer, but he also styles himself a materialist historian, breaking with an unhistorical essentialist humanism. Marx's materialist perspective was advanced by his study of political economy. The *Economic and Philosophical Manuscripts* interrogated and criticised the

For accounts of the Hegelian continuities in Marx's early and late works, see G. K. Browning (1996) 'Good and Bad Infinites in Hegel and Marx' in I. Hampsher-Monk and J. Stanyer (eds) *Contemporary Political Studies*, vol. 2, Exeter: PSA; (1993) 'The German Ideology: The Theory of History and the History of Theory', *History of Political Thought* XIV(3).

assumptions of the political economists. In a similar fashion, Marx's *Grundrisse* (rough draft of *Capital*) and *Capital* (1979) itself (the first volume of which was published in 1867) worked with but critically examined the assumptions of the political economists.

Marx's writings reflect the exigencies of political circumstances and the demands of movements, as well as the impact of philosophical and economic theorising. Examination of workers' conditions confirmed Marx's appreciation of the importance of the world of work and the interests of civil society as opposed to the formal political world which Hegel saw as the crowning glory of social and political life. The most famous single work of Marx and Engels is *The Communist Manifesto* of 1848, which in fact first appeared as a work written by the Communist League, a small political group of communists. It was published as a position statement for the group in the turbulent revolutionary atmosphere of 1848. Many of Marx's works respond similarly to specific circumstances and situations. For instance, Marx wrote *The Civil War in France* on behalf of the International of Working Men so as to memorialise the Commune of 1870 as a symbolic triumph for the working class.

Much of the difficulty of coming to terms with Marx's thought is to bring together and evaluate an enormous body of writings which were inspired by a diversity of contexts and which expressed a variety of purposes. *Capital*, for instance, is a work of immense theoretical energy devoted to unmasking the laws of motion of the capitalist political economy. Its scope and density contrast with those of journalistic pieces occasioned by political events in the British Empire and in British domestic politics.

## Marx's social and political theory

In the *Critique of Hegel's Philosophy of Right* (1843) Marx developed a sharp critique of Hegel's political philosophy. He criticised Hegel for supposing that the political activities of the state can be seen as superseding the private interests of civil society. For Marx, the private interests of bourgeois society are dominant, and the bureaucracy of the state, far from establishing a general, popular interest, distorts matters by operating in terms of its own separate interest. Marx advocated the overturning of bourgeois civil society and the establishment of a true democracy in which there would be popular control over social and economic activities. The radicalism of his critique of prevailing social and political life informs the *Economic and Philosophical Manuscripts*, where communism is seen as the radical antidote to the world of alienation set in motion by capitalist social relations.

Alienation is the key concept of this early critique of capitalist society. It is seen as being generated in the process of production, the crucial site of human interaction. Capitalist production is explained as setting human beings against the very process of production itself. Production, for Marx, is the sphere in which men and women can develop their humanity; human capacities can develop only by their use in productive activity, just as needs and powers only increase with the expansion of a productive system. But in a system of production where ownership is divorced from the act of production and objects are produced for profit in distant markets, those engaged in production neither flourish nor enhance their capacities. For Marx, workers under capitalism are alienated from the process of production, the objects they produce, their fellow human beings and their generic identity as creative beings who can produce freely and according to general, non-limited criteria. Marx's diagnosis of the alienation men and women suffer in the productive process and of the hegemony exercised by the owners of capital underpins his reading of the state which had been set forth in his *Critique of Hegel's Philosophy of Right*. The state and politics are seen in relation to the power and alienation prevalent in the economic sphere. Politics is the set of public power relations which underpins and supports the dominance of private, class interests in the economic sphere.

In *The Communist Manifesto* Marx and Engels set out a programmatic and propagandist account of history, society and politics which epitomises Marx's standpoint on power relations. Marx and Engels set out a theory of history in which changes in the sphere of production, and more particularly contradictions between the patterns of ownership and the forces of production, generate historical change. The capitalist mode of production is presented as obeying the general law of historical change; capitalist relations of production are held to have incubated a massive promotion of productive forces, but in so doing are shown to have dug their own grave. Capitalism, according to Marx, has produced a class of workers – the proletariat – which is a revolutionary force. The misery and the exploitation suffered by the proletariat are invoked to explain why the proletariat will break with prevailing social and economic conditions, and undertake a communist revolution after which the producers *en masse* will control society. The political dimension of this Marxist viewpoint is hammered home. Politics has hitherto reflected class interests, with the dominant class in production controlling the state. For Marx, the proletariat must take over the state to construct a communist society.

There are many questions which can be asked about Marx's theory of history and the state. The answers which have been offered are by no means definitive. In more particular writings on the state and on history, Marx qualifies the sweeping nature of the account of society and history given in *The Communist Manifesto*. The state is seen at times as the site for complex wrangles between classes, and history is also seen as allowing for a variety of types of cause. The broad vision of Marxism, however, remains constant. The proletariat has a mission to destroy capitalism and usher in a new world of communism. Likewise, his early account of alienation informs the understanding in his later writings of the distortions of capitalist society. In *Capital* Marx gives a detailed account of how profit represents the surplus value exploited out of labour power and of how capital is beset by inner contradictions exemplified in periodic crises and a declining rate of profit. Capitalism is portrayed as a decaying system to be replaced by the communal organisation and development of society, in which there will be no classes.

For the continuity of Marx's views on alienation, see Arthur (1986).

> The history of all hitherto existing society is the history of class struggles. Freeman and slave, patrician and plebeian, lord and serf, guild-master and journeyman – in a word, oppressor and oppressed, stood in constant opposition to one another, carried on an uninterrupted, now hidden, now open fight, a fight that each time tended either in a revolutionary re-constitution of society at large or in the common ruin of the contending classes.
>
> In the earlier epochs of history, we find almost everywhere a complicated arrangement of society into various orders, a manifold gradation of social rank. In ancient Rome we have patricians, knights, plebeians, slaves; in the Middle Ages, feudal lords, vassals, guild-masters, journeymen, apprentices, serfs; in almost all of these classes, again, subordinate gradations.
>
> The modern bourgeois society that has sprouted from the ruins of feudal society has not done away with class antagonisms. It has but established new classes, new conditions of oppression, new forms of struggle in place of the old ones.
>
> (Marx and Engels 1973: 67–8)

## Exercise

1 Express in your own words what Marx and Engels mean by class struggle.
2 How do Marx and Engels express the importance of history in their analysis?

## The limits of Western political thought

### Women and political thought

Gender is now considered to be an important aspect of politics, and it is relatively rare for contemporary theories of politics to ignore issues of gender. They are raised at all levels of political thinking. The British Labour Party has been exercised recently by the goal of promoting greater numbers of women MPs. Western institutions and practices are examined to ensure that they accord an equality of opportunity to women in relation to men. The order and conventions of family life have been challenged and changed. While only a minority of men and women would accept the radical feminist slogan that the personal is the political, questions of power and authority in relationships and families are now debated. Moreover, the 'patriarchal' bias of the law is the subject of contemporary debate. The treatment of domestic violence and the punishment of rapists are areas of the law which are seen as raising gender issues.

*See the discussion of feminism in Chapter 8.*

The contemporary impact of feminism has led political theorists to consider the issue of gender equality in an explicit way, which contrasts with the tradition of Western political philosophers. Hobbes and Locke, for example, assumed that the social contract is a device operated by men and they reserved political power for men without explicit justification of this restriction. Indeed, Pateman, a contemporary feminist, has observed that the gender inequalities entertained by Hobbes and Locke are at odds with the principle of equality they maintain explicitly (Pateman 1991). This discrepancy is to be explained by the contextual influence of a patriarchal social order whose assumptions were accepted by the theorists. The distinct context of contemporary feminist historians of political thought allows for an interrogation of past Western political theory and practice which reveals the gender bias unthinkingly entertained by past theorists. Okin, for instance, has observed the limitations of past theorists by exploring how their texts and arguments might have been different if gender equality had been accepted. In this light, Rousseau's espousal of participatory democracy is seen to trade upon women undertaking time-consuming domestic tasks (Okin 1980).

The current sensitivity to the prevalence of gender inequalities also engenders a reassessment of past theorists who argued for sexual equality. Mill, for instance, has been seen as a feminist, but from the standpoint of late twentieth-century radical feminism his easy acceptance of differentiated lifestyles for men and women points up the limits of his feminism. Again, Marx urged that men and women should be equal, but feminists today have criticised his failure to see gender as an irreducible category of social inequality.

The gender partiality of past theorists in the Western political tradition signals the contextual limits in which political thought takes place. Assumptions about gender are not universal; they reflect thought and practice at particular times and places. A feature of the tradition of Western political thought is that it has become increasingly sensitive to issues of gender. The correlation of changing patterns of thought to changing contexts of social and political life corroborates the standpoint of contextualist historians of political thought. It also illustrates the significance of the context of an historian of political thought, and the insights into questions of gender and political organisation generated by feminist rereadings of past male theorists attests to the significance of past political thought for today's political questions.

---

**THINK POINT**
- Given the feminists' recognition of the political dimensions of practices and institutions previously not seen as political, do you think we should adopt a broader notion of what should count as political thinking and the history of political thought?

---

## Islam

A relatively unexamined feature of most histories of political thought is their exclusively Western orientation, reflecting Western contexts of authors and markets, and assumptions of Western political and intellectual dominance. The assumptions arise out of the Western development of key features of the 'modern' world. The Western path to modernity, incorporating industrialisation, continuous technological development, assiduous promotion of market values and the ascendancy of secular political ideologies, has been followed by a range of non-Western nations, such as China, India, South Korea and post-colonial African regimes. The world today, however, is reverberating with the challenge of a distinct pattern of political thought, political Islam, which is non-Western in its provenance and in its general character.

Islam is the second largest religion in the world; it is growing rapidly and shapes the politics of Iran, a decidedly anti-Western nation, and is a major political force in Iraq, Pakistan and Algeria, as well as exerting an influence in the USA and a variety of other European, Asian and African nations. The anti-Western tenor of much of contemporary political Islam highlights the specifically Western character of the tradition of political thought in the West. While Islam is a religion, it differs from the Christianity of contemporary Western states by making holistic claims upon individuals which are to be achieved through political regulation.

All Muslims are fundamentalists in that they follow the words and doctrines of the Koran, but the distinguishing aspect of self-styled Islamic fundamentalists is that they see Islam as a dynamic force to shape all contours of political life. They wish to see a zealous religious spirit dominate and renew political life. In so far as fundamentalist political Islam challenges the prevailing order and looks for a spiritual and practical rebirth, it necessarily challenges the prevailing order which has been shaped by Western dominance. Political Islam and its fundamentalist spirit challenges the liberal temper, global capitalism and its socialist critique. The anti-imperialist character of political Islam was seen at the beginnings of the revival of fundamentalist Islam in the aims of the Muslim Brotherhood which was set up in Egypt in 1928. The Muslim Brotherhood sought a revivified Islamic faith to break with neo-colonialism and chart a socio-economic course distinct from Western forms of socialism and capitalism. It urged the revival of non-Western traditionalist patterns of family and social life.

Fundamentalist political Islam made relatively little headway in the Arab world until the 1970s and the discrediting of neo-socialist Arab regimes due to their inability to defeat Israel and continued dependence on a Western economic order. In the aftermath of the successful Iranian revolution of 1979, the spiritual and political hegemony in Iran exercised by Ayatollah Khomeini provided a focus for the loyalties of political Islam. Iran became the centre of fundamentalist Shiite Islam. Shiite Muslims are distinguished from Sunni Muslims by their belief in the infallible Imam, who they claim possesses authority in an unbroken line of divinely inspired succession dating back to Mohammed himself. Political power in Iran became focused upon the Islamic Revolutionary Council dominated until his death in 1989 by the Imam, Ayatollah Khomeini. Draconian laws were introduced regulating all areas of social and political life. In stark contrast to the development of radical feminism in the West, the Iranian regime controlled how women should be dressed. The intransigent hostility of fundamentalist Islam to Western modes of political thinking was demonstrated in 1988 by Khomeini's issue of a fatwa (death sentence) against the westernised author Salman Rushdie.

*See Chapter 6 for a detailed analysis of the Rushdie case.*

While the radicalism of the Iranian regime has been tempered by the passage of time, political Islam continues to challenge the assumptions and insularity of Western political thought. Distinctive Western political values such as individual autonomy, participative democracy, freedom of speech and gender equality are shown to lack universality in relation to Islamic support for traditional forms of moral and social behaviour. The challenge presented by a radically distinct political tradition has inspired some subtle contemporary modes of political thinking in the West which want to take account of cultural differences (Parekh 1983; I. Young 1990). Again, the problems and challenges presented by non-Western cultures have contributed to the development of a postmodern rejection of Western rationalism and triumphalism (Lyotard 1984).

## Conclusion

The closing reference to postmodern political thought brings this study of political thought up to date. Postmodernism, is, amongst other things, a reaction against the supposed universalism of Western political philosophy. But this reaction against the Western political tradition does not mean that we can flourish without knowing that tradition. The tradition rests upon contingent contextual foundations which explain textual silences entertaining patriarchy and which ensure that the work of political philosophy ever remains to be accomplished. None the less, our understanding of political liberty, rights, the relationship between work and politics, democracy and the necessity of the state is deepened by an awareness of the political thinking of philosophers such as Mill, Marx, Rousseau and Hobbes.

## Further reading

It is recommended that students have a look at the classic texts of of political philosophy. These texts come in a variety of editions, which reflects their ageless popularity. In this chapter the following were discussed: Plato, *The Republic*; Hobbes, *Leviathan*; J. S. Mill, *On Liberty*; K. Marx and F. Engels, *The Communist Manifesto*; J. Locke, *Two Treatises of Government*; and J.-J. Rousseau, *The Social Contract*. The following classic political philosophers and texts should be added to the list: Aristotle, *The Politics*; Machiavelli, *The Prince*; G. Hegel, *The Philosophy of Right*. Other classic thinkers could be added. Below are listed some works on the nature of political thought and the history of political thought which will be interesting and useful.

Ball, T. (1995) *Reappraising Political Theory*, Oxford: Oxford University Press. A lively book which engages in critical reflection on the nature of political theory and also suggests the fascination that can be exerted by the rethinking of interpretation of political philosophers.

Hampsher-Monk, I. (1992) *A History of Modern Political Thought*, Oxford: Blackwell. An excellent, well-informed account of a number of classic political philosophers.

Lively, J. and Reeve, A. (1989) *Modern Political Theory*, London: Routledge. A selection of articles on classic political theorists put together with clear, straightforward introductions to those theorists.

Oakeshott, M. (1962) *Rationalism in Politics and Other Essays*, London: Methuen. A very lively set of essays which add up to an elegant defence of a particular philosophical reading of politics which is at once entertaining and provocative.

Plamenatz, J. (1961) *Man and Society*, 2 vols, London: Longman. A lively review of the thought of classic political theorists in which the texts of past theorists are seen as speaking for themselves, to the extent that they can be understood and appraised by philosophical questioning without resorting overly to their historical contexts.

Pocock, J. (1972) *Politics, Language and Time*, London: Methuen. An interesting collection of essays on the history of political thought, which advocates a plausible line on contextualism.

Tully, J. (1988) *Meaning and Context – Quentin Skinner and his Critics*, Oxford: Polity. A collection of important essays by Skinner on the history of political thought, and some critical essays on Skinner's work by leading critics.

Williams, G. (1991) *Political Theory in Retrospect*, Aldershot/Vermont: Edward Elgar. A short guide to classic political philosophy. It is well written but very introductory, and the big problems of interpretation are not dealt with.

# 8 POLITICAL IDEOLOGIES

*Gary K. Browning*

**Introduction**

**The nature of political ideologies**

**Political ideology and history**

**Left and right**

**Liberalism**

*The origins of liberalism*
*Liberalism in the twentieth century*

**Conservatism**

*The nature of conservatism*
*Styles of conservatism*
*The success of conservatism*

**Socialism**

*Forms of socialism*
*Socialism and its development*

**Fascism**

*The nature of fascism*
*The development of fascism*
*Fascism in Nazi Germany and Mussolini's Italy*

**Nationalism**

*The development of nationalism*
*Explanations of nationalism*

**Feminism**

*Liberal feminism*
*Socialist feminism*
*Radical feminism*
*Postmodern feminism*

**Ecologism**

*Varieties of ecological standpoints on society, economy and politics*

**Conclusion**

**Further reading**

# Political ideologies

## Introduction

In this chapter, political ideologies are examined. It begins by reviewing the nature of political ideology, considering the history of the term and significant theoretical accounts of its identity. Once a framework is established to understand the nature of **political ideologies** and to appreciate the contested character of their identity, the rest of the chapter is devoted to presenting short accounts of the most significant political ideologies. Evidently, in one chapter only a brief introduction to specific political ideologies can be given. Brevity, however, can be a virtue as well as a vice, and the object of this chapter is to enable students to have an overall view of political ideologies and of the leading political ideologies. This overview should help students see the wood for the trees, and subsequently they can consult some of the excellent detailed studies referred to during the chapter.

**Political ideologies** Sets of political beliefs involving programmes of political action which draw on large-scale views about human nature and/or historical development.

## The nature of political ideologies

Ideology is a disputed concept; its meaning is not transparent. In the past many prominent theorists and commentators on ideology have cast doubt on the worth and integrity of the language of ideology. Many theorists warn against taking ideologists at face value. Sophisticated theorists offer delicate theories to undermine the very possibility of making the universal claims about politics made by classical ideologists, and in the bruising business of everyday political rhetoric, ideology is seen as being a political recipe cooked up by fanatics of the left and right.

The word ideology first came to prominence in the work of Antoine Destutt de Tracy, a figure of the French Revolution and Napoleonic France. He shared the optimistic attitude of the Enlightenment and thought that life would be improved if we could become clear about ideas and reality. Ideology, for him, represented the scientific approach to ideas whereby their links to real needs could be made plain. His optimistic faith in ideas soon ran counter to the practical needs of Napoleon, who castigated the impracticalities pedalled by ideologists. The negative estimate of ideology and ideologists has been common since Napoleon's time.

Marx and Engels are perhaps the most famous of all theorists of ideology, and they were resolute in their deprecation of the status of ideology. For Marx and Engels, in *The German Ideology*, ideology represents a distortion of the relationships forged in the productive process, and an account of history which took seriously the pronouncements of ideology would be both abstract and misleading. Ideological positions function as smokescreens for material interests; behind pious prayers, legal codes and moralising sermons, tangible benefits to groups or classes are held to lie (Marx and Engels 1973b).

Likewise, for the modern conservative theorist Minogue, ideological language is a suspicious form of currency, and the irony here is that Minogue sees Marx and Engels as prime exponents of the dark arts of ideological manipulation (Minogue 1985). Minogue holds that ideology essentially represents the deployment of abstract theorising to the complex world of concrete political action and that this process is inevitably one in which there is alienation from the practical world in which human beings are at home. For Minogue ideology is a dangerous fantasy, an escape from the realities of practical life, in which concrete safeguards of human freedom and political action are set aside for the pursuit of imaginary utopias. For Marx and Engels ideology is the distorted world where real class interests are dressed up as norms and laws for societies where the majority has suffered hitherto from privileges afforded to ruling classes.

The problem with taking the resolutely negative stance on political ideology exemplified above is that the very language of ideological negation can itself be seen as ideological. Both Marx and Engels and Minogue are concerned to warn their audiences against styles of political argument which they stigmatise as ideological. Marx and Engels are opposed to injunctions to moral, religious and legal norms within societies they diagnose as harbouring structural inequalities of power. Minogue wants to persuade readers to accept a limited style of politics which takes much of contemporary political life as given; he eschews appeals to principle to justify radical change. Their respective standpoints, though, can be seen as ideological in that they are canvassing the acceptability of general ideas about politics. Marx and Engels argue against structural material inequalities of power and Minogue argues for the rule of law and a limited style of politics. Their arguments are classic statements of ideology.

Indeed, in recent years there has been a growing tendency amongst academic commentators on ideology to speak of political ideology in broad terms which encompass a wide variety of styles of thought. The tendency has been to see political ideologies as representing frameworks of thought about politics in which large-scale ideas about human beings and society support more specific ideas about politics which constitute the basis for considered political action. Eatwell's introductory chapter to the recent book *Contemporary Political Ideologies* exemplifies this trend (Eatwell and Wright 1993). He identifies ideologies as involving specific programmes of political action supported by general beliefs about human nature, the process of history and social and political arrangements.

The gathering trend of seeing political ideologies in a non-pejorative way as standing for sets of ideas about politics in which specific proposals are linked to general beliefs about the human condition does not dissolve questions about the legitimacy of ideological language. While political ideologies undoubtedly represent sets of belief of this kind, the character and viability of such ideas may still be questioned. Insofar as ideologies are in the business of framing specific proposals they are necessarily in the game of making value judgements. The criteria for deciding between values are notoriously indeterminate.

---

**THINK POINT**

Ideologies bring large-scale sets of beliefs to bear upon the world of politics. We can't live without these ideas, but we can't decide between them. Consider these beliefs:

- 'From each according to his ability to each according to his need';
- 'I wouldn't sacrifice any part of my personal freedom';
- 'National unity comes before all other values'.

---

In politics there is no clear, uncontroversial way of deciding on the right thing to do. A supporter of the free market, like von Hayek or Thatcher, might see the market as promoting individual freedom and observe the propensity of planning and intervention to lead to coercion and muddle, but a committed supporter of government intervention to supply a just distribution of welfare sees the logic and reasons underlying a different set of values. Just as there is no knockdown way of establishing the cogency of political values, so there is no easy way of disproving political values to which one is opposed. The fascist celebration of aggressive nationalism and elitism might repulse those who are committed to equality between people and nations, but there can be no easy discursive dismissal of the value of exulting a nation and an elite.

## Political ideology and history

Political ideologies, then, are sets of belief about politics incorporating specific proposals and general ideas about human beings. Political ideologists are necessarily involved in the business of making value judgements and supporting these values by argument in a practical world where their proposals about what to do are meant to be taken seriously. The involvement of political ideologies with the world of practice means that they are involved in a world of change. A condition of practical life is that it involves change. Experience is always present experience but it is a present which is constantly changing into the past. This link between political ideologies and a world of change means that political ideologies do not stand still.

Political ideologists are bound up with the business of persuading people of the soundness of their political ideas in a changing political scene. This context of ideological activity explains why political ideologies change over time. Circumstances change with the passage of time, and proposals and ideas canvassed at one time seem inappropriate at another. Practical circumstances also change from place to place, and so ideological views display a local variety. All of the above means that the identity of a political ideology is somewhat problematic for those who like to keep things neat and timelessly tidy. A political ideology like liberalism is not one unchanging essential thing. Mill, in his *On Liberty* (1859), was concerned to carve out an area of private life preserved from state interference, whereas liberals of a succeeding generation began to see the need for the government to intervene, as their most pressing concern, in areas of life traditionally designated as private.

## Left and right

**THINK POINT**
- Consider a range of national newspapers and place them on a political scale of left to right.
- Consider the following politicians and place them on a political scale of left to right: Nelson Mandela, John Major, Bill Clinton, Teng Tsiao Ping.

A changing political landscape and a corresponding ideological innovation lend spice to the language of ideology. Terms like renegade, loyalist, traditionalist, old guard and new guard can spin in the ideological air. Tony Blair can explicitly call for a reappraisal of socialism and of the constitution of the Labour party, but the world of political ideology is constantly undergoing reappraisal. This can be seen by the chequered history of those arch ideological labels 'left' and 'right'. In the nineteenth century the word left stood, among other things, for support for the removal of entrenched privileges and the freeing up of property. The free market was a goal for those who called themselves the left. By the end of the nineteenth century freedom of property was seen by the left as something entrenching inequality, which needed to be rectified by the state. Indeed, attitudes to the state underwent change. In the eighteenth and early nineteenth centuries the left saw the state as entrenching privilege and as inclined to be repressive, but by the end of the nineteenth century many on the left were coming to see the state as an instrument of freedom, as Eatwell has observed (Eatwell and O'Sullivan 1989).

Lukes, in the extract below, defines the left in such a way as to allow for this omnipresent factor of ideological change.

The Left in short denotes a tradition and a project born of Enlightenment and expressed in the Principles of 1789; to fulfil the promises implicit in these by progressively reinterpreting what they consisted in, and moving from the civil to the political to the economic, social and cultural spheres, through political means, by mobilising support and winning power. Often, too often, it has been abandoned or betrayed, by those claiming to pursue it. What I here seek to identify is an ideal-typical Left, the essential elements by virtue of which abandonment and betrayal can be identified as such.

It is a project which has been identified in various ways – in the language of rights, as a story of expanding citizenship or justice or democracy, or as a continuing struggle against exploitation and oppression, as it was by Karl Kautsky when he wrote that the goal of socialism was the 'abolition of every kind of exploitation and oppression be it directed against a class, a party, a sex or a race.' The Left we may say is committed to the progressive rectification of inequalities that those on the Right see as sacred, inviolable, natural or inevitable. It seeks to put things right: to remedy all disadvantages that are naturally or socially caused, as far as is possible and reasonable, so that all may have equal life chances.

(Lukes 1992: 10; reprinted by permission of Steven Lukes)

## Liberalism

A good case can be made for seeing liberalism as the dominant ideology in modern Western states. Indeed, Fukuyama has suggested in his recent work that the story of modern Western history can and must be told as one which recognises the triumph of Western liberal **capitalist** regimes (Fukuyama 1992). The birth and growth of liberalism certainly track the rise of Western powers to industrial, technological and global eminence. Liberalism, like all ideologies, however, has shown different faces of itself at different times and in different places. President Johnson's 'liberal' determination, in the USA of the 1960s, to achieve the Great Society whereby the state would ensure civil rights and social welfare throughout the nation contrasts with the concern to establish individual autonomy and to construe the social good as arising out of the pursuit of self-interest which characterises Adam Smith's (1976) 'liberal' vision of social and political life.

The very success of liberalism across time and space renders difficult the job of summarising its character in a crisp and manageable way. Liberals themselves have sought to characterise it in generally laudatory ways as conducive to the overall happiness and as promoting the independence and progress of men and, latterly, women. Marx and Marxists, on the other hand, have sought to identify the liberal concern to celebrate individuality as a way of diverting attention from the social bases of power. But protagonists and antagonists of liberalism tend to agree that liberalism stands for the organisation of a society which allows for and promotes individual freedom and development. New Deal American liberals and early twentieth-century British liberals may argue for significant state intervention. This intervention, though, is characteristically portrayed as *aiding* individual development; the individual is never considered to be fulfilled by the submerging of her/his individuality in a higher collective purpose. The liberal emphasis on individuality goes hand in hand with the notion that individuals are

**Capitalism** An economic system in which the means of production for the most part lie in private hands and goods and services are bought and sold according to prices determined by a market in which the aim of producers and providers is to make a profit.

231

pre-eminently rational. Individuals are considered to be of the highest value and their value is seen as being displayed in their rational capacities to order and shape their own lives. The rationality of individuals is also held to make a society allowing a maximum of freedom to individuals an efficient one. Liberalism then, is distinguished by its concern to promote a society in which rational individuals can flourish. Individual liberal ideologists, however, will depict this form of society in different ways and favour differing sets of arrangements.

A resounding statement of liberalism's concern to promote and safeguard individuality is given in J. S. Mill's classic account *On Liberty*. It is worth reflecting upon some of Mill's words to appreciate how individual autonomy has been seen as of the utmost importance.

> The object of this Essay is to assert one very simple principle, as entitled to govern absolutely the dealings of society with the individual in the way of compulsion and control, whether the means used be physical force in the form of legal penalties, or the moral coercion of public opinion. That principle is, that the sole end for which mankind are warranted individually or collectively, in interfering with the liberty of action of any of their number is self-protection. That the only purpose for which power can be rightfully exercised over any member of a civilised community, against his will, is to prevent harm to others. . . . The only part of the conduct of anyone, for which he is amenable to society, is that which concerns others. In the part which merely concerns himself, his independence is of right, absolute. Over himself, his own body and mind, the individual is sovereign.
>
> (Mill 1982: 68–9)

## Exercise

1  Consider how Mill is seeking to promote individual autonomy.
2  At the same time consider what criticisms could be laid against this liberal emphasis upon the individual.

### The origins of liberalism

To look for origins is in a sense to look for what cannot be found, as in history all events are connected to preceding and succeeding events. To single out occurrences as causal conditions or originary is to mislead by abstracting from an ongoing stream of events. None the less, to shed light on a set of events or phenomena it can be useful to focus upon a set of changes which can be shown to be important in shaping the identity in question. A significant set of events which are important to an understanding of how liberalism developed are those changes which reflect the demise of the feudal world and the traditional authority of the Catholic Church, the divine right of kings and lordship of feudal barons. The centralisation of monarchical authority, the Reformation and the development of a freer market in goods and labour set the conditions for the flourishing of a liberal society.

The lineaments of a liberal view of government and society can be seen in outline in the thought of Thomas Hobbes, whose great work the *Leviathan* was published in 1651 (Hobbes 1968). While Hobbes deflected to no one in his support for unqualified, absolutist rule, he none the less derived political authority naturalistically from the nature and motivations of individuals. The basis of authority was seen to reside in the needs of individuals to find protection so that their lives could be safeguarded; it was not seen as a privilege dispensed by a divine mandate to a traditional governing class. John Locke, a seventeenth-century philosopher and theorist of politics, can be seen as more clearly preparing the way for distinctively liberal ideas. In his *Two Treatises of Government*, published in 1689, he saw political authority as emerging as the result of a contract between individuals who entrust a government with authority to protect their natural rights (Locke 1963). This government, for Locke, should be representative of the individuals contracting to form a political state. Locke's concern to protect individual rights, his derivation of political authority from the decisions of individuals and his granting individuals ongoing representation all point to a liberal focus upon individuals and their autonomy. In contrast to many subsequent liberals, however, he does not spell out that all individuals should be involved in the process of government. The political rights of women do not receive consideration.

*See the discussion of Hobbes in Chapter 7, pp. 205–7.*

*See the discussion of Locke in Chapter 7, pp. 207–9.*

In the eighteenth century the word liberalism came into common usage; its precise point of origin has been traced to Spain during the Napoleonic wars. Adam Smith, the famous Scottish philosopher, emphasised the importance of a free market for ensuring efficient and effective economic behaviour. This insight into the potentially beneficial effects of the spontaneous, rationally self-interested behaviour of individuals has figured subsequently as an important dimension of liberal thought. It lies behind a liberal notion of the minimal state, in which the job of government is seen as simply upholding a framework of law and order so that individuals can undertake their activities.

Jeremy Bentham, at the turn of the nineteenth century, provided a specific, and influential, ideological endorsement of liberalism. He justified a state of affairs where as much freedom as possible was granted to individuals by arguing that this would promote the general happiness. Individuality and personal autonomy were valued for the beneficial social consequences they were seen as promoting, not because they were seen as valuable in themselves. Bentham's philosophy and defence of liberalism were modified by J. S. Mill, whose classic defence of a liberal society is set out in *On Liberty* (1859). This work is a hymn of praise for an open society in which freedom is granted to individuals to make up their own minds and forge their own lifestyles. Individuals, it is argued, should be released from undue interference by governments and from the weight of overbearing

*See the discussion of J. S. Mill in Chapter 7, pp. 214–16.*

public opinion. While Mill justifies his concern for individual liberty in utilitarian terms which echo Bentham, he takes his standard of utility to be one which recognises man as a progressive being, and in his praise of individuality he values autonomy as being of intrinsic worth (Mill 1982).

By the end of the nineteenth century, a liberal faith in a *laissez-faire* society where there was to be minimal governmental interference in the lives of individuals was shaken. Many liberals in Britain by this time were advocating a more positive role for the state. The state was seen as having a more extensive role in eliminating social evils, such as poverty, unemployment, sickness and ignorance, which were diagnosed as preventing individuals from becoming free. A key theorist who can be seen as developing the ideological basis of this **new liberalism** is T. H. Green, who saw the pursuit of the common good as an individual duty and as something which conduced to freedom. Likewise, the French solidarist thinkers, notably Durkheim, emphasised the state's role in providing social conditions in which freedom could flourish.

**New liberalism** Refers to a strand of thinking which rejected the negative concept of liberty and saw state intervention as expanding liberty in areas like factory legislation.

### Liberalism in the twentieth century

By the mid-twentieth century a vigorous tradition of interventionist liberalism had developed. Keynes and Beveridge were liberal architects of the welfare state in Britain. They were ideologists of the ideas of indicative economic planning and the provision of comprehensive welfare measures to ensure individuals have a secure platform on which to build their freedom. There continued to be advocates of a minimal state amongst liberal theorists, however, notably von Hayek, the Austrian economist and social theorist. He saw the market as the sole way of coordinating human decisions and actions on a social basis which would secure efficiency and freedom. His brand of liberalism, exemplified in *The Constitution of Liberty* (von Hayek 1960), has become fashionable again in the late twentieth century in the wake of misgivings about the effectiveness of Keynesian economic planning and the costs of welfare.

Nozick, in *Anarchy, State and Utopia* (1974), set out an articulate vision of a minimal state which was attractive to Reaganite America. His liberalism was self-consciously set out against the more interventionist liberalism of Rawls, whose *A Theory of Justice* (1971) had received much attention and praise amongst academic political theorists. Central to the vision of both Rawls and Nozick, and of many contemporary liberal ideologists, is the notion of the neutrality of liberalism. There is a contemporary tendency to see liberalism as justifiable because of its refusal to take sides in the disputed question of what counts as a good life; it is seen as allowing individuals to make up their own minds. It remains to be seen whether this defence of liberalism will be strong enough to resist other ideological pressures; there may be a need to justify personal autonomy as a substantive good.

*See the discussion of justice in Chapter 6, pp. 186–90.*

*See the comparative discussion of Rawls and Nozick on justice in Chapter 6, pp. 187–9.*

**THINK POINT**
- Consider what you take to be the major styles of liberal argument.
- What do you take to be the strongest appeal of liberal arguments?

# Conservatism

## The nature of conservatism

To talk of conservatism as an ideology is already to enter into dispute with noted conservative theorists. Gilmour, in *Inside Right*, has urged that conservatism is not a theoretical ideology but a practical attitude which is sceptical of full-blown ideological theories (Gilmour 1978). Oakeshott is a distinguished conservative philosopher who, likewise, has seen the essence of conservatism to reside in its scepticism about the power of ideas, and hence has spurned the ideological label for conservatism (Oakeshott 1962). While there is some basis for this conservative disavowal of ideology, conservatives since the French Revolution have been engaged in defending the established order by appealing to general arguments. Indeed, both Gilmour and Oakeshott can be characterised as being involved in this kind of activity.

Academics, in characterising the nature of conservatism, have often seen its essential character as residing in its recognition of the political significance of human beings' imperfection. Both Lord Quinton and O'Sullivan, in their studies on conservatism, have seen a concern with imperfection as being of moment to conservatives (O'Sullivan 1976; Quinton 1978). It is certainly true, the evident differences between expressions of conservatism notwithstanding, that conservatives are generally keen to decry utopianism or even reformist activity in the name of a practical respect for the inevitable imperfections of human beings. Oakeshott's delicate but sophisticated brand of conservatism is designed to respect the distinctions between theory and practice. For Oakeshott (1962), to look for guidance from an abstract political doctrine is akin to begin cooking armed only with a recipe. The practical activity of cooking demands practical know-how, just as the very practical business of politics demands skills which cannot be translated into an abstract perfectionist theory.

The link between a respect for human imperfection and a distrust of abstract political doctrines had been observed in Burke's famous conservative broadside against the French Revolution.

Conservatism, then, can be seen as an ideology which views human imperfections as laying down limits to political activity, though it must be admitted that there are some conservatives of a liberal persuasion, such as the British Conservatives Peel and Heath, and indeed Thatcher, who are prepared to see politics as a rational activity insofar as it is designed to maximise human freedom. There are also critics of conservatism on the left, from Paine and Marx to Habermas and Rawls, who claim that conservative pessimism provides a cover for acquiescence to fundamentally unfair arrangements benefiting a privileged few.

> The nature of man is intricate; the objects of society are of the greatest possible complexity; and therefore no simple disposition or direction of power can be suitable either to man's nature, or to the quality of his affairs. When I hear the simplicity of contrivance aimed at and boasted of in any new political constitutions, I am at no loss to decide that the artificers are grossly ignorant of their trade, or totally negligent of their duty. The simple governments are fundamentally defective to say no worse of them. If you were to contemplate society in but one point of view, all these simple modes of polity are infinitely captivating. In effect each would answer its single end much more perfectly than the more complex is able to attain all its complex purposes. But it is better that the whole should be imperfectly and anomalously answered, than that while some parts are provided for with great exactness, others might be totally neglected, or perhaps materially injured, by the over-care of a favourite member.
>
> (Burke 1982: 150)

## Exercise

What does Burke consider to be the defects of 'simple' political constitutions which lay down regulations on a reasoned view of human nature?

### Styles of conservatism

Academic commentators on conservatism are united in recognising a number of distinct styles of conservatism. Conservative theorists display distinctive styles in different countries. German conservatives have often adopted a philosophically nuanced form of conservatism which displays a metaphysical and often romantic character. Hegel may be seen as a conservative of this type, constructing an imposing edifice of theory, charting a crisscrossing set of interdependencies between man and nature, and man and man, to point up the need to respect the actual achievements of political life. In France there has been a vigorous tradition of reactionary, religious conservatism such as the ideological formulation offered by de Maistre (1965). The conservative reliance on a notion of human imperfection can lend itself to a religious underpinning. After all, the Bible sees human imperfection in Adam's fall from grace. Religious conservatism is evidenced in the remark-able success of postwar continental Christian democracy – though it must be acknowledged that Christian democracy draws on non-conservative ideologies. This religious conservatism combines a Christian recognition of the limits of human political activity with a Christian-inspired social doctrine which sees a need for the political provision of welfare.

British conservatism reveals a range of different styles. Indeed, a sharp line could be drawn between liberal and one-nation traditions of British conservatism. At the beginning of the nineteenth century paternalistic

Tories like Oastler and Sadler opposed the prevailing harsh conditions in factories and recognised the duty of the social elite to care for the poor and unfortunate. This benevolent and nostalgic conservatism was invoked in mid-nineteenth-century England in the ideas of the Young England Group, whose most famous member was Disraeli. Disraeli, himself, when in office (1874–1880) instituted a whole series of social reforms which testified to his belief in a one-nation conservatism, in which the nation would be united behind a benevolent hierarchy catering for the interests of all. This strand of interventionist conservatism can be seen in the policies of Chamberlain and Baldwin in the interwar years. While their foreign policy of appeasement has been criticised, one of the reasons they were adept at gaining votes within a democratic franchise was that their conservatism appealed to all strands of society. The state assumed new responsibilities in their governments; for instance, new national corporations were set up. Macmillan, a conservative critic of governmental economic policies in the interwar period, called for a new middle way in which governments would intervene to ensure full employment and social justice, thereby anticipating the postwar establishment of planning and an extensive welfare state. Postwar Conservative governments accepted the Keynesian vision of an economic world supervised by government to ensure efficiency and harmony. The full-blown welfare state set up by the postwar Labour government was accepted by these governments.

The one-nation tradition of British conservatism has, however, co-existed with a liberal tradition of conservatism. Peel, refashioning conservatism in the 1830s, accepted the need to reform to appeal to the emerging middle classes. He sought to free markets and rationalise administration, and hence adopted a different standpoint from more interventionist Tories. This liberal dimension of conservatism was given a further edge by the rise of the Labour Party and gathering fears of collectivism at the turn of the nineteenth century. Mallock railed against such dangers in his espousal of limited government. In recent times Powell and Thatcher have been eloquent protagonists of a libertarian form of conservatism. Indeed, Thatcher has helped set an agenda of new right belief in minimal government and free markets throughout the world.

---

**THINK POINT**
- Recall the forms of conservatism referred to in the above discussion. Can you distinguish additional types? Do the various styles of conservatism have very much in common?

---

## The success of conservatism

The electoral success of conservative parties in an age of democracy is in many ways remarkable and testifies to the resourcefulness of conservatism as an ideology. If the French Revolution ushered in the world of ideology, it seemed at the same time to spell the ruin of the *ancien régime* and conservatism. Burke's (1982) ideological *tour de force* in composing a powerful rhetorical counterblast to the forces of change, however, signalled that conservative ideologists were by no means without resources in responding to the challenge of presenting their ideas to a popular audience. Burke's defence of a practical and limited form of politics and his denunciation of the extravagances of radicalism represent styles of argument which have continued to be significant features of conservative ideology.

The secret of conservative electoral success in Europe and the USA in the nineteenth and twentieth centuries has resided in the adaptability of conservative parties and conservative ideology. Conservatives have defended a conception of the state as having a broad and varied role to play in uniting the nation and they have at times sought to popularise themselves by espousing the cause of freedom of the individual in which a very limited role is assigned the state. Again, conservatives have invoked religion, nationalism and authoritarianism to augment their arguments and popularity. Conservative adaptability and realism have ensured that conservatism's appeal remains viable in an age of mass democracy.

## Socialism

### Forms of socialism

Socialism as a doctrine was first explicitly referred to in a journal of the Owenite movement in Britain in 1827. Its roots, however, have been traced back a long way. Indeed, Gray has used the title *The Socialist Tradition From Moses to Lenin* (A. Gray 1968). The roots of socialism have often been seen as extending deep into the past because its emphasis upon cooperation, fairness and equality has long had a missionary appeal. However, its emergence in the direct aftermath of the industrial revolution should not be forgotten. It applied traditional egalitarian moral principles to the set of problems and injustices diagnosed as bedeviling the industrial world of the nineteenth century.

The industrial revolution was seen to have changed society dramatically, opening up new possibilities of wealth but imposing new disciplines and hardships upon the labouring population. The aim of socialism from the early days of the nineteenth century was to refashion industrial society so as to organise industry more rationally and distribute its wealth more fairly. Socialism's spirit of collectivism emerged out of its critique of a situation in which power and wealth were in the hands of relatively few people.

Socialism, however, has been defined in different ways at different times. Perhaps the most serious division in socialism has been between Marxist revolutionary parties and social democratic parties who eschew the use of force. Revolutionary Marxist parties such as the Bolshevik Party in Russia have seen force as a vital means of breaking with the past. They have also developed tightly organised parties committed to breaking with capitalism and all bourgeois political forms. Social democratic parties, on the other hand, have tended to seek an evolutionary development whereby capitalism gradually changes into socialism. Indeed, the post-Second World War German Social Democratic Party announced its acceptance of the capitalist economy in its Bad Godesburg programme and the British Labour Party has recently formalised its acceptance of capitalism. Reformist social democratic parties have been concerned to maintain freedom and establish interventionist measures to secure greater fairness within a basically capitalist framework.

In recent years the ideological condition of socialism has been somewhat uncertain. The rousing days of the New Left in Western countries in the 1960s, the prevalence of Keynesian economic orthodoxy and social democratic governments in Western European countries and the sheer presence of Soviet-style socialist regimes in Eastern Europe had combined to make socialism perhaps the dominant ideology in the first three decades after the Second World War. However, the combination of unemployment and inflation in the 1970s cast doubt over social democratic techniques of economic management and the fall of the Soviet Empire seemed to confirm the bankruptcy of Soviet-style socialism. The event which precipitated the most doubts in socialist heads is perhaps the fall of the Soviet Union. Economic planning has been undermined by the perceived disaster of the Soviet economy. Socialists of all persuasions are now still busy thinking through what economic measures might be able to deliver the promised land of economic efficiency, justice and fairness.

The extract below outlines the economic background to the fall of the Soviet state and President Gorbachev's attempts at reforming the system.

### The Rolling Economic Disaster

It was the First World War which precipitated the collapse of tsardom in 1917. In 1991, it was the union treaty which brought about President Gorbachev's fall. In both cases it was economic crisis that created the conditions for a coup. The real surprise is that Mr. Gorbachev has been able to survive for so long in the face of an economy which has been collapsing day by day and week by week.

Throughout history autocratic regimes have always been at their most vulnerable when they have offered a semblance of political liberalisation but have been unable to deliver higher living standards.

That – despite all the power-broking on the international stage – has been the reality behind the Gorbachev mask. The glasnost process was supposed to march hand-in-hand with perestroika, a fundamental restructuring of the economy. . . . History will probably show that he failed, not for being too radical but for not being radical enough. . . .

The background to the Gorbachev experiment was the growing realization within the political hierarchy that the country's enormous natural resources were being squandered by the inefficiencies of a centrally-planned system which was established by Stalin in the late 1920s and early 1930s and gradually ossified in the decades after the Second World War.

> By the early 1980s it was obvious that the Soviet Union was failing to make the transition from a fairly primitive stage of economic development based on exports of primary products into a modern Western-based economic system.
>
> (Larry Elliott, reprinted by permission of the *Guardian*, 20 August 1991)

## Exercise

1 What criticisms does it make of the Soviet Union and economic planning and President Gorbachev's attempts at reform?
2 Do you consider these criticisms undermine the case for socialism?

### Socialism and its development

Key influences on the development of socialism include the industrial revolution and the rise of capitalism; the simultaneous increase in wealth and productive power and the misery of a newly cohesive working people gave inspiration to a socialist creed demanding a reordering of society to make it fairer. At the same time socialists, from the outset, saw a future socialist society as a more rational one than hitherto existing societies. In their rationalist visions of the future, socialists shared an Enlightenment optimism about the possibilities of reordering society on a rational basis. Again, the example of the French Revolution and the overturning of an entire social and political order inspired many socialists with a sense of revolutionary optimism.

Early nineteenth-century socialists including Saint-Simon, Fourier and Owen were stigmatised as utopian by Marx, and the label has stuck to them. They can be seen as utopian in the sense that they project complex schemes of new social orders in which socialism can be realised. Saint-Simon was inspired by a rationalist vision of a society directed by a series of experts armed with technological and organisational knowledge. Fourier exemplifies a libertarian brand of socialism in that, for him, hitherto-existing society has been emotionally stifling as well as unfair and a future socialist society would be sexually and emotionally liberating. Owen represents a moral vision of a future society organised on a cooperative basis whereby all would share in the wealth of society.

*See Chapter 7.*

Undoubtedly, the central figure in any account of socialism up to the present day is Karl Marx. He is the inspiration for a diversity of socialist developments and styles of thought. He produced a large-scale theory encompassing a wholesale critique of capitalist society. Marx, explicitly in his early writings and implicitly in his later work, offered a theory of alienation whereby men and women were seen as alienated from one another, work, products and their own creative capacities under capitalism. This notion of alienation has subsequently been developed and expressed by a variety of socialists, including William Morris and the prophet of New Left libertarians Herbert Marcuse. Marx also set out a theory of history in which communism is seen as the necessary product of historical development and not as a utopian project. The determinism involved in Marx's sense of history has been criticised by socialists and non-socialists, but in practical terms it has certainly offered hope to a variety of socialists. Marx's theory of politics sees class as the determining factor in political behaviour. Politics, hitherto, is diagnosed as expressing class interests, though Marx envisages a radical form of democracy in which representatives would be directly responsive to electors. Marx's mature economic theory purports to offer a model of the inner dynamic of the capitalist system, spelling out its inevitable downfall. The labour theory of value has been much disputed but the overall historical sense of the growth and development of capitalism has been very influential.

**THINK POINT**
- Does Marx have anything to offer to contemporary socialism?

Since Marx, an important development within socialism has been the emergence of revisionism at the end of the nineteenth century. In 1899 Bernstein produced *Evolutionary Socialism*, which challenged some of the central Marxist tenets of the German Social Democratic Party (Bernstein 1961). Bernstein repudiated the need for a violent break with capitalism to achieve socialism. He saw workers as benefiting from piecemeal advances under capitalism which shouldn't be squandered for participation in an uncertain revolution. He maintained that social justice could be achieved through redistribution under capitalism.

From 1919 there was a split in the world of socialism between highly disciplined Marxist parties following the example of the Bolsheviks and reformist social democratic parties who refused to accept Bolshevik-style discipline and tended to accept an accommodation with liberal capitalist regimes. In Western Europe the social democratic parties tended to flourish, whereas revolutionary Marxist parties were imposed upon Eastern European countries in the wake of the expansion of the Soviet Union. In China and Cuba and some parts of the third world, Marxist revolutionary parties prevailed but usually in the wake of the disorder following war or civil war.

The contemporary doubts about socialism emerge from the evident failure of Marxist regimes in the Soviet Union and Eastern Europe and the faltering ideological voices and electoral performances of reformist parties in Western Europe. The hesitation in the contemporary world of socialism informs the doubts surrounding Tony Blair's project of making the British Labour Party a vehicle for government. The Labour Party achieved successes in the post-Second World War world; the governments of 1945–51 and 1964–70 brought about changes in society developing the welfare state and achieving a measure of social justice. But doubts emerged about the corporatism and state spending associated with these governments and Blair, in remodelling the Labour Party to make it acceptable in the 1990s, is trying to rethink the terms of socialism.

## Fascism

### The nature of fascism

The ideological status of fascism is controversial. Fascism is often used as a term of abuse and nothing more. Bureaucrats and parents are on the receiving end of such abuse, as well as dictators like Hitler and Mussolini. Again, defining fascism is difficult because of the variety of the regimes and movements identified as fascist. The peasant-based Christian Iron Guard of interwar Romania, the reactionary Catholic Action Française of early twentieth-century France and the atheist, racist regime of the Nazis have all been labelled fascist. Despite the profound differences between 'fascist' movements, there have been a number of attempts to identify fascism as an umbrella ideological term.

One way of theorising fascism is to emphasise its negative character, the way it is opposed to enlightenment ideas such as reason, rights, freedom and democracy. It was also opposed to democracy and internationalism. The upshot of this approach, evidenced in the speeches of both Mussolini and Goebbels, is that fascism is presented as an essentially reactionary ideology, reacting against what are usually termed progressive currents of thought.

Some theorists of fascism bow to the difficulties involved in the enterprise, and see fascism as an amalgam of different elements which are arranged distinctly and unevenly in different fascist movements. Eatwell, for instance, sees fascism as assimilating diverse currents evident in other ideologies (Eatwell and Wright 1993) and Wilford stresses its syncretic character (Wilford 1994). These interpretations allow for the specific emphasis upon racism in the Third Reich, the marked statism and corporatism of fascist Italy and the syndicalist currents within interwar Spanish fascism.

Griffin has presented a challenging new interpretation in which fascism is seen neither as a merely reactionary ideology nor simply as a progressive, modernist ideology, but rather as incorporating both of these elements (Griffin 1991). He sees fascism as embracing a form of ultra-nationalism in seeking to refashion the nation through its own dynamic activity. He designates the fascist project of national regeneration as evoking past national glories within a modern context, in that fascist renewal employs forces of modernity such as advanced technology. Griffin's perspective, which centres on the emotive aspects of the fascist project of renewal, allows him to appreciate the mythic dimensions of fascism.

---

**THINK POINT**
- Consider fascist attitudes to the past and the future. Can a case be made for seeing fascism as a progressive force?

---

All of the above perspectives have something to offer. Fascism is certainly an ideology which picks up on a variety of themes and is not instantiated in one set way in all its manifestations. Again, it has mythic dimensions, and fascism derives much of its force from its emotional impact. Also, fascism is undoubtedly defined to some extent by its negation of Enlightenment doctrines. The various definitions examined here should not be seen as exclusive. Populist ultra-nationalism is a concept which, if unpacked, can be seen as involving a rejection of Enlightenment notions. Similarly, a model of fascism must allow for differences of emphasis to accommodate the variety of fascist movements.

## The development of fascism

The history of fascism must recognise the interwar years as crucial. It was in this period that self-styled fascist movements in Italy and Germany came to power. What promoted the rise of fascism in this period were the problems which bedeviled the modern age and which were becoming increasingly apparent by the end of the nineteenth century. The experience of industrialisation and imperialism had brought wealth and glory but, at the same time, had promoted discord, resentment and problems. The grand Enlightenment vision of a rational world of states and peoples in harmony with themselves and one another and who were committed to the peaceful resolution of disputes was threatened by the persistence of discord and the growth of social divisions.

The very ideal of rationality as the emblem of the distinctiveness of humans was being challenged. Nietzsche (1967), most notably, had questioned the disinterestedness of reason in the name of the ubiquity of the will to power. Others had looked to the elemental sense of the nation as the major force in life, and some, such as Chamberlain and Langbehn, had seen race as the primal force of human life. Similarly, the liberal ideal of personal autonomy had been challenged by those who looked to the nation to build up national wealth, in a statist reading of human life in which individuality was downgraded. Fichte (1968) can be seen as a nineteenth-century advocate of this autarchic nationalism.

## Fascism in Nazi Germany and Mussolini's Italy

The divisive and dissonant forces at work in modernity can be seen to have promoted fascism in interwar Germany and Italy. In both regimes there was a deprecation of reason. Force was praised; youth movements and shock troops represented incarnations of the vitality of force. Violence was inflicted upon internal opponents of the regimes, and war was celebrated as the quintessential activity of the nation. Both regimes exemplified an overheated nationalism in which the pursuit of glory justified aggression and violence. Both regimes' aggressive nationalism, cult of the leader and celebration of force were responses to the demands for unity, purpose and strength thrown up by divided and demoralised societies. Both Italy and Germany in the immediate post-First World War period suffered from the anguish of either defeat in the recent war or disappointed victory. Democracy struggled in both countries as social division and economic anxieties mounted.

The affinities between the two regimes and their histories indicated above notwithstanding, there were distinct differences between fascism in Germany and Italy. In Nazi Germany the driving ideological force of the regime was racism. The German nation was organised by an elite and a leader who were determined to achieve a 'true' community of Aryans. The establishment of such a community involved the systematic persecution and subsequent planned extermination of the 'alien' race, the Jews. Jews were depicted as the dark side of the light shining on the Aryan race, and they were excluded from influence and positions within society and were liable to be arrested and sent to concentration camps. The repression and terror exerted against the Jews was of a piece with the dictatorial measures taken by the Nazis to ensure that power in society was concentrated in their hands.

Soon after coming to power the Nazis, under Hitler's leadership, undertook a policy of *Gleichschaltung*, whereby society was coordinated to allow for a concentration of purpose and the elimination of dissent. The ideological aims inspiring the Nazi domination of society were the development of the racial power of the Aryans through internal purification and external expansion through a series of wars. While the power of the Nazis rested upon the force and repression underlying the regime, they also appealed positively to the German people through their promotion of a strong foreign policy maximising the image of German strength and through internal measures designed to boost employment and working conditions.

Fascism in Italy differed from Nazism primarily due to the relative insignificance attached to race as an ideological force within the movement. While in the latter period of Fascist rule and under Nazi influence racist persecution of Jews took place, the regime was not mobilised by the overriding concern to order the social and political world on racist lines. Fascism under Mussolini combined a number of disparate forces: **syndicalism**, a form of socialism where the role of unions is pronounced; **futurism**, an artistic movement celebrating dynamism; recent aggressive Italian nationalism; and more conservative **corporatist** doctrines. The range of influences points to a difficulty in identifying the nature of Italian Fascism; it was an opportunistic movement which under Mussolini's leadership was primarily concerned to gain and maintain power.

What can be said about the ideological distinctiveness of Italian Fascism is that it developed an elaborate version of the corporatist state. Before the end of the Second World War the Italian Parliament was swept away, to be replaced by a system of representation through corporations. While the representative character of the corporatist state was a fiction beneath which lurked the power of the Fascist state and a tyrannical regime, the emphasis upon state organisations in defining the purposes of the individual marks out a distinct expression of fascism. Mussolini and Gentile, the philosophical

*Gleichschaltung* The process whereby all institutions and organisations were coordinated to serve the purposes and goals of the Nazi state.

**Syndicalism** A form of revolutionary trade unionism in which the overthrow of capitalism is seen as arising out of direct action by workers. Sorel, an influential syndicalist, argued for the revolutionary potential of the general strike.
**Futurism** An early twentieth-century movement in the arts which glorified technology, industry and factories.
**Corporatism** The doctrine that major economic interests, such as business and trade unions, should be incorporated into the system of government.

ideologue of Italian Fascism, both identified the Fascist regime as totalitarian, by which they meant to convey the all-encompassing power of the Italian state over the lives of individuals.

What Italian Fascism shares with its Nazi counterpart is elitism, state authoritarianism, an aggressive nationalism promising renewal, and an antipathy to liberal democratic and socialist ideals. The existence of these common ideological values, in combination with a recognition of differences, points up the worth of the general viewpoints on fascism discussed at the outset of this analysis. There is a point to regarding these fascist regimes as exemplifying forms of populist ultra-nationalism in which the rebirth of the nation was seen in emotional terms. The negative standpoint adopted to other ideologies and enlightenment notions is clear and there is a range of values which the two regimes combine in distinct ways.

The commonalities exhibited between Nazism and Fascist Italy justify seeing fascism as a general ideology, differences between its national expressions notwithstanding. The varying extent to which regimes display these features enables the distinction of neo-fascist from fascist regimes. For instance, while the elitism and populist nationalism asserted by the National Front in France are distinctly fascist, its adherence to democracy and the French Constitution qualify its fascism; hence it is more appropriate to label the National Front neo-fascist.

Now the truth is that the State in itself has nothing whatsoever to do with any definite economic development. It does not arise from a compact made between contracting parties, within a certain delimited territory, for the purpose of serving economic ends. The State is a community of living beings who have kindred physical and spiritual natures, organised for the purpose of assuring the conservation of their own kind and to help towards fulfilling those ends which Providence has assigned to that particular race or racial branch. Therein, and therein alone, lie the purpose and meaning of a State. Economic activity is one of many auxiliary means which are necessary for the attainment of those aims. But economic activity is never the origin or purpose of a State, except where a State has been originally founded on a false and unnatural basis. And this alone explains why a State as such does not necessarily need a certain delimited territory as a condition of its establishment. . . . People who can sneak their way like parasites into the human body politic and make others work for them under various pretences can form a State without possessing any definite delimited territory. This is chiefly applicable to that parasitic nation which, particularly, at the present time preys upon the honest portion of mankind; I mean the Jews.

The instinct for the preservation of one's own species is the primary cause that leads to the formation of human communities. Hence the State is a racial organism, and not an economic organisation. The difference between the two is so great as to be incomprehensible to our contemporary so-called 'statesmen'. . . . The sacrifice of the individual existence is necessary in order to assure the conservation of the race. Hence it is that the most essential condition for the establishment and maintenance of a State is a certain feeling of solidarity, grounded in an identity of character and race and in a resolute readiness to defend these at all costs.

. . . the völkisch concept of the world recognizes that the primordial racial elements are of the greatest significance for mankind.

. . . By its denial of the authority of the individual and its substitution of the sum of the mass present at any given time, the parliamentary principle of the consent of the majority sins against the basic aristocratic principle in nature.

(Hitler 1969: 22–5)

## Exercise

1 What 'positive' appeal might Hitler's ideology have had for the German people?
2 What does Hitler mean by 'the völkisch concept of the world'?

## Nationalism

Nationalism is a disputed but undeniably potent ideology of the modern world. Across the globe, political passions are continuously excited by the call of national allegiances. War and civil war in Rwanda, Ireland and Bosnia testify to the impact of the destructive and passionate force of nationalism. The history of the modern world bears witness to the terrible conflicts emerging from the heart of Europe over disputes about national identity and integrity. While disinterested academics (like Kedourie in his book *Nationalism* (1966), might point up the fuzziness of nationalist accounts of political legitimacy, the flesh and blood populations of states are still swayed by appeals to their national character. Part of the suspicion with which nationalism is viewed resides in its capacity to excite passion, myth and emotion, which play unpredictable but significant roles in the economy of human existence.

As a political ideology nationalism must be understood as making claims about politics and how states should be organised. This political doctrine or ideology of nationalism is linked with general patriotic and nationalist notions of support for nations. The ideology of nationalism itself, though, is concerned with the bases of political organisation and government; humanity, for nationalists, is conceived as being divided up into groups, and the nation is taken as the unit for government and political organisation. Hence, the characteristic principle of nationalism is 'national self-determination'.

The central concept of the nation is problematic. It allows for no straightforward definition. A range of diverse criteria are invoked to explain and justify the notion of a nation. Nations are defined in terms of race, culture, religion, language and history. The profusion of constituent ingredients of nationhood tends to reinforce the suspicion that there is no clear way of distinguishing and defining nations. The nationalist move of identifying nation with state presumes that nations should be the appropriate building blocks for territorial units of political life. However, nations and nation-states are often in dispute over territories, and peoples of diverse ethnic allegiances are often set in the same states and intermingle in countless ways; these things render the prospect of states exemplifying a single national identity implausible in the extreme.

## Tragic History Repeats Itself

The war in Bosnia has been raging for two years, but the Balkan peninsula has been a cauldron of ethnic and religious unrest for centuries. The first Croatian areas were unified by King Tomislav (910–28). During the following century, to the east of the river Drina a Serbian state began to expand. An Orthodox Christian Serbian Empire was proclaimed by Stefan Dusan (1331–55), but after his death it fell apart.

Bosnia thrived in the vacuum created by the eclipse of Roman Catholic Croatia and the break-up of Serbia. The Bosnian nobles adhered to a Christian doctrine known as Bogmilism, which was fiercely persecuted by the Catholic Church. By the end of the 14th Century the Turkish or Ottoman empire had advanced into the Balkans, which it occupied for five centuries. The Croats were driven north but most of Bosnia's Bogomils converted to the Turks' Muslim Faith and were left to run their own affairs. Eventually the northern Balkans came under the control of the Austro-Hungarian Habsburg empire and the Balkan people – known as the Southern Slavs – became pawns in the wars between the Ottomans and the Habsburgs.

In 1829 after a war between Russia and Turkey, the Serbs, with Russian support, established a small independent state which they gradually enlarged. To quash nationalist ambitions in the Balkans, the Habsburgs occupied Bosnia-Herzegovina in 1878 and, 30 years later, formally declared it part of Austria-Hungary.

In 1912 the Ottomans were defeated in a war with Serbia, Montenegro, Bulgaria and Greece, and Serbia doubled its size. The Austro-Hungarian government was livid. When, in 1914, a Bosnian Serb assassinated the Archduke Ferdinand, heir to the Habsburg throne, in the Bosnian capital, Sarajevo, Austria-Hungary declared war on Serbia.

Tensions between countries supporting either side led to the outbreak of the first world war, which ended in 1918 with the defeat of Germany and Austria-Hungary. The Southern Slavs combined to form the Kingdom of Serbs, Croats and Slovenes, which changed its name in 1929 to the Kingdom of Yugoslavia (literally the Kingdom of the South Slavs).

In 1941, Hitler's Germany invaded Yugoslavia and left the Ustase, an extreme Croat nationalist movement, in charge of a puppet state that included Bosnia-Herzegovina. The Ustase moved to rid Greater

Croatia of Serbs, Jews, gypsies and anti-fascist Croats by expulsion, mass murder and religious conversion. They were resisted by the Cetniks – committed to Serbian dominance of Yugoslavia – and the Partisans, led by Marshal Josip Broz, a communist, who was later known as Tito. After Germany's defeat in 1945, Yugoslavia was re-established, with Tito as its unchallenged ruler.

After his death in 1980, however, politicians began to use ethnic divisions to claim power. When Slobodan Milosevic gained power in Serbia in 1987 he determined to control all the land where Serbs lived. Ambition to gain access to the rich coastal areas may also have been involved. The first serious sign of Serb expansion was the annexation of the predominantly Albanian province of Kosovo and the illegal installation of governments in the broadly Serbian or Serb-supporting areas of Vojvodina and Monetenegro.

In 1990 an authoritarian nationalist, Franjo Trudjman became leader of Croatia, and in June 1991, Slovenia, in the north-west of Yugoslavia, and Croatia declared independence. Britain and France believed that to recognise Croatia would provoke an escalation of the war. But, by December 1991, the EC gave in to German pressure for recognition, after Croatia gave vague safeguards over minority rights.

However, the Yugoslav army and the Croatian Serbs joined to fight a bloody war in Croatia, in which atrocities were committed by both sides. Areas were 'ethnically cleansed' with people being killed or forcibly removed from their homes and villages. The fighting continued until January 1992 when a ceasefire, patrolled by United Nations peace-keeping forces, was finally put into effect. By then much of Croatia was under Serb control.

Meanwhile a multi-ethnic Bosnia had been moving towards an independence that would be hard to uphold with a Serb–Croat war in progress. Radovan Karadzic, the leader of the Bosnian Serbs, warned that insistence on sovereignty would lead the republic 'into a hell in which the Muslims will perhaps perish'. In April 1992, the EC recognised the new state of Bosnia-Herzegovina, but the weapons of its territorial defence forces had been confiscated by the Serb-controlled army. Hundreds of thousands of Muslims were swept from their homes. Meanwhile, from their hilltop positions, the Serbs rained shells on Sarajevo. At the same time Muslims in Northern Bosnia were being herded into mass prisoner-of-war camps.

Caught between Serbian and Croatian forces carving up most of their country, the Bosnians who remain have been concentrated in five supposedly 'safe' areas, including Sarajevo. There, the UN has sought to provide humanitarian aid, but international uncertainty has allowed a war in which aggression is rewarded to continue up until the present and only partial ceasefire. [The present here is 1994. Since this article was written a USA backed peace initiative has succeeded in maintaining a fragile peace based upon the division of Bosnia.]

(Tony Craig, reprinted by permission of the *Guardian*, 1 March 1994)

## Exercise

1  What do you take to be the main sources of conflict in Bosnia over the centuries?
2  Why do you think ethnic cleansing took place in the states of the former Yugoslavia?
3  Could anything have been done at an early stage by the international community to prevent trouble and war in the former Yugoslavia?
4  Does the fate of the Republics of the former Yugoslavia suggest the utility of strong, authoritarian rule such as that exerted by Tito?

## *The development of nationalism*

Nationalism is a contentious subject, and the history of nationalism is controversial. Kedourie has observed that nationalism is a doctrine invented in Europe in 1789 and spread through the French Revolution (Kedourie 1966). However, the history of nationalism has also been traced back to the great process of nation-building that went on in the early modern world when the European nations of France and England were being consolidated. What can perhaps be said most accurately is that nationalism emerges as a full-blown political ideology at the end of the eighteenth century but that the development of the nation-state in the preceding centuries had prepared the way for its emergence.

The subsequent history of nationalism testifies to its power and variety. Nationalism has developed in a number of different directions and it has been used by a variety of political actors: communists, fascists, liberals, conservatives, imperialists and anti-colonialists. In fact, nationalism epitomises the general trait of adaptability which characterises ideologies. The French Revolution at its outset in 1789 bore liberal political credentials as it called for representative government and respect for individual rights. At the same time it was claimed that sovereignty was vested in the nation; dynastic authority yielded to rule by the nation. The French Revolution set off a series of nationalist revolts in Europe. The association of nationalism with liberal ideas, however, is not inevitable. Ideologies change according to the circumstances of time and place.

The changing face of nationalism can be seen in the history of the turbulent world of interwar Europe. The demands of national self-rule and aggrandisement had been satisfied for successful imperial powers such as France, Britain and Russia. Germany's dissatisfaction with its imperial spoils, coupled with its determination to dominate the heart of Europe, was an important cause of the First World War. Germany's defeat in that war and the subsequent hardships experienced by Germans in the Weimar Republic incubated the aggressive form of nationalism which inspired and was subsequently fostered by the Nazis. Fascism incorporated an intense, aggressive form of nationalism as one of its central features, and this mode of nationalism is quite distinct from more liberal forms of nationalism which respect the civic freedoms of individuals irrespective of their ethnic status.

The Janus-like face of nationalism can be seen in the way nationalism has been invoked by imperialist and anti-imperialist powers. The music halls of England in the late nineteenth century echoed to jingoistic tunes which celebrated nationalism and tales of imperial glory. Russian nationalism demanded imperial conquests, just as the fascist powers sought national redemption in dominance and control over other states. In the aftermath of the Second World War, however, indigenous populations in Asia and Africa sought to free themselves from imperial rule by appealing to the doctrines and myths of nationalism which had been propagated by the imperial powers. The fall of the Soviet Empire was effected by the vibrant force of nationalism which erupted throughout the empire, acting as a fierce rejoinder to the communist project of incorporating disparate nations within a union serving and masking Russian nationalism.

### Explanations of nationalism

There are a number of distinct types of explanation of nationalism, reflecting the variety of explanations which are invoked to explain social and political phenomena. One significant type of explanation is that proposed in different idioms by Gellner (1983) and Giddens (1990). Both see the roots of nationalism as lying in the psychological problems of identity posed by the modern world. For Gellner, modernisation undermines traditional face-to-face relations within societies as centralising technological forces break down the distances between peoples but at the same time destroy specifically local allegiances. He sees the prospect of cultural breakdown being averted by states constructing national identities based on linguistic identities for their own purposes of self-legitimation. Giddens sees nationalism as being promoted by the contemporary impact of globalisation. Technology links up all parts of the globe and compresses both time and space, but at the same time unleashes countervailing forces of opposition to this process. For Giddens, nationalism is a significant force resisting globalisation but being pulled in its wake.

Marxists take a different view of nationalism. Marx saw the development of nation-states as part of the process of constructing capitalism, observing the nation-state's role in securing markets and centralising communications. Nationalism, according to this logic, is the ideology equipped to justify the nation-state, which develops for essentially economic reasons. Lenin's theory of imperialism is a development of this theme. For Lenin, nation-states, in so far as they are concerned to promote economic development within their states, come into conflict with other nation-states as they scour the world for markets and raw materials. Imperial wars are therefore testimony to the destructive force of nationalism and developed capitalism.

The Marxist account of nationalism has the evident merit of linking the phenomenon of nationalism with processes of modernisation and economic development. Economic interest often lies behind nationalist rhetoric. The

USA's concern to maintain freedom and ward off the threat of communism after the Second World War was not disinterested. It had much to do with the economic interests of large corporations within the USA. The Marxist tendency to discount the political imperative to express and organise institutional representation of culturally recognised affinities between people, however, is unconvincing in the light of inter-class expressions of cultural solidarity amongst people of the same nation or culture.

Kedourie's famous book on nationalism emphasises the power of ideas in politics in that it points up the fatal attractiveness of nationalist ideas, notwithstanding the impossibility of fixing upon an uncontroversial account of the nation. Other accounts of nationalism, such as Antony Smith's (1971), point up the role of politics in explaining nationalism. Nations and nationalism, in this perspective, are promoted by political actors to provide coherence and purpose for political movements and states. Hobsbawm (1990) has written persuasively to support the notion that myths and conceptions of nationality are often the product of political engineering.

The truth about nationalism is not easily expounded. It is a political phenomenon which has been expressed in a variety of ways; its protean character testifies to its power and impact. Given its variety and fecundity no single explanation can account for it. Economic, political, ideological and cultural forces can be seen to contribute to its development and continued impact. The processes of globalisation which are deepening and facilitating communication between parts of the world exemplify the complex forces promoting nationalism. The increasingly global nature of economic and cultural activity has promoted supranational political initiatives such as the European Union, but it has also inspired cultural resistance to globalism, which has entrenched nationalist politics in Britain just as it has in Iraq. Globalisation therefore exhibits an intricate pattern of economic, political and cultural interaction which both opposes and promotes nationalism.

---

**THINK POINT**
- Consider the explanations of nationalism set out above. What are their main strengths and weaknesses?

---

## Feminism

Feminism is an ideology which has made an increasing impact on the modern world. While the origins of feminism can be traced back far into the past, and can certainly be seen in clear outline in the writings of eighteenth-century writers such as Mary Wollstonecraft, the late twentieth century has witnessed feminism's ideological flourishing and its profound legislative impact in Western countries. Feminism can be seen as a post-materialist ideology in its concentration upon the style and quality of life.

It has extended the reach and scope of politics, coining the phrase 'the personal is the political', which pithily and dramatically demands the extension of political analysis and contestation to 'personal' realms such as relationships and childcare. Feminism has questioned one of the central pillars of liberalism and the liberal state: the divide between the public and the private. This divide has been challenged from both sides, in that feminists have argued that the public world is devalued by its exclusion of women and private concerns from its purview, and that the private world has suffered by the exclusion of men from domestic duties and child-rearing.

While generalisations can be made about the nature of feminism and the impact of feminism on politics, there is a significant variety of expressions of feminism. To some extent this variety follows a chronological pattern, in that the first wave of feminism – up to the early part of the twentieth century – concentrated upon either achieving political representation or yoking feminism to socialist emancipation, whereas late twentieth-century feminism, the second wave, has set out a radical agenda in which the emancipation of women in all spheres of life has been supported and the pervasiveness of patriarchy has been opposed. Towards the close of the twentieth century various forms of feminism can be discerned. Liberal feminism accepts the liberal assumptions about the value to be accorded individuality and freedom, but campaigns to achieve their equal realisation for women as well as men. Socialist feminism, while pursuing traditional socialist goals of equality and fairness, sees gender as an important source of existing unfairness. Radical feminism embraces a variety of standpoints, but all variants challenge existing divisions of the public and the private, and see patriarchy as of fundamental importance. Postmodern feminism is a recent phenomenon, in which postmodern scepticism about the substantiality of selves, and doubt about the bases of explanation and liberation have combined to decentre feminist ideology, so that women are not seen as forming an unproblematic essentialist category and the feminist agenda is characteristically seen as deconstructing male universalistic linguistic paradigms.

> An important area of agreement [i.e. among feminists] is an increasingly general acceptance of the radical feminist claim that the 'personal is the political', and that power relations are not confined to the 'public' worlds of law, the state and economics, but that they pervade all areas of life. This means that such issues as childcare or domestic violence are redefined as political, and can be the focus of collective feminist action; it means too that politics is not simply something 'out there', but a part of everyday experience. At the same time, it is becoming clearer that gender issues cannot be isolated from their socio-economic context, and that apparently moderate feminist demands may come into conflict with dominant economic interests and assumptions.
>
> Disagreements remain over the role of men in aiding or opposing feminist goals. Liberal feminism started from the premise that all will gain if society is based on principles of justice and equal competition,

for men as well as women will be able to realize their full individuality, and society will benefit from the talents of all its members. Marxists and socialists too have argued that there is no fundamental conflict of interest between men and women, for the ending of sex oppression cannot be disentangled from wider social progress. In this sense, therefore, many liberal, Marxist and socialist writers would agree in principle that men as well as women can be feminists. At the same time, however, radical feminist theories and the experience of feminist politics have produced an increasingly widespread perception that men as a group are privileged by existing inequalities, at least in the short term, and that they therefore have an interest in maintaining them.

(Bryson 1993: 67)

## Exercise

1 What is meant by the expression 'the personal is the political'?
2 What is the socio-economic context of gender issues?
3 Can men be feminists?

### Liberal feminism

Liberal feminism conceives of politics in individualistic terms and looks to reform present liberal practices in Western countries rather than advocating wholesale revolutionary change. Liberal feminism's long historical pedigree is exhibited in the works of Mary Wollstonecraft, who wrote the celebrated *Vindication of the Rights of Woman* in 1792. Wollstonecraft argued for the fundamental equality of men and women. She saw both women and essentially rational creatures whose common rational qualities were overlooked on account of the education and socialisation of women, which contrived to render them coquettish, emotional creatures. Wollstonecraft recommended educational reform, some female representation and companionate marriages, but she was still prepared to countenance significant differences in the lifestyles of men and women. She thought that only a relative minority of women would pursue professional careers, that many women would undertake domestic work and that the majority would find satisfaction in their domestic labours and child-rearing.

Likewise, J. S. Mill, in the nineteenth century, emphasised the essential equality of men and women, explaining their common nature as deriving from their shared rationality. He argued for feminism on utilitarian grounds, for he calculated that society as a whole was losing out if it did not make good use of the rational qualities of women as well as of men. Mill's sensitivity to the harmful effects of uncriticised conventions enabled him to imagine the possible improvements to the human condition consequent upon general acceptance of the rational character of women. Mill was appalled by the domination over women which most men exerted in marriages. He considered that a more equal relationship between marriage partners would ameliorate the quality of life for both men and women. To promote equality of status in marriage Mill advocated reform of the property laws so that women retained rights to their property after marriage. Though Mill was a determined advocate of the feminist cause, he followed Wollstonecraft in assuming that most women would be able to find satisfaction in the private world of the family and a companionate marriage.

The most celebrated of latterday liberal feminists, the American Betty Friedan, resembles Mill and Wollstonecraft in so far as she does not want to overturn contemporary liberal society. Rather, she argues that women should not be excluded from the liberal dream of autonomy and self-determination. She advocates specific remedial measures such as widespread access to crèche facilities to enable women to combine effectively professional careers and family responsibilities. Like other liberal feminists, however, she does not seek to overturn conventional notions of gender in contemporary society, and accepts prevailing patterns of relationships between men and women and the appropriateness of the nuclear family.

## Socialist feminism

*See the discussion of equality in Chapter 6, pp. 183–6.*

Socialist feminism rejects the individualism of liberal feminism and aims to achieve the goals of substantive equality between men and women and a cooperative sense of community between all members of society. Fourier argued a case for socialist feminism at the outset of the nineteenth century, elaborating a version of socialism, based upon equality between men and women, which emphasised its emotionally liberating qualities. According to Fourier, men and women should live together polygamously in phalansteries, with children being reared collectively. Engels, in *The Origins of the Family, Private Property and the State*, provided a classic Marxist account of gender relations, which purported to explain the basis of gender inequality (Engels 1968). He argued that the origins of sexual inequality may be traced to the establishment of patrilineal descent which arose with the advent of private property as a mechanism to ensure property remains with male descendants. For Engels, the arrival of socialism would abolish both private property and the domestic servitude of women. Latterday socialist feminists like Juliet Mitchell characteristically see production as a central factor in the oppression of women but, unlike Engels, allow for the importance of other factors, notably the roles women have played in the reproductive and nurturing processes.

## Radical feminism

Radical feminism emerged in the period after the Second World War and is characterised by its emphasis upon the importance of patriarchy in maintaining a male domination of society and by its call for a radical overturning of gender oppression. The agenda of radical feminism is visibly present in Simone de Beauvoir's study *The Second Sex*, published in 1949 (de Beauvoir 1968). The theme of the work is the dependent, derivative status of women as the second sex. For de Beauvoir, women are defined dialectically and existentially as the other of men. She urges that women should undertake an existential reorientation and redefine themselves so as to transform their status and lifestyles across all social and cultural reference points. Eva Figes, in *Patriarchal Attitudes*, highlights feminity as a socially produced phenomenon created by men, and urges that women must be liberated from the gender straitjackets of marriage and motherhood (Figes 1970).

Germaine Greer, in *The Female Eunuch*, launched a savage critique of received notions of femininity. She castigated conventional notions of women as sexless and passive creatures, urging, instead, that women should be sexually assertive and energetic creators of their own destiny (Greer 1971). Kate Millet, in *Sexual Politics*, developed a comprehensive theory of patriarchy in which society, its structures and values were depicted as hostile to women on account of their explicit and tacit male dominance (Millet 1970). For Millet, the locus of male power is the nuclear family, which restricts the sexual and social possibilities of women to the demands of one man and his children and removes reproduction and nurturing from the public domain. She prescribes the destruction of the nuclear family if women are to achieve freedom. Since 1970, radical feminism has taken diverse directions, prompting some commentators to emphasise diversity rather than coherence in the women's movement. Some feminists, such as Mary Daly (1978), rejecting androgyny and the notion of pure equality between men and women, have favoured a pro-woman position in which the special qualities of women have been lauded. A radical expression of a pro-woman standpoint is Ti-Grace Atkinson's political lesbianism.

## Postmodern feminism

Postmodern feminism, as the name suggests, derives intellectual inspiration from postmodernism. It shares in the general postmodern critique of rationalism and progress, and is prepared to accept irresolvable difference and perspectivism in place of the contested universalism of modernity. The intellectual perspective of postmodern feminism harmonises with a gathering appreciation of the diversity of the women's movement, whereby the nature of woman itself is problematised. In France postmodern feminism has sought to deconstruct the symbolic order of a language construed as a male appropriation of experience. The general thrust of postmodernism to resist closure and systematisation has led feminists to recognise a diversity which has been discussed insufficiently in the classics of feminist literature. Wollstonecraft and Mill entertained easy generalisations about the essential rationality of women, but assumed uncritically that women of differing classes would adopt differing styles of life. Radical feminists like de Beauvoir and Greer have stigmatised prevailing sexual conventions and images of women, but have not reflected convincingly upon the contrasts between women in radically distinct situations such as those prevailing for a white professional woman in a Western country and a poverty-stricken Muslim woman in Iran or Iraq. While the tendency of postmodern feminism to recognise difference is salutary, the deconstruction of a general notion of woman threatens to disrupt the power of feminism as a focused political movement engaging in a clearly defined struggle.

**THINK POINT**
- What are the main differences between the types of feminism discussed above?
- With which form of feminism are you most sympathetic?

## Ecologism

Ecologism is a contemporary ideology in that it has, since the late 1960s, developed a strong profile, figures prominently in political discourse and has influenced other more traditional ideologies. Like feminism, it can be seen as a post-materialist ideology concerned not so much with the generation and distribution of wealth but with the quality of life.

The modern environmental movement dates from the early 1960s, but there is a longer tradition of environmental concern which reaches back to ancient pagan religions and 'romantic' reactions against industrialisation. There are a variety of forms ecologism can take. Historically, for example, there have been rural conservatives, blood-and-soil Nazi ideologues and back-to-the-land environmental anarchists. In the contemporary world, there are market environmentalists and ecologists of anarchist, socialist and feminist persuasions.

One useful way to thread a path through the variety of attitudes and positions which are associated with ecologism is to distinguish between environmentalism and ecologism as terms of ideological discourse. Environmentalism is a broad umbrella term which is generally understood as covering a great range of attitudes and approaches expressed within the environmentalist movement. It includes those who wish to remedy specific environmental problems, environmental reformers in traditional political parties and radicals who identify themselves as 'green'.

Ecologism as a term is usually reserved for a distinctive set of radical views about how human beings must relate to their environment. However, there is a diversity of outlook between those who call themselves ecologists. Dobson distinguishes between 'minimalist' and 'maximalist' views (Dobson 1990). Minimalist ecologists want to ameliorate the environment and minimise damage perpetrated upon it, and they view environmental concerns from the utilitarian perspective of human beings. Maximalist ecologists, in contrast, do not privilege the perspective of human beings. They adopt a holistic perspective, aiming to maintain and develop a harmonious set of inter-relationships between living things and their environments. The maximal perspective of deep ecology embraces an ecocentric viewpoint rather than an anthropocentric one. The viability of the ecosphere as a whole is the overriding ethical objective.

This deep ecological perspective challenges Enlightenment orthodoxy, namely the notion that reason is an uncomplicated and key resource of human beings in the planning of their lives. Likewise, it challenges the rationalist view that progress can be measured in terms of technological and material advance. The holistic perspective of deep ecology, as embraced for example by Lovelock (Lovelock 1979), sees nature as a living developing set of relationships rather than as a dead, inert machine.

The extract below is from a book by Jonathan Porritt, a leading exponent of ecologism in contemporary Britain.

### Reason, Sweet and Sour

That the green perspective does have a different view of reason or rationality is hardly surprising, for its critique of industrial society is radical in a remarkably literal way. By refusing to abstract our human concerns from the web of life that is our biosphere, it seeks to examine the very roots of human existence. Simply 'getting the facts right' is a much more complex business than today's rationalists would have you believe, and no judgement can ever be 'value-free'.

In his quite excellent pamphlet for the Green Alliance, *Economics Today: What do we need*?, eco-philosopher Henryk Skolimowski reminds us of the memorable scene in Brecht's play *The Life of Galileo*, where Galileo pleads with the courtiers and the scholars just to look into the telescope and see for themselves the proof that the world goes round the sun rather than the sun going round the world. But they wouldn't, for they were simply incapable of coping with any new facts that might overthrow the existing order of things. After all, they saw themselves as 'defenders of the faith'. Kids today are always taught to admire Galileo and his courageous stand against the reactionaries and religious bigots who put him on trial, without so much as a passing awareness that it is now the world view of Galileo and others like him that has become the dominant orthodoxy, and that it is now suppressing a different vision and a different interpretation of human destiny.

The dominant world view, the consequences of which we shall consider in detail in the next part, has come to the end of its useful life, not least because its notion of rationality is so woefully lacking. We like to think that ours is the supremely rational civilization, but does that claim really stand up to any kind of examination? Instead of looking into space through Galileo's telescope, let us look down at ourselves. Imagine, if you will, the proverbial little green person from Mars taking stock of Planet Earth, and the UK in particular. Having anticipated a model of rationality, might 'our Martian' not be surprised to find:

- that it's apparently possible to keep the peace only by threatening the total annihilation of the planet;
- that it's possible to achieve 'progress' and further growth only by the wilful destruction of our life-support systems;
- that so civilized a nation bats not an eyelid as it inflicts terrible suffering on its fellow creatures;
- that we obsessively promote the most expensive and most dangerous energy source to the exclusion of all others;
- that millions remain unemployed when there's so much important work crying out to be done;

- that millions more carry out soulless, mind-destroying jobs that make nothing of their resources and creativity;
- that we ravage our best farming land to grow food surpluses that are then thrown away or sold off cheap to the 'enemy';
- that we consider the best use of the proceeds of North Sea oil is to keep people on the dole;
- that in one part of the world millions die of starvation, while people here die of over-indulgence;
- that we spend as much on useless weapons of war as we do on either education or health;
- that our 'planners' have allowed rural communities to waste away, while making inner cities uninhabitable;
- that we pollute the planet in the very process of trying to get rich enough to do something about pollution?

> Now that's just the first 'dirty dozen' out of our little green Martian's notebook, and the list would go on and on. It's hardly a prima facie case for a rational, civilized society. So bear with me if I go on a bit about just who is rational and who is irrational in this crazy world of ours. Ecologists get very emotional about rationality! We've had our fill of the Rothschilds and the Paul Johnsons, who disparage what they can't comprehend and mock what they can't live up to. Though we would never be so foolhardy as to assume that reason alone is sufficient to build a caring, civilized society, the politics of ecology is none the less profoundly rational.
>
> (Porritt 1984: 18–19; reprinted by permission of Blackwell Publishers)

## Exercise

1 Why do you think that Jonathan Porritt is critical of the view of reason held by 'today's rationalists'?
2 What does Galileo represent for Porritt? Do you think that a case could be made for the Catholic Church's treatment of Galileo?
3 Examine one item of the 'dirty dozen' attributed to the little green Martian. Consider the reasons why it could be seen as signifying the irrationality of contemporary society. Do you think any of the items on the martian's list can be defended?
4 Do you think that there has been 'progress' over the last 200 years? Make a list of positive and negative factors which have developed over those years. How would you undertake an overall evaluation of the changes that have taken place?

### Varieties of ecological standpoints on society, economy and politics

One strand of ecology which has been influential is eco-socialism. It often bears a Marxist influence, as exemplified in Rudolph Bahro's *Building the Green Movement* (1986). For eco-socialism, human labour and natural resources are seen as being exploited in a class-based drive for profit. Eco-socialists differ over the nature of political organisation; some, like Bahro, favour small-scale communities, others, like Martin Ryle in *Ecology and Socialism*, envisage a continued role for the nation-state in dealing with large companies (Ryle 1988).

Anarcho-environmentalism forms another significant part of the ecologist movement. It favours natural spontaneity, harmony and a balance to be achieved without external controls. Its advocates favour decentralisation whereby small-scale communities can provide settings enabling people to live close to nature without the bureaucratic and technological paraphernalia associated with large conurbations. The anarchistic dimension of this form of ecologism explains its commitment to spontaneity and its revulsion against elaborate, contrived modes of political regulation.

Eco-feminism, whose standpoint is well represented by Judith Plant's collection of essays *Healing the Wounds* (1989), see the feminine character as a figure harmonising with nature. Women, on this view, are close to nature through their life-giving and nurturing roles. The devaluation of these roles in industrial societies is taken as reflecting the alienation of patriarchal cultures from their ties with the natural environment. Eco-feminists, in contrast with mainstream post-Enlightenment thinkers, value the traditionally feminine qualities of empathy and intuition over traditionally male attributes such as reason and energy. Eco-feminism is opposed to women achieving equality with men on terms which mean the surrender of these traditionally feminine values. Rather, they wish these traditionally feminine values to become dominant in society.

Not all of those wearing a 'green' label in the contemporary world are radical critics of contemporary patterns of social and political life. There are also 'green' capitalists who rely on taxation to promote desirable 'green' outcomes. An exemplar of green consumerism is the body shop.

---

**THINK POINT**
- Think over what you take to be the main differences between the types of ecologism discussed above.

---

## Conclusion

This brief review of political ideologies should make clear their significance and interest. In the early 1960s ideology was declared to be dead (Bell 1962), and Fukuyama, more recently, has written of the ideological victory of Western liberalism (Fukuyama 1992). Our preceding survey, however, has highlighted that a variety of political ideologies are alive and influential. An economic and cultural context of continuing change and development renders conservatism's respect for order and continuity appealing. Ecologists and feminists contribute to the language in which current politics is conducted. Nationalism is a powerful force throughout the globe, and fascism is not to be dismissed, despite the havoc it wrought in the interwar years. While the project and character of socialism are objects of debate, its commitment to equality and social justice in the context of enormous global and national disparities of wealth and opportunity signals its continuing relevance.

## Further reading

Bernstein, E. (1961) *Evolutionary Socialism*, New York: Schocken Books. A landmark book in stating the case for reformist socialism.

Burke, E. (1982) *Reflections on the Revolution in France*, Harmondsworth: Penguin. A famous statement of conservatism, set against the background of the French Revolution.

Dobson, A. (1990) *Green Political Thought*, London: Unwin Hyman. A clear account of the varieties of Green political thought.

Eatwell, R. and Wright, A. (eds) (1993) *Contemporary Political Ideologies*. London: Pinter. An assortment of contemporary writers discuss the leading ideologies. Good, clear writing.

Engels, F. (1968) *The Origins of the Family, Private Property and the State*, in K. Marx and F. Engels *Selected Writings*, London: Lawrence & Wishart. A classic Marxist statement on the nature of gender inequality.

Fukuyama, F. (1992) *The End of History and the Last Man*, London: Hamish Hamilton. A very modish book which talks in grand terms about the end of history. It argues that liberal capitalist democracy has succeeded in solving social, economic and political problems.

Gellner, E. (1983) *Nations and Nationalism*, Oxford: Blackwell. An influential book on nationalism by a respected scholar.

Giddens, A. (1985) *A Contemporary Critique of Historical Materialism*, Cambridge: Polity. Lively critique of Marxism by a prolific author.

Giddens, A. (1990) *The Consequences of Modernity*, Cambridge: Polity.

Greer, G. (1971) *The Female Eunuch*, London: Paladin. A classic statement of assertive feminism by a prolific and provocative author.

Griffin, R. (1991) *The Nature of Fascism*, London: Routledge. A fascinating overview of fascism which pursues an original line in modelling fascism.

Hitler, A. (1969) *Mein Kampf*, London: Hutchinson. The classic statement of Hitler's beliefs.

Kedourie, E. (1966) *Nationalism*, London: Hutchinson. A classic work written in a magisterial and highly readable style. It is suspicious of nationalist claims.

Marx, K. and Engels, F. (1973b) *The German Ideology* London: Lawrence & Wishart. The first section is read to the general exclusion of other sections, but the whole of it is a key text for Marx's beliefs as he blends philosophy and history.

Millet, K. (1970) *Sexual Politics*, London: Virago. A classic statement of second-wave feminism, urging a total overhaul of gender identities.

O'Sullivan, N. (1976) *Conservatism*, London: Dent. A plausible overview of conservatism, which sees a belief in imperfection as a central part of conservatism.

Oakeshott, M. (1962) *Rationalism in Politics and Other Essays*, London and New York: Methuen. Wonderful essays of a sceptical conservative turn of mind.

Porritt, J. (1984) *Seeing Green: The Politics of Ecology Explained*, Oxford: Blackwell. A lively and engaging statement of Green politics from a famous ecologist.

Ryle, M. (1988) *Ecology and Socialism*, London: Radius. A lively ecological work offering a particular perspective.

# PART 3      POLITICS IN ACTION

# 9 THE NATURE OF THE STATE

*Richard Huggins*

# The nature of the state

## Introduction

> The State, what is the State? The State is a lie!
>
> Nietzsche, *Thus Spake Zarathustra* (1883–5)

We live in a world full of states. It is a term we are all familiar with and often use. However, we often use it blindly, and it is relevant to ask some questions when we think of the state. What do we really mean? To what extent does it effect our lives? When do we come into contact with it? What is our relationship to it? In the contemporary period the answers to these questions are complex and extensive. In most advanced societies the state has become a consistent presence that affects our daily lives almost constantly. We have our births recorded and certified by the state, and our marriages authorised and enacted by the state; our education is often state-funded and almost certainly state assessed. Many countries have a state media system. We pay taxes universally, carry the passports of territorial states, and in an increasing number of instances the state watches over us – quite literally – with surveillance technology. Our lives are governed by the extensive laws of our state, which tell us how long we can work for, at what age we can engage in certain types of behaviour and, in some states, whom we can marry, how many children we may have and what type of food we can eat. Now, clearly implied in this opening statement is the link between state and nation, but we will not be exploring this relationship directly here (it is covered in Chapter 15). However, it is difficult not to reflect on the close realtionship between the two concepts of nation and state, and indeed the territoriality of the state is seen by many as part of its defining nature (A. J. Hall 1994). So, although this chapter is not about the nation-state, the implicit and explicit nature of the relationship between the two concepts is acknowledged.

This chapter sets out to explore the identity and nature of the state in both general and specific ways. Thus, general observations regarding the state are made in order to identify features of the state that might be said to be characteristic of this term across time and space. However, in order to illustrate such characteristics further and to explore the nature of the state more fully we will also consider the state in specific forms such as the *liberal state*, the *fascist state* and the *communist state*.

---

**THINK POINT**
- In what ways have you come into contact with the state today?

---

## The state: problems of analysis

The nature of the state has been subject to considerable scholarly attention in the twentieth century (A. J. Hall 1994), but despite such interest the concept of the state remains vague and obscure. This is due, in part, to the multitude of ways in which the word 'state' is used and, indeed, we would do well to remember Vincent's observation that 'the state is certainly not one thing' (Vincent 1987: 43). The nature of the state is difficult to identify clearly. Sometimes the state, or certain of its institutions and components, is more visible than at others. Some elements of the state may indeed be hidden and 'secret', some elements may be present in the analysis of one group of theorists but absent from another. The permutations are almost endless.

As is not unsual with terms in social science, discussion is complicated by the fact that the term 'state' is so much a part of the vocabulary of both political and social scientists and everyday communication. Political scientists and and non-academics alike use this term constantly and often in rather indistinct ways. So we talk of the 'welfare state', a 'police state', 'state control', the 'nanny state' or 'state education'. But what we actually mean by these terms is often far from clear, and how much they actually relate to any form of social reality – rather than a representation of social arrangements and relationships – is often a cause of considerable confusion. Indeed, the terms themselves contain deeply normative or value-laden notions of what the relationship between the individual and the state *ought to be* and thus cloud our understanding further.

In addition, we often say, 'The state should do something about it!' Again, what do we mean? Do we mean the ruling party of government? The monarchy? The political elites? Ourselves? To put this another way, who or what bodies constitute the state? Who does the state represent? What happens when individuals come into conflict with the state? Different theoretical and ideological conceptions of the state advance different answers to these questions and this chapter seeks to explore some of this analysis. Like any concept or term that occupies both specialist and general circulation and is in constant use, the terms 'state' and 'individual' have taken on a multitude of meanings – often competing and contradictory.

*As students of politics and society you must be clear what you mean by these terms when you use them.*

There is also a further difficulty of analysing the nature of the state and it is worth considering the quote from Nietzsche's *Thus Spake Zarathustra* (1883–5) that opened the chapter. Whatever else we may say or think about the state, we must remember that it is primarily an *abstract idea*. It is a way of conceptualising a network of agents, agencies and institutions that gives to this network a more solid appearance. However, this idea is a **social construction**. Although we can clearly identify the institutions and procedures of the state – in the form of parliaments, legal systems, elections, public events and so on – the state remains, in Nietzsche's words, a lie. Now, if it is a lie it is so because it does not exist in any total and tangible sense. Its nature and existence are networks, interrelationships and processes that ultimately come together at the level of social construction and convention.

If we take this analysis a little further we can conceive of the state as one way in which the social is made tangible or recognisable. It might be argued that human existence, or social life, is overwhelmingly complex. It is, in the main, unstable and contradictory, and its purpose is highly questionable. It would seem that all human beings crave nothing more than they crave order. In order to function we desire the world to be ordered either by us or, in the main, for us. These take the form of norms, values and beliefs that may be found in myths, religious beliefs, political ideologies or group rituals, for example. In addition to the totalising systems of ordering that are conveyed by, say, religious beliefs, we have a whole range of smaller systems for making sense of our lives – these include schools, universities, the legal system, family relationships and so on. So, in some ways I am arguing that the notion of the state is a way of ordering an otherwise unorganised set of experiences. Thought of in this way, the study of the state becomes more of an exercise in understanding competing social explanations than one of more familiar notions of politics. Nevertheless it adds weight to the interesting notion of the state as a fiction, abstraction or social construct.

**Social construction** The idea that value, perception and reality are constructed and given meaning through and in shared social understanding rather than existing in an objective reality or through natural development.

## The state: an overview

To ask why I am to submit to the power of the state, is to ask why I am to allow my life to be regulated by that complex of institutions without which I literally should not have a life to call my own, nor should be able to ask for a justification of what I am called upon to do.

(T. H. Green (1941) *Lectures on the Principles of Political Obligation*, p. 122)

What we need now is a far greater degree of personal responsibility and decision, far more independence from the government, and a comparable reduction in the role of government.

(Margaret Thatcher)

Discussion frequently occurs, especially in the Western tradition of political thought, between those who advocate a minimal role for the state and those who advocate a more interventionist role for the state. The minimal-role approach is identified with various strands of liberalism and, most recently, the New Right in many countries, including Britain, the USA and New Zealand. This approach maintains that the state should avoid intervening in the lives of the people as much as possible. This is argued for a variety of reasons. First, it is argued, the state cannot make appropriate choices for all of its citizens and therefore that which is provided by the state will be, at best, the state's concept of what the people need or want. Second, the state, by suggesting or maintaining that it can provide a whole range of services and contributions to social life and social organisation, extends the expectations of the people beyond that which the state can actually deliver – this creates future difficulties for the state in the form of a 'legitimation crisis'. Third, the provision of social and welfare reform, in particular, by the state can, it is argued, have the affect of discouraging and demotivating the individual, who becomes reliant upon state provision. This may also manifest itself in the destruction of 'community', self-help provision and other 'virtues' which are held to be characteristic of societies in the pre-welfare-state era. In this model the state aims to maintain a legal framework through which individuals can attain their true potential as directed by their individual motivation and choice. Whilst there exist other arguments in favour of a minimal state, these three provide a brief introduction to this set of ideas.

In opposition to the minimal-state thesis is the assertion that the state has a positive role to play in enhancing the life of the individual and, in turn, the function and 'success' of society. This set of ideas is often associated with the social reformist or social democratic traditions of thought. Here it is argued that certain problems – especially poverty – can be overcome only by the direct action and intervention of the state, and that if such problems are left unchallenged the individual and the community will suffer and social, economic and political inequalities will increase. This conception of the state has been used to justify the extension of the role of the state into a whole range of areas and activities that were previously seen as beyond state concern. Thus, throughout the twentieth century most advanced capitalist societies have set about the task of creating 'welfare states' in which state provision and organisation of healthcare, education, unemployment benefit, childcare provision and provision for the elderly have increased. In Britain this developed through waves of legislation, most notably from 1906 to 1914 with the emergence of 'new liberalism' within the British Liberal Party, and was influenced by the work of T. H. Green (1941), Hobhouse (1994) and Hobson (see Allett 1982). It is seen as having reached its zenith in the post-1945 consensus and acceptance of the Beveridge Report (Beveridge 1944) as a foundation for 'cradle to grave' welfare provision. In recent years extensive debate has arisen over the 'proper' extent of this provision and serious threats have been made to the level of

For an interesting and comprehensive survey of the development of the welfare state in Britain, see D. Fraser (1984) *The Evolution of the British Welfare State*, 2nd edn, Basingstoke: Macmillan.

provision by welfare states with the extent and cost of the welfare state being a prime target for the attention of the **New Right**.

Both of these conceptions of the state still conceive of the individual as the primary unit of interest, and the state is, theoretically, subservient to this unit. Although the social reformist argues that the state has an obligation to eradicate the worst excesses of poverty, poor education and ill health, for example, and therefore has the right to intervene, the justification for this intervention is that it will allow individuals to reach their full potential. Despite this, these accounts differ primarily in emphasis. They both maintain that there ought to be a space for individual activity that is free of state interference and does not depend on the state in any sense. There exist, for such analysis, three spheres of human activity. The political sphere, the private sphere and the **public sphere**.

The political sphere is that space in which political decisions are reached and political actions enacted. The private sphere concerns private desires and experiences. The public sphere is that area of public life which is not governed by state action but is open to public view, discussion and action. In some ways, it is best conceived of as the sphere in which we are citizens. A considerable academic literature has developed on the notion of the public sphere in the last two decades. The existence and maintance of a 'healthy' public sphere – with its attendent characteristics of critical reason, informed debate and free exhange of information between individuals – is seen as central to democracy and the 'success' of democracy. The exact characteristics of the public sphere and the relationship and balance between the public, private and political spheres continue to attract considerable debate and discussion. Nevertheless, whatever balance and emphasis are argued for by those competing political positions outlined above, the basic belief that there ought to exist both public and private spheres of activity free from state intervention is upheld.

A concept closely related to the notion of the public sphere is that of **civil society**. Civil society consists of the non-state – the market, private or voluntary organisations, activities and associations. Discussion of the nature of civil society and its 'proper relationship' to the state and the extent of state power has recently received increased attention, especially with the developments in the post-communist world (Keane 1988).

Other conceptions of the state, however, place greater emphasis on the primacy of the collective – often the national, ethnic or religious group – over the individual and would argue, to a greater or lesser degree, that no sphere is closed to the influence of politics and in particular, the central political authority of the state. Some theorists have argued that the state is itself an 'Ethical Idea', as conveyed in the works of Hegel (1975) or Rousseau (1973b), in which rather abstract notions of the ideal community are put forward. In other conceptions emphasis is placed on the more extreme forms of ultra-nationalist community found in fascism. In these conceptions of the state the individual can find meaning only through the collective unit, and this is most likely to manifest itself through or in the state. This is

**New Right** The term associated with a resurgence of the right in Western politics since the late 1970s. The New Right, drawing inspiration from the works of (amongst others) von Hayek and Friedman, demonstrates three key characteristics: first, a commitment to a *laissez-faire* attitude to state, society, market and individual that seeks to eliminate state intervention in all aspects of life; second, a reaffirmation of traditional values with regard to certain aspects of social life and social organisation, especially the family and community; third, a libertarian strand which stresses the need for individual liberty and responsibility. The New Right has been seen as highly influential in the administrations of President Ronald Reagan (1980–8) in the USA and the Conservative governments of Mrs Thatcher (1979–90) in the UK.

**Public sphere** The realm of social life in which information, opinions and critical discussion take place, thus allowing for public questions to be formed.

**Civil society** The sphere of society in which individuals freely associate in relationships, actions and organisations that are not dependent on state intervention, institutions or regulations.

characteristic of fascist states, communist states and certain religious states.

These two broad conceptions of the state provide some general statements of characteristic differences between certain ideas of the relationship between the state and the individual. In practice, outside radical conceptions of the state such as fascism, states often demonstrate elements of both minimal intent and maximum intervention, and how much the frontiers of the state can be 'rolled back' – especially in advanced capitalist states – is an area of serious dispute. The following quote from John Gray demonstrates some of the complexities of this debate:

> The scope of government activity in Britain remains vastly over-extended. The autonomous institutions of civil society are today threatened by an invasive state whose size and arbitrary power have not substantially diminished, and in important respects have indeed been enhanced, after over a decade of rule by a Conservative administration avowedly dedicated to whittling down government to its most indispensable functions.
>
> (J. Gray 1993: 2)

## Exercise

Consider whether the professed aim of 'rolling back' the state was actually achieved by the Thatcher administrations of the 1980s.

Indeed, despite claiming to reduce the size and function of the state, Mrs Thatcher's Conservative administrations witnessed a huge expansion of secondary legislation, the growth of quangos, and even increases in the size of state bureaucracy (J. Gray 1993). Perhaps most interestingly, in some areas the role and power of the state has been significantly extended.

## The state: towards a definition

> The State is considered the sole source of the 'right' to use violence.
>
> (Max Weber, 'Politics as a vocation', in H. H. Gerth and C. Wright Mills (eds) (1991) *From Max Weber: Essay in Sociology*, London: Routledge, p. 78)

A. Giddens (1985b) *The Nation-state and Violence*, Vol. 2 of *A Contemporary Critique of Historical Materialism*, Cambridge: Polity.

> A state can be defined as a political organization whose rule is territorially ordered and which is able to mobilize the means of violence to sustain that rule.
>
> (Giddens 1985b: 20)

So far we have argued that the identity of the ~~of the~~ state is complex and elusive. It is not surprising that this is reflected in the definitions and arguments contained in the academic literature. However, John Hall (1994) usefully identifies three elements that should be included in any composite definition:

> **The state – elements in a composite definition**
> 1 The state is a set on institutions, the most important of which are those concerned with violence and coercion.
> 2 These institutions are located within a geographically-bound territory.
> 3 The state monopolises rule-making within its territory
>
> *Source*: adopted from J. Hall (1994)

The state refers to all the institutions, agencies and agents that operate within a given territiorial space, have legitimate power and authority over us, and can legitimately utilise force as an (ultimate) sanction against us if we fail to accept its laws or orders or resist its actions or act against it. Indeed, this characteristic of the state as the body that is the sole legitimate user of force is a common theme in the literature. But the literature tells a limited tale, for, quite clearly, the recourse to violence in many states is rare, and state systems can maintain legitimacy through force for only a limited length of time and cannot maintain their authority through force alone.

However, the state is almost always ready to use force and coercion against sections of its people if they act against either the laws of the state or accepted norms of behaviour. Thus, the execution of criminals is accepted as legitimate in many states, the persecution of ethnic or religious groups may well be sanctioned by the state, and even those who dissent in terms of social norms and values may find considerable force exerted against them by the state. In Britain the case of 'New Age travellers' is one such example; considerable levels of state violence have been employed against the individuals concerned and the law has recently been strengthened – with this group, among others, in mind – by the Criminal Justice and Public Order Act of 1994.

In addition to possessing the power and authority to employ violence legitimately, the state can be characterised as consisting of a number of agents and offices. Thus, within the state a whole range of offices and agents – government ministers, judiciary, bureaucrats, army, police, education and local government – can be identified. In this sense the state is an umbrella term that covers all offices that make and enforce the collective decisions and rules of a society (Hague *et al.* 1992). Once again the emphasis is on the ability to make collective decisions and *enforce* them.

But the exact nature of the state remains to some extent ambigious and this ambiguity is conveyed well by Edelman when he states: 'the state benefits and it threatens. Now it is 'us' and often it is 'them'. It is an abstraction, but in its name men are jailed, or made rich on defence contracts, or killed in wars' (Edelman 1964: 1). One important consideration is that the state is a broader concept than government, and although the terms are often used as if they were interchangeable, they should not be. The most significant difference between the state and a government is the permanence of the state over time. Thus, the personnel and the institutions of the state – such as the bureacracy, army, police force and so on – fulfil these roles on a more permanent basis than the politicians who form the government of the day.

## Theories of the state

### Feudalism

Feudal society possessed no notion of the state as we conceive it today but it did develop a series of power relationships within a complex social structure. The key to this area is that what might be considered as constituting the state is best conceived of in organic terms, as a structure in which all parts were balanced in a relationship of mutual dependency. Thus the vassal, lord and king were linked in terms of duty and obligation, and the exercise of power was constrained by such relationships. As Dyson argues, it was 'possible to conceive of the king as a member of the feudal community and of the "law of the land" as the product of counsel and consent and as common for kings and barons' (Dyson 1980: 53). This system suggests that the rights of individuals were not a key consideration in political organisations. Instead the political system reflects the nature of a highly organic and interdependent society in which the rights and obligations conferred by membership of an economic and social class are the key determinant of status and rights. This system has been interpreted as a beneficial, or at least just, system (particularly by eighteenth- and nineteenth-century democrats), and has been conceptualised as an ascending pyramid.

### Divine right and absolutism

> The state of monarchy is the supremest thing upon the earth. For kings are not only God's lieutenants upon earth, and sit upon God's throne, but even by God himself they are called gods.
>
> (James I, *A Speech to the Lords and Commons of the Parliament at White-Hall,* 1610)

In this conception of the state, absolute power is vested in the sovereign – almost certainly the monarch. Individual rights are minimal and the individual has no choice but to submit to the will of the all-powerful sovereign. Justification of this state of affairs was made by appeals to divine power. Monarchs were God's representatives on earth and, as can be seen from the statement by James I, they ruled by virtue of divine right. In such a political system limited scope exists for dissent and individual expression. But the period of absolutism and divine right was relatively short-lived and it was soon challeneged by the assertions of contract theory and early liberalism.

## Constitutions and constitutionalism

### Declarations of rights

Although declarations of rights and bills of rights amount to very much the same thing, we will consider some early declarations of rights here and return to bills of rights later in the chapter. There exist numerous such statements and declarations of rights that indicate *how* the relationship between the state and the individual ought to be organised and what – in principle at least – the most important rights of the individual are. These statements began to appear in the eighteenth century and reflect an Enlightenment and liberal conception of the individual and of individual human rights. The emphasis is on the rights held by individuals by virtue of their possession of reason, property (in the shape of the individual physical self) and other 'natural' rights. Two of the most famous and indicative examples of this are the Declaration of Independence drafted by Thomas Jefferson for the thirteen American colonies in July 1776 and the French Declaration of the Rights of Man and the Citizen of 26 August 1789. Both documents are clearly a product of the continued development of liberal individualism and Enlightenment thought that characterises the political thought of the eighteenth century. They seek to define what the rights of individual (although in this case only male) citizens are. As such, the rights outlined are those identified as central to individual freedom and human rights, and the French Declaration of 1789, in particular, reveals strong similarities in wording, value and sentiment when compared with later declarations regarding human rights, such as the United Nations Charter of Human Rights.

In the following extract from the Declaration of Independence the values of liberal individualism are clearly evident. The authors of this statement are attempting to establish the form and nature of **limited government** as opposed to the oppresive and unrepresentative forms of government found in the European monarchies.

**Limited government**
Government in which the sovereign or executive power is limited by law, constitutional roles or institutional organisation. See also **separation of powers**.

### Declaration of Independence, July 1776

We hold these Truths to be self-evident, that all Men are created equal, that they are endowed by their Creator with certain unalienable Rights, that among these are Life, Liberty and Pursuit of Happiness. That to secure these Rights, Governments are instituted among Men, describing their just Powers from the Consent of the Governed that whenever any Form of Government becomes destructive of these Ends, it is the Right of the People to alter or abolish it, and to constitute new Government.

## Exercise

1  What are the main rights of the individual identified in this extract?
2  Are those truths that are identified as significant actually self-evident?

This statement clearly outlines the contractual nature of the relationship between the state and the individual. Furthermore, the individual retains the right to withdraw consent to be governed in the event of the government failing in its obligations and duties. This concern with the liberty and rights of the individual is further developed in the French Declaration of the Rights of Man and the Citizen of 1789. So far the statements we have considered have been general comments on the nature of the relationship between the state and the individual and, as such, often represent the first principles and the key intentions of the authors. Such sentiments and ideas can be developed further by a consideration of constitutions.

## Constitutions

We the People of the United States, in order to form a more perfect Union, establish justice, insure domestic tranquility, provide for the common defense, promote the general welfare, and secure the blessings of liberty to ourselves and our posterity, do ordain and establish the Constitution for the United States of America.

(The Constitution of the United States, Preamble, 1790)

Constitutions are one of the most readily identifiable methods of regulating the relationship between the state and the individual. They set out the rules by which the state is organised and operated; they formally enshrine rights, duties and obligations, and establish or formalise the relationship between the central political authority and the people.

However, there is a limit to how much a study of constitutions can tell us. Whilst the study of such documents and formal statements of intent can reveal the values believed to be important by the authors, it may be that the statement of intent differs markedly from the actual political situation in a country. Indeed, to grasp fully the workings or failings of a constitution we need to consider the concepts you studied earlier when you looked at political socialization, political culture and political behaviour (Chapters 1–4).

In many cases the formal document tells us only how, *in an ideal situation*, the relationship between individual and state ought to work. We also need to take into account the role of political socialisation and political culture in any assessment of the extent and expression of rights, freedoms and the workings of the political system. For example, although most countries accept that freedom of demonstration and expression are important individual rights, attitudes towards those who participate in politically motivated demonstrations vary considerably across cultures and social groups. Other points to consider are that certain political freedoms and rights might be relatively meaningless in cases of extreme poverty, high crime or on a larger scale, the status of the nation within the global economy and world order.

Furthermore, some constitutions are more explicit in their formulation of the organisation of the state and state power than others. In the case of the USA a formal document exists which specifies the role of each of the institutions of the state, the power and responsiblities of these institutions and the rights and obligations of the people with respect to these institutions. There also exists a process of regulation and appeal when the constitution and the rights enshrined therein are compromised or breached. Thus, the individual has recourse to the Supreme Court and this court can make binding rulings regarding the constitutional rights and freedoms of individuals.

In Britain no such constitutional organisation of the state machinery and its relationship to the people exists. Although neither of the popular assertions regarding Britain's constitutional arrangement – that Britain does not have a constitution or that the constitution is 'unwritten' is correct, identification and interpretation of the British constitution is highly complex because of the absence of a single constitutional document. Britain's constitution is characterised by a whole host of legal acts, conventions and practices. No formal separation of powers, no equivalent of the Supreme Court and no right of constitutional appeal exist. A Bill of Rights from 1689 does exist but this is a legal enactment which can be overruled by further legislation rather than a set of constitutionally guaranteed rights and freedoms. Although individuals can seek a judicial review, this is a ruling on the legality of an act or a piece of legislation rather than any attempt to rule on its constitutional validity. This means that the rights enjoyed by the people of Britain are legal rather than constitutional rights. Thus although the legal and conventional position is that elections are held every five years in Britain, this could be altered by law and the people would not have any constitutional document to appeal to nor any channel for such an appeal. This has led many critics of the British system to suggest that individuals enjoy not citizen's rights, or indeed citizenship, but the rights and obligations of subjects. However, it is equally valid to ask whether the people of Britain are impoverished in any way by this situation.

This discussion should alert us to the fact that constitutions do not always take the same form or exhibit the same concerns. Indeed they can differ markedly. Elazar (1985) has argued that constitutions can be classified according to five types, paraphrased below:

1 A loose frame of government which subsequently requires a considerable amount of adaptation and interpretation. A good example of this would be the constitution of the United States of America, which has undergone considerable revision and adaptation through the intervention of the Supreme Court.

2 A strict state code in which detailed rules and relationships are specified. This is more characteristic of the situation in some Western European states, most notably France.

3 A revolutionary manifesto which sets out a programme of considerable social, economic and political reorganisation. This is clearly conveyed in the constitutions of the former Soviet Union.

4  A statement of political ideals or an image of the world as it might or ought to be. This is common amongst new and emerging states and developing states, especially those gaining independence from colonial powers.

5  An embodiement of an ancient source of authority. This is characteristic of Israel's constitution which is based upon the sovereignty of the Knesset and derives from the Torah, the Jewish holy book.

---

**THINK POINT**
- Which of the five types of constitution outlined above would the state you originate from fit into?

---

The constitutional documents considered above are concerned with the limits of state power over the individual. Indeed they are documents which place at the centre of their political concerns the rights and liberties of the individual. But as we have argued they do not, in themselves, guarantee the rights they argue should exist. This has led commentators to argue that the functioning of constitutional government is dependent as much on political culture as on constitutional documents. This has led to the assertion that in order for constitutional government to work a further characteristic must be present; this is known as constitutionalism. Thus a set of values and political attitudes must exist amongst political agents and citizens in order for the values conveyed in the constitutional document to be enforced. Furthermore, the existence of constitutionalism helps to explain how countries without formal constitutional documents can still exhibit strikingly consistent constitutional procedures and outcomes.

### Bills of rights

The first ten Amendments of the Constitution of the United States of America constitute a Bill of Rights that offers additional and specific guarantees for the individual and defines certain aspects of the relationship between the individual and the state.

---

### The First Ten Amendments to the Constitution of the USA (Bill of Rights)

1  Congress shall make no law respecting an establishment of religion, or prohibiting the free exercise thereof; or abridging the freedom of speech, or of the press; or the right of the people peaceably to assemble and to petition the Government for a redress of grievances.

2  A well regulated militia, being necessary to the security of a free State, the right of the people to keep and bear arms, shall not be infringed.

3  No soldier shall, in time of peace, be quartered in any house, without the consent of the owner, nor in time of war, but in a manner to be prescribed by law.

4  The right of the people to be secure in their persons, houses, papers, and effects, against unreasonable searches and seizures, shall not be

---

violated, and no warrants shall issue, but upon probable cause, supported by oath or affirmation, and particularly describing the place to be searched, and the persons to be seized.

5 No person shall be held to answer for a capital, or other infamous crime, unless on a presentment or indictment of a grand jury, except in cases arising in the land or naval forces, or in the militia, when in actual service in time of war or public danger; nor shall any person be subject for the same offence to be twice put in jeopardy of life or limb; nor shall be compelled in any criminal case to be a witness against himself, nor be deprived of life, liberty, or property, without due process of law; nor shall private property be taken for public use, without just compensation.

6 In all criminal prosecutions, the accused shall enjoy the right to a speedy and public trial, by an impartial jury of the State and district wherein the crime shall have been committed, which district shall have been previously ascertained by law, and to be informed of the nature and cause of the accusation; to be confronted with the witnesses against him; to have compulsory process for obtaining witnesses in his favour, and to have the assistance of counsel for his defence.

7 In suits at common law, where the value in controversy shall exceed twenty dollars, the right of trial by jury shall be preserved, and no fact tried by a jury, shall be otherwise re-examined in any court of the United States, than according to the rules of the common law.

8 Excessive bail shall not be required, nor excessive fines imposed, nor cruel and unusual punishments inflicted.

9 The enumeration of the Constitution, of certain rights, shall not be construed to deny or disparage others retained by the people.

10 The powers not delegated to the United States by the Constitution, nor prohibited by it to the States, are reserved to the States respectively, or to the people.

(ratified 15 December 1791)

We have considered quite extensively the traditions of thought and state theory that have tended to conceptualise the relationship between the state and the individual in terms of protecting the individual from the worst excesses of state power and manipulation and to place ultimate value on the individual. In this model the state, in theory, is surbordinate to the individual and the rights and liberties of the individual are considerably more important than the powers of the state. Any power that the state does hold it does so in trust, and the extent of the state's power is limited. As we have seen, this model of the relationship is founded on concepts of limited government, constitutionalism and responsible government. It has been argued that this is a theory associated with liberalism and liberal constitutionalism. However, we should now turn to some further and different conceptions of the state.

## Marxist theories of the state

Although it is often pointed out that Marx did not produce a detailed analysis of the state, the impact of Marx's own work and its legacy on theories of the state is extensive. But partly because he did not produce a single and coherent statement of state theory and partly because he was such a prolific thinker and writer, Marx's legacy is open to a range of interpretations. Jessop (1990) identifies six ways in which the state can be categorised. First, the state is seen as essentially parasitic. Second, the state is characterised as an epi-phenomenon in which state power is a surface reflection of the economic struggle between classes. Third, the state can be seen as a factor of social cohesion, regulating conflict and attempting to maintain social order and stability. Fourth, the state acts as an instrument of class rule, in that the state, its institutions and personnel act to promote, protect and maintain the interests of the dominant economic (and hence political) class. This is the most readily identifiable notion of the state in Marxist analysis and finds a clear statement in *The Communist Manifesto*, where Marx and Engels argue that 'the executive of the modern state is but a committee for managing the common affairs of the whole bourgeoisie' (Marx and Engels 1973b). Fifth, the state is a set of political institutions. Sixth, the state is a system of political domination that has specific effects on the class struggle. The most significant conception and function of the state is either to reflect or to reinforce the nature of class divisions in society or to act in a way directly beneficial to the dominant economic class, thereby making the state an instrument of class rule. The idea that the state acts in the interest of a particular class was the most significant idea of Marx's concerning the nature of the state and was readily accepted and further developed by others such as Lenin. In classical Marxist analysis the forms that the state takes in liberal, parliamentary democracy – whilst promoting the image of democracy and universalism and allowing for certain concessions and 'victories' for the masses – are really just articulations of class interests and class power and actually inhibit the possibility for democracy and equality.

### The fascist state

In an earlier section of this chapter we argued that the political theories and ideologies associated with liberalism and social democracy stress the positive position of the individual in relation to the state. In this conception, we argued, the individual enjoys primacy (in theory if not in practice) and society is governed and organised through political institutions and rules that respect and even promote the individual's rights and freedoms.

This is, of course, only one particular way of seeing the state and its relationship with those who live under its jurisdiction, and there exist many others. For some Marxists the state within liberal capitalist democracies, though apparently concerned with the rights and freedoms of the individual, is actually concerned with the maintenence of capitalist power and economic relationships. Thus the state is ultimately an oppresive machine that upholds capitalism and acts in the interests of capital and those who belong to the capitalist class. In other words, the 'freedoms' and 'rights' of the individual are ultimately fictions. But in this conception the state is part of a larger delusion of the masses which takes place through a whole complex of processes identified as occurring in the notion of 'false consciousness'. Though the state may well be directly repressive and act in the interest of specific groups within society – the capitalist class – the state possesses no real independent identity; the state has a function only in that it acts in the interests of individuals – not all individuals, but members of a designated social group.

In fascist ideology the state, or rather the collective as manifested through the political body, is the location of primacy and not the individual or class. It is important to recognise that the scholarly discussion of fascism as an ideology and a political movement, as you will have seen in Chapter 6, is a deeply complex one.

However, in fascism the relationship between the state and the individual is less one of rights and freedoms than one of obligations and duties. Little is made of the freedoms and rights of individuals, and a limited amount of documentary space is given up to constitutions that formalise and protect such rights. The concern for fascists is the creation of a new society, a new order, in which the total loyalty of the individual and the total authority of the state are accepted. Fascism became a potent and established political force in Europe between the two world wars and fascist states took power in Germany and Italy. The following statement on the nature of the fascist state was written by Mussolini and Giovanni Gentile for the *Enciclopedia italiana* in 1932.

## The Fascist State

Against individualism, the Fascist conception is for the State; and it is for the individual in so far as he coincides with the State, which is the conscience and universal will of man in his historical existence. It is opposed to classical Liberalism, which arose from the necessity of reacting against absolutism, and which brought its historical purpose to an end when the State was transformed into the conscience and the will of the people. Liberalism denied the State in the interests of the particular individual; Fascism reaffirms the State as the true reality of the individual. And if liberty is to be the attribute of the real man, and not of that abstract puppet envisaged by individualistic Liberalism, Fascism is for liberty. And for the only liberty which can be a real thing, the liberty of the State and of the individual within the State. Therefore, for the Fascist, everything is in the State, and nothing human or spiritual exists, much less has value, outside the State. In this sense Fascism is totalitarian, and the Fascist State, the synthesis and unity of all values, interprets, develops and gives strength to the whole life of the people.

(Benito Mussolini and Giovanni Gentile, *Enciclopedia italiana*, 1932)

Here the emphasis is very different to that of the liberal conception of the state. For Mussolini, the state is a total organisation which is the only thing through which individuals can find their true reality and destiny. In this sense, the relationship between the individual and the state is one of dependence – without the state the individual has no real identity or value.

### The communist state

Since 1989 communism in Europe, at state level, has been in crisis. The fall of the Berlin Wall in 1989, the disintegration of the former USSR and the subsequent banning of the Communist Party of the Soviet Union symbolised the end of a significant political and social experiment in Europe and parts of Asia. The division between state and society is less clear than in the liberal state, in which the aim of politics is to regulate the proper relationship between the individual and the state and limit the scope, range and power of the state in respect of individual liberty and freedom. In communist states the public sphere is not distinct from the political sphere and poilitics permeates all aspects of life.

We will now consider now some extracts from the The Constitution (Fundamental Law) of the USSR, 1977, and consider their implications.

### The Constitution (Fundamental Law) of the USSR, 1977

The Great October Socialist Revolution, made by the workers and peasants of Russia under the leadership of the Communist Party headed by Lenin, overthrew capitalist and landowner rule, broke the fetters of oppression, established the dictatorship of the proletariat, and created the Soviet state, a new type of state, the basic instrument for defending the gains of the revolution and for building socialism and communism. Humanity thereby began the epoch-making turn from capitalism to socialism.

1). **Principles of the Social Structure and Policy of the USSR**

**Chapter 1 – The Political System**

*Article 1.* The Union of Soviet Socialist Republics is a socialist state of the whole people, expressing the will and interests of the workers, peasants, and intelligentsia, the working people of all the nations and nationalities of the country. . . .

**Chapter 3 – Social Development and Culture**

*Article 19.* The social basis of the USSR is the unbreakable alliance of the workers, peasants, and intelligentsia.

The state helps enhance the social homogeneity of society, namely the elimination of class differences and of the essential distinctions between town and country and between mental and physical labour, and the all-round development and drawing together of all nations and nationalities of the USSR. . . .

Chapter 7 – The Basic Rights, Freedoms, and Duties of Citizens of the USSR

*Article 60.* It is the duty of, and a matter of honour for, every able-bodied citizen of the USSR to work conscientiously in his chosen, socially useful occupation, and strictly to observe labour discipline. Evasion of socially useful work is incompatible with the principles of socialist society. . . .

*Article 67.* Citizens of the USSR are obliged to protect nature and conserve its riches. . . .

*Article 68.* Concern for the preservation of historical monuments and other cultural values is a duty and obligation of citizens of the USSR.

These extracts convey a very different view of the relationship between the state and the individual. Here the role of the state is far more extensive and the concern is to promote the social cohesion and social project of socialism in all realms of human experience. The constitution was a very long document with twenty-one chapters and 174 articles. These cover not just the institutional arrangements of party, state and government, but include, as can be seen from the extract, statements about social life, the environment and cultural preservation. They are concerned less with individual liberties than with the collective dimension of life and with obtaining collective aims through the state or by state mobilisation. Thus the constitution makes pronouncement on the family, wages and the standard of living, relationships between ethnic groups and the historical mission of the USSR. This constitution is as ready to speak of the obligations of the citizen as of the rights. Some of the rights enshrined in this constitution are from the same areas of individual rights as those in the constitutions we have already considered, including freedom of religious conscience, inviolability of the person and home, privacy in personal communications. But, in the main, the section of the constitution entitled 'The State and the Individual' is more concerned with collective social and economic rights. Thus the constitution affirms that women and men have equal rights, that citizens have the right to work, rest and leisure, the right to health protection and housing. Furthermore, citizens have the right to education, cultural benefits and, as seen above, they also have an obligation to preserve the environment. Article 66 affirms that citizens of the USSR are obliged 'to concern themselves with the upbringing of children, to train them for socially useful work, and to raise them as worthy members of socialist society. Children are obliged to care for their parents and help them.'

However, it is important to remember that constitutional documents do not, in themselves, guarantee anything. A glance at the works of, for example, Alexander Solzhenitsyn, and especially his 1963 publication *One Day in the Life of Ivan Denisovich*, illustrate how brutal this regime could be.

## Conclusion

In this chapter we have looked at the relationship between the state and the individual from a variety of perspectives. We have argued that a number of key themes and characteristics can be isolated and analysed. We have also argued that the term 'state' is complex and obtuse. In summing up here I would like to introduce one further complication.

The notion of the state explored here is very much one in which the state provides a space and the boundaries for a particular type or model of politics that can be characterised as one of the processes of modernity. The connection between state-building and modernity is marked and is worth reflecting on – albeit briefly – here. Increasingly, commentators argue that the political forms and practices that emerged in the modern era are under threat. Certain political, social and economic certainties of the modern era – nation-state, progress, scientific rationalism – are being eroded or at least challenged by new forms of politics, social organisation and economics. Considerable attention is paid to such developments later in the book, particularly in Chapter 16, 'The processes of globalisation, but brief commentary is required here. The central point is that the notion of sovereign states – which control spaces and territories and enjoy exclusive and specific relationships with their citizens – is being challenged, which means at least one element of Hall's composite definition (p. 273) is being seriously challenged (J. Dunn 1994). Although assertions that the nation-state is in crisis may be overstated (Hont 1994), there do seem to be two particular processes that are eroding the certainty that the nation-state once signified. First, the process of integration, most readily identified in the development of the European Union and the integration of the global economy, is undermining the efficacy and possibly the legitimacy of the nation-state. Second, fragmentation, in the form of greater autonomy or demand for autonomy by smaller units of society is increasingly important. This process has been most devastating in the former Yugoslavia. But some commentators have argued that the crisis of the nation-state is also manifest in the re-emergence of the phenomona of city-states as centres for policy and the articulation of demands (Worpole 1994). The key is no longer sovereignty over space but rather the sovereignty of flows – flows of information, money, people and so on. The flow of information on the 'information superhighway' and the proliferation of communications technology in the form of faxes, cellular phones and PCs is changing the speed and flow of information and diluting the boundaries of the state. All of these developments are affecting and will continue to affect the nature and extent of the state, in terms both of physical boundaries and of influence.

## Exercise

Design a Bill of Rights for the people of a newly independent state.

Give your document a title and a date.

Your document should have a Preamble to establish first principles and the bill should not extend beyond ten clauses.

When you have completed the draft Bill discuss it with a fellow student to see what differences and similarities there are between your two documents.

Then re-draft your Bill of Rights to include any major omissions.

What have you had to leave out?

How will your state enforce this document?

Will it work?

# Further Reading

Gibson, W. (1993) *Virtual Light*, London: Viking. A recent addition to the genre of dystopic visions of the state; a bleak but often humorous tale set in California in the not too distant future of 2005.

Giddens, A. (1985) *The Nation-state and Violence*, Vol. 2 of *A Contemporary Critique of Historical Materialism*, Cambridge: Polity. Comprehensive and sophisticated analysis of the nation-state.

Hall, A. J. (1994) *The State: Critical Concepts*, London: Routledge. This three-volume collection of essays and articles about the origins, extent and nature of the state is an excellent source for students.

Held, D., Anderson, J., Gieben, B., Hall, S., Harris, L., Lewis, P. and Parker, B. (1983) *States and Societies*, Oxford: Blackwell. A comprehensive and interesting collection of both primary and source materials, from Machiavelli to von Hayek, supported by a good range of analytical pieces by a range of scholars.

Huxley, A. (1977) *Brave New World*, London: Panther. A useful fictional portrayal of the relationship of the state with those under its control and jurisdiction.

Nabokov, V. (1974) *Bend Sinister*, London: Penguin. A satirical tale of an oppressive state run by the 'Average Man' party, which attempts to stamp out individualism and freedom.

Orwell, G. (1951) *Animal Farm*, London: Penguin. One of the most famous fictional presentations (certainly in the UK) of the relationships between the state and those it rules.

Orwell, G. (1983) *Nineteen Eighty-Four*, London: Penguin. Another of the most famous fictional accounts.

Zamyatin, Y. (1983) *We*, London: Penguin. Less well known but more chilling than either Huxley's or Orwell's work, this fictional account explores the nature of state power and control.

# 10 THE POLITICS OF NATIONAL GOVERNMENT (1)

*Richard Huggins*

# The politics of national government (I)

People means Parliament and, in our view, whomsoever the Parliament approves is a virtuous man or woman. I am suggesting many ways to ensure that the voice of Parliament is really the voice of the people and not that of hired voters. With this end in view I am looking for a device which will enable us to listen to the voice of the entire people. All systems are bound to be defective. We are looking for a system which will yield maximum benefit to India.

(Mahatma Gandhi, 24 August 1924[1])

Scarcely had the executive government become really responsible to the House of Commons, when it began to appear that the House of Commons was not really responsible to the nation. Many of the constituent bodies were under the absolute control of individuals; many were notoriously at the command of the highest bidder. . . . Thus while the ministry was accountable to the Parliament, the majority of the Parliament was accountable to nobody.

(Thomas Babbington Macaulay, *The Edinburgh Review*, October 1844)

## Introduction

In Chapter 9 we examined the nature of the state and considered the state as a set of institutions, actors and relationships that influence, restrain and ultimately coerce the individual members of a society. In this chapter we will consider more fully the construction, composition and role of those institutions and bodies that constitute the state and the relationships which exist between these bodies. In doing so, we will be looking at institutions such as parliaments, or other legislative assemblies, heads of state, presidents and prime ministers, and other forms of executive bodies, legal systems and courts or judicial bodies. Furthermore, we will consider what the functions of these institutions and bodies are. However, in doing so we will notice how these functions change over time, often overlapping, or how the same function may well be performed by different institutions in different states. This chapter, then, is concerned primarily with the three

**Executive** The apex of power in a political system, at which policy is formed and through which it is executed, for example the President in the USA or the Prime Minister and Cabinet in Britain.

**Legislature** The body within a political system that makes the laws. This is likely to be the national assembly, for example Parliament in the UK or Congress in the USA.

**Judiciary** The body charged with enforcing laws and, in some states, upholding the constitutional rules.

*Mahatma Ghandi (1869–1948), the leader of the independence movement in India. Ghandi advocated a policy on non-violent opposition to British rule. He was assassinated in 1948.*
*Thomas Babbington Macaulay (1800–59), Whig politician and historian.*

*Charles Secondat, Baron de Montesquieu (1689–1755), French political theorist and author of* Esprit des Lois *(1748).*

**Separation of powers** The doctrine that maintains that the three elements of government – executive, legislature and judiciary – should be separate in role and responsibility and that such a separation will ensure good and just government.

central elements of government – the **executive**, the **legislature** and the **judiciary**.

In considering these elements of the political system we are really asking a related set of questions which can usefully be outlined at the start of this chapter and which will act as a guide to understanding the comments that follow. In some ways this chapter asks the following questions: how are people governed? What formal machinery exists to govern? Who governs? What power do those who govern or the institutions that govern possess? How is this power related to the people and from where does the authority to govern derive? Some of these questions were asked by Ghandi and Macaulay. For Ghandi the aim was to construct a parliament through which the voice of the people could be heard. For Macaulay, the concern was to ensure accountability and responsibility within an institutional framework. These are key issues for this chapter. The struggle for responsible and accountable government has a long and often violent history throughout the world and remains for those countries engaged in processes of democratisation (the former communist states in Europe, for instance) a key question. Even in the established democracies of the West, the quest to ensure delivery of these criteria still occupies a good many politicians and scholars of politics.

The aim in this chapter is to avoid focusing unduly upon the organisation of government in liberal democratic states and to move beyond considerations of the type of organisation found in parliamentary or popular assembly political systems to other models of governance such as authoritarian or monarchical ones. But, that said, it is important to point out that considerable attention, be it explicit or implicit, is paid in such discussion to what form government *should* take. This normative question strikes at the very heart of the concern. Many scholars of politics take as self-evident the moral superiority of liberal democratic politics and the types of governmental structures, institutions and organisation that accompany this ideological position. It is important to bear this in mind when considering the formal organisation of politics and to remind oneself that this model is only one of many.

In considering the three branches of government – the executive, legislature and judiciary – it is impossible to avoid the classic doctrine identified with Montesquieu, the **separation of powers**. This doctrine is held up as an important organising principle of liberal democratic government and is enshrined in various constitutional arrangements, most notably in France and the USA.

Although the idea of a separation of powers has a long history and can be observed in the work of Aristotle and Locke the clearest and most explicit statement is associated with the writings of Montesquieu. This doctrine argues that in order to avoid a concentration of power in the hands of a minority in a political system the three principal constituents of government – the executive, legislature and the judiciary – should be separate and enjoy equal power and independence. This should guarantee a series of checks and balances that protect the people from authoritarian or arbitrary rule. This doctrine has been very influential and is also explored in the writings of James Madison and Simon Bolivar. For Montesquieu the problem could be summed up as follows:

> When legislative power is united with executive power in a single person or in a single body of the magistracy, there is no liberty, because one can fear that the same monarch or senate that makes tyrannical laws will execute them tyrannically.
>
> Nor is there liberty if the power of judging is not separate from legislative power and from executive power. If it were joined to legislative power, the power over the life and liberty of the citizens would be arbitrary, for the judge would be the legislator. If it were joined to executive power, the judge could have the force of an oppressor.
>
> (Montesquieu (1748) *Spirit of the Laws*)

We can see, then, that the prime concern of Montesquieu was to avoid the excess of political power which might occur if too much power was concentrated into the hands of one area of government. There was a risk of arbitrary and 'tyrannical' rule, and so the structure of government and the way in which the elements of the structure related to each other were of key importance for thinkers in the liberal tradition who were concerned to establish the limits of government power and its relationship to the people.

For thinkers in this tradition, including John Locke (1963), Montesquieu (1989) and John Stuart Mill (1982), the key point is to guarantee non-arbitrary and *just* government which is responsible to the people (however defined), limited in its extent and accountable both through reference to an electorate and through the organisation of government institutions and the relationship between these insitutions. The aim was to arrive at an organisation of the political system that produced limited, responsible and accountable government. In this respect the analysis of the relationships that exist between the executive, legislature and judiciary provide us with an important insight not only into the structure of government but also into the nature of the political system.

*James Madison (1757–1804), a key figure in the struggle for independence from Britain of the thirteen colonies and one of the Founding Fathers of the United States of America. Along with Alexander Hamilton and John Jay, Madison was the author of* The Federalist or the New Constitution.

*Simon Bolivar (1783–1830), key figure in the struggle for independence from Spanish rule in South America, and responsible for the liberation of five South American nations.*

*John Stuart Mill (1806–1873), British political philosopher and key contributor to the nineteenth-century discussions on representative democracy and the nature of liberty.*

## Executives

The executive is that body which initiates and administers policy within a state. There are two important points to make here. First, we need to distinguish between the political executive, those politicians who hold the office of executive – prime ministers, presidents, chancellor, Taoiseach – and the non-political executive or the civil service. In this chapter we are concerned with the first category – the political executive. Second, we can identify two principal types of executive: unipersonal executives, such as the president of the United States; or collective, or plural, executives, such as Cabinet government in Britain.

Whilst it is important to remember that alternative models to those of

Britain and the USA exist, it is also true that these two countries have provided a blueprint for many of the political systems of the world. Indeed, Britain's political system provides an ideal case study of the parliamentary executive form and the USA an ideal case study of the presidential executive, so consideration of these systems is a central focus of this chapter.

In the case of the parliamentary executive – which is the most common form of political executive in the world – twenty-six of the nations who have this type of political executive were formerly part of the British Empire and are now members of the Commonwealth. Although the Westminster model has not remained unchanged or unaltered in those countries who have adopted it, the model provided by the British system does make consideration of this system sensible.

### Parliamentary executives

These are characterised by a range of features that distinguish them from presidential executives, and we can use the work of D. V. Verney to guide us through this section. Verney's important book *The Analysis of Political Systems* (1959) is a seminal study of the differences and distinctions between parliamentary executives and presidential executives.

---

#### Characteristics of parliamentary government

1. The assembly becomes a parliament.
2. The executive is divided into two parts.
3. The head of state appoints the head of government.
4. The head of government appoints the ministry.
5. The government is a collective body.
6. Ministers are usually members of parliament.
7. The government is politically responsible to the assembly.
8. The head of government may advise the head of state to dissolve parliament.
9. Parliament as a whole is supreme over its constituent parts, government and assembly, neither of which may dominate the other.
10. The government as a whole is only indirectly responsible to the electorate.
11. Parliament is the focus of power in the political system.

Source: Verney (1959)

---

Crucially important here is that the role of head of state is separate from that of the head of government. In Britain, the head of state is the monarch, at present Queen Elizabeth II. The role of the monarchy in British politics is now purely symbolic and ceremonial and, although there remain residual powers for the monarchy, the long history of stuggle between democratic representation and monarchical power has resulted in these powers being purely procedural. The monarch still appoints the Prime Minister after a general election, although in reality this is always the leader of the party which has secured the highest number of seats in the first chamber of the legislative assembly. All legislation passed through parliament in Britain has to obtain royal assent – but again it is impossible to imagine a situation in which the monarch could or would withold consent. The British political system possesses a range of conventions and traditions that echo the long history of political development in the country – the prime minister still holds a weekly audience with the monarch, and members of the central executive are still referred to as 'king's' or 'queen's' ministers. In this sense, the monarchy is said to rule through parliament, and certainly the role of the monarchy cannot be ignored in British politics (or indeed in those countries where the British monarch is also the head of state, for example Australia). But there exists no real independent political power for the monarchy in the political system. The cultural, historical and symbolic role of the monarchy is, however, still important, and considerable passion is encountered in Britain and other countries when the possibility of abolition is raised. This possibility seems to be increasingly likely, certainly in some Commonwealth countries, and in Britain ever louder and more vocal calls are heard for abolition or at least significant reform of the monarchy are heard.

A second key pair of characteristics of parliamentary systems is that the executive is drawn from the national assembly and, crucially, its ability to hold on to power is dependent on legislative confidence. The location of the executive within the legislative assembly means that the executive – in the case of Britain, the prime minister and Cabinet – has to retain the support of the legislative chamber in order to be able to pass its legislative proposals and govern. In Britain, this system operates within a strong two-party system, which tends to mean that the executive can command legislative confidence in direct relation to the parliamentary strength of the dominant party. In recent years – since 1979 – the Conservative Party in Britain has enjoyed electoral dominance, with the three administrations of Mrs Thatcher enjoying relatively large majorities in parliament. This electoral dominance has led some observers to argue that the relationship is weighted in favour of the executive, which enjoys too much power in times of electoral dominance, and that the effectiveness of the legislature, as a chamber of scrutiny and representation, is too limited in relation to executive power.

In a parliamentary executive, such as Britain, the executive consists of the prime minister and a Cabinet which is responsible for policy formation and for the administration of the various government departments. Ministers are either heads of government departments – for example the Minister for Agriculture, Home Secretary (Home Office) or Chancellor of the Exchequer (Treasury) – or they may be appointed to a ministerial role for a particular purpose for the life of a parliament (or a shorter period). There are approximately twenty to twenty-four members of the Cabinet in contemporary Britain. This body meets on a regular basis to discuss policy and government business and acts as the core executive in the parliamentary system. This means that a parliamentary executive is a plural executive, in which bargaining, cooperation and interdepartmental considerations and rivalries play a considerable role in the formation and management of policy initiatives. However, this plurality of executive composition is given the image of unity through the existence of the convention known as collective responsibility; by this means decisions taken in Cabinet are portrayed as collective decisions which all members support and agree with. The justification for this is that such collective decision-making ought to guarantee balance and moderation. However, critics argue that it may instead be little more than a sophisticated method of maintaining party discipline and managing the party.

Figure 10.1 gives a diagrammatic representation of a parliamentary executive system; you should note the fusion of executive, legislature and judiciary and the location of the symbolic head of state. As we saw in Chapter 9, Britain lacks a formal constitutional document and one consequence of this is that the roles and powers of institutions and actors are ill defined,

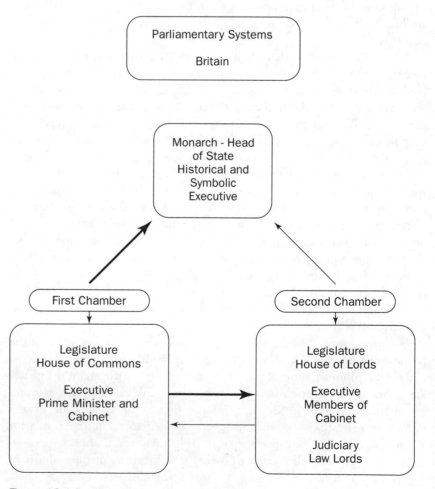

*Figure 10.1* Parliamentary systems: Britain

change over time (the monarchy for example) and develop their identity through conventions and practice rather than binding constitutional rules.

Another distinctive feature of the British system is that no clear separation of powers exist and indeed the executive is located primarily within the legislature. This makes analysis of the location of power arguably more difficult than in some other systems.

---

**THINK POINT**
- Do you think a fusion of executive, legislature and judiciary – as in the case of Britain – is a satisfactory situation?

---

## Presidential executives

Again, we can usefully employ Verney's (1959) categories here to identify the central characteristics of a presidential executive:

---

### Characteristics of presidential government

1. The assembly remains an assembly only.
2. The executive is not divided but is a president elected by the people for a definite term.
3. The head of government is the head of state.
4. The president appoints heads of departments who are surbordinates.
5. The president is sole executive.
6. Members of the assembly are not eligible for office in the administration and vice versa.
7. The executive is responsible to the constitution.
8. The president cannot dissolve or coerce the assembly.
9. The assembly is ultimately supreme over the other branches of government and there is no fusion of the executive and legislative branches as in a parliament.
10. The executive is directly responsible to the electorate.
11. There is no focus of power in the political system.

*Source*: Verney (1959)

---

Of central importance here is the clear separation of powers between executive, legislature and judiciary. We should note, however, that many would argue that the political system of the USA is, in reality, dominated by the president, who as the focus of popular attention can appeal to the public directly in a way that the other elements of the system cannot (McKay 1992).

A second key difference is the centrality of the constitution in allocating and specifying roles and functions of the constituent parts of the political system. A third key difference is the direct election of the executive by the electorate and the fact that this removes the reliance of the executive on legislative confidence. Figure 10.2 presents a model of a presidential executive. Here we clearly see the doctrine of the separation of powers enshrined in the institutional arrangements of the political system of the USA. The constitution not only identifies the three arms of government but specifies their relationship to each other and their respective powers and responsibilities.

### Semi-presidential systems

We have considered the parliamentary executive system in the form of the British political system and we have considered the presidential executive system in the form of the USA political system. Interestingly, there exists a third form, which is best conceptualised as a mixture of elements from both of these two forms. The most accessible example of this is France, but it is also characteristic of other countries, including India, Ireland and Iceland. This system is known as semi-presidential government or dual leadership. The key characteristic here is the existence of both a president

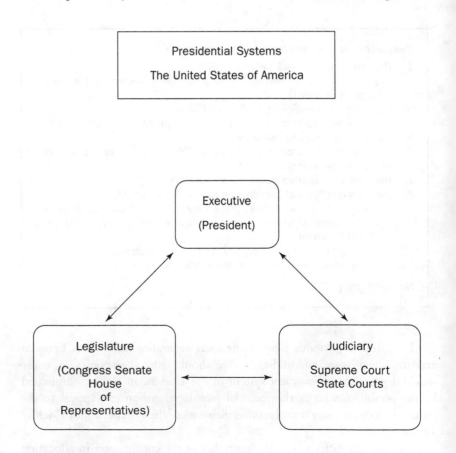

Figure 10.2 Presidential systems: the USA

and a prime minister (or equivalent). The power relationship between the two offices will vary – in France, for example, the president enjoys supremacy, in Ireland the Taoiseach and in Portugal a balance seems to exist.

Communist executives demonstrate different characteristics. In the former Soviet Union the Council of Ministers formed the executive body of the USSR. The Chairman of the Council was the prime minister and there were 130 members in total, including heads of all the Soviet ministries, high-ranking officials, and Chairs of the Union Republic Councils of Ministers (D. Lane 1985).

Other types of executive also exist and these take a range of forms. There is, of course, the unlimited presidential executive found in countries like Iraq, Angola and Syria. Countries where unlimited presidential executives exist tend to be one-party states and are characterised by strong individual leadership which often borders on 'cult of the leader' characteristics. There is usually greater authoritarianism, greater control of the media, opposition and dissidence, and often greater concern with the maintenance of cultural, religious or ethnic homogeneity. Some countries possess military executives and these have been particularly prevelant in South American countries and a number of African states. Here the political system is dominated by senior military officers, who frequently hold power for long periods of time and are often removed only by the actions of rival military leaders. Again, the tendency has been toward authoritarian and often reactionary government and, in South America in particular, the use of military force against civilian targets has been common. The list of human rights violations by South American governments is very long and includes the banning of opposition groups and freedom of speech, and the use of violence and death squads against individuals enaged in the most moderate of activity. For example, following a coup in Chile in 1973 a military junta took power under the leadership of General Augusto Pinochet, who governed until a new constitution was in place in 1990. Pinochet called his system of government 'authoritarian democracy'; political parties were banned, dissent stifled and political opponents 'disappeared'.

## Assemblies

Assemblies are diverse in structure and in name. They can consist of one chamber (unicameral) or two chambers (bicameral), and membership can be elected or appointed. They can be politically powerful or seemingly politically weak. They can be symbolically important and bond the nation in unity or they can be the location of division and confrontation. They are known by many names: parliament, congress, senate, national council, national assembly or more nationally specific names such as Sejm (Poland), Storting (Norway) or the Majlis (Islamic Consultative Assembly).

Although formally known as the legislature, this part of the political system is today not so concerned with law-making as with law-enacting.

There are some exceptions to this – such as the United States Congress and the Senate in Italy – but, in the main, the law-making capability of these bodies has been eroded over the years. There seem to be several reasons for this – and, of course, these are contested explanations – but it would seem that an erosion of the power of assemblies (in law-making terms) has taken place due to three main developments. First, the strengthening of the executive arms of government as law-makers and policy-initiators (Britain's prime minister). Second, the growth of strong party systems (particularly those containing two parties). Here, the existence of strong party discipline, party manifestos and platforms, party recruitment and financing of those seeking political office have all tended to undermine the independence of individual assembly members and almost guarantee that the party with a majority in the assembly will suceed in any legislation it initiates. It follows, of course, that those political systems where the assembly still has a signifi-cant role in the making of laws are found in those countries where party allegiances are comparatively weak, for example the United States, or where the electoral system tends to result in a relatively large number of competing parties, such as the Senate in Italy.

The third factor affecting the role of the assembly has been the increasing importance of mass media, and in particular television, in the political life of the nation. In this case, commentators have argued, the role of assemblies has been usurped by the media and the populace look to the media for their contact with politicians and what they say. Furthermore, politicians have increasingly prefered to address the nation, make policy statements and conduct other political business through the camera rather than in their national assembly.

If, then, law-making is no longer the primary aim of the legislative chamber what is its role? The focus of the assemblies' power has become legislative influence and scrutiny, which in many instances has been increasingly strengthened in recent years. Thus, as a chamber of popular representation, the legislature debates legislation introduced into it by the executive and encourages amendments, revision and consideration. Futhermore, the development of committee systems of scrutiny in many democracies has enhanced this role of the assembly.

We need now to consider further the functions or roles of assemblies in political systems. It would seem that there are three principal roles that are fulfilled by assemblies in political systems.

First, the assembly presents an opportunity for the people to be represented in the political system. Through the election of members to the assembly the people become involved in the political process. Clearly, this represen-tative function is likely to be a more complete process in a country where free and competitive elections occur – in other words, in a country subscribing to some form of representative democratic political system in which choice between political representatives is possible and parties compete for power. If the assembly does carry the voice of the people to the executive, then, one might argue, this is a crucial and valuable role for the assembly. This might be challenged, however, on the grounds that it is only really worth carrying the voice of the people to the executive if the legislature has sufficient power to affect executive power and decisions.

It is also worth making some observations about the role of the individual member who is returned on behalf of the people to the assembly in question. If the individual is a representative, then not only does s/he represent the political sovereignty of those that elected her/him, but s/he does so in a way that means between each election s/he is free to indulge her/his own political judgement rather than seek recourse to those who elected her/him originally (although if they act without consideration to those who originally elected them they run the risk of losing at the next election). This contrasts with delegates who are mandated to follow specific paths and plans of political action when they are returned by those who elect them.

Second, as the legislative assembly provides for the representation of the people (through the systems and procedures that the assembly adopts) the whole political process is granted a level of legitimacy in that it is not conceived of as arbitrary or unrepresentative. In particular, such legitimacy is passed on to individual pieces of legislation so that new laws and policy initiatives are accepted by the people, not necessarily because they agree or desire them, but because they do accept, at least, the legitimacy of the process and the decisions produced by it.

Third, the assembly functions, as we have seen, as a chamber of scrutiny, a debating chamber to which the executive is answerable and which can either prevent abuses of power through its powers of scrutiny or react to them by uncovering the existence of abuse or calling attention to it. This will, however, depend largely on the independent political power of the legislature to deliver such a critical role. In Britain, for example, in recent years the ability of the legislature to fulfil such a role has been challenged by the failure of the Nolan enquiry into standards in public life and, more damningly, by Sir Justice Scott's enquiry into breaches of power by politicians in the core executive. Neither of these cases, despite covering areas of particular public concern and sensitivity and involving very serious allegations of political wrongdoing and corruption, resulted in significant censure of any individual or in any significant changes to the political system to prevent repetition of the alleged occurrences.

# Mountain over molehill

When King Kong loomed over the Manhattan skyline, the citizens behaved like demented ants. Men dived into cars and crashed into lamp-posts. Policemen screamed and waved their arms. Beautiful girls tore their underwear. The monster smiled at them all and wrecked the Empire State Building.

Thus Downing Street in advance of yesterday's Scott report. This entire fiasco was almost vindicated by the handling of its climax. A Government pleading respect for Parliament insulted Parliament. Ministers desperate to wrongfoot their opponents handed them a gift on a plate. A Whitehall machine eager to dismiss the Scott inquiry as so much judicial self-abuse made it seem a noble crusade against men with something nasty to hide. As for the excuse that every government conceals reports until it can rebut them, that is hokum.

Why the fuss? Sir Robert Scott let them all off the book, albeit a book of *papier maché*. He was asked to answer two modest questions put to him in 1992 by the Prime Minister. One was about the status of government documents in criminal trials. The other was about the disclosure to Parliament of changes in arms trade policy. Both had caused ministers some embarrassment and arose from that bugbear of all governments, espionage. All Whitehall's great traumas from Vassall and Blunt to Franks and *Spycatcher*, have arisen from the antics of spies. It is a wonder nobody thinks to abolish them.

For some reason Sir Richard was seized by pretentions to grandeur. He set out to build a mountain over a molehill. He abandoned all sense of proportion and adopted the mien of a self-contessed 'naive' outsider. Theatrical public hearings were staged at which he and his assistant, Presley Baxendale, mimicked American courtroom dramas. They treated the highest in the land like defendants in a criminal trial. With the luxury of unlimited time and the right to summon paper they roamed free over such arcane concepts as ministerial responsibility, Civil service loyalty, judicial discretion and official secrecy. They hinted at deep constitutional thoughts and duly became the despair of Whitehall and darlings of the media and even the London stage.

The molehill remains a molehill. After the ballyhoo of his 'trial of ministers' and his leaked draft report. Sir Richard found himself backtracking on his wilder initial allegations. He is not a malicious man. Section D of his report indicates a clear misleading of Parliament about the nuances of non-lethal arms exports to Iraq, but it accepts that there was no bending of the formal arms policy. His conclusion rightly asserts that where a measure of secrecy is required by policy and where ministers

are relying on official advice, there is an obligation to be as frank as possible. (Ian Lang's summary of these passages yesterday was woefully partial). Yet Sir Richard detects no insincerity, no conspiracy to mislead and no hanging offences to be laid at the door of Lord Howe, William Waldegrave or their officials. There was only the usual obfuscation of parliamentary intercourse. In other words, the fault lay with the process and not the processors. In this he is wholly convincing.

As for the public interest immunity certificates, I remain baffled by the furore In a disclosure unthinkable in any of our trading rivals, ministers sent a judge in a criminal trial a mass of documents concerning commercial espionage. Had they not wanted them disclosed, they would not have sent them. The meaning of their action was to let the trial judge decide on disclosure. In the event he agreed. He passed documents to the defence, which showed them to the press. For the defence lawyer, Geoffrey Robertson, now to howl about 'gagging orders' is absurd. Thanks to these documents, he was given the opportunity to tear the veil from the entire 'arms to Iraq' affair, which he gleefully accepted. Nobody gagged him. His clients, men patently involved in making arms for the odious Saddam Hussein, got off.

A system designed to protect the activities of British spies from disclosure, yet not so as to lead to a miscarriage of justice, surely achieved its goal. Paul Henderson, a man whose business activities might have earned him the excoriation of Mr Robertson and *The Guardian*, emerged from their embrace a 'brave

M16 agent' (which he was not) and an idol of the Left. Indeed one of the many warped consequences of Sir Richard's *modus operandi* was to make public heroes of the two individuals most culpable in this silly affair, Mr Henderson and the former minister, Alan Clark. They have given new meaning to 'Scott free'. Those who had to mop up after them were cast as knaves (not least in the BBC's biased dramatisation).

So much for the molehills. What of Sir Richard's mountain, a veritable Ste-Victoire in its range and colouring, and in its creator's ambition? What justified three years work, three years of turmoil, publicity and anguish? Reading Scott I had an eerie sense that he had been passed a dummy. I would have welcomed his views on substantive matters such as the ethics of the arms trade, the efficacy of the House of Commons or the future of judicial review. Instead we have five volumes almost entirely filled with historical material on arms deals, parliamentary exchanges and commercial case law. There can be nothing left to learn of the nuances and compromises of 'grey area' machine tools licensing. But after 2,000 pages and a broad exoneration, we are hardly the wiser. It is as well Sir Richard was not directed at the Pergau dam scandal. There real clashes of trade and foreign policy were at stake, and ministers were unquestionably culpable of deception. Pergau remains the one that got away.

The Scott report ends with a dying fall. It illustrates what practitioners of government know well, that theirs is a difficult calling. Wrangling ministers and officials are not inept schemers seeking to evade Sir Richard's stern reprimand.

They represent real interests in real contention. Their accountability to Parliament, as to the press and the law, is foggy, since – especially in foreign affairs – there has to be a premium on confidentiality. Their chief enemy is time. Expecting them to cover all their traces against a Scott inquiry is like expecting Sir Richard himself to give his report in two weeks flat, with no mistakes and subject to public scrutiny of his every move, I imagine he would not like that.

Unlike the law, government takes place in real time. Lord Franks, reporting on the intelligence failures prior to the Falklands invasion, did so quickly and incisively in one short volume. Sir Richard's raw material was paltry, a few fudged parliamentary answers, the failed conviction of three arms dealers and some ministerial red faces. He should have spent six weeks on the job and gone back to his courtroom. I disagree with Lord Howe when he says the Scott technique was unjust. Politicians sometimes deserve a rougher ride than the stagey banter of Parliament. But the report's lack of proportion and dilatoriness was grotesque.

The test of an exercise in hindsight is whether those involved would, in retrospect, have behaved differently. The thinness of Sir Richard's recommendations suggests not. There will always be a tension between sensitive policy changes and their public presentation. Ministers will always seek to shield their disagreements from the public. Water will always flow downhill. The report leaves the P11 procedure (with some technical reforms) in place. It accepts commercial and security confidentiality. It agrees that ministerial responsibility is diluted by the complexity of government. The mountain reduces to eight final pages, wishing that ministers be more 'forthcoming with information'. The coda is a pious wish that politicians might behave less like . . . politicians.

This inquiry was begun after an executive, not a legal, failure. MPs Question Time and letters are not adequate properly to scrutinise modern government. Parliament hired an outside inquisitor to do this job for it, rather than delegate it to a select committees (as Congress would have done).

This is a poor comment on Parliament. I read to the end of the report for advice on how better to order these things in future. I read in vain.

(*The Times*, 16 February 1996)

## Unicameral or bicameral?

How many chambers an assembly should have is a question that has occupied many a political scientist and political activist and the number of chambers remains an important point of comparison between different assemblies and political systems. In the nineteenth century the discussion regarding the number of chambers in a political system was particularly marked in Britain, especially in the more radical Whig circles, where concern preceded the Parliamentary Reform Act of 1832. The central concern, though remaining with balance and a balanced constitution, is the number of chambers required to guarantee balanced government. An example of this discussion is found in the work of the Whig adviser John Allen (1771–1843), who was an adviser to the Whig peer Lord Holland and well known in Whig political circles for his knowledge and understanding of the constitution. In a short phamplet entitled *Suggestions on the Cortes* (1809), Allen outlines his views on how a parliament should be formally and institutionally constructed, while making suggestions for a reform of the Spanish parliament. In this approach, a parliament that consisted of only one chamber was rejected on the basis that, as no other chamber existed, the single-chamber parliament would be inattentive to form and procedure, inconsistent in its decisions and less concerned with justice and equanimity than it ought to be. In short, the single chamber would enjoy unchallenged power that would corrupt the quality of governance delivered. However, multiplication of chambers was not likely to provide good government either. A tricameral system, rather than introducing more checks and balances into the system, was likely to encourage inefficient government through excessive delay and the protection of public and legislative business. There also existed the possibility that two of the three chambers could 'gang up' on the other one and coerce its decisions. Therefore the best system available would be the bicameral one.

## Bicameral systems

These are systems in which the assembly possesses two separate chambers, each of which has specific and separate roles, different powers and different membership. The two chambers can be very similiar, with an almost balanced relationship in terms of power, as in the case of Belgium, or quite dissimiliar, as in the case of Britain, with its uniquely large second chamber based on hereditary and nominated membership.

Britain is a bicameral system, as are the USA and a whole range of other states, including Brazil, France, Canada, Australia and many others. But the reasons for retaining two chambers outlined above are not the only reasons that might exist. For instance, bicameral systems often fulfil a particular role within federal systems of government. In federal systems the membership of the second chamber will often attempt to reflect regional, cultural and ethnic differences and identities in order to underpin the federation of the state and to allow for local representation within the federal government system. Examples of this type of organisation can be found in a number of countries, including the USA, Canada, Argentina and Australia.

In other countries, such as Britain, the membership of the second chamber may reflect certain social and economic positions. Membership of the House of Lords consists of those who have a hereditary right to sit in the second chamber (Hereditary Peers), those nominated by the executive to become members of the upper house (Life Peers), and bishops (the Lords Spiritual).

Bicameral systems of government consist of two chambers. The membership of the chambers is normally based on different criteria, and tenure of each chamber is normally different. The argument is that two chambers can act as a balance to avoid an undue amount of power accumulating in one

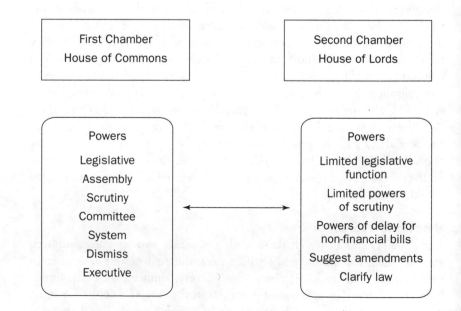

*Figure 10.3* Bicameral systems: Britain

part of the political system. However if the balance of power is equal, then legislative inaction and impotence may result. If the balance of power is unequal, then the reason for having a second chamber at all is undermined. In the case of Britain serious concern is frequently voiced over the effectiveness of the House of Lords (in addition to questions of democratic legitimacy) to act as an effective second chamber as its powers are so limited. Indeed Mrs Thatcher's governments were defeated in the Lords over 100 times between 1979 and 1990 – to little effect.

This concentration of power in the first chamber is, in part, a result of the political struggles that took place in the nineteenth and twentieth centuries between the democratically elected House of Commons and the hereditary House of Lords. Many feel that the balance works well and should be preserved, that the House of Lords represents an important part of British society and history. Others argue that it is archaic, limited and anti-democratic, and call for systematic reform of the assembly, either to abolish the House of Lords and replace it with another second chamber, differently constituted, or to create a unicameral system in Britain. There are important points on both sides, and what reforms could be made are hotly disputed.

Although few countries carry the role of nomination and privilege quite as far as Britain in membership of the second chamber, it is not unusual for attempts to be made for the membership to reflect certain specific characteristics. The most common is maturity, with relatively high qualifying age restrictions placed on intending candidates. Thus an individual must be over forty years of age to sit in the Senato in Italy and over thirty to sit in the Senate in the USA. This qualification, it is argued, allows members to bring greater experience and maturity to their office (often accompanied by political experience in other parts of the political system) and allows for more considered judgement and 'wisdom'. (You will note from my quotation marks that this is an argument that I do not wholly agree with.)

Another interesting characteristic of second chambers is that the length of office often varies from that of the first chamber. In Britain this is clearly the case, as membership of the House of Lords is lifelong. In countries where members are elected, the length of time they are elected for can vary: nine years in France, eight in Brazil, and six in the case of Japan, India and the USA. Interestingly, some of these countries also stagger the election of members to the Upper House; for example, in France a third of the membership retires every three years and in the USA a third retires every two years. The existence of a staggered term of office, coupled with age and other 'qualifications' for office, is designed to encourage a different balance of members and a different institutional culture with greater consistency and overlap between membership and executive administration. The longer period of office is also designed to reduce some of the concern with party politics and politics of the immediate present, which often, understandably, characterise lower chambers.

## The judiciary

Once again, the emphasis is on the independence of the judiciary from direct political influence, and in particular the executive. The role of the judiciary is to enforce the laws made by the executive and legislature and to enforce the rules of the political system. How this is actually achieved varies, however, from political system to political system. In the United States, the Supreme Court can rule unconstitutional and therefore invalid an act passed by the president or Congress. Indeed this is an important role for the Supreme Court in the USA. It not only represents a 'watchdog' role in regard to the power located in the other arms of the political system, but also shows how the Constitution of the United States is kept 'alive' and reinterpreted to adapt to changing social, economic and political conditions. Throughout the last two centuries, the judiciary in the USA has been highly significant in shaping the way in which an individual citizen's rights have developed and what the relationship between state and individual is. In this sense, the judiciary is *making* laws as much as it is enforcing them. In the 1950s and 1960s the decisions taken under the leadership of Chief Justice Warren established a series of precedents and vitally important decisions regarding the issue of black civil rights. In this sense the Supreme Court is a political body – or at least a body performing a political role – as much as a judicial one.

In Britain, no such consitutional power exists for the High Court or the House of Lords' Law Lords, but they can rule on whether or not an act is lawful. In the following extract we can see how this happened to the Home Secretary, Michael Howard, over his recommendations regarding the length of time to be served by the children found guilty of the killing of James Bulger in Britain in 1993. In this sense the role of the judiciary, is, perhaps, less openly political than in the USA. However, the judiciary still makes law through its interpretation of existing statute and through judicial precedent.

Since the role of the judiciary is very important to the functioning of a democratic state, the issue of the selection of the members of the judiciary is an important point for consideration. In particular the issues of independence and accountability are of a central importance. Of course, one might argue that if the law is neutral and the role of the judiciary is to enforce the law it should not matter greatly how judges are appointed. But as we have noted, judges, particularly at the most senior constitutional level, have as important a role in making laws as in interpreting them, and therefore their independence (or otherwise) from the political system becomes a question of crucial importance. Different countries appoint judges by different means. In Britain, and the USA in the case of Supreme Court, judges are appointed by the executive, and many would argue that this procedure opens up the possibility of 'political' appointments which might be sympathetic to the executive. The defence of such a system of appointment used to be that as judges often remain judges for a long time and political administrations are

**Bulger Case:** Home Secretary swayed by popular pressure

# Another page in history of conflict with judiciary

**PATRICIA WYNN DAVIES and KATE WATSON-SMYTH**

No one can dispute the intense public pressure for life to mean life after the convictions of Robert Thompson and Jon Venables for one of history's most horrific and troubling crimes.

One petition was signed by almost 300,000 people and another by nearly 6,000. Readers of the *Sun* sent in more than 20,000 coupons. More than 75,000 daytime TV viewers swamped a switchboard to demand that the two boys stay locked up.

Michael Howard, the Home Secretary, seemed more than willing to respond to the public outcry, apparently seeing the Bulgar case and the sentencing of the two boys as a central plank in his law and order platform, a chance to demonstrate heavy sentencing for serious crimes. Instead it has proved his undoing.

For Lord Woolf the case marks his first big battle with the executive since his appointment as Master of the Rolls, and he did not shrink from the task. While holding back from re-writing the law, Lord Woolf says Parliament must now reconsider how it deals with juveniles who commit serious crimes. He went as far as he could, constitutionally, in spelling out his backing for a more flexible, responsive regime for dealing with the uncertainties thrown up by cases involving child murderers. He also made plain his distaste for the 'tariff' system that has come to treat juvenile and adult killers as indistinguishable, despite legislation intended to handle children differently.

Like the Home Secretary, the Master of the Rolls was aware of the force of public opinion. In giving his ruling he considered that it could well provide part of the explanation for the 'striking difference' in the tarrif figures of the judiciary and the Home Secretary for the penal element of the sentence. But it was only at the point of possible release that public opinion could lawfully be brought into play.

But running a campaign to increase punishment in a particular case could amount to interference with the administration of justice, Lord Woolf said. 'This being the position as to the courts, I find it difficult to see the justification for the Home Secretary taking a different view.'

There was some small comfort for Mr Howard in that two out of the three judges were prepared to accept – provided it was done lawfully on the basis of relevant considerations – that 'tariffs' could be ordered for both adults on mandatory life sentences and children held at Her Majesty's Pleasure, the indeterminate and compulsory sentence for juvenile killers.

But if the House of Lords agrees with that, the case will inevitably go to the European Court of Human Rights in Strasbourg. Only last week, Mr Howard bowed to a Strasbourg court ruling in the cases of Prem Singh and Abed Hussein that decisions over the actual release on parole of offenders held at Her Majesty's Pleasure should be by a court-like body, without a politician having the final say.

If the House of Lords or, as is more likely, the European Court, strips a British Home Secretary of his power to set minimum terms, it would mean that child killers would have their cases regularly reviewed, heralding a return to the idea of 'juvenile justice' and leave the entire process in the hands of judges and an independent body such as the Parole Board.

An earlier European Court ruling, in 1990, abolished the Home Secretary's powers to decide on the release dates for prisoners serving discretionary life sentences – life terms for serious crimes other than murder. Some human rights campaigners predict that it is a matter of time before the final say in the release of those serving mandatory life sentences is also removed from politicians.

This is unlikely to faze Mr Howard – battling with the judiciary has become a hallmark of his three years as Home Secretary.

He has been accused of acting unlawfully, unjustly and unfairly with grim regularity. He has constantly batted back, insisting he feels 'no personal remorse' over court rulings that he has exceeded his powers.

He declared in a speech to law students: 'A number of decisions that have been taken recently would have amazed people a few years ago.'

Outside the courts, he is currently on a collision course with the legal establishment over his plans for tough minimum sentences.

Immigration has been another battlefield. In March a judge at an immigration appeal tribunal blocked moves by the Home Office to expel the Saudi dissident Mohamed al-Masari. The Government was forced into another embarrassing climbdown last month when Judge Pearl, the chief adjudicator, ordered Mr Howard to reconsider the deportation decision.

In 1994, the High Court ruled unfair his denial to convicted criminals of access to new evidence. That opened the way for at least 200 offenders to receive information on why their cases have not been sent for appeal, including Jeremy Bamber and those convicted of murdering the newspaper boy Carl Bridgewater.

None of this is likely to cause the Home Secretary sleepless nights, according to penal affairs sources. Denise Bulger, the murdered child's mother, yesterday called on the Home Secretary to 'stay on our side' as she renewed her protests against the original, eight-year, recommendation. 'What the judges are trying to say is that a kid can murder another kid and get a stupid sentence like eight years,' she said. The Home Secretary is more likely to take heed of her words than those of Lord Woolf.

*(Independent, 31 July 1996)*

by comparison relatively short-lived there should exist a 'healthy' overlap between the judges appointed by one administration and the next. This justification might be a little dated now, especially with the recent experience of Conservative Party executive dominance in the United Kingdom, and the system could still be criticised as being unfairly weighted in favour of the executive. The experience of the USA is equally unclear. Although Supreme Court judges are appointed by the president (subject to approval by Congress), seemingly political appointees have often asserted their independence once in position; this was the case with the Warren Courts of the 1950s and 1960s. Against this, however, it has to be said that the Supreme Court judges of the 1980s demonstrated considerable levels of conservatism in their rulings, which might have been a reflection of the political stance of those who appointed them.

At the other extreme of executive-appointed judges is the appointment of judges by popular election, which also takes place in some states in the USA. This form of judicial selection does allow for public responsiveness and makes the judiciary at this level more responsible to the people. Critics argue, however, that this responsiveness is achieved at too high a cost to impartiality and independence as popular concern compromises judicial integrity.

## The European Union – a new model?

The insititutional arrangements of the European Union provide a further interesting and illustrative case study of the relationship between government, state, nation and individual. The important point here is that this organisation is both inter-governmental and in some ways (although as you will have seen earlier in this book there exists a huge debate about this) federal. But the nature of the European Union produces some interesting points for consideration: first, there is no single head of state – rather a collective leadership through the European Council and Council of Ministers; second, a separation of powers and responsibilities is clearly at work and considerable tension, underlined by the clash between national and federal interests, is present within the system; third, the European Union is such a highly populated geo-political area (and one growing all the time) that issues of responsibility, accountability and democratic deficit are of key interest; fourth, this is a set of institutions and institutional relationships that are in the process of being formed (and re-formed) and this adds to the uniqueness of the process. Figure 10.4 shows the main bodies of the European Union and indicates the relationships between them. The institutional arrangements of the European Union provide an interesting case study of what government structure might look like in a multi-lateral organisation. Here there is no single head of state and a split executive with a complex relationship having developed between the European Council or Council of Ministers and the European Commission – both of which can be said to possess executive roles. The European Parliament takes an extremely limited legislative role and acts almost exclusively as a debating chamber. Although the power of the European Parliament has been strengthened by the Maastricht Treaty it remains a limited legislature and as such adds little to the European Union in terms of democracy or representation.

The European Commission, which holds that its first task 'is to initiate new European policies', positions itself as the executive body of the European Union. One might argue, however, that the power of the European Council and Council of Ministers also renders these bodies executive ones. More clearly, the European Parliament performs the legislative function of the European Union, although here, more than in many legislatures, the ability of the European Parliament to make law is extremely limited and although its powers are increasing it remains primarily a chamber of debate and scrutiny. The European Court of Justice fulfils the judicial role for the European Union but is a much more powerful body than the judiciaries found in many member states. The Maastricht Treaty and

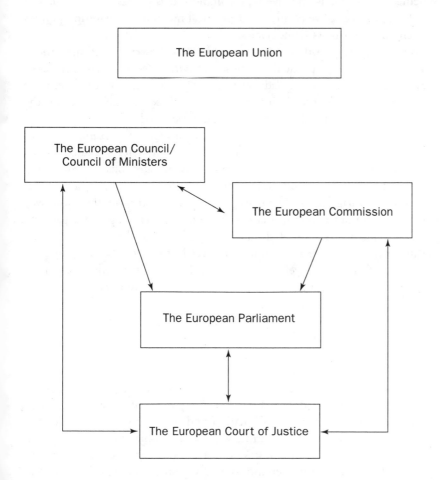

*Figure 10.4* The European Union

the Intergovernmental Conference in 1996 have altered, and will continue to alter, the roles of these institutions and their relationship both to each other and to the insitutions of the member states.

## Virtual government?

Our discussion here has focused upon how political systems are organised and what institutions exist to exercise and limit political authority. The aim or indeed the necessity of these systems is to render governable large numbers of people. In a country such as the United Kingdom, with a population of 56 million, it is clearly impossible to operate any form of direct democracy, and therefore systems of governance have to be found that allow such a large number of people to be represented at a political level while ensuring that those who represent the people are held accountable through regular and free elections and through the operation of responsible government. Whether or not this is effective representation, it is at least functional, and it is difficult to conceive of any other practical method of organising politics in such large and mass democracies.

As we have seen in other chapters in this book, however, the implications of new technologies – particularly those involving telecomedia – interactive television, home-computing, advanced digital telecommunications and the Internet – pose the possibility of increased direct participation of the citizenry in the political process. An increased level of direct electronic democracy could take a number of forms. In Sweden, for example, recent elections were carried out by electronic information systems, including the use of interactive technology in local and national elections (Sweden), the development of information and community service centres (Scandinavia) or electronic village halls (Denmark). The point is that in the same way that new communications media can be said to be eroding the organising principles and institutions of the nation-state they can be said to threaten the integrity and future of national political institutions. So, although we might well witness the development of alternative but sympathetic channels for political communication, as in the case of Sweden, we might also witness the development of something very different altogether.

Let us engage in a little futurology. The technology is available for homes in countries such as the USA and Britain to have an almost limitless number of television channels and already local cable-television networks are providing the means and systems for local and localised programming of a highly select nature. It is possible that in the not too distant future local authorities will operate their own interactive public information channels, which could provide service information and local information, and offer a two-way communication system between local people and local authority. Either through the television or, less extensively, through electronic networks operating through the Internet and located within public buildings, such as town halls, libraries and municipal car parks, the local authority could consult much more effectively with its local electorate and community. Consultation about local planning initiatives, provision of services and so on could be put to the popular note on a much more regular and frequent basis. Once again, a sympathetic and service-enhancing application of the new technology could operate hand in hand with the present systems and institutions of local authority already in place.

But other more problematic visions are available. Once again, if we engage in some futurology we might envisage a different world, one much more problematic for politicians and established political institutions. In many advanced capitalist countries it has already become common for television programmes – such as *You Decide*, with Jeremy Paxman, in Britain – to carry out telephone polls on certain subjects such as the availability of abortion, the reintroduction of the death penalty and more trivial items such as who should manage the English national football team. As yet these polls are small and by and large insignificant, but imagine a time in which, through access to interactive television and armed with the digital telephone, the nation can be consulted on major issues and political questions. Take, for example, a situation where the House of Commons in Britain is about to have a free vote on the reintroduction of the death penalty. (Debate and votes on the death penalty in the House of Commons are recurrent events in British politics and the issue is always voted on according to conscience rather than along party lines. The death penalty is a topic where many believe that the popular voice would support its reintroduction, while the political system rejects it.) It would be possible for all adults to vote in an unofficial referendum on the same day, at the same time as the politicians at Westminster were voting. The result of the MPs' division is a rejection of the death penalty by a clear majority of 150 MPs. But what if the popular vote – recorded by computer and flashed up on the television at exactly the same time as the official result – demonstrated that 77 per cent of the adult population wanted the reintroduction of the death penalty? What if this began to happen on more and more frequent and highly visible occasions? How would a minister respond when asked by a television presenter 'But our survey of the 13,000,000 car drivers demonstrates that they do not want to pay more road tax but favour an increase in the price of a gallon of petrol' or 'As we have been speaking, Prime Minister, 12,000,000 people have recorded a statement that you should resign'?

Electronic anarchy? Maybe. Such advances are certainly not without problems. Would people be any more likely to vote electronically than otherwise? How would we know that the vote was not made up of the same callers calling over and over again? But the principle – that mass communication through new technology could be used to present mass public opinions directly to the political elite almost instantaneously – creates a range of problems for the formal institutions of the political system. How, for example, could those in power justifiably resist such popular calls? Placed under such pressure what would the formal institutions of government do? The concerns of the elites – always frightened by radical direct democracy – would resurface. The 'tyranny of the majority' would once again become a real fear for parliamentarians and intellectuals alike. The people might actually be heard. The possibility of manipulation of public opinion would be vast. Who would ask the questions and what questions would be set? Even if this idea were embraced as a potential enhancement of democracy by increasing the amount of direct reference to the people, who would choose – or more importantly, how would they choose – which issues and areas of concern would be referred to the popular vote? The problems of such a future are almost endless – but the principle remains the same. The technological innovation which is shaping and reshaping all of our lives will not spare the formal institutions of government. This may take many forms: an alternative virtual parliament of networks and interfaces, a virtual European Union or a mass plebiscite democracy. In each case the institutions would be shaken to their foundations and the political classes left stranded in cyberspace.

---

### What could be the tasks of political bodies?

In conclusion of the previous proposals and initiatives in the three major ICT areas of the world, we can state that there are basic similarities in the American and Japanese approaches and the desired approach for Europe.

These similarities are to:

a. ensure an open network system;
b. ensure access for all;
c. ensure reasonable tariffs;
d. stimulate user driven applications;
e. adapt to bottom-up developments;
f. provide good education and training with respect to new ICT.
g. develop a basic understanding and enhance approaches to ensure a proper follow-up to new social, economic, and political developments.

European Union politics do not necessarily have to play the central role in the development of GIS (Global Information System). Assuring basic norms and values, tariffs, accessibility and the required control mechanisms should be the EU's major concern. As governments are the largest users of the infrastructure, it must be possible to deal out good tariffs with the (privatised) providers of the networks and services. This approach could also provide a safe basis for citizens as well.

Furthermore, one of the major tasks of the political bodies is to develop clear concepts of conceivable and (socially/politically) desired futures. ICT will not solve all the current problems of our societies. Disintegration processes are continuing to proceed. At the end of the day, it is not whether the market should or should not do the job, but whether morally we do accept the changes.

### Democracy

Experiments in American cities show that political participation is rising as a result of digital accessibility. Despite this, the general conclusion of experiments was different. The participation raised in absolute terms, but in relative and quantitative terms the situation turned out to be a failure. Santa Monica, California has had an experiment going with a Public Electronic Network since 1989. Everyone could observe and participate in discussions on local policies. Access is possible via public terminals and via PCs at home and sometimes lead to tele-action groups. Although the participation of specific groups, which were previously not interested in policies, raised, this fact did not improve the democratic quality of the local policies. Telepolicy formed a new elite of freaks, professionals and for example homeless people. With their provocative comments they over-rule the rest. The professional policy-makers do not really feel comfortable in this situation of digital streetfighters. The initial situation of removing the filters between the information source and receiver turned out to be an endless discussion between a limited group of activists.

Whether the tele-democracy can become the modern version of the old roman tribunal of the people we cannot say. But for the sake of democracy everyone should be included if we follow this road. The problem there is that what interests people is not necessarily 'close' – in their legal community anymore. This is not a matter of pure geographical reasons, but more so due to the degree of relevance with people's lives.

Mitch Kapor, of the EFF, doesn't feel very comfortable with the idea of these new forms of democracy. He argues that the processes of moder-ation in democratic structures will break down. It may outline the way to new forms of totaliarism and authoritarian behaviour.

The social role of the companies is underdeveloped. The political role is changing from merely lobby activities to real campaigns during election time, to influence the candidates or political party programmes.

One of the major concerns of national, regional and international bodies should be guiding these developments in a desired election. This would imply a full understanding of the developments (which is not the case these days; mental gap), identifying aspects which can enrich our social, political and economic structures, determine basic values which should be safeguarded in the near future as well as on a long term basis.

It is therefore useful to start a discussion on the aspects which are basic, even after structural changes in society (see also chapter on Democracy and Cyberspace). What is the future role of politics in society? What information systems are required? Who controls the input and output flows? And of course questions like who is 'wired' and who is 'unplugged'? Beyond the boundaries of competition, there is a vast and rough landscape to discover. The least we should do is discuss it, if government is supposed to occupy certain aspects out there.

*Source*: van Bolhuis and Colom (1995), pp. 59–60

## Conclusion

We have seen then that there exists a considerable range of institutions and systems for organising and balancing the power and responsibilities of political institutions within political systems. However, we must always bear in mind the influences of other factors – political culture, political socialisation and political values – when attempting to understand how political systems and institutions work.

## Further reading

Bolhuis, H. van and Colom, V. (1995) *Cyberspace Reflections*, European Commission, DG XII, Social Research Unit. An interesting discussion of the myriad applications of new technology and virtual environments.

Gordon, C. (ed.) (1983) *Erskine May: Parliamentary Practice* (20th edn), London: Butterworth. A thorough guide to British parliamentary procedure.

Montesquieu, Charles Secondat, Baron de (1989) *The Spirit of the Laws*, ed. A. M. Cohler et al., Cambridge: Cambridge University Press. A classic prescription of how the institution of government should be organised and why.

Norton, P. (ed.) (1990) *Legislatures*, Oxford: Oxford University Press. This presents an excellent collection of pieces for the student of legislative institutions.

Sampson, A. (1992) *The Essential Anatomy of Britain: Democracy in Crisis*, London: BCA. An interesting look at some key political institutions in Britain.

Verny, D. V. (1959) *The Analysis of Political Systems*, London: Routledge & Kegan Paul. A classic statement of the nature of and differences between parliamentary and presidential systems.

You may also like to visit the Global Democracy Network @ http://www.gdn.org/ or the European Union Information Society Project Office at http: www.ispo.cec.be.

## 11 THE POLITICS OF NATIONAL GOVERNMENT (2)

*John Turner*

**The modern state**

**The concept of bureaucracy**

*The application of bureaucratic terminology*

**Bureaucratic behaviour and the bureaucratic state of mind**

*Bureaucratic culture*
*Bureaucratic selection and promotion*

**The structure of administration**

*The tension between policy and administration*
*Departmentalism*

**Bureaucracy in a unitary state: the case of the British administration**

*The cabinet system*
*The parliamentary system*
*Pressure groups*
*The media*

**Bureaucracy in a Federal state: the case of the United States administration**

*The Federal civil service*
*Political changes to the bureaucracy: the Reagan reforms*
*The public service ethos: the Volcker reforms of 1986*
*The bureaucracy and Congress*
*The bureaucracy and Presidency*

**Quasi-government**

*Executive bodies*
*Advisory bodies*

**Conclusion**

**Further reading**

# The politics of national government (2)

## The modern state

All modern states have grown in size and complexity in recent years. In this century most states have extended their roles and responsibilities from primarily defence and law and order concerns to concerns about everyday economic management, welfare services and the regulation of many aspects of social life. This expansion in the scale and scope of big government has been accompanied by larger budgets, bigger bureaucracies and increasing difficulties for politicians in controlling the complicated structures and procedures of officials who now administer the state system.

The modern state has developed a cadre of administrative officials who are given the task of supporting ministers, coordinating programmes across departments, clarifying policy and managing relationships between their politicians, other non-governmental administrative bodies, regional and local government, commercial organisations, and the public. The modern bureaucracy provides continuity and permanence, which often override the concerns of less permanently elected politicians.

Bureaucratic politics in a large modern state involves people inside the administrative and governmental process bargaining over complex issues of public policy. No politician or official is ever in a position to know and decide all issues, despite the fact that some political leaders claim to. The bureaucracy is therefore naturally fragmented between different departments, sections of departments, tiers of authority and levels of territorial responsibility. As such bureaucratic problems occur in any large organisation, whether public or private, with officials or managers adopting perspectives and roles based on their own organisational requirements and cultures. Administrators in a modern state are therefore often criticised as:

- too attached to continuity, the status quo and precedence;
- too remote from the rest of the political system and society in general;
- too narrowly selected from an unrepresentative band of society;
- inaccessible and unaccountable for actions and decisions taken;

- too secretive and supporting a closed culture where information is seen as power;
- too conservative and reactive, being less inclined towards risk-taking and innovation;
- preserving and defending bureaucratic objectives which remain relatively independent of the objectives of ministers and other political leaders;
- too concerned about ensuring the preservation of bureaucratic status and privileges;
- time-wasting and too ponderous in making decisions and responding to new demands.

The role of the official in relation to the politician and criticisms of the bureaucrat are portrayed in BBC TV's *Yes Minister*. The interaction between politician and bureaucrat is drawn well in the series. In one episode the minister, Jim Hacker, is introduced for the first time to his senior civil servant, Sir Humphrey Appleby, and is given a lesson in bureaucratic hierarchy. Hacker decides to ask Sir Humphrey who else is in the department.

SIR HUMPHREY  Briefly, sir, I am your Permanent Under-Secretary of State, known as the Permanent Secretary. Woolley here is your Principal Private Secretary. I, too, have a Principal Private Secretary, and he is the Principal Private Secretary to the Permanent Secretary. Directly responsible to me are ten Deputy Secretaries, eighty-seven Under-Secretaries and two hundred and nineteen Assistant Secretaries. Directly responsible to the Principal Private Secretaries are plain Private Secretaries. The Prime Minister will be appointing two Parliamentary Under-Secretaries and you will be appointing your own Parliamentary Private Secretary.

HACKER  Can they all type?

SIR HUMPHREY  None of us can type, Minister. Mrs. McKay types, she is your secretary.

HACKER  What a pity, we could have opened an agency.

(Lynn and Jay 1987: 14–15)

---

**THINK POINT**
- What are the main criticisms of officials in a modern state bureaucracy?

---

The development of studies of the administrative process has tended to concentrate on the concept of bureaucracy; the structure of administrative organisations, including institutions, processes and relationships; and the activities of public officials themselves, including perspectives, cultures and decision-making.

Table 11.1 illustrates the three main ways in which studies have focused

*Table 11.1* Modern bureaucracy and the role of the official

|  | Main role | Relationship in political systems | Organisational culture | Implications |
|---|---|---|---|---|
| Functional/ service role | Policy objectives Policy options Ministerial support | Manage legislature and politicians Manage media | Professional independence Generalist Elitist | Difficult to reform Non-specialist Notion of neutrality |
| Political role | Power bloc to politicians and ministers Promotion of bureaucratic interests Information networks | Manipulation of policy agenda Conservatism Support for the status quo | Cohesive social group Education Recruitment Socialisation | Powerful interest Lobby Permanent Agenda-setting |
| Bureaucratic role | Monopoly control over policy details Budget and control | Political support Notion of objectivity | Rules Procedures Secrecy | Over-supply Defensiveness Duplication |

on the modern bureaucracy and the role of officials. It outlines functional, political and bureaucratic roles. In their functional and service roles, the traditional view of civil servants in relation to their minister is that:

- civil servants *advise*;
- ministers *decide*;
- parliament *approves*;
- civil servants *execute*.

The public administration or functional model therefore concentrates on civil servants as coordinating policy, supporting ministers, clarifying options, managing relationships with parliament and managing relationships with the media and public. Here the key cultural factors are the civil servants' professional independence and administrative generalisation rather than specialisation.

The implication of this view is that officials are politically 'neutral', staying out of the political debates and more controversial formulation stage of public policy. Of course, this functional perspective has been hard to challenge, and reform of the civil service in Britain has not been particularly successful. Often reforms have been interpreted by the administration as political interference.

This model also establishes a false dichotomy between policy formulation and implementation and the role of politicians and officials. Figure 11.1 shows the traditional way in which roles have been separated. The traditional view of the relationship between ministers and civil servants is that of master and servant; politicians decide policy and officials carry it out. Such a model is based on the rational and democratic principle that ministers and politicians are elected and civil servants are permanently employed to use

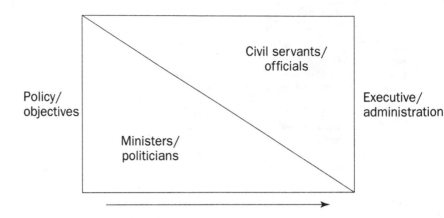

*Figure 11.1* Roles of politicians and officials

their expertise in executing decisions. As one moves along Figure 11.1 from the policy and political objectives end, so the political role of ministers and politicians is replaced by the administrative role of execution. However, administrative detail gradually shades into policy-making and ministers also have a role in execution. All the way along the figure politicians and officials are involved in policy-making and execution, but to varying degrees.

An illustrative example of this grey area between policy and operations centred on the relationship in Britain in 1996 between the Home Secretary, Michael Howard and the chief of the prison service, Derek Lewis over an increase in prison escapes. The latter accused the minister of interfering too much in the operation of the service, whereas Howard maintained that he had a responsibility for ensuring that government policy was carried out. Of course, in this case the prison service and law and order policy had a high profile in the Conservative Party and Lewis was finally forced to resign as the escapes were attributed to poor operational not policy procedures.

A second interpretation of the role of the official concentrates on the more political model of the power bloc. Studies have pointed to senior officials as composing a cohesive occupational group, selected and recruited from a privileged social elite and from similar social backgrounds. Officials are mainly educated in the same way in the same schools and universities and are socialised to have distinctive values which have emphasised a conservative, secretive and centralising perspective.

This model emphasises the fact that officials do form a powerful grouping within a political system and have a vested interest in pursuing their own 'political' interests and self-interest. They work together to lobby for specific projects and set the framework for policy decisions made by politicians.

The third way in which officials have been analysed is in their bureaucratic role. Like the power bloc model, the bureaucratic view emphasises the officials' monopoly over information within the government machine. Civil servants will support larger budgets for their respective departments and will expect ministers to argue their case in government. This leads to what is called an over-supply problem: too many civil servants, the growth in services and larger budgets. In the 1980s the Thatcher Governments attempted to deal with these issues by rationalising departments, creating non-ministerial bodies and privatising certain services.

## The concept of bureaucracy

Like many other terms we come across in the study of politics, the term '**bureaucracy**' does not have a clear and unambiguous meaning. There are various ways in which the term has been used in political analysis.

The term 'bureaucracy' has been used to describe rule-driven organisations. In this sense, many organisations, including those outside the public sector, can be called bureaucracies. Many large corporations (including multinational companies) have the characteristics of bureaucracies.

In government, bureaucracy refers to administrative procedures where officials have an important influence over the decision-making process.

The term 'bureaucracy' is also used to describe certain types of political behaviour. We often hear public complaints about 'faceless bureaucrats' and 'red tape', usually in reference to a situation where an official has taken some time in making a decision, not based on particular circumstances, but according to some general principle or rule which seems inflexible and unrelated to a particular circumstance. Usually, complaints such as this portray officials as aloof, uncaring and impersonal, and as taking too much time in arriving at a decision. Also the term may refer to the way in which decisions are often made in secret or according to an incomprehensible abstract formula.

Bureaucracy is also associated with the notion of performance. Today the term is often used synonymously with inefficient and cumbersome. For example, the formerly nationalised or publicly owned industries in Britain, including gas, electricity, railways, water and coal, were often attacked as being inefficient because they had bureaucratic structures and decision-making procedures. The term is often used to refer to all people working in public sector organisations. When privatising these industries, ministers have argued that once they were unconstrained by bureaucratic procedures these companies were able to innovate and modernise.

The term 'bureaucracy' is also used to refer to the roles of people who work in departments of state. More generally, it can be applied to any official working in bureaux (offices). More specifically, it refers to civil servants and government officials who are professionals with some degree of independence and elite status. Senior civil servants are seen as forming their own social group, supporting and defending their own administrative

**Bureaucracy** Government by permanent officials. The word is often used in a pejorative way to imply the tyranny of the office. Its main characteristics include a hierarchy, rules, merit appointments and rationality in decision-making. The term can be applied to private as well as government organisations.

and bureaucratic interests. This notion has already been discussed as the power bloc model. It means that studies have examined the role of officials in the political process, their recruitment, education, promotion and social values. In Sweden, for example, civil servants are not expected to be politically neutral and often bureaucrats subsequently embark on political careers.

The most influential writer on the subject of bureaucracy was Max Weber. He used the term as an ideal type, developing the concept of bureaucracy against which real organisations and procedures could be compared. Weber constructed three ideal types of authority system:

M. Weber (1947) *The Theory of Social and Economic Organisations*, Glencoe, IL: Free Press.

1 Charismatic authority based on personal attributes.
2 Traditional authority based on precedent and 'immemorial order'.
3 Rational-legal authority based on bureaucracy.

The rational-legal basis of legitimacy involves the acceptance of formal and legal definitions of power and a structure of rules and procedures which are applied uniformly across society and between different social groups. Bureaucracy is implemented through an administrative staff of officials. In its pure form, therefore, a bureaucracy might be compatible with a variety of political systems, including monarchies, one-party states, liberal democracies and totalitarian states. The differences lay in the type of laws, rules and procedures laid down in each system, not in the means of legitimacy through bureaucratic structures themselves.

Weber argued that administrative staff have certain characteristics because of the bureaucratic form of organisation. These include:

1 The bureaucratic career – officials are appointed on the basis of a legal contract and are paid a salary based on a clear job description. They have a clear career path involving a system of promotion based on merit and opportunities for training.
2 Administrative forms of behaviour – officials cultivate the notion of administrative neutrality and highlight the impersonal nature of rules and procedures. The concern is for general principles rather than specific circumstances, and knowledge and expertise have become the basis of power.
3 Structure of administration – there is a clear division of labour, clear lines of responsibility and clear hierarchical relationships.

Weber also contended that bureaucracy had become the main system of rule in modern states. He put forward a number of reasons for this development:

- the formation of larger states with larger populations;
- the extension of state activities, including the extension of state provision of welfare and economic management;
- the development of capitalism, which has placed new demands upon the state;

- the concentration and centralisation of finance and the development of a money-based economy;
- the levelling of social differences and the erosion of traditional social and class divisions.

### The application of bureaucratic terminology

Often the term 'bureaucracy' is used as a form of political abuse, pointing to the level of inefficiency and ineffectiveness of an institution or organisation. In recent years, the term has often been applied to the institutions and procedures of the European Union, often by those who have criticised aspects of European policy. Critics have pointed to the number of officials employed and the size of the organisation. A picture is conjured up of many officials engaged in repetitive and inefficient clerical tasks. Indeed, 'Brussels bureaucrats' are accused of wasting time by using too much 'red tape' to restrict national policy and employing excessive time in implementing decisions.

The Union employs about 25,000 employees, about 15,000 in the Commission (about one-fifth as linguists), 4,000 in the Parliament, 2,000 in the Council and 1,000 in the Court of Justice. The administrative cost of the Union's bureaucracy is about 5 per cent of its total budget, not an excessive figure.

Critics also point to the Union's protracted way of making decisions. However, bureaucratic procedures are often inevitable when dealing with a supranational organisation, when decisions have to be constantly referred back to national governments before being decided upon by the Union. Indeed, on the issues of the Single European Act, the Maastricht Treaty and future monetary union, it could be argued that decisions have been made effectively, on time and with the minimum of delay. Of course, future debates will be held regarding the degree of intervention and regulation imposed by the Union on member states, especially as regards social policy and fiscal policy. The moves to qualified majority voting and transitional opt-out procedures are attempts to reduce decision-making delays within such a large organisation.

---

**THINK POINT**
- What are the key elements of Weber's model of bureaucracy?
- Why has the modern state developed into a bureaucracy?

---

## Bureaucratic behaviour and the bureaucratic state of mind

It is important to consider the effect of a rule-driven organisation, with its formal procedures and hierarchies, on the personalities of the people working

R. K. Merton (1957) *Social Theory and Social Structure*, Glencoe, IL: Free Press.

in such organisations. Merton, for example, has argued that the bureaucratic organisation engenders a bureaucratic personality.

### Bureaucratic culture

C. Handy (1985) *Understanding Organisations*, London: Penguin.

Authority and control systems within a bureaucracy ensure subordinates remain submissive and are conditioned by what Handy has called a *role culture*, which is mediated through adherence to rules and procedures.

> In this culture the role, or job description, is often more important than the individual that fills it. Individuals are selected for satisfactory performance of a role, and the role is usually so described that a range of individuals could fill it. Performance over and above the role prescription is not required, and indeed can be disruptive at times. Position power is the major power source in this culture, personal power is frowned upon and expert power tolerated only in its proper place. Rules and procedures are the major methods of influence. The efficiency of this culture depends upon the rationality of the allocation of work and responsibility rather than on the individual personalities.
>
> The role organisation will succeed as long as it can operate in a stable environment. When next year is like this year, so that next year's tested rules will work next year, then the outcome will be good. . . . So the civil service, the automobile and oil industries, life insurance companies and retail banking are usually role cultures and successful ones.
>
> (Handy 1985: 190–1)

Merton (1957) analyses Weber's notion of the ideal model of bureaucratic organisation, arguing that any advantages of bureaucratic forms of organisations are outweighed by the internal strains and stresses generated by those working in such bureaucracies. Importantly, officials use bureaucratic structures and procedures to protect their own social positions and roles within an organisation. As such, formal rules and procedures are also used informally as a way of enhancing status, protecting officials from conflicts and so securing a safe zone protected from both politicians and the public.

Merton (1957) argues that public officials are placed in ambiguous and difficult positions. Often they disagree with their political masters and, at a more devolved level, there may be frustration in not always being able to respond to the genuine needs of clients. Officials are also accountable and open to public scrutiny, but within a constrained political context this usually leads to a defensiveness and a tendency to play safe. In recent years in Britain there has been a tendency for officials who feel there is a conflict between their administrative and political roles to leak official information to the media. Recent cases involving civil servants, including Sarah Tisdale and Clive Ponting, showed how personal and moral positions were placed before party political considerations. When Ponting was taken to court the jury accepted his plea that his concern for the public interest overrode the more narrowly defined government interest.

See C. Ponting (1986) *Whitehall: Tragedy and Farce*, London: Hamish Hamilton.

### Bureaucratic selection and promotion

Within bureaucratic organisations there are usually clearly defined career paths which officials can follow. Job descriptions, public appointments and competition for posts have created what Ridley calls a 'system of regularised promotion'. However, given the organisational constraints of a bureaucracy, as Handy indicated, behaviour tends to become 'satisficing' rather than risk-taking and innovative. Indeed, creative behaviour will be actively discouraged given the political penalties incurred if mistakes are made. Thus, recruitment and promotion tend to follow clearly defined paths, where patronage is less prevalent, but where conformity is encouraged.

F. F. Ridley (1983) 'Career Service: A Comparative Perspective on Civil Service Promotion', *Public Administration* 62(2).

Thus, the role culture of a bureaucracy tends to lead to conformity, where a safe pair of hands in ensuring the proper rules are followed is more highly regarded than risk-taking. Security is valued more highly than large rewards, as in a commercial organisation. Indeed, there are political demands which ensure that the administrative process does conform to such consistent values. Ministers in government will want officials to conform to their political objectives and will often protect themselves when mistakes are made by pleading that they either were wrongly informed or were not told of particular procedures. Politicians often hide behind the anonymity of bureaucratic procedures when their more political positions are questioned.

The particular perspectives engendered by bureaucracies have important implications for the people entering administrative careers. However, recently there has been a tendency to introduce new approaches to public administration and an emphasis has been placed on new ways of working. Many administrative functions have been devolved to agencies outside mainstream departments. The process of privatisation has taken some functions away. Today officials are encouraged to adopt behaviour more in keeping with that of private commercial organisations. Instead of administration, officials should think in terms of management, with clients being considered more as customers or consumers of services. This process has disturbed the usual stable environment of administration, with greater competition, risk-taking and pro-active management being encouraged. In Britain the traditional public service ethos has been challenged and market-oriented perspectives have been encouraged.

The British civil service conforms to Weber's ideal model, although in recent years politicians have been appointing more political advisers and experts from outside the career service. In the United States the career administrative system involves a much larger number of non-career political executives appointed directly by politicians. In the United States this process reflects the general political system and the role of political patronage in the presidential system of government.

In 1977 Heclo found that 97 per cent of Executive Schedule Officials were political appointees, although lower down the service political appointees are less numerous. As party has become less important in the political system, so the White House has become increasingly dominant regarding appointments. Recent presidents have chosen, to work in the administration, officials whom they can trust and who are more sympathetic with their political and ideological positions. Unlike Britain, where the

H. Heclo (1977) *A Government of Strangers*, Washington, DC: Brookings Institute.

conventional difference between administrative and political roles is upheld, in the United States the distinctions are much more blurred.

Direct political appointees to the administration come from many quarters and include political activists and experts brought in because of their specialist knowledge of particular policy areas. Whereas the Carter Presidency tended to choose recruits from the South with more liberal perspectives, Reagan chose appointees from the West with important roots within more conservative networks.

In the United States the selection of career civil servants used to be undertaken by a Civil Service Commission, although since 1978 there is an Office of Personnel Management and Merit System Protection Board which operates at a departmental rather than central level. In Britain recruitment to senior administrative posts, like under-secretary, deputy-secretary and permanent secretary, has traditionally been made on the basis of performance at lower administrative levels. In general, politics only plays a marginal role in this process, although under the Thatcher governments of the 1980s many permanent secretaries were removed and replaced by more politically supportive officials who either shared her ideology or had a commitment to more innovative policies. Usually senior officials are appointed by means of an extensive consultative process within departments, involving the permanent head of the civil service, the Cabinet Secretary, senior Cabinet ministers and the prime minister. Other permanent secretaries have a role in stating preferences, although the final choice is made by the prime minister following advice from the permanent head of the civil service.

In Britain there was a major review of the civil service in the late 1960s and the Fulton Report was published in 1968. It criticised the service for tending to promote those with a rather narrow social and elite educational background. The fast-track system for administrative trainees is dominated, at 63 per cent, by Oxford and Cambridge University graduates. Schemes to promote able administrators within the service were recommended, but the difference between the fast track and other promotions remains. The Thatcher premiership has certainly disturbed the system of senior appointments. She took a much more interventionist role in appointments policy. Consequently, the British system has moved closer to the American system.

The French administrative system again combines both career and political dimensions. Ministers nominate senior officials, like *directeurs*, within departments. However, senior officials resent too much political interference and both president and prime minister are wary about intervening too much in political appointments. In the main, politicians find it difficult to impose political appointments on the administrative system, tending rather to select people from amongst the career ranks of senior officials.

Administrative recruitment in France is similar to that in the British system in conforming to Weber's bureaucratic ideal-type model. Senior officials are recruited from the Grands Corps de l'État. In France there is a system of *corps* from which particular administrative posts are selected. For example, there is the Corps d'Inspection des Finances, which provides

See J. L. Bodiguel (1983) 'A French-style Spoils System', *Public Administration* 61(3).

officials for the finance and other economic ministries, and a Conseil d'État Corps, which provides administrators for legal posts. Access to these corps is through specialist administrative schools, the Grandes Écoles, and especially through the École Polytechnique. Good performances in examinations, the *concours*, provide access to further training and ultimately access to the elite administrative École Nationale d'Administration (ENA). Usually access to ENA is through the Institut d'Études Politiques, which has centres in Paris and Grenoble.

The German system of appointments allows greater intervention, with ministers having the power to remove senior administrators by right of constitutional law. This allows incoming ministers to change top civil servants, although a consultative process does take place through personnel councils, *Personalrate*. In Germany studies have shown that there is a high correlation between administrative appointments and promotions and party political membership. Again, there are exams, the *Staatsexamen*, which trainees need to pass before they can undertake a probationary period in a ministry. Promotion tends to take place within departments, not across the whole service, and promotion tends to follow seniority.

See Mayntz, R. and Scharpf, F. W. (1975) *Policy-Making in the German Federal Bureaucracy*, Amsterdam: Elsevier.

In these countries a university education is paramount for recruitment into senior positions and there is a bias towards elite educational establishments and high-status social groups. Table 11.2 indicates the educational background of top administrators in Britain, Germany and the United States.

*Table 11.2* Educational backgrounds of senior administrators

|  | Britain | Germany | USA Career | USA Political |
|---|---|---|---|---|
|  | % | % | % | % |
| No university | 16 | 1 | 0 | 3 |
| Law | 3 | 66 | 18 | 28 |
| Humanities | 40 | 2 | 6 | 7 |
| Social Science | 12 | 17 | 29 | 38 |
| Technology | 26 | 14 | 42 | 10 |
| Unknown | 2 | 0 | 5 | 15 |
| Total | 99 | 100 | 100 | 101 |
|  | N = 91 | N = 94 | N = 65 | N = 61 |

*Note*: N = number of administrators.

*Source*: J. D. Aberbach, R. D. Putnam and B. A. Rockman (1981) *Bureaucrats and Politicians in Western Democracies*, Cambridge, Mass.: Harvard University Press.

**THINK POINT**
● What are the main differences in the recruitment and appointment of officials in Britain, the United States, France and Germany?

# The structure of administration

## The tension between policy and administration

The tension between a policy-making role and an administrative implementation role has already been discussed and follows from Weber's (1947) notion that politicians decide and bureaucrats carry out the order of their masters. However, as Chapter 14 indicates, and as Pressman and Wildavsky make clear, policy implementation often determines the nature of the decision-making process itself. In this sense officials can be seen as policy-makers, including those officials lower down in the hierarchy who have more face-to-face contacts with clients.

Barrett and Fudge see the distinction between policy and implementation as misleading. Clearly, officials do shape policy and their general perspectives also provide the context in which politicians operate. For example, there is evidence from the United States that administrators were very influential in formulating and implementing welfare programmes, and the work of Richardson and Jordan shows similar influences in the British case. In Mrs Thatcher's period in office she wanted to ensure that officials were not obstructive to her particular policies. At the beginning of her premiership she considered many Treasury officials to be steeped in a Keynesian perspective which would ultimately prevent the implementation of her more monetarist economic strategy. This was a recognition that civil servants did have power over both policy-making and implementation.

## Departmentalism

Weber's analysis of bureaucracy also places emphasis on the **division of labour** in organisations and the division of responsibility in hierarchies. These divisions are underpinned by a rational-legal bureaucratic system of powers and obligations. For politicians, such a hierarchy provides legitimation for political decisions and provides channels through which decisions can be implemented.

Hood and Dunsire have argued that there is no such thing as a typical department. However, it is possible to distinguish between the following:

- ministerial or executive departments – key administrative units operating under the direct control of a minister;
- non-ministerial departments – operating under a non-executive control, although normally accountable to ministers;
- semi-autonomous agencies and **QUANGO**s – increasingly important bodies operating independently of ministers – which may be staffed by civil servants, but many of which include political appointees. (These will be discussed more fully later in the chapter.)

This ambiguity of definition is further complicated by recent trends which have seen the privatisation of certain public-sector functions and the 'hiving-

J. Pressman and A. Wildavsky (1973) *Implementation*, Berkeley, CA: University of California.

S. Barrett and C. Fudge (1981) *Policy and Action*, London: Methuen.

A. G. Jordan and J. J. Richardson (1987) *British Politics and the Policy Process*, London: Allen & Unwin.

**Division of labour** The division of tasks and functions, often leading to specialisation and increased productivity, but associated with alienation and fragmentation.

C. Hood and A. Dunsire (1981) *Bureaumetrics*, Farnborough: Gower.

**QUANGO** Non-governmental organisations given operational autonomy. Used with the term 'quasi-government' about organisations with an arm's-length relationship with government. There is concern that such organisations have been unaccountable and open to political patronage.

off' of units. The notion of central administration also now includes many organisations at the periphery of government.

The greatest extent of administrative fragmentation and complexity is found in the United States. There is a vast range of federal organisations and also a wide range of different types of unit. In one study it was found that central administration in the United States included 14 executive departments, 10 offices under the president, 25 independent agencies, 2 foundations, 17 institutes, 2 claims commissions, 13 regulatory commissions, 45 governmental corporations, 6 inter-agency boards, 4 statutory advisory bodies, 4 joint executive–congressional commissions, 13 intergovernmental organisations, 13 organisations in the 'twilight zone' and 14 institutions organised for contracting purposes by the federal government.

H. Seidman (1980) *Politics, Position and Power*, Oxford: Oxford University Press.

European administrative systems are less fragmented, although the growth of QUANGOs has made the notion of departmentalism more complicated. Greenwood and Wilson use three important features to identify departmental organisations, including size, the degree of decentralisation and the extent of bureaucracy.

J. Greenwood and D. Wilson (1984) *Public Administration in Britain*, London: Allen & Unwin.

### Size

Most ministerial or executive departments are large, thus increasing the complexity of organisations through a more extensive division of labour. Weber's (1947) notion of hierarchy, codified rules, clear procedures and roles can be applied most appropriately to these kind of departments. Communications and control systems are more formalised and effective management and coordination of administration are made more difficult. However, size is not necessarily a function of power. In Britain the Treasury is relatively small but very powerful, whereas the Department of Social Services is a huge organisation and has a vast budget, but relatively less power. Size reflects the scale of work, with service-providing departments like Social Security, which is more labour intensive compared with the policy-formulating role of the Treasury. Size will also reflect the degree to which the department has a diverse geographical location. With many local offices, the Department of Social Security decentralises most of its activities.

### Decentralisation

In the United Kingdom some administrative services are organised on the basis of constituent territories, like Scottish, Welsh and Northern Ireland Offices. Others are British-based, for example the Department of Health, while still others are organisations based on the country as a whole, like the Inland Revenue or the Foreign and Commonwealth Office. In these cases, departments operate through local offices, which involves territorial decentralisation. In a unitary state like Britain, decentralisation has occurred in a pragmatic way, based on the type of service and the most effective method of service delivery. In federal systems, decentralisation is more formal and states or regions have constitutional powers with clear demarcations between central administration and peripheral responsibilities.

See D. Pitt and B. C. Smith (1981) *Government Departments: An Organisational Perspective*, London: Routledge & Kegan Paul.

### Bureaucratic organisations

Usually these are top-down, hierarchical organisations which are constrained by three important factors:

1 Public accountability to parliament, ministers and indirectly to the public. Administration is governed by statutory powers and rules of conduct, with public accountability tending to reinforce hierarchical structures.

2 Equity in treatment given similar circumstances. This can be built into the organisational culture of a department, thus ensuring adherence to a unified set of principles. The notion of equity has been particularly important in tax departments, like the British Inland Revenue. Equity is seen by officials as a guiding principle acting as a bulwark against politicians who would wish to manipulate the tax system for ideological purposes. (See A. Robinson and C. Sandford (1983) *Tax Policy-Making in the United Kingdom*, London: Heinemann.)

3 Specialisation as part of a wider division of labour that involves both staff functions, like personnel and financial management, and operational functions related to specific policy areas. Changing methods of management have attempted to integrate issues related to service across the administration, but departmentalism is politically defended by civil servants.

---

**THINK POINT**
- What are the main differences between the bureaucratic structures of Britain and the United States?

---

### Conflicts between departments

Modern administrations have a complex division of labour, represented by relatively independent and fragmented departments which may have their own distinct perspectives, subcultures and policy interests. This may lead to interdepartmental and, in very large departments, intradepartmental conflict between competing interests. Each department will have its own interests to defend; with rivalry and competition centring on spending and policy influence.

Weber (1947) recognised that large bureaucratic organisations had a tendency to fracture into conflicting power groups or blocs. Bureaucracies should therefore not be seen as inevitably unified, monolithic top-down organisations. Instead, there may be a number of centres of power, where policy is a matter of negotiation and bargaining between different interests.

Figure 11.2 is a simplified illustration of the British departmental structure. The main spending departments are shown on the left, with central control being provided by the prime minister, Cabinet and Treasury. High-spending departments like Health, Social Security and Education may fight with the Treasury over their share of the public expenditure budget.

In this struggle there may be a large amount of **logrolling** involving trade-offs, coalitions and compromises. The net result for the Treasury's budgetary plans may be directly related to the shape of these departmental conflicts and the degree to which ministers take up their departmental cases.

Conflicts also arise regarding spheres of influence over policy, with departments coming into conflict over responsibility for certain services and spending. For example, in the British case there may be conflicts between the Home Office and the Ministry of Defence on the priority and expenditure given to civil defence, or between the Navy and Royal Air Force and the Ministry of Agriculture, Fisheries and Food regarding fisheries protection. It is obviously in the interest of the Services and the Ministry of Defence to have some military spending paid for through another department's budget.

Ponting (1986), writing as an experienced former civil servant with inside information, shows how intradepartmental conflicts can arise over arms sales. First, there is usually a conflict between the sales division within Defence and the Services. This is because weapons sales may divert resources from domestic needs and the Services may be potential enemies. Recent revelations about arms sales to Iran and Iraq highlight these conflicts. Second, a coalition of departments may be formed as the process of logrolling begins.

**Logrolling** The bargaining and coalition-building that takes place between departments in order to obtain resources.

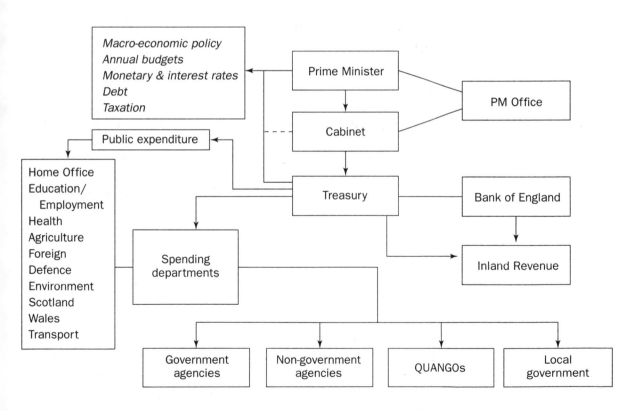

*Figure 11.2* The British departmental structure

The Department of Trade and Industry may line up in support of such export sales and the Department of Employment may see the venture in terms of increased employment. The Foreign Office will also have an important view and will advise on the basis of suitability in relation to Britain's wider international and diplomatic positions. Third, the Treasury will become involved, especially as the Export Guarantee Department may be asked to provide a cheap loan to subsidise the sale. This loan may be resisted by a Treasury wanting control over general public spending.

These conflicts within the bureaucracy may then spill over into the political sphere, with ministers taking up positions in the dispute. This battle will now be fought out in Cabinet and Cabinet committees, and may only be resolved by the intervention of the prime minister. Ministers are acting as arbiters in a longstanding conflict between different departmental or sectional interests within the administration.

---

**THINK POINT**
- Explain, with examples, why conflicts between and within departments arise?
- How are such conflicts resolved?

---

## Bureaucracy in a unitary state: the case of the British administration

### The cabinet system

The Cabinet is composed of some twenty to twenty-five ministers, and is itself a fragmented body, with political rivalries and conflicts which weaken its overall coherence. Ministers are particularly dependent on officials to brief them on issues and ministers may have only a fleeting knowledge of a policy problem, especially if it does not fall within the sphere of their own department's interests. Much work is devolved to Cabinet committees comprising ministers with specific interests in policy areas.

In the diaries of his time as a Labour Cabinet Minister, Richard Crossman reflects that he was really a captive of the administrative machine and his own department's narrow interests. In this case he was able to gain extra funding for his ministry, although he feels a broader departmental approach would have led to a different result:

> The more I reflect on it the more uneasy I become. Of course, I shouldn't have been allowed to win. I had a strong case, but if there had been a collective Cabinet policy I wouldn't have stood a chance. Yet I felt no sense of responsibility for the general Cabinet policy and just pleaded my departmental case as well as I possibly could. In fact, I was not the least concerned about the good of the country. I was solely concerned with looking after my department.

(Crossman 1969: 126)

When presenting a policy paper to Cabinet, ministers do not usually give options. They make a decision based on the views of their own department and then the Cabinet is asked to agree with it. The technical information supporting such a paper is not necessarily distributed to all Cabinet ministers, nor do most ministers have the time to get to grips with detailed arguments concerning policy only marginally related to their own departmental interests. Hence, alternative Cabinet positions are rare.

Much control over the Cabinet system is managed through the civil service's system of communications using Cabinet minutes. Minutes of ministerial meetings are circulated among senior civil servants on a limited basis, so that hardly any ministers obtain a complete record of meetings.

## The parliamentary system

Information about policy detail is also kept away from Parliament by Whitehall. In any appearance in the House of Commons or Lords a minister will be accompanied by officials who have already drafted parliamentary replies to questions, but who are also at hand to draft instant replies if they are needed. A minister's private secretary will have worked up a huge file of background policy material. Civil servants ensure that the opposition is in a weak position as regards holding ministers accountable. Civil service support for ministers treads a thin line between dissembling and prevarication to deliberately misleading Parliament. There is an old Westminster joke which sums up this civil service role:

> A Cabinet minister has been to visit a government institution in the West Country accompanied by his principal private secretary. Returning that night in the black government Rover across the rain and gales of Dartmoor, a bedraggled figure flags them down. 'I'm lost', he cries, 'can you possibly tell me where I am?' 'You're on Dartmoor,' replies the civil servant briskly and drives on. After a while, the minister enquires why he had behaved in such a way. 'Well minister,' says the civil servant, 'it was the perfect answer as far as I was concerned. It was entirely truthful, and gave away the minimum information.'
>
> (quoted in Leigh 1980: 8)

There is an imbalance between the power of ministers and their departments on the one hand and Parliament on the other. Again, it was Richard Crossman, in his diaries, who commented on the effectiveness of Parliament to scrutinise him as a minister.

> There is no effective Parliamentary control. All this time I have never felt in any way alarmed by a Parliamentary threat . . . I can't remember a single moment in the course of legislation when I felt the faintest degree of alarm or embarrassment and I can't remember a Question Time, either, when I had any anxiety.
>
> (Crossman 1969: 158)

In 1980 Parliament set up a system of Parliamentary Select Committees for each Whitehall department in order to shadow its activities. However, much is kept confidential from such committees, including advice to ministers, the level at which decisions are taken, information about discussions between departments, how consultations take place between Cabinet colleagues and how Cabinet Committees reach decisions. Select Committees do not have an automatic right to see civil service papers and are a pale imitation of the Congressional Committees in the United States. They are dominated by considerations of party politics, have few specialist advisers and are particularly weak in investigating politically controversial issues.

---

**THINK POINT**
- What are the main impediments to ministerial and parliamentary control of the civil service?

---

## Pressure groups

Civil servants have continuous contacts with important pressure groups who gain access to decision-making through government departments. Indeed, departments see pressure groups as an important source of information and support and in return provide channels for consultation on policy which affects them. Figure 11.3 contrasts those pressure groups seen by the administration as 'safe', respectable 'insider groups' and those seen as 'outsiders'. There are also those groups which employ tactics and show a willingness to cooperate with government in order to gain access to the administration. The insider groups are those that departments need for support in formulating and implementing policy. They will be part of the policy-making process and will have a close working relationship with officials. The most important groups in the British case are the Confederation of British Industry (CBI), representing the company sector; the British Medical Association (BMA) representing doctors; and other commercial and professional groups like the House Builders' Federation, the National Farmers' Union (NFU), the British Road Federation and the Brewers' Association.

| Outsider groups | Groups wanting to be insiders | Insider groups |
|---|---|---|
| Anti-nuclear groups | Transport 2000 | NFU |
| | | CBI |
| CND | Friends of the Earth | House Builders' Fed. |
| | | British Road Fed. |
| Greenpeace | RSPCA | County Landowners' Ass. |
| | | |
| | | World Wildlife Fund |
| PROP | ASH (anti-smoking) | Multi-nationals |
| | | Civic Trusts |
| Tenants' groups | FOREST (tobacco) | BMA |

→ Access to Officials →

*Figure 11.3* 'Insider' and 'outsider' groups

In the Home Office, for example, officials will provide access to insider groups like the National Association for the Care and Resettlement of Offenders and the Howard League for Penal Reform. However, outsider and more radical pressure groups like Prisoners' Rights groups (PROP) will be excluded. Equally, the Department of Transport will curry favour with the powerful British Road Federation, but will cold-shoulder anti-roads environmental groups. Again, the National Farmers' Union is a powerful employers' organisation which is highly influential within the Department of Agriculture. As in the case of the health scare over BSE, cattle departmental policy was highly influenced by the consultations with the NFU and lobbying from the industry.

Figure 11.4 illustrates the close relationship which exists between the Department of Trade and Industry and the oil industry. There are key mutual interests in this close relationship.

## The media

Another important function of officials is to run the government's information machine, releasing material to the media for public relations and **propaganda**. Each department has its own public relations officers, who are usually distanced from the main policy work of the department. Many are specialists recruited from the ranks of former journalists. Civil servants in Britain hardly have direct contacts with the media, instead publishing press releases and background information through their press offices. In the case of the Foreign Office the Head of Information is a career diplomat, and the Treasury press office is run by a career official. It is interesting to

**Propaganda** The term originally referred to propagation of the faith in Catholicism, but refers today to the way in which governments subordinate knowledge and information to state policy.

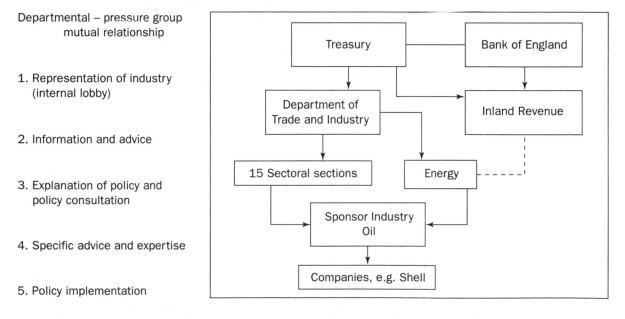

Departmental – pressure group mutual relationship

1. Representation of industry (internal lobby)

2. Information and advice

3. Explanation of policy and policy consultation

4. Specific advice and expertise

5. Policy implementation

*Figure 11.4* Relationship between the DTI and the oil industry

note the normal separation of press and information management from the work of the rest of the senior civil service. Information is something which has to be processed and separated from policy development work. Indeed, the information coming out of departments is regarded as sensitive material, likely to embarrass a government if handled ineffectively.

Within government departments, just as they deal with insider pressure groups, officials usually deal with a set of insider journalists. These are journalists specialising in defence, environment, transport issues, etc., and, again, close relationships between the media and officials are formed. Attempts have been made to coordinate public relations and media activities, although the fragmented departmental system persists. In the 1980s the Prime Minister's Press Secretary tried to develop a coordinated approach by regularly meeting with departmental information officers, ensuring that the public relations initiative remained with him and the Number 10 Press Office.

The administration also releases information in a much more insidious way, by planned leaks through the lobby system (see M. Cockerell, P. Hennessy and M. Walker (1985) *Sources Close to the Prime Minister*, London: Macmillan). Certain elite journalists form the lobby, as accredited journalists who can be trusted and held to account by the administration. Departments will brief such lobby journalists with background information on policy and will stipulate whether or not information can be published or broadcast. All lobby contacts with officials are non-attributable, and the source of such briefings is never discussed. Press and broadcast reports refer to 'senior Whitehall sources' or 'sources close to the prime minister'.

Officials have a complex system for classifying information based on the level of sensitivity. The publication papers and documents is graded according to the following definitions:

- Restricted: undesirable in the interests of the nation
- Confidential: prejudicial to the interests of the nation
- Secret: serious injury to the interest of the nation
- Top secret: exceptionally grave damage to the nation

Secrecy is used not only to protect national security, but also to avoid political embarrassment. If any civil servant leaks information then s/he is liable to criminal prosecution. Two contrasting views of the role of the civil service regarding the flow of information are provided in the next two extracts. The first is by a former Deputy Secretary in the old Civil Service Department and the second by a former Cabinet Minister.

> It is in theory and in principle, a very democratic system. The authority to determine how civil servants shall behave is totally vested in the elected representatives of the people; there is no basis on which the civil servant, the appointed official, can seek to impose his own values on the course of Government in action. . . . It is a very tight and rather closed system. There is equally no room in it for the character who is known in American literature on the subject as the whistle-blower. In Britain, the aspiring whistle-blower

is blocked. And the reason why he is blocked is not fundamentally, and never has been, the Official Secrets Act – that doubtful prop of the British Constitution. It is the fact that if he blows the whistle, the player against whom he is registering a foul is his fully responsible Minister. He is therefore committing a politically hostile act, and ipso facto, doing something inconsistent with his civil service status. The whistle-blower in this country must blow his whistle in the privacy of the Minister's room. If that is ineffective, he should resign his post before he blows it publicly.

(Wilding 1979: quoted in Leigh 1980: 33)

Wilding's view also supports information sharing within the service, including warning other permanent secretaries about what your minister is proposing to do and informing other civil servants about future departmental plans. This is different from secrecy to the outside world. The second extract takes up this latter view:

Unless this process is stopped in its tracks, Britain could be governed by a commission of permanent secretaries reducing ministers to ciphers only able to accept or reject what is put before them, and the House of Commons will be a consultative assembly which will be able to express its opinions but do little more.

Over all that I have described, an official curtain of secrecy is supposed to be maintained. Why? It is in the interests both of weak ministers and strong public servants, both of whom prefer to keep the public in the dark. Weak ministers because they dare not invite challenges to their policy which they fear they could not answer; strong civil servants because their strength lies in that they cannot be challenged if they can remain anonymous.

I have reached the solemn conclusion that what we have constructed in Britain is the embryo of a corporate state that more resembles feudalism than the democracy of which we often boast.

(Tony Benn; quoted in Leigh 1980: 35)

**THINK POINT**
- What are the main differences between these two views and what assumptions about the role and duties of civil servants lie behind such perspectives?

## Bureaucracy in a Federal state: the case of the United States administration

The Federal structure of government in the United States, with its separation of powers makes its bureaucracy fragmented, decentralised and complex. Unlike the centralised departmental system in Britain, the Federal bureaucracy is mainly organised as a system of semi-autonomous agencies, with separate influence being applied by the Presidency, Congress and pressure groups. The lack of a powerful central state ensures that the Presidency has only weak powers in influencing political appointments and the level of bureaucratic resources. The nominal 'neutrality' of British civil servants is replaced by a much more open system of relative influence and competition amongst different institutions in the United States political system.

The constitutional separation of powers ensures that the Federal government has no centre of power like that of the centralised British unitary state. In the United States officials openly compete for resources and influence over policy, with party politics cutting across administrative agencies. Federal executive departments are not hierarchical in the Weberian (1947) sense of bureaucratic structures. The myriad agencies are overseen by separate Congressional Committees and Subcommittees, the shape and scope of an agency being dependent on the decisions made by particular Congressional Committees and agency clients. In the United States the growth in the size of the bureaucracy has occurred because of three main developments: the increase in welfare and educational spending, the growth in Federal regulation and a vast increase in military and defence spending. The growth in the administration of policy has occurred since the 1930s under Roosevelt's Presidency, there being one civil servant for 280 Americans in 1933 compared with one for every 80 in 1953. The New Deal and Great Society programmes of the 1930s and 1960s have led to a large increase in employment in state and local government. Most Federal funding is spent by lower-level government organisations and other agencies, with most Federal employees working outside Washington.

### The Federal civil service

Patronage is still important at Federal, state and local levels, with elected politicians attempting to put in place their own political appointees. There are about three million Federal officials, although the more fragmented administrative system means that there is no government-wide career structure. With specialist and relatively autonomous agencies there are different patterns of administration, with different career structures and subcultures. Agencies are dominated particularly by technocratic and professional expertise, which acts as a bulwark against more overtly political interference and policy dominance.

### Political challenges to the bureaucracy: the Reagan reforms

The New Right agenda in the United States and the Reagan Presidency maintained a sustained attack on what was perceived as an ineffective and inefficient bureaucratic system of administration. In 1981 Reagan launched his programme of reform based on the assumption that the competitive element of private-sector management had to be injected into administrative behaviour. Pay cuts and changes in the conditions of service led to a fall in morale in the administration, with the gap between private-sector and public-sector pay widening by some 20 per cent. Similar policies were adopted in Britain under Thatcher, but it could be argued that the more unified civil service in Britain, especially at the higher level, was better able to resist such challenges. Both British and American governments nevertheless shared this antipathy towards the public service and the role of administration in government.

### The public service ethos: the Volcker reforms of 1986

In 1986 the National Commission on the Public Service was set up under Paul Volcker to examine the problems facing the civil service. He examined public perceptions of the service, the recruitment, education and retention of officials, pay and conditions of service and the relationship between political and non-political appointees. He recommended improved pay and conditions and a reduction in the number of political appointments available to the president. The Commission argued that the administration should be valued and held in higher esteem.

### The bureaucracy and Congress

The Congress facilitates, finances and oversees the Federal bureaucracy and devolves powers to departments and agencies where appropriate. This delegation of authority varies and there may be some conflicts between the Congress and the Presidency over appropriate responsibilities. Congress ensures that executive agencies comply with Congressional demands; the scope of the functions of agency regulation are determined and their effectiveness is then monitored and evaluated. Congress ensures that its objectives are complied with through the confirmation of presidential nominees to official posts, through appropriation and authorisation committee hearings and through the legislative veto. Powers of scrutiny over the bureaucracy are therefore much more extensive than those of the British Parliament. The separation of powers and the party competition that exists at different levels of the American system ensures that Congress can maintain scrutiny over the executive and administration. In Britain, the dominance of party government ensures parliamentary scrutiny tends to follow partisan lines.

### The bureaucracy and Presidency

The scrutiny of presidential nominations to political positions in Executive departments is an effective check on presidential influence. Few nominees are rejected; rather presidents tend to want to avoid disputes over nominees and therefore refrain from putting up the names of those they know will be rejected. Soundings are taken about the acceptability of nominees, their background, character and politics being considered before they are appointed to a key administrative post. In recent years the time spent on procedures surrounding hearings has increased, partly as Congress has become more mistrustful of the executive. Increases in resources, staffing, background expertise and general autonomy for such committees have placed a curb on the executive's fiscal and foreign affairs powers. Congress retains its authority to examine the implementation of policy. Executive officials, like higher ranking civil servants in Britain, do not tell committees all they need to know, but the more extensive system of scrutiny in the United States curbs executive administrative power.

## Quasi-government

In recent years there has been a tendency to distance areas of administration from direct political control. Quasi-government operates in a no-man's land, occupying an increasingly crowded territory between central government and regional or local administration. Institutions so defined can be government-created, semi-autonomous and semi-private. They include public, private or voluntary organisations. These organisations vary according to structure and role, but usually have a more specific administrative and policy remit than central government organisations.

Quasi-government in Britain goes back to the 1940s, and in 1968 the Fulton Report of the civil service supported the idea of 'hiving off' the work of departments to more specialist non-departmental units. In Britain, examples of such organisations include the Health and Safety Commission, set up as a statutory body by Parliament; the BBC, which was established by Royal Charter; the University Grants Committee, established by the Treasury; and the National Consumers' Council, which is a non-profit-making company.

It is difficult to distinguish between non-government and government organisations. Such organisations can be placed on a simplified continuum with central departments at one end and private companies at the other (see Figure 11.5). A key issue for quasi-government is the degree to which organisations are accountable to the public or to political process of election. As QUANGOs have grown in number, so central and local government have been increasingly sidelined. Of course, this may be in the interests of politicians who want services taken out of the political process, and certainly the former nationalised industries now act like large monopolies. One consequence, for example, has been the public disquiet over the water companies' ability to provide adequate services. There is no political recourse in this area now, much to the relief of politicians, who now can blame years of low public investment on the privatised companies.

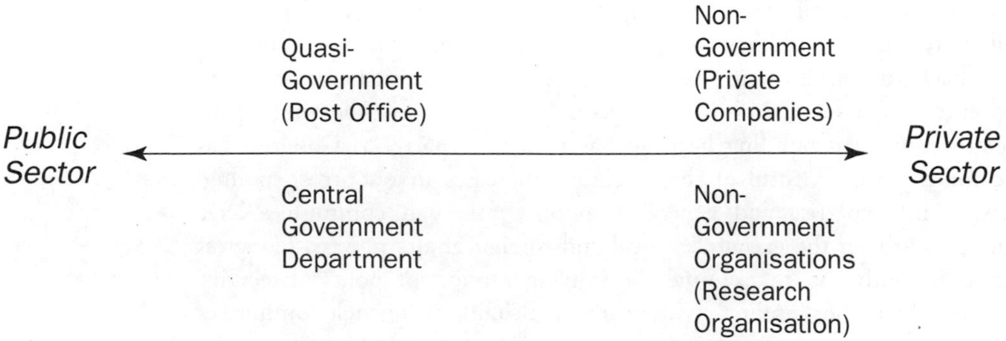

Quasi-
Government
(Post Office)

Non-
Government
(Private
Companies)

Public
Sector ←————————————————————————→ Private
Sector

Central
Government
Department

Non-
Government
Organisations
(Research
Organisation)

*Figure 11.5* Non-government and government organisations

There are a many different types of QUANGO:

- executive bodies;
- advisory bodies;
- tribunals;
- administrative agencies;
- public corporations;
- regional or local administrative bodies.

The two main organisations to consider are executive bodies and advisory committees.

## Executive bodies

The rationale for such organisations is that they can deliver services more effectively when they are distanced from central government. The functions of such bodies include:

- work which does not require day-to-day ministerial control and political interference;
- work which can be done more effectively by a single-purpose organisation rather than a large and multipurpose department;
- work which involves people from outside the public sector and government administration who are able to look beyond the confines of government and politics;
- work which can be distanced from direct political control.

## Advisory bodies

These bodies incorporate outside representation and their roles include:

- providing advice where a department is unable to do so, which may involve some specialist expertise and specific consultative process;
- providing access for people with other non-governmental knowledge and expertise, which is often necessary in relation to particular policy development.

With all QUANGOs, three important factors must be taken into account when considering their effectiveness. How are they controlled? How are they made accountable? How are people appointed to such bodies?

## Control

Ministers often try to distance themselves from the control of such bodies and the services they provide. This may be because they operate in sensitive policy areas, although ministers will become involved with overall spending issues and wider policy ramifications if they should arise.

## Accountability

Relatively autonomous bodies are responsible for their own management, with ministers being accountable only to Parliament for their own relationships with such QUANGOs. In Britain most are not answerable to Parliament. It has been argued that if they were, ministers would inevitably become more involved and the very rationale for such autonomous bodies would be lost.

Some QUANGOs have their accounts audited centrally, and there are judicial rules governing maladministration and some aspects of public redress, although legally the position of QUANGOs is confused. Some QUANGOs do give evidence to Parliamentary Select Committees, although the matters usually discussed centre on overall administration rather than operational effectiveness.

### Patronage

The growth in the number of QUANGOs in recent years has resulted in a great deal of public controversy over appointments made by ministers. The political appointment of members to these bodies has raised the issue of patronage and many posts involve pecuniary benefit. The civil service ethos of neutrality and of appointments based on merit has been eroded by political appointments based on support of the government in power. Parliamentary control over such appointments has been minimal and there is evidence that appointees have had close political connections with the party in power. Patronage has given ministers increasing influence over the activities of QUANGOs while formally seeming to give them less.

In Britain, the issue of patronage and membership of QUANGOs was specifically looked at by the Nolan Committee in 1996. The report of the Committee on Standards in Public Life recommended that there should be an end to payments for those sitting on public bodies. A sense of public duty rather than financial gain should be the underlying principle of membership. In a report in *The Guardian* (11 April 1996), it was revealed that the Chairman of the Port of London Authority received a payment of £4,000 a day for twelve days a year and the Chairman of the Dover Harbour Board received £1,500 a day for ten days work a year. Nolan also looked at the issue of conflicts of interest, and recommended that there should be firmer controls on political appointments. The Conservative landowner Lord De Ramsay is reported in *The Guardian* as receiving a £50,000 per year salary for a two-and-a-half day week, with former Conservative Environment Minister Lord Bellwin receiving £27,380 a year for a two-day week as Chairman of the North Hull Housing Action Trust.

---

**THINK POINT**
- In what ways have QUANGOs been criticised?

---

# Conclusion

Questions about the effectiveness and success of any administrative system must be placed in the context of the wider political system, its constitution, institutions and procedures. Bureaucratic politics has also to be placed in the context of wider policy-making processes and considered in relation to the capabilities of the political leadership in power. As has already been shown, the differences between the British and United States bureaucracies are very much a function of the very different political systems, with different emphasis on the nature of executive power, legislative scrutiny, decentralisation and devolution of powers.

Frequent criticisms of administrative systems point to the slowness, caution and lack of innovation within institutions. However, such complaints have to be placed beside public service qualities such as equity, fairness and even-handedness. There has, more recently, also been criticism about the lack of entrepreneurship in administration. These arguments point to the need for public servants to emulate managers in private-sector commercial organisations, and others point to the need for officials to become more proactive in a political way, responding to the party and ideological needs of politicians.

Again, these differences of approach can be seen in the United States and British examples. In Britain there has been a trend towards more political appointees, as in the American example, and commercial procedures have been brought into departments artificially, by means of the greater use of more autonomous agencies. The benefits of a more neutral, impartial and permanent administrative system have to be set against the possibility that a more politicised and entrepreneurial public service may lead to lower morale, higher turnover of staff and subsequent fragmentation and discontinuity in public policy.

## Further reading

Lynn, J. and Jay, A. (1987) *The Complete Yes Minister*, London: BBC Books. A humourous glimpse into the world of the administrator inside the fictional Department of Administrative Affairs.

Crossman, R. H. S. (1975, 1976, 1977) *The Diaries of a Cabinet Minister*, London: Hamish Hamilton and Jonathan Cape. This time the real thing, with poignant and perceptive reflections on the work of a British Cabinet minister pushing forward policy initiatives inside the administration during the 1970s.

Hennessy, P. (1989) *Whitehall*, London: Secker & Warburg. Well-written and perceptive analysis of the Whitehall bureaucracy.

# POLITICS BELOW THE NATION-STATE

*Alan Grant*

**Introduction**

**The territorial distribution of power**

**Federalism**

*The requirements of federalism*
*Developments in federal governments*
*Conclusions on federalism*

**Local government and politics**

*Constitutional and legal status*
*Structure and responsibilities*
*Internal organisation*
*Central–local relations*

**Conclusion**

**Further reading**

# Politics below the nation-state

## Introduction

Within nation-states policy-making and administration on a range of significant issue areas takes place at sub-national level. There may be a number of tiers of government co-existing with that of the central or national administration. A wide range of territorial units – states or provinces, regions and various levels of local government such as counties, cities, districts and small-scale parishes and communes – have been established in different countries and play an important role in the political life of their societies. A tradition of local self-government goes back to the seventeenth or eighteenth centuries or even earlier; for example, monarchs granted cities the power to run their own affairs in a number of European states. In liberal democracies the existence of active sub-national governments with their own powers was seen as an important means of maintaining democracy and in sharp contrast to the centralisation of authority seen in autocratic states. After both the Second World War and the collapse of communism in Europe after 1989, emerging democracies sought to establish a pattern of decentralised government as a vital part of their new constitutional structures.

However, patterns of local democracy vary according to national history, traditions and culture. In some countries, particularly geographically large ones, federalism developed as a way of dividing sovereignty and law-making authority between central government and territorial units known as states or provinces, which had their existence and powers guaranteed constitutionally. On the other hand, within unitary states where there was only one government with law-making power, decentralisation has taken the form of delegation of policy-making to various regional and local government authorities. This chapter examines the relationship between territory and power within nation-states, the relationship between different levels of government and the working of sub-national politics.

## The territorial distribution of power

The distribution of power between the central and other tiers of government varies from state to state, and indeed over time. Even where a constitution establishes a particular division of powers, relationships may well change because of economic, social and political developments. We must also be wary of assuming that a written constitution describes the reality of how relationships operate in practice; for example, the Soviet Constitution of 1936 appeared on paper to promise a federal structure with fifteen republics having their own decentralised powers in important policy areas. In reality the dictatorship established by the Communist Party meant that there was a highly centralised political system, with the powers of the Party dominating and controlling the official state structure.

Therefore a spectrum of relationships exists, with, at one extreme, a highly decentralised confederation with little power granted to the central government and virtually autonomous states or provinces, and, at the other, a very centralised unitary state with weak local authorities acting principally as administrative agents. The vast majority of nation-states cannot be categorised as falling at the extreme ends of this spectrum but, rather, can be located somewhere along the decentralisation–centralisation axis. Given the huge diversity in geographical size, from Luxembourg to China, the social compositions of the populations and the histories and cultures of nation-states, it should not surprise us that there is no easy rule of thumb that can be used to guide us in predicting the degree of decentralisation in particular countries. However, if would seem that at least in liberal democratic states, a very large geographical territory encourages the development of a decentralised structure, both for representational reasons and for the practical reasons of ensuring effective government; for example, four of the largest states by area in the world – Australia, Brazil, Canada and the United States – are federal systems.

What, then, are the advantages and disadvantages of decentralised government with significant sub-national policy-making? The arguments used in such debates tend to focus on two main issues: what is best for the proper representation of the people in a responsive democratic state and what is necessary for the efficient and effective administration of government. Sometimes the answers to these two questions are not the same and some sort of trade-off, balancing the requirements of democracy and efficiency, is sought.

First, it is often argued that a concentration of power in the hands of one person or group is dangerous; this is best expressed in Lord Acton's aphorism that power tends to corrupt and absolute power corrupts absolutely. Therefore, for a liberal democratic state to prosper power needs to be devolved to other territorial units. In this way the authority of central government can be checked and balanced by the authority of these bodies. Relationships between the centre and localities, regions or states therefore inevitably involve tension and conflict but this, it is argued, should be seen as creative and therapeutic for the body politic overall.

Second, proponents of decentralisation believe that more efficient and satisfactory administration of government happens when government is carried out closer to the people who are affected and when those with local knowledge are involved in making the decisions. It is not sufficient to have central government and civil servants implementing policies from regional or local offices (what is known as 'administrative deconcentration'), because their priorities still reflect those of the centre rather than the people living in the area; the power to decide policies must be in the hands of democratically elected representatives of the people, or, in some cases, power must be wielded by the people directly, through devices such as referenda.

It also can be argued that giving people the right to make decisions that affect them in their own areas has an important educative purpose. John Stuart Mill believed that the development of a responsible citizenry who become aware of the problems and limitations of government comes from this involvement at local level. What is more, politicians who have gained experience at local or state level, dealing with small-scale problems, can 'learn the ropes', even making mistakes which would affect only a relatively small number of people, before graduating to national-level policy-making.

Sub-national governments are also often seen as laboratories of democracy or centres of experimentation where new ideas can be tried out and, if they are seen to work and be popular, can then be applied on a national basis later. Sometimes such policy innovations may be initiated independently by the individual lower-tier authority (such as welfare reforms in some American states or the sale of council houses to tenants by particular English local councils), or the central government may encourage some units to participate in pilot schemes in order to assess both the benefits and practical difficulties of a complex new policy before implementing it more widely.

It has been claimed that another advantage of decentralisation is that it can take some of the administrative burdens from central government. In modern states there are so many demands made on government to solve society's problems and to respond to all sorts of issues that there is a danger that its desire to act exceeds its capacity for effective delivery; it suffers from what we call 'administrative overload'. One way of dealing with this problem is, of course, to do what many conservatives in Western states demand, which is to allow government to do better by doing less and leave some areas to the market and non-government bodies. As Ronald Reagan said in his inaugural address (1981), 'Government is not the solution to the problem: Government is the problem.' An alternative is for government to devolve some responsibilities to other tiers of the administration. In the United Kingdom one of the major arguments used by supporters of devolution to Scotland and Wales and possibly English regional assemblies is that greater efficiency of government overall would be achieved as a result. These people also contend that areas of policy carried out by agencies and

QUANGOs such as the National Health Service and a range of welfare, economic and cultural services would be made more accountable to elected representatives of the public through the new assemblies.

Advocates of public choice theory, supported by New Right politicians, have also seen advantages in decentralised structures; they have argued that public bureaucracies, at both national and local level, have a built-in tendency to be inefficient, to grow and to attempt to maximise their budgets. Such organisations are often heavily influenced by pressure groups and insensitive to the interests of the consumers of their services. They advocate more competition for contracts between public-sector bodies and private companies, greater choice for consumers and the break-up of monopoly provision by state bodies. They believe that decentralisation can lead to competition between territorial units wanting to attract and retain business and people in their areas as ways of boosting their economic prosperity. To keep taxes and government costs low and provide good services, particularly in areas such as infrastructure and education, competition works to counter some of the detrimental effects of public-sector organisation.

It can be said that decentralised forms of administration are more accessible to the people; their representatives have smaller constituencies than national legislators and usually live within the communities they represent; in many cases their services are the ones people use most often – for example schools, libraries and transport – and they do not appear to be as 'remote' as central government. This 'remoteness' is a relative and subjective phenomenon. In the United States, Washington, DC, the focus of national power, is 3,000 miles away from the residents of West Coast states such as California; those Scots who claim London is a remote capital city are only a few hundred miles away, but the feeling may be genuine all the same. Capitals are in many respects the symbols of what is seen as unresponsive central authority.

Finally, decentralisation may give distinct social groupings based on ethnic, racial, religious, national or language identity some degree of self-government if these social cleavages coincide with geographical settlements. In such cases it is argued that the political stability of the state is enhanced. (See discussion of federalism below, pp. 350–6.)

Because decentralisation of power is often seen as 'a good thing' there have been more advocates of the case than of centralist arguments. However, it can be legitimately stated that devolving authority to sub-national governments inevitably increases the degree of inequality in society, in the sense that people in different parts of the nation-state receive different levels of service in terms of quality, volume or kind. For example, parents' access to nursery education for their children may well depend, not on the need for the service or their income, but on which local or state area they reside in. If equality of provision is regarded as a high priority, then decentralising policy-making (as opposed to the administration) of the service makes little sense.

Second, it can be argued that while decentralisation may help check the opportunity for a tyranny to develop at national level, there is no guarantee that it will help protect the rights of individuals or minority groups against oppressive policies carried out by sub-national governments. For example, in the United States the case for 'states' rights' was advocated most vociferously, although not exclusively, by white Southerners who wanted to maintain racial segregation and other discriminatory practices against black people until the national government intervened in the 1950s and 1960s to protect the civil rights of these citizens. Therefore, in some cases the national government has to act to police the way sub-national governments are behaving with respect to their own communities. Even if the sub-national governments are not carrying out discriminatory or repressive policies, it can be argued that in some respects they may be far from ideal models of democracy at local level (Dunleavy 1980). They may consist of un-representative elite groups protected by large majorities in a principally one-party system or of a rather too cosy relationship with powerful interest groups dominating the local economy and society. Lack of effective competition electorally and weak opposition may also lead to inefficiency in government and the possibility of corruption. What is more, elections for sub-national levels of government may be said to be weak in terms of ensuring the accountability of local politicians when voters are heavily influenced by national politics and particularly the popularity (or lack of it) of the central government.

Third, it may be that inequalities in size and resources between the constituent units leads to the necessity for some central intervention in order to ensure that at least minimum standards of service are provided to all the people within a nation state. Central governments normally have access to the most lucrative sources of tax revenue (such as income tax or a national sales tax) and can channel grants to sub-national governments, thus re-distributing resources from the richer to the poorer areas and supplementing locally raised revenues.

National governments also often claim that they have a broader mandate from the people as a whole to make policy for the whole country. National elections attract more media coverage, there is more interest, voter turnout is often higher, and parties and leaders elected to power may argue that they have a superior claim to carry out their policies, even though at sub-national level leaders and parties elected by smaller and different electorates are opposed. The debate, therefore, is over who really represents the people in a particular area. In Britain in the 1980s local councils controlled by the urban left argued that they had a mandate to develop socialist policies in direct conflict with the right-wing programme of Mrs Thatcher's central government.

Finally it can be argued that decentralisation of power can actually encourage political instability, even leading to the disintegration of the nation-state altogether. By weakening the centre's authority, pressures for greater autonomy, particularly when the sub-national units' boundaries coincide with ethnic and cultural identities, can exacerbate divisions in society, leading to increased conflict and eventually fragmentation. This view sees increased decentralisation of power as a 'slippery slope' to the dissolution of the existing state and the breakdown of the governement's ability to govern.

Some commentators have suggested that territorial decentralisation is based on the assumption that people living in a particular area or locality have certain interests in common, and thus require representation through a formal government structure based on geography. However, they argue that such a system ignores the fact that in many modern polities people's interests are more likely to be based on common identities of a social or cultural nature, which are often not concentrated geographically, and that it is more important for the state to find arrangements that promote responsiveness to these groups (for example, consociationalism or other forms of pluralistic representation) than to rely on traditional territorially based institutions.

---

**THINK POINT**
- Where do you think the country you originate from stands on the decentralisation/centralisation spectrum?

---

## Federalism

As we have seen, a confederation is a weak form of political union between sovereign states. It goes further than normal international treaty arrangements because a form of central government authority is established, but this body does not usually have its own powers to tax the people directly and its decisions normally have to be made by the unanimous agreement of the representatives of the states. Confederations have often not provided a satisfactory balance of power between central and state authorities and either have developed into stronger unions through the establishment of a federation, as in the United States in 1787, or have effectively dissolved so that the constituent states become fully independent, as happened with the Commonwealth of Independent States (CIS) set up in 1991 after the collapse of communism and the Soviet Union.

**Federation** 'An institutional arrangement, taking the form of a sovereign state, and distinguished from other such states solely by the fact that its central government incorporates regional units in its decision procedure on some constitutionally entrenched basis' (Preston King).

The term '**federation**' derives from the Latin *foedus*, meaning a league, pact or covenant; federal systems are those based on the idea of a permanent compact between political bodies that creates a new political entity while not abolishing the original constituent units. Murray Forsyth describes this as a 'state of states' (Forsyth 1994: 15). A federal system can be regarded as a compromise form of unity which allows a balance between the need for union in some areas and the wish for diversity in others. Daniel Elazar sees a federation as being 'self rule plus shared rule' (Elazar 1987: 12). According to the constitutional theorist A.V. Dicey, an essential element of federalism is that the people desire an equilibrium between the forces of centralisation and decentralisation and that they 'must desire union, and must not desire unity' (Dicey 1908: 141). The concept of territory and the recognition and protection of minority and territorial interests are also central to an understanding of federalism. The term 'federalism' is one that has been used flexibly to refer to certain types of government structures or political processes, or to a set of political doctrines or an ideology. Some political scientists have argued that a distinction should be made between the term 'federalism', which they see as an ideology, and 'federation', which describes a federal system of government (Burgess 1993: 3-13).

M. Burgess and A. G. Gagnon (eds) (1993) *Comparative Federalism and Federation*, Hemel Hempstead: Harvester Wheatsheaf.

While accepting that it cannot be seen as a free-standing ideology, unlike liberalism or socialism, Burgess believes that federalism should be taken to mean the recommendation and (sometimes) the active promotion of support for federation. It is ideological in the sense that it can take the form of an overtly prescriptive guide to action, and it is philosophical to the extent that it is a normative judgement on the ideal organisation of human relations and conduct (Burgess 1993: 8). Graham Smith argues that 'federalism can be considered as an ideology which holds that the ideal organisation of human affairs is best reflected in the collaboration of diversity through unity' (G. Smith 1995: 4). Some writers see federalism as either a form or a sub-category of pluralism. Preston King argues that 'pluralism reflects a much broader theoretical concern than federalism. But federalism can still be fitted within it' (King 1982: 75). Forsyth, however, suggests that restricting use of the term federalism to refer to an ideology is illogical and impractical. Just as terms such as 'feudalism' and 'capitalism' are describing not just political ideals but concrete political and economic structures, so federalism can be used in a broader sense (Forsyth 1994: 14).

## The requirements of federalism

There is general agreement that certain characteristics distinguish federal systems from other forms of government. Preston King has advocated a conception of federation containing four essential features (King 1993: 94).

*In this section 'national', 'federal', 'general' and 'central' government are used as alternative ways of describing the central authority, while 'state' and 'province' are terms applied to the major sub-national units in a federation.*

1  Its representation is preponderantly territorial.
2  This territorial representation is characteristically secured on at least two sub-national levels which he refers to as 'local' and 'regional' government.
3  The regional units are incorporated electorally, or perhaps otherwise, into the decision procedure of the national centre.
4  The incorporation of the regions into the decision procedure of the centre can be altered only by extraordinary constitutional measures, not, for example, by resort to a simple majority vote of the national legislature or by the autonomous decision of the national executive.

King sees this last point about legislative entrenchment of the rights of the regions as the truly distinctive feature of federations. Because of it the nature and scale of the divisions of powers between the centre and the region can be distinguished from other forms of devolution or regionalism by the fact that regional autonomy and representation are not only more devolved but also constitutionally guaranteed. The centre does not have the right to abolish or amend the boundaries of the territorial units. It is also the case that a written constitution has to be accepted as supreme so that a body, such as a Supreme Court, is recognised as being able to settle authoritatively disputes about the meaning of the constitution, particularly with regard to the division of powers between the centre and the territorial units. The entrenchment of the regions' position may be protected by granting them a formal role in the process of amending the constitution. For example, in the United States, whereas a constitutional amendment is initiated at national level (in practice by a two-thirds vote in both houses of the US Congress), it has to be ratified by three-quarters of the states (usually by their legislatures).

A major feature of federal systems is that the territorial units are incorporated into the policy-making process at national level. Citizens in federations typically vote for their own state legislature and the national legislature. Within the national legislature, the upper chamber is designed to reflect the interests of the states in general and to protect the position of the smaller units in particular either by equal representation regardless of population or by granting additional members to those warranted by their size. In one sense this is, of course, highly undemocratic if we compare it with the democratic principle of one person, one vote and all votes carrying equal weight. In the United States the fifty states have two members each in the US Senate, which means that the twenty-six smallest states, with less than one-fifth of the population, have a majority of seats. However, in the Canadian appointed upper house Ontario and Quebec have twenty-four members each, while Newfoundland and Saskatchewan have only six each, and Prince Edward Island four. This still gives the smaller provinces proportionally a very favourable position relative to their populations. In Germany the upper chamber (the Bundesrat) allows six members for large states like Bavaria and Baden-Württemburg, while Saarland and Bremen have three each; this despite the fact that Bavaria, for example, has eleven times the population of Saarland. It is worth noting that the German Bundesrat consists not of directly elected members from the states or Länder, but of representatives of the governments of those states. This Federal Council has a very important role and possesses an absolute veto in all legislative matters affecting the interests of the Länder. It is able to bring the views of the governments of the Länder directly into the policy-making process at federal level, while promoting intergovernmental cooperation.

Relations between legislature and executive at state level tend to reflect those at national level in federal systems (see Chapter 10). For example, in the USA the fifty states each elect a governor separate from the legislature, while in Australia and Canada parliamentary systems exist at sub-national level.

## Developments in federal governments

According to K. C. Wheare, in his classic study *Federal Government*, the federal principle is 'the method of dividing government so that the general and regional government are each, within a sphere, coordinate and independent' (Wheare 1963: 10). In other words the constitution divides the powers of government between two tiers so that each is of equal status and can act independently within its own area of authority, a form of divided sovereignty. Wheare's view was that some political systems, while apparently federal in form, were not in practice because the balance did not allow for coordinate and independent status. One tier (normally the centre) could intervene in the jurisdiction of the other and therefore the latter tier was in reality subordinate and dependent. A constitution or political system could have federal aspects without being a truly federal system; India would be an example, in both its 1935 Constitution and its political experience since. Neither can federalism co-exist with autocratic control of power; the USSR, Yugoslavia and Czechoslovakia were what can be called 'pseudo-federations', because the unity of their ethno-regional parts was maintained from above and a complex array of techniques of coercion ensured compliance with the centre (Duchaek, cited in G. Smith 1995: 8).

An emphasis on the division of powers and separate authority of the tiers has led to the term 'dual federalism'. However, as we noted earlier, inter-governmental relations can change over time and each federal system has established its own particular balance bearing in mind its own history, culture and social structure; what remains true is that, while one in ten of the world's present-day polities claim to be federations, on investigation we would find that in practice many could not easily be distinguished from unitary systems of government.

Federal systems came into being either because previously independent states agreed to unite for certain purposes while retaining their sovereignty in other areas or via the disaggregation of a previously unitary state. The motives for such unions have often been related to defence requirements, the desire for economic development and increased trade or the need to find a way of protecting minority interests within a wider political system. Over a period of time political, social and economic changes can lead to a marked shift in the balance of power between federal and state governments. Developments such as improved communications and media, growing trade across state boundaries, stronger national identity fostered perhaps by foreign wars and crises, population growth and mobility and the effective assimilation of minority groups are factors that may well lead to a changed political culture making the growth of federal government power acceptable to the people. The citizens of such a state may well look increasingly to the federal government rather than their state capital for political answers to their problems. On the other hand, failure of federal policies, a sense of injustice by sections of the population based on territorial interest or an enhanced sense of identity based on cleavages such as race, religion or language within a territorial context may well lead to demands for greater state autonomy or even secession from the federation.

The United States (since the Civil War in the 1860s) would be an example of the former and Canada of the latter situation. In the US the federal government has increased its role and powers, particularly since the New Deal period of the 1930s. Political scientists argued that dual federalism had been replaced by 'cooperative federalism', where the various levels of government are seen as related parts of a single government system which is characterised more by shared functions and partnership in providing services than by a neat division of responsibilities. In this system the federal government has increasingly taken the lead in areas of domestic policy that were traditionally the preserve of the states, setting out standards and rules such that some writers have more recently described as 'coercive federalism' (Kincaid 1994: 205–16). The balance has been altered by constitutional amendment, by interpretations of the constitution by the Supreme Court which favour the national government and by the financial power of Washington in distributing grants to the states with conditions attached to them (Grant 1994 : 280–5). 'Dual federalism', however, still has a strong normative appeal to conservatives in the United States and proposals in 1995 by the Republican-controlled Congress were intended to devolve important powers to the state level.

Canada's Constitution of 1867 has elements of strong national authority such that Wheare described it as a 'quasi-federal' constitution (Wheare 1963: 19), while recognising that in practice it was federal because no national government attempting to stress the unitary elements would survive. Canada in fact has been unusual in that the power of the centre has weakened since the union's inception. Since the 1960s tensions have increased between Quebec province, with the rise of French-Canadian nationalism promoted by the Parti Québécois, and the rest of the Canadian federation. Attempts were made to satisfy their demands by the adoption of official bilingualism and biculturalism, by the removal of the remaining influence of the UK Parliament on the Canadian Constitution and the Meech Lake Accord in 1987, which recognised Quebec's special status and desire to be regarded as 'a distinct society'. However, some of the other provinces were becoming increasingly resentful at the concessions being granted to Quebec and they refused to accept the Accord. A further proposal, the Charlottetown Accord, which featured a new directly elected Senate in which all provinces would be equally represented while recognising Quebec's special position, was rejected by a national referendum in 1992 by 54.4 per cent to 44.6 per cent, with Quebec's rejection reflecting a similar division of opinion. In 1995 Quebec held its own referendum on whether it should break with Canada and become an independent state; with a 92 per cent turnout among Quebec voters the proposition failed by a margin of only 1 per cent, thus ensuring that the issue would remain a major destabilising question hanging over Canada's constitutional and political future. (See box for key dates.)

> **Key dates for Canada: The Quebec issue**
>
> | | |
> |---|---|
> | 1535 | French explorer Jacques Cartier claims territory |
> | 1759 | English defeat the French and take over territory |
> | 1960–8 | Terrorism by extreme nationalists |
> | 1967 | Parti Québécois formed. President de Gaulle of France declares: 'Vive le Québec libre.' |
> | 1968 | Canadian Prime Minister Trudeau calls out army after kidnapping of British consul and murders |
> | 1977 | Provincial government bans shop signs in English |
> | 1980 | First referendum: Quebecers vote 60:40 against a mild form of separation |
> | 1987 | Meech Lake Accord recognises Quebec's special status but this not accepted by all the provinces |
> | 1990 | Bouchard forms Bloc Québécois. Gains seats in federal Parliament |
> | 1992 | Charlottetown Accord: national referendum rejects the agreement 54:46 |
> | 1993 | Bloc Québécois becomes official opposition |
> | 1994 | Hardline separatist Jacques Parizeau elected Quebec's premier |
> | 1995 | Parizeau calls for referendum on separation; support soars after Bouchard takes over campaign but Quebecers reject proposal by less than 1% |

## Conclusions on federalism

Federal systems may promote many of the benefits set out in the previous section on decentralisation; for example, policy innovation at territorial level and the protection of minority interests. Federations may also succeed in regulating and managing social conflicts by easing tensions and being sensitive to diversity. We should not expect federal arrangements to eliminate conflict altogether, any more than conflicts are eliminated in unitary states, but by creating the environment and processes for managing clashes of interests federations can promote political stability. However, it may also be argued that federations have a built-in tendency to disequilibrium and some may appear to be in a state of perpetual crisis. 'Paradoxically, the capacity of a federal system to reflect diversity constitutes a built-in weakness since it allows for conflicts to emerge and be politicised' (Gagnon 1993: 18).

Margaret Covell observes that:

> Many writers on Canadian federalism argue that the existence of a provincial level of government has exacerbated the country's regional and language divisions by giving groups involved an institutional power base and creating political elites with a vested interest in bad relations with the national government.
>
> (Covell, cited in Gagnon 1993: 18)

It may also be argued that federalism has created a form of territorial corporatism, with the national government forced to bargain with representatives of entrenched geographical interests while paying less attention to the important social cleavages which do not coincide with state boundaries.

While there are numerous examples of failed federations – the West Indian Federation (1962), the Central African Federation (1963), the withdrawal/ expulsion of Singapore from the Malaysian Federation (1965) and, more recently, the break-up of Yugoslavia in 1992 – Preston King (1993) argues that these are failures of particular experiments in federation, not of federation as such. He suggests that there is no basis in fact for the belief that federations are somehow less permanent in form than non-federal states, and that the history of federations is at least as much one of success as of dissolution. Given particular difficulties such as territorial size and ethnic particularism, they can often be said to have succeeded where no imagined alternative would have done. Federations such as Switerzland, the United States, Australia and Germany are examples of stable and successful federal systems (King 1993: 96–7). The Federal Republic of Germany, of course, particularly since the reunification in 1989, has been a prime mover – some would say *the* prime mover – in promoting the vision of a federal Europe based on the European Union (EU). Chapter 15 looks at the development of supranational institutions making policy which applies across the EU. Here we only need to note that the confederal aspects of its institutions (the Council of Ministers, representing the national governments of the fifteen members, as the key policy-making body and the fact that the EU acts principally through the member governments) are increasingly being balanced by federal features such as the greater use of majority voting in the Council and the growing powers of the European Parliament. Different interpretations of the meaning of federalism and whether it is a centralising or decentralising concept have resulted in opposition to the development of a clearly federal Europe being greater in Britain than in most continental European nations.

## Local government and politics

Whether a state is federal or unitary in structure there will be in liberal democratic polities a pattern of local government with elected councils having responsibility for policy-making and administration over a range of services. Exactly what shape this system takes, how many and what type of local councils exist and how they relate to the rest of the government structure, depends of course on the history, constitution and political developments that have taken place in the particular state. There is, however, widespread recognition that a viable system of local self-government is an integral part of what makes a liberal democratic state work in a representative and responsible way. In Central and Eastern Europe it is acknowledged that the development of local democracy is a necessary step in the transfor- mation from the old communist regimes. Local authorities, by being elected representative institutions, enjoy a degree of legitimacy and electoral support which distinguishes them from other forms of administration.

Studies of comparative local government suggests that they can be categorised into a number of broad groups based on similarities and differences over a wide range of factors such as constitutional status, structure, powers, relations with central government, party systems and so on. In a comprehensive survey of sub-national institutions in Europe, North America and Japan, Alan Norton suggests that there are five broad groups: South European, North European, British, North American and Japanese. Table 12.1 demonstrates the characteristics of these categories. Norton says that:

A. Norton (1994) *International Handbook of Local and Regional Government*, Aldershot: Edward Elgar.

> On nine of the thirteen characteristics in the table the North American systems match the British, but there are major differences: not least in degrees of party politicisation, pluralism, the relative weakness of central government and the form of executive. There is a concentration of central power in the United Kingdom that is now alien to most European Latin systems as well as to the American. The North and South European groups stand together in ten characteristics but differ from the British in about half

*Table 12.1* Characteristics of world systems of local government

| | Britain | USA & Canada | France & Italy | Sweden & Denmark | Japan |
|---|---|---|---|---|---|
| Constitutional status | creature of parliament | state constitutional | national constitutional | national constitutional | national constitutional |
| National structure | mixed | mixed | 3 tier | 2 tier | 2 tier |
| Powers | limited by statute | limited by statute | general competence & statute | general competence & statute | general competence |
| Control of legality by | courts | courts | regions & courts | state & courts | state & courts |
| Control of local policy | low | low | interlocked | interlocked | interlocked |
| Control of local policy historically | low | low | high | high | high |
| Local functions 1949–89 | reduced | various | increased | increased | increased |
| Local authority expenditure as (UK) % of GDP* | 12% | 11%, 9% | 9%, 15% | 28%, 30% | 18% |
| Public expenditure as % of GDP* | 44% | 35% | 49%, 50% | 57%, 60% | 29% |
| Local executive authority | council | mixed | mayor or president | mixed | mayor or governor with board |
| Representational system | majoritarian | majoritarian | proportional representation | proportional representation | majoritarian |
| Party system | strong two-party | weak two-party | strong multi-party | strong multi-party | strong multi-party |
| Participation at elections | low | low | high | high | high |

* Figures from Poul Erik Mouritzen and K. H. Nielsen (1988) *Handbook of Comparative Urban Fiscal Data*, Odense: DDA.

*Source*: Norton (1994)

> of these. Japanese structures are clearly a modern synthesis from two conti-
> nents working in an often awkward relationship with national traditions.
>
> (Norton 1994: 13)

### Constitutional and legal status

In most liberal democratic states a written constitution provides for and
protects the principle of local self-government. Although this is different
from the constitutionally entrenched position of the states in a federal system
(see the section 'The requirements of federalism', pp. 351–2), Clarke and
Stewart argue that the provisions are still significant:

> The importance of the support given in constitutions to local government is
> not that it formally prevents the abolition of local authorities, but rather that
> it gives an established status to local government as part of the system of
> government.
>
> (Clarke and Stewart 1991: 14)

In almost all the states of continental Western Europe local government's
position is guaranteed in the national constitution or basic laws with its
rights defined in Germany, for example, as governing and regulating its own
affairs. In federal systems the state constitutions rather than the national
one may establish the powers and responsibilities of local government (e.g.
USA). In the case of the United Kingdom the 'unwritten constitution'
and tradition of parliamentary sovereignty means there is no constitutional
protection for local government nor any limit set to centralisation; new
laws abolishing particular types of authority (e.g. metropolitan counties),
individual authorities or affecting the financing, the powers or boundaries
of local councils can simply be passed by parliamentary simple majority,
even if they do have the effect of altering the overall system of government.
In most European states the doctrine of general competence applies; this is
the principle that local authorities have a general power of jurisdiction
over the affairs of their areas and inhabitants in so far as the law does not
explicitly provide otherwise. This is in direct contrast with the British
doctrine of *ultra vires*, whereby local authorities may carry out only those
responsibilities that are specifically assigned to them by Parliament (although
the 1972 Local Government Act introduced a limited exception to this
principle). In practice the general competence power may not actually lead
to more real powers for local government because they may lack the
resources to do more, and it can be argued that British local authorities
have traditionally had a broad range of well-defined responsibilities with
often substantial discretion. However, the general competence authority is
important symbolically and psychologically in that it enhances the concept
of the local government as a general political authority in its own right
which is fostering the welfare of the people and as the corporate expression
of the local community. From this also follows the European tradition
that local authorities are representative bodies articulating and speaking on
behalf of the general interests of their residents in the form of community

government as well as being involved in a wide range of functions, even though they may not carry them out directly or exclusively. The British tradition, on the other hand, has tended to emphasise the role of authorities as the providers of specific services within delegated powers from central government, while downplaying councils' wider community and representative roles.

## Structure and responsibilities

The simplest structure for local government is a single tier of all-purpose authorities. The attractions of such a system are that there is clear accountability and that the public should be in no doubt as to who is responsible for local services; it should be possible for the authority to plan and integrate its policies effectively. All-purpose authorities should also be able to determine overall priorities, avoid the possibility of duplication and overlap with other authorities and speak on behalf of the community with one authoritative voice. In Britain the county boroughs in the cities and larger towns, until they were abolished in 1974, were examples, and in the 1990s structural reforms have led to the creation of a number of unitary all-purpose councils to replace a two-tier structure in some parts of the country. However, this form of sub-national government is relatively rare; only in small countries like Iceland and Luxembourg is it the universal pattern, while Australia and Switzerland have single-tier structures within some of their member states. In a number of countries, including the USA, Germany, Canada and Sweden, general-purpose councils can be found, mostly in city areas. Because of the size of such authorities it has been felt necessary for some functions that are most efficiently carried out over a wide geographical area to be administered by joint boards made up of representatives of a number of authorities, thus in practice blurring responsibility.

Multi-tier systems of local government predominate in the vast majority of countries. Such systems provide for a division of powers so that the smaller units and those most accessible to the citizens can carry out a wide range of functions, while other responsibilities are administered by larger-scale authorities that can achieve greater effectiveness and efficiency through economies of scale, the employment of specialist staff and equipment and a wider strategic perspective. The multi-tier structure may also lead to the avoidance of joint bodies, unsatisfactory amalgamations of smaller authorities and direct provision by central government departments or appointed agencies.

Although a bewildering array of different types of local authorities with different names exist, according to Norton they can be categorised into three main groupings (Norton 1994: 34–5):

1 Basic level: examples would include non-metropolitan districts in England and Wales, municipalities/towns in the USA, communes in France, *Gemeinden* in Germany and *comuni* in Italy.
2 Intermediate: counties in England and Wales and in the USA, *départements* in France, *Kreise* and *kreisfreie Städte* in Germany and *provincie* in Italy.

Table 12.2 Government units in the United States

|  | Units |
|---|---|
| Federal | 1 |
| States | 50 |
| Total local governments | 84,955 |
| Counties | 3,043 |
| Municipalities | 19,279 |
| Townships | 16,656 |
| School districts | 14,422 |
| Special districts | 31,555 |
| Total | 85,006 |

Source: Statistical Abstract of the United States 1996, p. 295

3  State or region: in federal systems these would include the fifty states in the USA and sixteen Länder, including three city-states, in Germany. In unitary states, there are twenty-two *régions* in France and twenty *regioni* in Italy, but there is no regional level in the UK.

The range of population covered by local authorities varies widely, particularly at basic level. Whereas there have been reorganisations of local government in Germany and Scandinavia which have resulted in larger authorities the Mediterranean countries have in general shown considerable resistance to increased scale. In France over 36,000 communes have an average population of only 1,500. In Britain, where parish and town councils at this level of population have negligible functions, basic local authorities are unusually large, with English shire districts averaging populations of 127,000. This means that districts in Britain as a whole are thirteen times as large as the average German or Italian municipalities, which themselves are five times the size of the average French commune. It can be argued that in Britain the criteria for reorganisation have been based on the idea of streamlining for efficiency along with issues relating to service delivery at the expense of local community identity. Britain is also unusual in the European context in that, compared with countries of a similar size, it has no regional level. Although this is strongly opposed by the Conservatives, Labour and Liberal Democrat parties are committed to introducing assemblies for Scotland and for Wales with devolved powers. Apart from those bodies that exist within federal structures, Italy and Spain have autonomous regional authorities protected by constitutional guarantees and endowed with broad legislative powers. In France all regions have the same legal status as local authorities and are relatively weak in terms of their responsibilities (Blair 1991: 55).

A 1988 Council of Europe survey found that there was 'a certain homogeneity' between the functions performed at the basic level of local government, regardless of whether councils have a general competence power or a list of specific responsibilities. The position is complicated by the fact that local councils may have mandatory functions, and also

R. Batley and G. Stoker (eds) (1991) *Local Government in Europe: Trends and Developments*, London: Macmillan.

discretionary functions which they do not in fact carry out. Also, some responsibilities are shared between different tiers of local government or with central government; in some cases the amount of discretion is very limited. Given the very small size of some basic-level authorities, working with other councils is inevitable if provision is to be made on a reasonably efficient basis. In North America some services that in Europe are carried out by multipurpose authorities are often administered by directly elected special-purpose bodies such as school boards or directly by the states or the provinces.

Typically local governments are responsible for such services as primary and secondary education, roads, local planning, refuse collection, libraries, recreational facilities, personal social services, subsidised housing, fire services and environmental protection. In many countries they are also responsible for the police, vocational and adult education, promotion of the local economy and employment, social assistance, health services, and the running of public utilities (Norton 1994: 60–7). Clarke and Stewart point out that the education responsibilities of local authorities in Britain have been greater than in some European countries, but on the other hand it is common to find European local government having a greater role in health care, which in Britain is run by non-elected agencies, and in the administration of public utilities (gas, water, electricity), which they exercise through jointly owned companies, whereas in Britain they have been the responsibility of first nationalised and then privatised corporations (Clarke and Stewart 1991: 19).

Local authorities can carry out their responsibilities in a number of different ways. In Britain the tradition has been one of self-sufficiency, so that councils have been large enough to run the service by themselves and usually through directly employed staff. Direct provision through local government departments with their own managers or officers in control and accountable to elected members was the accepted norm at least until the 1980s. In many European states there has long been a more pluralistic approach, with the use of public enterprise companies, voluntary bodies, private organisations working under a franchise agreement, and joint local authority provision.

In the 1980s the Thatcher government in Britain required local authorities to conduct compulsory competitive tendering exercises over a range of services to test the cost-effectiveness of direct provision by council work-forces. Although private companies won only a minority of contracts in such areas as refuse collection, school meals provision and cleaning, competition itself did lead to significant changes in the management of local authorities and, its advocates claimed, savings in the costs of running the services. The Conservative government also emphasised 'the enabling authority' concept, which envisaged a much smaller role for local authorities in direct provision of services and greater partnership with the private sector, voluntary bodies and other non-government agencies. Councils would spend more time ensuring that services were provided and regulating and inspecting the provision and less time actually providing services themselves. This approach in some respects brought Britain closer to the more diverse patterns of provision in Europe, but critics pointed out that the compulsory element in contracting out was unusual, that local authorities were at the same time losing responsibility for services such as further and higher education altogether, and that there was also considerable growth in the number of non-elected QUANGOs, bodies with increasing powers in areas traditionally the preserve of local government.

Britain is not alone in reviewing and reforming methods of service delivery in order to improve efficiency and increase responsiveness to more demanding consumers, but it appears that it has been unusual in the degree of partisan and ideological controversy engendered. Decentralised service delivery and management, user panels and surveys of opinion have been common in many countries. Richard Batley identifies three main types of reform: first, to expand the role of local government and free it from restrictions, the most dramatic of which are the deregulation and 'free commune' experiments in Scandinavia; second, to improve public service practices by simplifying complexity that results from shared responsibilities, setting performance standards, improving staff training and decentralising management; third, to incorporate business methods and competitive practices into the public sector through such methods as devolving budget responsibilities and contracting out (Batley 1991: 216).

Despite recent changes, a survey in the early 1990s indicated that direct provision by local authorities through their own staff remains the norm. Excluding teachers and police to enable the figures to be more nearly comparable, France, Britain, the United States and Italy all had between 3.0 and 3.7 persons in every hundred in local government employment (Norton 1994: 70).

### Internal organisation

The representative nature of local government is embodied in the assembly or council, consisting of members directly elected by the citizens. Election may be by the first-past-the-post system or proportional representation. The electoral system has important effects on the nature of party politics and the areas represented by councillors. Elected members make policy, pass local laws and ordinances, determine local tax levels, act as 'watchdogs' on behalf of the public over the authority's administration and serve as forums for debate on local issues. Unless the executive is directly elected the council will also be responsible for the appointment of the executive. The size of such bodies varies considerably; in North America many councils are very small, with as few as three to five members, while at the other extreme the highest numbers were to be found in Sweden (149) and the combined department and commune in Paris (163) (Norton 1994: 96). In Britain there is a tendency for councils to be bigger in size than their European counterparts, reflecting their larger geographical areas they cover. However, because there are far fewer local authorities, the ratio of citizens to councillors is much higher. Discounting parishes, there is one councillor to every 1,800 electors in England and Wales, while in most European countries there are between one in 250 and one in 1,000 (Clarke and Stewart 1991: 15).

Very small assemblies may be more efficient in terms of making decisions but they obviously do not score so highly in terms of representativeness. Most countries operate through a committee system structured around the main service areas for which the council is responsible. Chairs of committees are often very influential and act as spokespersons, presenting committee policy proposals to the full council for its approval. Where party politics is prevalent, which has increasingly been the case in many countries, committee membership is usually divided proportionately according to the political balance of the council overall. Committees enable members to develop specialist interests and expertise, although it is sometimes argued that this can detract from their ability to consider the corporate interest of the council as a whole and encourages them to work in alliance with departmental officers and related pressure groups in giving priority to protecting the interests of particular services.

In Britain the full council is the sole source of authority and there is no distinction between legislative and executive responsibility. Unlike constitutional practice nationally, where the executive has a separate existence and identity within parliament, councillors are not only policy-makers but also responsible, in theory at least, for carrying out those policies. In practice, of course, the paid-officer administration of the authority implement the decisions of elected members and senior officers with professional expertise advise committees on policy issues. However, the British model of local government does not have a clear-cut executive and this does affect the way councils operate as well as reducing the visibility of their leadership to the public. Local councils may develop a form of 'submerged executive' consisting of party political leaders and committee chairs within the formal structure.

In many countries local authorities have clearly identified political executives in addition to their elected assemblies. They may be directly elected by the public, chosen by the council or even appointed at national level in agreement with the local authority. Executives are responsible for the administration of the authority as well as for preparing policy and budgetary proposals for the council. The existence of a strong mayor can affect the popular perception of the municipality, personifying the local authority and increasing interest in local elections. Mayors in countries such as the United States and France often have influence on a wider state or national basis. In France senior government ministers, including Prime Minister Alain Juppé, may continue to have a local power base by being mayor of their local government while concurrently holding national office. President Jacques Chirac held the office of mayor of Paris prior to being elected President in 1995. In the United States President Clinton's cabinet appointed in 1993 included the former mayors of San Antonio and Denver. Whereas in Britain a number of MPs have had experience as local councillors, it is extremely rare for a politician to hold national and local office simultaneously, and generally local politicians are not known widely even in their own areas. In some countries there is much greater overlap and interaction between national and local politics.

We should also distinguish between what are known as dual and fused systems, which affect intergovernmental relations between the centre and localities. The English tradition has been for local authorities to operate separately from the central government. Indeed not only is there a separation at the political level but recruitment practices for civil servants and local government officers have been very different. This is a dual system and, although of course central government influences and intervenes extensively in local government affairs it is through many different departments and officials (see section on 'Central–local relations', pp. 364–6). However, under a fused system best exemplified in France the two levels are joined in an office such as a prefect (now called Commissioner of the Republic), who is a central appointee with broad powers of oversight of administration in a particular local area. This official reports to the Ministry of the Interior and acts as the focus of a two-way process of intergovernmental communication. The commissioners for the departments are very important and influential individuals, although decentralising reforms in France in the early 1990s transferred some of their functions to the elected councils.

---

**THINK POINT**
- Do you know the names of any local council members in your area?
- If so, what positions do they hold?

---

## Central–local relations

It is beyond the scope of this chapter to attempt to describe the vast array of different forms of relationship between central and local government that exist in various political systems. Suffice to say, the history, political culture and constitutional developments of individual countries make for a diverse range of interactions and arrangements. There have been attempts to portray central–local relations by way of models or analytical frameworks intended to simplify and explain complex and multidimensional phenomena. For example, the agency model pictures local authorities as subordinate bodies with little or no discretionary power whose role is to act as agents of central government in implementing its policies. The power dependence model put forward by Rhodes, however, stresses that both levels of government have resources – legal, financial, political, informational and so on – and that bargaining between them is an important feature of the relationship (Rhodes 1981). However, Norton cautions us to be wary of such models, particularly in the context of comparing different political systems:

> There is a simple model of two pole central–local relations which bears little resemblance to reality. Each level of government is fragmented and complex. Relations cross each other in what is a diagonal and tangled pattern rather than a vertical one. Given the great variety and complexity of the institutions at any one level of government, the range of channels and the modes of communication that can be used downwards and upwards in any one case and the extent to which many of the channels used are invisible to researchers as well as to the general public, it is clear that even if a study is sharply focused, light can only be thrown on limited aspects of interaction.
>
> (Norton 1994: 51)

We may therefore draw attention to some of the factors that will affect central–local government relations, a number of which have been referred to earlier in the chapter.

1 Whether the system is a federal or unitary one; in the former the existence of a state tier affects the constitutional relationship between national and local levels and the degree of interaction directly between them.

2 How many tiers of local government exist and the number and size of local authorities with which the centre has to interact.

3 Whether the local authorities have a general competence or are restricted by the *ultra vires* rule.

4 The range of local government services and the proportion of public spending and GNP that expenditure on these services constitutes; if local spending is a significant percentage then central government is more likely to wish to influence or control it as part of its overall economic policy and its attempt to restrain public expenditure.

5 The organisation of central government; is there a Ministry of the Interior and a fused system with a prefect having overall supervisory responsibilities over local authorities? It is also important to remember that central governments are not monolithic entities; they consist of different departments with often different traditions and ways of dealing with local authorities in relation to the services for which they are responsible. The departments are also usually reliant on local government for the effective implementation of national policies.

6 The form of local government finance; how far local authorities are dependent on central government grants for their resources; whether the grants are general revenue that can be used at the authorities' discretion or specific grants limited to use on certain functions; what independent tax sources local authorities have and whether there are any central restrictions on their tax-raising powers. (Property taxes are the most common form of local tax but sales taxes, local income taxes and business taxes are also frequent sources of income.)

7 The type of relationship that exists between national and local politicians and administrators.

8 The nature of party politics and how far central–local relations are affected by strong party and ideological differences.

9 How far central government consults with and takes notice of the views of interest groups, professionals operating in different policy networks and bodies representing local government such as local authority associations.

Philip Blair draws attention to another important point to be considered when we attempt to analyse and contrast central–local relations in different countries.

> When comparing trends in different countries with regard to local autonomy, it is important to bear in mind the quite different starting-points from which each system is evolving. Decentralising tendencies may be observed in some traditionally highly centralised systems which may still leave them more centralised than some countries in which local autonomy is being eroded. The problem, however, is that the actual degree of local autonomy in different countries is not easy to compare, depending as it does on the interplay of a large number of factors which are often difficult to measure.
>
> (Blair 1991: 41)

In Scandinavia, Italy, France, Spain and Portugal, for example, there have been decentralising reforms with central government reducing the degree of regulation. Although in some cases, such as those of Spain and Portugal and perhaps France, where there was a tradition of highly centralised government, it can be argued there was only one way to go and although the degree of real antonomy created by such reforms can be debated, there is little doubt that the trend in Europe has been towards decentralisation. In Britain by contrast, local government has been subject to more detailed regulation than ever before. Between 1979 and 1992, 143 Acts of Parliament (58 of them major) were enacted which affected local government (Wilson and Game 1994: 95). The Thatcher governments of the 1980s were particularly concerned with restricting local government spending as part of their overall economic policy but they also, in line with New Right thinking referred to above (p. 348), saw local authorities in many ways as inefficient and wasteful providers of services. In answer to the charge that the government was centralising to an unprecedented level in modern times, Conservatives argued that the national government had a broader mandate, that it had a responsibility for ensuring national standards (for example, with the creation of the National Curriculum for schools) and protecting citizens from irresponsible local authorities by such measures as capping local government budgets. The government also argued that it was in many cases decentralising power by devolving decisions away from government to individual citizens by, for example, selling council houses to tenants and allowing parents more choice over which school their children attended.

## Exercise

1 Take the local council in the area you live in (choose one if there is a multi-tier system). Find out what services the council provides (maybe by obtaining information from the authority itself).
2 What percentage of its budget goes on the various services?
3 What other functions currently carried out by other bodies could it take on if a decision was made to reorganise and decentralise responsibilities?

## Conclusion

This chapter has demonstrated that, although most studies of political systems tend to concentrate attention on national government institutions and policy-making, an understanding of the nature of political activity at sub-national levels is essential if we are fully to appreciate the complexities and subtleties of how these systems work in practice and the way people govern themselves on a day-to-day basis. There is continuing discussion in most countries about the proper distribution of power between the central administration and other tiers of government, a debate that is increasingly affected in Europe by arguments over whether there should be a devolution of policy-making in some areas down to regional bodies while other responsibilities are simultaneously transferred to the supranational authority of the European Union.

## Further reading

Batley, R. and Stoker, G. (eds) (1991) *Local Government in Europe: Trends and Developments*, London: Macmillan. A comparative analysis of recent changes in local government in European political systems.

Burgess, M. and Gagnon, A. G. (eds) (1993) *Comparative Federalism and Federation*, Hemel Hempstead: Harvester Wheatsheaf. An important work by leading experts on federalism which provides a range of perspectives and approaches.

Norton, A. (1994) *International Handbook of Local and Regional Government*, Aldershot: Edward Elgar. A major reference book which provides a wealth of data and information about local government in Europe, America and Japan.

Wilson, D. and Game C. (1994) *Local Government in the United Kingdom*, London: Macmillan. A comprehensive textbook with an attractive format which examines the workings of local government in the UK and recent developments in a lively and interesting way.

# 13 THE POLITICS OF INFLUENCE AND CONTROL

*Richard Huggins and John Turner*

# The politics of influence and control

## Introduction

This chapter considers the way in which certain groups, individuals and actors seek to influence the political system, agenda and process. In particular it considers the aggregation of interests through pressure or interest groups. It also considers the role and function of the mass media in constructing and delivering political messages and communications. The chapter begins with a consideration of the organisation of political parties, the nature of party ideology and a survey of the pattern of political party competition. It then moves to a consideration of interest group politics and considers the characteristics of interests groups, their functions and status in political systems and considers some examples of interest groups operating within and across national boundaries and political systems. The third section of the chapter considers the role, organisation and function of the mass media in contemporary society. In particular, by way of illustration, the chapter analyses the role of newspapers in British election campaigns, television in election campaigns in the USA, and the use of images in politics in various political systems. Furthermore, it considers the crucial area of global media systems and the emergence of new forms of media as we enter the new millennium.

## Political parties

Political parties are often assumed to be a self-evident part of all political systems and as such are often taken for granted. For many people, parties are not particularly popular, especially when they are involved in the cut and thrust of everyday party politics, involving rhetoric, and claim and counter-claim. Parties are often perceived as railroading elected politicians, enforcing a discipline and control on politicians in the name of some wider ideology. For others, parties can appear dangerous and ineffective, especially where there are military leaders, for example, who are prepared to remove them by military force. People also notice parties and regard them in a dubious light when their leaders use patronage to promote their supporters and financial backers.

The development of modern democratic states has been paralleled by the emergence of mass political parties. Parties have become the principal way in which demands and expectations in society can be expressed and channelled. They are also the main way in which elites are recruited and new forces and movements integrated into the existing political system. Parties have become more important with the development of the wider franchise and electoral system. They are the main mobilising force behind elections and party organisation is a prerequisite for gaining support and ultimately power.

### Models of political parties

Political parties are very complex organisations. They are rarely monolithic and homogeneous, but rather a coalition of contending interests and ideas brought together at particular times based on wider social forces such as class, ethnicity, regionalism, religion and economic interests. Parties play an important function in transmitting and reinforcing cultural values and political assumptions. There are four models of parties which can be considered:

1  Undeveloped loyalty model – exists where a party expects its supporters to show a high level of loyalty and consistent following. This would become manifest in support for the leader and the party at elections. Loyalty in this sense has no real material or political benefits.
2  Developed loyalty model – exists where a party demands a great deal of loyalty and where there is a structured system for promotion and material and political rewards.
3  Developed non-loyalty model – exists in large countries where there are complex relationships between different states or regions. Party loyalty is relatively weak and there are developed bureaucratic, lobby and governmental institutions.
4  Undeveloped non-loyalty model – exists where parties are weak or do not exist at all. In countries with elements of such a model solidaristic corruption may occur, with those in government providing rewards for family and friends. Older cultural and social loyalties dominate and the differences between the state and civil society are blurred.

---

**THINK POINT**
- Consider these four models and try to apply each to countries you know.
- What are the main reasons for the differences between parties in these different countries?

---

### Functions of parties

A rather artificial distinction is often made between political parties and interest groups, which will be discussed later in the chapter. This distinction is often defined as the difference between interest aggregation, in the case of parties, and interest articulation, in the case of interest groups. These distinctions are especially highlighted in the literature on North American politics. Politics in the United States has a plethora of lobbyist groups which are assumed not to be seeking office and are therefore contrasted with parties. Parties are distinguished essentially as organisations seeking power and government, although even here the distinctions are often blurred. In modern societies there are many centres of power, and many parties not only compete in elections and hold power, but also represent political interests. For example, the green movement originally emerged out of a relatively heterogeneous set of interest and pressure groupings. Their main tasks were to influence environmental policies and campaign on particular green issues. However, today, throughout Europe there are green parties competing against more traditional parties in elections.

Parties are organised to compete in elections, aiming to gain power through representation and office. Parties fulfil four main functions:

1  The identification, development and espousal of a political ideology through policy programmes.
2  The mobilisation and socialisation of support, especially through election campaigns and party organisation.
3  The articulation and aggregation of social and economic interests.
4  The recruitment of elites and the formation of governments.

Clearly these functions are not all encompassing. Some parties never have enough support to form governments, while others may be revolutionary and therefore may reject the goal of office altogether.

---

**Models of political parties**
Most Western European countries have an undeveloped loyalty model (i); communist parties of the former Eastern European states had a developed loyalty model (ii); the United States can be said to have a developed non-loyalty model, with much weaker support and more switching between the parties at presidential elections (iii); and the undeveloped non-loyalty model can be applied to many less developed countries of the Third world (iv).

---

## The emergence of parties

Parties developed in Europe and the United States in the early part of the nineteenth century. In the twentieth century parties have taken hold in Central and Eastern Europe, Asia, Africa and South America. Very few countries have never had some kind of political party. A few states, like Saudi Arabia and other countries in Asia, remain non-party states.

Today, mass parties attempt to regulate and control other social institutions, like trade unions and the media. Modern party machines mobilise

R. Michels (1962) *Political Parties*, New York: Collier.
M. I. Ostrogoski (1902) *Democracy and the Organisation of Political Parties*, London: Macmillan.

**Oligarchy** Government by the few; Michels argued that even in parties which claimed to have democratic internal structures there was a controlling elite pursuing its own self-interest.

**Patronage** The distribution of political favours to government or party followers in return for political support.

**Adversarial politics** The confrontational style, especially of British politics, where political positions tend to become polarised.

R. Rose (1984) *Do Parties Make a Difference?*, Basingstoke: Macmillan.

thousands of members and millions of supporters, the modern political system being structured and shaped by parties. As mass parties became more important at around the turn of the century, so the first criticisms of them were made by such writers as Michels and Ostrogoski. Both described the modern party as oligarchical rather than democratic, bureaucratic rather than participative. Parties tended to exclude more people than were given access to decision-making within their organisations. Michels argued that parties were the main force behind the 'iron law of **oligarchy**'.

There are three criticisms usually levelled at the role of parties in modern political systems:

1  Tendency towards oligarchy – parties tend to concentrate power in the hands of an elite of party leaders who are difficult to replace. There is also a tendency for a clique or faction within leadership to emerge in order to make decisions for the party. **Patronage** and strong party discipline ensure that parties remain oligarchical.
2  Tendency towards **adversarial politics** – as factions parties tend to pursue their own sectional interests rather than wider national or social goals. Much time is spent in party squabbles and the pursuit of narrow party political advantage. Political virility is measured in terms of the ability of party leaders to score points off each other and cling on to power.
3  Tendency not to implement declared policies – despite detailed policy programmes and election manifestos before elections, parties have a chequered history in actually doing what they say they were going to do. Policies are not followed through, as parties respond to other institutions, like interest groups, commercial interest and administrative concerns once in power. Rose has argued that the choice of party actually makes little difference, since they tend to follow the same basic policies despite the rhetoric.

### The role of parties

General and fundamental common goals for parties are difficult to define. Parties are groups, but there is an overlap between pressure groups and wider social movements. Figure 13.1 indicates the main roles of political parties, although some may not perform certain of these roles. For example, parties compete to win elections and organise government, although some parties may not participate in elections and will not want to form governments.

The key to success for any mainstream party is not simply its leadership, its beliefs and ideas, the clarity and comprehensiveness of its policies, or its general image, but whether it can win elections. Other facets of party politics flow from such electoral success.

### Winning elections

Clearly this is in most cases the prime purpose and ultimate sign of success for a party. In parliamentary democracies, gaining an electoral majority

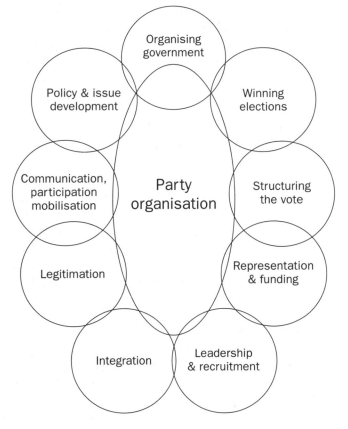

*Figure 13.1* Party organisation

ensures that a party's leaders can form a government and implement party policy. In the British case, the first-past-the-post electoral system has benefited two main parties, whether that was Conservative and Liberal at the beginning of the twentieth century or Conservative and Labour today. For the Conservatives in the 1980s such an electoral system split the non-Conservative vote, allowing the Tories to maintain power with about 43 per cent of the actual vote.

## Structuring the vote

This relates to the electoral system and the political geography of a country and the ability of a party to ensure that over time different classes and other social groups supply it with continuous support. Again using the British case, it is clear that the Conservative Party has been the most successful party in Europe, if not the world, in ensuring that its support has been maintained. This has meant that the party has at times changed in order to ensure that people still identify with it as a party.

Today the media play a much more profound role in shaping people's perceptions of parties, and the public in general respond to images and labels built around a general view of what a party is perceived as representing. As such, parties do transform themselves, reconstituting their images and messages, appealing to new voters, addressing new public concerns. Historically, all modern parties have had to adapt to a changing electorate. Franchise reform has meant that the electorate has vastly increased in size and has changed in composition, involving a much wider cross-section of social classes.

Again taking the example of the British Conservatives, it is possible to trace the way in which they have modified their policies as the franchise was extended in 1867, 1884 and 1918. In the 1980s the party, under Mrs Thatcher, was able to gain the support of skilled working-class voters as well as its natural constituency of middle-class support. Mrs Thatcher's Tories consciously attempted to restructure allegiances and so ensure support for a new party political agenda. Crewe has illustrated the way in which the working-class vote was restructured during the 1980s, using election results from 1983, with what he calls an 'old working class' still allied to Labour, but with a 'new working class' attracted to the Thatcher agenda (see Table 13.1).

### Representation and funding

Parties are also the focus for wider political participation. All parties represent particular interests, with some parties linked to organised labour, others to the Catholic church, some to business, others to environmentalist groups. Parties reflect the wider divisions which exist in society and attempt to build support around certain social and economic values. In more traditional societies, where there is much more social cohesion, parties have less of a role. Historically, where there has been a high degree of autoritarianism parties either have not existed or have been persecuted.

Parties help to structure the form and expression of these divisions in society, institutionally integrating such conflicts within a constitutional and legal framework. Parties also represent social classes. For Marxists, **class-consciousness** is a prerequisite for social and political action. Parties which have been formed out of class conflict need people to perceive that conflict as fundamental to their position in society. For example, for parties on the

**Class-consciousness** The awareness of social divisions in society and the acceptance that class strongly determines life chances.

Table 13.1 Restructuring of the working-class vote in the 1980s

| | The new working class | | | | The old working class | | | |
|---|---|---|---|---|---|---|---|---|
| | Lives in South | Owner occupier | Non-union member | Works in private sector | Lives in North | Council tenant | Union member | Works in public sector |
| | % | % | % | % | % | % | % | % |
| Conservative | 46 | 44 | 40 | 38 | 29 | 25 | 30 | 32 |
| Labour | 28 | 32 | 38 | 39 | 57 | 57 | 48 | 49 |
| Liberal Democrat | 26 | 24 | 22 | 23 | 15 | 18 | 22 | 19 |

left in Europe, the perception that class is less important as a determinant of social and economic organisation has de-aligned working-class support. As such, parties of the left have reinvented themselves, moving away from a rhetoric based on class divisions and towards notions of social mobility.

Parties themselves stimulate conflicts in society. Parties may wish to accentuate latent divisions in order to generate support. In 1982, in the war between Argentina and Britain, governing parties in both countries used nationalism and patriotism as a way of staying in power. Parties in a single-party political system may choose to highlight one paramount conflict in society. As with war, a common threat can act to galvanise support, although, as in the case of former Yugoslavia, ethnicity and race are also often used.

Linked to representation is funding. Some states, like the United States and Germany, for example, have some state funding for parties, although more commonly parties receive funds from their main supporters, either through membership contributions, or through donations from big business or trade unions. It is particularly important for parties to raise money at the time of elections, with huge amounts being spent on media and advertising campaigns. It is estimated that the two main parties in Britain spent in the region of £30 million at the 1992 General Election.

## Leadership and recruitment

Access to political positions within political systems is provided almost exclusively through political parties. A political career was once described by Disraeli as a climb up a 'greasy pole', the pole being the political party itself. Access through the party usually begins at the local level, or through work for the party machine. Working in the party bureaucracy provides a means of political preferment.

## Integration

Parties also play an important role in bringing together what would otherwise be divergent or conflicting interests. Political parties attempt to overcome public apathy, alienation and frustration with the political system by providing a home for disaffection. Parties are made up of factions which represent ideas from different strands of party thinking over time (see Rose 1974). Parties can also be the focus for new movements, giving political expression to a newly emerging labour or peasant movement. Without an expression such groups might become revolutionary and work outside constitutional arrangements. Parties integrate these forces and provide access for such views and leadership within existing political arrangements.

R. Rose (1974) *The Problem of Party Government*, London: Macmillan.

## Legitimation

An important function of parties is to legitimise belief in the party system itself and in its own leadership. The leadership of a party will need to develop policies which are broadly supported by its membership and potential supporters. In a loose coalition of interests, the leadership may be forced to compromise its position on a number of issues in order to gain consent.

For example, it may need to establish a balance between the views of its nationally and locally elected politicians, grassroots membership, corporate clients and media organisations. Sometimes such interests become so disparate that their views become irreconcilable and major divisions occur within the party.

One consequence of this may be a public perception that the party is not united and therefore legitimacy to hold power is questioned. Leaders will also look beyond the confines of their own party. They will also need to respond to the expectations and aspirations of a wider electorate, which may be much more fickle in its support. For example, a governing party on the left may need to adopt more centrist policies in order to retain the support of a less leftist electorate. This is also the case where there is a coalition of parties, perhaps in a multi-party system, where a party of the right or left may need the support of a third party.

### Communication, mobilisation and participation

In fostering wider support, parties face the problems of organisation and leadership. As Michels (1962) indicated, parties tend to be oligarchical, with decision-making controlled at the top and most decisions being made by a relatively small number of leading politicians and party officials. However, all parties need followers and supporters, some being more active than others. A party develops when supporters of a faction become followers. Support may come for a variety of reasons. Groups and individuals may want to change existing social relationships by gaining greater access to political power and economic resources. However, some parties have found it difficult to mobilise mass support. Traditional barriers of ethnicity or class have meant that some modernising parties have been unable to gain deeper grassroots support. In such regimes, more authoritarian political leadership may choose to repress party development. Parties create situations where strength supposedly derives from the size of their support. Modern democratic parties claim that participation in party decision-making is open, although differences may exist between the notions of representation and mobilisation. A representative party tends to put forward the views of its supporters as its paramount aim. Party policy shifts as the views of its supporters change, and organisational procedures will be established to ensure the party's rank and file are allowed to participate in decision-making. As such, leaders will claim that they are in touch with their members and that they represent their views. Most Western parties are built around the assumptions of this representative model.

Mobilising parties are organisations which place the conversion of people to their cause as a main priority. This may involve increasing awareness among the public of issues which the party wants to address. It may highlight certain divisions within society, certain injustices or economic inequalities. Latent demands are tapped, with parties raising consciousness of issues and proactively generating support.

## Policy and issue development

A major task of parties is to formulate and implement policies. Policies are shaped by the wider conflicts in society, and party ideologies are influenced by the way in which the electorate perceives these divisions. Policies emerge as a consequence of demands, expectations and perceptions, although parties will attempt to build an agenda around their core values. Parties attempt to sell their ideology and claim support for it through wider electoral appeals.

Leaders need to respond to the demands of party members generated from within the party. Within a party a range of policy papers, pamphlets and position documents feed into the preparation of the party's election programme. Policy development also involves groups from outside the party, including academics, experts and wider pressure groups. Insider groups play an important part in generating new ideas and policies relatively independently of permanent government officials in the administration.

## Organising government

This is the ultimate prize for parties in winning elections and taking office. Britain's first-past-the-post electoral system has created a two-party system which has tended to centralise power. Compared with the United States, Britain does not have a clear separation of powers. The degree of separation is very much dependent on the party system. Britain in the 1980s was dominated by the Conservative Party in power and this has had the effect of drawing together other parts of the governmental system.

## Party organisation

These different aspects of party politics are drawn together by the party's organisation. In examining party organisation, again it is useful to look at the structure of the successful British Conservative Party. Unlike its main rival, the Labour Party, which has a federal party structure, the Conservative Party has a hierarchical structure based on the three pillars of the parliamentary leadership, the party bureaucracy and the party in the country. At ward or constituency level the party is organised to mobilise support, delivering votes, raising funds and recruiting new members. However, power is wielded by a top-down leadership underpinned by a general party ethos of loyalty and deference, rather than formal accountability and open decision-making. The party is structured around its main rationale of achieving power and other considerations are secondary to this. For example, if a leader is thought to be unable to deliver another election victory the party usually ensures that leader is removed.

Formally, the party in the country and the party's annual conference are subordinate to the leadership. Figure 13.2 gives a simplified illustration of the party's structure, showing the three pillars of party organisation which have been so effective in allowing the party to achieve power.

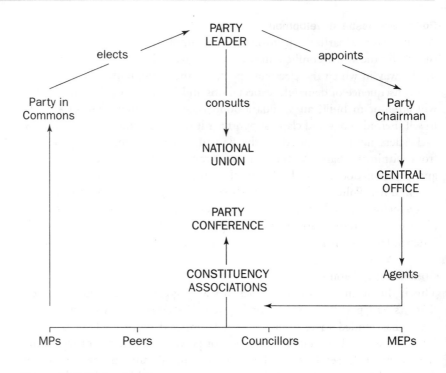

*Figure 13.2* Party structure

---

**THINK POINT**
- Consider these different roles of a leading political party in your country.
- Write a note on each role and evaluate how effectively the party is organised.

---

## Constraints on political parties

In general it can be argued that party leaders and members claim too much regarding parties' ability to influence and change society. There are a number of constraints which limit the scope of party activities and influence.

### The wider political culture: the social and economic environment

Countries have different political traditions and histories, which in turn affect their cultures. For example, revolutions in France and Russia have determined the scope, support and relative power of parties, whereas the continuity of British institutions has led to the emergence of a two-party system integrated within relatively conservative political structures. Attempts have been made to copy party systems. For example, after Independence, Nigeria adopted a Westminster-style constitution with similar party-political assumptions. In Nigeria's case the heterogeneous nature of ethnic and regional differences did not make this imitation a success. Civil strife and a post-colonial history of military coups have partly been a consequence.

Social divisions are reflected in party structures and ideologies. Religious parties will not develop if religious conflicts do not exist; whereas the development of a large industrial working class has allowed working-class parties to emerge. Communist parties have found it difficult to establish themselves in agrarian societies, where an urban working class is small. Much of the success of the Communist Party in establishing itself in China was a consequence of the anti-Japanese nationalistic position it took.

The social and economic environment of a country will determine the type of party system, which in turn will determine the kind of parties which will emerge. For example, a tradition and culture of political tolerance will allow a party system to emerge where there is a high-level agreement on pluralist values. However, a high degree of repression in society will allow authoritarian parties to emerge.

## Limits on party influence

Parties are also limited by the scope of their organisations and their ability to make contact with the wider population. Today, electronic media allow party leaders to communicate with millions, although whether their messages are understood or believed is another matter.

There is no hard evidence that parties, their ideologies and policies can actually change people's attitudes and behaviour. For example, party leaders often claim that they intend to change hearts and minds, although evidence suggests that this is rarely achieved. For example, in Britain Mrs Thatcher did change many institutional arrangements, but whether she actually changed people's more fundamental beliefs is more difficult to assess. Many opinion polls have suggested that attitudes are very similar now compared with when Mrs Thatcher came to power.

The ability of parties to mobilise people tends to decline as a political system develops. Propaganda has a limited effect, given wider changes in the social and economic environment. For example, at the end of the 1980s it became increasingly difficult for parties in Eastern Europe to mobilise people and retain party legitimacy. As consumerism developed in other parts of Europe it became increasingly difficult for communist parties in Hungary, Poland, Czechoslovakia, Romania and East Germany to retain control and legitimacy.

## Policies, organisation and leadership

A further constraint on parties is the relationship between organisation and policies. For example, Blondel (1969a) has argued that what a party gains in support or organisation it often loses in policies or programmes. He argues that there is a trade-off between accommodating grassroots members and attracting new supporters.

## *Political parties, power and support*

To examine how parties come to power given different social and economic circumstances it is important to take a wide and more specific view of different political systems. Firstly, there are general factors, related to how parties develop, and, secondly, there are the specific circumstances related to how parties emerge within specific countries and political cultures. Parties which gain wide social support tend to have policies, an organisational structure and a leadership which meet the political aspirations of people. However, these factors may be in part culturally specific, so some parties may do better in some societies and political cultures than other parties. The amount of support for a given party often determines the strength of such groups, although this does not always follow. Support itself will vary. In relation to a party it might mean that there are both active and passive members. Support may vary from active participation in fund raising and campaigning to occasional support sometimes delivered at election time.

Support for a given party may be due to a number of factors. Someone may support a party because they identify with what the party says and does. The emphasis here is on what the person perceives to be the case rather than what the reality might be. Party images, especially as portrayed in the media, are important here. A distinction can be made between types of support for a party: *communal support*, based on the basic values and way of life of the supporter; and *associational support*, based on activities and wider objectives. Support can be placed on a continuum between these two positions (see Figure 13.3). The degree of support determines the strength of allegiance of an individual to a party. In turn the degree of allegiance determines its legitimacy. The more communal the support the less the party's leaders are constrained by the views of its members. Leaders may attempt to foster group or communal feelings so that they can become freer to act and less constrained by the individual views of members. For example, the solidarity and ideological underpinning for socialist ideas may provide the leadership of left parties with the freedom to pursue more moderate, centrist policies, designed electorally to win over essentially non-socialist voters.

### Electoral systems and the development of party politics

The details of a discussion of policies, organisation and leadership will depend upon the type of political environment in which parties are operating. Clearly, the other parties against which it has to compete are a major challenge to any political party. The effect on a party will be greatest where this competition is toughest. Party structures, ideologies, policies and leaders will vary according to the view the party has of its main rivals for power. A situation where there is acute rivalry between parties will generate political activities which are very different from a situation where one party

| Family | Church | Charity | Sports Club | Political Party | Motoring Organization |

Communal ———————————————————————————————————— Associational

*Figure 13.3* Party support continuum

dominates all others. Thus we need to consider *party systems* as well as parties.

The level of conflict in a party system may determine the nature of party competition. The degree of conflict is shown in the continuum in Figure 13.4. There are three variants here: first, traditional party systems where competition between parties is low; second, representative party systems where party competition is normal and permanent; and, third, mobilising political systems where tough competition between parties gives power to a single party, which may then repress all competition, hold power for a long time and take control of all state institutions.

Multi-party systems socialise party competition and institutionalise it. Complex rules and guidelines are created to regulate party competition and party rivalry is kept within bounds. Key guidelines for party systems with more than one party include:

- the control of bribery and physical violence;
- the establishment of electoral rules of fairness and equality;
- the acceptance of the electoral result;
- the establishment of equality of opportunity including access to the media.

There is also a relationship between a party system and an electoral system. In a simple majority system the candidate with most votes is elected, although two issues follow from such systems: first, the larger the number of seats, the more distortion in result; second, if there are more than two parties, third and fourth parties remain underrepresented. Third parties will only gain seats in a majority system where they are geographically concentrated. A majority system is used in Britain.

In a two-ballot system only candidates with over half the vote are elected. Second preferences are taken into account if a candidate fails to win an outright majority in the first ballot. This system has been used recently in presidential elections in France.

In proportional representation systems the votes of extremely popular and extremely unpopular candidates are redistributed to next preferences. In proportional list systems each party will have a list of candidates and electors vote for one list or another. Seats are allocated on the basis of the proportion of votes each list obtains.

There has been much discussion about whether simple majority systems lead to two-party systems, squeezing out and underrepresenting third parties. In Britain, the third party, the Liberal Democrats, rarely achieve more than twenty Members of Parliament out of 650 on around 20 per cent of the

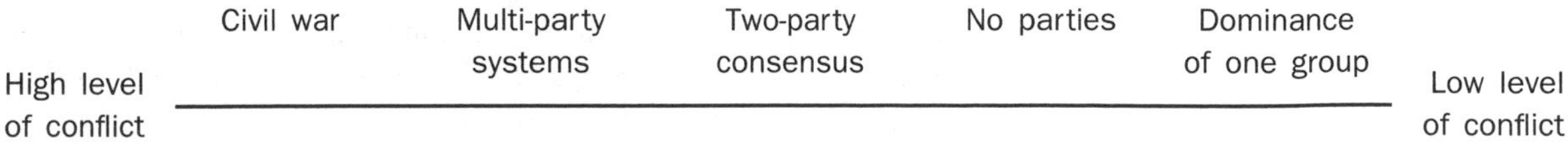

| High level of conflict | Civil war | Multi-party systems | Two-party consensus | No parties | Dominance of one group | Low level of conflict |
|---|---|---|---|---|---|---|

*Figure 13.4* Party conflict continuum

vote. The electoral system has the effect of squeezing out the Liberal Democrat vote because it is less concentrated. However, the two-party system has been in decline since the 1950s in Britain. In the 1950s the two main parties gained around 90 per cent of votes; today that figure is nearer 75 per cent.

Equally, it has been argued that proportional representation leads to multi-party systems. Smaller parties have a greater chance of representation in a PR system, and PR may encourage factions within parties to break up as a consequence. However, other factors must be taken into account. A two-party system dominates where there is a single cleavage, perhaps along class lines. However, with the breakdown of traditional attitudes built around class, the two-party system declines as well. The dealignment of working-class voters from parties of the left is an example of this. Two parties may exist where there are a large number of divisions which in turn are too small to form parties. Left–right party systems, representing progressives and conservatives may operate to draw together disparate groups.

### The future of parties

Criticism of parties is widespread and longstanding. The legitimacy of party politics and its dominance, especially in Western political systems, has been questioned. The continued dominance of elites, low membership and participation, party dominance over legislatures and electoral systems which seem to perpetuate single- or two-party rule has raised questions about their future role.

There have been a number of criticisms:

1 The tendency towards oligarchy – parties have become increasingly bureaucratic and unrepresentative, often with questionable if not un-democratic structures and procedures. Questions have been posed as to how parties give members access to decision-making, how they elect party leaders, how they raise finance, how they recruit and promote people within the parties and on the widespread use of patronage.

2 Parties have tended to fossilise old social and political divisions and perpetuate them in the name of power. This has involved emphasis-ing adversarial conflicts rather than areas of consensus. Hence, parties tend to highlight differences rather than similarities. The decline in class, ethnic and regional differences has challenged the basis of party organisation and ideology.

3 Linked to the previous point is that parties tend to find it hard to meet new demands and expectations. The new politics built around ecological issues and greater political participation has not been encompassed by traditional party machines.

4 Parties have seen the growth of factionalism and hence political fragmentation, usually as groups within parties have pursued narrow ideological self-interest in the name of the public interest.

5 Parties have also had a chequered history in implementing programmes

and policies which they have promised at elections. Parties have tended to make only marginal policy adjustments, despite the claims of party manifestos and election campaigns.

These general criticisms must be placed alongside the fact that parties have grown in importance over the past century and in Western countries remain the main channel of political communication and the main route to power. As Blondel has concluded:

J. Blondel (1963) *Voters, Parties and Leaders*, London: Penguin.

> Like other human organisations, parties deserve neither praise nor criticism which they periodically receive. It may be unrealistic to expect parties to unite a divided country, genuinely represent the population, and provide the basis for social and economic development. The oscillation between cynical criticism and exaggerated hopes may simply reflect the failure of observers to recognise that a human institution can only achieve limited results in a short period of time.
>
> (Blondel 1963: 162)

## Interest groups

Interest groups – or pressure groups as they are sometimes known – seek to influence the political process so that the interests they represent gain some form of improvement in or retain undiminished their social, political or economic position, or achieve some particular aim or vision of how society ought to be organised. They have become an increasingly important characteristic of contemporary politics, which has led some to argue that these organisations now characterise politics and that their proliferation and increasing importance represents a shift to *single-issue* politics. Furthermore, the effect of interest groups on the workings of democracy is contested, with some arguing that their existence and power within the political process equate with an erosion of democracy and others arguing that these organisations – by mobilising a plurality of views and by making complex issues comprehensible to the general public – enhance the political process. As with most things the truth is somewhere between the two.

Although governments have always had to reconcile different interests within the society they govern – if only to achieve a level of governability – many would now argue that our societies have grown more complex, more diverse and contain more interests than was once the case. The effect of this has been to give rise to a greater number and diversity of interest groups.

***THINK POINT***
- What interest groups do you belong to?
- What did you answer? Many of you may well have said none and could justifiably point out that you do not belong to Amnesty International, Greenpeace, the National Trust or any other specific group. But you might want to think again. If you are attending a British university, the chances are that you are a member of the National Union of Students (NUS). If you own or drive a

> car you may well belong to a motorists' organisation such as the Royal
> Automobile Club (RAC) or the Automobile Association (AA). The fact is that
> interest groups are so prolific and commonplace that we sometimes forget or
> fail to realise that we are members. But our membership is significant. It
> provides money and resources to the group to which we belong and it allows
> that organisation to claim our voice in support of its aims.

### Sectional or promotional groups

Interest groups may be divided into two main groups (although groups may
overlap or change their location within this classification over time). Sectional
groups are those that promote or protect the interest of certain sections
of a society. These groups are almost always concerned with protecting or
promoting the economic and status interests of their membership and
as a consequence their membership consists almost exclusively of those
who seek protection or promotion. This group contains organisations such
as employers organisations, for example the Confederation of British Industry
(UK); trades unions and their 'peak' organisations, such as the Trades Union
Congress (UK); or the Deutscher Gewerkschaftsbund (Germany). This group
also contains professional associations which promote the economic interest
and professional integrity and 'rules' of their profession – such as lawyers,
doctors, engineers, dentists and accountants.

Promotional groups are not centrally concerned with the protection of
the economic or status interests of their membership but rather with securing
either particular aims – in which case the life of the group will be pretty
much limited to the securing of that end (for example the anti-apartheid
movement) – or the promotion of an image of society or the creation of a
different type of value system. Thus the human rights organisation Amnesty
International campaigns for the release or more humane treatment of political
prisoners. There are a fantastic number of promotional groups around the
world promoting all sorts of causes and values for all sorts of people. Some,
like Amnesty or Greenpeace, are concerned with global issues and are global
organisations with a global membership. Others operate on a national basis:
Liberty (UK) campaigns for the protection and extension of civil liberties in
Britain, whilst Gingerbread campaigns for the interests of one-parent families,
again in the UK. But action and organisation may well take place at a highly
local level where specific issues are at stake and organisations are formed to
apply pressure at a local level to achieve, usually, a specific aim. Thus in
Henley-on-Thames, Oxfordshire (UK), local business and media interests
combined with local inhabitants to form the Save the Regal campaign when
the local cinema – the Regal – closed in 1986.

Amnesty International is clearly a promotional group seeking to secure
certain ends, not, on the whole, for its members but in accordance with
the value systems that its members would appear to have. Another set of
highly visible organisations which are attempting to promote a certain worldview are those concerned with environmental and ecological issues.

**Promotional groups – Amnesty International**

This organisation campaigns for the release of political prisoners around the globe. By a combination of letter-writing campaigns (fax and e-mail are also used), special reports, an Urgent Action network, affiliation through group membership, and individual membership subscription, this organisation seeks to heighten awareness of human rights abuse around the globe and to bring direct influence to bear on governments who contravene the United Nations Human Rights Charter. Releases are, not surprisingly, celebrated, as this extract from an Amnesty *Newsletter* demonstrates:

*Haiti*

The 2 men arrested in Port-au-Prince on 31/7/1994 whilst accompanying 3 US journalists in Haiti airport were reportedly released several days after Urgent Action appeals were generated. Sources in Haiti have told the researchers that the releases were directly due to AI's action on their behalf.

(*Newsletter*, Winter 1994: 6)

*Table 13.2* Growth and membership wealth of environmental interest groups

|                    | 1981   | 1993    |
|--------------------|--------|---------|
| Greenpeace         | 18,000 | 120,000 |
| Friends of the Earth | 30,000 | 410,000 |

## Exercise

1 How far do you think these groups are responsible for the increased interest and concern for protection of the environment?
2 Do you belong to any of them?

One of the most startling success stories for interest groups would seem to be the transformation of groups like Greenpeace – which was once seen (in Britain) as a radical, direct-action minority interest group – into organisations that command the apparent respect of senior politicians, mass support and sympathy, and the reinvention of their activists as 'eco-warriors'. The reasons for this are no doubt many, and certain key events must have been particularly significant in this development. The growing weight of scientific evidence of environmental damage (disputed, it has to be said) has no doubt contributed to both the growth in membership of environmental groups and greater awareness of the potential for ecological damage. Some examples of environmental damage are: depletion of the ozone layer;

the sinking of *Rainbow Warrior* agents by French government and the resulting death of a Greenpeace activist in New Zealand; a series of high-profile environmental disasters in the shape of Bhopal, Prince William Sound and Chernobyl; and the environmental cost of the Gulf War.

However, we must also recognise the central importance of the success of these groups in gaining publicity for their activities – often through the dramatic nature of their direct-action initiatives, which do make captivating television, and through the alliances they have built with certain sections of the entertainment media and actors within it. In 1988, for example, a double album entitled *Rainbow Warriors* was released featuring various musicians and rock groups, and some of the proceeds went to Green-peace. This represents a range of interesting developments. First, it reflects the increased importance and possibility for communication and visibility that contemporary media allow for. Second, it trades on a number of developments which would appear to be part of the processes known as **globalisation**. Third, it demonstrates both the global nature of the issue area – environmental protection and ecological damage – and the global reach of mass media. It is, of course, still pertinent to ask how successful these groups are in securing lasting and significant change in relation to environmental law and ecological protection.

**Globalisation** The process by which the world is being made into a single place, not just politically, but economically and culturally too.

### Power and interest groups

Quite clearly, not all interest groups meet with the same success and various factors can be advanced as to why this is the case. This is not a matter of size of membership or of the 'importance' or gravity of the issue area, but rather has more to do with the nature of the relationship of the interest group concerned to the political and social structure it operates within. We can outline some key factors influencing the success of an interest group.

### Finance

Although it is not simply a case of money generating power, adequate resources clearly help a group get its message across to both the general public and the decision-makers. In recent years this has become an increasingly important aspect and the use of professional lobbyists – who often enjoy a wide network of contacts within the political system – has become more commonplace.

### Public status

The power of an interest group will be influenced by the image that group enjoys in the wider society. If a group possesses public esteem and is respected by the population its voice is more likely to be heeded by government than if if is either poorly understood or held in lower esteem.

### Membership

The membership of the group – particularly the active membership – can be very important in determining the level of access that the group has to the decision-makers. The sharing of norms, values and backgrounds – such as educational – by the membership of a group and those in government and state bureaucracy may assist a group to achieve its ends and gain representation of its views within government circles. But, equally, membership can prove problematic in terms of providing funding and so on. The UK-based environmental group ARK has abandoned membership in favour of raising funds (and awareness) through its range of domestic and industrial cleaning products.

### Ideology and aims

Not surprisingly, the aims or ideological stance of the groups concerned will have an influence on the success that they enjoy. The further apart government and group ideology are, the less chance there is of finding common ground and, subsequently, the less the chance for accommodation between them.

These types of criteria have led commentators such as Grant (1989) to suggest that interest groups enjoy either *insider* or *outsider* status. Insider groups are likely to be 'inside' the political system or at least enjoy greater links with those who are within it – this would include many employers' federations, trades union organisations and others such as the National Trust in Britain, which seeks to preserve the British nation's architectural and landscape heritage. These groups get themselves heard most readily, have the right sort of contacts and are seen as legitimate players in the political system, and it is these groups which are most likely to succeed in meeting their objectives. On the other hand, outsider groups are those which do not enjoy such close links with or privileged position within the establishment, and as a consequence they are likely to find many routes of influence closed off to them. Whether or not a group is an insider or outsider group is not specifically related to the issue area that concerns it. If, for example, we consider the issue areas of animal welfare we can see that a group such as the Royal Society for the Protection of Animals is an insider group with a high level of public support and strong contacts with the establishment in Britain. On the other hand, the Animal Liberation Front – another group concerned with the welfare of animals – does not enjoy such a status and is very much outside of the established political process.

## Interpreting the role of interest groups

There are a number of different theoretical perspectives on how interest groups fit into the political process. We will consider two of the most significant here. The first is *pluralism*, which, on the whole, maintains that interest groups serve a useful purpose in widening the representation of people's interests in political systems. The other is *corporatism*, which treats interest groups with greater ambiguity and has led to considerable criticism of the role of pressure groups in recent years, particularly from the New Right.

Pluralism is strongly associated with the work or Robert Dahl (1982); this approach maintains that groups increase the representative, and subsequently the democratic, nature of politics by giving voice and visibility to a wide range of diverse groups in societies. In this perspective government is seen as a (relatively) neutral referee or arbiter which delivers public policy that is the outcome of responses to the various and competing interest groups within the society it governs. The proliferation of groups, popular membership and competition between different groups – for members, resources and policy outcomes – helps ensure that no one group or interest dominates and that, overall, a balance between interests will be reached. It also holds that the popularity of ideas and values can be deduced from membership size and that highly motivated individuals – activists – can exert greater pressure on the political process than those who care less. The net outcome will be public policy that is moderate, balanced and 'fair' because government is forced to recognise competing interests and those competing interests are forced to bargain and compromise among themselves and with government.

---

**THINK POINT**
- Do you think that this model explains the role and value of interest groups sufficiently? How does it fit with the comments made earlier in this section about insider and outsider groups?

---

For many the pluralist model is misleading. Critics argue that public policy is not equitable and balanced and that it tends to favour certain interests over others, that equity of access to the political system does not exist and that government is not a disinterested or neutral referee. Furthermore, it can be argued that few groups are themselves internally democratic, that they add little to genuine political representation as a consequence and that they can be very secretive in their activities.

Corporatism provides a very different model of the role of groups in society and politics. Like pluralism, it maintains that groups are central to an understanding of the workings of politics and political processes. Unlike pluralism, it does not conceive of the government as a neutral player; nor does it conceive of interest groups as competing and enjoying reasonable levels of equity of access. This model maintains that groups work together, that government actively decides which groups will be consulted and what the aims of public policy should be. Furthermore, those groups who enjoy real access are likely to be limited – most likely to employers and labour – and they are likely to be welcomed into the policy-making process. This model was particularly relevant in Britain in the 1960s and 1970s during which time a system of *tripartism* – between government, employers and unions – was said to exist. In such an arrangement policy decisions would be the outcome of consultation and negotiation between the three groups.

Critics have argued that corporatism is deeply unrepresentative and leads to the constitutional arrangements that should oversee legislative and policy outcomes being bypassed. The groups who are inside this arrangement wo in reciprocal relationships with the government and in doing so help exclude other groups who might represent other interests or the sar interests differently. Certainly these were the types of arguments put forwa by the Thatcher administrations in Britain in the 1980s, and subseque steps were taken to break the tripartite model – especially with regard the role of trade unions. Interestingly, the New Right also attacked t pluralist model, arguing that too much consultation was taking pl between government and interest groups. This argument suggested tha *pluralist stagnation* had developed (Beer 1982) and that groups – particularly certain groups – should be excluded from the political process.

We can see, then, that interest groups are an important but contested part of the political system. They are channels for the representation of interests, but different interpretations exist regarding how representative they are, how effective they are and how 'valuable' they are to, in particular, democratic systems of government.

## Exercise

1 Imagine that you are the an activist for a particular promotional group (choose one or make one up). What are your key concerns and aims?
2 How will you get these heard?

## The mass media

The art of propaganda lies in understanding the emotional ideas of the great masses and finding, through a psychologically correct form, the way to the attention and thence to the heart of broad masses.

(Adolf Hitler, *Mein Kampf*)

### Introduction

This section looks at the role of the mass media in politics. The role, power and function of the mass media is an area of great debate and disagreement and, unfortunately, we can only consider some central points here. Indeed, discussion here will be limited to three main areas of interest:

1 The issue of newspaper bias.
2 The issue of image, form and content.
3 The emergence of global media systems.

These are important issues which effect a considerable area of politics, political theory and political debate. At stake are issues of democracy, control, manipulation, propaganda and emancipation. This section also touches directly on areas developed more fully elsewhere in the book; in particular the relationship between the media (particularly electronic media) and the process of globalisation is of considerable importance (see Chapter 16).

Of course, it is not new for politicians or those seeking to gain or retain power to use the media available to them. In the classical societies of Greece and Rome marble statues were often employed to denote power and portray superior human qualities in their representation of the military or political community of the day. Later, figures of the nineteenth century, the Emperor Napoleon or the Duke of Wellington, were not strangers to the power of the portrait to depict their power and military might (and, by implication, their nobility and command of 'rightness.') Indeed, representation of power and personality through the media of the day is nothing new. The key interest here is the specific development of **mass media** systems and products in the course of the twentieth century. In particular, we mean the development of mass circulation newspapers, radio and television broadcasting and, more recently, the development of new telecomedia forms in the shape of VCRs, PCs, cellular phones and the Internet. The significance of the development of such new communications technology is the way in which politicians and other political actors can reach a mass audience, a new collectivity. But these developments may mean more than this: it is also a way in which the new media and new channels of communication may bring new actors and groups into the political arena.

This process has accelerated throughout the twentieth century to the extent that we now live in media-saturated worlds. Some of the images that have been generated by and through the mass media have become embedded in our cultures: the assassination of John F. Kennedy, the white-suited image of Elvis Presley, Mickey Mouse, the beating of Rodney King by members of the Los Angeles Police Department (LAPD), the starving children of Ethiopia, the horrors of the former Yugoslavia – this list is endless. But the importance and centrality of the media to an increasingly large number of the world's population is a key development of the twentieth century. Indeed, so transformed and transforming are our cultures that some scholars are arguing that we now live in a media culture (Fiske 1994; Kellner 1995) and that in order to understand our societies we need to appreciate what it is to live in a media culture. This chapter asks in what ways the media has affected or altered the way in which politics, and particularly election campaigning, is conducted and it seeks to identify some of the characteristics of media-orientated politics. It also considers some of the implications and the type of assumptions made about such developments, as well as some of the implications of the increasingly rapid shifts in communication technology that are apparent in the contemporary world.

### The centrality of political communication

Communication is central to human experience, understanding and society, and indeed without communication human society could not exist. By extension we could argue that without political communication there could

**Mass media** Media that disseminate usually undifferentiated popular forms of output (reflecting the mass nature of the audience) to a mass audience. For example, this would include the popular tabloid press, television, cinema and book publishing.

not be any politics, for politics is as much about getting your message across as about having a message in the first place. The impact of the proliferation of mass communications technology has, however, led to a far greater diffusion of political messages into all areas of life. Take, for example, the picture shown in figure 13.5. This poster is a striking image of the well-known British politician and wartime hero Sir Winston Churchill. On one level it is a plea for voters to vote for Churchill as the leader of a National (coalition) Government. True, it attempts to trade on Churchill's wartime success ('help him finish the job') and the picture draws attention to Churchill's perceived personal strength and integrity. Nevertheless, it is a formal and readily decoded piece of political communication. Today, in our media-saturated environments, the situation has grown infinitely more complex. Politicians appear in the most unexpected of places – pop videos, sports programmes, MTV, advertisements for bank cards and television comedy shows. Likewise media personalities are found in the company of politicians and sometimes in the institutions of government themselves. The filmstars Ronald Reagan (Vaughn 1994) and Clint Eastwood and the musician Sonny Bono in the USA are the most notable examples. Sonny Bono was the Sonny half of 'Sonny and Cher', the 1960s pop duo who sang, among other songs, 'I Got You, Babe'. Sonny Bono is now a politician in the USA.

In this sense the roles of political communications and the accomplished communicator have become increasingly central to the activities of the politician. Gone are the days when the politician could afford the sentiments expressed by Canadian Premier Louis St Laurent when he gave his first television interview to answer questions (which were submitted in advance):

> They even wanted to know what I had been thinking about. I answered, perhaps a bit sharply, that I was responsible to the public for what I did as a result of my thinking but only to my conscience for the thinking itself until it became translated into acts.
>
> (L. St Laurent; quoted in Seymour-Ure 1989: 307–25)

Such coyness would not go unchallenged today (unless one assumes it was a cleverly constructed media-invented innocence designed to illicit an appropriate response from the electorate). In addition to the growing centrality of communication to the role of the politician, the role of media, marketing and communications professionals (often known as 'spin doctors') has become increasingly important to the political process. The developments outlined above have encouraged an extended debate about whether these tendencies are a 'good' thing or a 'bad' thing, whether or not they inhibit democracy or 'real' politics and whether they distort the relationship between politician and citizen (Keane 1991; Jamieson 1992a; Franklin 1994).

Certainly the media have had a considerable effect on the operation of politics in advanced societies and a number of key developments have been identified by commentators. It has been argued, for instance, that the mass media have taken the place of political parties in organising, motivating and

*Figure 13.5* 'Help him finish the job' poster

mobilising political participation. It has also been argued that television has removed the focus on legislative assemblies and traditional channels of political communication by allowing a direct route from the prime minister or president to the public. Another important development has been that governments are increasingly prepared to use the mass media – and especially television – to 'sell' their policies. In Britain this development has been most striking in relation to the privatisation policies of the Conservative administration throughout the 1980s and 1990s. Indeed, between 1979 and 1989 the government expenditure on television advertising rose from £35 million to £150 million (Franklin 1994).

## Newspapers

In order to illustrate some key points about the nature of the media it is useful to take as an example the British tabloid press. In attempting to evaluate the influence of the press, however, and in particular the mass-circulation tabloid press, on the outcomes of elections, we encounter great difficulty. On the commonsense level, a great many individuals believe and argue that the Conservative-supporting press contributed both directly and significantly to the result of the 1992 election. That bias in favour of the Conservative party affects electoral outcomes is also something that, clearly, some politicians believe, as Kinnock's post-1992 defeat comments testify. The question is, however, infinitely more complex than the commonsense perception and the comments of defeated politicians suggest. The question 'Was it the Sun wot wonit ?' (*Sun* headline, 10 April 1992) really consists of a range of questions and assumptions that need far greater consideration and unpacking than is usually afforded such questions.

## Negative campaigning

The argument is that the reliance on negative image management, dirty tricks, stunts and the deeply personal nature of the campaign obscure the real issues that real politics ought to be about. In this analysis the media dilute and deform the process and operation of democracy by obscuring or ignoring the real issues and presenting a set of irrelevant criteria and information to the electorate (see Figures 13.6 and 13.7).

## Partisanship

One cannot, and indeed would not seek to, deny that the newspaper press is deeply partisan. However, this has always been true. The press In Britain, unlike television, is not bound by laws regarding impartiality and can – and does – clearly take positions over whom we should vote for. We can express this through a number of statistical comments and examples (see tables 13.2, 13.3 and 13.4).

In media theory we can identify two broad conceptualisations of the role of the media in society. For liberal theory (see pp. 231–5) the media act or should act as the 'fourth estate', a watchdog that helps expose excesses, restrain or expose corruption, give vent to public concern and anger and so on. In this conceptualisation a free market (or a relatively free market) in media allows for the representation of a plurality of ideas and views and the role of the state is to regulate legally the media market so that the fourth estate can function to the best of its ability.

Critics – and particularly those of the left – argue that the media act against the interests of the people. Either through sympathy to certain dominant groups, or because of the highly capitalist nature of the media industry

Figure 13.6 'Page 3 under Kinnock'
Reproduced by permission of the *Sun* newspaper

**Dominant ideology** Sets of social values, norms and expression dominate all others at given points in the development of society. In particular, the dominant ideology that characterises a particular historical epoch will tend to reflect the class interests of the social group that is economically dominant. Furthermore, this dominant ideology will seek to mask the 'real' nature of the economic and exploitative relationships on which society rests.

and the concentration of ownership among a small number of people, the media favour certain political positions and groups. Ultimately in Marxist theory the media are seen as supporting the **dominant ideology**, reinforcing the experience of people with false consciousness and ultimately reinforcing the hegemony associated with certain dominant groups in society.

Certainly press ownership is highly concentrated in Britain. In 1992 57 per cent of daily sales and 66 per cent of Sunday sales were enjoyed by newspapers owned by two large news groups, News Corporation, headed by Rupert Murdoch, and Mirror Group Newspapers – an overwhelmingly Conservative bias – with only the *Daily Mirror* regularly supporting the Labour Party.

*Figure 13.7* 'If Kinnock wins today …'
Reproduced by permission of the *Sun* newspaper

So we can identify a pattern of attack politics and 'dirty tricks' in the media and a pattern of partisan alignment and support, but to what extent does this type of coverage affect voting behaviour and ultimately the outcome of elections? Such a link is highly disputed.

For Dunleavy and Husbands (1985), a study of the 1983 election provides clear-cut evidence of press influence because the Conservative vote was 30 per cent lower among those primarily exposed to a non-Tory press than those exposed to a Tory press. For Harrop (1986, 1987), however, this is best explained as a process of reinforcement of tendencies already present in the electorate and not in the production of new voters.

*Table 13.3* Major group ownership of national daily and Sunday newspapers, 1947–94

| Group | Number of titles and percentage of circulation | | | | | | | | | | | |
|---|---|---|---|---|---|---|---|---|---|---|---|---|
| | 1947 | | 1957 | | 1967 | | 1977 | | 1987 | | 1994 | |
| *National dailies* | | | | | | | | | | | | |
| Associated Newspapers (*Mail*, etc.) | 1 | 13 | 2 | 21 | 2 | 19 | 1 | 13 | 1 | 12 | 1 | 13 |
| Beaverbrook (*Express*) | 1 | 24 | 1 | 25 | 1 | 25 | - | | - | | - | |
| Mirror Group (*Mirror*, etc.) | 1 | 23 | 1 | 28 | 2 | 41 | - | | - | | 2 | 20 |
| Kemsley (*Sketch*) | 1 | 5 | - | | - | | - | | - | | - | |
| Odhams (*Herald*) | 1 | 14 | 1 | 10 | - | | - | | - | | - | |
| Thomson (*Times*) | - | | - | | 1 | 2 | 1 | 2 | - | | - | |
| New International (*Sun*, etc.) | - | | - | | - | | 1 | 27 | 3 | 32 | 3 | 38 |
| Reed (*Mirror*) | - | | - | | - | | 1 | 28 | - | | - | |
| Trafalgar House (*Express*) | - | | - | | - | | 1 | 17 | - | | - | |
| Maxwell (*Mirror*) | - | | - | | - | | | | 1 | 21 | - | |
| United (*Express*, etc.) | - | | - | | - | | | | 2 | 19 | 2 | 15 |
| Total, 3 largest | 3 | 61 | 4 | 74 | 5 | 85 | 3 | 72 | 6 | 72 | 7 | 73 |
| *National Sundays* | | | | | | | | | | | | |
| Associated Newspapers (*Dispatch*, etc.) | 1 | 8 | 1 | 8 | - | | - | | 1 | 10 | 1 | 12 |
| Beaverbrook (*Express*) | 1 | 9 | 1 | 12 | 1 | 17 | - | | - | | - | |
| Mirror Group (*Mirror*, etc.) [a] | 1 | 15 | 1 | 20 | 2 | 45 | - | | - | | 3 | 31 |
| Kemsley (Various) | 4 | 18 | 3 | 15 | - | | - | | - | | - | |
| News of the World | 1 | 29 | 1 | 25 | 1 | 25 | - | | - | | - | |
| Odhams (*People*) | 1 | 17 | 1 | 17 | - | | - | | - | | - | |
| Thomson (*Times*) | - | | - | | 1 | 6 | 1 | 7 | - | | - | |
| News International (*N.O.W.*, etc.) | - | | - | | - | | 1 | 26 | 2 | 36 | 2 | 38 |
| Reed (*Mirror*, etc.) | - | | - | | - | | 2 | 42 | - | | - | |
| Trafalgar House (*Express*) | - | | - | | - | | 1 | 17 | - | | - | |
| Maxwell (*Mirror*, etc.) | - | | - | | - | | - | | 2 | 33 | - | |
| United (*Express*) | - | | - | | - | | - | | 1 | 13 | 1 | 10 |
| Total, 3 largest | 6 | 64 | 3 | 62 | 4 | 87 | 4 | 85 | 5 | 82 | 6 | 81 |
| *National dailies and Sundays* | | | | | | | | | | | | |
| Associated Newspapers | 2 | 10 | 3 | 13 | 2 | 8 | 1 | 6 | 2 | 11 | 2 | 13 |
| Beaverbrook | 2 | 15 | 2 | 17 | 2 | 20 | - | | - | | - | |
| Mirror Group[a] | 2 | 18 | 2 | 23 | 2 | 43 | - | | - | | 5 | 26 |
| News of the World | 1 | 18 | 1 | 16 | 1 | 16 | - | | - | | - | |
| Kemsley | 5 | 13 | 3 | 10 | - | | - | | - | | - | |
| Odhams | 2 | 16 | 2 | 14 | - | | - | | - | | - | |
| Thomson | - | | - | | 2 | 5 | 2 | 5 | - | | - | |
| News International | - | | - | | - | | 2 | 26 | 5 | 34 | 5 | 38 |
| Reed | - | | - | | - | | 3 | 36 | - | | - | |
| Trafalgar House | - | | - | | - | | 2 | 17 | - | | - | |
| Maxwell | - | | - | | - | | - | | 3 | 27 | - | |
| United | - | | - | | - | | - | | 3 | 16 | 3 | 12 |
| Total, 3 largest | 5 | 52 | 5 | 56 | 5 | 79 | 7 | 79 | 11 | 77 | 13 | 76 |

*Note*: omits small circulation papers or groups.
*Sources*: Royal Commission on the Press, 1947; Press Council Annual Reports.

*Table 13.4* Circulation of national daily newspapers, 1945–94

| Newspaper (launch date) | 1945 | 1950 | 1955 | 1960 | 1965 | 1970 | 1975 | 1980 | 1985 | 1990 | 1994 |
|---|---|---|---|---|---|---|---|---|---|---|---|
| 'Qualities' | | | | | | | | | | | |
| *Daily Telegraph* (1855) | 822 | 976 | 1,055 | 1,200 | 1,337 | 1,409 | 1,331 | 1,433 | 1,202 | 1,076 | 1,041 |
| *The Times* (1785) | 195 | 254 | 222 | 260 | 254 | 388 | 319 | 316 | 478 | 420 | 545 |
| *Financial Times* (1888) | (35) | (57) | (80) | 122 | 146 | 170 | 181 | 196 | 234 | 290 | 292 |
| (Manchester) *Guardian* (1821) | (80) | (140) | (156) | 212 | 270 | 304 | 319 | 379 | 487 | 424 | 401 |
| *The Independent* (1986) | - | - | - | - | - | - | - | - | - | 411 | 281 |
| Total | 1,017 | 1,230 | 1,277 | 1,794 | 2,007 | 2,271 | 2,150 | 2,324 | 2,401 | 2,621 | 2,560 |
| (%) | (8) | (7) | (8) | (11) | (13) | (15) | (16) | (16) | (18) | (19) | |
| (including *Financial Times* and *Manchester Guardian* | (1,132) | | (1,427) | | (1,513) | | | | | | |
| 'Middle market' | | | | | | | | | | | |
| *Daily Express* (1900) | 3,239 | 4,116 | 4,036 | 4,270 | 3,987 | 3,563 | 2,822 | 2,194 | 1,902 | 1,585 | 1,338 |
| *Daily Mail* (1896) | 1,752 | 2,225 | 2,068 | 2,825 | 2,464 | 1,890 | 1,726 | 1,948 | 1,815 | 1,708 | 1,774 |
| *Daily Herald/Sun* (1912) | 2,000 | 2,017 | 1,759 | 1,418 | 1,273 | - | - | - | - | - | - |
| *News Chronicle* (1930) | 1,454 | 1,534 | 1,253 | - | - | - | - | - | - | - | - |
| *Today* (1986) | - | - | - | - | - | - | - | - | - | 540 | 597 |
| Total | 8.445 | 9,046 | 9,116 | 8,513 | 7,724 | 5,453 | 4,548 | 4,142 | 3,717 | 3,833 | 3,709 |
| (%) | (68) | (60) | (57) | (53) | (49) | (37) | (32) | (28) | (25) | (27) | (27) |
| 'Mass market' tabloids | | | | | | | | | | | |
| *Daily Mirror* (1903) | 2,000 | 4,567 | 4,725 | 4,649 | 5,019 | 4,570 | 3,968 | 3,625 | 3,033 | 3,083 | 2,494 |
| *Daily Sketch/Graphic* (1908) | 883 | 717 | 950 | 1,075 | 844 | 785 | - | - | - | - | - |
| *Sun* (1970) | - | - | - | - | - | 1,615 | 3,446 | 3,741 | 4,125 | 3,855 | 4,078 |
| *Daily Star* (1978) | - | - | - | - | - | - | - | 1,034 | 1,455 | 833 | 744 |
| (*The Post* [1988]) | - | - | - | - | - | - | - | - | - | - | - |
| Total | 2,883 | 5,344 | 5,675 | 5,724 | 5,863 | 6,970 | 7,41 | 8,400 | 8,613 | 7,771 | 7,316 |
| (%) | (23) | (32) | (35) | (37) | (38) | (47) | (53) | (56) | (58) | (55) | (54) |
| *Daily Worker/ Morning Star* (1930) | 115 | 115 | ? | 60 | ? | ? | ? | 33 | ? | ? | ? |
| Total (including *Daily Worker*) | 12,345 (12,460) | 16,520 (16,717) | 16,068 (16,304) | 16,031 | 15,594 | 14,694 | 14,112 | 14,886 | 14,731 | 14,225 | 13,585 |

*Guardian* and *Financial Times* not counted as national dailies until 1960. *Daily Mirror* excludes *Scottish Daily Record.* *Sources:* Audit Bureau of Circulations, Press Council Annual Reports; individual newspapers. Some figures are part-year averages.

Bill Miller (1991) argues that the evidence from the 1987 election in Britain demonstrates that 'Political attitudes were very largely determined by partisanship but not completely. Even with stringent controls for partisanship and ideology, multiple regression analyses show that the press, but not television, had a significant influence on voter preferences (W. Miller 1991)' Curtice and Semetko argue that the evidence from the 1992 election in Britain demonstrates that

> The message is clear. Neither *The Sun* nor any other of the pro-Conservative tabloid newspapers were responsible for John Major's unexpected victory in 1992. There is no evidence in our panel that there was any relationship between vote switching in the election campaign and the partisanship of a voter's newspaper.
>
> (Curtice and Semetko 1994: 55)

Table 13.5 Circulation of national Sunday newspapers, 1945–94

| Newspaper (launch date) | 1945 | 1950 | 1955 | 1960 | 1965 | 1970 | 1975 | 1980 | 1985 | 1990 | 1994 |
|---|---|---|---|---|---|---|---|---|---|---|---|
| 'Qualities' | | | | | | | | | | | |
| Independent on Sunday (1990) | - | - | - | - | - | - | - | - | | 352 | 324 |
| Observer (1791) | 299 | 422 | 564 | 738 | 824 | 830 | 730 | 929 | 736 | 551 | 493 |
| (Sunday Correspondent [1989–90]) | - | - | - | - | - | - | - | - | | 197 | - |
| Sunday Times (1822) | 460 | 535 | 606 | 1,001 | 1,290 | 1,439 | 1,380 | 1,419 | 1,251 | 1,165 | 1,236 |
| Sunday Telegraph (1961) | - | - | - | - | 650 | 764 | 752 | 1,003 | 686 | 594 | 650 |
| Total | 759 | 957 | 1,170 | 1,739 | 2,764 | 3,033 | 2,862 | 3,351 | 2,673 | 2,859 | 2,703 |
| (%) | (4) | (3) | (4) | (6) | (12) | (13) | (14) | (18) | (15) | (16) | (17) |
| 'Middle market' | | | | | | | | | | | |
| Reynolds' News/Sunday Citizen (1850) | 580 | 705 | 579 | 329 | 233 | - | - | - | - | - | - |
| Sunday Chronicle (1885) | 1,150 | 1,118 | 830 | - | - | - | - | - | - | - | - |
| Sunday Dispatch (1801) | 1,372 | 2,378 | 2,549 | 1,520 | - | - | - | - | - | - | - |
| Sunday Express (1918) | 2,114 | 2,967 | 3,235 | 3,706 | 4,190 | 4,263 | 3,715 | 2,989 | 2,449 | 1,664 | 1,511 |
| Mail on Sunday (1982) | - | - | - | - | - | - | - | | 1,631 | 1,903 | 1,959 |
| (News on Sunday (1987)) | - | - | - | - | - | - | - | - | | | |
| (Sunday Today [1986–7]) | - | - | - | - | - | - | - | | | | |
| Total | 5,216 | 7,168 | 7,193 | 5,555 | 4,423 | 4,263 | 3,715 | 2,989 | 4,080 | 3,567 | 3,470 |
| (%) | (26) | (24) | (24) | (20) | (18) | (18) | (16) | (23) | (22) | (21) | (22) |
| 'Mass market' | | | | | | | | | | | |
| Empire News (1884) | 1,812 | 2,085 | 2,049 | 2,100 | - | - | - | - | - | - | - |
| News of the World (1843) | 5,000 | 8,444 | 7,971 | 6,664 | 6,176 | 6,229 | 5,479 | 4,198 | 5,103 | 5,056 | 4,791 |
| People/Sunday People (1881) | 3,447 | 5,089 | 5,075 | 5,468 | 5,538 | 5,140 | 4,188 | 3,846 | 2,962 | 2,566 | 2,029 |
| Sunday Graphic (1915) | 1,026 | 1,169 | 1,220 | 893 | - | - | - | - | - | - | - |
| Sunday Pictorial/Mirror (1915) | 2,500 | 5,094 | 5,539 | 5,461 | 5,082 | 4,826 | 4,251 | 3,831 | 3,009 | 2,894 | 2,562 |
| Sunday Sport (1986) | - | - | - | - | - | - | - | - | | 402 | 290 |
| Total | 13,785 | 21,881 | 21,854 | 20,586 | 16,796 | 16,195 | 13,918 | 11,875 | 11,074 | 10,918 | 9,672 |
| (%) | (70) | (73) | (72) | (74) | (70) | (69) | (68) | (65) | (62) | (63) | (61) |
| Total | 19,760 | 30,006 | 30,217 | 27,880 | 23,983 | 23,491 | 20,495 | 18,215 | 17,827 | 17,344 | 15,845 |

News on Sunday and Sunday Today lasted only for a short time, with circulations of 100,000–200,000. The Sunday Correspondent is included in 1990 but ceased publication on Nov. 27. The figure shown is its final sales. It began publication on Sept. 17 1989.

Sources: Audit Bureau of circulations; Press Council Annual Reports.

The evidence is at best contradictory. It would seem that many voters appear to view newspaper reports (and watch television news) through a partisan filter that enables them to ignore politically uncongenial messages. Indeed, many individuals buy papers that support their political views rather than purchasing papers in a politically neutral way.

### Television, image and politics

Television provides an equally complex and interesting area of discussion for students of politics. The role of television as a channel for political communication and disseminator of political values, ideas and images is increasingly central to an understanding of politics in advanced societies. In some ways politics is now everywhere. This proliferation of sophisticated media coverage has resulted in the production of an era of 'metacoverage' (Gitlin 1991) in which every political move and word is planned, rehearsed and delivered by an all-pervasive mass media. It is now commonplace for election campaigns in the US to be carried out through the 'entertainment' genres of television and radio, especially talk shows and even MTV.

Political communication and marketing now occupy a central position in the political landscape, but curiously the academic study of elections has tended to neglect this development, or else to note with disdain the emergence of a market-orientated politics. In the literature political marketing is approached in two ways (O'Shaughnessy 1990). First, there is the tendency to note the emergence of heavily marketed campaigns. This type of study involves recording the strategies of marketers and image-makers and cataloguing the techniques they employ. Since Nixon's 'Sweaty Lip' and running 'Lazy Shave' (Bruce 1992) in the 1960 US presidential campaign and the Saatchi and Saatchi-led 'Labour isn't Working' campaign for the Conservatives in 1979 we have become increasingly familiar with the processes and techniques of a heavily marketed politics. These include not only the specific techniques of brand management, negative and positive advertising, the sound bite, the photo opportunity and the press conference, but also the key device of news and agenda management. These descriptions are often accompanied by pessimistic comments on the dire catastrophe for 'real politics' and democracy. Consider this extract from Kathleen Hall Jamieson's book *Dirty Politics* (1992a):

> Michael Dukakis looked 'like Patton on his way to Berlin', observed NBC's Chris Wallace (September 13, 1988). '(A) Massachusetts Rambo on the prowl,' noted CBS's Bruce Morton the same evening. Footage of that ride was resurrected by a Bush attack ad that pilloried Dukakis's supposed positions. 'Dukakis opposed virtually every weapons system developed,' declared the ad in the first of its false statements about the Democrat. The Massachusetts Democrat responded with an ad in which he turned off a set showing the Bush ad. 'I'm fed up with it,' said Dukakis. 'George Bush's negative ads are full of lies and he knows it. I'm on record for the very weapons systems his ad says I'm against.'
>
> By the campaign's end, the tank ride had appeared in news, the news footage had appeared in a Bush ad, the Bush ad had appeared in a Dukakis ad, and the Bush and Dukakis ads had appeared in news. The *New Yorker* cartoon showing a man watching a television set had prophesied the endless loops through which the image passed. In the set in front of him, the man sees himself watching the television set. In that set is another image of himself watching the set. Images of images damaged Dukakis's campaign. One poll indicates that 'voters who knew about the ride were much more likely to shift against the Democrat than toward him.'
>
> (Jamieson 1992a: 3)

Jamieson's argument is clear. Media-driven politics distorts political communication, the integrity of the message and ultimately the democratic process. Certainly the landscape is different and somewhat disconcerting, but is it all so negative and bleak?

Maybe not. John Fiske (1994) makes a useful contribution to this debate. He comments on the mixing of reality and fiction in *Murphy Brown*, a prime-time US sitcom in which the central figure, Murphy Brown, took the decision to become a single mother, describing her action as 'just another lifestyle choice'. This became a totemic act during the 1992 US Presidential elections, when politicians of the right argued that the show challenged the social value of the family and the role of the father within it. In TV land the fictional Murphy Brown watches the news report of the 'real' Dan Quayle criticising her single motherhood. Later the same day 'real' television news carries pictures of Dan Quayle surrounded by single mothers watching Murphy Brown watching Dan Quayle. The real news report ends with the information that Quayle has sent the fictional child a real toy and thus consciously implicated himself in the storyline. Characters in the show are also pictured reading both real and fictional newspaper reports of the incident in the programme itself (Fiske 1995). This conflation of the 'real' and the 'fictional' is now a routine formula in entertainment products and can be seen in the film *Dave* and in Neil Kinnock's appearance in the television comedy *Drop the Dead Donkey*. For Fiske the key to this is that

> The structural difference, for instance, between information and entertainment television (roughly, between fact and fiction), is a residue of modernity that contains the hierarchical evaluation that the former is superior to the latter.
>
> (Fiske 1995: 63)

FEMALE TELEVISION ANCHOR
Presidential politics and TV entertainment blended together today in the season's opener of *Murphy Brown*. Last summer, the pregnancy of the show's unmarried title character became a rallying point in the issue of 'family values'. Tonight, the man who led the charge against the show watched it in the company of single mothers in Washington, D.C. Quayle said earlier that he had respect and understanding for single mothers; he also said he sent Murphy's baby a card and a toy elephant, hoping to make him a Republican.
Here in the Twin Cities, supporters of Democrat Bill Clinton used tonight's *Murphy Brown* as an excuse for a fund raiser, charging $15 for the chance to watch the show in the proper political company. The evening raised $2,000 dollars.
MALE TELEVISION ANCHOR
Earlier today, someone asked a member of Dan Quayle's staff why did the vice president send a real toy to a fictional baby. He answered, 'You tell me where fiction begins and reality ends in the whole business.'

(local news report in the USA, cited in Fiske: 26)

But Fiske maintains that this development does not represent a simple corruption of political communications. Rather it is an example of a shift in the political landscape. It is evidence of how different goups can be brought into the arena of political struggle and how the media can play a crucial role in giving a voice to groups and raising issues that are not normally raised in this way or with this high a profile.

Certainly the impact of an image-based politics changes the nature of political communication and complicates interpretation of the political. Take one further example, the Solidarity poster reproduced in Figure 13.8. Ask yourself why Gary Cooper is prepared to vote for Solidarity in this election. What other messages are conveyed by the use of a cultural icon of American cinema, taken from the film *Gunfight at the OK Corral*? This type of political communication is becoming far more commonplace and locates the content and form of political communication very much within other cultural and political discourses (Wernick 1991).

*Figure 13.8* Polish election campaign poster 1989

### Global media and new media

> We have a sense, we know we exist because there we are on the screen, and if you do not appear, you or your people do not appear on the screen, or only appear in certain roles, it diminishes you, you are diminished by that.
>
> (Professor Brian Groombridge; cited in Dowmunt 1993: 175)

In addition to the ideas outlined above we are witnessing significant structural shifts in the organisation of the mass media around the world which will have a significant impact on politics and society in the twenty-first century. We are seeing the development of 'global media' in at least two senses. First, in the emergence of global communication networks, systems and technology. The most relevant example of this is clearly the television and communications empire headed by Rupert Murdoch, although other examples, such as Berlusconi in Italy and the Brazilian network GLOBO also illustrate this tendency.

In addition to the emergence of global media systems we can also see the emergence of global markets and global cultural media products. This is a result, and a cause, of many processes, but in particular of the merging of media types and the process of globalisation. These developments have massive implications for notions of democracy, power, identity and voice. Many commentators are concerned about the levels of cultural homogeneity, and in particular the possibility of an 'Americanisation' of global and indigenous cultures.

News Corporation

**US:**
Twentieth Century Fox
Fox Broadcasting Company
Fox Affiliated Stations
US Pay TV Network
Partnership with News Datacom
NTL
Constream

**UK:**
50% of BSkyB
Increasing links with the terrestrial broadcasters
Partnership with British Telecom/Cable Network

**Europe:**
Association with Kirch Corporation
Association with PRO 7

**Australia:**
15% of the 7 Network
Pay TV national satelite system

**Asia:**
63% of Hutchvision

**Africa:**
Sky News Broadcasts

*Figure 13.9* Rupert Murdoch's media empire

Whatever the implications of these developments, we are witnessing a significant shift away from national broadcasting provision and systems towards global ones. There has been a decline in the legitimacy of monopolistic arrangements which tended to support public broadcasting systems such as the BBC in Britain. Greater recourse to market solutions with a commensurate level of deregulation and a subsequent emergence of new media outlets, new media moguls and alternative strategies has occurred. These developments, when taken together, have led to a very different media and communications world, and the implications for politics and political communications have yet to be fully appreciated. Various theories have been put forward to interpret these developments. **Technological determinism** argues that all these changes are inevitable under the impact of new technologies. **Free-market positivity** maintains that new technologies bring new commercial opportunities which must be exploited to the full. This can be achieved only through the market – hence the need for radical deregulation leading to consumer abundance. **Free-market negativity** argues that these developments more or less herald the end of world as we know it and that our futures as well as our political and communication freedoms are under threat. Postmodern theory argues that maximum exploitation of opportunities provided by the developments of computation and electronic communications will lead to the destruction of old constraints of time and space, change the basis of (economic) reality, dissolve old conflicts in society, and make possible a radically pluralistic society where all voices can be heard. We wait to see. Perhaps we can leave the last comment on the matter to Jean Baudrillard, the French philosopher of postmodernism, who maintains that we already live in media- and image saturated societies in which reality as we once might have known it has disappeared:

> Everything is destined to reappear as simulation. Landscapes as photography, women as the sexual scenario, thoughts as writing, terrorism as fashion and the media, events as television. Things seem only to exist by virtue of this strange destiny. You wonder whether the world itself isn't just here to serve as advertising copy in some other world.
>
> (Baudrillard (1983) *Simulations*, New York: Semiotexte)

## Information superhighways

Most of this chapter has concentrated on the relationship between the mass media of television and newspapers and politics. There is, however, a very new development in the arena of communications technology that will provide both new challenges and new opportunities for politicians and citizens in the coming years – the Internet. The creation of 'information superhighways' is now at the centre of policy aims for a number of national governments – most notably in the USA – and some transnational bodies, for example the G7 group of nations and the European Union (Bangemann Report 1994). The growth of electronic democracy, electronic town meetings and the possibilities for disseminating vast amounts of information are very real developments that accompany the shift to an 'information age', and

**Technological determinism** An approach which argues that the development, use and proliferation of technology influences social change and interactions to the extent that technological revolutions can lead to social ones. Put another way, this approach argues that the social organisation of society is determined by the technology in place.

**Free-market positivity** A defence of the application of free-market concepts to the media marketplace. This approach argues that through a combination of new technologies, deregulation and market forces not only will the audience and the public get more media content to consume but that this content will be 'better', in that it will be more responsive to audience choice and more varied, and will allow for greater audience choice and difference.

**Free-market negativity** An attack on the application of free-market concepts to the media marketplace. It argues that the valuable public service broadcasting ethos characterised by 'protected' and to some extent non-market institutions such as the British Broadcasting Corporation (BBC) cannot be matched in a free media market in which all values will be subject to the needs of profit, and that quality will be reduced in the pursuit of cheap programming and copy. Furthermore, the promise of choice offered by the market will, in reality, mean choice between one thing and more of the same.

these developments will allow citizens to be more fully informed and possibly more directly linked to each other and to the political process at local, national and even global levels. The US Democratic Party employed this type of technology during the 1996 Presidential election campaign, issuing daily press releases and campaign updates, and posting a Bob Dole 'gaff' line to any e-mail address registered with the campaign headquarters. This sort of development will become more commonplace and will open up new arenas for political campaigning, advertising and argument. In addition to this, the Internet provides a new forum for opposition groups – not just the formal opposition of organised political movements, but any which have access to a PC, a modem and a telephone line. Thus, anti-roads campaigners in Britain can use this technology to get their message across. Web sites can be set up by pressure groups, political activists and groups hithero bypassed or marginalised by the more 'traditional' media.

## Conclusion

In this chapter we have considered the ways in which groups and individuals seek to influence the political system, agenda and process. We have explored the nature of political parties, interest groups and the mass media. Of course, covering such complex topics in a single chapter has led to a compression of the discussion. However, what you must concentrate upon is the different and often competing interpretations of the organizations and groups we have looked at and the way in which social, economic and technological change is influencing the formation, action and power of political parties, interest groups and the mass media.

## Exercise

1 Imagine you are an advertising and marketing specialist engaged by a political party to create a new image for them. The party has been out of power for a number of years and requires a complete image overhaul. What sort of political adverts would you recommend and why?
2 Design a newspaper advert to reassure the populace about the safety of beef products within the European Union.

## Further reading

Blondel, J. (1969) *An Introduction to Comparative Government*, London: Weidenfeld & Nicolson.

Bradbury, M. (1976) *Fahrenheit 451*, London: Grafton. This is an excellent and haunting look at the way ideas and the written word can affect society and those within it.

Dowmunt, A. (ed.) (1993) *Channels of Resistance: Global Television and Local Empowerment*, London: British Film Institute. A fascinating collection of pieces from media professionals, individuals and media activists giving a very different perspective on the digital and media revolutions.

Duverger, M. (1964) *Political Parties: Their Organisation and Activity in the Modern State*, London: Methuen.

Finer, S. (1974) *Adversary Politics and Electoral Reform*, London: Wigram.

Fiske, J. (1994) *Media Matters: Everyday Culture and Political Change*, Minneapolis: Minnesota Press. An excellent and absorbing study of the media and politics in a postmodern age.

Ingle, S. (1987) *The British Party System*, London: Blackwell.

Keane, J. (1991) *The Media and Democracy*, Cambridge: Polity. A seminal statement of the relationship between the media, democracy and the citizen from a liberal perspective.

Mair, P. (ed.) (1990) *The West European Party System*, Oxford: Oxford University Press.

Michels, R. (1962) *Political Parties*, New York: Collier.

Ostrogoski, M. I. (1902) *Democracy and the Organisation of Political Parties*, London: Macmillan.

Rose, R. (1974) *The Problem of Party Government*, London: Macmillan.

Rose, R. (1984) *Do Parties Make a Difference?*, London: Macmillan.

Thompson, S. (1994) *Better than Sex*, London: Black Swan. A very funny and irreverent look at what political junkies do *after* the campaign trail is finished.

Vaughn, S. (1994) *Ronald Reagan in Hollywood: Movies and Politics*, Cambridge: Cambridge University Press. An instructive and fascinating study of the relationship between the movie industry and politics in the USA through the lens of Reagan's film and political career.

# 14 THE POLICY PROCESS

*John Turner*

**Introduction**

**The study of policy**

**A model of policy-making: Easton's input–output model**

**The policy process and the state**

*Pluralist explanations*
*Neo-pluralist explanations*
*Corporatist explanations*
*Marxist explanations*
*Neo-liberal explanations*

**Theories of decision-making**

*Rationality and decision-making*
*Cost-benefit analysis*
*Modified rationality*
*Disjointed incrementalism*
*Innovation and mixed scanning*
*Organisational and bureaucratic models of decision-making*
*Ideology and decision-making*
*Implementation models of policy-making*
*Advocacy coalitions and negotiated orders*
*Policy communities and networks*

**Case study in the policy process: policy learning and the Brent Spar decision**

*Introduction*
*The initial policy decision*
*Widening the policy environment: a global dimension*
*The German connection*
*The organisational context: the corporate culture at Shell*
*The organisational context: Greenpeace and the politics of protest*
*Crisis politics: policy in reverse*

**Conclusion**

**Further reading**

# The policy process

## Introduction

Explaining how policy is made provides a good guide to how a political system operates as a whole. In other words, policy brings together different aspects of a political system and the various political issues and concepts discussed in the chapters of this book. To understand how policy is made in one country as opposed to another is to understand that country's specific political characteristics, including the interaction of its political system with other systems such as its social and economic environments. Policy also helps us to study the way in which these characteristics come together and are integrated through processes of decision-making and the implementation of policy.

We talk of policy in a general way. We hear people say 'Why don't politicians do something about that problem?', 'Why did the government make that decision?' or 'I'm going to stop the government from doing that'. They are all referring to policy, whether that relates to how issues get put on the political agenda, how policy is formulated, who makes the key decisions and how they are implemented, or why some policies seem to fail and other policies evolve and are modified.

Essentially, policy is about three processes:

- the intentions of political and other key actors;
- the way decisions or non-decisions are made;
- the consequences of these decisions.

In examining any political system we can ask ourselves four key questions about the nature of the political and policy-making process. We will have the opportunity of considering these questions when we examine a case study at the end of this chapter.

1. What are the dominant values of key social and political actors in society? How are these values expressed and how are such wider cultural values modified and changed? For example, what are the dominant values which underpin attitudes towards the state intervention,

including public policy in the areas of welfare, defence, the economy? How are resources, like income and wealth, distributed between different social groups? How far are market, rather than state, solutions favoured?

2 Who has most power in the policy-making process and how is that power distributed in relation to particular decisions? For example, which groups have most power and influence over decisions? Does public policy tend to favour certain groups and vested interests? Does some groups get preferential access to policy-making? Are decision-makers more receptive to certain interests than others?

3 How constrained are policy-makers by their wider social, economic and political environment? For example, how far is domestic policy-making affected by changes in public opinion? In what ways do the media, the press and television in particular, influence policy and decisions? How does the electoral system, and in particular the proximity of elections, affect decision-makers? How do international factors constrain national policy-makers, for example global economics, other national governments or international organisations?

4 How is policy affected by administrative and bureaucratic processes? For example, how do officials constrain the party programmes of governments? How do administrative concerns affect the implementation process? How are individual decisions constrained by technical, scientific or legal concerns? How does the organisation of government itself, with its structures and procedures, affect decision making?

These key questions must be asked of any political system and answers will vary according to the particular institutions and processes within different political systems. Therefore there are certain generic questions which need to be posed about the policy process, although a study of policy will also highlight the way in which different political systems operate.

## The study of policy

There is no universally accepted definition of the term policy. The field of policy studies is filled with competing definitions. However, in recent years there has been a growing interest in the study of the policy process. Lasswell (1951) called for a policy dimension to political studies in 1951 and policy studies developed in the United States in the 1960s and has become increasingly important in political studies since then. Initially, such studies borrowed from a range of different disciplines, including management studies, organisational analysis, decision-making techniques and more theoretical studies of values. The current interest in policy has come about because of a number of factors.

1 The growing scale and complexity of modern government have posed increasing problems for policy-makers. The study of policy has

attempted to define and understand this change in scale and complexity.

2 Politics has been increasingly analysed from the point of view of outputs rather than through analyses of structures and institutions. Here individual and collective decisions are analysed and studies attempt to explain differences between political systems by reference to policy outcomes.

3 There has been a greater emphasis on how decisions are made and on the techniques used in solving problems. In a more prescriptive way, some policy studies have suggested better techniques for problem-solving and decision-making.

4 Policy studies has also been encouraged by the drawing together of different academic disciplines to show how decisions are made in an integrated way.

5 Policy analysts themselves have been increasingly drawn into politics, offering advice and consultancy in government departments, agencies and organisations.

Hugh Heclo has attempted to demarcate the policy field and has pointed to the fact that policy is not a self-evident term. It can, for example, involve a course of actions or inactions. According to Richard Rose (1980), policy represents a long series of related activities, and for Etzioni (1967) policy is a system of generalised decision-making in which decisions and contexts are reviewed. Policy can be interpreted as an empty shopping basket ready to be filled with policy goodies. Braybrooke and Lindblom (1963) use the term to indicate consciously made decisions and the course policies take as a result of the interrelationships among decisions. Policy involves a process whereby policy-makers attempt to deal with a problem, defining options, making decisions and implementing possible solutions.

In Figure 14.1 it should be noted that there is a policy process and a policy outcome. All policy is continuous. Problems are not so much solved as superseded or redefined by policy-makers. Outcomes are impacts of policy affecting people in direct and indirect ways and posing future problems in terms of their unintended consequences. This simplified model also involves

H. Heclo (1972) 'Review Article: Policy Analysis', *British Journal of Political Science* 2.

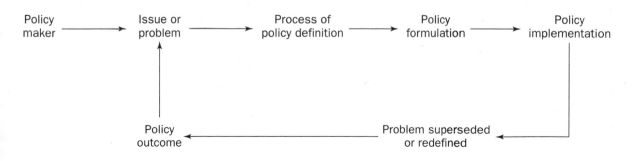

Figure 14.1 The policy process

policy definition and the motivations of policy-makers. Often policy can be seen as responding to particular problems, although decisions can also be based on ideology and the need for internal party support, or it can arise for more general symbolic reasons.

---

**THINK POINT**
- Examine an area of policy which has recently been reported in the press.
- Can you see any of the above factors playing a part in this particular area?

---

## A model of policy-making: Easton's input–output model

D. Easton (1953) *The Political System*, New York: Knopf; (1965) *A Systems Analysis of Political life*

David Easton's pioneering work on the policy process is important because it sees policy as a process involving the interaction of policy-makers with their policy environment. Easton's model is fairly simple, but should be seen as an ideal-type model which attempts to explain conceptually complex relationships. Easton's model has always been seen as important and innovative in that it emphasises policy as an interactive process. He also attempts to disassemble the policy process and separate it into key stages or components which have different impacts on the process as a whole. Attention is also given to the relationship between the political system and

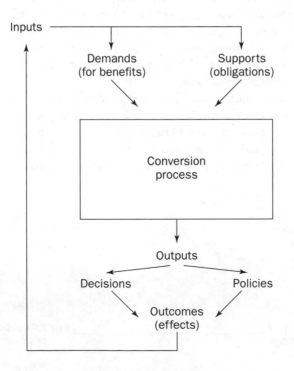

*Figure 14.2* Easton's input–output systems model

other systems. Wider environments, including the social, economic and cultural, are affected by public-policy outcomes.

Criticisms levelled at Easton's input–output model have pointed to its simplicity and its attachment to rationality in the policy process. The model itself is borrowed from the physical sciences, with policy and the political process being analysed like a technical system. For example, many of Easton's categories overlap. Political demands do not arise only from outside the black box or 'conversion process' of decision-making. Politicians and key decision-makers also have demands, and via ideologies and electoral strategies often attempt to manufacture demands through emotive appeals and create policy agendas accordingly and on their terms.

Other critics have pointed to Easton's rather vague notion of this 'conversion process'. Again, there is an assumption that political actors act in rational ways in converting demands into outputs and decisions. Looking inside the black box of decision-making involves looking at the way public officials, elite politicians and other insider groups affect outcomes. Often their influence is hidden from public scrutiny and involves contradictory positions. In a sense, Easton's model also assumes that there are clearly defined objectives and goals. This is rarely the case. Government ministers may have a number of contradictory objectives, including meeting the demands of their party, their perception of the needs of public opinion, the views of their officials and reconciling demands from interest groups and other institutions of government.

Easton's model, therefore, is fairly simple, although it is difficult to envisage more complex models which are not more complicated and less readily understandable. Easton's input–output model creates a cycle through a feedback loop, with policy outcomes affecting future demands. Policy can be seen as a cycle or a staged process involving five key stages which are rarely segmented. They are:

1 Deciding to decide in issue recognition.
2 Formulating alternative options.
3 Making decisions.
4 Implementation.
5 Correction and supplementation.

This cycle emphasises the dynamic nature of the political process and highlights the way in which policy can be understood as a learning process. Hogwood and Gunn have developed this model as a framework for decision-making. Their policy sequence is portrayed in Figure 14.3.

As a learning process policy can be seen as a way in which decision-makers come to terms with issues, consider different forms of action, put them together in a formulation package and then make amendments in the light of their experience of implementing policy.

B. W. Hogwood and L. A. Gunn (1984), *Policy Analysis for the Real World*, Oxford: Oxford University Press.

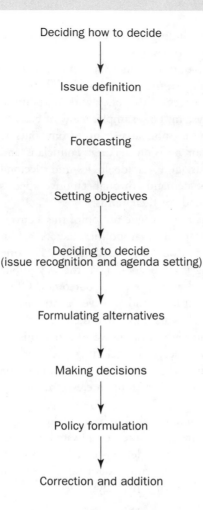

Deciding how to decide

↓

Issue definition

↓

Forecasting

↓

Setting objectives

↓

Deciding to decide
(issue recognition and agenda setting)

↓

Formulating alternatives

↓

Making decisions

↓

Policy formulation

↓

Correction and addition

*Figure 14.3* The Hogwood and Gunn policy sequence

## The policy process and the state

As the previous chapter indicated, the modern state has a fundamental affect on people. Wars, intervention in economic and industrial policy, and the development of welfare programmes have all extended the role and scope of the state. As the state has become more interventionist through increasing government legislation and regulation, so the study of policy has become more important. Policy and the way it is made can tell us a great deal about the organisation and processes of the modern state. The way in which state institutions formulate and implement policy can tell us a great deal about the state's values, political institutions, political culture and political processes.

The state can be defined in terms of the institutions and processes which oversee the development of policy. The key institutions in this process are shown in Figure 14.4. The degree to which these institutions overlap is important for an understanding of the different ways in which policy is formulated and implemented. For example, the United Kingdom is a unitary state where there is no formal constitution and where there is an overlap between these institutions. However, the United States is a federal state with a formal constitution clearly setting out the separation of powers between institutions, with autonomous state and regional powers.

Individuals are affected in nearly all parts of their lives by the activities of the state. In modern society this is particularly the case with:

- the provision of public services in the form of welfare programmes, including health care, pensions, education, income support and housing;
- the intervention of the state in economic policy through budgets, with taxation, public spending and borrowing and in industrial policy, including regional policy, investment incentives and subsidies.

We can consider five theories or explanations of the relationship between state and society. Each explanation can be applied to policy-making processes in different countries.

### Pluralist explanations

The concept of pluralism centres on the notion that power is dispersed in society and that the activities of the state are for group influence checked by the countervailing influence of groups. A wide range of policy outcomes can be accommodated by this explanation given the assumption that there are several sources of power in society. Of course, power is not equally dispersed and some groups have greater access to policy-making circles and have greater opportunities for affecting policy outcomes. Pluralism emphasises the facts that there are multiple centres of power and that policy

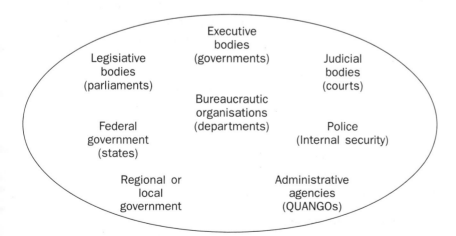

*Figure 14.4* State institutions

development comes from the results of competition between contending groups.

Such groups are said to form policy communities, policy emerging from the bargaining and negotiation between groups. Lively has developed a useful distinction in such relationships between what he terms 'arena' and 'arbiter' pluralist approaches:

> The arbiter theory envisages government as standing above the group battle, settling ground rules for the conflict (particularly those determining what groups and what modes of action are legitimate), ensuring the enforcement of those rules, and perhaps correcting imbalances if there is a danger of particular groups growing into over-mighty subjects. The arena theory, in contrast, sees politicians merely as co-equal participants in the group.
>
> (Lively 1978: 191)

Both arbiter and arena definitions have implications for how the policy process operates. Arbiter pluralism sees the state as holding the ring and only inviting groups into the policy arena when required, setting ground rules and procedures. However, arena pluralism sees policy as a matter of mutual negotiation and bargaining between the state and interested groups. In the arena model, government needs the support of such groups in order to implement its policy. Governments and officials need to build a coalition of support for their policy proposals.

### Neo-pluralist explanations

**Neo-pluralism** has adapted the pluralist model by emphasising the unequal distribution of power between groups. Power and influence over the policy process are controlled by a small elite. According to writers like Mosca, this elite of party politicians, government ministers, officials, lawyers, military leaders, media owners and powerful business interests directs and controls power which essentially supports their own interests and their hold over power. In policy terms the emphasis has been placed very much on top-down approaches, emphasising the role of elite decision-makers. Neo-pluralist explanations would support such a perspective, while not ignoring the view that there are contending and competing elites.

For writers like Weber, power is increasingly located within large bureaucracies. The growth of big government, large business corporations and large-scale military establishments has been accompanied by the growth of rule-driven bureaucracies, again controlled by a relatively small number of administrative elites. Others have pointed to a power elite which now dominates government, business and the military. In a study of the United States C. Wright Mills emphasised the interrelationship between leaders and institutions. In the policy arena different elites operate in relation to different issues and are constrained by conflicting interests between elites.

### Corporatist explanations

Pluralism and corporatism are similar models in many respects. At its heart corporatism attempts to explain tendencies of the state towards intervention,

J. Lively (1978) 'Pluralism and Consensus', in P. Birnbaum, J. Lively and G. Parry (eds) *Democracy, Consensus and Social Contract*, London: Sage.

**Neo-pluralism** A variant of pluralism which recognises the development of elite groups with more access to power.

G. Mosca (1939) *The Ruling Class*, New York/London: McGraw-Hill.

M. Weber (1947) *The Theory of Social and Economic Organisation*, Glencoe, IL: Free Press.

C. Wright Mills (1956) *The Power Elite*, New York: Oxford University Press.

intermediation and incorporation. Winkler has argued that the modern state has had to intervene as economic circumstances have deteriorated in countries. The development of global markets, greater industrial concentration and higher unemployment has meant that the state has had to intervene with policies designed to support and gain the cooperation of corporate interests.

Governments have attempted to develop a tripartite set of relationships, institutionalising the cooperative relationship between the state, business and organised labour. Corporatist explanations would point to the loss of control of such groups as they are incorporated into the decision-making process at the expense of relative autonomy.

A useful distinction has been made by Schmitter (1979) between state corporatism and social corporatism:

> State corporatism tends to be authoritarian and anti-liberal as in the political regimes of fascist Italy or Nazi Germany. Social corporatism tends to develop as pluralist arrangements break down and the state has to intervene in the face of economic and industrial decline.
>
> (Schmitter 1979: 64)

J. Winkler (1974) 'Corporatism', *Archives Européennes de Sociologie* XVII (1).

## Marxist explanations

Marxist analyses take as a starting point the development of two social classes, the proletariat and bourgeoisie, formed as a consequence of the development of the capitalist mode of production. Essentially, a strong link exists between political power and economic power, with the most dominant economic class exercising political control. In this sense the state is not seen as holding the ring between different interests, but rather as actually representing the most dominant class. This argument is similar to the neo-pluralist interpretation, which sees the development of elites.

Marxists see state intervention as a way of ensuring that capital accumulation continues and existing social relationships are preserved. In policy terms this means the state intervening to pick up the social costs of production, or subsidising capital, or ensuring that organised labour is controlled.

The relationship between economic and political power is not a simple one and cannot be understood in a deterministic way. For example, different factions within elites may exist representing, for example, different elements of capital, like finance and manufacturing. Such factions may compete for political control and the state takes its form from the struggle between such factions and classes. Poulantzas has argued that the state and economy are relatively autonomous, with the state often intervening in the longer-term interest of the dominant class, despite short-term compromises having to be made.

N. Poulantzas (1973) *The Problem of the Capitalist State.*

## Neo-liberal explanations

**Neo-liberal** explanations became increasingly dominant in the 1980s. For example, proponents of the New Right, including Reagan and Thatcher in

**Neo-liberalism** A theory which place market efficiencies as the foundation for political freedom and argues for a limited role for the state.

**419**

government, have argued for the rolling back of the state and the breaking up of corporatist vested interests. Writers like Olson (1965) have emphasised that corporatist and pluralist perspectives have actually damaged society, the alternative being policies of deregulation and privatisation to favour market-led rather than state-led policy solutions.

## Theories of decision-making

Theories of how decisions are made in political systems are important because they provide us with a framework for understanding the complex relationships which surround policy-making. The detail and volume of empirical evidence can be placed within a pattern of relationships by using such theories. They help us to explain where power lies and how political systems process information and attempt to deal with issues and problems.

Theories tend to be oversimplified models of political relationships and also tend to be abstract. However, they do provide organising principles and can help us understand the way in which issues are processed. An examination of such theories can help us understand the way political decisions are made and we will apply them to a case study involving a range of political actors and issues.

### Rationality and decision-making

A rational model of decision-making centres on the assumption that the policy-maker already has clearly defined goals and a range of tools for obtaining such objectives. The decision-maker is assumed to be seeking solutions to well-defined problems and employing the optimal means for achieving clearly defined ends. Rationality refers to the normative nature of the process and the means adopted in arriving at decisions.

**Rationality** A concept which places the individual actor at the centre of analysis, policy-making being determined by individual choice.

Models which consider that there is a high degree of **rational** decision making assume that there are clear stages in the decision-making process. From the outset the policy-maker is identified as defining the issues; once this has been accomplished the next stage involves determining the key goals and then evaluating alternative methods for achieving them. The final stage involves the decision-maker choosing the most appropriate means by which policy can be enacted.

---

**THINK POINT**
- Think of a decision you have recently made in your personal or social life.
- Do you feel you made decisions according to the criteria laid down by rational theory?

---

Rationality in social choice theory assumes that the individual:

- can always make a decision, given a range of options;
- can prioritise these different options and decide on which is the most preferred;

- can rank other solutions in order of importance;
- can choose solutions which are the best;
- can make similar decisions given similar options.

---

**THINK POINT**

- Reflecting on the questions above, were you aware of the range of options available?
- Did you have enough information?
- Were you aware of the implications of available options?
- What criteria did you use to define 'the best' option?
- Were you in a position to make the decision alone, as an individual, or did the decision involve others (i.e. was it contingent on how others would decide and react to your decision)?

---

The media also tend to interpret policy through the lens of these rational assumptions. Journalists will locate responsibility for a policy and make judgements about its success or failure using such rational criteria. The rational theory is less messy and complicated than more complex alternative explanations. Electorates find it comfortable to assume that there is a president or prime minister making rational decisions based on the fullest information and the widest options in the best interest of the community. However, in politics it is rare for decisions to be made in such an autonomous and isolated way. Usually, decisions are made collectively, involving a wide range of governmental, non-governmental and voluntary bodies. Decisions, rather than being made on the basis of rationality, are made through compromise, bargaining and negotiation and there is always a strong injection of ideology involving a clear judgement about goals which are seen as good and those which are seen as bad.

### Cost-benefit analysis

A prominent method using this rational approach is **cost-benefit analysis** (CBA), which attempts to asses and prioritise all aspects of a problem. CBA is often used by politicians to make decisions about public projects such as a new road, dam, airport or housing project. It will take into account economic costs and then set them against the economic benefits that are expected in the medium to long term.

CBA tends to assume that all issues can be quantified and measured in this way, and it also assumes that comparisons can be made between very different factors and priorities. For example, a new motorway may involve a calculation of (i) the economic benefit of locating it in a particular terrain against (ii) the social cost that it may run close to a densely populated housing district or conservation area. Comparisons between such alternatives often become rather superficial and dependent on the relative weight given to such costs and benefits.

Neo-liberal perspectives have attempted to assess public services in this way. Welfare, housing, education and defence projects have been assessed

**Cost-benefit analysis** A method for balancing and assessing policy options according to their costs and benefits.

M. Olson (1965) *The Logic of Collective Action*, Cambridge, Mass. Harvard University Press.

**Public choice** Theories which argue that people make choices according to economic scarcity based on marginal utility.

**Market testing** A process whereby publicly provided goods and services are compared according to cost and quality with those provided by the private sector.

using this quantifiable method. Relative costs and benefits are then placed in the wider context of political and economic demands on resources. The New Right's **public choice** theory stems from assumptions about rationality and especially rational consumer behaviour given market conditions of perfect competition. Projects are then assessed against such ideal-type criteria. If private market initiatives can provide a more cost-effective service, then policy would indicate public projects need to be abandoned. In recent years in Britain, for example, services provided by local government have undergone **market testing** and many large national projects like the Channel Tunnel have been financed solely by the private sector. Economic theory, especially micro-economic assumptions about perfectly competitive markets, now plays an increasingly important part in political policy-making.

---

**THINK POINT**
- Consider a national or local project which involves key decisions about costs and benefits.
- Draw up a sheet placing costs on one side and benefits on another.
- Now try to weight each item on a scale of 1 to 10.
- Why did you weight the items as you did and what assumptions lay behind your decisions?

---

Rational models have therefore been crucial in the development of studies about decision-making and policy development. However, it is important to consider the wider political assumptions which underlie such approaches:

- hierarchies in organisations tend to determine the decision-making process;
- there are clear demarcations between command and communications in such organisations;
- information can be processed in a clear and logical way;
- expertise and knowledge will be held at a premium;
- non-rational attitudes and behaviour will be marginalised;
- rational planning and decision-making will find it more difficult to deal with sudden and unexpected crises;
- the policy process will tend to be divided into key stages;
- the scale and complexity of problems may lead to decisions being based on rational methods like CBA, which simplifies and quantifies the choices which ultimately have to be made;
- decision-making may become routinised and creative thinking may be rejected as non-rational or illogical;
- ultimately politics will intrude, with decisions about options coming down to party ideologies or electoral politics.

### Modified rationality

The issues raised by a rational model of decision-making have led writers to consider modifications which bring the theory more in line with empirical evidence from the real world of politics. It is generally accepted that policy-makers will not choose all options available to them, and clearly some options will conflict with more deeply entrenched ideological positions. Indeed, some decisions will have unintended consequences which cannot be rationally predicted or planned for.

The policy maker may also make decisions which conflict with the wider values of the organisation. Organisational structures, procedures and cultures may determine the type and scope of decisions being made and set limits to the options available. Simon, for example, argues that decision-makers are constrained by their personal values, the structure and culture of their organisations and the unpredictability of a complex political environment. Given the problem of the unintended consequences of decisions, there are important constraints on such a rational perspective.

H. A. Simon (1957) *Administrative Behaviour*, Glencoe, IL: Free Press.

For example, clearly the building of major roads has been a priority for governments in reducing congestion, urban blight and pollution. However, many roads experts would agree that more roads actually attract traffic and hence the problem which was supposed to be solved by the original policy is in fact exacerbated by its implementation. This modified view of rationality also contends that the policy makers themselves import their own value judgements into the decision-making process.

## Disjointed incrementalism

Alternative models of decision-making have differed from these rational and modified rational approaches. Braybrooke and Lindblom have argued that, in practice, decision-makers are rather conservative about the decisions they make. Indeed, they make small decisions, testing the water or taking one step at a time, rather than following a more fundamental and comprehensive rational approach. They argue that decision-making involves incremental adjustments to existing policy.

C. E. Lindblom (1968) *The Policy Making Process* Enlgewood Cliffs: Prentice Hall.

Fundamental decisions are therefore rare. Generally, an organisation will decide on a policy and decisions will then follow within this context. Policy develops in a piecemeal and gradual way or through ad-hoc changes as circumstances change. There will be continuity when policy will change little, but there will also be times of flux or crisis when policy will change but not necessarily in any clear direction. Policy initiatives therefore tend to arise from existing mainstream policies and from orthodox perspectives, and change only occurs gradually over time.

Braybrooke and Lindblom have used a diagram (reproduced in Figure 14.5) to explain the nature of this disjointed incremental approach to policy. They argue that quadrants A and B are rare in politics. Quadrant A relates to situations where there is fundamental change with visionary decision-making, whereas B involves revolutionary or crisis decision-making. Most policy making in a political system involves small decisions related to quadrants C and D. Quadrant C is dominated by rational decisions where one has clearly defined goals and options. This area is also rare in the real world, where politicians do not have adequate information and knowledge

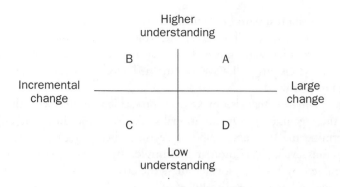

*Figure 14.5* Braybrooke and Lindblom's policy-making continuum
*Source*: Braybrooke and Lindblom (1963: 67)

to adopt such a rational approach. Instead, Braybrooke and Lindblom argue that a more realistic position for policy-makers is in quadrant D, where decisions involve small changes and where there is a limited amount of information and knowledge.

Disjointed incrementalism therefore involves a modified view of policy making. Instead of a process conceived in well-defined stages, Braybrooke and Lindblom argue that policy is continuous and cumulative. Policy-makers often attempt to avoid innovative policy initiatives because they are too risky and potentially very costly, especially if they go wrong. Policy-makers attempt to minimise or avoid problems rather than address issues directly.

C. E. Lindblom (1959), 'The Science of Muddling Through', *Public Administration Review* 19.

Lindblom has called this incremental theory 'the science of muddling through'. However, muddling through is a more accurate description of how policy is made than the more simplistic and unreal rational approaches. Given that policy is made in a fragmented way, without full knowledge and a centralised and authoritative rational mind, muddling through provides us with a messier but more accurate interpretation of how public decisions are actually made.

Lindblom's notion of partisan mutual adjustment involves an acceptance that policy derives from the interplay between contending interests within a more fragmented framework. Normatively, such a view suggests a more democratic and participative ethos, involving bottom-up as well as top-down decision-making. As Lindblom has argued:

> The connection between a policy and good reasons for it is obscure, since the many participants will act for diverse reasons. In many circumstances their mutual adjustments will achieve a co-ordination superior to an attempt at central co-ordination, which is often so complex as to lie beyond any co-ordinator's competence.

(Lindblom 1979: 516)

Critics of Lindblom have picked up on this notion of participant mutual adjustment of policy. They point to the underlying conservatism of such an approach in that it assumes that groups have open access to policy-making and that the status quo is the preferred position given that political stability is formed around it and any changes are small incremental adjustments to it. Such small adjustments seem to rule out more radical changes. The model also appears to eschew any form of strategic planning. It has also been criticised for underestimating the frequency of crises in politics which force governments to make fundamental decisions. In a more global and complex political environment governments find it increasingly difficult to deal with issues in a piecemeal way.

## Innovation and mixed scanning

Dror, for example, has argued that Lindblom's 'muddling through' hypothesis tends to reinforce the pro-inertia view of modern government. He recognises that there is continuity in the problems facing governments, although Dror reinjects a notion of rationality into the policy-making process. He believes there has to be both 'realism' and 'idealism' in understanding how policy is made. There is muddling through and incrementalism, but there is also some appraisal and evaluation of options and objectives. Alongside piecemeal decision-making Dror places creative and innovative methods such as brainstorming. Together they represent both rational and idealist approaches, permitting innovation and creativity in policy to break through the piecemeal nature of incrementalism.

Dror Y. (1964) 'Muddling Through – Science or Inertia?', *Public Administration Review* 24.

Etzioni has also criticised the notion of incrementalism, arguing that 'muddling through' seems to suggest a lack of direction and policy making which is disconnected. Instead, he argues that a model of 'mixed scanning' needs to be considered involving policy-making where fundamental decisions are important in that they provide a context for more incremental approaches. A policy-maker attempts to gain a comprehensive view of issues, which provides a shape for the more specific and ad-hoc decisions which are then made on an everyday basis. Etzioni argues:

A. Etzioni (1967) 'Mixed Scanning: A "Third" Approach to Decision-Making', *Public Administration Review* 27.

> both elements of mixed scanning help to reduce the effects of the particular shortcomings of the other; incrementalism reduces the unrealistic aspects of rationalism by limiting the details required in fundamental decisions, and contextuating rationalism helps to overcome the conservative slant of incrementalism by exploring longer term alternatives.
>
> (Etzioni 1967: 390)

A problem for Etzioni's approach is in deciding between incremental and fundamental decisions, especially given politicians' use of rhetoric in making more of out of a policy than is justified by the substance of the decision made. Often, fundamental notions are used to justify incremental decisions when they are deemed to have been successful.

## Organisational and bureaucratic models of decision-making

In examining any policy decision the organisational context has to be considered. As Elmore has indicated, 'only by understanding how organisations work can we understand how policies are shaped in the process of implementation' (Elmore 1978: 187).

R. Elmore (1978) 'Organisational Models of Social Program Implementation', *Public Policy* 26.

Weber (1947) studied the bureaucratic nature of administration in the modern organisation. Central to his concerns was the notion of formal rationality. The modern bureaucracy is a continuous organisation dominated by functionaries with specific roles, pursuing rules and routine procedures within a structured and consistent organisational framework. Modern organisations are based on a formal hierarchy with clearly defined levels of authority and control.

The implication must be that policy itself is placed within the context of the organisation's objectives, overall strategy and structures. To understand how public policy is made one must therefore look to the departments of state, with their officials who formulate and implement policies. There has been a growing interest in the study of organisations and their role in mediating policy. However, in the 1950s a critique of this rational bureaucratic model of policy-making was developed by writers like Merton and Gouldner. They pointed out that a conflict can exist between an organisation's formal system of control and the individual positions of officials within the organisation's hierarchy. For example the formal authority of the organisation can come into conflict with the particular specialisms and expertise of officials within the organisation. In large government departments, like education and health, there may be a clear division between different staff, for example between officials and health and educational professionals with contending perspectives and professional values. The goals of the organisation may be translated by those with particular concerns about the nature of the policy being decided.

R. K. Merton (1957) *Social Theory and Social Structure*, Glencoe, IL: Free Press.
A. W. Gouldner (1954) *Patterns of Industrial Bureaucracy*, Glencoe, IL: Free Press.

Another aspect of Weber's work which has been studied in relation to policy-making is the concept of 'organisational culture' (Weber 1947). Organisations pursue wider values and socialise the officials who work within them. These values are reinforced by organisational control and regulation and by a structure which rewards conformist behaviour. This wider culture will also provide a context in which decisions are made and will determine the way in which the organisation responds to its environment.

Allison's analysis of the Cuban missile crisis indicated that policy was developed in response to the bargaining and negotiation between key officials and political actors in the policy-making process. These officials represented the interests of different departments within the bureaucratic structure and forwarded certain policies and rejected others on the basis of narrow departmental interests. Hence, decisions were made as a consequence of which departments had most power and which departments could form coalitions in powerful mutual support of certain policy positions.

G. T. Allison (1971) *Essence of Decision*, Boston: Little, Bown & Co.

Bureaucratic politics in modern states constrains elected politicians. An incoming government may be provided with limited policy options and a continuation of existing policy is often the norm. Policy change can be very slow, especially if policy initiatives are opposed by senior officials within the bureaucratic structure. Often departments will have longstanding semi-autonomous policy positions with which they will try to influence incoming politicians. Officials will also have ready access across the administrative

P. Dunleavy (1981) 'Professions and Policy Change: Notes Towards a Model of Ideological Incorporation', *Public Administration Bulletin* 36.

system, with senior officials often meeting independently of ministers to discuss the framework and development of policy. This process is underpinned by the fact that many senior officials will come from similar social and educational backgrounds, developing close working relationships as they move up in their careers. Officials will also have the advantage of controlling the detail of policy. Elected politicians often find it difficult to cover all aspects of policy detail, so inevitably many decisions will be delegated to officials. Bureaucracies also attempt to 'capture' ministers. Ministers are socialised into the culture of the department and the process of interdepartmental rivalry creates a team attitude, with ministers overidentifying with their departments. This process of 'going native' leads ministers into defending a departmental view against the political views of their government colleagues.

## Ideology and decision-making

Political decisions clearly are not made simply on the basis of rational or optimal choice. Political parties and politicians are thrust into power by purporting to hold a set of core beliefs and ideas in the form of ideology. Such ideologies often have the effect of excluding ideas, information and empirical evidence when they fail to support the political party's core beliefs. Policy-makers may therefore hold prejudicial views which run in the face of clear evidence related to issues. They support a partial interpretation of events, ensuring there is not a dissonance between perceived reality and their given ideological position on an issue. Shared values can form around important misconceptions. Janis has coined the term 'groupthink' in examining the psychological basis of these misconceptions. He argues that policy-makers tend to develop conformist behaviour in order to ensure amicable political relationships. In this way conflict and alternative views are excluded. The tendency for policy-makers 'not to rock the boat' is often legitimised through constitutional conventions like collective Cabinet responsibility, which ensures that the 'outside world' sees the government in power as united and undivided by policy conflicts.

I. Janis (1972) *Victims of Groupthink*, Boston: Houghton-Mifflin.

The use of ideology and power can also lead to issues failing to enter the political agenda and decision-making process. Interest groups with powerful access to government may want to ensure that policy is not formulated and implemented against their interests. The art of non-decision-making is therefore as politically significant as positive decision-making. Bachrach and Baratz have analysed the issue of non-decision-making. Instead of simply concentrating on policies where there is a visible decision, process and outcome it is equally important to discern where decisions are not made and where conflicts are hidden, demands remain latent and certain interests are excluded.

P. Bachrach and Baratz (1963) 'Decisions and Nondecisions: An Analytical Framework', *American Political Science Review* 57.

> **THINK POINT**
> • Think of an issue where key policy decisions have not been made and where you think government action should be taken. For example, you may think of issues like more rigorous curbs on tobacco, smoking or alcohol; tougher enironmental laws; more proactive public transport policies; or aid policies for developing countries.
> • What are the main reasons why you feel governments have been reluctant to make decisions in these areas?

## Implementation models of policy-making

More recently the focus of analysis has concentrated on the implementation phase of the policy process. Emphasis has switched from an analysis of rational policy objectives to policy outcomes. Easton's (1953) model already discussed made the distinction between policy formulation, policy implementation and outcomes. These were arranged in terms of inputs and outputs being processed by a black box of decision-making. In politics much can go wrong between the policy formulation stage and the outcomes of policy. Pressman and Wildavsky have analysed the limited success of policy implementation in the United States. Policy objectives were ultimately confounded by difficulties in practically implementing policy through a complex political system. They argue that successful policy development depends upon the creation of a network of related institutions in the policy process.

J. Pressman and A. Wildavsky (1973) *Implementation*, Berkeley, CA: University of California Press.

> **THINK POINT**
> • Consider a recent example of a public policy which was deemed to have been unsuccessful or to have failed to meet its objectives.
> • List the reasons why the policy failed?
> • At what stage – formulation or implementation – did the policy fail?

B. W. Hogwood and L. A. Gunn (1981) *The Policy Orientation*, Glasgow: University of Strathclyde Press.

Hogwood and Gunn, following on the work of Pressman and Wildavsky, have outlined the key preconditions for the successful implementation of policy. Although they imply a top-down approach, and a set of criteria which can rarely be completely achieved, these 'perfect' conditions for policy success include:

- the lack of external constraints;
- the need for adequate time and resources, especially at each stage of the implementation process;
- better understanding of the relationship between cause and effect in relation to policy issues;
- the lack of intervening factors which can push the process off course;
- the need for a single clear implementing body not dependent on other agencies or departments;
- key policy objectives are known and shared by policy-makers;

- each stage of the implementation process can be demarcated and defined;
- the need for full commitment amongst those involved;
- agreement on policy control and lines of communication.

Critics of top-down approaches argue that policy is the outcome of negotiations and bargaining between groups which attempt to forge a policy consensus on an issue. Barrett and Hill argue that policy involves a bargaining process whereby compromises are made between different values and interests inside and outside the formulation and implementation process. Policy-makers have to reconcile the key differences between policy stakeholders and must take into account the latent value and interests in the wider political environment.

Barrett and Fudge have argued that policy involves a process of continuous movement, with implementation as a policy–action continuum in which negotiation and compromise between interested parties structure the substance of policy itself. In this sense, the rationalistic concern for policy objectives seems less important, if not irrelevant, given the view that the way policy is implemented determines the substantive nature of policy content itself. Within the field of policy studies emphasis has thus shifted to bottom-up approaches. For example, Elmore (1978) has argue that the study of policy involves a process of 'backward mapping', moving from effect to cause and concentrating on those network of agencies most involved in the implementation process.

S. Barret and C. Fudge (1981) *Policy and Action*, London: Methuen.

Barrett and Hill (1981b) put much of the blame for top-down approaches on the legacy left by the influence of administrative and managerial perspectives of the policy process. Increasingly, the complexity of the interaction of groups involved in the policy process must be analysed and policy should be seen as a continuous shifting of contending interests placed within the context of a more difficult wider environment.

## Advocacy coalitions and negotiated orders

Attempts have been made to draw together many of the ideas already discussed, including an approach which makes use of many aspects of rational and non-rational approaches. Sabatier, for example, has attempted to develop a general model of the policy-making process which draws together concerns about resources, interest groups, information and ideologies.

P. Sabatier and D. Mazmanian (1979) 'The Conditions of Effective Implementation: A Guide to Accomplishing Policy Objectives', *Policy Analysis* 6(3).

Sabatier has developed a model of 'policy subsystems' comprising not only interest groups, politicians and bureaucrats, but groups such as policy analysts, journalists, researchers and specific policy professionals. Within policy sub-systems are 'advocacy coalitions' made up of those who share common beliefs and attitudes towards policy formulation and implementation, but who may be located in different parts of the policy-making network. There are also 'policy brokers' who attempt to keep order and attempt to develop compromises around policies which can be meaningfully implemented.

Sabatier's model recognises the dynamic nature of policy-making and the shifting pattern of policy coalitions which forms around different issues. Rather than taking a more institutional view of policy-making, he sees policy subsystems as flexible and reaching across traditional areas of the political system. Coalitions are underpinned by shared ideological beliefs and the need for policy outcomes to reflect these core beliefs. Sabatier argues that there are three layers of belief which these advocacy coalitions develop and share:

1. Application of policy related to specific issues
2. Basic political values and strategies
3. Deep core beliefs and fundamental ideas

It is easier to change and negotiate positions at the surface level of policy application related to specific problems. However, it is harder at the deeper levels to compromise on ideas regarding basic political values and core beliefs. It is also these deeper core beliefs which will hold together different advocacy coalitions, with some being more powerful than others.

Sabatier's model also takes account of external factors which come to influence and provides context for the decisions made within the policy subsystems. In what he calls 'stable system parameters' we find factors which do not change radically over time. These include economic and social circumstances, technological innovations and changes in politics. External factors also include policy outputs from other subsystems and feedback from previous decisions.

Policy change occurs through what Sabatier calls 'policy learning', which involves the interplay between members of advocacy coalitions, including policy brokers. For example, members of the policy community will respond to evidence of economic and social change through new research ideas. Power holders will interpret such information, taking it on board if it concurs with existing thinking, while modifying their existing ideological positions if empirical evidence raises insurmountable contradictions. Sabatier has developed a model of these relationships, which is shown in Figure 14.6.

With policy subsystems there will be a number of advocacy coalitions. There will be a stable and consistent difference between contending groups regarding core beliefs, although there will be less stability at the basic political values level and even less agreement at the level of policy application. Policy brokers will attempt to mediate between these coalitions and ensure policy can be implemented in an agreed and effective way. Generally, there will be one dominant and powerful advocacy coalition within the subsystem, although relative power positions may change as external circumstances alter. Although the most powerful group may dominate in terms of core beliefs, nevertheless there will be compromises and policy learning takes place as the policy decision develops towards implementation. Groups which respond to the environment and learn faster and more effectively will tend to influence policy even though they are in a minority and play no part in the dominant coalition.

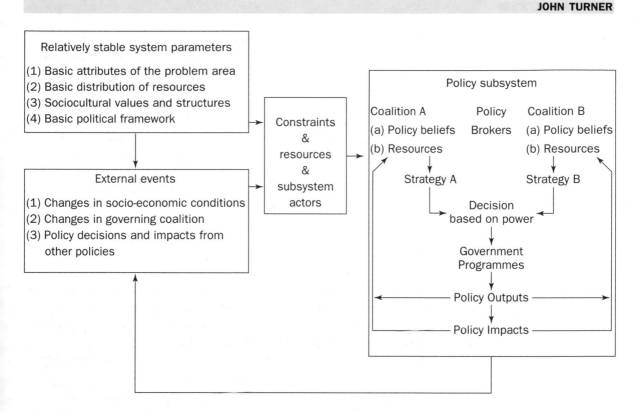

*Figure 14.6* Sabatier's policy learning model

For example, in the 1960s ideas relating to Keynesian demand management dominated treasury thinking in governments throughout the world. With changes in the external economic environment and major contradictions in Keynesian policy, minority coalition groups put forward alternative explanations which attempted to make sense of new economic and political realities. By the 1980s most advanced economies had modified their Keynesian core beliefs for some form of monetarism. Even where core beliefs had not changed, policy was changed pragmatically at the policy application level.

It was the application of policy which was the first to change, although such changes finally allowed new dominant advocacy coalitions to emerge and so win the ideological battle over core beliefs. However, that policy battle is clearly far from over.

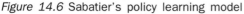

*THINK POINT*
- Think of an area of policy, like health, education or economic and industrial policy.
- Which groups would Sabatier include as advocacy coalitions in these areas of policy?
- Are there natural coalitions which would form built around shared common beliefs about particular policies?

## Policy communities and networks

The sectorisation of policy is a consequence of the complexity and size of modern government. It remains very difficult to coordinate policy across all policy areas. Richardson and Jordan have referred to the British administrative and departmental system as 'departmental pluralism' or as a 'collection of separate fiefdoms' which tend to dissolve into factionalism.

The notion of policy communities and networks shows how policy is fragmented and how different structures and relationships are formed by the stakeholders with an interest in particular policy areas. Boundaries between different government departments and other administrative bodies are ambiguous and will change according to particular policy issues. Writers have developed the notion of *policy space* to describe the way in which policy responsibilities and interests can overlap between different organisations. Space is defined by the degree of organisational interdependence. Policy space is related to the concept of policy territory, with departments and other public bodies defending their policy preserves and resisting the challenges from other parts of the administrative system. One can talk of departments at the periphery where policy influence is marginal and locations so far away that influence is non-existent.

Policy networks have been analysed in relation to five key dimensions:

1 Constellation of interests, including the interests of stakeholders, which may vary according to territory, expertise or service area.
2 Membership, including those elites seen as a traditional part of a policy sector made up of administrators, business people, professionals, trade unionists and consumers.
3 Vertical interdependence involves relationships between central and subcentral policy-makers and implementers. For example, such relationships may cover the policy concerns of central and regional or local government.
4 Horizontal interdependence involves relationships between different networks, breaking down the boundaries between different government departments.
5 The distribution of resources within the administrative system affects the relative power and influence of different networks both vertically and horizontally.

Policy communities exist where there is some degree of stability and where relationships and responsibilities are continuous over a period of time. There is a process of sharing in terms of responsibility, common objectives, implementation processes and general culture. Communities are also strong where there is some autonomy from other governmental institutions. The least integrated networks are those based around general issues where there are many stakeholders and interested parties and where there is a high dependence on other networks. There are also networks formed around producer and professional interests. Economic and industrial policy is dominated by networks which incorporate commercial interests and depend

J. J. Richardson and A. G. Jordan (1979) *Governing Under Pressure: The Policy Process in a Post-Parliamentary Democracy*, Oxford: Martin Robertson.

See R. A. W. Rhodes (1988) *Beyond Westminster and Whitehall*, London: Allen & Unwin.

on the acquiescence of corporate interests for the implementation of policy. Professional groups dominate health care and educational policy agendas, where the medical profession and educational establishment are crucial to policy formulation and implementation. In the case study which follows the close relationship between government and the oil industry was crucial in determining particular policy positions.

## Case study in the policy process: policy learning and the Brent Spar decision

At the beginning of this chapter policy was defined as involving three processes: the intentions of key political actors; the way decisions or non-decisions are made; and the consequences of these decisions. In examining decisions regarding Brent Spar we can address the four key questions also posed at the start of this chapter. What are the dominant values of the key actors and how far are they modified? Who has most power in the policy-making process? How constrained are the policy makers? How is policy constrained by administrative and bureaucratic processes?

As was indicated in the preceding section, policy can be seen as a web of interrelated decisions and actions, and the Brent Spar case study illustrates a situation where policy makers failed to appreciate the interrelated nature of the decision-making process, the wider environmental framework and the power of bottom-up challenges to the legitimacy of this particular policy approach.

### Introduction

The Brent Spar incident started with a rather inconsequential policy decision by the British Government to give permission to Shell UK to proceed and decommission an old oil storage platform by sinking it in the North Atlantic. This decision came after a three-year period of lobbying by Shell and after submissions from technical and scientific experts. This seemed like a rational policy decision, made fairly secretively by the British Energy Minister, but with multilateral departmental support from the Ministry of Agriculture, Fisheries and Food, the Department of the Environment, the Scottish Office and the Department of Trade and Industry. However, after the initial publicity about this decision, the subsequent three months saw an unprecedented furore ending in the reversal of policy which in turn contributed to the decision of the British prime minister to submit himself to re-election as Conservative Party leader.

The assumption behind the initial policy decision was that a rational decision had been made based on the fullest scientific information and according to the most up-to-date technical data. The political decision rested on, first, the weight of existing scientific evidence and, second, the least-cost option, it being estimated that the cost of disposal at sea would be one-fifth of the cost of disposal on land. Interestingly, it was also the case that once the decision had been made both the British government and Shell UK kept doggedly to their position, despite growing opposition within the wider policy network.

There are a number of reasons why such an issue came to destabilise policy makers. What on the face of it seemed a straightforward, un-complicated and rational decision ran into many of the problems which this chapter has discussed in relation to the policy-making process. The issue raised questions about how policy-makers seemed to have lost the power to make decisions, so forfeiting their legitimacy and wider credibility.

### The initial policy decision

The initial decision about Brent Spar illustrates Allison's (1971) three models of decision-making: the rational actor, organisational and bureaucratic models. The British government, working closely with the oil multinational Shell, assumed that the objectives of the exercise were clear and that implications, options and alternatives had all been carefully considered. Interestingly, in defence of their decision, the government and Shell reiterated the point that formal procedures had been properly followed. Both legal and technical concerns had been investigated and addressed. However, using the bureaucratic model, it is true that the original decision had been made by a relatively small number of officials, oil company executives and departmental scientists.

In the section on 'Corporatist explanations' (pp. 418–19) we came across the notion of 'corporatism', pointing to the way in which transnational companies like Shell have a large influence over policy related to their area of commercial influence.

In the preceding discussion of rationality and decision-making (pp. 420–1) emphasis was placed on a process which highlighted the importance of hier-archy and informed expertise underpinned by optimal methods and routines which rejected notions of 'non-rational' attitudes and behaviour. Rationality allowed government ministers to defend their original decision by reference to statements like 'this is the only logical way' and 'there are no other viable alternatives based on the logic of evidence'. It also led ministers to under-estimate the power of what were seen as non-rational ideas.

In the section which discussed ideology and decision-making (see pp. 428–8) it was suggested that some issues fail to get onto the policy agenda because certain groups are excluded. A similar point is made by Sabatier in discussing weaker advocacy coalitions (pp. 429–31). In the Brent Spar case the key decision-makers tended to underestimate the importance of ecological concerns and the green political agenda. They were put on the defensive by the organising abilities of Greenpeace and their vocal and active tactics, like seizing the media agenda and occupying the oil storage plat-form itself. Much policy is mediated through television, radio and the press, with public understanding emanating from visual images and messages.

### *Widening the policy environment: a global dimension*

The decision on decommissioning Brent Spar started as a relatively local decision made in London by representatives of the British government and Shell UK. As the dispute over implementation continued, so the issue became part of a much wider environment, being placed first in the context of a global ecological agenda and then within a more European political environment. Greenpeace ensured that 'dumping an installation in any ocean' was a matter of international concern and consequently the British government was forced to defend its original decision within a wider European Union (EU) context, and Shell UK within the context of its own global organisation. Despite the parochial and limited nature of the original decision, nevertheless, as Sabatier (1987) would put it, the policy subsystem now had new advocacy coalitions, including powerful foreign governments and the EU Commission. It is important to emphasise that such issues do have global significance given the ever increasing political interrelationships. It is difficult for individual governments to make autonomous decisions, given the global economic and political systems of which nation-states have become part.

### *The German connection*

The issue of sinking Brent Spar in the North Atlantic was a much more important political issue in Germany, Holland and Scandinavia than in Britain. As a member of the EU the British government came under increasing pressure not only from partner governments, but from the Commission and European Parliament as well. Green groups were able to exploit this widening of the policy agenda and used the Conference on the North Sea in Copenhagen to publicise their views. The German government also used a G7 summit of leading industrial nations to raise the issue and put pressure on the British prime minister to reverse his government's original decision.

Again, it is the interdependence of nation-states within supranational bodies like the EU which must be considered in relation to contemporary policy. The British government found that it was unable to decide on such an issue without support from its political partners. This tends to confirm the pluralist view that there are numerous sources of power and, in this case, that power was not evenly distributed between the contending interests (see the section on 'Pluralist explanations', pp. 417–18, and 'Neo-pluralist explanations', p. 418).

In Germany the ruling Christian Democrats were concerned that the issue should not further the election hopes of the Green Party, pushing the government's coalition partners, the Free Democrats, into fourth place and opening up the possibility of a Social Democratic Party-led coalition with the Greens. Leaders of all main German political parties criticised Shell UK, and the German media were far less equivocal than their British counterparts. The turning point was the realisation that Shell Germany was losing 30 per cent of its sales.

### *The organisational context: the corporate culture at Shell*

To understand how decisions were made in this case study it is important to consider the Shell organisation, its wider culture and its decision-making processes (see the section on 'Organisational and bureaucratic models of decision-making', pp. 425–7).

It has been said of Shell that the 'organisation is like one of its super-tankers; once the corporation's course is set it is difficult to stop or turn about' (Gurdon 1995). To appreciate how decisions are made in Shell it is important to consider its 'corporate culture'. The global nature of Shell's business is indicated by its £4 billion income in 1995. It is Europe's largest company and has a history going back to 1907. The Dutch own 60 per cent of the company assets and the UK branch the rest.

The company has a devolved, fragmented and autonomous structure, with central control in the hands of four directors – two in Holland and two in the UK. This structure posed particular problems for Shell during the crisis. At times it was clear that certain parts of the organisation, mainly in Holland and Germany, felt that they had not been adequately briefed and consulted by Shell UK.

In organisational and public relations terms this culture has important consequences too. The decision to decommission Brent Spar at sea was made by Shell UK on behalf of its exploration and production business, Shell Expro. It took a legalistic and technical view of the problem and was accused of hiding behind official procedures and scientific evidence. It failed to scan its own environment in political and ethical terms, remaining inward-looking and mistrustful of a more open PR approach.

### *The organisational context: Greenpeace and the politics of protest*

It is also important to consider the nature of the other main player in this policy arena, Greenpeace. It also has a global organisation. Greenpeace is itself big business, with a global income of £131 million, with reserves of £72 million; it employs 1,000 people, with 30 worldwide offices and 411,000 supporters in the UK and over 3 million worldwide. Brent Spar provided the opportunity for the organisation to reinvolve and motivate its flagging membership. Greenpeace tactics, such as lobbying, public relations with the Greenpeace brand, advertising, protests, boycotts and disciplined direct action were organised by a fairly small number of professional activists at the top of the organisation. For example, one innovative Greenpeace slogan stated, 'If you come back as a whale, you'll be glad you put Greenpeace in your will.'

Another reason why Brent Spar was important to Greenpeace was that for a number of years grassroots activists had thought the leadership had become too professional and lobbyist rather than favouring direct action. The occupation of the Brent Spar platform and the counter-action of Shell in removing protesters gave a fillip to the rank and file and allowed the organisation to reclaim much of its grassroots credibility.

### Crisis politics: policy in reverse

Important national newspapers pointed to Brent Spar as an illustration of 'This crisis-prone Prime Minister' (*Daily Mail* headline, 22 June 1995) and referred to 'This Shell-shocked Prime Minister' ('Shell U-turn Sinks Major', *Daily Mail*, 21 June 1995). This policy controversy came at a politically sensitive time for the British prime minister, given the parliamentary divisions within the Conservative Party over Europe and its general unpopularity because of the most prolonged economic recession in Britain since 1945.

The policy reversals on this minor area of policy nevertheless had major ramifications for the prime minister. The Brent Spar policy decision brought this to the fore. Questions were asked about a government in crisis, and specifically about why ministers took such a high profile in defending their original decision. Also, questions were asked as to why Britain seemed to have fallen out with the German government on the issue. Above all, Brent Spar was interpreted by the media as a public humiliation, the cost of which the British taxpayer would have to meet.

Ultimately, Shell reacted to public opinion, a carefully orchestrated PR campaign, European pressure and market signals, whereas the government found itself unable to back down.

## Conclusion

At the beginning of this chapter the point was made that a study of the process of policy-making can tell us a great deal about the way in which different political systems operate. This chapter has attempted to show why the study of policy has become an expanding field within political analysis, and why the relationship between the policy process and the state is important. We have looked at decision-making, and the think points asked you to try to apply some of these different theories to particular policies enacted in your own political systems. Finally, the case study on the decision made about Brent Spar highlighted the complexity of even a relatively small decision and showed how such an issue can involve a wide web of interested groups and stakeholders.

With a single case study like this it is always difficult to generalise about political relationships. However, it does help us try to ground some aspects of these decision-making theories and it is possible to draw some general conclusions about the need for a policy approach in political analysis.

Clearly the main reason why the original decision (however rational) was overturned was that it was so strongly challenged. There were multiple goals involved, as Simon's (1957) notion of bounded rationality would suggest. Green issues, goals related to acceptability to public opinion and media interpretations all combined to make this a much more complex and difficult issue. Shell UK executives freely admitted that they had underestimated the more 'emotive' issues. 'We underestimated the objectives related to hearts and minds' was one such response (Chris Fay, Chairman of Shell UK, quoted in *The Battle of Brent Spar*, BBC TV, 3 September 1995).

The Brent Spar issue also illustrates the close relationship which exists between corporate interests and governments. This single decision was made as part of a longstanding and ongoing relationship between Shell UK, the oil industry in general and the UK government. The substance and form of the Brent Spar decision are clearly the product of organisational factors. The administrative procedures and working relationships of government departments, and the organisational cultures of Shell and Greenpeace were major determinants of how and why such decisions were made.

The Brent Spar case also indicates the importance of the relationship between ideology and belief systems and the policy process. Clearly, what interested parties felt 'ought' to be the case very much determined the nature of the evidence and tactics they used. Ends tended to justify means on both sides of the argument. Greenpeace had finally to admit that it had made important errors in its calculations of data on which its evidence was based. However, winning the argument over implementing the Brent Spar decision was seen as a priority.

Sabatier's (1987) model attempts to integrate several features of these other theories of decision-making. Sabatier developed his model through the examination of a specific area of American public policy, although it can be generally applied in the Brent Spar context. Coalitions clearly did emerge, including Shell UK/British government, Greenpeace/green groups and European governments/European Union. Other coalitions might include the media, church groups and consumer groups. There was also some policy brokering taking place. Shell Germany and Dutch Shell headquarters acted as brokers in recognising the political need for reversing the decision and then selling the idea to their British subsidiary. The relatively stable parameters of the corporate relationship between Shell UK and the British government were thrown into some disarray by external events related to the impact of the Brent Spar decision and the implementation process. These constraints and the coalition battle fought out in the media, inside Shell and within the decision-making process of the EU transformed the nature of the policy itself.

Politics is essentially a clash between competing interests. In this case study of Brent Spar, the essence of politics can be understood through an analysis of how policy was made and its relationship to the policy that was finally implemented.

## Further reading

Easton, D. (1965), *A Systems Analysis of Political Life*, New York: Wiley. A very prominent and influential systems approach, often cited as the foundation for further studies of policy-making.

Greenaway, J., Smith, S. and Street, J. (1992) *Deciding Factors in British*

*Politics*, London: Routledge. A useful text which uses a range of case studies to demonstrate how theories of decision-making can be applied.

Heclo, H. (1972) 'Review Article: Policy Analysis', *British Journal of Political Science* 2. A wide-ranging and influential article setting out the boundaries of the policy studies discipline.

Janis, I. (1972) *Victims of Groupthink*, Boston: Houghton-Mifflin. An interesting work which applies ideas from the area of psychology to the policy-making process, the outcome of policy being explained in terms of decision-makers conforming to group pressures.

# PART 4    POLITICS BEYOND THE NATION-STATE

# 15 POLITICS ABOVE THE NATION-STATE

*Ben Rosamond*

# Politics above the nation-state

## Introduction

A glance at a map of the world shows that the globe is divided over virtually all of its surface into **nation-states**. When we draw mental maps of Europe, Africa or South America, we are inclined to think of the ways in which those continents are carved up into distinct national units called things like 'France', 'Nigeria' or 'Brazil'. The division of the world in this way is, of course, a fundamentally political phenomenon and major political upheavals such as the collapse of communism in Eastern Europe are symbolised (eventually) by the redrawing of maps as new countries emerge. But while the precise configuration of the world will change from time to time, there can be little doubt that the *idea* of the nation-state is the key organising principle of global politics. This suggests, as Benedict Anderson argues, that 'nationness is the most universally legitimate value in the political life of our time' (Anderson 1991: 3).

This legitimacy of the idea of nationhood manifests itself in two key ways. First, the actors who constitute the political world – 'ordinary' citizens as well as politicians and bureaucrats – almost always see themselves as in some way representative of or affiliated to a national identity. Politicians may go to the negotiating table in international bodies such as the United Nations or the European Union to defend their perceived national interest. In a cosmopolitan setting – say a tourist resort or a university – individuals are likely to identify themselves with phrases such as 'I am French' or 'I come from Nigeria'. It is not surprising to find such mindsets at work. To think in this way seems to be in tune with the natural order of things. This is a way of thinking about the world which is underpinned by very deep assumptions. In his book *Nationalism*, Elie Kedourie argues that it is generally supposed that 'humanity is naturally divided into nations, that nations are known by certain characteristics which can be ascertained, and that the only legitimate type of government is national self-government' (Kedourie 1966: 9).

Second, it is fair to say that nationhood is the primary way in which the world has been conceived through the lens of modern political analysis.

**Nation-state** The governmental and administrative apparatus of a bounded national territory. The term is often used as a synonym for 'country'. The most recent way in which human politics has been organised, and now thought by some to be under considerable threat.

B. Anderson (1991) *Imagined Communities*, London: Verso.

E. Kedourie (1966) *Nationalism*, London: Hutchinson.

**445**

If we consider theoretical concepts such as freedom, rights, justice, power and democracy, it is clear that these are usually understood as matters which are contested within nations. Indeed, 'the state' – that core concept at the heart of the study of politics – is more often than not seen as a national entity, hence the phrase 'nation-state'. 'Nationness' and 'stateness' are frequently thought of as virtual synonyms. This assumption is often reflected in the way in which politics is taught. University departments all over the world run courses which are called things like 'the Government and Politics of France' or 'British Politics' and which study institutions, policy-making and political behaviour within the confines of these bounded territories. The point is that the idea of the nation-state provides a powerful organising framework for understanding the way in which the world works politically, as well as socially and economically.

This chapter will attempt to show why the idea of the nation-state is so pervasive and reflects upon the debates within political science concerning the adequacy of nation-state-centric approaches to politics in a world which is undergoing rapid and far-reaching political change. It is a world which is characterised by a variety of international regimes and organisations; a world increasingly subject to what some might call 'global governance'. At the root of this analysis lies a simple yet critically important question: is the nation-state still of primary importance to the practice and the study of politics, or is politics 'above' the nation-state becoming more important?

## Nationhood and sovereignty

**Sovereignty** The idea of ultimate political authority. A body is fully sovereign if there is no higher or lower power. Sovereignty has been the basic ground rule for the conduct of the business of international relations. The widespread legitimacy of the idea of sovereign statehood has hindered the development of authoritative institutions above the nation-state.

Before it is possible to address these questions, we need to pay attention to the concept of **sovereignty**, which underpins the whole idea of nationhood. Few politicians have been as vociferous in their championing of sovereignty as Margaret Thatcher, the British Conservative prime minister of 1979–90. In her memoirs she writes about the dealings of her government with the European Community (now the European Union) and explains her fear that a more fully integrated 'Europe' would pose a severe threat to some cherished principles:

> Not only were . . . nations functioning democracies, but they also represented intractable political realities which it would be folly to seek to override or suppress in favour of a wider but as yet theoretical European nationhood.
>
> (Thatcher 1993: 743)

In her famous speech to the College of Europe in Bruges in 1988, Thatcher used the following formulation:

> We have not successfully rolled back the frontiers of the state in Britain only to see them reimposed at a European level, with a European superstate exercising a new dominance from Brussels.
>
> (cited in Thatcher 1993: 742–3)

Thatcher's primary complaint here is that the drift of EC policy is very much out of step with the professed anti-statism of her government. She fears the evolution of a powerful, interventionist state at the European level. An emergent European government would threaten to undermine much of what she sees as the Thatcherite achievement in the United Kingdom. But her comments also reveal a more principled objection to the evolution of *any* form of authority at a level above national government. While it is not explicitly mentioned in the two passages above, Thatcher is displaying considerable reverence for the idea of *national sovereignty* or the notion that ultimate authority ought to reside at the level of national government.

Sovereignty is one of the most written about political concepts. It is the subject of both philosophical discussion and political jousting of the sort illustrated above by Margaret Thatcher. Sovereignty is in essence about the power to make laws and the ability to rule effectively. The concept throws up the obvious connotation of rule by a monarch (a sovereign) who would be, as Foster puts it, 'invested with an authority which confers the force of the law upon whatever he wills' (Foster 1942: 165). This perspective of the all-powerful sovereign was given its most powerful theoretical justification by the English philosopher Thomas Hobbes in the seventeenth century. Hobbes's sovereign need not be a single person; what he is really advocating in *Leviathan* (1651) is that the state be invested with absolute power. Hobbes reasons that left to a situation of *individual* self-government, people would engage in the relentless pursuit of their own interests. This would lead to a perpetual power struggle, a 'warre of every one against every one' as Hobbes puts it. The only rational course is for individuals to surrender their rights to an authority which is able to act on their behalf as well as to make them keep to the various contracts and deals they may make with each other. The state must be sovereign so that its citizens are protected.

What we can take from Hobbes is the notion that sovereignty is deemed to be essential to the prosperity of the human race and that it ought to reside in public institutions. Indeed to speak of state sovereignty nowadays is to think about different configurations of institutions – legislatures, executives and judiciaries – which together wield political power.

Over whom is this power exercised? It is at this point that we must introduce the spatial aspect of sovereignty. In modern political discourse the word 'sovereignty' is usually used to denote the combination of *political power* and *territorial space*, where that territory is a nation. In other words, sovereignty is said to be an attribute of nation-states, where a country's governing institutions exercise power and control over their allotted domain. Sovereignty is normally understood as possessing two distinct aspects: internal and external. A state which possesses internal sovereignty is one which has the authority and ability to exercise command over its society. In this situation there are no alternative sites of authority *within* the nation. Externally, a state is sovereign if no higher body has authority over that state's assigned society.

The external dimension of sovereignty alerts us to the role played by sovereignty in the global order. If we think about it, the comment made by James that 'sovereignty is the ground rule of inter-state relations' (James 1984: 2) conveys a very profound truth about the political organisation of the world. The Treaty of Westphalia (1648) provided the first statement of the way in which the principle of sovereignty should order the international environment. Violation of the internal affairs of a country was defined as a breach of this nascent international law. Ever since, especially as the world – driven by the forces of nationalism outlined in Chapter 8 – has become divided into nation-states, the axiom of *sovereign statehood* has been the keystone of world politics. As empires have waned and major global conflicts have been resolved over the course of the twentieth century, so the idea of 'national self-determination' has been the aspiration (if not the reality) of global political organisation. For example, why did forces under the aegis of the United Nations go to war with Iraq in 1991? This is a contentious question. But it is worth remembering that the legitimacy in international law of the allies' action derived from the claim that by invading Kuwait in August 1990 Iraq had infringed the sovereign status of an independent nation-state.

Legitimate nations, it would appear, have a right to be sovereign. What constitutes a legitimate nation is, of course, an altogether more difficult issue. Ask anyone living in Catalonia, Northern Italy, Scotland, Quebec, Tibet or the Punjab (see also Chapter 12).

---

**THINK POINT**

- How sovereign is your country?
- We have seen that sovereignty is an extremely important organising principle in global politics. It provides theoretical justification for the idea of nationhood and legal support for the division of the world into national territorial units. Before we move on we need to reflect on the passages above by asking how *realistic* the principle of sovereignty is.
- Think about your own country. In the terms defined here is it sovereign both internally and externally?
- Write down a list of constraints which you think prevent countries from being sovereign in modern conditions?

---

## *Inter*-national politics

Much of the foregoing hints at something rather obvious but very important for the student of politics to bear in mind: politics is not simply those processes of conflict and collective decision-making which occur *within* nation-states. Events and procedures which are manifestly political take place at a higher level, particularly within formal and relatively informal institutions which bring together representatives of national governments.

Politics of this kind is not new. The practice of diplomacy in various forms – in particular the exchange of the envoys of sovereigns – is as old as politics itself. The same is true (of course) of war. The nineteenth-century military theorist Carl von Clausewitz famously wrote:

> [War] is only a branch of political activity . . . it is in no sense autonomous. It is of course well known that the only source of war is politics – the intercourse of governments and peoples; but it is apt to be assumed that war suspends that intercourse and replaces it by a wholly different condition, ruled by no law but its own. We maintain, on the contrary, that *war is simply a continuation of political intercourse, with the addition of other means.*
>
> (*On War*, 1832; cited in Luard 1992: 244; emphasis mine)

Indeed, we might go on to define diplomacy as the main political means by which states have sought to settle disputes and thereby avoid war. It is important to note that, like all legitimate political activity, diplomacy requires mutually recognised ground rules or norms. Therefore, before diplomacy – as a form of politics above the nation-state – can take place, all involved actors need to be conversant with and prepared to accept a set of common procedures.

So far we have sought to avoid using the word 'international' to denote such politics. This may seem curious at first, but it is worth bearing in mind that the term 'international' is suggestive of a particular set of *agents* who are most important in political processes above the nation-state (i.e. nation-states themselves). The word 'international' is a relatively recent invention. As the *Concise Oxford Dictionary* points out, the word is suggestive of activity 'existing, or carried on between different nations'. So to speak of 'international politics' or '**international relations**' is to project definitions of 'politics' on to the processes which occur between and among nation-states. Thus directed, it is easy to see that relations between national governments are the most visible form of international politics.

**International relations**
Formally, the conduct of politics among nation-states, but also the study of international political interaction, which has more recently begun to include the analysis of non-state as well as state actors and forces.

### The fall-out spreads: France and the Pacific

Does Paul Keating, the Australian prime minister, hate France? According to a pro-government French daily newspaper, Le Figaro, he has a 'fetishist hatred' of the country. In reality, he probably admires the French, to judge from his collection of French clocks. But in the quarrel over France's decision to resume the testing of nuclear weapons in its Pacific island of Mururoa in September, normal discourse between the two countries has been replaced by venom.

The Figaro's editor, Franz-Olivier Giesbert, an ally of the French president, Jacques Chirac, said Australia was attacking France over the tests to salve its conscience about the 'ethnic cleansing' of aborigines. Mr Keating's spokesman found the accusation 'offensive'. As it was, but no more so than an open letter to Mr Chirac from a church in Tahiti, in French Polynesia, that compared the tests to the deportation of French Jews in the second world war.

At a more sober level, New Zealand said on August 8th that it would seek an interim order at the International Court of Justice in the Hague to stop France from going ahead with the underground tests. Australia said it would support this challenge, although earlier it had said the action had little chance of success. Both countries launched actions against France at the court in 1973, when the French were conducting tests in the atmosphere at Mururoa. Those cases never moved to a conclusion, because Paris announced during the proceedings that from 1975 it would do its testing underground. Technically, New Zealand appears to be in a better position than Australia to revive its 1973 case, which covered nuclear contamination generally. Australia's action dealt specifically with atmospheric tests. Even so, Jim Bolger, New Zealand's prime minister, admits that his country's case is not a strong one. Strong or not, France said in 1974 that it would not recognise the international court's authority in the issue. New Zealand, though, is happy to take a stand, in line with its general anti-nuclear policy. In the 1980s it upset America by banning visits by nuclear-armed ships.

Trade and business ties between France and Australia have managed to survive the nuclear quarrel, but only just. An estimated 40,000 jobs in Australia are directly linked to trade in French goods and products. The Australian government has stood back from imposing economic sanctions and boycotts which could hurt Australians more than the French. But when the government barred a French company, Dassault, from bidding for a contract to supply jet trainers to the Australian air force, France said it would reconsider its imports of Australian coal and uranium.

Even though the uranium consignments to France are earmarked solely for electricity generation, they are causing Mr Keating's Labor Party government considerable embarrassment. The party's left wing and the Australian Council of Trade Unions have called for a halt to the exports. If that happened, France might even be pleased. Australia has a contract worth almost ADollars 80m (Dollars 60m) to supply uranium to France up to 2001. At present spot prices, France could replace its Australian supplies for half the cost.

(reprinted by permission of *The Economist*, 12 August 1995)

The example given here is typical of the sorts of engagement between governments that characterise the day-to-day practice of international politics. Notice also the vocabulary used to describe such politics. More often than not, we are told that the government of 'A' (or perhaps just 'A') does 'x' to advance its interests, thereby eliciting responses from governments of 'B', 'C' and 'D' which in turn derive from the interests of 'B', 'C' and 'D'. Disagreements and conflicts may occur, alliances may form and machinery for international conciliation may have to be used.

International society, then, is most frequently portrayed as the interaction of states, usually through the medium of governments. Yet, it is also necessary to attend to the array of non-state actors which are also present in the processes of global politics. These include international organisations of various sorts, such as the United Nations and the European Union (both discussed below), various transnational interest groups (for example, Greenpeace), as well as the groups located domestically which colour the perceptions and influence the choices of national governments. Thus, accounts of international politics which are concerned with the various actors involved are compelled to take account of the whole array of agents.

Of course, alternative theoretical perspectives tend to give weight to different actors in the processes of international politics. The close relative of political science, international relations, has been consumed by such debates. Broadly two schools of thought, realism and idealism (or liberalism), have vied for dominance in the discipline as the twentieth century has progressed (see Kegley 1995a).

The *realist* account of politics above the nation-state develops from a number of core assumptions:

1  The international system is *anarchic*, that is to say, there is no central authority capable of settling feuds.
2  The main actors in this anarchic system are nation-states, which are guided by the *rational* logic of their national interests.
3  These national interests are determined predominantly by a rational analysis of the state's place in the international system. They are much less likely to derive from domestic pressures on national governments.
4  States are engaged, then, in the rational pursuit of power and security, which induces a Hobbesian struggle for power at the international level: one state's quest for security may leave other states insecure.
5  Stability and the avoidance of war are not the consequence of the existence of international organisations or systems of international law, but the development of a *balance of power* either through the formation of alliances or through the sheer dominance of a single *hegemonic* power.

These core assumptions mean that scholars from the realist school depict the game of world politics as one in which there is little place for moral principles, ethics or idealism. In addition, the imperative of self-help in pursuit of security lends credence to the doctrine of sovereignty. Sovereign governments have, in theory at least, the capability to undertake those actions which are necessary for the advancement of national interests (see the key texts of realist international relations, particularly Morgenthau 1985 and Waltz 1979). Such thoughts are projections of realist views of human nature which, as Kegley suggests, see people as essentially 'sinful and wicked . . . no sins are more prevalent, inexorable or dangerous than are their instinctive lust for power and their desire to dominate others' (Kegley 1995b: 5).

The *idealist/liberal* version of international politics is rooted in an alternative set of propositions:

1  Human nature does not necessarily conform to the pessimistic scenario offered by realists. People are capable of acts motivated by altruism as well as those motivated by the pursuit of power.
2  Much that is 'bad' about the way people (and states) behave is a consequence of the way in which institutions are structured.
3  International conflict and war, then, are not the inevitable consequences of rational, selfishly motivated power politics, but of the structural condition of 'anarchy'.
4  The route to stability and peace in the world consists in the construction of institutions, laws and frameworks of cooperation which are designed to eliminate the condition of anarchy.

C. Kegley (ed.) (1995) *Controversies in International Relations Theory: Realism and the Neoliberal Challenge*, New York: St Martin's Press.

H. J. Morgenthau (1985) *Politics Among Nations: The Struggle for Power and Peace*, 6th edn, New York: Knopf.

K. W. Waltz (1979) *Theory of International Politics*, Reading, Mass.: Addison Wesley.

5  States are by no means the only key actors in world politics. A variety of non-state actors partake in the international political game, which is not solely concerned with the quest for power and security but with a host of economic, political, social and ecological issues.

Unlike realism, which only really developed as a solid – though massively influential – account of world politics in the twentieth century, liberalism has a much longer and messier ancestry. As a consequence it has multiple strands, which emphasise different aspects of the liberal international vision. Generally though, as Zacher and Matthew argue:

> liberalism is committed to the steady, if uneven, expansion of human freedom through various political and economic strategies, such as democratization and market capitalism, ascertained through reason and, in many cases, enhanced by technology.
>
> (Zacher and Matthew 1995: 111)

Routes to international stability may include the construction of international organisations such as the European Union (EU). Indeed, early proponents of European integration were strong advocates of the view that the atomistic interaction of nation-states could be overcome by large-scale engineering. In his book *A Working Peace System* (originally published in 1943), David Mitrany (1966) outlined a strategy for developing a network of functional agencies which would lead to the inexorable intertwining of national polities. National divisions would cease to be important. Other liberals emphasise less direct routes to global stability, such as the pacifying impact of the spread of democracy across the globe and the complex interdependence wrought by the globalisation of economic activity.

D. Mitrany (1966) *A Working Peace System,* Chicago: Quandrangle Books.

---

**THINK POINT**
Which model of international politics?
- Realism and liberal idealism offer two powerful scripts for the depiction of the way in which politics above the nation-state operates.
- Select an issue in international affairs from a newspaper and produce a short summary of the ways in which each of these perspectives might explain the events that you have selected.

---

The models of realism and idealism outlined above, it should be understood, are ideal types which few modern scholars would accept in their pure form. As the study of international relations has developed, so the insights of both schools have been refined and there has been a good deal of productive cross-fertilisation. For example, many recent realist thinkers (in the guise of neo-realism) have tried to locate their state-centric approach within the boundaries provided by the existence of international institutions and regimes. States may continue to be the primary actors within international organisations, but those institutions (or structures) may revolve around norms and rules which either limit the range of possible state strategies or may even contribute to the reformulation of 'national interests'. Inter-state cooperation may also coax states away from the international politics of power, security and militarism.

## The end of sovereignty?

It is not just the character of inter-national politics that is thought to be changing. In recent years the idea that nation-states are able to be sovereign has been the subject of serious challenge. For increasing numbers of analysts, the study of a nation's politics in isolation from the broader global environment has become impossible. This is based on observations such as the view that a country's politics may be affected by political events in other nations. Obvious questions about the external sovereign status of nations are raised. A further observation is that forms of authority above the nation-state have come into being and, as we just noted, politics takes place in various forms *above* the nation-state. Again, the external dimension of sovereignty appears to be threatened by forces apparently beyond the control of national governments.

One of the principal political theorists of this transformation is David Held. He points out that

> there are disjunctures between the idea of the state as in principle capable of determining its own future, and the world economy, international organizations, regional and global institutions, international law and military alliances which operate to shape and constrain the options of individual nation-states.
>
> (Held 1991: 212–13)

D. Held (1991) 'Democracy and the Global System', in D. Held (ed.) *Political Theory Today*, Cambridge: Polity.

Much of this is bound up with the processes of globalisation which we will address in Chapter 16. Here we need to identify the kinds of things which threaten the external sovereignty of nation-states and which might also help our understanding of the creation of international and potentially supranational bodies which exercise authority above the nation-state. What we need to understand is the processes which 'alter the range and nature of decisions open to political decision makers within a delimited terrain' (Held 1991: 213).

The most obvious of these factors is the operation of the *world economy*. In the same way that we regularly speak of nation-states, so we also refer to national economies and assume that it is possible for governments to possess programmes of economic, monetary and industrial policy. The rules of the political game in democratic polities demand that parties vying for public office make promises about the ways in which they will, if elected, improve the economic fortunes of their respective nations. If governments preside over economic failure they risk electoral catastrophe. The built-in assumption here is that nation-states possess economic sovereignty; that the governments of Australia or the Netherlands are able to control the collective economic fate of Australians or the Dutch.

W. Hutton (1995) *The State We're In*, London: Cape.

However, with the increases in multinational production, the rise in the global flows of goods and services, advances in communications and information technology and the growth of global financial exchange, serious doubts have been raised about the ability of governments to maintain control over the economic determinants of their countries' well-being. These dilemmas are expressed well by the British economist Will Hutton:

> The world financial system is spinning out of control. The stock of cross-border lending now exceeds a quarter of the GDP [Gross Domestic Product] of all industrialised countries. International bank assets are double the value of world trade. The volume of business in the currency futures markets exceeds even that generated by daily trade flows. . . . Not even the US, German or Japanese governments have the financial clout to deal with the new volume of speculative flows – while many developing countries lack enough reserves to cover the purchase of eight weeks' imports.
>
> (*Financial Times*, 25 January 1995)

In addition there exist a range of *global institutions* which appear to promote a particular international economic orthodoxy and therefore allegedly force governments to pursue particular patterns of policy. The operation of the International Monetary Fund (IMF), which was founded in 1945, provides a good example. The IMF was designed with the aim of creating a more stable international economic order so that trade and economic development in the postwar world would not be threatened by major upheavals in international money markets. Member countries would be able to draw on the Fund's resources when confronted with domestic economic difficulties such as heavy balance of payments deficits and currency crises. The aim was to avoid the situation just before the Second World War when the world capitalist economy was hit by a series of tit-for-tat devaluations which had the effect of stultifying trade. However, there would be a price to pay for any country which drew on the IMF's reserves of international liquidity. The IMF was empowered by its founders to dictate policy restrictions on large borrowers, usually in the form of public expenditure cuts and deflationary packages. In effect, therefore, an international institution appeared to have the power to intervene directly in the economic policy-making of nation-states.

This fact has not been lost on politicians. Lawrence Harris quotes the exasperated response of the Finance Minister of West Bengal to the IMF loan given to India in 1981:

> Over the period during which the loan is to be disbursed, India's monetary and fiscal policies – including the size of the internal money supply, the structure of taxation and the quantum of budgeted deficits – would be formulated not in New Delhi, but in Washington; never mind the Industrial Policy Resolution and several declarations of national intent in the National Development Council, parliamentary resolutions and Five-Year Plan documents . . . , the Union Government has agreed, in conformity with the Fund's wishes, to accord special privileges to the private sector, including foreign investors, and to reverse the policy of import substitution and allow imports of even such banned items for which we have built adequate productive capacity in the country.
>
> (Ashok Mitra; cited in Harris 1984: 80)

Mitra's comments reveal a serious concern about the ability of the various layers of government in India to follow the policies which they have a legitimate right to pursue. He suggests that institutions such as the IMF are the tools of powerful – 'hegemonic' – countries which seek to impose their interests on the world. One interpretation of the rise of such constraints, then, is that they are the product of a rather pernicious form of power politics, where states still matter but the most (economically) powerful states matter most. Others would see the operation of the IMF as a symptom of the 'embedding' of a particular set of economic ideas in the global economy. The first interpretation offers a nation-state-centric version of the constraints on states, whereas the second emphasises the more abstract – but no less powerful – logic of the global capitalist economy.

Governments are further constrained by the systems of collective decision-making which have emerged in the context of *international organisations*. As Held (1991) notes, such organisations range from technical and uncontroversial bodies such as the World Meteorological Organization and the International Telecommunications Union to the likes of the United Nations (UN) where major debates about the propriety of states surrendering sovereignty are played out.

More is said below about two examples of international organisations, the European Union and the United Nations. But one notable side-effect of the growth of international organisations and institutions is the emergence of bodies of *international law* which set in place the principle that in some instances nation-states cease to be the highest form of authority for citizens. Of particular importance have been attempts to produce binding international commitments on the protection of human rights. Declarations such as the Council of Europe's European Convention for the Protection of Human Rights and Fundamental Freedoms (1950) are premised on the view that human rights *transcend* national boundaries and that the appropriate definitions of rights and freedoms are not the business of national authorities. The European Convention opens up the possibility that citizens can take their own governments to the European Court of Human Rights.

The appearance of international law raises fascinating questions about *transnational justice*. The trials of alleged Nazi war criminals at Nuremberg in 1945 and the subsequent prosecutions of similar suspects in Israel raise fascinating questions about the relationship between the state and its citizens, the right of national courts to prosecute citizens of other countries and, in the case of the two Israeli cases, the right of a nation-state to adjudicate on crimes which did not take place within its territory. As Held notes, the Nuremberg tribunals set down the principle that 'when *international rules* that protect basic humanitarian values are in conflict with *state laws*, every individual must transgress the state laws (except where there is no room for "moral choice")' (Held 1991: 220; emphasis in original).

A further incentive for governments to emerge from the cocoon of sovereignty concerns the perception amongst significant actors that genuine *global issues* have emerged. The recognition that the world was on the verge of a serious ecological crisis became a widespread component of mainstream political discourse in the mid-1980s. Politicians and opinion-formers alike began to propagate the view that the only way to address this issue was through some form of international cooperation at the very least. The appearance of issues such as ozone depletion, global warming, acid rain and pollution illustrates very effectively the juxtaposition of the doctrine of national sovereignty and the global ecological totality.

Two analysts of the diminution of sovereignty use the example of the accident in 1985 at the Chernobyl nuclear power plant in the Ukraine (then part of the USSR) to illustrate this point:

J. Camilleri and P. Falk (1992) *The End of Sovereignty? The Politics of a Shrinking and Fragmenting World*, Aldershot: Edward Elgar.

> As the fire raged and then smouldered, over some ten days vast quantities of radioactive gases poured into the air. The plume of radioactive gases swept across Scandinavia, then spread southwards over other parts of Europe, moving on to contaminate parts of England and then dispersing over an even wider area causing significant increases in radiation levels as far afield as Japan. A number of governments were forced to introduce emergency measures – from monitoring radiation levels to withdrawing certain foodstuffs or advising communities to change their diet. . . . What became clear from the first few days was that although national governments might construct nuclear reactors and even lay down various regulations intended to make their operation safer, the actual risk they posed extended beyond the control of any single state.
>
> (Camilleri and Falk 1992: 177)

Ecological issues highlight two very different ways of conceptualising the world which have vital political implications:

1 The view of the world as a single place, where actions in one part of the globe can have profound consequences in distant locations.
2 The view of the world as consisting of individual territorial units, each with its own legitimate jurisdiction.

The pervasive doctrine of sovereign statehood, argue Camilleri and Falk, poses a serious threat to a sustainable global ecology. Firstly, the idea of sovereignty tends to separate the state from the ecological consequences of its actions. Secondly, different regulatory standards in different countries will allow polluters to operate in areas where legislation is less rigid. Thirdly, adherence to the idea of nation-states as the primary makers of world politics ignores the forceful dynamics of global political and economic power which induce environmental damage. Finally, they argue that powerful allegiance to the doctrine of sovereignty blinds us to the cooperative procedures and institutional developments which are necessary for the resolution of environmental crises.

## A supranational state? The European Union

The European Union (EU) provides us with an excellent case study of the debates which rage over the principle of sovereignty as well as an instance of the development of institutions and norms which denote the evolution of political and decision-making processes above the nation-state. It possesses a mature set of institutions and is by some distance the most advanced project of **regional integration** in the world. More prosaic perhaps, but of no less importance, is the fact that EU-related matters are increasingly pivotal in the day-to-day political debates of its member states. The fractious debates within the British Conservative Party about the proper relationship between the UK and the EU provide an obvious illustrative example.

The EU would seem to be something special. Citizens of the member countries of the EU may from time to time be bewildered by the complex workings of the Commission and the Council of Ministers, but it is clear that the EU is not an obscure organisation to which national governments periodically send delegates to discuss obscure matters of the highest politics. Its very existence and the decisions which are made under its auspices are deeply embedded in the politics of member and even non-member states.

**Regional integration** The processes by which states in particular regions of the world come to bring together aspects of their economies and politics. There is much debate about the stimulus for such developments, with some seeing the cause as residing in the more or less sovereign preferences of states themselves. Others argue that integration occurs because of the operation of powerful dynamics beyond the control of nation-states.

### European integration since the second World War: a brief chronology

1947 Establishment of 'Benelux' customs union involving Belgium, Netherlands and Luxembourg. Beginning of 'Marshall Aid' (American financial assistance for the economic reconstruction of European countries.

1948 Organisation for European Economic Cooperation (OEEC) founded.

1949 Establishment of North Atlantic Treaty Organisation (NATO).
Ten countries sign statute of the Council of Europe.

1951 'Benelux' countries plus France, Germany and Italy sign the Treaty of Paris, forming the European Coal and Steel Community (ECSC), the product of the 'Schuman plan' of the previous year.

1954 Treaty for a European Defence Community rejected by French National Assembly.

1955  Messina conference convened by the ECSC 'Six' to discuss further European integration.

1957  Treaties of Rome signed by the 'Six' to establish the European Economic Community (EEC) and the European Atomic Energy Community (Euratom).

1960  Convention of the rival European Free Trade Association (EFTA) signed by Austria, Denmark, Norway, Portugal, Sweden, Switzerland and the UK.

1961  The UK, Denmark and Ireland begin negotiations to join the Community (Norway follows a year later).

1962  Agreement for framework for a Common Agricultural Policy (CAP).

1963  The French President Charles de Gaulle vetoes British membership.

1965  The three communities formally merge.

1966  French boycott of EC institutions because of feared supranational developments is resolved by the 'Luxembourg compromise' which enshrines the veto on vital national interests into EC practice.

1967  The four applicant states reapply for EC membership, but French opposition to UK membership prevents the renewal of negotiations.

1970  Membership negotiations begin with the 'four'.

1972  Norwegian referendum produces majority against EC membership.

1973  Denmark, Ireland and the UK formally join the EC.

1975  Meetings between heads of government in the EC are formalised with the first meeting of the European Council.

1979  Establishment of the European Monetary System (EMS). First direct elections to the European Parliament.

1981  Greece becomes the tenth member state of the EC.

1983  Agreement on Common Fisheries Policy (CFP).

1984  Establishment of free-trade area between EC and EFTA.

1985  Plans to complete the EC's internal market are approved in the form of the Single European Act (SEA), which vows to accomplish the task by the end of 1992.

1986  Portugal and Spain join the EC.

1987  SEA comes into force.

1989  'Delors report' offers three-stage plan for progress towards full economic and monetary union (EMU) within the Community. European Council accepts a Commission 'social charter' to complement the economic measures outlined in the SEA.

1990  Former German Democratic Republic becomes part of EC following German reunification.

1991  European Council meets at Maastricht in the Netherlands, producing the Treaty on European Union (TEU). The final TEU excludes a 'social chapter' (due to the insistence of the UK government) and contains opt-outs for Denmark and the UK on membership of a full EMU. The TEU creates a European Union based on three 'pillars': the European Communities, Common Foreign and Security Policy, and Co-operation in Justice and Home Affairs.

1992  Narrow rejection of TEU in Danish ratification referendum.

1993  Second Danish referendum produces majority for ratifying the TEU.

1994  Norwegian referendum rejects EU membership.

1995  Austria, Finland and Sweden joint the EU.

The space available here does not allow for a detailed discussion of the workings and scope of the EU (for which see in particular Nugent 1994). Our job here is to explore the Union as a case study of the operation of politics above the nation-state. With that brief, several questions come to mind:

- What is European integration and why has it taken place?
- Do the factors which account for the genesis of what we now know as the EU still explain the Union's dynamism?
- To what extent have particular/unique patterns of politics evolved within the EU's institutions?
- Is the EU emerging as a new form of government/state?
- Does the development of the EU demonstrate the decline of the nation-state as the key unit/focus of political activity in the contemporary world?

N. Nugent (1994) *The Government and Politics of the European Union*, 3rd edn, Basingstoke: Macmillan.

## European integration

There is no easy definition of 'integration'. The word is used frequently by politicians, academics and journalists alike, and is usually used as a synonym for what goes on within the European Union. Political scientists should be more interested in establishing a general definition of integration. This would allow judgements to be made about the extent to which 'Europe' has undergone a process of integration and it would be a basic requirement for the meaningful comparison of instances of integration in different times and/or places.

When political scientists speak of international integration, they have in mind something along the lines suggested by Reginald Harrison:

> Integration is evidently a process of political, but also far-reaching, social transformation. The integration process . . . may be . . . defined . . . as the attainment within an area of the bonds of political community: of central institutions with binding decision making powers and methods of control determining the allocation of values at the regional level and also of adequate complementary consensus-formation mechanisms.
>
> (Harrison 1974: 14)

Integration, in this sense, appears to be about the manufacture of the attributes of a political system from two or more previously separate systems. This involves both the creation of common institutions and the development of adequate levels of public support to ensure that the new system is endowed with legitimacy. It might be argued, then, that international integration is analogous to the process of nation-building, but on a much grander scale.

However, such definitions presuppose a particular destination for a successfully 'integrated' European Union. Is it really the case that an integrated Europe will be one which possesses a set of institutions which give it the attributes of statehood? Other scholars have different views on what integration entails. Economists tend to understand integration as a five-stage

W. Wallace (1991) 'Introduction: The Dynamics of European Integration', in W. Wallace (ed.) *The Dynamics of European Integration*, London: Pinter/RIIA.

process whereby separate economies gradually gather the characteristics of a single economy (Table 15.1). Others prefer to see integration as a cultural phenomenon: the development of intensive patterns of interaction amongst previously separate peoples through forms of communication (e.g. computer technologies, tourism). This has led some to offer yet more generic definitions of integration. William Wallace describes it as 'the creation and maintenance of intense and diversified patterns of interaction among previously autonomous units' (Wallace, 1991: 9)

Wallace goes on to make an important distinction between *formal* and *informal* integration. Formal integration is the deliberate creation by governments in concert of institutions, norms and procedures via treaties, regulations and decisions, whereas informal integration consists in the growth of networks of interaction without the conscious intervention of governments. Again we find ourselves in a debate about the role to be attributed to the agency of the nation-state in the development of politics above the nation-state. Are major advances in European integration to be understood as the result of member states pursuing their national interests? Or does the very existence of regional integration denote the weakening of the power of nation-states?

In any case, we need to be cautious about whether we understand integration as a *process* (or a set of processes) or as a particular *outcome* or end-point. Again, different perspectives emphasise different key variables

*Table 15.1* Stages of economic integration

| Stage | Title | Attributes |
|---|---|---|
| 1 | Free-Trade Area | Removal of tariffs between two or more economies |
| 2 | Customs Union | Imposition of common external tariff by all members of the free trade area |
| 3 | Common Market | Removal of all barriers to the free movement of goods, services and persons amongst member states |
| 4 | Economic and Monetary Union | Development of a single currency and a common monetary authority |
| 5 | Total Economic Integration | Single economic policies; attributes of a single economy |

*Table 15.2* Alternative accounts of European integration

Integration as process

(a) Political variables
   *Key issues:* which are the main agents of integration, nation-states or non-state actors such as the European Commission or transnational interest groups?

(b) Structural stimuli
   *Key issues:* what external economic, social and technological variables drive the integration process? Do they work independently of governments, or do they act as agenda-setters for intergovernmental business?

Integration as outcome

(a) State models
   *Alternatives:* a centralised, authoritative set of institutions at the European level; a European 'federal' system, with a layering of power between Europe, nation and sub-national region; a supranational network involving the interaction of state and non-state actors.

(b) Community models
   *Alternatives:* a European security community; a European socio-psychological community; the enhanced interaction of the peoples of Europe.

*Source:* adapted from Pentland (1973)

involved in the processes of integration and depict very different integration outcomes. When we examine an organisation like the EU, it is as well to be conversant with the various alternative accounts of what drives it and where it might be going. Some of these are summarised in Table 15.2.

### The origins of the EU

Projects of one sort or another to 'unify' Europe are certainly not new (den Boer 1995; Heater 1993), and projects for something analogous to a 'united states of Europe' were especially prevalent in the period after the First World War (Bugge 1995). Such ideas were also part of the political *zeitgeist* of the late 1940s, as several major European politicians were persuaded of the need for some form of European unification as a means to prevent further conflict between nations on European soil. So while ideas were important, they were given credence by the security dilemmas which confronted European politicians and publics in the aftermath of the Second World War. Two particular security questions were of importance. Firstly, it was felt that the avoidance of war on the European continent would turn on the resolution of the historical antagonism between France and Germany. This was the rationale behind the so-called Schuman Plan of 1950 (named after the French Foreign Minister Robert Schuman), which led to the creation among six European states of the European Coal and Steel Community (ECSC) in 1951. The ECSC was based on a very deliberate political strategy. Its first act would be the creation of a common market in commodities such as coal, steel and iron ore. This would be presided over by newly created *supranational* institutions. By bringing together these crucial economic sectors, it was hoped that three things would occur:

1 The creation of a state of interdependence between member countries, thereby reducing the propensity for conflict between them.

2 The initiation of an integrative logic that would compel other economic sectors to be drawn into the process.

3 The consolidation of central institutions which would emerge as the most important focal points of political loyalty in the new community.

The key lesson here is that the integration of economies was an element in a much longer-term political strategy. To render countries economically interdependent was to lay the basis for their eventual political union.

The second main security concern was the development of the Cold War. The postwar political map of Europe was characterised by a clear east–west division separated by what Winston Churchill memorably called the 'Iron Curtain'. The division of Europe into the communist east under the influence of the USSR and the liberal democratic west was consolidated by developments such as the US government's Marshall Aid programme to non-communist European states, which began in 1948, and the foundation of the North Atlantic Treaty Organisation (NATO) in 1949. This meant that Western European states had acquired a rationale for closer links beyond their geographical proximity.

The influence of the United States as a 'hegemonic power' in the Western world was clear from the vantage point of postwar security dilemmas. It could also be argued that US influence was decisive in the drive towards the creation of an integrated European economic region. After all, the US had emerged from the war with its domestic economy intact and a global economic regime (the Bretton Woods system) which was conducive to American dominance of world trade. Western Europe could then be understood as one of the US's most viable markets, but one which required urgent reconstruction. This could be galvanised through integration.

---

**THINK POINT**

- Reread the above section on 'The origins of the EU (pp. 461–2). How would thinkers from the realist and liberal-idealist schools understand the development of the institutions of European integration in the immediate postwar years?
- Do you think that this section has been written in the language of either perspective?

---

The foregoing should be understood as more than a history lesson. The beginnings of postwar integration are studied so intensively precisely because they are thought to hold important lessons for the analysis of the contemporary situation. Two particular concerns come to mind. Firstly, there is the matter of whether the dynamics which initiated the EU can still explain its maintenance and its trajectory. After all, the 'geopolitics' of Europe have changed considerably in recent years. The security condition which some say was the primary force behind integration has been transformed by the collapse of communist regimes in the USSR and Central and Eastern

Europe. This poses a whole series of questions, most notably whether deeper economic integration is any longer possible in the context of a host of potential new members of the EU with diverse histories and disparate levels of economic development.

The second matter raises comparative issues. The EU is a longstanding example of regional integration. Can we generalise from the European experience to develop a general understanding of the conditions for and the dynamics of regional integration elsewhere in the world? In particular, analysts are drawn to consider whether fruitful comparisons can be made between the EU and developing instances of regionalism elsewhere in the global political economy such as the North American Free Trade Agreement (NAFTA) and the Asia Pacific Economic Co-operation Forum (APEC) (Higgott 1995). The sceptical view is that such comparison is pointless because the European experience is so particular, especially in terms of the institutions and patterns of politics which have been built on top of various forms of economic cooperation. It is these to which we now turn.

## Patterns of politics

The set of institutions which characterise the modern EU bear a marked resemblance to those which were designed for the six-member ECSC in 1951. The main institutions of the EU are described in Table 15.3.

It is difficult to do justice to the complexities of the EU system here, but it is worth making a few observations about the development of political processes within this environment. The central issue from the point of view of this chapter is whether the operation and interaction of these institutions has produced a new form of politics above the nation-state. The growth of the political science of European integration in recent years has certainly been founded on the idea that the EU is best understood as a functioning political system with patterns of political exchange and networks of interests. The opposing view incorporates the argument that the EU remains above all an experiment in international politics. At the heart of this polarity is once again the question of the significance of the nation-state as an actor.

The **intergovernmentalist** position can be summed up as follows. In terms of formal decision-making the Council of Ministers is still the final port of call for any piece of significant EU legislation. That means that national governments must be the pivotal actors in the policy process. Moreover, the EU has developed a number of institutions which consolidate the power of member states. Council agendas are prepared by national officials in the Committee of Permanent Representatives (COREPER), which essentially intercepts and moulds Commission initiatives. The European Council now appears to guide the direction of EU activity and represents a direct challenge to the agenda-setting powers of the Commission. An influential school of thought argues that integration progresses only when national governments will it. The American scholar Andrew Moravcsik (1991, 1993) has produced work which suggests that

K. Middlemass (1995) *Orchestrating Europe: the Informal Politics of the European Union, 1973–1995*, London: HarperCollins.

H. Wallace and W. Wallace (eds) (1996) *Policy-Making in the European Union*, Oxford: Oxford University Press.

**Intergovernmentalism** The view which argues that the development of international institutions and regimes tends to be shaped by the actions of and convergences among nation-state actors.

A. Moravcsik (1991) 'Negotiating the Single European Act', in R. O. Keohane and S. Hoffmann (eds) *The New European Community: Decisionmaking and Institutional Change*, Boulder, Col.: Westview.

*Table 15.3* Institutions of the European Union

*The European Commission*
Consists, at the highest level, of 20 Commissioners appointed by national governments, but who are sworn to pursue European rather than national interests. Each is allocated one or more policy portfolios. Beneath this level sit a series of Directorates General (DGs), each charged with a particular area of policy (for example DGVI deals with agriculture). Each DG is staffed by officials with particular consultative and bureaucratic functions. The Commission has a number of roles in the EU system. It is the formal initiator of policy in areas where the EU has competence to legislate (it is expected to consult widely with interested parties before doing this); it is responsible in some areas for monitoring the extent to which EU directives and regulations have been implemented in the member states; it represents the EU externally, particularly in international economic negotiations.

*The Council of Ministers*
Traditionally, while the Commission is said to propose legislation, the Council of Ministers (or the Council) decides. The Council consists of representatives of the member state governments of the EU. The relevant ministers attend according to the policy area under discussion. Meetings are chaired by a member state government and this presidency rotates in six-month cycles. The agenda for Council meetings is prepared by a Brussels-based Committee of Permanent Representatives (COREPER) which consists of nationally appointed officials.

*The European Council*
Began as rather *ad hoc* summit meetings of heads of state and governments of the member states in the late 1960s, but is now formally recognised as a formal institution of the EU. The European Council, which now meets twice a year, has evolved an agenda-setting forum for the EU.

*The European Parliament*
The only body in the EU system that is directly elected. Elections take place every five years; the method of election varies from member state to member state. Seats are allocated roughly in accordance with population size. While Members of the European Parliament (MEPs) are usually elected on conventional national party platforms, they organise in transnational party groups in the Parliament itself. The Parliament's formal powers are much weaker than those of any national legislature, although revisions to the founding treaties have taken the institution well beyond its original role as an advisory body. It now has powers of co-decision with the Council in some instances. The Parliament has acquired a reputation as a lobbyist for deeper integration and substantial institutional reform.

*The European Court of Justice*
Not to be confused with the European Court of Human Rights, the ECJ consists of judges and advocates-general appointed by the member states. The ECJ is charged with the interpretation and enforcement of the ever-growing body of law made within the EU's policy process, the *acquis communautaire*. The ECJ is significant for the judgements that it makes about the application and interpretation of European law, as well as for the principles it has laid down more generally about the primacy of the *acquis* over national law.

major advances in integration have reflected the convergence of the national interests of the most powerful member states. His famous analysis of the negotiation of the Single European Act of 1987 (which set in motion the completion of the Community's single market) suggests that the idea of market liberalisation had come to dominate the policy agendas of the most powerful member-state governments (notably West Germany, France and the UK). In effect, what was visible was not the unfolding of some integrative logic sponsored by the European Commission, but the convergence of national interests.

The case against, which we might call the **supranationalist** argument, would tend to emphasise a series of formal developments which mean that national governments do not have decisive control in the EU system. In particular, the growth of qualified majority voting in the Council appears to be a direct challenge to the idea that states can remain sovereign in the EU system. The occurrence of majority voting in the key decision-making forum suggests that national interests might be overridden. The growth of the powers of the European Parliament following recent treaty revisions might be taken as the development of a significant hindrance to the operation of an EU system based predominantly on the negotiation and exchange of national interests.

To many the EU appears to be a paradigm of 'complex' or 'multi-level' policy-making. The complexity is enhanced by two factors. Firstly, the Treaty on European Union (the Maastricht Treaty of 1992) specifies the appropriate formal policy procedure for each area of policy in which the Union has competence. This means that the formal decision-making patterns and the involvement of institutions differ from policy sector to policy sector. Secondly, the EU policy process is – like all policy processes – composed of a host of formal and informal actors. The key difference is that these actors are located at a variety of levels (the global, the European, the national and the sub-national). To map and to analyse the interaction of these interests and to ascertain the central issues of interest articulation, influence and power is a fiendishly difficult process for the interested political scientist. Let us take the example of interest groups which, as we saw in Chapter 13, are often taken to be central to the understanding of the political process. Conventionally, interest groups focus their activity on national governments. The emergence of a European level of authority raises new strategic dilemmas. Should interests continue to lobby national governments in the hope that they will be able to influence positions which are taken at the European negotiating table? Or should they seek to alter the focus of their lobbying activity from national institutions to European institutions? (And if so, which ones?) Or should they seek to combine with other national interests in cognate areas and form transnational interest groups?

The EU may provide a good case study for political scientists of the role of institutions. When we speak of institutions we are referring not only to formal bodies such as the European Commission, but also to patterns of rules, norms and mutual expectations that may develop in particular settings. Such factors may transform the behaviour of actors located in these institutional settings. So, we could still argue that the EU is a predominantly intergovernmental organisation, but it might well be that the nature of that intergovernmentalism is bounded by institutional norms.

**Supranationalism** The development of executive and binding authority at levels higher than the nation-state. The term is used by some to describe complex networks of interaction among policy actors in international relations.

### European integration and the end of the nation-state?

One of the most frequently voiced concerns in contemporary European politics is the idea that the EU is becoming a kind of 'superstate' which is draining the lifeblood from the European nation-states via its relentless accumulation of powers (see, for example, the comments of Margaret Thatcher quoted above, p. 446). This is a fiendishly complicated question to address.

The work of the international relations scholar John Ruggie (1993) suggests that to approach European integration as a matter of whether or not the EU will become a 'state' (and thereby deprive national administrations of their 'sovereignty') sets up a false debate. Just because the EU does not achieve the common attributes of nation-statehood, this does not mean that it has 'failed' as a project of integration. The common mistake highlighted by Ruggie is that we assume that any evolving form of political authority above the nation-state must assume the characteristics of the state's national institutional form. The fact that debates about the EU are often framed in this manner demonstrates again the alluring power of sovereignty as a 'social episteme' which shapes the imagination of citizens and politicians alike about the possible forms of political community.

Other writers have suggested that the fears of losing sovereignty to the EU are quite misplaced. The economic historian Alan Milward has argued in a series of books (particularly Milward 1992) that the EU is best understood as a project to *rescue* the European nation-state. Milward's idea is that modern nation-states are held together not by the symbols of nationhood or by coercion, but by the successful implementation of national policy programmes designed to provide material benefits to particular groups within the national territory. The experience of the twentieth century, argues Milward, demonstrated to states that forms of international cooperation would be necessary if national policy programmes were to continue to deliver the necessary rewards. Integration, therefore, is a rational response to the circumstances of a group of Western European states in the immediate aftermath of the Second World War. They chose to cede a limited amount of sovereignty so that they would remain cohesive entities which continued to attract the loyalties of their citizens.

Three elements of the relationship between European integration and national governments are worthy of mention:

1 Governments may use the development of a European-level politics to insulate themselves from the pressures of national politics. If states are understood to be entities which seek policy-making autonomy, then the relative lack of accountability afforded by the EU system may be a means by which national governments can liberate themselves from constraints from below.

2 On the other hand governments are confronted with a seemingly insoluble dilemma: the recognition of the need for integration as a means to achieve prosperity versus the continued expectation that

J. G. Ruggie (1993) 'Territoriality and Beyond: Problematizing Modernity in International Relations', *International Organization* 47(1),

A. S. Milward (1992) *The European Rescue of the Nation State*, London: Routledge.

governments should be autonomous and sovereign. As a result, 'national political leaders have found themselves caught between electoral fears of lost autonomy and electoral demands for the economic growth that only further integration can provide' (Wallace 1994: 8).

3 If integration is seen as a threat to nationhood from above, then it should also be said that the territorial integrity of nation-states is increasingly being interrogated from below by sub-national groupings seeking autonomy and independence. Forces such as North Italian, Catalan and Scottish nationalism have placed the question of the legitimacy of existing systems of territorial rule squarely on the respective political agendas of Italy, Spain and the UK. Also, in each of these cases movements for sub-national independence have tended to articulate their demands within the context of a wider integrated Europe. For some, therefore, an integrated 'Europe of the regions', with an associated weakening of the power of national governments, is a tantalising political vision.

## Global governance? The United Nations

While it may be criticised for lack of effectiveness, there can be no ignoring the United Nations (UN). A glance at any news bulletin or any newspaper provides an instant demonstration of the significance of the UN in world affairs. In particular, the UN is associated with global security and the prevention of war, or with 'peacekeeping', to use the UN's own parlance. What also renders the UN significant is the near universality of its membership. It is important because virtually every nation-state on the globe is part of the 'United Nations system'. The world environment is characterised by the existence of a multitude of nominally sovereign nation-states, virtually all of whom subscribe to the principles laid down in the UN Charter. This suggests that the UN has a legitimacy like no other body; it lays down and seeks to enforce a set of precepts which govern international politics. As one pair of commentators put it, 'the political, economic, social, ideological and cultural structures of the post-1945 world were embedded in the UN system as constitutive principles and underlying ideas' (Krause and Knight 1995: 9).

### The origins of the UN

The United Nations Organisation emerged in the aftermath of the Second World War as a body designed to consolidate world peace and to promote stable underlying socio-economic conditions. Its immediate origins lie in a series of agreements made between the Allied Powers during the war with a view to envisioning the shape of the postwar international order. The UN Charter was signed by some fifty countries at San Francisco in June 1945.

The UN is not the only attempt to secure global peace and security in the twentieth century. Most analysts understand the UN to be the offspring of the ill-fated League of Nations, which appeared in 1920 as a response to the decimation wrought by the 'Great War' of 1914–18. The League's aims were the achievement of international peace and security and the promotion of international cooperation. The Covenant establishing the League (which was part of the Treaty of Versailles) created a set of institutions which would seek to safeguard the political independence and territory of nation-states from external aggressors. In addition, the Covenant provided for sanctions to be taken against states which resorted to war unlawfully and for procedures designed to resolve disputes between countries peacefully. The explanation of the League's failure is the subject of much historical conjecture, but it failed to acquire the legitimacy that an organisation with its purposes clearly needed, not least from its own members (see Walters 1952).

Scholarship on the League and the UN also recognises medium- and long-term historical antecedents to those organisations. Chadwick F. Alger (1995) suggests that we need to go beyond the founding conferences of the UN and the League to understand the origins of their momentum. For instance, the main organ of the League of Nations, the Council, represented a direct evolution of the Concert of Europe which had been initiated by the Congress of Vienna (1815). Procedures for undertaking the peaceful resolution of conflicts had been agreed at two conferences held in the Hague in the late nineteenth and early twentieth centuries. Thirdly, the idea that humanity was faced with common problems which transcended national boundaries had found institutional expression in a number of 'public international unions' dating from the nineteenth century. Finally, the elimination of war had been a longstanding project of political philosophers and legal scholars. A steady stream of so-called 'systems of universal peace' had been produced since the fourteenth century (see Luard 1992: 400–23).

### Features of the UN system

Article 1 of the UN Charter lists the purposes of the UN:

1 To maintain international peace and security, and to that end: to take effective collective measures for the prevention and removal of threats to the peace, and for the suppression of acts of aggression or other breaches of the peace, and to bring about by peaceful means, and in conformity with the principles of justice and international law, adjustment or settlement of international disputes or situations which might lead to a breach of the peace.
2 To develop friendly relations among nations based upon respect for the principle of equal rights and self-determination of peoples, and to take other appropriate measures to strengthen universal peace.
3 To achieve international co-operation in solving international problems of an economic, social, cultural or humanitarian character, and in promoting and encouraging respect for human rights and for fundamental freedoms for all with distinction as to race, sex, language, or religion.
4 To be a centre for harmonising the actions of nations in the attainment of these common ends.

(cited in Roberts and Kingsbury 1993: 500–1)

A. Roberts and B. Kingsbury (eds) (1993) *United Nations, Divided World: The UN's Role in International Relations* 2nd edn, Oxford: Oxford University Press.

In addition, the UN Charter established six 'principal organs', which are detailed in Table 15.4. Beyond the formal organs of the UN lies an impressive array of UN agencies which would appear to have arisen, according to Alger, as responses 'to the accelerating need for institutions for *human* governance' (Alger 1995 10). These are listed in Table 15.5.

It is worth reflecting on the values which the UN seeks to promote. In other words, what is the vision of global politics which the UN Charter propagates? First, and most notably, the UN seems to give rise to a paradox. An institution which seeks to establish a global form of authority is deeply bound up with a world system of sovereign states. The UN – as its very name suggests – is the product of the near-universal reach of the nation-state as a form of governance. The ideas of self-determination and sovereign statehood are aspects of that system and the UN could be read as an attempt to impose such values on a world characterised by the structures of anarchy. Second, the institutional framework of the UN, and in particular the

*Table 15.4* The institutions of the United Nations

The UN Charter established six 'principal organs'

*The General Assembly*
gathers together all of the UN's membership in plenary meetings. It is charged with approving the UN's budget and acts as a forum for international debate on a wide range of issue areas. It is empowered to set up international conferences and has a substantial committee structure like most parliaments.

*The Security Council*
is composed of fifteen member states of whom five (France, China, Russia, the United Kingdom and the United States) are permanent. Each of the permanent members has the power of veto. The remaining ten members are elected for two-year terms by the General Assembly. The Security Council is charged with responsibility for international peace and security and therefore attends to armed conflicts and international disputes. Its powers are wide-ranging and include the ability to call for military action on the UN's behalf. It also establishes the UN's peacekeeping forces, which are stationed in trouble spots around the globe.

*The Secretariat*
would appear to be the oil which allows the UN machine to run smoothly. It is headed by the Secretary-General, which over the years has become a pivotal post in world diplomacy.

*The International Court of Justice*
based in the Hague in the Netherlands, is able to issue binding decisions in cases where countries have consented to its jurisdiction.

*The Trusteeship Council*
is now more or less obsolete, but was intended to act as the UN body which oversaw the development of self-government in former colonial territories.

*The Economic and Social Council,*
as its name suggests, is responsible for overseeing the UN's work in the economic and social spheres. It consists of fifty-four states elected by the General Assembly.

*Table 15.5* UN agencies

*Created by and Reporting to the General Assembly*

Office of the UN Disaster Relief Coordinator (UNDRO)
Office of the UN High Commissioner for Refugees (UNHCR)
UN Centre for Human Settlements (Habitat)
UN Children's Fund (UNICEF)
UN Conference on Trade and Development (UNCTAD)
UN Development Fund for Women (UNIFEM)
UN Development Programme (UNDP)
UN Environment Programme (UNEP)
UN Population Fund (UNFPA)
UN Institute for Training and Research (UNITAR)
UN Relief and Works Agency for Palestine Refugees in the Near East (UNRWA)
UN University (UNU)
UN International Research and Training institute for the Advancement of Women (INSTRAW)
World Food Council (WFC)
World Food Programme (WFP)

*Specialised Agencies*

Food and Agriculture Organisation of the UN (FAO)
International Bank for Reconstruction and Development (IBRD) (World Bank)
International Civil Aviation Organisation (ICAO)
International Development Association (IDA)
International Finance Corporation (IFC)
International Fund for Agricultural Development (IFAD)
International Labour Organisation (ILO)
International Maritime Organisation (IMO)
International Monetary Fund (IMF)
International Telecommunications Union (ITU)
UN Educational, Scientific and Cultural Organisation (UNESCO)
UN Industrial Development Organisation (UNIDO)
Universal Postal Union (UPU)
World Health Organisation (WHO)
World Intellectual Property Organisation (WIPO)
World Meteorological Organisation (WMO)

*Other Autonomous Affiliated Organisations*

General Agreement of Tariffs and Trade (GATT)
International Atomic Energy Agency (IAEA)

*Source*: Alger (1995: 11)

operation of the Security Council, would seem to support the view that governance by the 'great powers' is legitimate. Third, the UN's activities in the security sphere also lend credence to the view that war can be a valid means of settling international disputes. The Charter is also a statement which espouses a Western liberal individualist understanding of 'human rights'. Fourthly, many agencies of the UN such as the IMF and the World Bank are clear institutional props of a global capitalist economic system. Finally, the proliferation of UN agencies in areas such as population control, arms limitation and environmental protection suggests that the UN is infected with the view that certain global issues are not amenable to resolution by a system of states located in an anarchic environment.

However, although this set of principles would appear to be enshrined in the various aspects of the UN system, they are all, without exception, the subject of furious debate within the UN (Krause and Knight 1995: 9). A good example is the concept of human rights, where complex legal argument and political expediency would seem to have created a formidable cocktail of disagreement (see Farer and Gaer 1993). Three kinds of argument seem to have been prevalent. First, the formulation of worldwide standards on human rights is contrasted with the right of sovereign states to do as they please within their own territorial boundaries. Second, there is an argument about the notion of human rights which ought to be adopted. What are often understood to be core human rights – freedom of speech, freedom of expression, freedom of association and so on – are often criticised as being Western conceptions. To impose such schemes on other culturally specific areas of the world is seen as an act of power. Third, different conceptions of human rights could be said to derive from different sorts of political framework. Early negotiations in the UN system about human rights revealed a cleavage between the preference of 'Western' countries' liberal freedoms and the social and economic rights favoured by members of the communist bloc.

Article 2(7) of the UN Charter prohibits the United Nations from intervening 'in matters which are essentially within the domestic jurisdiction of any state' (cited in Roberts and Kingsbury 1993: 501). This would seem to offer decisive support for the concept of sovereign statehood. Yet later sections of the Charter sanction a mediating and peacekeeping role for the UN, as well as allowing for the use of force and the imposition of mandatory sanctions. 'Peacekeeping' is defined by the UN Secretary-General Boutros Boutros-Ghali as:

> the deployment of a United Nations presence in the field, hitherto with the consent of all the parties concerned, normally involving United Nations and/or police personnel and frequently civilians as well. Peace-keeping is a technique that expands the possibilities for both the prevention of conflict and the making of peace.
>
> (Boutros-Ghali 1993: 475)

Recent years have seen a notable upturn in the peacekeeping role of the UN. Thirteen peacekeeping forces were deployed by the UN between 1945 and 1987; twenty-three new peacekeeping operations were created in the eight years after 1987. There are multiple explanations for this (Morphet 1993), but most commentators would attribute the greater success of the UN in this department to the demise of the Cold War and the consequent removal of superpower vetoes in the Security Council.

## Implications

All of the foregoing might lead us to the conclusion that the UN only works when the state system allows it to. In times of major superpower conflict, runs the argument, the UN is a prisoner of that hostility. However, this type of argument does rather suggest that the world system is a very static one. Many of the challenges to effective state sovereignty discussed earlier in this chapter have become apparent during the short fifty-year lifespan of the UN. It is also true that the UN has evolved significantly during this period, as global developments such as the Cold War and extensive and rapid decolonisation have unravelled. So while the principles of statehood have continued to define the basic ground rules of world politics, the global agenda has altered remarkably and the UN is intimately bound up with that agenda shift.

Indeed, as Krause and Knight argue, 'the UN system has . . . been an arena for competition between alternative "transformational" visions of world politics that are directed at changing the existing order' (Krause and Knight 1995: 13). In other words, the UN system has created the conditions for diverse forms of international politics to flourish. Its existence has created a real focal point for the activities of various non-governmental organisations in areas such as human rights and environmental protection. There is a danger perhaps of regarding the UN as a set of formal institutions which do things. This sort of argument, on the other hand, identifies the less tangible aspects of the UN system: mutual understanding between actors, which facilitates the operation of an embryonic global politics.

C. C. O'Brien and F. Topolski (1968) *The United Nations: Sacred Drama*, London: Hutchinson.

Conor Cruise O'Brien drew attention to the importance of mythology in the United Nations. What was significant, he argued, was not the fact that the UN at best muddled through and succeeded or failed according to the whims of the most powerful member states, but rather the role of the organisation as a repository of global myths and principles of *how things should be*. It was much less important that these principles were at variance with the way that things are.

The use of the concept of *governance* (the activity of government rather than the institutions which perform that activity) is helpful in understanding the UN system. It is perhaps better in the light of the discussion above to understand the UN as a project of global governance rather than as one of *global government*. The key here is to see the UN as an agreed arena for the resolution of common human problems without the formal creation of powerful institutions which supersede nation-states.

## Conclusion

Nation-states clearly still matter. They are the sources of authority with which most people readily identify; an international system of interacting sovereign states is an image which seems plausible and in tune with the practice of politics at the global level. But as this chapter has tried to show, there is a serious and growing debate about the possible obsolescence of the nation-state as the most effective way of ordering human relations. Confronted with the emergence of genuinely transnational dilemmas and the seemingly irresistible power of international financial markets, many have begun to argue that the traditional nation-state needs to be complemented, perhaps even replaced, by something else. Indeed, it could be argued that the growth of bodies such as the EU and the UN, as well as the proliferation of more issue-specific international organisations and regimes, constitutes a conscious and deliberate policy response to such dilemmas. But the existence of such organisations itself provides a stimulus for both the emergence of nascent forms of transnational politics and the appearance of sustained debates about some quite fundamental questions. The appearance of institutions of regional and global governance has resuscitated debates about sovereignty, democracy, rights and so on. The nation-state may be dead or dying, but politics is alive and well.

Perhaps a better way of thinking about these problems is to argue that the traditional barrier between domestic and international politics is in the process of dissolving; that the local and the global are so inexorably inter- twined that there is no longer any discernable analytical distinction between the two domains. This is where the next chapter takes up the story by considering the ways in which the world is being transformed by the processes of globalisation.

## Exercise

This chapter has explored the pressing question of the extent to which national governments are still the focal point of political activity in the modern world. Is global politics still a matter of 'politics among nations' and have key functions of governance been transferred to authorities higher than national governments?

The task here is to explore these issues with reference to your own country's government. To help your enquiries, it is suggested that you consider the answers to the following questions:

1  To what major international organisations does your government belong? What are the powers of these international organisations?
2  Is membership of these institutions a matter of domestic political debate? If so, what are the parameters of that debate?
3  Has your government been an active sponsor of international collaboration of any sort? If so, what are the arguments used by leading politicians to justify such activity?
4  Do governing elites in your country think that they still possess sover- eignty? Or do they admit that there are certain forces beyond their control?

If you prefer, you can focus on a particular issue area. Engagement in regional economic blocs or attitudes to global environmental cooperation spring to mind as good case studies. The point of this exercise is to think not only about the *objective* questions of sovereignty, but also about the *subjective* side of the argument. Is the *discourse* of sovereignty still present or is it being undermined?

## Further reading

Anderson, B. (1991) *Imagined Communities: Reflections on the Origins and Spread of Nationalism*, 2nd edn, London: Verso. A brilliant essay on nationalism and its constitution.

Camilleri, J. and Falk, P. (1992) *The End of Sovereignty? The Politics of a Shrinking and Fragmenting World*, Aldershot: Edward Elgar. A clear analysis of the challenges to a world order based on sovereign statehood.

Kegley, C. (ed.) (1995a) *Controversies in International Relations Theory: Realism and the Neoliberal Challenge* (1995), New York: St Martin's Press. A thoroughgoing set of essays which map the parameters of the dispute in contemporary international relations between realist and liberal paradigms.

Kegley, C. and Wittkopf, E. (1995) *World Politics: Trend and Transformation*, 5th edn, New York: St Martin's Press. A very reliable and comprehensive introduction to the main issues in international relations.

Nugent, N. (1994) *The Government and Politics of the European Union*, 3rd edn, Basingstoke: Macmillan. A clear, accurate account of the EU's institutional architecture and formal policy processes.

Roberts, A. and Kingsbury, B. (eds) (1993) *United Nations, Divided World. The UN's Role in International Relations*, 2nd edn, Oxford: Oxford University Press. Practitioners as well as analysts discuss the role and schievements of the United Nations

Strange, S. (1994) *States and Markets*, 2nd edn, London: Pinter. A superb introduction to the study of international political economy.

Wallace, H. and Wallace, W. (eds) (1996) *Policy-Making in the European Union*, Oxford: Oxford University Press. Contains detailed anaysis of the EU's policy process, including some thoughtful pieces on how best to conceptualise contemporary Euroepan integration.

Waltz, K. (1979) *Theory of International Politics*, Reading, MA: Addison Wesley. Seminal and controversial restatement of the realist theory of international relations.

# The processes of globalisation

## Introduction

In this final chapter of the book we will examine the concept of globalisation and discuss why it is now of such interest to academics, journalists and politicians, as well as to people in business. A good starting point is the message from the previous chapter, that some of the more conventional ways of thinking about and describing political life need to be modified in the light of developments in what is often called *international* politics. The theme of this chapter is that terms like *transnational*, or even *postnational*, may be more applicable to the changing condition of world politics. Because of what we are about to discuss, the importance of the distinction between these two concepts should not be underestimated, and before taking the discussion further we should think about what the terms mean.

The idea of international politics is quite accepted in everyday language, suggesting a world ordered through bilateral or mutilateral relations between nation-states, perhaps as treaties or trade agreements, or through agencies established by formal agreements among nation-states. The United Nations clearly falls into this category, as does the General Agreement on Tariffs and Trade (GATT). So, on some accounts, does the European Union (EU). But the EU occupies a rather uneasy position between the claims and aspirations of those called *intergovernmentalists*, and others who see it as a new sort of supra- or postnational institution of governance.

But the nub of the idea of **transnational politics** is that political activity is conducted *across* national boundaries, for example when non-governmental organisations like the Red Cross, Amnesty International and Greenpeace create a politics – of human rights or of ecology – which is not tied to specific territories, histories or cultures. James Rosenau's (1990) description of a 'multi-centric' world in which there are many different sorts of actors and a consequent dispersal of political and economic power makes much of the growing significance of transnational forces and actors in world politics which are outside the remit and the control of any one nation-state. He says that transnationality is apparent in the activities of:

*Look back to the extended discussion of the EU in Chapter 15, where we examined attempts to classify that set of institutions.*

**Transnational politics** Political activity conducted across national boundaries.

1 *Transnational organisations* – commercial ones like Nissan or Nestlé, cross-national professional bodies like the International Political Science Association, various social movements such as the women's movement, the networks of global shopping clubs like Amway, and through organisations like Friends of the Earth.

2 *Transnational problems* – like those of political refugees, labour migration, global warming, or AIDS, which expose us to risk, regardless of who we are and where we live.

3 *Transnational events* – made immediate by the reach of global news media. Events like the major earthquake in Kobe in Japan in 1995, the Bosnian crisis or the Rwandan famine become global rather than local issues through the mediation of the news media, especially the electronic media. Whether saturation coverage makes us just voyeurs, enjoying the immediacy of satellite broadcasting of world disasters in the same way that we enjoy soap operas, or perhaps intimates a sense of global citizenship in a world society is, of course, a debatable point.

4 *Transnational communities* – for example religious communities, both mainstream and orthodox religions like Islam, and cultist 'New Age' religions. This category also includes environmental organisations and the 'virtual' communities established by users of the Internet.

5 *Transnational structures* – of production, certainly, and also finance, but increasingly the mechanisms (hardware and software) for storing, retrieving and disseminating information, for example through commercial and public-access data bases.

Of course the idea of transcending national boundaries (psychological and cultural as well as physical) is still a fairly neutral way of putting it. The really potent charge attached to the concept of transnationality, and especially to that of postnationality, is that the nation-state is becoming irrelevant to the actual flows of political, economic and cultural activity and to the formation of political identities. Look at the following précis which discusses some ideas on the 'cyber-economy', which William Rees-Mogg, writing in *The Times* of 31 August 1995, believes will have a great impact on the independence of the modern nation-state.

### The Global Cyber-Economy and the Nation-state

Writing about the state of the world economy in the year 2025, Rees-Mogg argues that great changes will have taken place, largely because of the impact of information and communications technologies upon many areas of life. He identifies three main themes:

i) the acceleration of social and economic change in what he terms the second stage of the revolution in electronic communications

ii) the rise of Asia relative to the Western economies, and

iii) the weakening of the nation-state relative to global economic forces, but also relative to the citizen.

He argues that while many people predicted the communications revolution, they often made the assumption that its main effect would be to give a competitive advantage to large-scale organisations, particularly international businesses and strong governments. The twentieth-century nation-state was built, at least in part, on the ability to tax and spend a large proportion of national income, for the most part on defense and on welfare. Developments in communications technology by the year 2025 will, says Rees-Mogg, make it much more difficult for states to raise tax revenues, because many taxable transactions will have been shifted into cyberspace, and thus become virtually, beyond regulation. The modern nation-state will starve to death as its tax revenues decline, although small nations, like Bermuda, may be able to adjust to the changed circumstances, as their economies are already based upon fluid financial transactions and, presumably, because they do not carry with them the enormous apparatus of government, in the shape of a welfare state or the burden of sustaining an independent defence capability.

But the most successful 'country' of all, says Rees-Mogg, will have no geographical location. It will consist of networks of specialist users of the new technologies, cyber-elites in commerce, finance, the arts and so on, who interact and transact outside existing jurisdictions. By 2025 this cyber-country, will have, on his reckoning, at least 250 million citizens, with the cyber-rich earning great wealth, and the cyber-poor subsisting on incomes of less than $200,000 pa. It is this cyber-country, rather than new territorial contenders for world power, like China, which will be the greatest economic phenomenon of the next three decades.

---

**THINK POINT**
- How persuasive do you find these arguments? Is Rees-Mogg's vision of a cyber-future one with which you are in sympathy?

---

One of the aims of this chapter will be to examine the claim that the nation-state is 'dying', to adopt Rees-Mogg's language, since this has a direct bearing on the issue which is the main focus of the chapter, namely the concept of *globalisation*.

## From beyond the nation-state to global politics?

It is a commonplace that political life is something that takes place within and sometimes between political and societal units that are *territorial* units, and that the modern nation-state is predominant among these. So in modern times politics and political identities, as well as the study of these phenomena, have been closely connected with questions of geography or of place, and the same is often true of cultural identities. One consequence of the spread of the territorial nation-state around the globe has been to put spatial and conceptual boundaries around two of the most fundamental attachments of modern life – national identity and citizenship. In other words, it is very hard to think about these concepts other than in the context of this or that country. Because of this, many people would describe them as the 'natural boundaries' of a political community and thus the most obvious boundaries for social analysis as well. As a consequence, the study of politics, even what is sometimes described as 'world politics' or 'international relations', has been very much centred on the nation-state.

Now in one sense this is hardly surprising, because the territorial nation-state is the typical 'modern' political form seen across the world. States are found everywhere, and even where they are not they often lay claim to a territory, or to a part in policing what have become known as the 'Global Commons', those areas – Antarctica, the ocean deeps, 'the final frontier' of outer space itself – which are not recognised as part of the jurisdiction of any one state. But it is important to remember that from an historical perspective the nation-state itself is a relative newcomer in world politics, being part of a political landscape set down at the Peace of Westphalia in 1648, consolidated in Europe and North America in the century following the French Revolution of 1789, and exported to the rest of the world largely in the twentieth century. It is true that the nation-state and national societies are the characteristic political forms in which the world has become modern, but we must not fall into the trap of assuming that their centrality is given, or that they are the only way to imagine and to conduct political life and governance. As we shall see below, the autonomy and power of the nation-state are being eroded and new forms of what some people call 'de-spatialised' or non-territorial politics and government are increasingly visible. These, too, are part of the process of globalisation and, as we discussed in Chapter 4, they have the effect of making the discussion of central political concepts like citizenship, or democracy, much more complicated. Policy-making too, of the kind examined in Chapter 14, is given a new dimension by the appearance of global actors, like transnational corporations and interest groups and transnational institutions of economic governance like the World Trade Organisation, set up under the Uruguay Round of trade talks which ended in 1994.

But a commonsense response to the question of whether there is such a thing as global politics would be to say that of course there is not, at least not in the way that people normally mean when they talk about politics. There is no world political system in the way that there are national systems of government and international and even supranational institutions like the United Nations or the European Union, both of which perform at least quasi-governmental functions, still have problems in securing compliance and attracting loyalty precisely because they lack the legitimacy of most national governments. We should not be too surprised at this. Generally speaking, people do not think of themselves as global citizens, or even citizens of the European Union, and in the case of the latter they experience few of the ties of loyalty that bind individuals to particular nation-states or national identities. So, to reiterate, for most people, politics is seen as something that goes on 'inside' territorial units called sovereign states, except when it refers to the sort of exchanges that take place *between* them. But if there is no world political system beyond the interstate system, or the activities of transnational pressure groups like Greenpeace, what do we mean when we talk about globalisation, and is it useful to use the expression at all?

# The concept of globalisation

It is possible to identify a number of usages of the concept globalisation. The definition in the margin of p. 388 is a no-nonsense one. We will have to examine the definition carefully in order to evaluate its worth. Let us start by looking at the processes involved in making the world a single place. There are a number of possibilities:

## Globalisation as growing interconnectedness

The first is the relatively simple idea of globalisation as the 'multiplicity of linkages and interconnections that transcend the nation-state' (McGrew 1992: 65). This definition is a straightforward affirmation of the growing volume of goods, services, capital and people flowing across national boundaries. There are numerous examples of this phenomenon: for example, Table 16.1 shows the volume of exports from major trading nations in the period 1913 to 1984. With some variation and with significant pauses due to war and worldwide economic depression, the overall trend in the period was to expand the world trading economy.

There is also that interconnectedness which is a result of the globalisation of communications technology, for example in multimedia fields, perhaps bringing the prospect of the global 'information superhighway' much closer. As Mcgrew says, all these flows constitute a process through which 'events, decisions and activities in one part of the world can come to have significant consequences for individuals and communities in quite distant parts of the globe' (McGrew 1992: 65). The more potent implication of this is that global interconnectedness leaves the territorial boundaries of the nation-state less and less coincident with the changing patterns of life, and this is a theme stressed by a growing number of commentators from various academic disciplines and with different concerns. For example, the following is an extract from a work on the creation of global markets carried out by a well-known management consultant, Kenichi Ohmae. Here Ohmae is talking about the creation of consumers of global products:

*Table 16.1* Trade as an indication of the growing interconnectedness of the world economy: volume of exports, 1913–84 (1913 = 100)

| year | France | Germany | Japan | Netherlands | UK | USA |
|------|--------|---------|-------|-------------|-----|-----|
| 1913 | 100 | 100 | 100 | 100 | 100 | 100 |
| 1929 | 147 | 92 | 258 | 171 | 81 | 158 |
| 1938 | 91 | 57 | 588 | 140 | 57 | 126 |
| 1950 | 149 | 35 | 210 | 171 | 100 | 225 |
| 1960 | 298 | 155 | 924 | 445 | 120 | 388 |
| 1973 | 922 | 514 | 5,673 | 1,632 | 241 | 912 |
| 1984 | 1,460 | 774 | 14,425 | 2,384 | 349 | 1,162 |

*Source:* Maddison (1987: 694)
*Note:* figures rounded to nearest decimal point

### Borderless World: The Interlinked Economy

You have read enough about 'global' products to realise that few of them exist. But there are emerging global market segments; many of them centred in specific countries. For example, the market for off-road vehicles is centred in the United States, with incremental sales elsewhere. What is important to understand is the power of these customers vis-à-vis manufacturers. Part of that power comes from their lack of allegiances.

Economic nationalism flourishes during election campaigns and infects what legislatures do and what particular interest groups ask for. But when individuals vote with their pocket-books – when they walk into a showroom anywhere in Europe, the United States, or Japan – they leave behind the rhetoric and the mudslinging.

Do you write with a Waterman or a Mt Blanc pen or travel with a Vuitton suitcase out of nationalist sentiments? Probably not. You buy these things because they represent the kind of value you are looking for. At the cash register, you don't care about country of origin or country of residence. You don't think about employment figures or trade deficits You don't worry about where the product was made. It does not matter to you that a 'British' sneaker by Reebok (now an American owned company) was made in Korea, a German sneaker by Adidas in Taiwan, or a French sneaker by Rosignol in Spain. What you care about most is the product's quality, price, design, value and appeal to you as a consumer. Young people of the advanced countries are becoming increasingly nationality-less and more like 'Californians' all over the Triad countries – the United States, Europe and Japan – that form the Interlinked Economy.

(Ohmae 1989: 16. Reproduced with permission from HarperCollins Publishers.)

---

**THINK POINT**
- As a consumer, do you think that Ohmae is right?
- Are you aware of the 'national' origins of products?
- If so, which ones?
- Do you think that there are any truly global products?

---

A. Giddens (1990) *The Consequences of Modernity,* Cambridge: Polity.

Of course, Ohmae is not saying that the availability of global products homogenises tastes, but rather that the irrelevance of the origins of a product to consumers in different countries and different cultures is an important aspect in the making of a 'borderless world'. The sociologist Anthony Giddens, writing in 1990, offers a further and deceptively simple gloss on the idea of interconnectedness, which is that global flows serve to link people (and organisations) who were previously separated and insulated by time and space. He says that interconectedness is part and parcel of the 'stretching' of economic and social relations across the globe.

---

**THINK POINT**
- What do you think Giddens means when he talks about time and space insulating people?
- What sort of effects might follow from the removal of spatial and temporal barriers to personal and other sorts of relationships?

---

At root, Giddens wants to emphasise the increasing interpenetration of the modern world through a dramatic reordering of time and space, including changing the ways in which people think about the concepts, thus altering the meanings they attach to them and the constraints which are related to them. In this reordering, two processes are paramount. The first, which he calls 'deterritorialization', involves things like the massive growth in cross-border transactions and collaborations taking place between businesses, the movement of people between countries and regions of the world economy, the creation of truly global markets in areas like finance and telecommunications and the establishment of networks of professionals who communicate through technical language irrespective of national origins and cultures. The second, called 'disembedding', refers to all sorts of social relations being 'lifted out' of local contexts of interaction and reorganised across much larger spans of time and space. Giddens (1990) sees this process at work in an increased use of what he calls 'symbolic tokens' – money or trading in government bonds would be good examples – which serve as universally accepted ways of effecting transactions among agents widely separated in time and space. But the process is seen also in the routine use of 'expert systems', like computerised data bases, or the fax and modem systems now common in many areas of everyday life. It is also seen, of course, in the behaviour of Ohmae's consumers who have stripped their purchases of any meaningful association with particular places and cultures. The combined effect of these two processes is to enlarge the scope for social relations or interactions which are not limited by the need for personal presence or tied to a specific location.

The growing connectedness of the globe is easily demonstrated, but before we can talk of these processes making the world a single place we need to examine the ways in which actors (both individually and collectively) think and feel about globalisation, and thus how they experience it.

### Global consciousness, or thinking globally

The processes referred to above are more than just flows of what the sociologists Scott Lash and John Urry (1994) call 'objects and subjects', mainly goods, services, money, images and, of course, people, and include the orientation of different actors – individuals, groups, communities, corporations and states – towards the features of globalisation. Orientations refer to people's psychological make-up and to the mental equipment they use to make sense of the world. Only by understanding these orientations is it possible to assess the fragility or strength of global institutions and processes and to say if the world is becoming one place. Some individuals may begin to 'think globally' rather than as nationals or aboriginals and this modifies certain aspects of their behaviour, but whether their identity (that is, their sense of who they are) is changed too, so that their personalities and interests are redefined, is a much more contentious point. For example, businessmen and women are often advised to 'think globally and manage locally'. This means that, at the very least, they should be aware of the global forces operating on them, and at most that they should look at the world as a potential operational whole, adapting their strategies and company cultures accordingly. This is one sense of what is meant by the phrase, 'global consciousness'.

R. Robertson (1992)
*Globalization: Social Theory and Global Culture*, London: Sage.

In his interesting book *Globalization: Social Theory and Global Culture* Roland Robertson talks about individuals and groups, but also whole communities and even nations, being 'constrained to identify' with what he calls the 'global circumstance' (Robertson 1992). These are rather unwieldy phrases, but what Robertson means is that for a variety of reasons – a growing awareness of population issues, famine in Rwanda, the takeover of one's place of work by a multinational company with the consequent loss of job security, the collapse of a currency in the face of intense speculation by the money markets, or just watching *Home and Away* or *Roseanne* on television – people develop a greater awareness of the world and a greater consciousness of the influence of global factors on the quality and conduct of everyday life.

---

**THINK POINT**
- From your own perspective, could you identify any global factors which affect the way you live, or does Robertson's argument strike you as too simple?

---

From a more narrowly political standpoint, growing awareness of globalising forces can produce quite different responses. These may be to 'go global' and to adopt a global mentality, like the managers referred to on p. 483, or like the proponents of a single world government. It might mean adjusting to changing circumstances in the manner of national governments struggling to contain or regulate the power of financial markets; or it might impel individuals or groups who feel threatened by exposure to global forces to try to diminish their impact on them or, as in the following extract, on whole civilisations.

### Local Cultural Resistance to the Power of the Internet

In a recent article in the *Sunday Times* (News Review, 3 September 1995), Stuart Wavell looks at the ways in which what he calls 'closed societies' are being exposed to, and opened up by, the Internet. The freedom to 'surf' the Internet, or to ride its information superway, presents both issues of morality and questions of regulation to the rulers of authoritarian countries like Saudi Arabia, which until recently had traditional and relatively simple methods for dealing with dissent and imposing censorship. When Western magazines featured pictures of women who were completely or partially undressed, the censors simply blacked them out prior to sale. Even satellite television is subject to control through restrictions or complete bans on the sale of receiver dishes, which both Iran and the Saudis have imposed.

But the Internet presents much more difficult problems of control for closed societies and autocratic regimes. Regimes have little or no control over what flows between terminals in the form of digital codes, and at least some of what flows is going to be irrevelant, maybe even seditious. The Saudis have tried to keep control by granting access by special permission

only to universities and hospitals. Furthermore, the penalties for unautho-
rised use are very severe. Try ordering a *Playboy* centrefold over the NET,
and you risk imprisonment.

Wavell says that Iranian censors from the Ministry of Culture and Islamic
Guidance are fighting a battle with thousands of 'hackers' (that is, computer
users who illegally access information) in the country, while the Chinese
authorities have been reduced to cutting off the power connections to users
trying to download what they consider sensitive materials.

At the same time, as Wavell acknowledges, at least some of these
'closed societies' have ambivalent attitudes towards the use and spread of
information technologies. The Saudis, alarmed by the uncontrollable nature
of the Internet, are also anxious to depict themselves as in the forefront
of the use of high-tech goods and services.

Wavell says that in the long term all these regimes are facing a terminal
crisis for censorship.

This is a useful example of what is meant by globalisation and by global
consciousness. What is most interesting about it is that while the unifying
and homogenising power of information technology is shown as penetrating
closed societies, or as tearing down the barriers created by time and space,
to make the world one, the process also generates strong forces of opposition that are committed to defending cultural, religious and linguistic
boundaries and economic interests, or the idea of national sovereignty, sometimes to the point of violent conflict. We can see this sort of response in
those regimes which wish to hide from permissive or potentially destabilising global influences like those mentioned in the extract, or in the brutal
regime of the Khmer Rouge in Cambodia in the 1970s, which sought to
reverse all modernising trends in that country. It is visible, too, in the politics of some of the more open and apparently stable liberal democracies. In
France, political elites continue to defend a particular model of 'Frenchness'
by trying to protect the language and French culture from the ravages of
American English and forms of popular entertainment like *Baywatch*, while
in the United Kingdom 'Eurosceptics' in the Conservative Party (that is,
those opposed to the principle of ever closer union in the Europe) seem to
have been successful in reopening the question of Britain's continued
membership in the European Union, on the basis of the claim that it is
injurious to national prosperity and national traditions of government and
public law. In 1996 the Community of Portuguese-Speaking Countries was
formed to contest the spread of the 'global' languages of English and Spanish.

There are many more examples of sheer bloody-mindedness or cultural
resistance in the face of globalising (or, in the case of the EU, regionalising)
pressures, but regardless of the case in question, there are two key points
to bear in mind.

The first is that although they are all in some way opposed to globalisation, each example of cultural resistance is also defined in relation to it,
or given a rationale because of it. Many concerns with the defence of national
identity, or with religious purity, become politicised largely as a result of

actors being 'constrained to identify' with the global condition and to support or oppose some of the features found there. A further example may clarify this difficult point. Much of the discussion of globalisation presents it as the diffusion of Western (for which read American and Western European) values, institutions, products and practices to other parts of the world, with a resulting erosion of local tastes, traditions and identities. In this sort of interpretation, the opening of the first McDonald's restaurant in Moscow might be seen as an increment in the homogenisation of consumer tastes around the world and an implicit attack on authentic Russian traditions. In 1995 a number of Russian entrepreneurs took a commercial, but also an implicitly political stand, against this threat by opening the first in a chain of Russian fast-food outlets, specialising in the sale of vodka and Russian cabbage. The point is that this particular expression of Russian identity is only really comprehensible when seen as a deliberate counterweight to the import of a foreign product which is an icon, perhaps *the* icon, of Americanised global cultures and tastes, although it may be an optimistic attempt to establish a niche market as well. 'Constrained to identify' with the global condition in the guise of sesame-seed buns, meat patties and chocolate 'shakes', the Russian patriot as entrepreneur rediscovers seemingly more authentic fare, both as a culinary statement and as a defence of indigenous culture.

---

**THINK POINT**
- Can you think of other examples of what could be called anti-global politics, or the politics of cultural resistance? Like the Russian example these need not always be in the less-developed parts of the world.

---

The second point is that because of instances like this the processes of globalisation must be seen as contested. So the idea of a single place does not, indeed cannot, imply complete homogeneity, with the elimination of local traditions and identities, but a much more pluralistic condition, where competing and sometimes fundamentally conflicting ideas about the global circumstance – capitalism versus communism, Islamic versus Judeo-christian, or national versus both supranational and communitarian – abound. This, too, is a crucial observation, because instead of a world becoming one willy-nilly, through the integrative force of market capitalism and the power of clever machines like computers or video telephones to 'compress' our sense of time and space, we are faced with a much more pluralistic 'totality' or, in some instances – the case of fundamentalist Islamic ideals may be a case in point – quite different visions or models of what a single world should look like.

This may seem an obvious point to make – after all the world is full of variety – but it is useful to remind ourselves that the process of globalisation is often a matter of conscious decision and struggle by individuals and groups in support of, but also against, powerful transnational and postnational economic and cultural forces, as well as an unconscious adoption or assimilation of these same forces into our lifestyles. Thus, while it is clear that many consumers would be hard put to identify the local origins of a lot of products and couldn't care less, the same is almost certainly not true of their choice of politicians or political parties. So, when individuals buy a car whose parts have been sourced from around the world and which has no obvious national provenance – for example, the Ford Mondeo, marketed as a 'world car' – they have been implicated in the processes of globalisation just by being there, through behaving routinely as buyers and sellers.

On the other hand, when these same people, or others like them, protested at the French government's decision to resume underground nuclear testing in the Pacific during 1995, they chose to support a globally sanctioned ideology of eco-protection. The force of such ideologies, circulating at the level of popular opinion, via global media outlets and through the agency of multilateral organisations like the United Nations, can, and sometimes does, create a global constraint on the actions of individual states. On the other hand, as French intransigence in the face of world opinion demonstrated, sometimes it does not. Even so, it may be quite appropriate to talk about the existence of a world civil society and, with regard to issues like this, even an emerging global moral order.

### *Global compression*

All this suggests that the changing experience of time and space spoken of by Giddens (1990) does not, or need not, proceed in a linear fashion or towards a predetermined goal – say, one-world government or global capitalism – precisely because of the different perceptions and experiences of those caught up in it and because of the new forces at work within it. So while there may be what the geographer David Harvey calls a dramatic speeding up or intensity of 'time–space compression' (Harvey 1989), the relationships between the constituent units of the global system display no neat functional unity.

There are two main reasons for this. The first is suggested by the anthropologist Arjun Appadurai (1990) who points to some major 'disjunctures' at work in the global cultural economy which are the result of different and competing 'logics' of integration – most notably, the universalistic logic of capitalist markets versus the particularistic logic of individual nation-states and national identities. Appadurai provides a useful insight into some of the 'fundamental disjunctures' between economic factors and politics and culture, when he describes a world and a process of globalisation which move to the fluid and unpredictable interaction of different global 'scapes'. These are:

1 *Ethnoscapes* – the landscape of persons who make up the shifting world in which we live. Tourists, migrants, refugees and, if we are to believe the novelist David Lodge (1984), delegates at international conferences, are all part of the make-up of this mobile universe.

2   *Technoscapes* – the global configuration of technology and technological innovation, now increasingly indifferent to conventional boundaries and to the need for particular sites for the production of goods and the delivery of services.

3   *Finanscapes* – the highly fluid world of global finance – money markets, futures, commodities broking, portfolio investments, all moving too fast for easy regulation by national regimes.

4   *Mediascapes* – the electronic dissemination of information and images and its organisation in multimedia forms quite unlike the older divisions between print and broadcast media.

5   *Idioscapes* – the rapidly expanding or even exploding world of political ideas and slogans which inform and legitimate new kinds of political forces and social movements – feminism, ecologism and survivalism are good examples, along with the organisation of indigenous peoples like Native Americans or Australian Aborigines.

The second reason is the related fact that actors in world politics are all players in it, but players who have been schooled in different traditions and perspectives; that is, they already have a sense of their own interests and histories, maybe even their own sense of destiny. The processes of globalisation do not write upon these individuals, groups and communities as if they were blank pages in an exercise book, and because of this the interplay of global forces with individual or local identities is often more reciprocal than a simple model of global dominance or of local subservience to global scripts. This brings us to a further nuance in the concept of globalisation.

### Globalisation as relativisation and indigenisation

The introduction of certain kinds of consumer products, like satellite TV dishes or contraceptive devices, into a previously closed society may have the effect of undermining or **relativising** existing identities and practice, as well as challenging established political interests. But this challenge to local practice is seldom uncontested. In Algeria in recent years, the attempt to modernise the country under a succession of socialist and quasi-military regimes has been contested by those often called Islamic fundamentalists, notably the Groupe Islamique Armé (GIA), whose primary aim lies in the eradication of what it sees as the corrupting influence of Western culture on the purity of Islamic thought and custom. Such reactions can and do produce violent challenges to the introduction and use of outside influences and artefacts, leading to the tearing down of TV satellite dishes or, as we saw earlier, banning *Baywatch*, as happened in Iran. It can also produce challenges to the legitimacy of the modernising elites who encourage them.

Less dramatic, although typical of the relativising power of global forces, are what we may call *world cultural scripts*, like Conventions in international law, or UN Declarations on the rights of workers or women or children. These provide a framework of expectations (a script, in other words) to

**Relativisation** The process whereby the integrity, wholeness or absolute quality of an identity is diluted by the power of global forces.

which individual countries often feel obliged to conform in full or in part. Such scripts are really models or guides for national policies and national profiles of appropriate development. Adherence to the norms circulating in the global system establishes and reinforces the legitimacy of a particular regime and also contributes to the shape and solidity of the emerging world society. Sometimes these scripts are embodied in what students of international relations call 'regimes', like the agreements on the environment which arose from the 1992 Earth Summit in Brazil. We will look at this phenomenon more closely when we examine international relations theory below (pp. 497–8). As the execution in 1995 of the Nigerian poet Ken Saro-Wiwa shows, some regimes can and do choose to ignore such constraints, at least with regard to particular cases, even if they feel obliged to pay lip service to the ideals. On the other hand, pressure from the world community, organised through the international force in Bosnia, forced the Bosnian Serb leader Radovan Karadic to step down from public office in 1996, in recognition of widespread criticism over his conduct of the civil war in Bosnia.

The consequences of the relativising power of global forces for local identities may be:

1 Their complete erosion through cultural homogenisation or assimilation; that is, the local identity becomes swallowed.
2 The reaffirmation or entrenchment (sometimes called the retraditionalisation) of existing identities in the form of religious orthodoxies or other types of fundamentalism;
3 Their replacement by 'hybrid' cultures or identities, the result of some accommodation between the local and the global, involving the fusion of different cultural traditions. Stuart Hall (1992) writes persuasively that hybrid identities, often found among migrant communities, are not simply a variant of 1 or 2 above, but, as Monty Python said, 'something completely different'.

---

**THINK POINT**
- Can you think of any examples of hybrid identities? For example, when someone is described or describes herself as a 'Polish American', or when people in Western countries wear 'ethnic' dress from non-Western societies, these are both instances of hybridity.

---

Where there is evidence of straightforward resistance, or hybridisation of identities, this introduces a cautionary note into arguments which depict the process of globalisation as a simple diffusion of Western cultural values, and sometimes as an unmediated flow of influence from the West to the rest. By contrast, the geographer Doreen Massey has spoken of the need to assess what she calls the 'power geometry' in the relationships involved, and part of her interesting argument is reproduced below.

### A Global Sense Of Place

Imagine for a moment that you are on a satellite, further out and beyond all actual satellites; you can see 'planet earth' from a distance and, rarely for someone with only peaceful intentions, you are equipped with the kind of technology which allows you to see the colour of people's eyes and the numbers on their numberplates. You can see all the movement and tune in to all the communication that is going on. . . . Some of this is people moving, some of it is physical trade, some is media broadcasting. There are faxes, e-mail, film-distribution networks, financial flows and transactions. Look in closer and there are ships and trains. . . . Look in closer and . . . somewhere in sub-Saharan Africa, there's a woman on foot who still spends hours a day collecting water.

Now I want to make one simple point here, and that is about what one might call the 'power geometry' of it all, the power-geometry of time–space compression. For different social groups and different individuals are placed in very distinct ways in relation to these flows and interconnections. This point concerns not merely the issue of who moves and who doesn't, although that is an important element of it; it is also about power in relation to the flows and the movement. Different social groups have distinct relations to this . . . some people are more in charge of it than others; some initiate flows and movement, others don't; some are more on the receiving end of it than others; some are effectively imprisoned by it.

(Massey, D. (1995) *Space, Place and Gender*, Cambridge: Polity Press, pp. 146–56)

Massey draws our attention to various instances of the power geometry found in different kinds of flows and movements. Migrants and refugees are not 'in charge' in her sense of the expression, while business travellers are. An elderly person eating a meal from a Chinese takeaway while watching an American film on television is just a passive recipient of global fare, whereas virtual travellers on the Internet are conscious and probably willing participants in the compression of their own world. Massey's idea of the 'power geometry' contained in a relationship or transaction also reminds us that the processes of globalisation take place within pre-exisiting social relationships. In her version, the rich go on getting rich and the poor get *Dallas*. But the idea of power geometry also highlights the second of the two concepts dealt with in this section, that of **indigenisation**. Here is an example of indigenisation:

**Indigenisation** The adaptation of alien practices to local circumstances and to meet local needs.

### Western Culture in Japan

In recent years there has been a remarkable influx of Japanese Manga cartoons into countries in the West. These cartoons, which are often full-length, adult animation films, along with cyberpunk movies constitute a uniquely Japanese contribution to the global culture of the late 1990s. Tom Hiney (*The Sunday Times, News and Travel*, 2 Jan 1994, p. 14) suggests that we should 'forget bullet trains and company anthems', or even samurai and tea houses as expressions of Japanese life and culture. He says that Manga is 'the subversive imagination of a new, streetwise Japan'. At the same time, Japanese directors not involved with animation, he says, are reviving tired Hollywood genres. *Violent Cop*, a motion picture released in the UK and USA, was directed by and also starred 'Beat' Takeshi, an actor hailed by reviewers as the Japanese 'answer to Clint Eastwood'.

Now, in this extract, we not only have the indigenisation of a notable Western cultural form (animation) by the Japanese, but its reinvention and re-export to achieve cult status in the West. What does this tell us about the relations between the local and the global?

First, it shows us that Western artefacts can be entirely assimilated into local practices. Yet at the same time, the particular form and indeed the specific usage referred to is meaningful only when seen as part of the localisation of thoroughly global practices.

Second, it shows us that we should be very careful about any claim that the 'relativising' of the world by global processes annihilates local cultures, while acknowledging that these same global forces are making it much harder for local identities to survive intact. Indeed the very meaning of locality or 'place' may undergo change in a world linked by fibre-optics and the suspicion that a visit to McDonalds really can make your day, regardless of the time zone or the place. The other side of Japan's confident reinvention of American cartoon culture to reflect its own cultural traditions is the fear among some intellectuals that 'Japlish' (English words rendered into Japanese) is leading to the corruption of the Japanese tongue. Often cited is the fad among young people for saying 'sankyoo' (thank you) instead of 'arigato' and 'bye-bye' for 'sayonara'.

## *The idea of a global system*

Global processes like changes in communications technology or new production techniques and also the spread of 'global' ideologies like the UN Declaration of Human Rights provide constraints or models of acceptable national, local or organisational development, what Ien Ang calls 'cultural frames', in relation to which 'every identity must define and position itself' (Ang 1991: 7). To reiterate the point, this is not a simple matter of the 'Westernisation' or Americanisation of the world, but a much more complex and interactive process.

So what can we conclude about the idea of the world as a single place, a global system where local actors and global structures interact? First, that globalisation is a process which is made and not given, and made through the interaction of various situated actors (individuals, localities, groups, organisations, etc.) with a variety of more encompassing structures and flows. Second, that at the heart of this idea of a single place is the realisation that the world is undergoing a process of growing interconnectedness, so that it is becoming irrelevant to talk about separate national economies, or national companies, but it is still necessary to talk about national and local identities. Third, globalisation is not producing a homogenised world; indeed, it may be that a heightened consciousness of global pressure triggers a renewed sense of personal, local or civilisational identity. Finally, as Anthony Giddens says, it suggests that the process of making the world a single place links people previously separated by time and space (Giddens 1990). Social relations are not only stretched, as he puts it, across the world space but, on occasion, made 'virtual' by the technologies of transnational media.

All this paints a rather complicated picture, and suggests a theory of globalisation in which larger-scale processes and structures, involving, for example, changes in the ways in which people communicate with each other or in where and how consumer products are produced and sold, are only one side of the equation. The other side sees these same structures and processes affected by the resilience of local identities and traditions, and finds them interpreted, often idiosyncratically, by actors as they go about the everyday business of living. So globalisation is a complex process which moves to no unique logic nor to unstoppable laws of history. But other theories are much less catholic on the nature and direction of globalisation and on the sort of historical forces which are driving it. Some of these are examined below (pp. 493–9), in part to draw attention to the marked differences between them and between all of them and the richer concept of globalisation outlined above. Needless to say, what follows only summarises complex arguments.

*You will remember that we talked about these in Chapter 5, citing the work of Francis Fukuyama and Marx, among others.*

## Theories of globalisation

Globalisation is widely discussed these days, sometimes as part of ideologically committed accounts of the need for a single world government, in the discussion of possible resolutions to 'global' problems like climate change, or in the language of specialist groups like users of the Internet and the managers of large companies. Most such discussion is not really concerned with explaining the phenomenon of globalisation, just with describing its features. Because of this there is a relative dearth of theoretical accounts. In this section we will set out some of the main arguments from various disciplines, bearing in mind that they often start from different intellectual positions, work with different concepts and have different images for what is taking place. Most recognise that there are now various worldwide fields of interaction, but what these refer to can be either the more traditional image of international society – a global system of nation-states – some form of world economy in which states struggle to maintain their control over key areas of economic life or, as one branch of theorising puts it, an integrated *world-system*.

The imperatives or logics which are said to drive globalisation are also in dispute, with some authors seeing the world becoming one through the powerful force of capitalist markets, while others stress the historical importance of factors like war or conquest. Economic and political forces are usually given prominence in these accounts, with cultural factors seen as secondary, although this view is changing under the impact of recent work from cultural studies, geography and anthropology.

As most of these theories confirm, globalisation is not a new phenomenon, even if its pace has increased dramatically of late. In the distant past, empires like that of Alexander the Great, which spread out from the Mediterranean core of the old world to span parts of what is now the

Middle East and South Asia, also served to compress the world. During the Middle Ages, the concept of 'Christendom' and the universalising mission of the Catholic Church were premised on the assumption of a world unified by faith and reinforced by the writ of papal authority. For all this, globalisation is an essentially modern process (in much the same way we used the term 'modern' in Chapter 5) and refers to the (contested) spread of Western influences (most obviously capitalism, the nation-state and the secular doctrines of the Enlightenment) across the globe over the last few centuries. At least some accounts of globalisation are directly concerned with the impact of the industrialized nations of the West on what we now call the 'Third World' and also on the erstwhile 'Second World' of state socialism. The following theoretical perspectives all say different things about these forces and relationships, and for the sake of convenience we will group them as modernisation theory, dependency theory, world-system analysis and international relations theory.

### Globalisation and modernisation

Globalization is a feature of modernity, and modern institutions like the nation-state and liberal economics, with its emphasis on the creation of markets, have become the means through which the world is being made one. Theories of modernisation deal with the processes and institutions through which societies become modern. Much work in this area was done in the United States in the period between the 1950s and the 1970s, when students of economics, sociology, international security and comparative politics were particularly concerned with the division of the world into two armed blocs, each dominated by a superpower, and by the prospects for economic development and political democracy exhibited by various Third World countries in the process of being freed from colonial rule. Although theories of modernisation have been more exercised by societal development than by ideas about globalisation, there is much in this work that has relevance for the latter theme.

One of the key characteristics of modernisation theory, and one which it shares with Marxism, is the idea of social evolutionism. Social evolutionism offers a view of the evolution of societies and, by implication, of the way in which the modern world was made, in which modernisation is seen as a progression through a number of necessary stages of development. The economist Walt Rostow, in a famous book called the *The Stages of Economic Growth* (1960) talks about the universal stages of economic development that all societies must pass through before they achieve a fully modernised form. These are: traditional or agricultural societies, a stage involving the laying down of the preconditions for economic 'take-off', actual take-off, where full commercial and industrial structures are set down, sustained economic growth and, finally, the mature high mass-consumption society, which is the completion of social evolution. Talcott Parsons (1967) gives a rather different gloss to this process, with a greater emphasis upon the achievement of democratic institutions and the importance of social and

*We first looked at this in Chapter 5 as a way of understanding social and political change, noting writers like Talcott Parsons as key contributors to the debate.*

political elites who are willing to embrace societal innovation rather than kick against it.

Societies which leave or are forced to diverge from this linear path, like the former Soviet Union – which in terms of modernisation theory underwent a seventy-year experiment in societal engineering and thus missed out on the critical transformation of Russian society to the point where it could 'take off' economically – are either marginalised in world-economic terms or experience major social calamities. In other words, the message is that societies cannot short-cut history without incurring major social and political costs. These sorts of claim struck many commentators as at least inaccurate, or very biased, as they seem to describe historical progress as the dissemination of Western institutions and practices to the rest of the world. The Soviet route to modernity, or alternative versions of that path now being travelled by countries like Singapore, South Korea or even the Chinese People's Republic, are not easily accommodated in conventional modernisation theory. Of course, like the collapse of the Soviet Union, it may well be that history will have the last word and that these maverick contenders for full modernisation will also fall by the wayside.

Such at any rate appears to be the message of Francis Fukuyama, whose seminal work *The End of History* (1992) is an attempt to rescue modernisation theory from its detractors and to resurrect a 'directional' or, as it is sometimes called, a teleological theory of history. Fukuyama's thesis, which we examined in Chapter 5, is easily caricatured, and because of this it is worth repeating here. He argues that History (the capital 'H' is deliberate) has come to an end because, with the collapse of state socialism, there are no longer any serious global contenders to liberal democracy and market capitalism. But history with a small 'h' goes on, characterised by death and destruction and by debate over the *means* of politics. Ethnic cleansing in Bosnia or Rwanda is part of history with a small 'h' and so is disagreement over the powers of the European Commission in Brussels. But they are not seminal disputes, because History has evolved to a point where the *ends* of politics are no longer an issue. Interestingly enough, Fukuyama's vision of what the world will look like at the end of History is that it will resemble a rather unflattering portrait of the European Union – integrated, bureaucratised, regulated and ineffably boring. Here is a brief statement of Fukuyama's credo:

> The collapse of communism and the end of the Cold War have not, as many commentators have asserted, lead to a global upsurge of tribalism, a revival of nineteenth century nationalist rivalries, or a breakdown of civilization into anomic violence. Liberal democracy and capitalism remain the essential, indeed the only framework for the political and economic organization of modern societies. Rapid economic modernization is closing the gap between many former Third World countries and the industrialized North. With European integration and North American free trade, the web of economic ties within each region will thicken and sharp cultural boundaries will become increasingly fuzzy. Implementation of the free trade regime of the Uruguay Round of the General Agreement on Tariffs and Trade (GATT) will further

> erode interregional boundaries. Increased global competition has forced companies across cultural boundaries to try to adopt 'best practice' techniques like lean manufacturing from whatever source they come from. The worldwide recession of the 1990s has put great pressure on Japanese and German companies to scale back their distinctive cultural and paternalistic labour policies in favour of a more purely liberal model. The modern communications revolution abets this convergence by facilitating economic globalization and by propagating the spread of ideas at enormous speed.
>
> (Fukuyama 1995: 353. Reproduced with permission from Hamish Hamilton Publishers)

By now you should have no difficulty in recognising that these are still very contested ideas.

## Imperialism and dependency theory

Like modernisation theory, Marxism is also a theory of historical evolution, though with quite different motive forces and stages. For Marx, the socialist society is the alternative end of history, reached because capitalism self-destructs under the logic of its own internal contradictions. Marxism is also a theory of social evolution, but in Marx's partial treatment of colonialism, and in Lenin's much more developed critique of imperialism as a necessary phase of capitalist expansion, the Marxist theory of history becomes a theory of the development of global capitalism, a system based upon the uneven development of colonial and metropolitan powers and on the systematic impoverishment of what we now call the Third World. In today's world the processes of direct imperialism, through military conquest and administrative rule, have been replaced by forms of *neo-imperialism*, carried on through the imbalance of trade between the First and the Third Worlds and by the power of transnational corporations with their roots in the First World to dictate the terms of world trade and investment.

V. I. Lenin (1975) *Imperialism: the Highest Stage of Capitalism*, Moscow: Foreign Language Press.

The work of dependency theorists builds on these insights to portray a single global capitalist economy grounded in the systematic exploitation of the periphery (Africa, most of Asia and Latin America) by the core (North America, Western Europe and also Japan). In a phrase first used by economist Andre Gunder Frank (1969) the rich core is said to 'underdevelop' the periphery, whose progress towards full modernisation is stunted by the need for metropolitan capital – through traded goods and investment opportunities – to expand. Underdevelopment of the periphery produces a global division of labour between rich and poor countries, in which the latter mainly supply raw materials and some labour to the core economies, but the former produce and supply most high-value goods to Third World consumers, thus draining off capital which might otherwise be used to fund domestic investment and industrial modernisation.

Of late, critics of the underdevelopment thesis have argued that it has taken no account of the ability of peripheral countries to break out from dependency and to develop indigenous manufacturing capacity and technical expertise sufficient to challenge metropolitan capital in its own markets

(Warren 1980). The recent economic success of the so-called 'tiger' economies of the Pacific Rim – Hong Kong, Singapore, South Korea and Taiwan – has influenced a school of 'dependency reversal' analysis. In many ways this sort of thinking parallels Marx and Engels' own ideas on the 'powerful engine' of colonialism (Marx and Engels 1972), which sometimes had beneficial effects upon the economies of peripheral countries. For Marx, India was a case where colonial rule and capitalist expansion set what he understood as a backward country on the road to modernity.

### World-system theories

I. Wallerstein (1974) *The Modern World-System, Volume 1*, New York, Academic Press.

World-system analysis, which is most closely associated with the work of Immanuel Wallerstein, is a critique of both modernisation theory and dependency theory, rejecting the teleology of the former and the theoretical pessimism of the latter. There are various strands of world-system analysis, with Wallerstein's being the most embracing and persuasive, even though it relies upon basically economic criteria to explain the functioning of what he calls the *modern world-system*. Wallerstein argues that it is wrong to analyse national societies without understanding the links they have to transnational and trans-societal networks of exchanges, which he calls world-systems. In fact he distinguishes historically between two sorts of world-systems: *world empires*, like the Chinese, the Inca or the Egyptian, which were often culturally and economically diverse, but held together by a single administrative and legal framework; and *world-economies*, which have a unified economic division of labour and multiple states or other units of rule. In the modern world there is only one world-system, the capitalist world economy, which has been spreading out from northwest Europe since about the sixteenth century. Today it is a global system, or, in Marxist terms, a global *mode of production*, and there is nowhere that is exempt from its embrace. States which try to remain outside the orbit of the world economy find that they are unable to do so for any length of time, being dependent upon it for trade, investment, technical assistance and aid. Even those countries which adopt a worldview completely opposed to the principles of the capitalist world economy, for example the former USSR and post-revolutionary Iran under Ayatollah Khomeini, find themselves drawn into its toils through the need for aid, technology transfers and inward investments. In Robertson's (1992) phrase, they too are 'constrained to identify' with the global system.

The capitalist world economy is made up of what Wallerstein (1984) calls 'commodity chains' of producers and consumers, sellers and buyers, linking countries in the core of the world economy – like Britain, Germany and the United States and Japan – with economically weaker countries in the semi-periphery (for example some Mediterranean economies) and even weaker, still mainly agricultural economies in the periphery of the world-system (most of Africa, Latin America and Asia). The relationship between these zones of the world economy is basically exploitative in the way argued by dependency theorists. In the world-system economic power equates with political and strategic clout, but in fact there is a kind of dynamism built into the system which is absent in most dependency theories, so that countries can and do move between zones. For example, Argentina was almost a core power in the 1920s, but has slipped back since then, and really dominant or hegemonic powers – of which the modern world-system has seen three: the United Provinces (what we now call the Netherlands), Britain and the United States – are also subject to cyclical forces which assist their rise, but also precipitate their fall. Wallerstein (1984) is unsure about the prospects for some kind of radical transformation of the world economy, although he sees various 'anti-systemic' forces, like Green activists, feminism, the political movements of indigenous peoples like Native Americans, even new forms of organised labour, or student activism, as all struggling to challenge the dominant ideology (he calls it the 'geoculture') of the world economy, market liberalism. More recently other strands of world-system analysis reject even the Wallersteinian conception of a modern world created in the image of Euro-America, preferring to locate these developments in a longer world-historical cycle stretching back to the Asia-centred world of medieval times and before (Frank 1995).

## International relations theory

Marxist attempts to build a theory of world politics and the world economy through concepts like imperialism tend to treat politics within and between states as secondary to the influence of economic forces. By contrast, international relations theory places much greater emphasis upon the importance of political and strategic issues in affecting the pattern of world events. Until recently the *realist* school of international relations described a world in which antagonism and conflict between independent nation-states was the driving force of international politics. States are seen as completely egoistic actors in world politics, always trying to protect and promote the national interest and suspicious of the equally self-interested behaviour of others. Because of this, cooperation between states, in the form of treaties, trade pacts and so on, can be justified only to the extent that it contributes to national goals, and this might include forming an alliance to prevent a powerful rival from becoming dominant. In this version of world politics, the international system of states survives through a collective belief in institutionalised anarchy, with cooperation and forms of international regulation being kept to the minimum necessary to ensure the balance of power.

H. Morgenthau (1985) *Politics Among Nations*, 6th edn, New York: Knopf.

Of course, a belief in systemic anarchy makes it very hard to explain why states cooperate with each other, and even harder to comprehend why they would voluntarily choose to surrender some part of their autonomy to international or supranational institutions like the North Atlantic treaty organisation (NATO) or the EU. Some commentators, who muster under the name of 'institutionalists', have tried to modify the realist obsession with raw self-interest, emphasising the growing trust between state actors, which is fostered and maintained by various international institutions or *regimes*. Regimes are arrangements which institutionalise cooperation in a particular area or field of activity. Some, like the GATT, may be fully institutionalised, others, like the Climate Agreements which followed the Earth Summit in 1992, less so. Regimes lay down rules or expectations about how states should behave and a regulative framework that is both practical and moral. Because of this, they ameliorate the anarchy of the international system and provide a framework for self-interested behaviour, but also for cooperative actions which are not predicated solely on the need to ensure survival or the ambition to maximise power. In the debate over the 'true' nature of states much has been made of the argument that, contrary to the assumption of inherent conflict between states, democracies do not appear to go to war with each other.

> ### International Political Economy: Abiding Discord
>
> The compelling empirical testimony presented by liberal analysts, is the relationship between democracy and war. Democracies have not fought each other, though they have fought non-democracies. The explanation for this finding has been provided by Kant and his successors. Although the validity of the claim that democracies have not fought has been challenged on the basis of classification [should Germany be counted as a non-democracy at the outbreak of the First World War?] and the small number of available cases . . . the fact remains that the absence of war among democracies is an exceptionally powerful finding in a field where unambiguous evidence is hard to come by.
>
> (*Review of International Political Economy* 1(1) (Spring) 1994: 17)

*Immanuel Kant was an eighteenth-century philosopher whose works on the supreme principles of morality were key texts in the working out of Enlightenment thought.*

Further modifications to the basic realist or state-centred position take account of the significance of other features of a globalised world – transnational economic arrangements, the activities of 'global' companies and so on – and qualify the realist assumption that only security matters control the policy agendas of states. In these versions of international politics, cooperation replaces conflict as the engine of world politics. The stable anarchy of the realist model of international relations gives way to a picture of a much more fluid, unpredictable but still dangerous global political economy.

### Final thoughts on theory

While it is clear that each of the approaches outlined above provides some insights into the origins and processes of globalisation, there are problems with all of them. Modernization theories, especially those grand theories from Talcott Parsons (1967), Rostow (1960) or Fukuyama (1992) paint too neat and deterministic a picture of world history and of the process of modernisation, whereas different brands of Marxism, including dependency theory, are too heavily reliant upon economic factors and are also too deterministic in their insistence that states in the core and periphery are locked into given patterns of development and underdevelopment. World-system analysis also suffers from some of these faults, although its insistence on dealing with global phenomena rather than with the societal level of analysis is a major advance in social theory. Realist conceptions of global order and disorder offer a more politically oriented approach than is found in the others we have canvassed, but only by reducing the international system to conflicts between self-interested nation-states. In fact, all of these approaches lack the means by which to analyse the more contested and open version of globalisation which we covered earlier in the chapter (see pp. 481–92), where human agents are not just supine in the face of global forces and where economics, politics and culture are all important factors in creating a globalised world.

---

**THINK POINT**
- What, if anything, do these approaches have in common?
- What are the major factors which distinguish them from each other?

---

## The forces and features of globalisation

The complexity of the process by which the world is being made into one place beggars any simple description or cataloguing of the main features of globalisation. However, we can identify some of the primary 'sites' at which a contested globalisation is being fashioned:

### The world economy and the new international division of labour

The collapse of state socialism seems to herald the completion of a truly worldwide capitalist economy, although the speed with which countries like Poland, Russia, Mongolia or Cuba will be fully integrated into a system founded on market economics is still open to question. Furthermore, the marketisation of the world economy still leaves many countries in the Third World, and the even poorer Fourth World of sub-Saharan economies, still very marginal in economic terms. Most financial markets, and, increasingly, those concerned with communications and the processing and dissemination of information, now inhabit what Kenichi Ohmae calls a 'borderless world' (Ohmae 1989), with which the traditional mechanisms of national regulation and control are out of kilter. The new world economy is one in which success is based more and more on the production of information and the marketing of services rather than on making things. In this sort of economy, which some people call 'post-Fordist' (to distinguish it from the highly industrialised mass-consumption form of capitalism called 'Fordist'), place and labour power are no longer the most salient factors in economic success. With new forms of information technology guiding production, goods can be produced almost anywhere, with little need for labour-intensive methods of production or for the social and political structures which attended them, like organised trades unionism. Flexibility in production techniques and in working practices and the overall impact of information technologies are transforming the meaning of work for many people in the core states of the world economy, but also contributing to

*Named after Henry Ford, the car-maker and pioneer of mass-production techniques in manufacturing industry.*

the rapid integration of peripheral economies like the 'intelligent island' of Singapore into the mainstream of the world economy in key growth sectors like micro-electronics. Taken together, these developments have important effects on another central institution of a globalised world, the nation-state.

### The world political order

Much of the discussion of globalisation takes place in terms of its adverse effects upon the sovereignty and autonomy of the nation-state. Despite this, the sovereign state is still the principal actor in world politics, but its centrality appears much more fragile than in the recent past, for example with regard to the ability of national governments to implement policies which may run counter to the interests of world markets. Even membership of international regimes like the European Exchange Rate Mechanism (ERM) is not proof against the power of financial markets to undermine a government's attempts to achieve currency stability, as Britain, Italy and France found in 1991 and 1992, when intense speculation on these currencies lead to the first two countries leaving the ERM. In addition, the ability of national governments to regulate the flows of information and entertainment now available online or down-line is becoming increasingly tenuous when so many images and messages can be carried on the virtually uncontrollable Internet and its clones.

*The ERM is a system for establishing and maintaining currency stability between EU trading partners, by restricting movements in the exchange rate value of currencies within specified 'bands'.*

Membership of multilateral and supranational bodies like the EU is also compromising the status of the nation-state as the expression of national unity and identity and as the focus of demands and support from individual citizens and organisations. We should be careful not to overstate this, but, by way of illustration, it is apparent that a growing number of organised interests now routinely lobby Brussels or Strasbourg, seeing European institutions as increasingly central in the policy process which affects them, and sometimes as the means by which to bypass national decision-makers who are less sympathetic to their claims. It may be that the leaders and membership of such groups do not consider themselves to be Europeanised as a result of these activities and feel themselves to be no less French, Italian, Dutch or British because of what they are doing, but, at the very least, the stretching of political activity across borders is contributing to a redefinition of what we mean by domestic politics. At the other extreme, it may be part of a process in which political identities are being changed radically, such that these groups become truly Europeanised, although to date there is very little corroborating evidence.

Of course, realist models of international relations would point to the continued salience of states in the conduct of areas like economic management and emphasise the undoubted resources of most individual states relative to those of even the largest business corporation. Work done by students of international management, like Michael Porter (1990), also stresses the importance of peculiarly national factors in explaining the global success of companies.

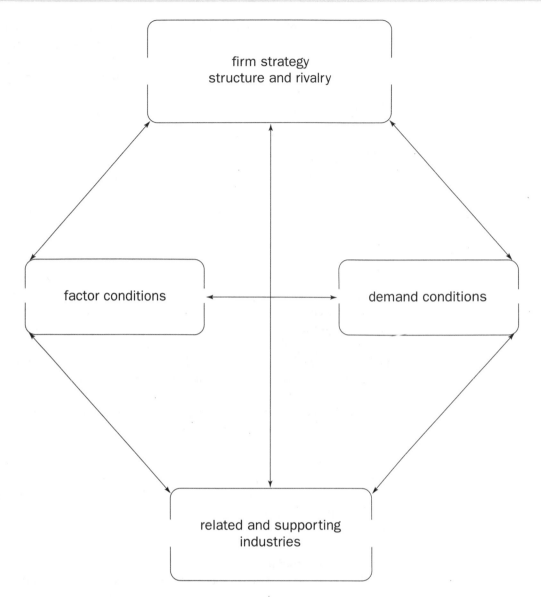

*Figure 16.1* Porter's (1990) model for global success of countries
Reproduced with permission from Macmillan Publishers

When you look at Figure 16.1, which stresses the critical importance of 'national' factors, remember Ohmae's argument about the 'borderless world' and the growing irrelevance of nation-states to the real flows of economic life (Ohmae 1989). Overall, these discussions suggest that under the impact of globalising forces the 'architecture' of world politics and of the world economy is changing quite rapidly (Cerny 1990). John Ruggie, a student of international relations says that rather than the absolute decline or even the complete dissolution of the nation-state, globalisation is bringing about

*In Figure 16.1 'factor conditions' refer to things like skilled labour and a good communications structure; 'demand conditions' to the nature of home demand for the industry's product or service; 'related and supporting industries' to the competitive quality of supplier industries; and 'firm strategy, structure and rivalry' to the rules and norms governing the setting up and managing of companies.*

a 'rearticulation of international political space' (Ruggie 1993), and the nation-state is just one of the components of that emerging structure, the others of which include multilateral institutions like the United Nations, forms of regional government like the EU, transnational interest groups and social movements, and the changing culture of the world polity, which is allowing new kinds of political demands and issues onto the agenda while marginalising older ones.

### Global cultures

The idea of global or cosmopolitan cultures strikes some people as a contradiction in terms, because they say that 'real' cultures are those which bind people to particular places. National cultures are 'real' in this sense, full of imagery, symbolism and meaning for people, because of the myths of origin, the flags, the language and so on, which provide them with a context for knowing who they are. Global cultures, on the other hand, are none of these things, arising out of the general availability of global products and the pervasiveness of images carried by advertising and by the increasingly global entertainments industries. It is quite right to point to these features of global culture and even to suggest that they may be eroding more traditional and local identities. But, as we have seen, this is not a one-way process, and it often spawns a politics of resistance and the reaffirmation of alternative worldviews in a politics of re-traditionalisation. In addition, it could be argued that the separation of culture and identity from place which is implicit in the idea of a global culture, is part of the dialectic which will produce de-spatialized cultures in the same way as it is producing de-territorialized politics.

The preceding features of globalisation reveal it as not only a multidimensional process, but one in which there are a number of tensions, all of which influence the contested making of the global system and underline the possibilities for increased diversity as well as greater homogeneity. These are outlined below.

### Order versus disorder

Teleological explanations of social change describe an historical process unfolding towards an inevitable goal or end-state. Obviously there are different versions of what this will be – a socialist utopia, the global triumph of liberal democracy or a single world community and government – but the ultimate order implied in all these positions seems markedly at odds with the highly contingent and disordered feel of contemporary world politics and of large areas of life. This is not just a matter of older certainties being undone, like the collapse of state socialism and the end of a bipolar world dominated by two superpowers, but also includes, for example, the personal and social dislocation attendant upon changes in employment prospects produced by digitalising production, or shifting assembly plants to another part of the world in order to reduce costs. Overall it seems that the processes of globalisation are speeding up the transformation of both individual and collective identities. People experience these changes sometimes as liberating but often as threatening, and their response may be to try to reinvent a more stable past through some political action or movement, thereby contributing to further disorder. A globalised world may not be a safer or more stable place than one riven by national conflicts or superpower rivalry.

## Globalisation versus localization

The effects of global processes and institutions is to relativise national and local identities and practices and to establish transnational and post-national forms (for example multilateral regimes, networks of professionals in business, finance, science and so on) which marginalise or bypass local rules. At the same time, many global practices are subject to an implicit, but sometimes an explicit, 'localization', to fit local tastes but also to protect local identities.

## Places versus spaces

The modern world and certainly the premodern world were worlds full of places with particular meanings for the people who inhabited them. Landscapes, images of nature, and the physical separation of one community from another were important elements in securing local and national identities. Globalization erodes the intimacy of place, partly because of the greater physical mobility allowed, partly because it permits interests and communities to form which are not tied to particular places and do not need face-to-face contact to sustain them, like 'virtual communities' on the Internet. For all this, nostalgia for 'real' places and the 'whole' lifestyles they supported remains strong and is in direct opposition to the fragmented patterns of living found by some observers in 'global cities' like London, New York or Rio.

## Homogenisation versus diversity

The key message about globalisation is that it does produce what Anthony McGrew calls an 'essential sameness' in the surface appearance of social and political life across the globe (McGrew 1992). However, the appearance of sameness can be deceptive: first, because it disguises a great deal of diversity and fudges the continued vitality of different worldviews; second, because it does not recognise that the process is both multilayered (multidimensional) and driven by a variety of conflicting forces. Because of this it is still a very contingent process.

# Vectors of globalisation

We have already questioned the idea that globalisation is producing a homogeneous world or moving towards an historically prescribed goal or end-state. Fukuyama's (1992) teleological theory of world history and

Wallerstein's (1974) treatment of the making of a capitalist world economy are important insights into aspects of the globalising process, but they underestimate the imponderables in a process that is nowhere complete or uncontested. Roland Roberston (1992) talks of the possibility of different trajectories of global change even at this juncture of world history, but what sort of futures are available?

## A world of nation-states

The future of the nation-state looks rather fragile in the increasingly inter-connected world. But states remain important actors in world politics, with the myth of sovereignty still a powerful constraint on how the international system functions. States are still critical in giving definition to national societies and cultures and are the focus for what Benedict Anderson calls the 'imagined community' of the nation (Anderson 1983). So it is highly unlikely that nation-states will disappear in the foreseeable future, but the meaning of territoriality and the state-centred nature of world politics is almost certain to be further eroded by transnational forces and institutions.

## A post-capitalist world economic order

Wallerstein says that we already have a post-capitalist world economic order and any doubts about its global reach have been removed by the fall of communism and by the frantic attempts of post-communist regimes to marketise their economies and societies. There are few places and few activities not penetrated by capital: tribes in the Amazon Basin, fighting a losing battle with hardwood logging companies, Saturday shoppers at the local hypermarket, boyz 'n' the 'hood, buying rap CDs of Snoop Doggy Dog, are all part of Wallerstein's (1984) global commodity chains. The Ford Motor Company, through its 'Ford 2000' programme, is busy transforming itself into a global organisation, selling global products, regardless of place. In fact the very idea of being a purely national company is becoming rapidly outdated for any business hoping to compete in world markets. Going into the twenty-first century, world trade will be increasingly dominated by big transnational corporations struggling to keep ahead of their rivals, especially in key sectors like telecommunications. In the new century, the shift will be completed from organised, national capitalism, based on national companies and mass production, to disorganised capitalism, where the emphasis is on niche markets, specialised and computer-aided production techniques, global marketing strategies and the provision of services rather than the production of things.

These developments problematise the question of governance, and especially the regulation of economic activity organised on a global scale. The independent nation-state is often simply unable to exercise control or require accountability from transnational organisations, and forms of co-operative regulation like the International Monetary Fund (IMF) or the EU may be better placed to ensure things like fair competition or the rights of consumers. In a globalised world the growth in the number and range of transnational non-governmental organisations (NGOs) working in areas like pollution control or other forms of environmental protection contributes to the essentially democratic function of monitoring powerful commercial and governmental bodies which have shed their own national identities, and also demonstrates the growing vitality of a global civil society.

### Global society

The implied and sometimes explicit universalism of organisations like Friends of the Earth suggests a growing sense of global unity or awareness of global risks, and is part of what we might call 'bottom-up' globalisation, as opposed to the 'top-down' version found in bodies like the United Nations. Perhaps somewhat curiously, this universalism also sanctions a growing respect for difference, or for the tolerance of differences. Global scripts like that of universal human rights underwrite a whole apparatus of regulations, sanctions, educational programmes and forms of political action devoted to achieving this goal. At the same time there is evidence that new and old forms of particularism (ethnic nationalism, racism, religious fundamentalism) are contributing to the destabilising of local and world politics, and that chaos, not order, may be the hallmark of the new century.

### Civilisational conflict

Some writers have even gone so far as to predict the emergence or re-emergence of older more elemental conflicts in the wake of the Cold War. The reference here is to tribalism or ultra-nationalism of the sorts found in Rwanda or the former Yugoslavia, but mainly to the threat of civilisational conflicts. The idea of civilisation used in this way means the broadest forms of cultural identity that bind people together, through history, language, custom or religion. The clear distinction between one civilisation and another is difficult, but writers like Samuel Huntington (1993) are prepared to identify a number of what he calls civilisational identities: the Western, the Confucian (Chinese) as well as Islamic, Hindu, Slavic-Orthodox, Latin American and possibly African. These, he says, constitute great 'fault-lines' across history, lines which were overlaid by the modern conflicts of left versus right, capitalism versus communism and superpower versus superpower, but which are appearing anew as history is released from its Cold War tutelage. These fault-lines will reappear because civilisational identities are more enduring and more authentic than those forged by modern political doctrines, including nation-state nationalism, and because they offer the promise of emotional, if not physical, security in an uncertain and globalised world.

Islamic fundamentalism and its growing appeal in modernised or modernising countries like Turkey or Algeria, along with its potential to disrupt the routines of political and social life in metropolitan countries like France, are often cited as a case in point. On some accounts, the conflict between Bosnian Serbs and Muslims is a local variant of these larger themes. There is undoubtedly a deep sense of 'otherness' or difference between

Islamic and Western worldviews. But apocalyptic visions of civilisational conflict should be modified in the light of the routine transactions which take place between Muslim and non-Muslim countries in the form of trade, tourism and cultural exchanges. No civilization is the monolith conjured up in this interpretation of world conflict. As the Gulf War coalition against the Iraqi invasion of Kuwait in 1991 showed, Muslim states, jealous of their national interests, were still prepared to take up arms against their co-religionists.

### Global chaos

Fukuyama's (1992) picture of the end of History and American President George Bush's prescription in 1990 for a 'New World Order' to be built on the ruins of the Cold War may both appear as far too benign visions of a global future. Much of what we have discussed above describes a world more unsettled, possibly more chaotic, than these pacific models suggest. In this world, which is more intensely localised and globalised, the permanence of some institutional forms like the nation-state and of corresponding identities like citizenship looks quite fragile. Of course, social scientists must always be cautious about how they interpret evidence and must strive to separate wishful thinking and mere speculation from good evidence. Given the scope and diverse nature of the process of globalisation, this task is made more difficult than usual. However, students of politics cannot afford to ignore the impact of politics and social forces which are not just above the nation-state but beyond it too.

## Conclusion

In this chapter we have explored the idea that the study of globalisation adds important new dimensions to the study and understanding of political and social life. First it draws attention to the links between politics, economics and culture in ways rarely seen in the study of national societies. While some accounts still trade on one causal factor in the making of a single world, it is very unlikely that such approaches can grasp the enormous complexity of globalisation as a multidimensional process. Second, it directs attention away from the national society as the focus for social analysis and the main container for social and political life, reflecting the

*This was a concept we first examined in Chapter 1 to explore the links between the individual and the social.*

stretching of social, economic and political relations across the globe. Third, it qualifies the tendency to analyse social and political relations through a concentration upon particular levels of analysis. Rather, the study of globalisation links the personal and the global, showing how individual perceptions and experience of globalisation can have significant effects upon the larger processes at work, as well as how these processes affect individual and collective identities. As with so much in the world of politics, many of the outcomes here have still to be decided.

# Exercise

One of the most important lessons of this chapter has been the idea that the process of globalisation problematises aspects of politics and other areas of social life previously taken for granted. Read the following extract by David Held and answer these questions.

1  What are the main points in Held's argument?
2  What does he mean by the term 'cosmopolitan democracy'?
3  How does this model depart from more conventional ideas about a democratic polity?
4  Does his argument strike you as convincing? In particular, does he underestimate the problems involved?

### *Democracy: From City-States to a Cosmopolitan Order*

Politics unfolds today, with all its customary uncertainty and indeterminatess, against the background of a world shaped and permeated by the movement of goods and capital, the flow of communication, the interchange of cultures and the passage of people.

In this context, the meaning and place of democratic politics, and of the contending models of democracy, have to be rethought in relation to a series of overlapping local, regional and global processes and structures: first, the way processes of economic, political, legal and military interconnectedness are changing the nature, scope and capacity of the sovereign state from above, as its 'regulatory' ability is challenged and reduced in some spheres; secondly, the way in which local groups, movements and nationalisms are questioning the nation-state from below as a representative and accountable power system; and thirdly, the way global interconnectedness creates chains of interlocking political decisions and outcomes among states and their citizens, altering the nature and dynamics of national political systems themselves. Democracy has to come to terms with all three of these developments and their implications for national and international power centres. If it fails to do so, it is likely to become ever less effective in determining the shape and limits of political activity. The international form and structure of politics and civil society has, accordingly, to be built into the foundations of democratic thought and practice.

Three distinct requirements arise: first, that the territorial boundaries of systems of accountability be recast, so that those issues which escape the control of a nation-state – aspects of monetary management, environmental questions, elements of security, new forms of communication – can be brought under better democratic control. Secondly, that the role and place of regional and global regulatory and functional agencies be rethought so that they provide a more coherent and useful focal point in public affairs. Thirdly, that the articulation of political institutions with key groups, agencies, associations and organisations of international society be reconsidered to allow the latter to become part of the democratic process – adopting within their very modus operandi a structure of rules and principles compatible with those

*See the discussion of models of democracy in Chapter 4.*

of democracy. How might this approach to democracy be developed? What are its essential characteristics? . . . [For] if the above arguments are correct, democracy has to become a transnational affair if it is to be possible both within a restricted geographic domain and within the wider international community. The possibility of democracy today must, in short, be linked to an expanding framework of democratic institutions and agencies. I refer to such a framework as 'the cosmopolitan model of democracy'. The framework can be elaborated by focusing initially on some of its institutional requirements.

In the first instance, the 'cosmopolitan model of democracy' pre-supposes the creation of regional parliaments [for example, in Latin America and Africa] and the enhancement of the role of such bodies where they already exist [the European Parliament] in order that their decisions become recognised, in principle, as legitimate independent sources of regional and international law. Alongside such developments, the model anticipates the possibility of general referendums, cutting across nations and nation-states, with constituencies defined according to the nature and scope of controversial transnational issues. In addition, the opening of international governmental organisations to public scrutiny . . . would be significant.

Hand in hand with these changes the cosmopolitan model of democracy assumes the entrenchment of a cluster of rights, including civil, political, economic and social rights, in order to provide shape and limits to democratic decision-making. . . .

In the final analysis, the formation of an authoritative assembly of all democratic states and societies – a reformed UN – or a complement to it, would be an objective.

(Held 1992: 33–4. Reproduced with permission from Basil Blackwell Publishers)

## Further reading

Axford, B (1995) *The Global System: Economics, Politics and Culture*, Cambridge: Polity. Looks at the various dimensions along which globalising pressures have emerged and stresses the cultural aspects of globalisation and of resistance to it.

Drucker, P. (1993) *Post-Capitalist Society*, London: Butterworth-Heinemann. A management guru's readable and thoughtful, if somewhat optimistic account of political, social and economic changes in the 'borderless world'.

Gibson, W. (1984) *Neuromancer*, London: Gollancz. The first cyberpunk vision of a post-apocalyptic, globalised world.

Hirst, P. and Thompson, G. (1995) *Globalization in Question*, Cambridge: Polity. Provides a critical and iconoclastic view of globalisation, suggesting that the idea of a globalized economy is a myth.

Kennedy, P. (1993) *Preparing for the Twenty-First Century*, London: Harper Collins. A historian's view of globalising tendencies, which looks at the impact of factors like environmental change on different parts of the world.

Naipaul, V. S. (1982) *Among the Believers: An Islamic Journey*, Harmondsworth: Penguin. A famous novelist's journey through post-revolutionary Iran and other Islamic countries, examining the tensions between globalising (Westernising) pressures and Islamic identity.

# Glossary

**adversarial politics** The confrontational style, especially of British politics, where political positions tend to become polarised.

**agents of socialisation** Those individuals, groups or institutions which are responsible for the transmission of the information through which people acquire their socialistion.

**anarchy** A term often used rather loosely as a synonym for disorder, but which in fact refers to the doctrine which counsels the absence of formal government.

**behaviouralism** A movement in postwar political science, concerned with both the generation of law-like generalisations about the political world and shifting the emphasis of political studies away from its traditional legal-institutional manifestation. With a focus upon individual behaviour, the 'behaviouralist approach', as it is called, is linked with quantitative rescarch techniques designed to generate testable hypotheses about measurable attitudes and observable behaviour, thus rendering the study of politics more scientific.

**bureaucracy** Government by permanent officials. The word is often used in a pejorative way to imply the tyranny of the office. Its main characteristics include a hierarchy, rules, merit appointments, rationality in decision-making. The term can be applied to private as well as government organisations.

**capitalism** An economic system in which the means of production for the most part lie in private hands and goods and services are bought and sold according to prices determined by a market in which the aim of producers and providers is to make a profit.

**citizenship** Literally, membership of a particular state and the rights attaching to that status, despite the fact that modern conceptions of citizenship stress universal rights and obligations and there is now a transnational doctrine of human rights.

**civic culture** The type of political culture thought by some to provide the best environment for stable democratic politics to occur. It combines the optimum mix of subject and participant political attitudes.

**civil society** The sphere of society in which individuals freely associate in relationships, actions and organisations that are not dependent on state intervention, institutions or regulations.

**class-consciousness** The awareness of social divisions in society and the acceptance that class strongly determines life chances.

**conceptual analysis** A practice and view of philosophy which takes philosophy to be concerned with the analysis and clarification of concepts rather than substantive issues.

**consociational democracy** A form of government said to characterise deeply divided, albeit stable, countries. It involves the creation of power-sharing institutions among coalescent political elites.

**contextualism** This stands for the view that the meaning of political ideas can be understood only by relating them to the historical contexts in which they were generated.

**corporatism** The doctrine that major economic interests, such as business and trade unions, should be incorporated into the system of government.

**cost-benefit analysis** A method for balancing and assessing policy options according to their costs and benefits.

**democracy** From the original Greek, the term means, literally, rule by the people, or by the many. In modern political systems the term is usually linked with universal suffrage, free elections and with notions like the consent of the governed. In terms of modern democracies, an emphasis on human rights and the rule of law would also be key elements of any definition.

**distributive justice** A theory which sees the distribution of wealth and goods in society as involving justice, and which sets out a 'just' scheme of distribution.

**division of labour** The division of tasks and functions, often leading to specialisation and increased productivity, but associated with alienation and fragmentation.

**dominant ideology** Sets of social values, norms and expression which dominate all others at given points in the development of society. In particular, the dominant ideology that characterises a particular historical epoch will tend to reflect the class interests of the social group that is economically dominant. Furthermore, this dominant ideology will seek to mask the 'real' nature of the economic and exploitative relationships on which society rests.

**elite** The best or the noble; in contemporary usage it is generally applied to those who have high status or high formal positions in politics, religion and society.

**empirical** A term meaning sense or understanding derived from experience.

**Enlightenment** The eighteenth-century Enlightenment 'project' was based on a belief in the universality of reason and the power of scientific explanation. The individual was at the centre of the philosophical and political project, with human emancipation seen as following from the spread of rational inquiry and decision-making.

**executive** The apex of power in a political system, at which policy is formed and through which it is executed, for example the President in the USA or the Prime Minister and Cabinet in Britain.

**false consciousness** A term associated with Marxist thought which maintains that individuals and the class to which they belong may well demonstrate a sense of social understanding that is predominantly 'false', in that it hides from them or prevents them from recognising the 'real' nature of their position within the social order and the extent to which they are exploited.

**federation** 'An institutional arrangement, taking the form of a sovereign state, and distinguished from other such states solely by the fact that its central government incorporates regional units in its decision procedure on some constitutionally entrenched basis' (Preston King).

**free-market negativity** An attack on the application of free-market concepts to the media marketplace. It argues that the valuable public service broadcasting ethos characterised by 'protected' and to some extent non-market institutions such as the British Broadcasting Corporation (BBC) cannot be matched in a free media market in which all values will be subject to the needs of profit and that quality will be reduced in the pursuit of cheap programming and copy. Furthermore, the promise of choice offered by the market will, in reality, mean choice between one thing and more of the same.

**free-market positivity** A defence of the application of free-market concepts to the media marketplace. This approach argues that through a combination of new technologies, deregulation and market forces not only will the audience and the public get more media content to consume but that this content will be 'better', in that it will be more responsive to audience choice and more varied, and will allow for greater audience choice and difference.

**functionalist** A term used to describe a range of theories which stress the extent to which norms and values underlie social and political stability. Stable societies are seen as being able to carry out the basic 'functional' imperatives – socialisation, reproduction, education and so on – necessary for their survival.

**futurism** An early twentieth-century movement in the arts which glorified technology, industry and factories.

**Gleichschaltung** The process whereby all institutions and organisations were coordinated to serve the purposes and goals of the Nazi state.

**globalisation** The process by which the world is being made into a single place, not just politically, but economically and culturally too.

**hegemony** A term used to describe the non-coercive aspects of domination, the diffusion throughout society of the value and knowledge systems of a ruling group.

**ideal type** A social scientific technique which imposes an analytical order on the social world and provides clear categories to guide further investigation.

**indigenisation** The adaptation of alien practices to local circumstances and to meet local needs.

**intergovernmentalism** The view which argues that the development of international institutions and regimes tends to be shaped by the actions of and convergences among nation-state actors.

**international relations** Formally, the conduct of politics among nation-states, but also the study of international political interaction, which has more recently begun to include the analysis of non-state as well as state actors and forces.

**judiciary** The body charged with enforcing laws and, in some states, upholding the constitutional rules.

**legislature** The body within a political system that makes the laws. This is likely to be the national assembly, for example Parliament in the UK or Congress in the USA.

**legitimacy** The procedures used by a party for maintaining a belief in the appropriateness and acceptability of the party system.

**level of analysis** For our purposes, the difference between studying individuals and collectives of different sorts. Choosing one level of analysis as opposed to another determines the sort of inferences which can be made from data of various sorts.

**liberal democracy** A doctrine, and sometimes a practice, which combines individual freedom with the idea of popular sovereignty.

**limited government** Government in which the sovereign or executive power is limited by law, constitutional rules or institutional organisation. See also **separation of powers**.

**logical positivism** A philosophical doctrine which maintains that a term is meaningful in so far as it is susceptible of verification.

**logrolling** The bargaining and coalition-building that takes place between departments in order to obtain resources.

**market testing** A process whereby publicly provided goods and services are compared according to cost and quality with those provided by the private sector.

**Marxism** There are various interpretations, although, essentially, emphasis is placed on the way in which the economic process shapes social and class relations and power in the policy-making process.

**mass media** Media that disseminate usually undifferentiated popular forms of output (reflecting the mass nature of the audience) to a mass audience. For example, this would include the popular tabloid press, television, cinema and book publishing.

**methodological individualism** A philosophical and empirical focus on the individual and individual behaviour.

**model** A representation of events and processes which focuses on key aspects of what is going on in them.

**modernisation** Literally, the processes whereby society becomes modern.

**modernity** The distinct way of life found in 'modern' societies. A process beginning in Western Europe in about the fifteenth century, the idea of modernity achieved an intellectual flowering during the Enlightenment. It is usual to tie modernity, or becoming modern, to the emergence of the nation-state, industrialism and the institution of private property. Modernity is also linked to the growth of bureaucratic organisations and secular and individualist ideas.

**modes of production** A phrase usually associated with Karl Marx, and which refers to the way production is organised in society. It focuses upon the technology and social relations of production. The most essential part of social relations is control over productive forces and resources.

**nation-building** The processes through which a sense of national identity and belonging are effected. Sometimes these involve deliberate policy on the part of rulers, sometimes they are instigated through things like threat of invasion.

**nation-state** The governmental and administrative apparatus of a bounded national territory. The term is often used as a synonym for 'country'. The most recent way in which human politics has been organised, and now thought by some to be under considerable threat.

**negative freedom** A term taken as meaning freedom from state interference. It assumes that individuals should have an area of life where they are free to make decisions and behave as they wish as long as they do not interfere with the freedom of others.

**neo-liberalism** A theory which places market efficiencies as the foundation for political freedom and argues for a limited role for the state.

**neo-pluralism** A variant of pluralism which recognises the development of elite groups with more access to power.

**new liberalism** refers to a strand of thinking which rejected the negative concept of liberty and saw state intervention as expanding liberty in areas like factory legislation.

**New Right** The term associated with a resurgence of the right in Western politics since the late 1970s. The New Right, drawing inspiration from the works of (amongst others) von Hayek and Friedman, demonstrates three key characteristics: first, a commitment to a *laissez-faire* attitude to state, society, market and individual that seeks to eliminate state intervention in all aspects of life; second, a reaffirmation of traditional values with regard to certain aspects of social life and social organisation, especially the family and community; third, a libertarian strand which stresses the need for individual liberty and responsibility. The New Right has been seen as highly influential in the administrations of President Ronald Reagan (1981–9) in the USA and the Conservative governments of Margaret Thatcher (1979–90) in the UK.

**normative** The prescription of what should or ought to be the case as opposed to what, descriptively, is the case.

**oligarchy** Government by the few; Michels argued that even in parties which claimed to have democratic internal structures there was a controlling elite pursuing its own self-interest.

**patronage** The distribution of political favours to government or party followers in return for political support.

**pluralism** The belief that there is, or else there should be, diversity. Political pluralism recognises and encourages variety in social, cultural and ideological forms and processes. Pluralist theories examine the influence of social groups in contributing and having access to the making of public policy, with competition for group influence.

**political competence** A person's political competence is both a formal status, in the sense that as a citizen one has the right to vote, and a practical skill, for example in terms of organising a demonstration or writing to a member of Congress or Parliament.

**political culture** The set of values, beliefs and attitudes within which a political system operates.

**political efficacy** The extent to which an individual feels that his or her political participation will be effective.

**political ideologies** Sets of political beliefs involving programmes of political action which draw on large-scale views about human nature and/or historical development.

**political participation** A term to denote the actions by which individuals take part in the political process. Debate centres on two issues: the value of political participation to individuals and the political system, and the causes of participation and non-participation.

**political socialisation** The process, or set of processes, through which people learn about politics and acquire political values. There is much dispute about which processes are significant and about when in the life cycle the most important socialisation takes place.

**political system** An expression sometimes used as a synonym for 'country', but which technically refers to the relationships, processes and institutions which make up a distinct political universe. Thus, the French political system consists of 'inputs' from society to the formal institutions of government, in the form of public opinion, pressure group activity and so on, while the institutions of government process these inputs to produce 'outputs' in the form of laws, policies and even norms and values.

**positive freedom** A view which sees freedom as a condition to be achieved through positive actions.

**postmodern** Literally, beyond the modern, and suggesting a fragmentation of modernist beliefs, identities and certainties.

**propaganda** The term originally referred to propagation of the faith in Catholicism, but refers today to the way in which governments subordinate knowledge and information to state policy.

**public choice** Theories which argue that people make choices according to economic scarcity based on marginal utility.

**public sphere** The realm of social life in which information, opinions and critical discussion take place, thus allowing public opinion to be formed.

**QUANGO** Non-governmental organisations given operational autonomy. Used with the term 'quasi-government' about organisations with an arm's-length relationship with government. There is concern that such organisations have been unaccountable and open to political patronage.

**rationality** A concept which places the individual actor at the centre of analysis, policy-making being determined by individual choice.

**regional integration** The processes by which states in particular regions of the world come to bring together aspects of their economies and politics. There is much debate about the stimulus for such developments, with some seeing the cause as residing in the more or less sovereign preferences of states themselves. Others argue that integration occurs because of the operation of powerful dynamics beyond the control of nation-states.

**relativisation** The process whereby the integrity, wholeness or absolute quality of an identity is diluted by the power of global forces.

**Renaissance** A sixteenth-century movement in Europe which brought a more questioning and secular approach to art and literature and thus to the place of humans in the order of things.

**revolution** A term which suggests profound change involving dramatic events over a short period of time, rather than evolution through stages or incremental adjustments to existing social, political and cultural arrangements.

**separation of powers** The doctrine that maintains that the three elements of government – executive, legislature and judiciary – should be separate in role and responsibility and that such a separation will ensure good and just government.

**social construction** The idea that value, perception and reality are constructed and given meaning through and in shared social understanding rather than existing in an objective reality or through natural development.

**sovereignty** The idea of ultimate political authority. A body is fully sovereign if there is no higher or lower power. Sovereignty has been the basic ground rule for the conduct of the business of international relations. The widespread legitimacy of the idea of sovereign statehood has hindered the development of authoritative institutions above the nation-state.

**state** A human association in which sovereign power is established within a given territorial area, and in which the sovereign power usually possesses a monopoly on the means of coercion.

**supranationalism** The development of executive and binding authority at levels higher than the nation-state. The term is used by some to describe complex networks of interaction among policy actors in international relations.

**syndicalism** A form of revolutionary trade unionism in which the overthrow of capitalism is seen as arising out of direct action by workers. Sorel, an influential syndicalist, argued for the revolutionary potential of the general strike.

**technological determinism** An approach which argues that the development, use and proliferation of technology influences social change and interactions to the extent that technological revolutions can lead to social ones. Put another way, this approach argues that the social organisation of society is determined by the technology in place.

**teleology** A theory of the final causes of things, a story unfolding to a predetermined end.

**totalitarianism** An all-encompassing system of political rule in which political control is exerted over all aspects of life.

**transnational politics** Political activity conducted across national boundaries.

**unit for analysis** The concrete object of inquiry: the individual, the primary group like the family, voluntary associations, formal organisations like political parties, whole societies, nation-states, even the world as a whole.

# General bibliography

Aberbach, J. D., Putnam, R. D. and Rockman, B. A. (1981) *Bureaucrats and Politicians in Western Democracies*, Cambridge, Mass.: Harvard University Press.

Alger, C. F. (1995) 'The United Nations in Historical Perspective', in C. F. Alger et al. (eds) *The United Nations System: The Policies of Member States*, Tokyo: United Nations University Press.

Allett, J. (1982) *New Liberalism: The Political Economy of J. A. Hobson*, Toronto: Toronto University Press.

Allison, G. T. (1971) *Essence of Decision*, Boston: Little, Brown & Co.

Almond G. A. (1980) 'The Intellectual History of the Civic Culture Concept', in Almond, G. A. and Verba, S. (eds) (1980) *The Civic Culture Revisited*, Boston: Little, Brown & Co.

Almond, G. A. and Verba S. (1963) *The Civic Culture: Political Attitudes and Democracy in Five Nations*, Princeton: Princeton University Press.

Almond, G. A. and Verba, S. (eds) (1980) *The Civic Culture Revisited*, Boston: Little, Brown & Co.

Althusser, L. (1969) *For Marx*, London: Allen Lane.

Althusser, L. (1971) *Lenin and Philosophy and Other Essays*, London: New Left Books.

Anderson, B. (1991) *Imagined Communities: Reflections on the Origins and Spread of Nationalism*, 2nd edn, London: Verso.

Appadurai, A. (1990) 'Disjuncture and Difference in the Global Cultural Economy', in M. Featherstone (ed.) *Gobal Culture: Nationalism, Globalization and Modernity*, London: Sage.

Aristotle (1958) *The Politics*, trans. Sir Ernest Barker, Oxford: Oxford University Press.

Aron, R. (1967) *18 Lectures on Industrial Society*, London: Weidenfeld & Nicolson.

Arthur, C. J. (1986) *The Dialectics of Labour*, Oxford: Blackwell.

Ashcraft, R. (1987) *Locke's Two Treatises of Government*, London: Macmillan.

Axford, B. (1992) 'Leaders, Elections and Television', *Politics Review* 1(3), pp. 17–20.

Axford, B. (1995) *The Global System: Economics, Politics and Culture*, Cambridge: Polity.

Axford, B. and Booth, J. (1995) 'Reflexive Modernisation and the Transformation of Identities: Management Education and Systemic Change in East-Central Europe', in V. Edwards (ed.) *Central and Eastern Europe: 5 Years On*, Chalfont St Giles: Buckinghamshire College.

Axford, B. and Browning, G. K. (eds) (1996) *Postmodernity: From the Personal to the Global*, Oxford: Oxford Brookes.

Axford, B. and Huggins, R. (1996) 'Media Without Boundaries: Fear and Loathing on the Road to Eurotrash or Transformation in the European Cultural Economy', *Innovations* 9(2).

Axford, B., Madgwick, P. and Turner, J. (1992) 'Image Management, Stunts and Dirty Tricks: The Marketing of Political Brands in Television Campaigns', *Media, Culture and Society* 14(4).

Bachrach, P. (1967) *The Theory of Democratic Elitism*, London: University of London Press.

Bachrach, P. and Baratz, M. S. (1963), 'Decisions and Nondecisions: An Analytical Framework', *American Political Science Review* 57.

Bachrach, P. and Baratz, M. (1970) *Power and Poverty: Theory and Practice*, Oxford: Oxford University Press.

Bahro, R. (1981) *The Alternative in Eastern Europe*, London: Verso.

Bahro, R. (1986) *Building the Green Movement*, London: GMP.

Ball, T. (1995) *Reappraising Political Theory*, Oxford: Oxford University Press.

Bardi, L. (1996) 'Anti-party Sentiment and Party System Change in Italy', *European Journal of Political Research* 29.

Barkman, K. (1995) 'Politics and Gender: The Need for Electoral Reform', *Politics* 15(5).

Barrett, S. and Fudge, C. (1981) *Policy and Action*, London: Methuen.

Barrett, S. and Hill, M. J. (eds) (1981a) *Policy and Action*, Methuen: London.

Barrett, S. and Hill, M. J. (1981b) *Report to SSRC Central–Local Government Relations Panel*, unpublished.

Barry, B. (1970) *Sociologists, Economists and Democracy*, London: Collier Macmillan.

Barry, N. (1981) *An Introduction to Modern Political Theory*, London: Macmillan.

Batley, R. (1991) 'Comparisons and Lessons', in R. Batley and G. Stoker (eds) *Local Government in Europe: Trends and Developments*, London: Macmillan.

Batley, R. and Stoker, G. (eds) (1991) *Local Government in Europe: Trends and Developments*, London: Macmillan.

Baudrillard, J. (1976) *Symbolic Exchange and Death*, London: Sage.

Baudrillard, J. (1983) *Simulations*, New York: Semiotext.

Baudrillard, J. (1987) *The Evil Demon of Images*, Sydney: Power Institute of Fine Arts.

Baudrillard, J. (1988) *Jean Baudrillard: Selected Writings*, ed. M. Poster, Cambridge: Polity.

Baudrillard, J. (1993) *The Transparency of Evil: Essays on Extreme Phenomena*, London: Verso.

Bauman, Z. (1987) *Legislators and Interpreters: On Modernity, Post-Modernity and Intellectuals*, Cambridge: Polity.

Bauman, Z. (1994) 'After the Patronage State. A Model in Search of Class Interests', in C. G. A. Bryant and E. Mokrzycki (eds) *The New Great Transformation? Change and Continuity in East-Central Europe*, London: Routledge.

Beck, U. (1996) *The Reinvention of Politics*, Cambridge: Polity.

Beer, S. M. (1982) *Britain Against Itself: The Political Contradictions of Collectivism*, London: Faber & Faber.

Bell, D. (ed.) (1962) *The End of Ideology: On the Exhaustion of Political Ideas in the Fifties*, New York: Free Press.

Bellah, R. M., Madson, R., Swidler, A. and Tipton, S. (1985) *Habits of the Heart*, Berkeley, Ca.: University of California Press.

Bellamy, R. (ed.) (1993) *Theories and Concepts of Politics*, Manchester: Manchester University Press.

Bentham, J. (1843) *The Works of Jeremy Bentham*, 2 vols, Edinburgh: William Tait.

Berger, P. and Luckmann, T. (1966) *The Social Construction of Reality*, Harmondsworth: Penguin.

Berlin, I. (1991) 'Two Concepts of Liberty', in D. Miller (ed.) *Liberty*, Oxford: Oxford University Press.

Bernstein, E. (1961) *Evolutionary Socialism*, New York: Schocken Books.

Beveridge, W. (1944) *Full Employment in a Free Society*, London: Allen & Uniwin.

Bhaskar, R. (1976) 'Two Philosophies of Science', *New Left Review* 94.

Birch, A. H. (1993) *The Concepts and Theories of Modern Democracy*, London: Routledge.

Blair, R. (1991) 'Trends in Local Autonomy and Democracy: Reflections from a European Perspective', in F. Batley and G. Stoker (eds) *Local Government in Europe: Trends and Developments*, London: Macmillan.

Birnbaum, P., Lively, J. and Parry, G. (1978) *Democracy, Consensus and Social Contract*, London: Sage.

Blondel, J. (1963) *Voters, Parties and Leaders*, London: Penguin.

Blondel, J. (1969a) *Comparative Government*, London: Macmillan.

Blondel, J. (1969b) *An Introduction to Comparative Government*, London: Weidenfeld & Nicolson.

Bodiguel, J. L. (1983) 'A French-style Spoils System', *Public Administration* 61(3).

Boutros-Ghali, B (1993) 'An Agenda for Peace', in A. Roberts and R. Kingsbury (eds) *United Nations, Divided World. The UN's Role in International Relations*, 2nd edn, Oxford: Oxford University Press.

Boyne, R. and Rattansi, A. (1990) *Postmodernism and Society*, Basingstoke: Macmillan.

Bradbury, M. (1976) *Fahrenheit 451*, London: Grafton.

Braudel, F. (1975) *Capitalism and Material Life 1400–1800*, New York: Harper.

Braudel, F. (1977) *Afterthoughts on Material Civilization and Capitalism*, Baltimore: Johns Hopkins University Press.

Braybrooke, D. and Lindblom, C. E. (1963) *A Strategy of Decision*, New York: Free Press.

Brennan, T. (1981) *Political Education and Democracy*, Cambridge: Cambridge University Press.

Browning, G. K. (1991a) *Plato and Hegel: Two Modes of Philosophising About Politics*, New York: Garland Press.

Browning, G. K. (1991b) 'Ethical Absolutism in Plato and Hegel', *History of Political Thought* XII(3).

Browning, G. K. (1993) 'The German Ideology: The Theory of History and the History of Theory', *History of Political Thought* XIV(3).

Browning, G. K. (1996) 'Good and Bad Infinites in Hegel and Marx', in I. Hampsher-Monk and J. Stanyer (eds) *Contemporary Political Studies*, vol. 2, Belfast: PSA.

Bruce, B. (1992) *Images of Power: How the Image Makers Shape our Leaders*, London: Kogan Page.

Bryant, C. G. A. and Mokrzycki, E. (eds) (1994) *The New Great Transformation? Change and Continuity in East-Central Europe*, London: Routledge.

Bryson, V. (1993) 'Feminism', in R. Eatwell and A. Wright (eds) *Contemporary Political Ideologies*, London: Pinter Press.

Bugge, P. (1995) 'The Nation Supreme. The Idea of Europe 1914–1945', in K. Wilson and J. van der Dussen (eds) *The History of the Idea of Europe*, London: Routledge.

Bulpitt, J. (1983) *Territory and Power in the United Kingdom*, Manchester: Manchester University Press.

Burger, T. (1976) *Max Weber's Theory of Concept Formation. History, Laws and Ideal Types*, Durham, NC: Duke University Press.

Burgess, M. (1993) 'Federalism and Federation: A Reappraisal', in M. Burgess and A. G. Gagnon (eds) *Comparative Federalism and Federation*, Hemel Hempstead: Harvester Wheatsheaf.

Burgess, M. and Gagnon, A. G. (eds) (1993) *Comparative Federalism and Federation*, Hemel Hempstead: Harvester Wheatsheaf.

Burke, E. (1982) *Reflections on the Revolution in France*, Harmondworth: Penguin.

Butler, D. and Kavanagh, D. (1992) *The British General Election 1992*, Basingstoke: Macmillan.

Butler, D. and Stokes, D. (1969) *Political Change in Britain*, Basingstoke: Macmillan.

Calhoun, C. (ed.) (1993) *Habermas and the Public Sphere*, Cambridge: Polity.

Calhoun, C. (1994) 'Social Theory and the Politics of

Identity', in C. Calhoun (ed.) *Social Theory and the Politics of Identity*, Oxford: Blackwell.

Camilleri, J. and Falk, P. (1992) *The End of Sovereignty? The Politics of a Shrinking and Fragmenting World*, Aldershot: Edward Elgar.

Cerny, P. (1990) *The Changing Architecture of Politics: Structure, Agency and the Future of the State*, London: Sage.

Chapman, J. (1993) *Politics, Feminism and the Reformation of Gender*, London: Routledge.

Childs, D. (1983) *The GDR: Moscow's German Ally*, London: Allen & Unwin.

Clarke, M. and Stewart, M. (1991) *The Choices for Local Government for the 1990s and Beyond*, Harlow: Longman.

Cockerell, M., Hennessy, P. and Walker, M. (1985) *Sources Close to the Prime Minister*, London: Macmillan.

Cohen, G. A. (1978) *Karl Marx's Theory of History: A Defence*, Oxford: Oxford University Press.

Collini, S., Winch, D. and Burrow, J. (1983) *That Noble Science of Politics*, Cambridge: Cambridge University Press.

Cox, R. (1987) *Production, Power and World Order*, New York: Columbia University Press.

Cox, R. (with Sinclair, T.) (1996) *Approaches to World Order*, Cambridge: Cambridge University Press.

Cranston, M. (1973) *What Are Human Rights?*, London: Bodley Head.

Crenson, M. (1971) *The Un-Politics of Air Pollution: A Study of Non-Decision-Making in American Cities*, Baltimore: Johns Hopkins University Press.

Crenson, M. (1987) 'The Private Stake in Public Goods: Overcoming the Illogic of Collective Action', *Policy Sciences* 20.

Crewe, I. (1984) 'The Electorate: Partisan Dealignment Ten Years On', in H. Berrington (ed.) *Change in British Politics*, London: Cass.

Crewe, I. and Harrop, M. (eds) (1986) *Political Communications: The General Election Campaign of 1983*, Cambridge: Cambridge University Press.

Crewe, I. and Harrop, M. (eds) (1989) *Political Communications: The General Election Campaign of 1987*, Cambridge: Cambridge University Press.

Crewe, I. and Gosschalk, B (eds) (1995) *Political Communications: The General Election Campaign of 1992*, Cambridge: Cambridge University Press.

Crossman, R. H. S. (1975, 1976, 1977) *The Diaries of a Cabinet Minister*, London: Hamish Hamilton.

Crozier, M. (1964) *The Bureaucratic Phenomenon*, Chicago: University of Chicago Press.

Curran, J. and Seaton, J. (1991) *Power without Responsibility: The Press and Broadcasting in Britain*, 4th edn, London: Routledge.

Curtice, J. (1994) 'Great Britain: Imported Ideas in a Changing Political Landscape', *European Journal of Political Research* 25.

Curtice, J. and Semetko, H. (1994) 'Does it Matter What the Papers Say?', in A. Heath, Jowell, R. and Curtice, J. (eds) *Labour's Last Chance? The 1992 Election and Beyond*, Aldershot: Dartmouth.

Curtice, J. and Steed, M. (1992) 'The Results Analysed', in D. Butler and D. Kavanagh, *The British General Election 1992*, Basingstoke: Macmillan.

Dahl, R. (1961) *Who Governs: Democracy and Power in an American City*, New Haven, Conn.: Yale University Press.

Dahl, R. (1971) *Polyarch: Participation and Opposition*, New Haven, Conn.: Yale University Press.

Dahl, R. (1982) *Dilemmas of Pluralist Democracy*, New Haven, Conn.: Yale University Press.

Dahlgren, P. and Sparks, C. (eds) (1991) *Communication and Citizenship: Journalism and the Public Sphere*, London: Routledge.

Daly, M. (1978) *Gyn/Ecology: The Metaethics of Radical Feminism*, Boston, Mass.: Beacon Press.

Davis, J. C. (1962) 'Towards a Theory of Revolution', *American Sociological Review* 27(1).

de Beauvoir, S. (1968) *The Second Sex*, Harmondsworth: Penguin.

de Maistre, J. (1965) *The Works of Joseph de Maistre*, London: Allen & Unwin.

den Boer, P. (1995) 'Europe to 1914: The Making of an Idea', in K. Wilson and J. van der Dussen (eds) *The History of the Idea of Europe*, London: Routledge.

Dicey, A. V. (1908) *Introduction to the Study of the Law of the Constitution*, London: Macmillan.

Dobson, A. (1990) *Green Political Thought*, London: Unwin Hyman.

Dogan, M. and Pelassy, D. (1990) *How to Compare Nations: Strategies in Comparative Politics*, 2nd edn, Chatham, NJ: Chatham House.

Domhoff, W. (1979) *The Powers That Be: Processes of Ruling Class Domination in America*, New York: Vintage Books.

Dowmunt, A. (ed.) (1993) *Channels of Resistance: Global Television and Local Empowerment*, London: British Film Institute.

Downs, A. (1957) *An Economic Theory of Democracy*, New York: Harper & Row.

Dowse, R. E. and Hughes, J. A. (1972) *Political Sociology*, Chichester: Wiley.

Doyle, M. (1983) 'Kant, Liberal Legacies and Foreign Affairs', *Philosophy and Public Affairs* 12 (summer).

Dror, Y. (1964) 'Muddling Through – Science or Inertia?', *Public Administration Review* 24.

Drucker, P. (1993) *Post-Capitalist Society*, London: Butterworth-Heinemann.

Dunleavy, D. and Husbands, C. T. (1985) *British Democracy at the Crossroads: Voting and Party Competition in the 1980s*, London: Allen & Unwin.

Dunleavy, P. (1980) *Urban Political Analysis*, London: Macmillan.

Dunleavy, P. (1981) 'Professions and Policy Change: Notes Towards a Model of Ideological Corporation', *Public Administration Bulletin* 36.

Dunleavy, P. (1990) 'Mass Political Behaviour: Is There More to Learn?', *Political Studies* 38.

Dunleavy, P. and O'Leary, B. (1987) *Theories of the State: The Politics of Liberal Democracy*, London: Macmillan.

Dunn, J. (1984) *The Political Thought of John Locke*, Cambridge: Cambridge University Press.

Dunn, J. (ed.) (1994) 'Contemporary Crisis of Nation State?', *Political Studies* 42 (special issue).

Duverger, M. (1955) *The Political Role of Women*, Paris: Unesco.

Duverger, M. (1964) *Political Parties: Their Organisation and Activity in the Modern State*, Methuen: London.

Dye, T. (1990) *American Federalism: Competition Among Governments*, Lexington Books.

Dyson, K. (1980) *The State Tradition in West Europe*, Oxford: Martin Robertson.

Dyson, K. (1994) *Elusive Union: The Politics of Economic and Monetary Union*, London: Longman.

Easton, D. (1953) *The Political System*, New York: Knopf.

Easton, D. (1965) *A Systems Analysis of Political Life*, New York: Wiley.

Easton, D. and Dennis, J. (1969) *Children and the Political System: Origins of Political Legitimacy*, New York: McGraw Hill.

Eatwell, R. and O'Sullivan, N. (1989) *The Nature of the Right: European and American Politics and Political Thought Since 1789*, London: Pinter Press.

Eatwell, R. and Wright, A. (eds) (1993) *Contemporary Political Ideologies*, London: Pinter.

Eckstein, H. (1966) *Division and Cohesion in Democracy: A Study of Norway*, Princeton: Princeton University Press.

Edelman, M. (1964) *The Symbolic Uses of Politics*, Urbana, Ill.: University of Illinois Press.

Elazar, D. (1985) *American Federalism: A View from the States*, Harper & Row.

Elazar, D. (1987) *Exploring Federalism*, Tuscaloosa, Alabama: University of Alabama Press.

Eldridge, J. (1993) *Getting the Message: News, Truth, and Power*, London: Routledge.

Elliott, L. (1991) 'The Rolling Economic Disaster', *Guardian* (20 August).

Elmore, R. (1978) 'Organisational Models of Social Program Implementation', *Public Policy* 26.

Elmore, R. (1980) 'Backward Mapping: Implementation Research and Policy Decisions', *Political Science Quarterly*.

Elster, J. (1985) *Making Sense of Marx*, Cambridge and Paris: Cambridge University Press.

Engels, F. (1968) The Origins of the Family, Private Property and the State, in K. Marx and F. Engels, *Selected Writings*, London: Lawrence & Wishart.

Etzioni, A. (1967) 'Mixed Scanning: A Third Approach to Decision-Making', *Public Administration Review* 27.

Etzioni, A. (1993) *The Spirit of Community*, London: Crown Publishers.

Eulau, H. (1963) *The Behavioural Persuasion in Politics*, New York: Random House.

Farer, T. J. and Gaer, F. (1993) 'The UN and Human Rights: At the End of the Beginning', in A. Roberts and B. Kingsbury (eds) *United Nations, Divided World. The UN's Role in International Relations*, 2nd edn, Oxford: Oxford University Press.

Featherstone, M. (ed.) (1990) *Global Culture: Globalization, Nationalism and Modernity*, London: Sage.

Featherstone, M. (1991) *Consumer Culture and Post-modernism*, London: Sage.

Feuerbach, L. (1966) *The Principles of the Philosophy of the Future*, New York: Random House.

Fichte, J. G. (1968) *Addresses to the German Nation*, ed. G. A. Kelley, New York: Harper Torchbooks.

Figes, E. (1970) *Patriarchal Attitudes*, London: Macmillan.

Finer, S. (1974) *Adversary Politics and Electoral Reform*, London: Wigram.

Filmer, Sir R. (1949) *Patriarcha and Other Political Writings*, ed. P. Laslett, Oxford: Oxford University Press.

Fiske, J. (1993) *Power Plays – Power Works*, London: Verso.

Fiske, J. (1994) *Media Matters: Everyday Culture and Political Change*, Minneapolis: Minnesota Press.

Forman, N. (1991) *Mastering British Politics*, Basingstoke: Macmillan.

Forsyth, M. (1981) *Unions of States: The Theory and Practice of Confederation*, Leicester: Leicester University Press.

Forsyth, M. (1994) 'Federalism', *Politics Review* (November).

Foster, M. (1942) *Masters of Political Thought*, vol. 1, London: Harrap.

Frank, A. G. (1969) *Capitalism and Underdevelopment in Latin America*, New York: Monthly Review Press.

Frank, A. G. (1995) 'The Modern World-System Revisited: Rereading Braudel and Wallerstein', in S. K. Sanderson (ed.) *Civilizations and World-Systems*, Walnut Creek: Altamira Press.

Franklin, B. (1994) *Packaging Politics: Political Communications in Britain's Media Democracy*, London: Edward Arnold.

Fraser, D. (1984) *The Evolution of the British Welfare State*, 2nd edn, Basingstoke: Macmillan.

Fukuyama, F. (1992) *The End of History and the Last Man*, London: Hamish Hamilton.

Fukuyama, F. (1995) *Trust: the Social Virtues and the Creation of Prosperity*, London: Hamish Hamilton.

Fulton, Lord (Chairman) (1968) *The Civil Service: Report of the Committee*, 4 vols, Cmnd. 3638, London: HMSO.

Gadamer, H. G. (1981) *Reason in the Age of Science*, Cambridge, Mass.: MIT Press.

Gagnon, A. G. (1993) 'The Political Uses of Federalism', in M. Burgess and A. G. Gagnon (eds) *Comparative Federalism and Federation*, Hemel Hempstead: Harvester Wheatsheaf.

Gellner, E. (1983) *Nations and Nationalism*, Oxford: Blackwell.

Genet, J. (1971) *The Miracle of the Rose*, London: Penguin.

George, S. (1994) 'Cultural Diversity and European Integration: The British Political Parties', in S. Zetterholm (ed.) *National Cultures and European Integration: Exploratory Essays on Cultural Diversity and Common Policies*, Oxford: Berg.

Gerth, H. H. and Wright Mills, C. (1991) *From Max Weber: Essays in Sociology*, London: Routledge.

Gibson, W. (1984) *Neuromancer*, London: Gollancz.

Gibson, W. (1993) *Virtual Light*, London: Viking.

Giddens, A. (1984) *The Constitution of Society*, Cambridge: Polity.

Giddens, A. (1985a) *A Contemporary Critique of Historical Materialism*, Cambridge: Polity Press.

Giddens, A. (1985b) *The Nation-State and Violence*, Cambridge: Polity.

Giddens, A. (1990) *The Consequences of Modernity*, Cambridge: Polity.

Giddens, A. (1991) *Modernity and Self-Identity: Self and Society in the Late Modern Age*, Cambridge: Polity.

Giddens, A. (1993) *New Rules of Sociological Method*, 2nd edn, Cambridge: Polity.

Giddens, A. (1994) *Beyond Left and Right: The Future of Radical Politics*, Cambridge: Polity.

Gill, S. (ed.) (1993) *Gramsci, Historical Materialism and International Relations*, Cambridge: Cambridge University Press.

Gilmour, I. (1978) *Inside Right: A Study of Conservatism*, London: Quartet.

Githens, M., Norris, P. and Lovenduski, J. (1994) *Different Roles, Different Voices: Women and Politics in the United States and Europe*, New York: HarperCollins.

Gitlin, T. (1991) 'Bites and Blips: Chunk News, Savvy Talk and the Bifurcation of American Politics', in P. Dahlgren and C. Sparks (eds) *Communication and Citizenship: Journalism and the Public Sphere*, London: Routledge.

Gouldner, A. W. (1954) *Patterns of Industrial Bureaucracy*, Glencoe, Ill.: Free Press.

Gramsci, A. (1970) *Selections from the Prison Notebooks*, trans. Q. Hoare, London: Lawrence & Wishart.

Grant, A. (1994) *The American Political Process*, Aldershot: Dartmouth.

Gray, A. (1968) *The Socialist Tradition From Moses to Lenin*, New York: HarperCollins.

Gray, J. (1993) *Beyond the New Right: Markets, Government and the Common Environment*, London: Routledge.

Green, T. H. (1941) *Lectures on the Principles of Political Obligation*, London: Longman.

Greenaway, J., Smith, S. and Street, J. (1992) *Deciding Factors in British Politics*, London: Routledge.

Greenstein, F., Herman, U., Stradling, R. and Zureik, E. (1970) 'The Child's Conception of the Queen and the Prime Minister', *British Journal of Political Science* 4(3).

Greenwood, J. and Wilson, D. (1984) *Public Administration in Britain*, London: Allen & Unwin.

Greer, G. (1971) *The Female Eunuch*, London: Paladin.

Griffin, R. (1991) *The Nature of Fascism*, London: Routledge.

Griffin, R. (ed.) (1995) *Fascism*, Oxford: Oxford University Press.

Guardian, (1991) 'The Rolling Economic Disaster' (20 August).

Guardian, (1994) 'Tragic History Repeats Itself' (1 March).

Gurdon, H. (1995), 'Four Men Changed Brent Spar's Course', *Daily Telegraph* (21 June).

Gurr, T. R. (1980) *Why Men Rebel*, Princeton: Princeton University Press.

Habermas, J. (1974) 'The Public Sphere: An Encyclopedic Article', *New German Critique* 3.

Habermas, J. (1987) *The Philosophical Discourse of Modernity*, Cambridge: Polity.

Habermas, J. (1989) *The Structural Transformation of the Public Sphere*, Cambridge, Mass.: MIT Press.

Hague, R., Harrop, M. and Breslin, W. (1994) *Comparative Government and Politics*, 3rd edn, Basingstoke: Macmillan.

Hall, A. J. (1994) *The State: Critical Concepts*, London: Routledge.

Hall, J. (1986) *Powers and Liberties: The Causes and Consequences of the Rise of the West*, Harmondsworth: Pelican.

Hall, S. (1988) *The Hard Road to Renewal. Thatcherism and the Crisis of the Left*, London: Verso.

Hall, S. (1992) 'The Question of Cultural Identity', in S. Hall, A. McGrew and D. Held (eds) *Modernity and its Futures*, Cambridge: Open University/Polity.

Hallin, D. (1994) *We Keep America on Top of the World*, London: Routledge.

Hampsher-Monk, I. (1992) *A History of Modern Political Thought*, Oxford: Blackwell.

Handy, C. (1985) *Understanding Organisations*, London: Penguin.

Harris, L. (1984) 'Governing the World Economy: Bretton Woods and the IMF', in D209 *The State and Society*, Block 6, Unit 25, Milton Keynes: Open University Press.

Harrison, R. J. (1974) *Europe in Question. Theories of Regional International Integration*, London: Allen & Unwin.

Harrop, M. (1986) 'The Press and Post-War Elections', in I. Crewe and M. Harrop (eds) *Political Communications: The General Election of 1983*, Cambridge: Cambridge University Press.

Harrop, M. (1987) 'Voters', in J. Seaton and B. Pimlott (eds) *The Media in British Politics*, Aldershot: Gower.

Harrop, M. (1990) 'Political Marketing', *Parliamentary Affairs* 43(3).

Harvey, D. (1989) *The Condition of Postmodernity: An Inquiry into the Condition of Cultural Change*, Oxford: Blackwell.

Hay, C. (1995) 'Structure and Agency', in D. Marsh and G. Stoker (eds) *Theory and Method in Political Science*, Basingstoke: Macmillan.

Heater, D. (1993) *The Idea of European Unity*, Leicester: Leicester University Press.

Heath, A. (1981) *Social Mobility*, London: Fontana.

Heath, A., Towell, R. and Curtice, J. (1994) *Labour's Last Chance? The 1992 Election and Beyond*, Aldershot: Dartmouth.

Heclo, H. (1972) 'Review Article: Policy Analysis', *British Journal of Political Science* 2.

Heclo, H. (1977) *A Government of Strangers*, Washington, DC: Brookings Institution.

Heclo, H. (1983) 'One Executive Branch or Many?', in A. King (ed.) *Both Ends of the Avenue*.

Hegel, G. W. F. (1971) *The Philosophy of Right*, ed. T. M. Knox, Oxford: Oxford University Press.

Hegel, G. W. F. (1975) *Lectures on the Philosophy of World History*, Cambridge: Cambridge University Press.

Held, D. (1989) *Political Theory and the Modern State*, Cambridge: Polity Press.

Held, D. (1991) 'Democracy and the Global System', in D. Held (ed.) *Political Theory Today*, Cambridge: Polity.

Held, D. (1995) *Democracy and the Global Order: From the Modern State to Cosmopolitan Governance*, Cambridge: Polity.

Held, D., Anderson, J., Gieben, B., Hall, S., Harris, L., Lewis, P. and Parker, B. (1983) *States and Societies*, Oxford: Blackwell.

Hennessy, P. (1989) *Whitehall*, London: Secker & Warburg.

Higgott, R. (1995) 'Economic Co-operation in the Asia-Pacific: A Theoretical Comparison with the European Union', *Journal of European Public Policy* 2(3).

Hiney, T. (1990) 'Tokyo? Yo!', *The Sunday Times*, Style and Travel section, 2 January.

Hirschman, A. O. (1970) *Exit, Voice and Loyalty*, Cambridge, Mass.: Harvard University Press.

Hirst, P. and Thompson, G. (1995) *Globalization in Question*, Cambridge: Polity.

Hitler, A. (1969) *Mein Kampf*, London: Hutchinson.

Hobbes, T. (1962) 'Elements of Law', in R. Peters (ed.) *Body, Man and Citizen: Selections from Hobbes's Writings*, London: Collier.

Hobbes, T. (1968) *Leviathan*, Harmondsworth: Penguin.

Hobbes, T. (1983) *De Cive*, Oxford: Oxford University Press.

Hobhouse, L. T. (1994) *Liberalism and Other Writings*, ed. J. Meadowcroft, Cambridge: Cambridge University Press.

Hobsbawm, E. (1990) *Nations and Nationalism since 1780*, Cambridge: Cambridge University Press.

Hobsbawm, E. (1992) 'Introduction: Inventing Traditions', in E. Hobsbawm and T. Ranger (eds) *The Invention of Tradition*, Cambridge: Cambridge University Press.

Hogwood, B. W. and Gunn, L. A. (1981) *The Policy Orientation*, Glasgow: University of Strathclyde Press.

Hogwood, B. W. and Gunn, L. A. (1984) *Policy Analysis for the Real World*, Oxford: Oxford University Press.

Hohfield, W. (1919) *Fundamental Legal Conceptions*, New York: Yale University Press.

Hood, C. and Dunsire, A. (1981) *Bureaumetrics*, Farnborough: Gower.

Howell, D. (1995) *Easternisation*, London: Demos.

Huntington, S. (1968) *Political Order in Changing Societies*, New Haven, Conn.: Yale University Press.

Huntington, S. (1993) The Clash of Civilizations, *Foreign Affairs* 72(3).

Hussey, G. (1995) *Ireland Today. Anatomy of a Changing State*, Harmondsworth: Penguin.

Hutton, B. (1995) 'Confucius to Beveridge – The Outline of a Welfare State is Emerging', *Financial Times* 26 January.

Hutton, W. (1995) *The State We're In*, London: Cape.

Huxley, A. (1977) *Brave New World*, London: Panther.

Hyman, H. (1959) *Political Socialization: A Study in the Psychology of Political Behavior*, New York: Free Press.

Ingle, S. (1987) *The British Party System*, London: Blackwell.

Inglehart, R. (1977) *The Silent Revolution: Changing Values and Political Styles Among Western Publics*, Princeton: Princeton University Press.

Inglehart, R. (1991) 'Postmaterialism', in V. Bogdanor (ed.) *The Blackwell Encyclopaedia of Political Science*, Oxford: Blackwell.

Jacques, M. (1993) 'The End of Politics', *Sunday Times* (18 July).

James, A. (1984) 'Sovereignty: Ground Rule or Gibberish?', *Review of International Studies*.

Jameson, F. (1991) *Postmodernism or The Cultural Logic of Late Capitalism*, London: Verso.

Jamieson, K. H. (1992a) *Dirty Politics*, New York: Oxford University Press.

Jamieson, K. H. (1992b) *Packaging the Presidency*, 2nd edn, New York: Oxford University Press.

Janis, I. (1972) *Victims of Groupthink*, Boston: Houghton-Mifflin.

Jaros, D. (1973) *Socialization to Politics*, New York: Praeger.

Jessop, B. (1990) *State Theory: Putting the Capitalist State in its Place*, Cambridge: Polity.

Johnson, C. (1966) *Revolutionary Change*, Boston: Beacon Press.

Jones, B. (1993) 'The Pitiless Probing Eye: Politicians and the Broadcast Interview', *Parliamentary Affairs* 46(1).

Jordan, A. G. and Richardson, J. J. (1987) *British Politics and the Policy Process*, London: Allen & Unwin.

Jordan, G. and Maloney, W. A. (1996) 'How Bumble Bees Fly: Accounting for Public Interest Participation', *Political Studies* 44(3).

Katz, P. and Mair, P. (1994) *How Parties Organise*, London: Sage.

Kavanagh, D. (1972) *Political Culture*, London: Macmillan.

Kavanagh, D. (1980) 'Political Culture in Great Britain: The Decline of the Civic Centre', in G. A. Almond and S. Verba (eds) *The Civic Culture Revisited*, Boston: Little, Brown & Co.

Kavanagh, D. (1983) *Political Science and Political Behaviour*, London: Allen & Unwin.

Keane, J. (1988) *Civil Society and the State*, London: Verso.

Keane, J. (1991) *The Media and Democracy*, Cambridge: Polity.

Kedourie, E. (1966) *Nationalism*, London: Hutchinson.

Kegley, C. (ed.) (1995a) *Controversies in International Relations Theory: Realism and the Neoliberal Challenge*, New York: St Martin's Press.

Kegley, C. (1995b) 'The Neoliberal Challenge to Realist Theories of World Politics: An Introduction', in C. Kegley (ed.) *Controversies in International Relations*

*Theory. Realism and the Neoliberal Challenge*, New York: St Martin's Press.

Kegley, C. and Wittkopf, E. (1995) *World Politics: Trend and Transformation*, 5th edn, New York: St Martin's Press.

Kellner, D. (1991) *Jean Baudrillard: From Marxism to Postmodernism and Beyond*, Cambridge: Polity.

Kellner, D. (1995) *Media Culture: Cultural Studies, Identity and Politics between the Modern and the Postmodern*, London: Routledge.

Kennedy, P. (1988) *The Rise and Fall of the Great Powers: Economic Change and Military Conflict from 1500–2000*, London: Fontana Press.

Kennedy, P. (1993) *Preparing for the Twenty-First Century*, London: HarperCollins.

Kerbel, M. (1994) *Edited for Television*, Connecticut: Westview Press.

Kincaid, J. (1994) 'Governing the American States', in G. Peele et al. (eds) *Developments in American Politics 2*, London: Macmillan.

King, P. (1982) *Federalism and Federation*, London: Croom Helm.

King, P. (1994) 'Historical Contextualism: The New Historicism?', *History of European Ideas* 21(2).

King, P. (1983) *The History of Ideas: An Introduction*, London: Croom Helm.

King, P. (1993) 'Federation and Representation', in M. Burgess and A. G. Gagnon (eds) *Comparative Federalism and Federation*, Hemel Hempstead: Harvester Wheatsheaf.

King, P. (1996) 'Historical Contextualism Revisited', *Politics* 16(3).

Kleinsteuber, H. J. (1995) 'The Mass Media', in M. Shelley and M. Winck (eds) *Aspects of European Cultural Diversity*, London: Routledge.

Kolarska-Bobinska, L. (1994) 'Privatization in Poland: The Evolution of Opinions and Interests, 1988–1992', in G. S. Alexander and G. Skapska (eds) *A Fourth Way? Privatization, Property, and the Emergence of New Market Economies*, London: Routledge.

Krause, K. and W. A. Knight (1995) 'Introduction: Evolution and Change in the United Nations System', in K. Krause and W. A. Knight (eds), *Society and the UN System: Changing Perspectives on Multilateralism*, Tokyo: United Nations University Press.

Kroker, A. (1992) *The Possessed Individual*, London: Macmillan.

Kuhn, T. (1970) *The Structure of Scientific Revolutions*, Chicago: University of Chicago Press.

Lane, D. (1978) *Politics and Society in the USSR*, 2nd edn, Oxford: Martin Robertson.

Lane, D. (1985) *Politics and Society in the USSR*, Oxford: Blackwell.

Lane, J. and Ersson, S. O. (1994) *Politics and Society in Western Europe*, 3rd edn, London: Sage.

Lash, S. and Urry, J. (1994) *Economies of Signs and Space*, London: Sage.

Laski, H. (1948) *The Grammar of Politics*, London: Allen & Unwin.

Laslett, P. (1956) 'Introduction', *Philosophy, Politics and Society* series, Oxford: Blackwell.

Laslett, P. (1963) 'Introduction', *Locke's Two Treatises of Government*, Cambridge: Cambridge University Press.

Lasswell, H. (1951) 'The Policy Orientation', in D. Lerner and H. Lasswell (eds) *The Policy Sciences*, Stanford: Stanford University Press.

Leigh, D. (1980) *Frontiers of Secrecy*, London: Junction Books.

Lenin, V. I. (1975) *Imperialism: The Highest Stage of Capitalism*, Moscow: Foreign Language Press.

Lerner, D. (1958) *The Passing of Traditional Society*.

Lijphart, A. (1975) 'The Northern Ireland Problem: Cases, Theories and Solutions', *British Journal of Political Science* 5(1).

Lijphart, A. (1977) *Democracy in Plural Societies: A Comparative Exploration*, New Haven, Conn.: Yale University Press.

Lijphart, A. (1980) 'The Structure of Inference', in G. A. Almond and S. Verba (eds) *The Civic Culture Revisited*, Boston: Little, Brown & Co.

Lijphart, A. (1991) 'Consociational Democracy', in V. Bogdanor (ed.) *The Blackwell Encyclopaedia of Political Science*, Oxford: Blackwell.

Lindblom, C. E. (1959) 'The Science of Muddling Through', *Public Administration Review* 19.

Lindblom, C. (1968) *The Policy Making Process*, Englewood Cliffs, NJ: Prentice Hall.

Lipow, A. and Seyd, P. (1996) 'The Politics of Anti-Partyism', *Parliamentary Affairs* (March).

Lipset, S. M. (1959) 'Some Social Requisites of Democracy: Economic Development and Political Legitimacy', *American Political Science Review* 53(1).

Lipset, S. M. (1960) *Political Man*, New York: Doubleday.

Lipset, S. M. and Rokkan, S. (eds) (1967) *Party Systems and Voter Alignments: Cross National Perspectives*, New York: Free Press.

Lipset, S. M., Seoung, K. R. and Torres, J. (1993) 'A Comparative Analysis of the Social Requisites of Democracy', *International Social Science Journal* 136.

Lively, J. (1978) 'Pluralism and Consensus', in P. Birnbaum, J. Lively and G. Parry (eds) *Democracy, Consensus and Social Contract*, London: Sage.

Lively, J. and Reeve, A. (1989) *Modern Political Theory*, London: Routledge.

Locke, J. (1963) *Locke's Two Treatises of Government*, ed. P. Laslett, Cambridge: Cambridge University Press.

Locke, J. (1971) 'An Essay Concerning the True Original, Extent and End of Government' (Second Treatise of Government), in E. Barker (ed.) *Social Contract*, Oxford: Oxford University Press.

Locke, J. (1975) *Essay Concerning Human Understanding*, Oxford: Oxford University Press.

Lodge, D. (1984) *Small World*, Harmondsworth: Penguin.

Lovelock, J. (1979) *Gaia: A New Look at Life on Earth*, Oxford: Oxford University Press.

Luard, E. (ed.) (1992) *Basic Texts in International Relations*, Basingstoke: Macmillan.

Lukes, S. (1974) *Power: A Radical View*, London: Papermac.

Lukes, S. (1992) 'What is Left?', *Times Literary Supplement* (27 March).

Lynn, J. and Jay, A. (1987) *The Complete Yes Minister*, London: BBC Books.

Lyotard, J. F. (1988) *The Differend: Phrases in Dispute*, Manchester: Manchester University Press.

MacCallum Jr, G. (1991) 'Negative and Positive Freedom', in D. Miller (ed.) *Liberty*, Oxford: Oxford University Press.

Machiavelli, N. (1950) *The Prince and the Discourses*, New York: The Modern Library.

McGrew, A. (1992) 'A Global Society?', in S. Hall, D. Held and A. McGrew (eds) *Modernity and its Futures*, Cambridge: Polity.

Macintyre, A. (1981) *After Virtue*, Duckworth: Guildford.

Macintyre, A. (1988) *Whose Justice? Which Rationality?*, London: Duckworth.

McKay, D. (1992) *American Politics and Society*, 3rd edn, Oxford: Blackwell.

Mackenzie, W. J. M. (1978) *Political Identity*, Manchester: Manchester University Press.

McLennan, G. (1995) *Pluralism*, London: Open University Press.

McLean, I. (1987) *Public Choice: An Introduction*, Oxford: Blackwell.

Maddison, A. (1987) 'Growth and Slow-Down in Advanced Capitalist Economies: Techniques of Quantitative Assessment', *Journal of Economic Literature* 2.

Madison, J. (1961) *The Federalist Papers*, ed. Clinton Rossiter, New York: New American Library of World Literature no. 10.

Mair, P. (ed.) (1990) *The West European Party System*, Oxford: Oxford University Press.

Mandela, N. (1995) *The Long Walk to Freedom*, London: Abacus.

Mandelson, P. (1996) *The Blair Revolution: Can Labour Deliver?*, London: Faber.

Mann, M. (1986) *The Sources of Social Power, Volume 1: A History of Power from the beginning to AD 1760*, Cambridge: Cambridge University Press.

March, J. and Simon, H. A. (1958) *Organisations*, New York: John Wiley & Sons.

Marx, K. (1967) *Capital*, vol. 1, New York: International Publishers.

Marx, K. (1973a) *Grundrisse: Foundations of the Critique of Political Economy*, Harmondsworth: Penguin.

Marx, K. (1973b) 'The Civil War in France', *Political Writings, vol. 3, The First International and After*, Harmondsworth: Penguin.

Marx, K. (1975a) 'Critique of Hegel's Philosophy of Right', *Early Writings*, Harmondsworth: Penguin.

Marx, K. (1975b) 'Economic and Philosophical Manuscripts', in *Early Writings*, Harmondsworth: Penguin.

Marx, K. (1979) *Capital*, Harmondsworth: Penguin.

Marx, K. and Engels, F. (1972) *Ireland and the Irish Question*, New York: International Publishers.

Marx, K. and Engels, F. (1973a) 'The Communist Manifesto', *Political Writings, vol. 1, The Revolutions of 1848*, Harmondworth: Penguin.

Marx, K. and Engels, F. (1973b) *The German Ideology*, London and Moscow: Progress Publishers.

Mayntz, R. and Scharpf, F. W. (1975) *Policy-Making in the German Federal Bureaucracy*, Amsterdam: Elsevier.

Melling, D. (1987) *Understanding Plato*, Oxford: Oxford University Press.

Merton, R. K. (1957) *Social Theory and Social Structure*, Glencoe, Ill.: Free Press.

Michels, R. (1962) *Political Parties*, New York: Collier.

Middlemas, K. (1995) *Orchestrating Europe: The Informal Politics of the European Union, 1973–1995*, London: HarperCollins.

Milbrath, L. (1965) *Political Participation: How and Why Do People Get Involved in Politics?*, Chicago: Rand McNally.

Milbrath, L. and Goel, M. (1977) *Political Participation: How and Why Do People Get Involved in Politics?*, 2nd edn, Chicago: Rand McNally.

Miliband, D. (ed.) (1994) *Reinventing the Left*, Cambridge: Polity.

Mill, J. S. (1964) *Autobiography of John Stuart Mill*, New York: Signet Classics.

Mill, J. S. (1972) *Considerations on Representative Government*, London: Penguin.

Mill, J. S. (1982) *On Liberty*, Harmondsworth: Penguin.

Mill, J. S. (1989) 'The Subjection of Women', *On Liberty and Other Writings*, Cambridge: Cambridge University Press.

Miller, D. (1991) (ed.) *Liberty*, Oxford: Oxford University Press.

Millet, K. (1970) *Sexual Politics*, London: Virago.

Mills, C. W. (1956) *The Power Elite*, New York: Random House.

Milward, A. S. (1992) *The European Rescue of the Nation State*, London: Routledge.

Minogue, K. (1985) *Alien Powers: The Pure Theory of Ideology*, London: Weidenfeld & Nicolson.

Minogue, K. (1990) 'Equality: A Response', in G. Hunt (ed.) *Philosophy and Politics*, Cambridge: Cambridge University Press.

Mitrany, D. (1966) *A Working Peace System*, 2nd edn, Chicago: Quadrangle Books.

Montesquieu, Charles Secondat, Baron de (1989) *The Spirit of the Laws*, ed. A. M. Cohler et al., Cambridge: Cambridge University Press.

Moore Jr, B. (1966) *The Social Origins of Dictatorship and Democracy*, Boston: Beacon Press.

Moravcsik, A. (1991) 'Negotiating the Single European Act', in R. O. Keohane and S. Hoffmann (eds) *The New European Community: Decision-making and Institutional Change*, Boulder, Col.: Westview.

Moravcsik, A. (1993) 'Preferences and Power in the European Community: A Liberal Intergovernmentalist Approach', *Journal of Common Market Studies* 31(4).

Morgenthau, H. J. (1985) *Politics Among Nations: The Struggle for Power and Peace*, 6th edn, New York: Knopf.

Morphet, S. (1993) 'UN Peacekeeping and Election Monitoring', in A. Roberts and B. Kingsbury (eds) *United Nations, Divided World: The UN's Role in International Relations*, 2nd edn, Oxford: Oxford University Press.

Mosca, G. (1939) *The Ruling Class*, New York and London: McGraw-Hill.

Mueller, C. (1988) *The Politics of the Gender Gap*, London: Sage.

Mulgan, G. (1994) *Politics in an Antipolitical Age*, Cambridge: Polity.

Nabokov, V. (1974) *Bend Sinister*, London: Pengiun.

Naipaul, V. S. (1982) *Among the Believers: An Islamic Journey*, Harmondsworth: Penguin.

Nietzsche, F. (1967) *The Will to Power*, New York: Random House.

Nietzsche, F. (1969) *Thus Spake Zarathustra*, London: Penguin.

Niss, H. (1994) 'European Cultural Diversity and its Implications for Pan-European Advertising', in S. Zetterholm (ed.) *National Cultures and European Integration: Exploratory Essays on Cultural Diversity and Common Policies*, Oxford: Berg.

Nordlinger, E. (1967) *The Working Class Tories*, Berkeley, University of California Press.

Nordlinger, E. (1981) *The Autonomy of the Democratic State*, Cambridge, Mass.: Harvard University Press.

Norris, P. (1996) 'Mobilising the "Women's Vote": The Gender-Generation Gap in Voting Behaviour', *Parliamentary Affairs*, vol. XXXXIX(3).

Norton, A. (1994) *International Handbook of Local and Regional Government*, Aldershot: Edward Elgar.

Norton, P. (ed.) (1990) *Legislatures*, Oxford: Oxford University Press.

Nossiter, T., Semetko, H. and Scammel, M. (1994) 'The Media's Coverage of the Campaign', in A. Heath et al., *Labour's Last Chance? The 1992 Election and Beyond*, Aldershot: Dartmouth.

Nozick, R. (1974) *Anarchy, State and Utopia*, Oxford: Blackwell.

Nugent, N. (1994) *The Government and Politics of the European Union*, 3rd edn, Basingstoke: Macmillan.

O'Brien, C. C. and Topolski, F. (1968) *The United Nations: Sacred Drama*, London: Hutchinson.

O'Shaughnessy, N. (1990) *The Phenomenon of Political Marketing*, Basingstoke: Macmillan.

O'Sullivan, N. (1976) *Conservatism*, London: Dent.

O'Sullivan, N. (1993) 'Political Integration, the Limited State, and the Philosophy of Postmodernism', *Political Studies* 41(4).

Oakeshott, M. (1962) *Rationalism in Politics and Other Essays*, London and New York: Methuen.

Ohmae, K. (1989) *Borderless World: Power and Strategy in the Interlinked Economy*, London: HarperCollins.

Okin, S. (1980) *Women in Western Political Thought*, London: Virago.

Olson, M. (1965) *The Logic of Collective Action*, Cambridge, Mass.: Harvard University Press.

Orwell, G. (1951) *Animal Farm*, London: Penguin.

Orwell, G. (1982) *The Lion and the Unicorn: Socialism and the English Genius*, London: Penguin.

Orwell, G. (1983) *Nineteen Eighty-Four*, London: Penguin.

Ostrogoski, M. I. (1902) *Democracy and the Organisation of Political Parties*, London: Macmillan.

Owen, D. and Dennis J. (1996) *Anti-partyism in the USA and support for Ross Perot*.

Parekh, B. (1993) 'The Cultural Particularity of Liberal Democracy', in D. Held (ed.) *Prospects for Democracy: North, South, East, West*, Cambridge: Polity.

Parekh, B. (1990) 'The Rushdie Affair: Research Agenda for Political Philosophy', *Political Studies*, xxxviii(4) (December).

Pareto, V. (1935) *The Mind and Society*, 4 vols, New York: Harcourt Brace.

Parker, M. (1993) 'Post-modern Organisations or Post-modern Organisation Theory?' *Organisation Studies* 13(1).

Parry, G., Moyser, G. and Day, N. (1992) *Political Participation and Democracy in Britain*, Cambridge: Cambridge University Press.

Parsons, A. (1994) *From Cold War to Hot Peace: UN Interventions 1947–1994*, London: Michael Joseph.

Parsons, T. (1967) *Sociological Theory and Modern Society*, New York: Free Press.

Pascale, R. (1990) *Managing on the Edge*, Harmondsworth: Penguin.

Pateman, C. (1971) 'Political Culture, Political Structure and Political Change', *British Journal of Political Science* 1(3).

Pateman, C. (1988) *The Sexual Contract*, Cambridge: Polity.

Patrick, G. (1976) *The Concept of Political Culture*, International Studies Association Working Paper no. 80.

Peake, M. (1972) *Titus Groan*, Harmondsworth: Penguin.

Peele, G. (ed.) (1994) *Developments in American Politics*, 2nd edn, Basingstoke: Macmillan.

Pentland, C. (1973) *International Theory and European Integration*, London: Faber & Faber.

Perryman, M. (1994) *Altered States: Postmodernism, Politics and Culture*, London: Lawrence & Wishart.

Phillips, A. (1994) *Democracy and Difference*, Cambridge: Polity.

Piccone, P. (1996) 'Postmodern Populism', *Telos* 103.

Pirsig, R. (1974) *Zen and the Art of Motorcycle Maintenance*, New York: Bodley Head.

Pitt, D. and Smith, B. C. (1981) *Government Departments: An Organisational Perspective*, London: Routledge & Kegan Paul.

Piven, F. F. and Cloward, R. A. (1977) *Poor People's Movements: Why They Succeed, How They Fail*, New York: Random House.

Plamenatz, J. (1963) *Man and Society*, 2 vols, London: Longman.

Plant, J. (1989) *Healing the Wounds*, London: Green Print.

Plato (1945) *The Republic*, trans. and with introd. by F. M. Cornford, Oxford and New York: Clarendon Press.

Plato (1961a) 'Apology', *The Collected Dialogues of Plato*, Princeton: Princeton University Press.

Plato (1961b) 'Letter VII', *The Collected Dialogues of Plato*, Princeton: Princeton University Press.

Plato (1961c) 'Crito', *The Collected Dialogues of Plato*, Princeton: Princeton University Press.

Plato (1961d) 'Laws', *The Collected Dialogues of Plato*, Princeton: Princeton University Press.

Plato (1961e) 'Statesman', *The Collected Dialogues of Plato*, Princeton: Princeton University Press.

Pocock, J. (1971) *Politics, Language and Time*, London: Methuen.

Ponting, C. (1986) *Whitehall: Tragedy and Farce*, London: Hamish Hamilton.

Porritt, J. (1984) *Seeing Green: The Politics of Ecology Explained*, Oxford: Blackwell.

Porter, M. (1990) *The Competitive Advantage of Nations*, London: Macmillan.

Poulantzas, N. (1974) *Classes in Contemporary Capitalism*, London: Humanities Press.

Pressman, J. and Wildavsky, A. (1973) *Implementation*, Berkeley, Ca.: University of California Press.

Prewitt, K. (1970) *The Recruitment of Political Leaders: A Study of Citizen Politicians*, New York: Bobbs-Merrill.

Quinton, A. (1978) *The Politics of Imperfection*, London: Faber.

Randall, V. (1987) *Women and Politics: An International Perspective*, Basingstoke: Macmillan.

Rawls, J. (1971) *A Theory of Justice*, Oxford: Oxford University Press.

Rawls, J. (1993) *Political Liberalism*, New York: Columbia University Press.

Rees-Mogg, W. (1995) 'The End of the Nations' from *The Times*, 31 August.

Reeve, A. and Ware, A. (1992) *Electoral Systems: A Comparative and Theoretical Discussion*, London: Routledge.

Rheingold, H. (1994) *The Virtual Community: Finding Connection in a Computerised World*, London: Verso.

Rhodes, R. A. W. (1981) *Control and Power in Central–Local Relations*, Farnborough: Gower.

Rhodes, R. A. W. (1988) *Beyond Westminster and Whitehall*, London: Allen & Unwin.

Richardson, J. J. and Jordan, A. G. (1979) *Governing Under Pressure: The Policy Process in a Post-Parliamentary Democracy*, Oxford: Martin Robertson.

Ridley, F. F. (1979) *Government and Administration in Western Europe*, Oxford: Martin Robertson.

Ridley, F. F. (1983) 'Career Service: A Comparative Perspective on Civil Service Promotion', *Public Administration* 62(2).

Righter, R. (1995) *Utopia Lost: The United Nations and World Order*, Twentieth Century Fund.

Riker, W. H. and Ordeshook, P. C. (1968) 'A Theory of the Calculus of Voting', *American Political Science Review* 62.

Roberts, A. and Kingsbury B. (eds) (1993) *United Nations, Divided World The UN's Role in International Relations*, 2nd edn, Oxford: Oxford University Press.

Robertson, R. (1992) *Globalization: Social Theory and Global Culture*, London: Sage.

Robinson, A. and Sandford, C. (1983) *Tax Policy-Making in the United Kingdom*, London: Heinemann.

Rorty, R. (1992) 'Cosmopolitanism Without Emancipation: A Response to Lyotard', in S. Lash and J. Friedman (eds) *Modernity and Identity*, Oxford: Blackwell.

Rose, R. (1974) *The Problem of Party Government*, London: Macmillan.

Rose, R. (1980) *Do Parties Make a Difference?*, London: Macmillan.

Rose, R. (1984) *Do Parties Make a Difference?*, Basingstoke: Macmillan.

Rosenau, J. (1990) *Turbulence in World Politics*, London: Harvester Wheatsheaf.

Rosenau, P. and Bredemeier, H. (1992) 'Modern and Postmodern Conceptions of Social Order', *Social Research* 60(2).

Rostow, W. (1960) *The Stages of Economic Growth: A Non-Communist Manifesto*, Cambridge: Cambridge University Press.

Rousseau, J.-J. (1911) *Emile*, London: Methuen.

Rousseau, J.-J. (1957) *Confessions of Jean-Jacques Rousseau*, Harmondsworth: Penguin.

Rousseau, J.-J. (1973a) 'A Discourse on the Origin of Inequality', *The Social Contract and Discourses*, London and New York: Dent.

Rousseau, J.-J. (1973b) 'The Social Contract', *The Social Contract and Discourses*, London and New York: Dent.

Rousseau, J.-J. (1973c) 'A Discourse on the Arts and Sciences', *The Social Contract and Discourses*, London and New York: Dent.

Ruggie, J. G. (1993) 'Territoriality and Beyond: Problematizing Modernity in International Relations', *International Organization* 47(1).

Rush, M. (1992) *Politics and Society. An Introduction to Political Sociology*, Hemel Hempstead: Harvester Wheatsheaf.

Rushdie, S. (1990) 'In Good Faith', *Independent* (11 February).

Ryan, M. (1988) 'Postmodern Politics', *Theory, Culture and Society* 5.

Ryle, M. (1988) *Ecology and Socialism*, London: Radius.

Sabatier, P. (1987) 'Knowledge, Policy-oriented Learning and Policy Change. An Advocacy Coalition Framework', *Knowledge, Diffusion, Utilization* 8(4).

Sabatier, P. and Mazmanian, D. (1979) 'The Conditions of Effective Implementation: A Guide to Accomplishing Policy Objectives', *Policy Analysis* 6(3).

Sandel, M. (1984) *Liberalism and its Critics*, New York: New York University Press.

Sanders, D. (1995) 'Behavioural Analysis', in D. Marsh and G. Stoker (eds) *Theory and Methods in Political Science*, Basingstoke: Macmillan.

Sandholtz, W. and Zysman, J. (1989) '1992: Recasting the European Bargain', *World Politics* 42.

Sartori, G. (1970) 'Concept Misinformation in Comparative Politics', *American Political Science Review* 64.

Schlozman, K. L., Berba, S. and Brady, H. (1995) 'Participation's not a Paradox: the View from American Activists', *British Journal of Political Science* 25.

Schmitter, P. C. (1979) 'Still the Century of Corporatism', in P. C. Schmitter and G. Lehmbruch (eds) *Trends Towards Corporatist Intermediation*, London: Sage.

Schumpeter, J. (1976) *Capitalism, Socialism and Democracy*, London: Allen & Unwin.

Seidman, H. (1980) *Politics, Position and Power*, Oxford: Oxford University Press.

Seymour-Ure, C. (1989) 'Prime Ministers' Reactions to Television: Britain, Australia and Canada', *Media, Culture and Society* 11.

Simon, H. A. (1957) *Administrative Behaviour*, Glencoe, Ill.: Free Press.

Singer, P. (1976) *Animal Liberation*, London: Jonathan Cape.

Sinnott, R. and Niedermayer, O. (1995) *Public Opinion and Internationalized Governance*, Oxford: Oxford University Press.

Skinner, Q. (1988) 'Meaning and Understanding in the History of Ideas', in J. Tully (ed.) *Meaning and Context – Quentin Skinner and his Critics*, Cambridge: Polity.

Skocpol, T. (1978) *States and Social Revolutions: A Comparative Analysis of France, Russia and China*, Cambridge: Cambridge University Press.

Skovmand, M. and Schroder, K. (1992) *Media Cultures: Reappraising Transnational Media*, London: Routledge.

Smart, B. (1992) *Modern Conditions, Postmodern Controversies*, London: Routledge.

Smelser, N. (1963) *Theory of Collective Behaviour*, New York: Free Press.

Smith, A. (1973) *The Concept of Social Change*, London: Routledge & Kegan Paul.

Smith, Adam (1976) *An Inquiry into the Nature and Causes of the Wealth of Nations*, Chicago: Chicago University Press.

Smith, A. D., (1971) *Theories of Nationalism*, London: Duckworth.

Smith, A. D. (1991) *National Identity*, Harmondsworth: Penguin.

Smith, G. (ed.) (1995) *Federalism: The Multiethnic Challenge*, London: Longman.

Solzhenitsyn, A. (1963) *One Day in the Life of Ivan Denisovich*, London: Penguin.

Sparkes, A. W. (1994) *Talking Politics: A Wordbook*, London: Routledge.

Stewart, J. and Stoker, G. (eds) (1995) *Local Government in the 1990s*, London: Macmillan.

Stoker, G. (1991) *The Politics of Local Government*, London: Macmillan.

Stoker, L. and Jennings, N. K. (1995) 'Life-Cycle Transitions and Political Participation: The Case of Marriage', *American Political Science Review* 89(2).

Strange, S. (1994) *States and Markets*, 2nd edn, London: Pinter.

Taylor, C. (1989) *Sources of the Self: The Making of the Modern Identity*, Cambridge: Cambridge University Press.

Thatcher, M. (1993) *The Downing Street Years*, London: HarperCollins.

Therborn, G. (1995) *European Modernity and Beyond: The Trajectory of European Societies 1945–2000*, London: Sage.

Thompson, H. S. (1994) *Better than Sex*, London: Black Swan.

Thompson, J. (1990) *Ideology and Modern Culture*, Cambridge: Polity.

Thompson, J. (1995) *Media and Modernity: A Social Theory of the Media*, Cambridge: Polity.

Tilly, C. (1975) *The Formation of National States in Western Europe*, Princeton: Princeton University Press.

Tilly, C. (1991) 'Does Modernisation Breed Revolution?', *International Social Science Journal* 134, 22–43.

Tocqueville, A. de (1947) *The Old Regime and the French Revolution*, Oxford: Blackwell.

Tocqueville, A. de (1954) *Democracy in America*, ed. P. Bradley, New York: Random House.

Toffler, A. (1971) *Future Shock*, London: Bantam Books.

Touraine, A. (1991) 'What Does Democracy Mean Today?', *International Social Science Journal* 128.

Tressell, R. (1965) *The Ragged Trousered Philanthropists*, London: Granada.

Trimberger, E. (1978) *Revolution from Above: Military Bureaucrats and Development in Japan, Turkey, Egypt and Peru*, New York: Transaction Books.

Tully, J. (1988) *Meaning and Context – Quentin Skinner and his Critics*, Cambridge: Polity.

Turner, B. (ed.) (1990) *Theories of Modernity and Postmodernity*, London: Sage.

Vattimo, G. (1992a) *The End of Modernity*, Cambridge: Polity.

Vattimo, G. (1992b) *The Transparent Society*, Cambridge: Polity.

Vaughn, S. (1994) *Ronald Reagan in Hollywood: Movies and Politics*, Cambridge: Cambridge University Press.

Verba, S. and Nie, N. H. (1972) *Participation in America: Political Democracy and Social Equality*, New York: Harper & Row.

Verba, S., Nie, N. H. and Kim, J.-O. (1971) *The Modes of Democratic Participation: A Cross-National Comparison*, Beverly Hills: Sage.

Verba, S., Nie, N. H. and Kim, J.-O. (1978) *Participation and Political Equality: A Seven Nation Comparison*, Cambridge: Cambridge University Press.

Verney, D. V. (1959) *Analysis of Political Systems*, London: Routledge & Kegan Paul.

von Beyme, K. (1996) 'Party Leadership and Change in Party Systems: Towards a Postmodern Party State?', *Government and Opposition* 3(2).

von Hayek, F. A. (1960) *The Constitution of Liberty*, Chicago: Chicago University Press.

Wallace, H. and Wallace, W. (eds) (1996) *Policy-Making in the European Union*, Oxford: Oxford University Press.

Wallace, W. (1991) 'Introduction: The Dynamics of

European Integration', in W. Wallace (ed.) *The Dynamics of European Integration*, London: Pinter/RIIA.

Wallace, W. (1994) *Regional Integration: The West European Experience*, Washington, DC: Brookings Institution.

Wallerstein, I. (1974) *The Modern World-System, Volume I*, New York: Academic Press.

Wallerstein, I. (1979) *The Modern World-System, Volume II*, New York: Academic Press.

Wallerstein, I. (1984) *The Politics of the World Economy*, Cambridge: Cambridge University Press.

Wallerstein, I. (1989) *The Modern World-System, Volume III*, New York: Academic Press.

Walters, F. P. (1952) *A History of the League of Nations*, London: Oxford University Press.

Waltz, K. W. (1979) *Theory of International Politics*, Reading, Mass.: Addison Wesley.

Walzer, M. (1983) *Spheres of Justice*, Oxford: Blackwell.

Ward, H. (1995) 'Rational Choice Theory', in D. Marsh and G. Stoker (eds) *Theory and Method in Political Science*, Basingstoke: Macmillan.

Warren, B. (1980) *Imperialism: Pioneer of Capitalism*, London: New Left Books.

Wavell, S. (1995) 'Closed Societies Opened by the Internet Genie', *The Sunday Times*, New Review section, 3 September.

Webb, P. (1996) 'Apartisanship and Anti-party Sentiment in the United Kingdom: Correlates and Constraints', *European Journal of Political Research* 29.

Weber, M. (1930) *The Protestant Ethic and the Spirit of Capitalism*, London: Allen & Unwin.

Weber, M. (1946) 'The Protestant Sects and the Spirit of Capitalism', in C. Wright Mills and H. Gerth (eds) *From Max Weber: Essays in Sociology*, New York: Oxford University Press.

Weber, M. (1947) *The Theory of Social and Economic Organisation*, Glencoe, Ill.: Free Press.

Webster, F. (1995) *Theories of the Information Society*, London: Routledge.

Weldon, T. D. (1953) *The Vocabulary of Politics*, London: Penguin.

Wernick, A. (1991) *Promotional Culture*, London: Sage.

Westlake, M. (1994) *Britain's Emerging Euro-Elite?*, Aldershot: Dartmouth.

Wheare, K. C. (1963) *Federal Government*, Oxford: Oxford University Press.

White, R. (1994) 'Audience "Interpretation" of Media: Emerging Perspectives', *Centre for the Study of Communication and Culture* 14(3).

Wilding, R. W. L. (1979) 'The Professional Ethic of the Administrator', *Management Services in Government* 34(4), Civil Service Department, London.

Wilford, R. (1994) 'Fascism', in R. Eccleshall et al. *Political Ideologies*, London: Routledge.

Williams, G. (1991) *Political Theory in Retrospect*, Aldershot and Vermont: Edward Elgar.

Williams, R. (1976) *Keywords. A Vocabulary of Culture and Society*, London: Fontana.

Wilson, D. and Game, C. (1994) *Local Government in the United Kingdom*, London: Macmillan.

Winkler, J. (1974) 'Corporatism', *Archives Européennes de Sociologie* XVII(1).

Winkler, J. (1977) 'The Coming Corporatism', in R. Skidelsky, (ed.) *The End of the Keynesian Era*, London: Macmillan.

Wolfe, T. (1970) *The Electric Kool-Aid Acid Test*, London: Fontana.

Wollstonecraft, M. (1992) *A Vindication of the Rights of Woman*, London: Everyman's Library.

Wright Mills, C. (1956) *The Power Elite*, New York: Oxford University Press.

Young, H. (1990) *One of Us*, London: Pan.

Young, I. M. (1990) *Justice and the Politics of Difference*, Princeton: Princeton University Press.

Zacher, M. W. and Matthew, R. A. (1995) 'Liberal International Theory: Common Threads, Divergent Strands', in C. W. Kegley (ed.) *Controversies in International Relations Theory. Realism and the Neoliberal Challenge*, New York: St. Martins Press.

Zamyatin, Y. (1983) *We*, London: Penguin.

Zetterholm, S. (ed.) (1994) *National Cultures and European Integration: Exploratory Essays on Cultural Diversity and Common Policies*, Oxford: Berg.

# Index